DATE DUE

YALE IN NEW HAVEN

VINCENT SCULLY

CATHERINE LYNN

ERIK VOGT

PAUL GOLDBERGER

Yale in New Haven
Architecture & Urbanism

YALE UNIVERSITY · NEW HAVEN · 2004

Library of Congress Control Number: 2004100158
ISBN 0-9749565-0-3

The paper in this book meets the guidelines for permanence and durability of the Committee on Production Guidelines for Book Longevity of the Council on Library Resources.

Produced under the direction of the Yale University Printer
Edited by Lesley K. Baier
Designed and typeset in Adobe Minion by Julie Fry and John Gambell
Prepared for production by Gist and Herlin Press, West Haven, Connecticut
Printed and bound in Singapore by CS Graphics

Acknowledgments

Many people helped in the production of this book. It was Penelope Laurans, Associate Dean of Yale College and Special Assistant to the President, who first suggested to Vincent Scully that he write a book about the history of the university's architecture. Linda Koch Lorimer, Vice President and Secretary of the University, quickly adopted the book proposal as part of Yale's Tercentennial celebrations. The support of Yale administrators, with the encouragement of President Richard C. Levin, has continued well past the tercentennial year, and we are grateful for it. Our primary thanks are due to their sponsorship of the evolving project, which was sustained through the enlistment of three additional authors along with an editor, Lesley Baier, and a designer, John Gambell, who called on their long experience in the Office of the University Printer to become essential contributors to the text and its illustrations, and who in turn called on Julie Fry to assist in designing the book. John Robinson, Rich Nesbit, and Beth Gilbert of Gist and Herlin Press have worked with them scanning numerous images for illustration and pre paring proofs and files for the printer, CS Graphics of Singapore. The compilation of the index was greatly facilitated by the efforts of David Baker. Lesley Baier's meticulous attention to every detail, large and small, would be hard to match anywhere. All of us owe her an enormous debt. Primary funding for this project has been provided by the Office of the Secretary. Additional funds to support printing costs were generously provided by A. Mark Novitch, M.D., Yale Class of 1954.

A great many members of the Yale community have been extraordinarily helpful, especially those in Manuscripts and Archives at Sterling Memorial Library, among whom Judith A. Schiff, Chief Research Archivist; William R. Massa, Jr., Public Services Archivist; Diane E. Kaplan, Head of Reference Services; and Kirsten M. Jensen, former Archivist, have been more than generous with their deep knowledge of Yale's history and buildings. For their patience in answering innumerable requests we thank Richard V. Szary, Carrie S. Beinecke Head of Manuscripts and Archives and University Archivist; Mary A. Caldera, Technical Services Archivist; Stephen E. Cohen, Archivist; Christine Connolly, Library Services Assistant; Michael Frost, Library Services Assistant; Dika Goloweiko-Nussberg, Library Services Assistant; Tom Hyry, Head of Arrangement and Description; Carter A. Jones, Computer and Information Systems Specialist; Nancy F. Lyon, Archivist; Danelle Moon, Public Services Manager; Kevin Moore,

Library Services Assistant; Anne Marie Phillips, Assistant University Archivist and Project Manager; Raman Prasad, Computer and Information Systems Specialist; Sheilah G. Robinson, Library Services Assistant; Sandra Staton, Library Services Assistant; and Christine Weideman, Assistant Head.

In Sterling Library's Map Collection, Margit Kaye located images for our use, as did archivists in other Yale collections, including Toby Appel, Research Affiliate in the History of Medicine at the Harvey Cushing/John Hay Whitney Medical Library, and Martha Smalley, Curator of the Day Missions Library at the Divinity School. In the Arts Library we received special help from Helen Chillman, Librarian, Visual Resources, and from Beverly Lett, Library Services Assistant. At the Beinecke Rare Book and Manuscript Library, Susan Brady, Assistant Head of Public Services, answered our questions about newly acquired drawings by A. J. Davis for a proposed Yale library. At Yale-New Haven Hospital, Bethany Hipple, Archivist, as well as Kristen Ostheimer and Allison W. Carboni, her predecessors, each located valuable documents and illustrations for our use.

From beginning to end, the Office of Facilities' Department of University Planning, headed by Pamela Delphenich, University Planner, has made its resources available to us. Initially Waltrude Woods, Senior Architect and Planner, opened her extensive personal research files on the history of Yale's architecture and planning for our use, and near the end of this book's preparation, she was of great assistance with picture research. Sean Dunn, Manager of Information Resources, found answers to many specific questions about Yale buildings. Others who were helpful within the facilities office include Faith Brown, Joe Hogan, Bev Joy, Robert M. Ponichtera, and Jayshree Pugh. Alexander Cooper, FAIA, and Jaquelin Robertson, FAIA, of Cooper, Robertson and Partners, the university's consultants for planning, contributed to our understanding of the shape of Yale's campus.

In the School of Architecture, Robert A. M. Stern, Dean, John Jacobson, Associate Dean, and Grazyna Kirsch, Registrar, supplemented our research on the school's early history with some intense delving into its early records. Additional picture research was undertaken by Graham Banks, a student in the School of Architecture. From the Divinity School, the Reverend Jaime Lara, Associate Professor of Christian Art and Architecture and Chair, Program in Religion and the Arts, contributed his important discoveries about John Davenport. In the Office of Development, Monica Robinson, Director, School of Architecture Capital Giving, and George Howard, Development Officer, Annual Giving, each undertook research in ancient files to clarify vexing questions. At the Yale University Art Gallery, Susan Matheson provided information based on her research for a show on the Gothic Revival, as did Elise K. Kenney from her studies of the Art Gallery's earlier homes. From the files of the *Yale Alumni Magazine* and his own recollections, Mark Branch retrieved arcane facts about ivy. Over several years, discussions with Gaddis Smith, Professor Emeritus of History, have enlightened our thinking about this book. Diane Torre,

Student Financial Services Counselor, has coached us in the use of the Internet for research, as has Beth Dunlop, Architecture Critic for the *Miami Herald*.

Patrick Pinnell, Architect and Town Planner, generously made his extensive research in Yale's architectural history available to us and contributed important photographs. His wife Kathleen Curran, Associate Professor of Fine Arts, Trinity College, was equally generous in making available her files on the architect Josiah Cleveland Cady. Kevin Roche, FAIA, graciously consulted with us about Eero Saarinen's plans for Yale. Anstress Falwell contributed information about Hillhouse Avenue, and Peter Hall led us to obscure early-twentieth-century publications that proved valuable. Brooks Kelley, a distinguished student of Yale's history, made us a present of his book while it was temporarily out of print. At the Connecticut Historical Commission, its incomparable former Director and State Historic Preservation Officer, John W. Shannahan, provided information about Yale's National Historic Landmarks, and David Poirier, Archaeologist, detailed current plans for the Adee Boat House.

Photographs of several Yale buildings were provided by Michael Marsland, University Photographer; Steve Conn, Director, Yale Sports Publicity; and Terry Dagradi, Photographer, MedMedia Group, Yale School of Medicine. Karen Clute allowed us to have photographs taken from her lofty office overlooking the campus and the town. Amy Trout, Curator, located essential images at the New Haven Colony Historical Society. Farther afield, at The Octagon, The Museum of the American Institute of Architects, Washington, D.C., Sherry C. Birk, Director of Collections, guided us skillfully through the archive of Richard Morris Hunt to important Yale-related material. Erica Stoller of Esto Photographics Inc. retrieved useful photographs of Yale buildings of the 1960s from the company's files. Other photographs have been generously provided by Coosje van Bruggen and Claes Oldenburg; Harold Roth, FAIA, of Roth and Moore Architects; Susan Scanlon, Public Relations Manager, Venturi, Scott Brown and Associates; and Eugenie Hoffmeyer Devine, Manager of Public Relations, Centerbrook Architects and Planners.

Perhaps our largest debt is to the generations of administrators, archivists, and chroniclers of Yale who maintained detailed records not only of the university's academic life, faculty, and students (whose lives they followed in published class histories until they died), but also of its building activities. These survive in the treasurers' files of business correspondence and other documents that include building contracts, receipts, drawings, and photographs documenting construction. Not all universities have done this. And our indebtedness is not least to the institution's willingness to make these unexpurgated resources available to researchers.

Yale in New Haven: An Introduction

VINCENT SCULLY

This book is about the architecture and planning of Yale University, especially as they relate to the architecture and planning of New Haven (FIG. 1). It is intended as a critical history rather than a definitive one, and it leaves many issues aside and neglects some fine buildings in order to focus upon what its authors believe to be one of the major issues facing Yale as it enters its fourth century: its relationship to the city of New Haven. Here we have been aided by a number of earlier publications: Brooks Kelley's history of Yale, Rollin Osterweis's of New Haven, Ben Holden's touching pictorial history with its enormously useful maps of the university, Elizabeth Brown's fine guide to New Haven, and Patrick Pinnell's admirably complete and critically astute guide to Yale, recently published by Princeton Architectural Press.[1] A new edition of *Buildings and Grounds of Yale University* is now in press as well.[2] These last two publications are especially recommended as chronological records of the development of Yale's architecture, and I feel that they leave my coauthors and me free to pursue those aspects of the architecture of Yale and New Haven which interest us the most and which, undoubtedly for that reason, we consider the most important. It will be obvious too that our interests differ, and we write about them in very different ways.

Erik Vogt, already a brilliant young architect, has now worked for some years on questions having to do with Yale and colonial New Haven, including the later developments of that relationship, and he is uniquely able to supplement his conclusions with magnificent reconstruction drawings of a type and quality we have never had available before. His solid textual and topographical analysis establishing New Haven as Ezekiel's New Jerusalem is especially moving to me, as are his descriptions of Yale's Brick Row and of the City Beautiful Movement of the end of the nineteenth century and the beginning of the twentieth, about which I take the liberty of making a few remarks of my own later on.

Paul Goldberger, at the very beginning of his distinguished career as historian and critic, wrote a senior paper for me on the architecture of Yale's residential colleges and the work of James Gamble Rogers in general.[3] It was the first modern study to value the colleges properly and to put them into their historical context. Here Goldberger returns to that topic some thirty years later, especially equipped to write about this major fact of the environment of Yale as we have all experienced it. Again I add a few comments. The reevaluation of Rogers and admiration for the beautiful Yale he created are sympathetic topics for all of us.

FIG. 1 *Yale and New Haven looking northeast toward East Rock.*

Catherine Lynn brings her special knowledge of nineteenth-century architectural theory and historic preservation to her study of those Yale buildings which are now gone and in particular to those periods in Yale's history, like the later nineteenth century, dominated by Ruskinian theory, of which the buildings have almost entirely disappeared, victims of that self-cannibalization for which Yale has always shown a lively taste. She also considers forgotten architects and examines Yale's style of patronage and real estate dealings. Beyond that, all of us have profited from Ms. Lynn's research and editorial skills, and she, too, helps us to understand just how admirable James Gamble Rogers's achievement was. We can now perceive that his work marked the high tide of architectural achievement at Yale and is coming into its own as a model of urbanistic excellence for the new city builders, the New Urbanists of the present day. The first of them, Andres Duany and Elizabeth Plater-Zyberk, were trained at Yale.

As for me, my topic of architecture since 1950 is one that I have lived through and with during my entire life at Yale, and I should perhaps apologize for the personal and rather familiar tone I employ in writing about it and its major personalities. It would have been difficult for me to write about it or them in any other way. But the topic is by no means simply personal or parochial. The architecture that developed after 1950 at Yale and because of Yale profoundly affected the architecture of the rest of the United States and to some extent that of the world as a whole. I am proud about that and happy to have been around to watch it happen. Recently, Andres Duany sent me a letter in which he wrote, "Last night I spent the entire night dreaming of the Yale campus. It was the most beautiful place in the entire world. I will describe it to you sometime." In fact, he has been describing it, praising it, in his work all along, and it has shaped all of us who have come in contact with it far more fundamentally than most of us have ever realized.

First of all, without attempting to preempt topics that others will be writing about in greater detail, I should like to give some general consideration to the architectural interaction between Yale and New Haven as it has developed since the seventeenth century. Today, that relationship is all too often seen in terms of Yale as a rich and rather alien force set in an old New England town which, like many of the industrial cities of the Northeast, has fallen on evil times. Indeed, if we stand on New Haven's incomparable Green we cannot help but feel the unified power of the long row of Yale buildings that crowns the high ground along College Street. It looms over the city. In contrast to the more diversified, more or less *ad hoc* development of City Hall and the other government buildings across the Green, it does seem to represent some overwhelming unity of purpose. But the relationship between the city and the university is much more complicated than that. Yale needs New Haven, might in fact fall if New Haven falls, and this is fair enough, because Yale was the first great achievement of New Haven's culture; it was brought into being by the Congregational program that shaped the city itself.

New Haven's plan of nine perfect squares with the open Green in the center was unique in the Anglo-American colonies. Its ancestors certainly include the gridded colonies of the Greek city-states and the squared-off colonial cities of Rome, as well as the numerous Ideal City projects of the Renaissance which were inspired by them. The British palisaded towns of the seventeenth century in subjugated Ireland have also been suggested as models. But the direct inspiration for New Haven was, I think, considerably nobler than that. It was surely Old Testament in origin. John Archer traced it to Villalpando's reconstruction, published in Rome in 1604, of Ezekiel's ideal city, his Jerusalem reborn.[4] Vogt agrees with Archer and, to go further, draws a strong connection between the ideal sacred landscape as described in Ezekiel and elsewhere and that of New Haven. At the same time, New Haven's square plan, with its central open space, is almost exactly that of all the Spanish towns of Latin America, laid out under the Laws of the Indies of 1573, whose provisions themselves derived from earlier reconstructions of Ezekiel.[5] So New Haven and Caracas, for example, were derived from the same biblical sources. And, surprisingly enough, John Davenport, the founder of the New Haven Colony, had a brother named Christopher, raised like him as an Anglican, who converted to Roman Catholicism, as he to Puritanism, emigrated to Spain, became a Franciscan monk, and eventually occupied a chair at the University of Salamanca. Professor Jaime Lara of the Yale Divinity School, who made me acquainted with that remarkable relationship, believes that correspondence between the brothers will some day come to light. Even so, this special Puritan link to the colonial urbanism of Catholic Spain, as to Ezekiel, seems securely forged.

In the famous sermon that he delivered on the brig *Arbella* as it approached the Massachusetts Bay Colony, John Winthrop said, "Wee shall be as a Citty upon a Hill."[6] But John Davenport's New Haven is conspicuously under a hill, the red escarpment of East Rock, which rises so splendidly above New Haven's harbor as one's ship comes in from the Sound. It blazes at sunset like a butte bursting up from Arizona to dominate the Connecticut shore. Ezekiel 40:1–3 reads:

In the five and twentieth year of our captivity,…in the fourteenth year after…the city was smitten,…the hand of the Lord was upon me, and brought me thither.

In the visions of God brought he me into the land of Israel, and set me upon a very high mountain, by which was as the frame of a city on the south.

And he brought me thither, and, behold there was a man…with a line of flax in his hand, and a measuring reed; and he stood in the gate.[7]

In the Wadsworth map of 1748 (FIG. 2) we first see the city Ezekiel then describes, much as Villalpando's reconstruction showed it, as made up of nine squares shaped by the symmetrically laid out encampment of the twelve tribes of Israel, each holding a gate, with the Levites divided into

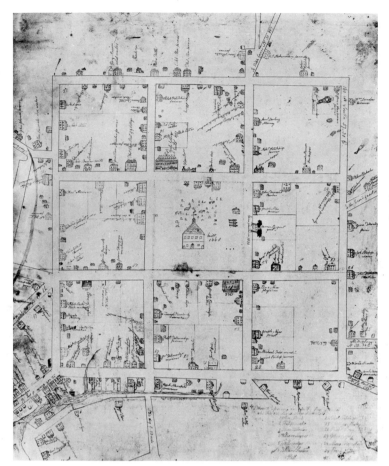

FIG. 2 *James Wadsworth, "Plan of the City of New Haven," 1748.*

four groups in the center as guardians of the tabernacle. In Davenport's New Haven, the gates become the streets, with the squares between them, and the central square is reserved as common land, eventually to be called the Green, with, as Ezekiel tells us, the sea beyond it to the south. It was out of the square adjacent to the gate that Ezekiel described as held by the tribe of Naphtali, on the west of the city, that the former acting president of Yale, the aged Naphtali Daggett, rode out against the British in 1779, and was so beaten about the body by their musket barrels that he died the following year.[8] For some reason not described, Villalpando shifts Naphtali's gate to the north side of the square (see FIG. 25).

The meetinghouse was at the center of everything, Ezekiel's Temple with God's entrance on the east:

And, behold, the glory of the God of Israel came from the way of the east…
And the glory of the Lord came into the house by the way of the gate whose prospect is toward the east.[9]

That is the prospect of the meetinghouse door, and I suspect that Wadsworth's map was oriented with west at the top, as most later maps of New Haven came to be, not only because that was Villalpando's orientation, clearly labeled by him, but also because it was the only way the eastern entrance of the meetinghouse, the sacred gate, could be shown right-side-up in the elevational convention used in the map. Vogt's reconstruction drawing beautifully presents the whole sacred landscape (see FIG. 20); it is Ezekiel's vision to the life, the nine-square city by the sea, the red mountain flaring. It is the new Jerusalem, the most perfect of all the Puritan towns.

In that first map, the Yale College House, over 170 feet in length, much bigger than the meetinghouse itself, already dominated the city, pressed close up to College Street, rising above

FIG. 3 *A. B. Doolittle, "A View of the Buildings of Yale College at New Haven," 1807.*

the Green. It was there because New Haven, after many false starts from Davenport's time on, had finally managed to secure Yale's presence, since only by training its own teachers could the Congregational community endure. Out of that beginning, Yale's wonderful Brick Row, designed by John Trumbull with James Hillhouse in 1792, eventually spread northward in a process well described by Vogt. It was set back behind the first College House — first built, first demolished — in a grand alternation of the horizontal house type and the vertically spired church type of colonial New England (FIG. 3). The whole embodied the grand simplicity and urban order that the direct employment and clear repetition of basic architectural types can best achieve. Simple and majestic, the Brick Row not only defined the Green and dominated it but faced it too, and could be entered from it. We are told that the townspeople could walk past the Yale Fence where it ran along College Street and go on through the college yard between the Fence and the Row and might even roam freely among the buildings themselves. The yard was beautifully planted with elm trees by James Hillhouse, as shown in Trumbull's plan, and Hillhouse planted elms on the Green itself and along the adjacent streets, and New Haven became the Elm City, which Charles Dickens was later to regard as one of the most beautiful in America. By 1800 or so Hillhouse had also been instrumental in subdividing the nine squares, and the Green was split by a north-south road called Temple Street, running just east of the place where the first and second meetinghouses had stood. The demolition of the second, the one shown in Wadsworth's map, surely represented New Haven's first serious break with the past. The town could never be so wholly unified again, and the simple, square building was at once succeeded by two churches and a State House whose spires joined those of the Brick Row in standing out

FIG. 4 *Whitneyville: detail from "The City of New Haven, Connecticut," 1879.*

in the sky before the mountain. When Temple Street appeared, three new churches were soon built facing it. They are still there, oriented eastward as the meetinghouse itself had been, and, especially considering the name of the street, like Greek temples as well.

That new enthusiasm for classicism and the picturesque alike was apparently also involved in the extension of the subdivided streets northward across the old fields: Orange Street aimed right at East Rock, visually emphasizing its direct relationship to the town. But the new, eponymous avenue that James Hillhouse laid out on picturesque principles began only at Grove Street rather than from deeper within the nine squares—a lack of integral connection with the old town that was to pose serious problems for Yale later. From Grove, Hillhouse ran his beautiful, parklike avenue directly to the foot of the north-south ridge called Sachem's Grove (or Wood, or Ridge). It was designed with broad grass verges and long rows of trees, and became a kind of model for some of the finest suburbs and garden cities in the United States, right through to Coral Gables in Florida, developed by George Merrick in 1922–26, which remains conspicuous among them. Picturesque mansions of a new suburban type flanked the avenue, culminating in a noble Greek Revival house designed by Ithiel Town and Alexander Jackson Davis in 1828 for James Hillhouse's son and set on the forward slope of the hill on the axis of the street.[10] The angle of Hillhouse Avenue off the nine squares was more or less repeated by that of Prospect Street west of it; and, in turn, the skewed grid of Grove Street Cemetery, also laid out by Hillhouse, soon filled the irregular space west of Prospect.

At the same time, Whitney Avenue diverged from the axis of Church Street in order to skirt East Rock at its base, just where little Mill River could be dammed to provide power for the first factory in America, perhaps in the world, to produce interchangeable parts on a large scale. That first step toward mass production distinguished Yale alumnus Eli Whitney's establishment for the manufacture of small arms; with its associated housing, it soon became Whitneyville, long preceding Colt's in Hartford as the first of Connecticut's mass producers of weapons (FIG. 4). Its factory and rooming houses were versions of the domestic type that had shaped Yale's Brick Row, but the frontal-gabled structures—they too essentially a Greek Revival adaptation, with the entrance in the narrow end—were now adapted to a narrow street frontage and as such were soon to become New Haven's major two- and three-family house type. Whitneyville

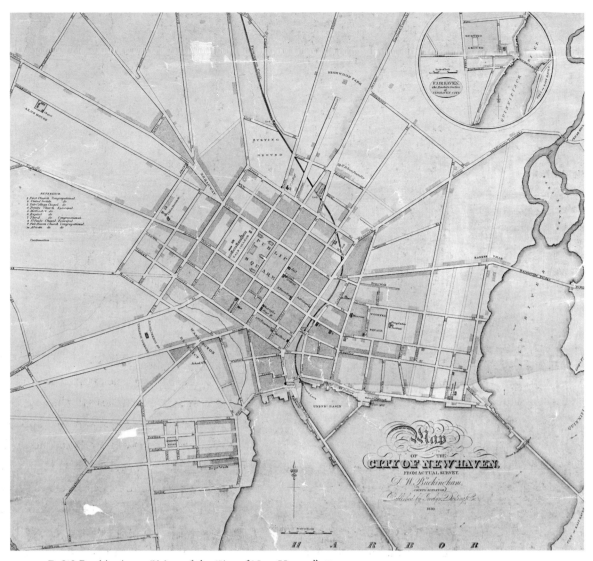

FIG. 5 *D. W. Buckingham, "Map of the City of New Haven," 1830.*

marked the beginning of New Haven's lively factory economy, which found its climax, and indeed almost its end, in the so-called Defense plants of the Second World War.

Industrial New Haven first came wholly into its own with the arrival of the railroad in the 1840s, which profoundly altered the social structure of the town. Right up through Buckingham's map of 1830 we are shown a New Haven Green wholly dominated by Yale and the rest of the old Protestant establishment (FIG. 5). On the east side, the city's side, along Church Street, there was basically nothing but a jail. In 1861, however, a new City Hall was built, designed by Henry Austin in what the city was proud to call "the Gothic Style" (FIG. 6). The building had a tower like the churches, but the city obviously wanted to think of it as something new and exotic and of a style different from that employed in older New Haven, though "well known in Europe." There was already, of course, a more or less "Gothick" church on the Green designed by Ithiel Town (1813–14), and Yale itself had built a picturesquely Gothic library, also by Henry Austin, well behind Brick Row, but the City Hall represented a newer, tougher, mid-century version of the revival. That was even truer of its Annex — the old County Courthouse, built in 1871 — which was intended to give it a "more imposing" presence on the Green, enough to enable the city to challenge Yale and the churches with some architectural authority.

FIG. 6 *New Haven City Hall, with the County Courthouse annex on the left, after 1871.*

FIG. 7 *Farnam and Lawrance Halls in 1888.*

New Haven as a whole, now full of immigrant Irish, with some Germans, and soon to be the home of Italians, Poles, and many other Europeans, was itself beginning to challenge Yale seriously by the time of the Civil War. There had always been trouble between the students and the tougher members of the community, with sailors especially, and eventually with the firemen who occupied the corner of High and Chapel Streets for some time. But this was a vaster change; Yale recognized it by the late sixties and responded to New Haven's Gothic City Hall with the immediate Gothic Revival fortification of the campus along College Street. Farnam Hall and its successors, all resembling the medieval castles published by Viollet-le-Duc, were pushed right up to College Street; their defensive towers replaced the Brick Row's entrances on that side (FIG. 7). The Yale Fence or its replacement was moved to the west side of the new buildings, which were eventually extended all the way to Chapel Street, shaping a new enclosure, scaled off from the Green except for a couple of gates and doorways, which became the Old Campus. Brick Row was torn down, piece by piece. Architectural theory played a significant part in that development. The newest buildings, like Street Hall on Chapel Street, were inspired primarily by the writings of John Ruskin. They represented high art, while the old brick buildings of the Row began to look too much like the factories that had risen in Whitneyville and across town. The old colonial type—one is tempted to say the old Puritan type—was no longer valued. Now the rather sinister determination to make each building different from every other began to dominate the thinking of the university, especially that of President Timothy Dwight,[11] who literally hated the Brick Row. It was the expressed disappointment of his life that he had never been able to demolish Connecticut Hall, the last of them all. But Dwight did succeed in pushing through the building of Osborn Hall, the most "artistic" of the new buildings, wonderfully brutal in its Richardsonian massing and rich, highly colored, Romanesque details. It completed the fortification of College Street and destroyed the last of the old Yale Fence at the corner of College and Chapel. The alumni raged but to the usual no avail.

So by the late nineteenth century Yale's campus had become consciously elite, separate from the town, a special community whose unique qualities were proclaimed by its monumental portals, like Phelps Gate, challenging the Green. It was only the idea of the enclosed quadrangle that controlled the rather anarchic high-artiness of the newly individual buildings, and it was that urban principle which eventually shaped most of Yale's future development. But not for some time, not until it was picked up again by Yale alumnus James Gamble Rogers in the Memorial Quadrangle, begun in 1917. It was only then that Yale began to explore the image of the secret garden—in effect something like that of its senior societies—upon which Rogers's colleges were to be based. In the interim, during the late nineteenth and early twentieth centuries, Yale built some courtyard types, like the Berkeley Oval (so-called) and the second Divinity School next to it on Elm Street, but only the latter was entirely enclosed, and that not until 1911. Yale also began a rather spotty development of individual buildings for the sciences along Hillhouse Avenue.

FIG. 8 *Woolsey and Memorial Halls, looking north toward the buildings of the Sheffield Scientific School on Prospect Street, ca. 1905.*

It was then that a certain difficulty of connection between north and south, occasioned by the awkward intervention of Grove Street Cemetery, began to be felt; and it was the City Beautiful architects of the beginning of the twentieth century, who were especially sensitive to such things, who first reacted to the problem, in their siting of the Bicentennial Buildings of 1901–2. Woolsey Hall and Commons were joined by Memorial Hall, placed right at the difficult intersection and designed so that its domed rotunda literally directed the diagonal movement across Grove Street that is required to link up with Prospect Street and Hillhouse Avenue (FIG. 8). That pedestrian axis runs right through Memorial Hall from Hewitt University Quadrangle and is distributed thence northeastward by the rotunda. Hundreds of students in introductory courses over the years have walked through it and described in their first short papers how its axial movement is encouraged and enlivened by stairs, vaults, domes, and columned screens. With its great concert hall, dining hall, and central quadrangle, the whole complex still furnishes the closest thing Yale has to a center for the university. Its architects knew exactly what they were doing in that critical place, if they were perhaps a little timid in the dimensions of their dome and its lack of a drum.

The Yale Bowl, which opened in 1914, was another conspicuous monument of the City Beautiful movement (FIG. 9). Like Harvard's colonnaded stadium of the same period, it was classically conceived as part of a general renaissance of American architecture. Harvard's stadium is much more Greek, and, though its spectators sit in hideous discomfort as the icy winds blow in through the open end on the Charles, they are much closer to the field of play than they are in the Bowl. On the other hand, the Bowl, dug into the earth, is truly expansive, more Roman; it has a gravitas all its own. Spectators sit well back in it, perhaps a little too much so, but the

FIG. 9 *Yale Bowl during the Yale–Harvard game in the 1970s.*

command of space is imperial, the setting majestic, with New Haven's other, less sacred red escarpment, West Rock, rising beyond the trees. (Less sacred, but part of the sacred landscape described by Vogt and carrying a megalithic pile of stones called a cave on its summit, where three of Charles I's regicidal judges are supposed to have hidden themselves.) Harvard Stadium and the Bowl attest to that late-nineteenth- and early-twentieth-century overemphasis on athletics of which both universities were supremely guilty. Indeed, they started the whole thing and can hardly sneer at the antics of the Big Ten and everybody else today. Yale, with Walter Camp and *Brek-kek-kek-kek-koax-koax* and all the rest of it, was, one suspects, especially obnoxious. But the Bowl brought New Haven closer to Yale than it had been since the 1840s. Sport really was king for a long time in twentieth-century America, and New Haveners of every kind identified with Yale during its great football days and rode out to the Bowl on the open trolleys of summer and wept real tears when their own Albie Booth whipped Army—it seemed to them, all by himself.[12]

The City Beautiful period of the early twentieth century marked New Haven's great days too. It was a prosperous factory town, with everybody working, though some of them were being encouraged to moisten with their lips the tiny brushes loaded with radium paint which they used to paint the faces of the watches and clocks they made. New Haven was well-off materially, and the last of its old Protestant elite was endowing it with the generous system of parks which is still one of its glories. Foremost among the civic-minded was George Dudley Seymour, not a graduate of Yale. But in New Haven it was Seymour who led the agitation of the City Beautiful movement for the kind of urban planning that was necessary nationwide to control

FIG. 10 *New Haven Free Public Library and New Haven County Courthouse from the New Haven Green, with the United Congregational Church on the far left, the Union Trust Company on the far right, and the Southern New England Telephone Company in the middle background.*

the rapid growth of American cities and to engage their large immigrant populations in their destinies. One of Seymour's first civic triumphs was the embellishment of the Green with the building that was, in my youth, by far the most important one on it. This was the new Public Library, by Cass Gilbert, of 1908 (FIG. 10). Its splendid portal, columned and staired, faces directly toward the Green at Temple Street, the very heart of the city. Through it my contemporaries and I were accustomed to troop, during the twenties and early thirties, rushing in to take out the five books we were allowed and rushing out again to devour them, to return as soon as possible for five more. What a gift it was, the best a city could give its children. During Redevelopment in the 1960s the library came within a whisker of being removed from that conspicuous, important place and hidden in an anonymous warehouse that was intended to be part of a new government center beyond what was to be left (not much) of City Hall. It was saved by Margaret Flint, director of the New Haven Preservation Trust, under circumstances best described later and representing almost the solitary time in its history when the Trust more than lived up to its responsibilities.

But in 1908 Seymour and Gilbert knew how a city was made and sustained. They understood that it was a continuing process, wherein each generation builds sympathetically in relation to what has gone before. The library, for example, was designed to get along with the churches closest to it on the Green. It employed their materials and their classical details and was at their scale, enlivened by its own dominant act, the emblematic door. Gilbert was soon to design the Woolworth Building in a totally different way. Like most of his contemporaries before the advent of modernism, he was secure enough in himself as an architect to shape and detail

FIG. 11 *United States Post Office and Courthouse from the New Haven Green, ca. 1918.*

each building differently according to its type and in relation to the place it occupied in the city. He was eclectic; he fit the style to the place. Later, some years after the library was saved by Margaret Flint, it received an addition by a modern architect who was apparently much less secure, refusing to employ Gilbert's forms and saying in effect that such could be done by any draftsman. He insisted on his own originality and produced a somber and rather brutal wing, primitively detailed and proportioned in relation to the original. Fortunately, though, the old building is mostly still there and continues to get along very well with everything around it (see FIG. 10): not only with the churches but also with the colonial and federalist buildings west of Temple Street, as well as with the considerably larger New Haven County Courthouse, of 1909–14. That, too, though bigger in scale, was designed contextually, seeming to grow naturally out of the library and to be part of the same urban order. True enough, the later Union Trust Company across Church Street is somewhat stretched in size for its Georgian style, but it holds the corner steady, while Douglas Orr's beautiful Art Deco skyscraper for the Telephone Company rises to the north, a real titan in the city. In comparison, the late modern New Haven Savings Bank facing the Green south of Elm Street jettisons most traditional architectural features such as doors, cornices, et al., and turns itself into folded cardboard, a thin abstraction related to nothing around it. The last of the City Beautiful buildings, though, was the Federal Post Office, in the center of the block on Church Street and James Gamble Rogers's first building in the city (FIG. 11). It sets up an eloquent urban contrast with the Gothic Revival City Hall to its north. The older building is dark and movemented, alive with gesture and jaggedly edged against the sky. The Post Office is just the opposite: white, strictly contained, symmetrical, and beautifully made.

FIG. 12 *Looking east from Harkness Memorial Tower toward the New Haven Green in 1942.*

FIG. 13 *Model of City Government Center Project and speculative office tower designed by I. M. Pei for the site of the United States Post Office and Courthouse, on Church Street facing the New Haven Green, 1966.*

But because both buildings are reasonably scaled and solidly put together and face the Green with equal authority, they get along very well: two images of the kinds of differences that make up a city, but can, with mutual confidence, be reconciled with each other. They set up architecture's best kind of conversation across the generations, enabling a city to endure beyond the lives of individual human beings (FIG. 12).

In 1928 there was a competition for a new City Hall — it was clearly hoped to make it more like the Post Office — and the best entry was by Paul Cret, who had taught Louis I. Kahn at the University of Pennsylvania in the years immediately preceding and was indeed employing him by that time. Cret's project was in his "Stripped Modern" or "Modern Classic" mode and would have fitted in very well with the Post Office, but we should probably be grateful that the old City Hall was not demolished to build it. The present contrast is surely better, with its resonance of different times and its celebration of variety. In 1967–68 Margaret Flint saved the Post Office from a catastrophic project (FIG. 13), but the Annex to City Hall was torn down shortly thereafter and, sadly, its successor, though it attempts to provide a reasonable contextuality, is not as strong. It doesn't seem to "face" the Green. Moreover, it could only be built — Redevelopment money being long gone by that time — by arrangement with a private developer who was allowed to build an enormous corporate skyscraper, thankfully set back a little, between City Hall and the Post Office. Perhaps not as awful as it might have been, that tower is still much too big, and now it rather than City Hall or the Post Office dominates the east side of the Green. It is a sad example of how urban victories can usually be only partial or impermanent. This one was a kind of standoff, but the two relevant buildings are at least still there, actively complementing each other and affirming the complex presence of civic government and federal authority.

Another of George Dudley Seymour's major achievements was the building of a new railroad station, designed by Cass Gilbert, some blocks south of the eastern edge of the nine squares. Gilbert's first design was much grander, more Baroque, than the simple brick block that was finally constructed, but that in itself is splendid enough. Its high-arched windows flood the expansive waiting room with a light that turns golden as it is reflected off the marble walls. In the 1950s the railroad boarded it up and left it to decay, substituting for it only a low metal and glass tunnel running down to the tracks, an odious hovel suggestive of a urinal and normally smelling like one. Huddled next to the masonry bulk of the old station, the thing looked like one of Pugin's angry *Contrasts* of 1836, between the good old England and the bad new. Again, it was Margaret Flint, in almost the last act of her career in preservation, who induced the railroad to restore the station to its original state. It serves New Haven beautifully once again, and causes all of us to wonder, not for the first time, at the crassness of postwar urbanism, which permitted Pennsylvania Station in New York to be demolished in 1963 and by that very act mobilized the American public to the creation of effective preservation law.

Seymour's culminating achievement was the proposal he put forward in 1910 to connect the railroad station to the Green at Temple Street by means of a leafy boulevard designed by Cass Gilbert and Frederick Law Olmsted, Jr. It was not to be a limited access, many-laned "connector," like the one that came to separate the nine squares from the railroad station under Redevelopment in the sixties. Instead it was intended to be a shaded roadway set in a park, and it would not only have moved traffic efficiently but would also have attracted people from both sides of it to itself, so enhancing and connecting, rather than degrading and ghettoizing, its surrounding neighborhoods. Other boulevards of the City Beautiful period had exactly those salutary effects in Chicago, Philadelphia, Cleveland, and many other places. The origin of these enormously civilized avenues radiating out across space was of course in the *allées* of the great French classic gardens such as Versailles, upon which the plan of Washington, D.C., itself had been based by L'Enfant in 1791, and which had inspired the boulevards of modern Paris in the middle of the nineteenth century. All of that culminated in the United States with the convention of the American Institute of Architects that was held in Washington in 1900. There the MacMillan Commission was set up, and monumental Washington was expanded by the reflecting pool and the Lincoln Memorial and, eventually, the Jefferson Memorial, and the City Beautiful movement came into its own all over the country. In it, the grid which had become the standard way of planning in nineteenth-century America was supplemented by the diagonal boulevards and urban squares of the French tradition, and always by the Olmsteds' wonderful parks. How each element supplements the other can be rather heartbreakingly seen in Olmsted's and Gilbert's drawings for New Haven. There is the perfect grid of the nine squares, the ideal Congregational neighborhood, just about a five-minute walk from its periphery to the Green. And there, from a new open plaza just outside the old grid at Temple Street, a new radiating avenue leads out across parklike space, expanding the city to the new twentieth-century scale of the train and the motorcar. It is a wonderful linking of a new world with an old, and it respects the special qualities of each. Again, contrast has to be made with the connectors of the 1960s, which isolated the old city and condemned it to be abandoned, and tore the new one apart.

Now the traditional urban elements of grid, avenue, and park, united with the five-minute walk as a determinant of the size of neighborhoods, have shaped the basic vocabulary of the self-styled New Urbanism of the present day. Its pioneers and most distinguished practitioners have been Andres Duany and Elizabeth Plater-Zyberk, who received their architectural degrees from Yale in 1974 and were steeped in the architecture of Yale and New Haven, and especially in the vernacular buildings, the "types," which made the town. They built, as so often in history, upon the incomplete experiences of the past, in this case upon the traditional American town making which had culminated in the City Beautiful movement and died with it. The beautiful expansion of the city which that way of planning had made possible represented New Haven's best opportunity to enter the new century properly, and it was missed completely.

Seymour was not supported by the city, and there was after all no massive federal funding to support urban planning at that time, as there was to be—unfortunately enough—during the period of Redevelopment later. But Yale lost a chance too. In 1919, while Seymour's proposals were still being debated by the city, Francis P. Garvan, an alumnus of Yale, engaged John Russell Pope to draw up a long overdue, sorely needed, comprehensive plan for the university. It was, to my knowledge, the first such plan attempted since Trumbull's, and its guiding principles were those of the City Beautiful movement. It employed three strong axes, one from the Old Campus to Hewitt Quadrangle, another crossing it from York Street to Temple, and a third running in a strong diagonal from Temple Street all the way to the summit of Science Hill. Here the decisive act was the perforation of the old nine squares from Grove to Temple. Hillhouse Avenue, which James Hillhouse had ended, or begun, at Grove Street, was to be pushed right through the block south of Grove to intersect the cross-campus axis at a new, very urban square extended west from Temple just far enough to receive it. For the first time Yale was to become one unified body north and south of Grove Street, which at that time also meant a stronger physical union between Yale College and the Sheffield Scientific School.[13] And at the exact spot where that connection would have taken place, right at Temple Street near the Green, a new monumental entrance to Yale was to have found a central and natural position.

It is important to imagine New Haven and Yale as they would have looked if Pope's and Seymour's projects had both been carried out. Vogt's drawing conveys the idea (see FIG. 240). The city and the university would have been effectively united, swept together into one generous urban order from the railroad station to the Green, and from there extended right through the campus and up Science Hill. The scale would have been sympathetic to pedestrians and vehicles alike, with New Haven's wonderful elms playing their essential part. Yale would have been more open to New Haven and New Haven more monumentally equivalent to Yale. City and university would have shared a common, rather splendid environment, and New Haven especially would have been spared some basic urban disasters later. But Yale's scheme was no more carried out than was New Haven's. It is clear that Yale's administration at the time did not want to be united with the city, and as the city's administration had shilly-shallied with Seymour so did Yale's with Garvan and the other backers of the plan. It finally turned the problem over to James Gamble Rogers for some kind of resolution. There can be no doubt that Rogers failed to meet the challenge, or perhaps simply gave Yale what it really wanted, not interaction with New Haven but seclusion from it. He blocked his own cross-campus axis at College Street and, most of all, failed to push Hillhouse Avenue through to Temple Street. Everything simply fell apart there at the critical point. There was no entrance to the university, and its backbone was broken. Its seems clear that Rogers did not have the backing, or perhaps even the inclination, to make the hard decisions, on the one hand revolutionary and on the other deeply traditional, that Pope's plan required. Certainly he himself had set Yale off in another direction through his design of the Memorial Quadrangle in 1917 (FIG. 14). There, as I noted earlier, the principle of the closed

FIG. 14 *Looking west over the New Haven Green and the Old Campus toward the Memorial Quadrangle, with the Divinity School, Berkeley Oval, and University Gymnasium on the far right, in 1925.*

quadrangle was picked up from suggestions offered by the Old Campus and was brought to its own kind of perfection. The whole block became one moated fortification, sealed off from the town as by military force. It would have been very difficult to integrate such a discrete unit into any open-axial general plan. Here, though, it is instructive to look at Pope's scheme to see how skillfully he handled that very problem, stringing open and closed quadrangles along the long axes, somehow enabling each principle to find its fullest expression within the larger whole. Rogers's conception was of a compartmentalized, reclusive Yale, and he became the consummate artist of quadrangular design. Memorial Quadrangle is the most beautiful of secret gardens, surprisingly soothing in scale. It is also full of variety, playing its small courtyards off against its large one, its frontal gables against its long sweeps of wall. It breaks big forms down into little ones and shapes everything with a masonry of wonderful richness and warmth, glowing as if with the patina of centuries. And, fortified or not, it is much gentler, infinitely more inviting, in relation to the streets it defines than the high blocky buildings of the previous generation, such as those of the Berkeley Oval, had been. It is above all more interesting, to use an old-fashioned critical word, more constantly attractive to the eye, more natural somehow, to employ the ulti-mate Picturesque term, because seeming to embody the massive irregularities and the endlessly varied details of Nature itself. It is indeed masterful in every way and is unmatched by any of the other Collegiate Gothic campuses of the twentieth century.

Rising effortlessly above it is its marking tower, intended to symbolize the new medieval Yale from afar, as do its bells. Frank Lloyd Wright was to say that the only place to live in New Haven was in Harkness Tower, where one need not look at it. But that was simply Wright being himself. In fact, after Harkness Tower was published in 1920 it had, I believe, a distinct effect upon the development of the stepped-back New York skyscrapers of the 1920s, beginning with Eliel Saarinen's entry in the Chicago Tribune Competition of 1922 and going on to Raymond Hood's American Radiator Building of 1924. The most creative architects of the time who were thinking about tall buildings clearly thought highly of Rogers's tower. And so should we. But it came at a price; it represents something gained and something lost. Certainly Memorial Quadrangle is one of the most important groups of buildings ever constructed at Yale, the distinct opposite of the old Brick Row. It formed the model for the closed and self-sufficient university that turned a well-tailored back on New Haven and created its own garden world in the twenties and thirties.

That world — it must be said once more — was a very beautiful one, and Rogers was its architect. He built all the colleges with the exception of Calhoun, by Pope, and Silliman, assembled last of all out of many different elements by Eggers and Higgins just before World War II. The fog laid down between Rogers's work and us by modernist criticism, which dismisses it as "historicist" and so on, should finally be blown away by fresher perceptions. It is absurd to judge it any longer according to modernist criteria which were at that time marginal at best, had nothing to do with Rogers's education or training, and have since turned out to be not overly intelligent or realistic anyway. Rogers needs no apologetics. Measured by any objective standard, he was an uncommonly sensitive and skillful architect, and he was at his absolute best at Yale, somehow above himself always. His sense of scale here was exact and humane. His quadrangles, though closed against New Haven's streets as the Corporation demanded they be, do not affront them. They create an overall university environment which, if undeniably fragmented, is rich in contrasted relationships and a special sense of place. Each college gets along well enough with all the others but is at the same time different from them in special ways. Each develops its own genial fantasies.

Branford is surely the most elaborately developed of them all and probably the most beautiful, and the incomparable metal gates by Samuel Yellin through which its courtyard can be seen are essential to it (FIG. 15).[14] I'd like to quote from an article I wrote about them some years ago:

Like all too many modern architects and historians, I have hardly looked at Yellin's great gates for Yale, though I have been passing by them every day for some fifty-five years. Perhaps it was

FIG. 15 *Memorial Quadrangle:
Samuel Yellin's gate for the
Memorial Gateway.*

*Modernism itself that blinded the eyes of people like me to Yellin's special powers. They have to do
with figural decoration after all, and with ancient techniques of hand craftsmanship; so while
we have been fighting our way out of Modernist abstraction and technological romanticism in other
aspects of architecture for over a generation it would appear that we are only now getting around
to architecture's metal grilles and pierced screens.*

*Yellin's gate under Harkness Tower is the greatest of them all at Yale. It is set below the
massive masonry of the pointed vaults that weigh down upon the void of the gateway, shaping it like
a cavern deep in the earth. In that dark void Yellin's iron leaps up like flame, the flame of the forge,
the fire out of the ground. Behind it the foliage in the courtyard echoes its shapes, but the iron fixes
that deeper pattern in one plane, one thin black web beaten by the hammer in the heart of the fire.
Almost nothing else in architecture or nature is so thin or so black as that hammered iron.*[15]

Beyond those mighty screens Branford's generous long courtyard, entered through a smaller,
paved court and flanked by others, is at once pastoral and urbane, and was never to be outdone.
Saybrook's, laid out on the dark north side of the Quadrangle, is positively tough by contrast,
restricted in size, largely paved, cast in winter shadow, and with its own rather surprisingly military aura, like the ancient stony home of some fashionable regiment (FIG. 16). Something of that
is also to be felt in Trumbull, which defines the north side of Elm Street across from Saybrook,
making that block the most solidly walled, the darkest and most portentous of all the sections
of street that Rogers defined. Inside, Trumbull hollows out a set of tight courtyards, walled in
by solid cliffs of building, with Sterling Memorial Library looming to the north over everything

FIG. 16 *Looking north from Harkness Memorial Tower over the courtyards of Saybrook and Trumbull Colleges toward Sterling Memorial Library in 1942.*

(see FIG. 16). The comparatively small court just to the left of Trumbull's main entrance on Elm Street is distinguished by a carved lintel, which graphically refers to the most tenacious myth of senior society ritual. The tone is almost savage, and all the courts, drained by corridors leading off to isolated rooms lost in the masonry masses, suggest those of a beleaguered citadel.

To the south of Branford, across Library Street — surely the gentlest of all Rogers's urban pathways and, like all of them, a delight to walk through — Jonathan Edwards stretches out below the dark hulk of Weir Hall and the Art Gallery. It is the most modest and smallest scaled of the colleges, rather touchingly thin in detail compared with Branford, disarming, and capable of inspiring a quite remarkable degree of collegial loyalty in its alumni. Across York Street, shaped on both sides by comparatively high Yale buildings, but still feeling like some kind of edge within the university, the whole panoply of Davenport and Pierson deploys (FIG. 17). It should no longer occasion special comment to note that Davenport, set back from York Street behind a wide, deep moat into which many distinguished persons have fallen, is sheathed in Gothic masonry to get along with Branford and Saybrook across the way but is detailed in Georgian brick and white trim around its big courtyard within. We go from dark to light; everything opens up; the space gets wider and higher. Stairs mount to a terrace on the north, and smaller courtyards filter out to Park Street on the western side. Along Davenport's south wall, the pedestrian passage to Pierson changes step by step from Gothic to Georgian, with wonderful Renaissance porticoes, rusticated as by Serlio, punctuating the way. The route is dominated by Pierson's clock tower, beneath which we enter the long courtyard of that college, opening

FIG. 17 *Looking west from Harkness Memorial Tower over Branford College toward Pierson and Davenport Colleges in 1942.*

FIG. 18 *Pierson College: "Slave Quarters."*

expansively to the south. It finally dwindles away in a gentle tangle of little buildings, once unhappily called "Slave Quarters," but in fact delightful in scale and giving the impression of a modest mews in an elegant eighteenth-century city (FIG. 18).

On Elm Street, Berkeley College shows us how Rogers's quadrangles might well have been adapted to the axial avenues of Pope's plan. It is divided in two by Rogers's own, more modest Cross Campus from Sterling Library to College Street. Its elevated courtyards look across it and are connected underground by Yale's extensive system of tunnels, much of which has been explored by generations of students seeking to escape the cold. Above ground, Sterling Library walls off the Cross Campus on the west. Its tower is two stories shorter than Bertram Goodhue's original project would have made it, apparently, we are told, because Rogers offered his client a choice between those stories and a richer sculptural embellishment of the entrance and the ground floor. It used to seem to me that this made the stacks too squat. Certainly their mass is less decisively vertical, less stern and upstanding than Goodhue's would have been—or than Pope's Payne Whitney Gymnasium so spectacularly came to be. But now I am not so sure. Tragic drama was not natural to Rogers; he preferred to qualify his effects in order to create an environment generally warm and harmonious, and his broader, lower tower probably does just that for the Cross Campus here. The library as a whole becomes a kind of cityscape, made up as it were of many massive buildings crowned with mysterious little settlements on their roofs. (And it was as a fantastic city, filling the horizon, that it was to serve as a backdrop for Yale's climactic Tercentennial speeches of 2001.) It is also time to stop making fun of the Gothic nave. It is a noble space by any reasonable standard and the heart of a cross-axial plan, largely Goodhue's, that still works very well.

Berkeley itself is the other major definer of the Cross Campus, and it is probably the most elaborately developed of all the colleges after Branford and Saybrook. It has the most impressive common room and dining hall, whose sequential relationship from one fine transverse space to another has been measurably injured by a recent remodeling which closed the central doors between them. Eastward, beyond Noah Porter Gateway, Calhoun is a solid block at the corner of Elm and College Streets, here a true edge to the university. Again, like Battell and Farnam and Durfee across the way, it is almost a fortified one. Calhoun itself suggests a compact gatehouse, a quality that did not prevent its invasion by rioting police officers on a sunny St. Patrick's Day in the early sixties. They were under the impression that the women students of Albertus Magnus College, on parade up Elm Street, had been insulted by cat-calls from Calhoun's windows. Yale had been similarly assaulted from Elm Street after a parade of veterans in 1919. Calhoun clearly has to stand firm at its corner, and it was Pope's forte, as shown again in his imposing gymnasium, to endow his buildings with a special density of mass.

FIG. 19 *Payne Whitney Gymnasium in the 1930s.*

Like Sterling Library, Payne Whitney Gymnasium has been the object of a great deal of loose-lipped derision over the years, as a "Cathedral of Sweat" and so on. But its long, high-towered, solid wall is a magnificent definer of Tower Parkway, a great mountain over the street, shaping the most monumental urban space at Yale (FIG. 19). Even more than the library, because ungentled by Rogers, the gym embodies the tough Gothicism, like that of Cram and Goodhue, which shaded over during the 1920s into that powerfully abstracted, fundamentally very modern architecture called Art Deco. As such its overpowering massing is much more Maya than European medieval, as was the work of Frank Lloyd Wright during those years, and we may legitimately feel that it is permeated by a love for the physical body like that exhibited by the Maya themselves. They of course liked it best in the contortions of their deadly ball games and the throes of terminal torture. Those qualities may be taken as romantic, but perhaps not inappropriate, images for a gymnasium—especially one like Pope's, surely the closest Yale has ever come to the Temple of King Jasaw Chan K'awiil at Tikal. And it is surely true that if Pope's plan had been adopted and its buildings built, Yale's environment as a whole would have been not only more unified but also sterner, harsher, and more stiffly monumental than Rogers permitted it to be. One must admit that we would probably not have liked it as well.

Timothy Dwight College is another thing entirely, with its decidedly Southern, ante-bellum air. It is true that its facade on Temple Street obliquely refers to the old Brick Row by jamming dormitory buildings together with a spired gatehouse between them, but their detailing is otherwise much more Southern than old New Haven. Rogers's real genius for softening big masses and gentling out their scale did in fact tend to lead him, in Georgian architecture, toward effects more characteristic of the colonial South than of New England. Expansive Davenport, lush Pierson, and Timothy Dwight with the little columned portico in its courtyard, are nothing like the tough red-brick barracks of the Harvard houses of that period. At the same time, they are very far from the straightforward builders' Georgian of Yale's Brick Row. In that sense, Harvard in the thirties was remaining much truer to its earlier traditions than Yale was. It also seemed to be affirming something that was probably true enough at that time: that it was in many ways a tougher-minded place than Yale, bigger, harder. Granted that, Silliman, the last of Yale's colleges of the thirties, has some of those qualities too. It is bigger than the other colleges but less homogeneous either than they or the Harvard houses, combining as it does hard-edged old Collegiate Gothic and generously classical buildings. But the new Georgian infills that complete its quadrangle, though shorn of their shutters, have a markedly Southern character. That is especially true of the chunky, high-hipped gatehouse over the entrance to the college, which is on axis with Hillhouse Avenue. Here the intention was clearly to suggest a kind of axial relationship with the President's House far up the street, newly remodeled (in 1937) with a similar high-hipped roof. Both buildings directly recall the Governor's Palace at Colonial Williamsburg, itself reconstructed only a short time before. The axis of Hillhouse Avenue, too, is used here to suggest a connection with Williamsburg's axial organization. So it again affirms the character of pre-World War II Yale with its romantic self-absorption and its tweedy Southern graces, and the contrast with New England's Harvard of the period holds very well. The environment that the colleges shaped was indeed a rather bucolic one — amazingly so considering their situation in the heart of the city. Distaste for New Haven's factories had contributed to the razing of the Brick Row. All that earlier connection with the city was now well in the past. New Haven was, symbolically, far away. Yale's new world was a comforting one, rich in elegiac associations, its architecture much more effective in creating its multiple illusions of cloistered peace than we who inhabited it then ever gave it credit for being. Rogers gave shape to that intention; even the few buildings he did not design himself, with the exception of the gymnasium, fundamentally reflect his tone. The university required of him that he wall it off from the city and transform it into a loose association of little paradises, and he did just that.

A New Heaven & a New Earth: The Origin and Meaning of the Nine-Square Plan

ERIK VOGT

THE GRAND ERRAND

Whereas it was the glorious publick design of our now blessed fathers in their Removal from Europe into these parts of America, both to plant, and under ye Divine blessing to propagate in this Wilderness, the blessed Reformed, Protestant Religion, in ye purity of its Order and Worship...We their unworthy posterity, lamenting our past neglects of this Grand errand & Sensible of our equal Obligations better to prosecute ye Same end, are desirous in our Generation to be Serviceable therunto — Whereunto the Liberal & Religious Education of Suitable youth is under ye blessing of God, a chief & most probable expedient.

Preamble to *The Proceedings of the Trustees for a Collegiate School,* Saybrook, Connecticut, November 11, 1701[1]

With this statement of purpose, the ten Congregational ministers who founded the Collegiate School of Connecticut, later christened Yale College, opened their first formal meeting. Their declared mission descended directly from the "Grand errand" that their exiled ancestors had undertaken: to propagate, in the American wilderness, the Puritan faith in its purest form. Indeed, they intended their school to redeem that errand and ensure, through the "Education of Suitable youth," that it remain a living tradition.

The Puritan faith was propagated through the founding of new townships, and only a congregation duly formed under the guiding hand of a minister could be charged with that task. Thus its continued growth depended on a steady supply of trained ministers. A college — or a "School of the Churches," as an early supporter of Connecticut's Collegiate School deemed it — was the best guarantor of such a supply. Although the Collegiate School undertook the broader aim of educating "Youth [that] may be fitted for Publick employment both in Church & Civil State,"[2] its foundation lay in ensuring that the aims of the original religious errand remained intact, forwarded by the generations of ministers who left the college sanctuary and shepherded the flocks of New England's faithful.

Just as Yale's founding was deeply rooted in the Puritan mission, so too was that of the town in which it would eventually settle. The New Haven Colony, established in 1638, was intended by its founders to be the leading exemplar of the Puritan communal ideal. As Cotton Mather wrote in 1701, they "endeavored...a yet stricter conformity to the *word of God*, in settling of all matters, both *civil* and *sacred*, than [they] had yet seen exemplified in any other part of the world."[3] It constituted, in the words of historian Perry Miller, "the essence of Puritanism, distilled and undefiled, the Bible Commonwealth and nothing else."[4]

That essence was manifested visibly in its famous nine-square plan. When the New Haven company, led by the minister John Davenport and the merchant Theophilus Eaton, established their settlement, they gave it a form and geometry unique among the New England colonies: nine perfectly square blocks, with the center square left open as a common, the whole encircled by a belt of agricultural fields that radiated out into the surrounding wilderness (FIGS. 20 & 21). The plan's origin and meaning have been the subject of numerous theories.[5] What has remained largely unexplored, however, is its relationship to the broader context of the Puritans' mission in the New World and New Haven's role in that mission. Although there were many reasons for

FIG. 20 *New Haven Colony around 1640. Drawing by Erik Vogt.*

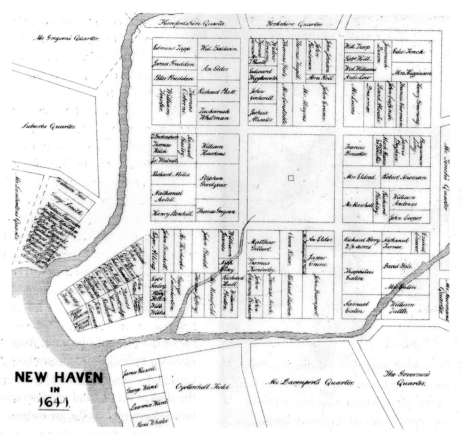

FIG. 21 *Plan of New Haven in 1641.*

the Puritans' exile, the overriding imperative was religious: they wished to restore in their own time a purified Christian church, stripped of all "humane inventions" and, in the words of John Davenport, adhering in "full and exact conformity with heavenly rules and patterns."[6]

Those rules and patterns could be found in the model of the so-called primitive church, specifically the Israelite nation of the Old Testament and the apostolic church as it existed in Christ's time and three hundred years after. At the heart of the primitive church, the Puritans believed, lay the congregation. Although English Puritans had propounded Congregational theory before the great migration to the New World in the 1630s, it was the New England exiles who developed it fully. Because they made the Congregational polity their organizing religious principle, by definition it became an overarching communal pattern, shaping the social, civil, legal, economic, and physical aspects of colonial life. In the nine-square plan, New Haven's founders rendered it as an explicit physical form; its geometry and organization derived from a divinely ordained pattern of settlement for God's chosen. What gave them the license, and indeed the imperative, to re-create this pattern was the theological doctrine of typology. Typology shaped the Puritans' view of

history and their place in it, and the nine-square plan represented an essential biblical type, recurrent throughout sacred and human history.

Both typological pattern making and the ideal of the Congregational community were to have profound effects on Yale as it defined its own mission and formed a sense of communal tradition and renewal. To understand better the roots of its institutional and physical character, one must look back to the founding of the New Haven Colony: the events that led to its planting, the motives of its leaders, and the very plan of its community. All point to the colony's crucial role in the "glorious publick design" that Yale's founders hoped to perpetuate in their School of the Churches.

———

Churches were gathered in a Congregational way, which that Mr. John Cotton *so approved that he wrote unto me, being then in* Holland, *to encourage my coming to* New England, *that the Order of the Churches and of the Commonwealth was so settled, by common Consent, that it brought to his mind, the New Heaven and New Earth, wherein dwells Righteousness.*

John Davenport, *A Sermon Preach'd at the Election of the Governour at Boston in New England,* 1669[7]

John Davenport arrived in Cotton's "New Heaven" on June 26, 1637, landing at Boston in the

FIG. 22 *"Cambridge around 1638, drawn by Erwin Raisz from data compiled by Albert P. Norris." Map reprinted by permission of the publisher from* The Founding of Harvard College *by Samuel Eliot Morison, p. 350, Cambridge, Mass.: Harvard University Press, Copyright © 1935 by the President and Fellows of Harvard College.*

Massachusetts Bay Colony. He made the crossing from England with his lifelong friend Theophilus Eaton and a close-knit company of several hundred men and women. As a group, they were wealthier and better educated than previous emigrants to the Bay. Most were Londoners with mercantile backgrounds, and many were members of Davenport's parish.[8]

Davenport (1597–1670) had attended Oxford and in 1624 settled as minister of the parish of St. Stephen's in London. Sympathetic to church reform and the developing tenets of Congregationalism, he gravitated toward Puritanism. However, by the late 1620s, nonconformists had come under a campaign of persecution by King Charles I and William Laud, the archbishop of the Anglican Church, and in 1633 Davenport felt compelled to flee to Amsterdam. While there, he corresponded with John Cotton, an English Puritan minister and colleague who had recently emigrated to Massachusetts Bay. Cotton convinced him that exile in New England was his

best, and perhaps only, opportunity to practice his beliefs freely. Davenport surreptitiously returned to England in the winter of 1636 and by early spring of 1637 had organized the crossing with Theophilus Eaton.

A successful merchant and member of Davenport's parish, Eaton (1591–1657) was devoted to the Puritan cause; he and Davenport had earlier contributed to the patent of the Massachusetts Bay Company. As the wealthiest of the New Haven company and closest to Davenport, he quickly became the lay leader of the group (and was to be elected civil governor of the New Haven Colony upon its settlement). Their partnership and respective roles reminded later Puritan historians of a similar pair of biblical leaders: Cotton Mather called them "the Moses and Aaron of the Christian colony," New England types of the Israelite saviors.[9]

John Winthrop, the governor of the Bay Colony, and John Cotton, minister of Boston's church, greeted the arrival of Davenport and Eaton with enthusiasm. One of the most highly educated Puritans in England or America, Cotton (1584–1652) had served as vicar of St. Botolph's Church in Boston, England, and had become a much respected leader of the Puritan movement; in 1630 he delivered the farewell sermon to Winthrop's Massachusetts Bay Company, one of the first and largest groups to emigrate to New England.[10] In 1632, threatened with imprisonment by Archbishop Laud, Cotton went into hiding in London. There he met with other Puritan ministers, including Davenport, and decided to resettle in the New World. Davenport and Cotton's conference in London was their first meeting, and although they went their separate ways at the time, they struck up a friendship that was to last until Cotton's death twenty years later. Close colleagues in New England, they were to become in the 1630s and 1640s the leading proponents of the "Congregational Way," which found its highest expression in the establishment of the New Haven Colony.

Since their arrival in 1630, the Winthrop company had not ventured far. Intending at first to settle as one town, they were forced by disease and the threat of attack by the French to scatter into half a dozen encampments around the Bay, which soon grew into permanent settlements.[11] These were largely unplanned, with the notable exception of Newtowne, established in 1631 (and later renamed Cambridge in honor of Harvard's founding in 1638). It was laid out as a small grid, fortified on one side with a palisade; contemporary observers praised it as "one of the neatest and best compacted towns in New England"[12] (FIG. 22). Although these original settlements absorbed the population increase in the first few years, by 1634 a shortage of farmland as well as an influx of newly exiled ministers accompanied by many of their congregants forced the Bay Colony to form new congregations, and thus new towns.[13]

In planning new settlements, the colonists had to confront conflicting needs: social cohesion necessitated compact towns, but expansion of agricultural land tended to disperse homesteads. An anonymous "Essay on the Ordering of Towns," submitted to the Colony Court around 1635, sought to reconcile the contradiction by prescribing town planning based on efficient concentric geometry: a three-mile square was to contain all the houses, "orderly placed about the midst to enjoy comfortable Communion" and centered on the meetinghouse. This square was to be surrounded by agricultural fields, enclosed in a larger six-mile square.[14] The "Essay" may have influenced the form of some communities; at least one, Concord—the first "frontier" town planted beyond the shores of the Bay—was laid out as a six-mile square with the meetinghouse at the center.[15] Nevertheless, the Colony Court felt compelled to address the issue of communal solidarity more directly. In 1635, it decreed that no new houses within a town could be built more than half a mile from the meetinghouse. This did little to mitigate the problem of dispersal, however, and the ministers charged with gathering their congregations lamented the attendant loss of spiritual unity.[16]

Other religious and social divisions began to plague the colony as well. In 1635, Roger Williams, one of its most prominent ministers, openly dissented with the Court and other ministers on the proper roles of church and civil government. Failing to dissuade him of his views, the Bay leaders ordered his expulsion, and Williams left to found the colony of Providence. Soon after, Thomas Hooker, the minister at Newtowne, requested that he and his congregation be allowed to leave the Bay Colony, citing a lack of adequate pastureland. The Court reluctantly gave its permission, and in 1636, Hooker led his congregation south to establish the Connecticut Colony. The Bay Colony considered this departure a providential sign of God's displeasure, a judgment on their failure to maintain themselves as a unified communal body.[17]

At the same time an even more serious threat to that body was developing: the so-called Antinomian crisis. In the fall of 1636, Anne Hutchinson, a member of Cotton's church in Boston, began to question the authority of God's moral law over worldly conduct. She and her followers developed a belief in personal revelation, whereby one could establish a direct connection with God. The Bay ministers argued with Hutchinson throughout the winter and spring of 1637. Davenport and Eaton, arriving from England just at this time, became witnesses to the colony's most serious internal crisis to date.[18] That it had evolved out of Cotton's church was ironic; although he placed great emphasis on personal salvation, he was also an ardent Congregationalist. Both he and Davenport wrote numerous tracts and sermons on the subject, often concentrating on its historical and theological foundations in the primitive church. Defining the congregation's specific nature and form was crucial not only to religious practice but also to their conception of the Puritan township and, ultimately, the communal order and physical plan of the New Haven Colony.[19]

A GARDEN IN THE WILDERNESS

Every Christian Church must have in it both matter and forme, and as matter by God's appointment are visible Saints, only so many as may meete together in one Congregation: So the forme is a uniting, or combining, or knitting of those Saints together into one visible body, by the bond of this holy Covenant.

John Davenport, *An Apologie of the Churches in New-England for Church Covenant*, 1643[20]

Here Davenport captured the essential qualities of the Puritan Congregational church. It was, above all, a corporate body: united, compact, and complete unto itself. Its member "Saints," bound by covenant and shepherded by their minister, formed a spiritual and physical community distinct from other congregations but sharing with them a common form and practice.[21]

In conveying these qualities to a lay audience, Davenport variously described the congregation "as the natural body of man...orderly joyning and firmly knitting the parts together"; "as a material house...built by orderly placing and firmly cementing [the stones] together"; and "as a city compact within its self, without subordination under any other."[22] He emphasized three fundamental characteristics that defined the congregation's nature as an organic whole: order and proportion among its parts and as a whole; compactness, as a body "joined" and "fitted" in close communion and limited in size; and, finally, autonomy. Autonomy was gained through the church covenant, which bound the congregation with God, who in turn rendered judgment on their faithfulness through visible signs, or divine providences, in the natural world.[23] The covenanted congregation was "the first subject of all

FIG. 23 *"The Garden of Canticles (Song of Solomon)," 1633. From Henry Hawkins,* Partheneia Sacra.

church power needful to be exercised within itself," Cotton wrote, "and consequently independent from any other church."[24] This was vital to the Puritans, as it represented a decisive break with the corrupted hierarchy of the Anglican Church.

The Puritans sought to restore the practices of Congregational polity and church covenant from the primitive Israelite and Christian churches. John Cotton's influential tract, *A Brief Exposition of the Whole Book of Canticles,* first composed in England but rewritten in New England around 1641, interpreted the Song of Solomon as a "historical Propheticall description of the estate of the Church," using verse passages to support the contention that "the primitive Apostolick Church [was] the most completely and abundantly fair of all that ever have been before it, or shall be after it, upon the face of the earth."[25] Cotton drew from the text a compelling image and apt allegory for this perfected church, one that resonated with the exiles' difficult life in the New World: "The estate of the Christian Church, in her primitive times, was as a Garden enclosed…A garden in the Originall Paradise, as if this were the Garden of *Eden.* All the world out of the Church is as a wildernesse…where all manner of unclean, and wilde beasts live and feed. Only the Church is God's Garden, as the Garden of Paradise" (FIG. 23). More pointedly, the primitive church was an "exemplary patterne to succeeding Churches," especially those of New England, where "all plantations and reformation of Churches duly gone about are attended according to [its] patterne." The Congregational township was thus to be planted as "a garden enclosed," restoring the primitive pattern in the wilderness of the New World.[26]

Cotton extended such a restoration to the civil commonwealth as well. In 1636, he drew up a legal code for the Bay Colony, dubbed "Moses his judicialls" by Winthrop for its emphasis on Israelite law. He presented these laws as divine ordinances, or "perpetual types," applicable to Puritan society because "God, who was then bound up in covenant with [the Israelites] to be their God, hath put us in their stead and is become our God as well as theirs, and hence we are as much bound to their laws as well as themselves."[27] He soon expanded on this argument in *A Discourse about Civil Government in a New Plantation whose Design is Religion,* believed to have been written in response to Davenport's plans for a new colony. Indeed, Cotton's primary assertion in the essay—that those who hold power in the commonwealth as either magistrates or landholding citizens should rightly belong to the church—was eventually incorporated into New Haven's civil code. No other colony, including Massachusetts Bay, was to adopt so strict a model.[28]

The Congregational pattern imprinted itself on the Puritans' civic life in other fundamental ways. The township system, which differed substantially from the hierarchical organization of parish and borough familiar to the English exiles, closely paralleled the church form. Settlers of new towns entered into plantation covenants, binding them together in the work of carving out a community in the wilderness. The town meeting, which shaped their political life, derived its distinctly democratic bent from Congregational principles. Insistence on the church's autonomy translated to the political realm as an emphasis on self-governance, with power residing ultimately in the body of the township, its citizens.

The pattern also guided the size and number of towns. In his civil code, Cotton legislated compactness, limiting to half a mile the distance between any dwelling and the meetinghouse. "All Civill affaires are [to be] ordered," he wrote, "so as may best conduce to the upholding and setting forward of the worship of God in church fellowship."[29] Restrictions on the size of a congregation — mandated by the practice of splitting off, or "hiving out," one congregation from another — guided the formation of new townships: "When a particular church of Christ shall grow so full of members, as all of them cannot hear the voice of their ministers," Cotton wrote, "then as an hive full of bees swarmeth forth, so is the Church occasioned to send forth a sufficient number of her members, fit to enter into a church state and to carry along church work amongst themselves."[30] Thus the continual subdivision of congregations into new townships was less the result of doctrinal schisms among ministers than a self-imposed system of organic growth, permitting the town and congregation to remain coherent and cohesive even as the number of settlers grew.[31] This system allowed Davenport and Eaton, faced with the crisis in the Bay Colony, to entertain the possibility of striking out on their own.

Wherein doth this work of God stand in appointing a place for a people? 1. When God espies or discovers a Land for a people, as in Ezek. 20.6… *And that is, when either he gives them to discover it themselves, or hear of it discovered by others. 2. After he hath espied it, when he carries them along to it, so that they plainly see a providence of God leading them from one Countrey to another.*
John Cotton, *God's Promise to His Plantations*, 1630[32]

Throughout the summer of 1637, the Bay ministers, now joined by Davenport, persisted in their attempts to dissuade Anne Hutchinson. By early August, they agreed to hold a synod, or conference, at the end of the month to clarify the theological ramifications of the crisis and outline their charges against the Antinomians. Shortly thereafter, Cotton and Davenport delivered sermons in the Boston Church condemning the dissension; Davenport "set forth the nature and danger of divisions, and the disorders which were among us," Winthrop noted in his *Journal*, "[and] clearly discovered his judgment against the new opinions and bitter practices which were sprung up here."[33]

As events unfolded in the Bay, another crisis beyond its shores was coming to a head. Since the fall of 1636, the Puritans had been engaged in the so-

called Pequot War, their first major skirmish with the Indian tribes of New England. Instigated by the murder of an Englishman by Narragansett tribesmen, the conflict was less a war than a punitive campaign waged by the colonists against the largely innocent Pequot and Narragansett tribes that ranged along the Connecticut and Rhode Island shores.[34] A series of raids by colonial militia throughout the winter and spring culminated in a decisive and infamous attack in late May 1637. Soldiers surrounded a Pequot fort at Mystic in Connecticut and massacred hundreds of men, women, and children as they slept in their tents. Through June and the first half of July, the militia pursued the remaining tribesmen west along the Connecticut shore and finally caught up with them on the plain of Quinnipiack. There, on July 13, the soldiers, "guided by a Divine Providence, came upon them…hard by a most hideous swamp," Winthrop recounted. "Into this swamp they were all gotten."[35]

During the campaign, colonial officers sent Winthrop detailed letters describing their progress and the territory into which they had ventured. The land that impressed them most was Quinnipiack. "It is beyond my abilities for the present to resolve you which is best…about planting Pecot [Pequot territory]," wrote Israel Stoughton, a captain in the Massachusetts Bay militia, on August 9, "yet the providence of God guided us to so excellent a country at Quaillipioak [Quinnipiack] river… I am confident we have not the like in English possession as yet. It is too good for any but friends." A week later, in another letter to Winthrop, he again extolled his "providential discovery:" "If you would enlarge the state, and provide for the poor servants of Christ…I must speak my conscience. I confess the place whither God's providence carried us, that is to Quillipeage River, and so beyond to the Dutch, is before this, or the bay either, [the most abundant]."[36]

Stoughton himself arrived back at the Bay in late August. Having already raised expectations in his letters, he must have delivered an even more compelling description of Quinnipiack in person, for on August 31 Winthrop recorded that "Mr. Eaton, and some others of Mr. Davenport's company, went to view Quinepiack, with intent to begin a plantation there."[37] Davenport himself stayed behind to participate in the synod. As he grappled with the Antinomian crisis's "divisions and disorders," Eaton's scouting party traveled south, eager to spy out the land where their tribal enemy had fallen, a place discovered for them by the providence of God.

And the Lord spoke unto Moses, saying

*Send thou men out to search the land of Canaan which
I give unto the children of Israel: of every tribe of their
fathers shall ye send a man.*

*So Moses sent them to spy out the land of Canaan, and
said unto them, Go up this way toward the South, and go
up into the mountaines.*

*And they went and came to Moses and to Aaron and unto
all the congregation of the children of Israel, and showed
them the fruit of the land.*

*And they told him, and said, We came unto the land
whither thou hast sent us, and surely it floweth with milk
and honey.*

Numbers 13:2, 3, 18, 26, 28[38]

Although there is no record of what Eaton's party observed, they must have deemed Quinnipiack a land well suited for a new plantation. As John Underhill, an officer in the Pequot War, recorded in his narrative of the conflict, "that famous place called Queenapiok… hath a fair river, fit for harboring of ships, and abounds with rich and goodly meadows."[39]

Davenport and Eaton began planning their move in the fall and winter of 1637. The Antinomian crisis was reaching its end; the ministers had solidified their position during the three-week synod and, in November, Winthrop and the Colony Court brought Anne Hutchinson to trial. They convicted her and eighteen followers, sentencing those who would not recant to banishment from the Bay.[40] Cotton, meanwhile, began to have serious misgivings about his role in the crisis, fearing that he was partly responsible. He considered an invitation from Davenport and Eaton to join them in their move to Quinnipiack but, assured that he was still welcome in the Bay Colony, chose to remain.[41]

Davenport and Eaton waited until the spring of 1638 to undertake their removal, a delay likely occasioned in part by the harsh New England winter. On March 12, they wrote a letter to Winthrop and the Court giving notice of their decision to leave the Bay. "Our desire of staying within this patent was real and strong," they declared, "if the eye of God's providence (to whom we have committed our ways, especially in so important an enterprise as this) had guided us to a place convenient for our families and for our friends."[42] Although the Court had offered them any unclaimed land in the Bay, as well as parcels in several existing townships, they were not able to find a place adequate to their needs. Davenport and Eaton made it clear that they

desired a site by the water; as a company largely composed of merchants, they required access to the shipping trade. Quinnipiack offered them unoccupied territory possessing both fertile lands and a harbor and river suitable for commerce. They had other reasons to leave as well. Winthrop noted in his *Journal* that it was not only "the fruitfulness of that place [Quinnipiack]" that prompted them but also the "danger of a general governour [from England], who was feared to be sent this summer."[43] Striking out from the Bay was thus a second exile of sorts, as the company sought a haven from English rule even as it threatened to extend to their new homeland.

But, beyond these immediate considerations, they may have also been impelled by something more fundamental to their beliefs: the desire to begin anew and restore the communal order that had clearly been shaken in the Bay. They interpreted the divisions of the Antinomian crisis as a divine judgment on the colony's erring ways. The threat of an English governor would have only seemed to confirm that judgment. And while such dire omens had marked their stay in the Bay Colony, other more hopeful signs had disclosed to them a redemptive path. The destruction of their Pequot enemy and the consequent discovery, by "divine providence," of a fruitful land were no mere coincidence. For the Puritan steeped in biblical history and driven to re-create its model, these events conformed with a readily discernible pattern.[44] As Davenport and Eaton declared in their parting letter to Winthrop, they chose to be guided by "the good hand of the only wise God, whose prerogative it is to determine the bounds of our habitations according to the ends for which he hath brought us into these countries."[45] On the plain of Quinnipiack, they were to acknowledge the signs that God had set before them and establish, as "the bounds of [their] habitations," the perfect pattern of his eternal type.

THE ETERNAL TYPE

So many things that literally concerned the Jews were types and figures, signifying the like things concerning the people of God in these latter days.

John Davenport, *An Apologie of the Churches in New-England for Church Covenant*, 1638/39[46]

Perceiving the events of 1637 as a divine pattern fit into the Puritans' overarching self-conception. Their "Grand errand" was a reenactment of biblical history, an Exodus to the New World: persecuted in their homeland and exiled into the wilderness, they would be guided by the providential hand of God toward redemption in the Promised Land. He had ordained them as latter-day incarnations of the Israelite nation, they believed, chosen as a people to restore the true Christian church.[47]

This belief in a reenacting pattern was grounded in the Puritans' adherence to the theological doctrine of typology. Although in its strictest sense typology was a mode of exegesis connecting the Old and New Testaments, it also represented a more comprehensive view of human history and the intervention of divine will in its course. First developed by early Christian scholars in the time of the New Testament, typology fell out of common use in the Middle Ages but was resurrected by Protestant reformers in the sixteenth century. The Puritans adopted it with particular vehemence, understanding it to be fundamental to the primitive Christian church. In its interpretation of history, typological exegesis also permitted them to connect their own circumstances in postbiblical history with the events of the Bible itself.[48]

According to typological doctrine, the persons and events contained in the Old Testament are at once historical realities in themselves and also prophetic signs, or types, which foreshadow the persons and events of the New Testament. The New Testament figures are in turn antitypes, fulfilling the promise of the earlier types. Resemblance, in both their real qualities and spiritual meaning, establishes the connection between types and antitypes. Thus Moses is a type of Christ, signified, among other correspondences, by his role as a savior to his people.[49] Events and places are also types: the Exodus prefigures the Christian Baptism, as a form of salvation, and the Garden of Eden at the beginning of time prophesies the New Jerusalem at the end of time, each comprising a physical and spiritual sanctuary from worldly sin.

Connecting the Old and New Testaments typologically permitted the Puritans to present them as a single, unified narrative of God's unfolding plan for human redemption. The Old Testament was both an essential part of that plan and a shadow, or prophecy, of Christ's incarnation and life. Typology thus performs a delicate balancing act between the authority of the two narratives. It imbues Hebraic history with a direct relevance to Christian belief but also dictates that the coming of Christ supersedes the Old Law and "perfects" its meaning as divine truth.

The essential quality of the biblical type, however, is not its occurrence as a single event but rather its recurring incarnation over time. Each recurrence

exhibits a similar, though not identical, pattern that refers it both backward to its preceding type and forward to its successor and, ultimately, to its antitype. So not only is Moses a type of Christ but also Adam before him and Solomon after. As Davenport made clear in one of his Congregational tracts, the divine covenant itself conforms with such a recurring pattern, exhibiting the type's paradoxical qualities of permanence and renewal: "The Covenant was first given to Adam in Paradise after his fall, afterward to Abraham, then to the people of Israel under types and shadows, and again after the coming of Christ… yet none of these doth disanull the former because it is still the same Covenant though renewed upon new occasions."[50]

It is God, existing outside time, who directs the renewal of the type according to his redemptive plan. He mandates it as a fixed event within historical time as well as a recurring pattern, divine and eternal. In this respect, the type embodies both a cyclical and linear conception of time. The former and more ancient of the two understood events as part of a repetitive and unchanging pattern immanent in the world, an "eternal return" to origins through the cycle of life. The conception of time as a progression of events, each one contingent on its predecessor, superseded this understanding and shapes our modern view of progress. Indeed, it was introduced by the Judeo-Christian tradition, with its biblical narrative forming a progressive history beginning with Genesis and ending in the final judgment of Revelation.[51]

The type, both contingent and eternal, synthesizes the cycle and arrow of time. It has a fixed beginning and end in history; and yet within that frame it spirals back, overlapping the present with the past even as it foreshadows the future. Every incarnation both recalls its primal origins and anticipates its destruction and renewal in the succeeding type, awaiting ultimate fulfillment at the end of time. An engraving from Thomas Burnet's *Sacred Theory of the Earth* (1681), a widely read account by an English theologian of the earth's formation according to the Bible, cleverly illustrates this synthesis in one image: the recurring cycle of time, represented by the circling and symmetrical phases of the earth, is directed by God, the "alpha and omega" of human history (FIG. 24). In the broader theological sense, this conception of progress was related to the Christian belief in a predestined pattern of fall and redemption, a cycle of degeneration in sin and regeneration through purifying renewal. Davenport and his company considered their mission to restore the primitive church just such a renewing act, with New Haven designated as its typological exemplar.

Though Moses was as well a great Prophet as a great Prince, yet God left no part of the building of the Tabernacle to his prudence, but limited him in all things to the pattern in the Mount. Nor might Solomon, though the wisest of meer men, act by his own wisdom in building the Temple, but he was guided therein by the perfect pattern…so concerning Christian Churches. Christ hath given his People a perfect pattern, which he requireth the Ministers to hold forth distinctly in every point of it, to his people.

John Davenport, *The Power of Congregational Churches Asserted and Vindicated*, 1648[52]

The perfect pattern for the community of God's chosen resides in the type of the Temple. It could be found in various incarnations throughout the Old Testament: the Garden of Eden in Genesis, the encampment of the Israelites in the wilderness (FIG. 25), their holy cities in Canaan, Ezekiel's vision of the restored Temple, and the Temple of Solomon (often conflated, by virtue of its typological resemblance, with Ezekiel's Temple). The New Jerusalem or "City of God," envisioned by John in Revelation, was the antitype, fulfilling the prophecy of the Temple type at the end of time.[53] The Bible contains lengthy descriptions of all these places, noting in detail their form and dimensions. Using such descriptions, numerous sixteenth- and seventeenth-century religious scholars illustrated their treatises with reconstructed plans and views. One of the best known such works is the reconstruction of the Temples of Ezekiel and Solomon (published in 1596 and 1604) by the Spanish Jesuit scholars Villalpando and Prado (FIG. 26).

The spiritual meaning of the Temple, as with all the biblical types, referred ultimately to Christ. Davenport, following Puritan doctrine, interpreted it as a "Reall type" of the savior, analogous to the body of Christ.[54] The type's temporal or earthly significance, meanwhile, derived from its status as a sanctified realm: it was "the place where God dwells." The final verse of Ezekiel conveyed the same when God, having set out the pattern of the Temple and city, declared its name to be "The Lord is There."

Protestant theological tracts produced in the early to mid-seventeenth century sought to establish the basic figural pattern underlying the recurring type. Joseph Mede, an Anglican scholar whose work influenced greatly the first generation of New England ministers, wrote his *Clavis Apocalyptica* (first published in 1627) as an attempt to unlock the mil-

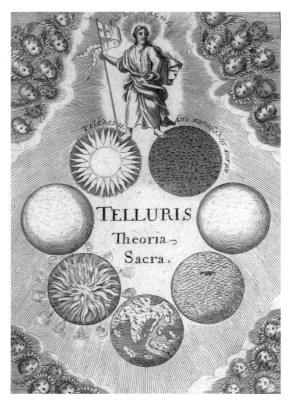

FIG. 24 *"Sacred Theory of the Earth," 1681. From Thomas Burnet,* Telluris Theoria Sacra.

lennial prophecies in the Book of Revelation.[55] In it, he argued for the correspondence of John's vision of the New Jerusalem with the Temple types of the Old Testament, beginning with the Israelites:

The Apocalyptick Theatre of the Church described [is] exactly framed according to the form of that ancient encamping of God with Israel in the wilderness…the throne answereth to the Tabernacle or Temple; the elders to the Levites and Priests; the four Beasts to the four camps of Israel; that is, the whole session [is] the type of the ancient encamping in the wilderness.

He saw the same resemblance in the Temple of Ezekiel. "The court of the Temple [of Revelation is] to be measured by the reed of God, setting forth the Primitive state of the Christian Church and exactly comformable to the rule of God's word," he noted. "Such a measure was propounded in the type, also, of an Angel measuring in *Ezekiel*, chap. 43: 'But thou sonne of man, show the Temple to the house of Israel, that they may be ashamed for their iniquities, and let them measure the pattern.'"[56]

Many Puritan scholars took up the argument for a common typological pattern. One of them, John Lightfoote, devoted a whole tract to the type in *The Temple* (1650). He analyzed biblical descriptions to arrive at the basic geometric order of concentric squares that underlay all of its various incarnations:

FIG. 25 *Juan Bautista Villalpando, "Encampment of the Israelites," 1596. Courtesy Colegio Oficial de Arquitectos de Madrid (COAM).*

There is intimation enough in Ezekiel, that the four living Creatures stood square; but in the Revelation it is yet more plaine, for there it is said the four living Creatures stood round about the Throne, which could not be but in a quadrature...The Throne then meaning the Temple as was showed before, this double quadrature about it doth call us to remember the double camp that pitched about the Tabernacle upon the four sides of it when the Lord did first platforme and order the incamping of Israel in the Wilderness. He pitched his owne Tabernacle in the middle, as that being the very Center, heart, and life of the Congregation...The outmost of all, in four main bodies on the four sides of the Tabernacle did the whole Congregation pitch...and so there were two quadratures, the Sanctuary and the Congregation.[57]

This double quadrature formed the eternal figure of the type. The tabernacle — God's throne — sat at the center of a four-square court or sanctuary, and about it the congregation — God's community — gathered, bounded as well by the geometry of the square. The whole comprised the Temple, united by covenant as a body both earthly and spiritual. Its precise dimensions and disposition varied in the type's incarnations through time, but the underlying

FIG. 26 *Juan Bautista Villalpando, "Plan of the Temple of Solomon," 1604. Courtesy Colegio Oficial de Arquitectos de Madrid (COAM).*

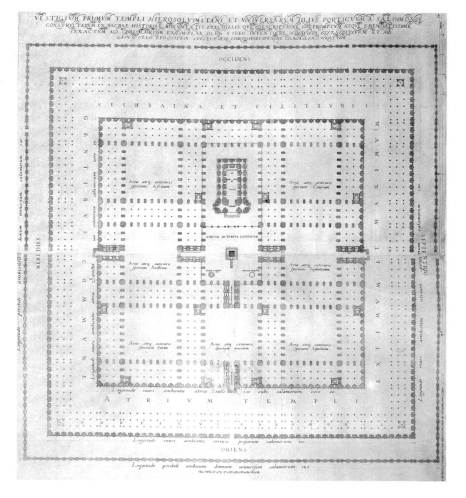

communal order of the double square—sanctuary and congregation—remained fixed as the eternal pattern. This can be seen clearly in comparing just two reconstructions from the early seventeenth century: Villalpando's illustration of the plan of the Temple of Solomon (see FIG. 26) and Mede's illustration of the court of the Temple from Revelation in his *Clavis Apocalyptica* (FIG. 27). Lightfoote acknowledged the paradoxical nature of the type as a form fixed in eternity but changing through time, remarking that "the Temple, though it were of a heavenly resemblance, use and concernment...yet being but an earthly building it was subject to the universall condition of earthly things, casualty [*sic*] and changing."[58]

Davenport and Cotton, immersed in this scholarly tradition, considered the Temple type to be the ordained pattern of the primitive church, not only relevant but indeed essential to the Puritan mission. "Whatsoever Ordinance of the Old Testament is not repealed in the New Testament...but was of moral and perpetual equity," Davenport wrote in 1638, "the same binds us in these days." The Temple possessed such equity and, in this respect, took on a symbolic

as well as typological significance: its moral equity resided in its role as an exemplar to be followed by the reforming Christian community.[59]

More to the point, it expressed the Congregational frame that the Puritans wished to restore. As Cotton had argued for the model of the "primitive apostolick church" in his exposition of Canticles, so he identified the type of the Temple with the primitive Hebraic congregation. While the New Jerusalem of Revelation "is a perfect pattern of a pure church," he wrote in 1643, "Ezekiel speaketh of the dimensions of any ordinary Jewish church of one congregation."[60] Thus the pattern of the Congregational church—the enclosed garden in the wilderness—lay in the divine prescription delivered by Ezekiel and perfected in the vision of John. Davenport was to state this even more explicitly in a tract from 1648. Here he distinguished the form of the congregation from the parish church of Anglican practice by virtue of its correspondence to the Temple type:

The Parish frame, as it was wont to joyn all the inhabitants within such a praecinct into one Church...is meerly humane, not being measured by the Golden Reed, which is the Church-measure, but by the Court-measure. [But] the Congregational frame of a Christian Church is no humane invention. That Members so qualified as Christ requireth should ordinarily meet together in one Congregation is the Ordinance of Christ, and according to the measure of the golden Reed, whereby the City and Gates, and the dimensions of the New Jerusalem are measured.[61]

His assertion established clearly both the origin of New Haven's nine-square plan and its meaning as a form: to restore the pattern of the Temple and signify the colony's intended role as an exemplar of the Congregational Way.

———

Behold, a King shall reign in justice and the princes shall rule in judgment

And that man shall be as an hiding place from the wind, and as a refuge from the tempest: as rivers of water in a dry place, and as the shadow of a great rock in a weary land.

And my people shall dwell in the tabernacle of peace and in sure dwellings, and in safe resting places

When it haileth, it shall fall on the forest, and the city shall be set in the low place.

Isaiah 32:1–2, 18–19

Although the Congregational polity formed the basis of every Puritan township, only in New Haven was it to be rendered as a figural type. The reason for this most likely arose from the biblical type's incarnation as a historical event, always tied to a

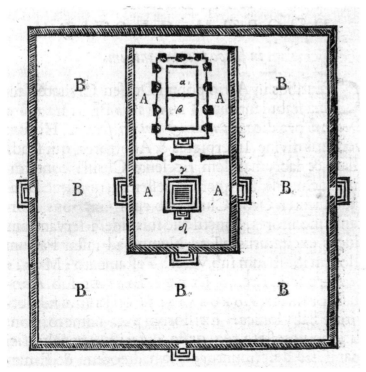

FIG. 27 *"Plan of the New Jerusalem of Revelation," 1627. From Joseph Mede*, Clavis Apocalyptica.

FIG. 28 *"New Haven, View from East Rock," 1872.*

Jehovah, speaking from the fiery mount of Sinai, had entered into covenant with the Israelites and decreed the pattern of their encampment. Later, he was to order Moses to ascend Mount Pisgah, above the plain of Moab, to view the Promised Land before striking him dead. The type repeated again with the Israelites' final settlement in Canaan; by divine ordinance they set out their four-square cities on the Jericho plain, overlooked by Mount Zion and divided by the River Jordan. So too did the sacred landscape accompany the visions of Ezekiel and John. An angel of God brought each to a "great and high mountain." Ezekiel was shown, spread out below him, "the building of a city, towards the South," and John bore witness to "the great city, holy Jerusalem, descending out of heaven from God."[62] It seems certain that New Haven's founders recognized the striking resemblance between their chosen place of settlement and this recurring scriptural landscape. If so, they could only have taken it as a providential sign; as Perry Miller observed, their doctrine of divine providence dictated that "in the face of every experience [the Puritan] was obliged to ask himself, What does this signify? What is God saying to me at this moment?"[63]

In the plan of their "holy city," the colonists answered God's call, visibly acknowledging the sacred landscape as the place of his covenanted elect. They laid out a compact square, half a mile long on its side, close by the harbor and nestled between two bending creeks (see FIG. 20). Even this placement between two creeks made reference to the Temple type; Joseph Mede, in comparing its incarnations, had noted that "new Jerusalem followeth Paradise, which having the tree of life in the middle, like Eden, a river doth environ on this side and that side"[64] (FIG. 30). Four intersecting streets divided the square's expanse, and four bounded its perimeter. These formed nine perfect, equal blocks, each measuring fifty-two rods, or 858 feet, on a side.[65] The settlers left open the inner central square as "common and undivided land," the communal sanctuary of the congregation. They designated the blocks around it as "quarters," which in turn were divided into "houselots" and assigned to, as well as named after, the appointed leaders of the colony.[66]

Both the concentric geometry and the method of assigning blocks by "tribe" were unique to New Haven. The typical Puritan township, while often nucleated, was loosely organized with little hierarchy of land divisions.[67] The precedent for such an order could be found not in previous New England plantations but in the Old Testament. There, in

specific time and place, as determined by the guiding hand of God. If the New Haven colonists had interpreted the confluence of events preceding their move as evidence of his will, then the description that Eaton's party brought back of their future home would have only confirmed those providential signs.

As Eaton viewed the plain of Quinnipiack, he was met with a sight that, to the discerning Puritan eye, clearly recalled a setting of biblical significance: the recurring sacred landscape where God had instituted the Temple type. To the north a ring of hills enclosed a low, broad plain, bordered on the south by the "inland sea" of Long Island Sound and run through with the snaking Quinnipiack River. Overlooking it all was the red mountain of East Rock, rising up and facing out on the great harbor that Davenport and Eaton had been seeking for their new colony (FIG. 28).

The figure of the rock presiding over the low plain called forth the type of God's holy mount, as it was to appear repeatedly in the Old and New Testaments (FIG. 29). It was on the Horeb plain that

Numbers, God decreed to the Israelites that "every man of the children of Israel shall camp by his standard, and under the ensign of their father's house; far off about the Tabernacle of the Congregation shall they pitch." Even the location of Davenport's and Eaton's houselots, to the east of the central common, conformed to this prescription: "Those that encamp before the tabernacle toward the east...*shall be* Moses and Aaron, keeping the charge of the sanctuary."[68]

Between the nine-square plan and the harbor, the colonists laid out what they called the "suburbs," a block and a half of tightly packed houselots bordering the creeks as they let out into the sea. The conscious distinction between the "city" proper— contained within the nine squares—and its outskirts was also unprecedented in Puritan town planning. But, once again, the model could be found in the Bible: for the Israelite cities of Canaan, God ordered that "the suburbs [shall be] from the wall of the city outward." Following that same commandment, the settlers arranged their agricultural fields, or "townlots," in a radial pattern, extending out from the "wall" of their nine-square city and divided into sections assigned to each of the quarters.[69]

Thus the nine-square plan formed the double quadrature of the Temple type, with its central sanctuary and surrounding congregation. Even the tripartite division of the outermost square into quarters had sacred significance. The sum of their outer sides numbered twelve, a figure that John Cotton considered essential to the primitive Congregational pattern. "The *Holy Ghost* leads us by the hand to consider," he wrote, "the whole Fabrick

of *Jerusalem* is 12, the foundation of the number is Apostolicall, it is numbered by 12 and multiplyed by 12. It ariseth still but to Apostolicall simplicity... [that] when you have summed it up to the highest, their Laws and Orders that they set up, you shall find 12 there, and you shall finde no more."[70]

In the fall of 1639, the colonists were to complete the pattern with the building of a wooden meeting-house. Located in the center of the common and measuring fifty-feet square, it re-created the construction of the Israelite tabernacle in its placement, materials, and even size.[71] Its single door faced east and so shared with the Temple of Ezekiel "the glory of the Lord [which] came into the house by the way of the gate, whose prospect is toward the East."[72] Marking the physical and spiritual center of town and congregation, the meetinghouse stood watch as a shepherd over God's flock as they gathered about the sanctuary. Compact within the half-mile limits of its nine-square plan, the congregation of New Haven rendered visible their covenant with God and with each other, planted as a garden enclosed before the fiery rock in the wilderness.

FALL AND REDEMPTION

It is the common Faith, wherein every Believer hath his interest in common with the rest; as all Planters or Inhabitants have in the Commons that belong to a Town, for which they will contend with any man that shall wrong them in that their interest.

John Davenport, *The Saints Anchor-Hold*, 1661[73]

The efforts of New Haven's founders to restore the "heavenly rules and patterns" of the primitive church

FIG. 29 *"East Rock and Meadows,"* 1872.

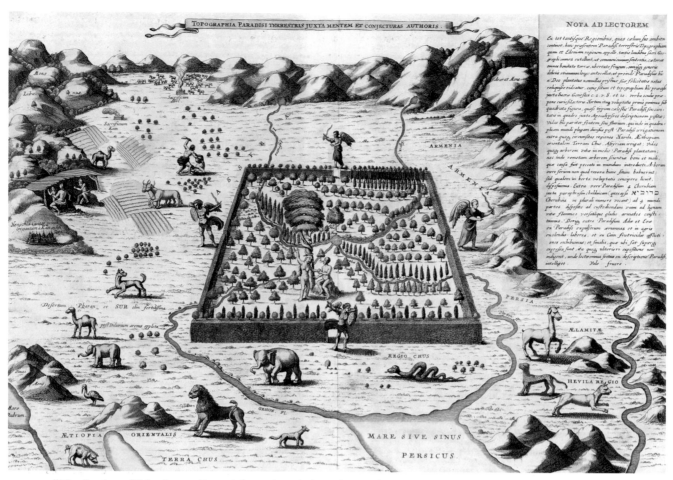

FIG. 30 *"The Garden of Eden," 1675. From Athanasius Kircher,* El Arca de Noe.

did not end with the plan of their town. The civil and ecclesiastical governments they established adhered more strictly to "the worde of God" than those of any other colony; as the settlers declared in their "foundamentall" meeting of June 4, 1639, the rule of Scripture "shall be the onely rule to be attended unto in ordering the affayres of government in this plantation." They restricted civil magistracy to church members only and required public testimony as a prerequisite for membership in the church of the visible elect. These were measures propounded by John Cotton for the Bay Colony, but only in New Haven were they adopted as a matter of course.[74] The Colony's constitution as a pure Bible commonwealth, physically embodied in the nine-square plan, ratified New Haven's self-conceived role as the redemptive inheritor of Puritan ideals.[75]

Davenport and his fellow founders sought one remaining element of that redemption: the establishment of a college. It was an endeavor essential to upholding and perpetuating the pure faith of the primitive ordinances. Yet despite repeated efforts during the colony's brief life as an independent body, they managed only to plant the seed of such a vision, never bringing it to fruition.

In 1647, having secured a measure of stability for their town, the Colony Court broached for the first time the idea of forming a college, "which they dissire maye bee set up so soone as their abillitie will reach thereunto."[76] Nothing came of this initial desire, however, and eight years passed before the Court considered it again. This time Theophilus Eaton, the governor, raised the prospect, prompted by changes at Harvard College in Massachusetts Bay. The New Haven Colony had more than a passing affiliation with the Cambridge college; preparations leading up to Harvard's formal opening in 1638 had coincided with the New Haven company's stay in the Bay Colony, and Davenport served as one of its first overseers. Since the colonists had settled in Quinnipiack, they regularly supported the institution with contributions of corn. But in

1654, Harvard underwent a change in leadership that, in the eyes of New Haven, signaled a threat to the teaching of the pure faith.[77] So they resurrected their plan for a college of their own, raised money, and mustered surrounding townships to the cause. But, as with the first attempt, they failed to build upon this initial impetus. In 1660, Davenport raised the issue again, this time instigated by a bequest of money from Edward Hopkins, a Connecticut colonist then living in London who intended it to help fund a school or college in New Haven. Davenport even chose a site — "Mrs. Eldreds lott," on the north side of the Green facing directly onto the center meetinghouse — but, once again, the colony did not follow through.[78]

In all of these attempts, New Haven seemed to lack the necessary money and resources to match its will and desire. It was a shortcoming caused, at least in part, by the economic struggles it endured during its brief existence as an independent colony. Despite the settlers' initial wealth, repeated setbacks in their efforts to establish a mercantile trade drained money and distracted attention from the collegiate campaign.[79] As it was, their independence was coming to an end by the 1660s; although Davenport tried to resurrect the college plan once again in 1664, an ominous turn of events had already taken place that was to seal New Haven's fate. In 1662, the Connecticut Colony, centered in Hartford, obtained a charter from England that included the territory belonging to the New Haven Colony, effectively annexing it to Connecticut. Having no prior knowledge and giving no approval of the act, New Haven, and especially Davenport, bitterly resisted the union. Many of its surrounding townships acceded, however, and New Haven found it increasingly difficult to support itself

as an independent community. In 1665, it submitted to the rule of Connecticut and abandoned its cherished autonomy.[80]

Davenport, newly subject to Hartford's less orthodox religious ways and no longer free to pursue his own vision, chose to return to the starting point of his New England mission. In 1667, he moved back to Boston, taking up the position of minister in its First Church, where his colleague John Cotton had presided until his death in 1652. Having heeded Cotton's call in 1635 to join him in "the New Heaven and New Earth" of New England, Davenport was to join him once again upon his death in 1670; at his request, he was buried with his friend and fellow divine. "Cotton and Davenport are together in heaven," wrote Cotton Mather in his biography of the New Haven minister, "as their bodies are now in one tomb on earth."[81]

Davenport's dream for a New Haven college, broken in the demise of his colony, was to be redeemed in time by his grandson-in-law, James Pierpont. In 1684, Pierpont made his home beside the Green, on the lot Davenport had chosen for the school in 1660, and took up the pulpit of the First Congregational Church. Beginning in 1701, he led a renewed effort to found a second New England college, this time finding success.[82] By 1717, the School of the Churches took its place beside the sanctuary of the Green, facing east to the meetinghouse of the congregation. In the world of the Puritan, it could only have been an act of divine providence; ordered in the types of Davenport and Pierpont, the redemptive pattern disclosed itself in the founding of Yale as surely as it did in the colony of New Haven. The promise of one "glorious publick design" found fulfillment in the other, restored in the spiral of time.[83]

Cultivating Types:
The Rise & Fall of the Brick Row

ERIK VOGT

Yale has a religion. The solution of the greatest problems is not sought, it is regarded as already discovered. The work of education is to instill these revealed principles and to form habits congruous with them. Everything is arranged to produce a certain type of man…There is sometimes a beautiful simplicity and completeness in the type which this ideal produces.

George Santayana, "A Glimpse of Yale," 1892[1]

HALL, CHAPEL, AND YARD

It may well have been a building that finally decided the location of Yale College in New Haven. In 1701 ten Congregational ministers—led by James Pierpont, successor to John Davenport's pulpit in New Haven—founded "a Collegiate School" in Saybrook, Connecticut. The site was a convenient compromise in distance between the Connecticut River towns, led by Hartford, and the Long Island shore towns, dominated by New London to the east and New Haven to the west. By 1716, quarreling among the minister trustees threatened the struggling school's survival, and the question arose of moving it to a more advantageous location. Split by local loyalties, they could not decide whether to stay in Saybrook or relocate to Hartford or New Haven, once separate colonies but now united as co-capitals of Connecticut.

After many acrimonious discussions, the trustees from New Haven took matters into their own hands: in September 1717 they sponsored the annual college commencement in the meetinghouse on the New Haven Green. Its success must have encouraged them because, two weeks later, they arranged to purchase a one-and-a-quarter-acre lot at the corner of present-day College and Chapel Streets, to build a new college house. New Haven's First Congrega-

tional Church, headed by Pierpont, conveyed the land to them, a gesture that expressed at the start the close relationship among town, church, and college.

On October 8, the New Haven trustees began construction of the college building. Their colleagues who still opposed the move protested to the Connecticut General Assembly, which ordered the ministers to meet in New Haven to resolve the issue. They again failed to come to an agreement, but the sights and sounds of construction a few hundred yards from their meeting place must have lent a sense of finality to the issue that no words could equal. On October 28, the Assembly issued a proclamation confirming the removal of the college to New Haven. The building had served its first purpose even before it was completed.[2]

———

We are in hopes of having shortly perfected our Splendid Collegiate House…We behold its fair Aspect in the Market-place of New-haven, mounted in an Eminent place thereof…all in a little time to be Splendidly compleated.

Letter from the Collegiate School Trustees to Jeremiah Dummer, English agent to the Connecticut Colony, October 31, 1717[3]

The site of the Collegiate House (it would be renamed the Yale College House in 1718[4]) was indeed eminent. New Haven's Green, or Market-place as the settlers had named it, sloped up dramatically from east to west.[5] The land leveled off west of the Green, and it was here—on a shelf overlooking the descending common—that the new building perched, facing east to the meetinghouse below (see FIG. 2). It was thus prominently displayed, especially to visitors and townsfolk who arrived from the east by highway or harbor. Yale was to exploit this "fair Aspect" to its fullest in later years.

FIG. 31 *Fence-sitting and the Brick Row from Chapel Street in 1872.*

The trustees' letter indicates that the building took less than a month to complete. Most likely constructed in a method similar to barn raising, it was little more than a wooden barracks (FIG. 32). Although decidedly domestic in character, resembling a colonial inn-house, it was extraordinarily long and narrow, only twenty-one feet wide but stretching out over 170 feet in length. As with the houses of its day, it pressed up close to the street. The plan, reflected in the ordered and repetitive facade, resembled three large central-hall houses joined side by side. Square student rooms flanked stair entries; and the library and recitation hall, located closest to the street corner, differed from the private chambers only in their greater length.[6]

An engraving of the College House from about 1745 compressed its length in an oblique side view and dignified it by enlarging the cupola and adding a nonexistent clock.[7] In doing so the view hinted at a probable model for the building: Harvard's Stoughton Hall, built in 1698. Based on an English dormitory precedent, Stoughton—the middle building in a view of 1726 (FIG. 33)—was also a simple gabled volume, one-room wide and served by lateral stair halls. Yale, founded by ministers who had graduated from Harvard, would naturally have taken a cue from the Cambridge institution. Established in

1638, it was the only other college in New England and thus an obvious model for the fledgling New Haven school.[8] Most remarkable, however, was the way that Yale's building deviated from the Harvard model in its astonishing length. It seems certain that this was, at least in part, a response to its site alongside the enormous Green, which measured over 850 feet on a side. Much as the square geometry and pyramidal roof of the meetinghouse pinned the center of the Green physically and symbolically, the stretched, taut volume of the College House held its edge; each in its own way emphasized the clarity of its form. This was the first of many times that New Haven's great communal meeting ground was to make its presence felt and inflect the course of Yale's campus building.

———

The college progressed steadily if modestly over the next twenty years; while only five students graduated in 1717, twenty-four did so in 1737. The relative calm was shaken, however, with the advent of the Great Awakening in 1740. This movement toward a more emotional and populist strain of Puritanism quickly gained popularity in the New England towns, dividing the Congregational Church between the established order, or Old Lights, and the New Lights of the Awakening. The split affected all of New England's

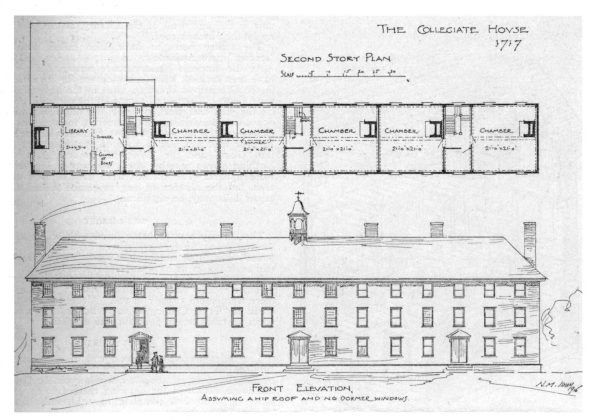

FIG. 32 *Yale College House: reconstruction of the plan and elevation.*

FIG. 33 *Harvard College in 1726. From left to right: Harvard Hall, Stoughton Hall, and Massachusetts Hall.*

FIG. 34 *Connecticut Hall in 1906: east (College Street) facade, with Vanderbilt Hall on the left.*

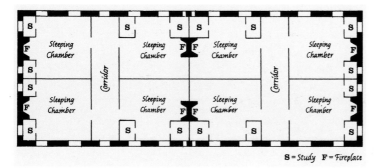

FIG. 35 *Connecticut Hall: plan of the ground floor, after a drawing by John Trumbull.*

institutions, not least Yale, which was to manifest it even in the character of its campus.[9]

The year 1740 also marked the beginning of the Reverend Thomas Clap's long and tumultuous reign as rector of the college (a title soon to be changed to president). Religiously conservative and aggressively autocratic, he gained few allies during his tenure but was effective in imposing his will on the institution. One of the college's most pressing needs was to provide housing on campus grounds for the growing student body, a measure intended to shield them from the corrupting temptations of town life. In 1747 Clap proposed building a new dormitory; as he later recorded in his *Annals or History of Yale College* of 1766, "the number of students being about one hundred and twenty, more than half of them were obliging, for want of room, to live out of the College; which was upon many accounts inconvenient. The President therefore projected a Scheme for building a new College House."[10]

The president's "Scheme" was not entirely his own invention. Clap wrote to President Holyoke of Harvard requesting information about Massachusetts Hall, a dormitory that the college had built in 1720 (see FIG. 33, on the right). Holyoke replied in a six-page letter, accompanied by plans that detailed the hall's construction and suggested minor improvements.[11] Clap followed his specifications closely, and Yale's new building (FIG. 34) varied only slightly from Harvard's model. It was named Connecticut Hall in recognition of the General Assembly's financial assistance. Clap described it upon its completion in 1752, two years after laying the foundation stone: "It is 100 feet long, 40 feet wide, and three story high…containing 32 chambers and 64 studies. It took about 230,000 bricks."[12] The plan type was similar to Yale's first College House, with lateral stair halls separating the student chambers, but now the rooms were doubled across the width, bringing the building's proportions back into line with the more conventional dormitory model (FIG. 35).

Clap placed the hall well back on the lot, behind and to the north of the first College House. The siting was part of a larger plan for campus growth, which he described in his *Annals*:

[*The new College House*] *makes a good appearance, and was set back in the Yard that there might be a large and handsome area before it, and toward the north side of the Yard, with a view that when the old College should come down, another College or Chapel or both should be set on the south of the present House; and additional lands were purchased on the north and on the west for better accommodation.*[13]

By setting the hall back and creating the "handsome" yard in front, Clap gave it a grander, more dignified presence. The placement also partook of a tradition of building and lot arrangement that was becoming common on New Haven's nine square blocks, whose enormous size meant that many of the lots were quite deep. Houses built from the mid-eighteenth century on began to take advantage of this, stepping back from the street to create spacious fenced forecourts, often planted as gardens with trees and shrubs. At least one contemporary observer saw the parallel with such a domestic arrangement; an anonymous eighteenth-century needlepoint depicted Connecticut Hall in an embellished landscape, fronted by a fenced Eden of flowers and trees.[14]

Clap had another reason for creating the yard, one related to the life of the college rather than its appearance. Shepherding the flock within the campus bounds was his paramount concern, as the construction of a college chapel in 1761 more fully revealed. Since Yale had moved to New Haven, its trustees—now constituted as a Corporation—had agreed that the students would attend all services at the First Congregational Church, in the meetinghouse on the Green. College and town shared a mutual bond: the church was entrusted with the students' spiritual guidance, and the students in turn fortified the congregational body of the town. The Great Awakening changed all that. During the confrontation between the Old and New Lights in the 1740s, Clap had initially supported the Reverend Joseph Noyes (B.A. 1709), the First Church's minister and a Yale Corporation member. By the 1750s, however, Clap signaled a retreat from the Old Lights and First Church. In 1755 he created the Livingston Professorship of Divinity and proposed that the students begin worshipping within the college rather than in the First Church. He also openly questioned the orthodoxy of Noyes's faith and began courting New Haven's New Light congregation. The reasons for his change of heart were never made clear, but it is apparent that Clap's inherent need for control, along with a disdain for Noyes's weak ministering, helped to set him on a path of defiance. Events came to a head in 1757 when the Corporation, bitterly divided, nevertheless approved the establishment of a church within the college, the first of its kind in America.[15]

Clap marked his newfound religious affinity in the building type that he chose for the new college chapel. In 1757, the First Congregational Church had replaced its seventeenth-century wooden meetinghouse with a much larger brick one. It was a rectangular gabled volume, its long side forming its front, with a brick steeple and wooden spire appended to the north-facing gable end (see FIG. 47). It was the latest model, as it were, in meetinghouses and was to be used by congregations throughout New England in coming years, including New Haven's Fair Haven Society Church of 1770, just to the north of the First Church.[16] The Yale chapel, completed in 1763, took a different tack. Turning ninety degrees, it fronted the yard and the New Haven Green beyond with its gable end and attached steeple (FIG. 36). In this orientation, it resembled not the First Church but the White Haven Society Church, belonging to the New Light congregation that Clap had been wooing for several years. Built in 1748, the White Haven meetinghouse faced the Green diagonally across from Yale, presenting its short steepled side toward the street, just as the chapel was to do (see FIG. 47). At a time when religious building types were as nuanced in their differences as the congregations they sheltered, the chapel's about-face could easily be taken as a further sign of Yale's defection from the church that had shepherded its move to New Haven forty years earlier.

The new chapel fell into line, literally and figuratively, with Clap's larger plan of campus growth. "It is set near the south end of the brick College," he wrote, "with a view that when another College is built, it will be set near the south side of the Chapel."[17] It was a puritanical brick box, forty feet wide by fifty feet long, with a double-height, galleried first floor for religious and academic services and a second story above housing the library. Pulling these functions out of Connecticut Hall began the process of segregating the college's public and private uses into separate buildings. The iconic types of chapel and hall expressed a sacred and secular split as well. The chapel was solid and upright, like the Puritan minister himself, while Connecticut Hall, punctuated by its many close-set windows, seemed to overflow with student energy. The future repetition of the two types, in what would come to be known as the Brick Row, only heightened this contrast.[18]

Although the building of the chapel constituted a real and symbolic break with the First Congregational Church, it did not sever the bond between town and college. Clap noted in his *Annals,* shortly after the chapel's completion, that "some gentlemen in New Haven have generously subscribed considerable towards erecting a spire upon it, for an ornament to the town, as well as the Chapel." The contribution suggested that New Haven's citizens regarded Yale's appearance and character as

inseparable from that of their town. They were to strengthen that connection twenty years later when the town renamed the two streets that formed the campus corner Chapel and College after the Yale buildings adjoining them.[19]

The creation of a college congregation and chapel made it clear that Clap intended to control the students' hearts, minds, and souls. He expressed this not only in the buildings but also in the college yard that fronted them. The great flaw of the original College House of 1717 was its proximity to the street. Students, merely upon crossing its threshold, could enter into the life of the town and fall prey to its temptations and distractions. Now, with a forecourt enclosed on three outer sides by a wood fence and on its fourth by the hall and chapel, they stepped from their rooms or classes into a protected realm, a sanctuary guarded under the minister's watchful eye. Clap codified behavior in the college yard with an elaborate set of rules and fines governing noise, conduct, and etiquette. The fence itself established a real and symbolic boundary between town and college; students who trespassed beyond its limits jeopardized their good standing. Within, the campus was to be a peaceable kingdom, a gathering place of pious repose where students were to conduct themselves with restraint and dignity. Reality, however, often fell short of this ideal. The strict regulations rarely contained the restless and sometimes rebel-

lious students, and Clap's autocratic style eventually turned them against him. Having already alienated half the Corporation, the congregation of New Haven's leading church, and many members of the General Assembly in the divisive battle to establish a college church, Clap retained few allies outside the school. By 1766, with students threatening open revolt, he finally resigned. Nonetheless, his built legacy long survived his ignominious exit. During his rule he had set in place the three elements—hall, chapel, and yard—that were to order Yale's campus for the next hundred years.

A PLAN FOR A UNIVERSITY

The minister who eventually took up Clap's legacy had belonged to his flock. Ezra Stiles (1726–1795) had been a student at Yale in the 1740s (B.A. 1746) and a tutor from 1749 to 1755. And although he was one of the few who had befriended Clap, his own temperament was very different. Tolerant and open-minded, Stiles had a voracious appetite for knowledge and indulged a wide array of interests. By the time of his death, he was widely considered the most learned man in America. Although influenced by Enlightenment thought, he was also a Puritan of New England. Caught between his religious faith and empirical bent, he struggled for a good part of his life to reconcile his engagement in the natural sciences with the received wisdom of divine revelation.

Nevertheless, the effort made him particularly suited to the task of leading a Puritan college in the late eighteenth century.[20]

In 1755, Stiles left his tutoring position at Yale to become minister of the Second Congregational Church in Newport, Rhode Island. He remained there for over twenty years, faithfully attending to his religious duties but also partaking of the prosperous seaport's cosmopolitan life. The start of the Revolutionary War interrupted this comfortable routine. When English ships threatened Newport with bombardment in 1776, many, including Stiles, chose to evacuate. He resettled temporarily in Portsmouth, New Hampshire, hoping to return soon to his home and congregation. But those plans changed when, in September 1777, he received word that the Yale Corporation had offered him the college presidency. Naphtali Daggett (B.A. 1748), the Livingston Professor of Divinity and college minister who had been serving as president *pro tempore* since Clap's resignation eleven years earlier, was stepping down, and Yale needed a strong leader to see it through the crisis of the war. Stiles was the ideal choice: a Connecticut native and Yale-educated minister in good standing. Equally important, his vast erudition and commitment to learning were essential to a college that aspired to greatness.

Stiles deliberated his response for several months. In November, he visited New Haven and met with the Corporation to discuss Yale's present state and future prospects. Although still undecided, he produced two important plans for the college as a result of the visit. The first, titled "Plan of a University" and drafted in December, was an ambitious program of academic expansion, outlining the additional areas of study that he felt were necessary to transform the college into a true university.[21] Stiles's other plan, although far more schematic, established a physical framework for his academic program. It was a sketch, hastily produced, that depicted not only the college's existing buildings and grounds but also new buildings, organized to yield a unified campus plan: a proto-master plan, as it were (FIG. 37). Undated, it was drawn on the envelope of the letter that Stiles had received in Portsmouth informing him of his nomination to Yale's presidency.[22]

In the upper center of the drawing, Stiles depicted Yale's grounds as a complete rectangle. To the left he showed the corners of the adjoining blocks on Chapel and College Streets, with the Yale president's house—including its floor plan and fence gate—fronting College Street. At the far lower right he drew the square of New Haven's First Church in the center of the open Green. Within the Yale rectangle, Stiles located the chapel in the center and, to its right, a schematic floor plan of Connecticut Hall, showing student rooms with the figure "70" just above, apparently a count of the students residing there.[23] On the campus edge facing the Green he drew the original College House, still in use. He exaggerated its long proportions and left its northern end open, perhaps a graphic notation of its state of disrepair and likely removal in the near future.[24]

Stiles drew additional forms to represent his design for an enlarged campus. To the left or south side of the chapel, he dotted in a dormitory hall, also annotated with the figure "70." This addition fell in line with Clap's vision, balancing Connecticut Hall to the north. Perhaps inspired by the symmetrical hall-chapel-hall composition thus produced, Stiles then made his most remarkable conceptual leap: he drew in two additional halls at right angles, flanking the college yard at both ends. The result extended the symmetry of halls and chapel around the yard, forming a great three-sided court with the steepled chapel marking the centerline (FIG. 38).

The open-ended court had a precedent at Harvard, where its three halls formed a small yard adjoining the street (see FIG. 33). Although Stiles may have had such a model in mind—and he certainly knew the Cambridge campus—his conception had much more power. It substituted for Harvard's *ad hoc* arrangement a formal clarity and symmetry that made the whole greater than the sum of its parts. What held the greatest implication for Yale, however, was its closed unity. By replacing the college yard's picket fence with the enclosure of the flanking halls, Stiles contained and completed the campus. As such, it seemed to withdraw somewhat from the Green, the presiding chapel less of "an ornament to the town" as the new halls folded it in their embrace. This turn inward was to resonate some years later, when Stiles was finally able to initiate his "Plan of a University."

———

Stiles accepted Yale's offer in March 1778. He had to forestall any expansion plans, however, because of the ongoing war with England; simply keeping Yale open occupied all his time. But even after the American victory he faced discouraging problems. A postwar recession, which hit New England especially hard, made it difficult to put the college on a solid financial footing. Compounding this setback, Yale's role as a ministerial school was decidedly unpopular at the time. The New Divinity movement, a highly intellectualized brand of Puritanism that had swept

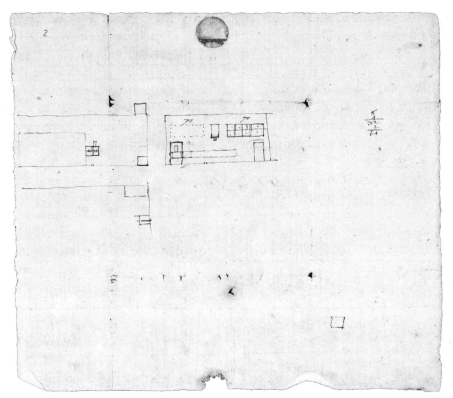

FIG. 37 *Ezra Stiles, "Plan for Yale College," 1777.*

over the Connecticut ministry in the 1770s, was alienating many congregation members, and the resulting backlash made the college a target of resentment. In addition, the influence of European Enlightenment ideals was causing widespread distrust of the church in general and Yale in particular.[25]

The public's anticlericalism worsened the college's already damaged relationship with the Connecticut General Assembly. Influenced by popular sentiment, the legislators offered much-needed financial assistance only on the condition that the Corporation include state-appointed laymen among its members. The minister trustees refused to comply, seeing it as an unacceptable incursion on their autonomy. This stalemate lasted until the spring of 1791, when the Assembly, again pressured by public suspicion, authorized a committee to review and report on the physical, curricular, and financial condition of the college. The Corporation feared the worst: the state

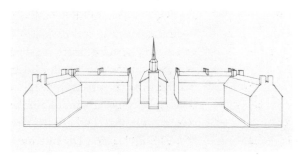

FIG. 38 *Perspective of the Stiles plan. Drawing by Erik Vogt.*

would insist on majority representation and effectively bring the college under secular control.[26]

The college's case was argued valiantly—and, it turned out, successfully—by James Hillhouse (B.A. 1773), Yale's treasurer and himself a former Connecticut assemblyman. The Assembly's audit praised the institution and recommended only a minority stake in its ruling body. This alone was cause for celebration, but the report—delivered to Stiles in June 1792—went further: Connecticut pledged to Yale $30,000 in tax arrears owed to the state by the federal government. After years of estrangement and financial deprivation, the college greeted the news with jubilation. The Corporation agreed immediately to the conditions, and Stiles exclaimed in his diary, "This is a grand and liberal Donation and a noble Condescension, beyond all Expectations! It will unite Moses and Aaron… and promote a friendly Disposition towards College throughout the State."[27]

With this windfall, his "Plan of a University," deferred for fifteen years, could finally begin to take shape. The first order of business was to build a much needed second dormitory, as Yale had torn down the decrepit College House in 1782. Stiles and the Corporation wasted little time; by mid-September 1792 they appointed a building committee and, on October 23, met to make final plans for the new college hall. As the records show, they proposed a last-minute change of course that would have great consequences for the future of Yale's campus.[28]

The first vote recorded that "the proposed Edifice be executed South of the College Chapel, the end next adjoining the Chapel at the same Distance from the Chapel as the East of the present College is from the Chapel north of it, the Fronts in a Line with the present College, 100 feet long, not less than 40 feet wide, and four stories high, upright with a flat roof."[29] This new hall fulfilled the plan that Clap had made thirty years before. It conformed with Connecticut Hall in all of its particulars and, most important, fell into its prescribed place on the chapel's south side (FIG. 39, top). But without explanation, the Corporation crossed out this vote and inserted, on an extra page, a very different version of the proposed building:

Voted that the proposed College Edifice be erected at the North Part of the College Yard, the length to be about 130 feet [and width about 30 feet], the Front being not far from the Line Place of the present College Fence and the South Westerly Corner in an exact Range with the North Easterly End and Front of the present College…the Building to be 4 stories high…and be built with Brick upon a Stone Foundation.[30]

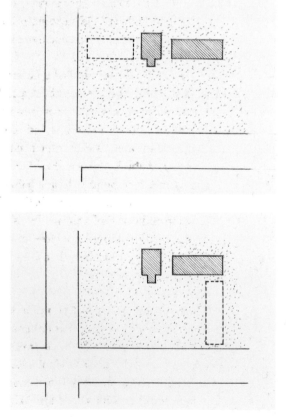

FIG. 39 *Building placement plans of 1792 as initially rejected (top) and approved (bottom) by the Corporation. Drawing by Erik Vogt.*

Thus they placed the hall, now much longer and narrower, to the north, at a right angle to the line of existing buildings (FIG. 39, bottom). The question remains, why did they have this seemingly last-minute change of heart, deviating from the straightforward logic of their first vote?[31]

Perhaps Stiles, recalling the sketch he had made for the campus in 1777, chose to forward his ideas at this opportune moment. The hall's new location, perpendicular to Connecticut Hall and closing off the yard's northern end, followed part of his design. But his sketch had also included a new hall south of the chapel, just as the Corporation's first vote proposed. This suggests that there may have been an extenuating circumstance that made the northern location preferable. And indeed there was: along College Street, to the north of the yard, a rather motley collection of buildings had accumulated, with functions that hardly comported with college life. "A grotesque group—generally of most undesireable establishments," Benjamin Silliman (B.A. 1796), Yale's renowned professor of chemistry, was to recall later, "among which were a barn—a barber's shop— several coarse taverns or boarding houses—a poor house and house of correction—and the public jail with its prison yard—and used alike for criminals, maniacs and debtors."[32] If the new hall could serve to wall off such "undesireable establishments" from the college campus, then locating it to the north would have an added benefit.

If the Yale Corporation was satisfied with its final decision, however, the citizens of New Haven were not. The reasons for public disapproval remain unknown. Surprise might have been a factor, for those who followed the college's progress may have expected the hall to be located where Clap had long ago proposed. And the concentration of disreputable establishments along Chapel Street was probably no less a source of concern to the town. New Haven was taking steps to improve the aesthetic character of the Green, and the citizenry may have counted on Yale's future expansion into this property as a means of removing the unwanted buildings. On a more fundamental level, the public may also have considered the development of a college quadrangle, even an open three-sided one, to be something of a step back from the town. Their consciousness of New Haven's close relationship with the college was likely more acute than the Corporation realized. The memory of Clap's retreat in the 1760s would have resonated as well, with this new move appearing to be another attempt by Yale, thirty years later, to turn inward.

Stiles conveyed the public's disapproval to the Corporation members in a letter sent in early December, a month and a half after their meeting:

Sir, the determination of the Corporation of Yale College at their last meeting to erect the new College Edifice at the North end of the old College and at right angles with it, seems as far as we have been able to learn not to accord with the public mind, and the Committee appointed by the Board to build the House are accordingly diffident as to proceeding in the Business at present, because they are confident that the Board being informed of the subsisting uneasiness would think it expedient once more to consider the Subject, and if possible to satisfy the wishes of the Public relative to the Situation & Form of the Building.[33]

Stiles accordingly asked the members to convene again on New Year's Day, 1793, to reconsider their decision.[34] And he turned once again for help to James Hillhouse, who only six months earlier had negotiated the compromise with the General Assembly. As the leading force in New Haven's civic improvement efforts at the time, Hillhouse shared the public's misgivings and saw an opportunity in Yale's dilemma. Out of it, he was to help produce the first campus plan in America, one which knit together college yard and town common, Yale and New Haven, into a greater urban whole.

———

Born in Montville, Connecticut, in 1754, James Hillhouse moved to New Haven in 1763 and graduated from Yale ten years later. He cut short a law career to join the Revolutionary War effort, during which he was elected to the Connecticut General Assembly. Hillhouse served there until 1789, when he was elected to the U.S. Congress as a Connecticut representative, serving three terms before moving up to the Senate. He finally retired in 1810 and thereafter lived full-time in New Haven. Time away from the city, however, had not prevented him from participating fully in its civic life. In addition to his federal duties, he served on New Haven's Common Council, and he oversaw Yale's finances for fifty years, from 1782 until his death in 1832.[35]

Hillhouse's career reflected not only his commitment to public service but also his status as a member of Connecticut's "Standing Order," a small circle of patrician elite who ruled the state during the Federalist era. His accomplishments in the civic improvement of New Haven, however, rarely arose from any elected office; there he built support by persuasion and by the example of his own tireless efforts. He conceived an undertaking and followed it through with dedication and care, often personally attending to its most mundane requirements.[36]

Hillhouse began his long campaign in 1784, when he and President Stiles led New Haven's successful effort to incorporate as a city. The same year, he organized a letter of subscription to enclose the lower, eastern half of the Green with a wooden rail fence.[37] It was a private agreement, approved by the city, whereby each signatory contributed money toward the task, and Hillhouse and two colleagues undertook the work. The improvement must have been judged a success, because in 1786 Hillhouse requested permission to plant a row of elm trees across Temple Street, a newly laid street that bisected the Green from north to south and fronted the two churches and State House then standing along the center (see FIG. 53). Thus he instituted the first organized planting of elms within the nine squares of New Haven, deploying them as an ornament to the city's public buildings.[38] The plan for Yale that he developed six years later should be understood as an integral part of, and evolutionary step in, Hillhouse's larger scheme of civic improvement. The design of the college yard in particular—a formalized space shaped by *allées* of trees and coordinated with the row of halls—partook of his work on the Green. It both related to his earlier effort on Temple Street and foreshadowed his more ambitious proposal, seven years later, to transform the town common into a true civic square.

Hillhouse was in Philadelphia attending to congressional duties in December 1792. With the Corporation meeting scheduled for January 1, time to produce a campus plan was critically short, and he enlisted the aid of an acquaintance from Connecticut, John Trumbull, who was also in Philadelphia at the time. Trumbull's skills as a painter and amateur architect complemented perfectly Hillhouse's vision and practical knowledge. As Hillhouse later remarked, Trumbull was to do "much to improve the great opportunities" that Yale's unexpected quandary presented.[39]

———

John Trumbull (1756–1843) was a native of Connecticut but not a Yale man. His father and brother would be future governors of the colony and state, and both played decisive roles in the Revolutionary War. Although Trumbull developed an interest in drawing and the arts at an early age, his father encouraged him to pursue a career in law or the ministry. To that end he attended Harvard, graduating in 1774. He joined the war effort with the rest of his family soon after and served in several capacities, most

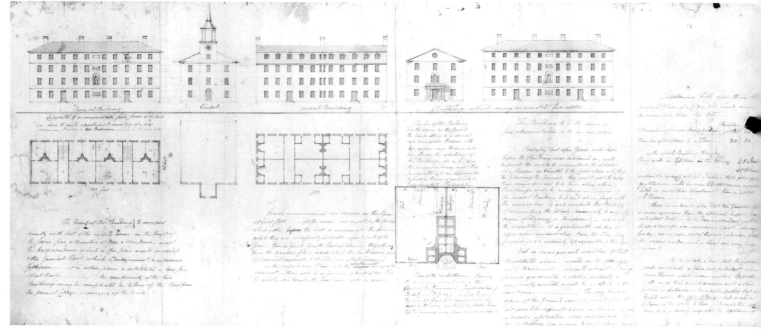

FIG. 40 *John Trumbull, "Plan and elevation for the development of Yale College," 1792.*

notably as an aide to General George Washington, for whom he formed a deep and lifelong admiration.[40]

Trumbull resigned his commission as a colonel in 1777 and returned to Lebanon.[41] He had not shaken his love for painting, despite his father's well-founded objections. To be an artist by profession was extremely rare in colonial America; there was practically no market for such work beyond the occasional portrait. For someone of the patrician class like Trumbull, the choice was more than rare — it was unique. Nevertheless, he so chose and was to suffer for it most of his life, struggling to find patrons in the new republic. However, his wartime service provided him with a newfound artistic purpose, one that he soon made the central focus of his career: to depict, as historical tableaux, the most important battles and events of the Revolution. Trumbull conceived their purpose to be monumental; as he later conveyed to Thomas Jefferson, they were intended to do nothing less than "preserve and diffuse the memory of the noblest series of actions which have ever presented themselves in the history of man."[42]

To further his studies, he knew that he had to find the company of fellow artists and so began a long and peripatetic career in search of such a community. After a brief stay in Boston, he moved to London and arranged to study with Benjamin West, but his family name, well known to those fighting the rebellion in America, soon attracted attention. The British government put Trumbull under house

arrest on the charge of treason. Nevertheless, he and his family had many well-placed friends who worked to secure his release. One of these was Edmund Burke, the English philosopher and statesman who had written a landmark essay on aesthetic perception, *A Philosophical Inquiry into the Origin of Our Ideas on the Sublime and the Beautiful* (1756). As Trumbull later recounted, it was Burke who steered him toward the study of architecture, admonishing him in a visit during the artist's confinement "that architecture is the eldest sister [of the arts]…be aware that you belong to a young nation, which will soon want public buildings; these must be erected before the decorations of painting and sculpture will be required."[43] While Trumbull did not turn away from his first passion, painting, he began to study architecture on the side, putting the skills to good use in coming years.

By 1782, he was released and allowed to return to America. Soon after the war, he made his way back to London to resume his studies. During this time he met Thomas Jefferson, then in Paris as a United States minister, who invited Trumbull to stay with him in the French capital. It was here that the artist began to compose his Revolutionary War series in earnest and, with Jefferson's advice, laid out his first and most famous scene, *The Declaration of Independence.*[44] The interlude in Paris was also to prove valuable to Trumbull's subsequent forays into architecture. Jefferson was embarking on his famous design for the Virginia State Capitol in Richmond.

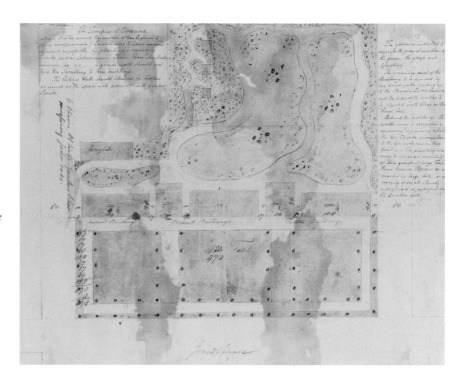

FIG. 41 *John Trumbull, "Landscape plan ('The Temples of Cloacina') for the development of Yale College," 1792.*

His final scheme, based on the Roman temple type, stood as a solitary building occupying its own block on an elevated ridge within the city's gridiron plan. The urbanistic strategy — a civic institution composed within a self-contained and elevated urban block — may well have come to Trumbull's mind when he later helped to design Yale's campus, a collection of public buildings, in Burke's words, intended to serve a young nation.[45]

In 1790, Trumbull returned to America to collect the portraits he needed for his war paintings. He settled in Philadelphia, then the national capital, where many who had led the war effort were now forging a federal government. The year he arrived, Congress had decided to create a new capital along the Potomac River. Trumbull, traveling often to and from Philadelphia between 1790 and 1793, was in a position to follow the planning of the new city, under the hand of Pierre L'Enfant, a French engineer. He even had occasion in 1791 to review the site with L'Enfant, riding on horseback over the marshy plains along the Potomac.[46] James Hillhouse would have been following L'Enfant's progress as well, given his own interest in urban planning and civic art. When Stiles asked for his help, he in turn looked to Trumbull for guidance. Together, and perhaps inspired by the farsightedness of L'Enfant's capital design, they set about composing not only a place for Yale's new hall but a plan for the college's growth well into the future.

THE COLLEGE SQUARE

Since my Arrival in [Philadelphia] I have taken all the pains in my power to obtain information on the subject of our New College and from that and my own reflections am led to conclude most decidedly against the location of the New College on the North side of College Yard.[47]

So began James Hillhouse's letter, which accompanied the campus plan he and John Trumbull had conceived for Yale. Stiles received these on December 31, 1792, the day before the emergency Corporation meeting.[18] Although Hillhouse and Trumbull had less than a month to work, they nevertheless produced a plan that not only convincingly argued against the proposed location of the "New College" but also fit that argument within a grander framework of campus expansion. They presented it on two sheets: one (13 x 30 inches) displayed the existing and proposed halls in plan and elevation, with explanatory notes and details below and on the far right; the other, half as wide (13 x 16 inches) was an overall site plan of the campus (FIGS. 40 & 41). The drawings, rendered by Trumbull in ink with washes of color highlighting landscape and building volumes, were elegant and economical. They conveyed a remarkable range of information, delineating not only the larger organizing vision but also relatively minor details that were, nonetheless, essential to the design's unity.

In the explanatory notes, Trumbull echoed the themes that Hillhouse touched on in his letter; the plan was assuredly a shared effort, "the result," Hill-house wrote, "of all our information and the full exercise of our joint deliberations and Judgment on the Subject." Without qualification, they argued that the new hall should be sited where the Corporation had first determined, mirroring Connecticut Hall to the south of the Chapel. "If the present building be placed at an angle with existing ones," Trumbull wrote, "it will preclude the possibility of reconciling the whole University to any degree of elegance or uniformity."[49] Indeed, the hall's placement to the south cleared the ground, literally and figuratively, for Trumbull and Hillhouse's larger plan. Suggesting to the Corporation that, "whether in placing the present [hall] they ought not to carry their views forward to a time when other buildings will be nec-essary," they proposed two additional halls to the north, ranged along the line of the existing buildings and repeating their types of gable-front chapel and lateral dormitory. These formed the row into a unified composition, rhythmically alternating long and short and symmetrically balanced around the now central Connecticut Hall. The proposed build-ings were "not necessary at present," Hillhouse explained in his letter, "but in my apprehension will be wanted much sooner than is generally expected… I have very raised expectations of the future growth and prosperity of our College and do not think it chimerical to suppose that all the Building repre-sented upon the plan will in fact be erected within the term of 20 Years." Using the array of new and existing halls as a compositional basis, Hillhouse and Trumbull further extended the architectural order into the front and rear campus yards. They formalized the enlarged college yard with walks and *allées* of trees that aligned with the halls; and in the rear yard they designed a picturesque garden of meandering paths and informal plantings.

A larger conception of the campus established the framework for the overall design. Although not remarked upon in previous studies of the plan, it was perhaps its most radical feature. Trumbull and Hillhouse proposed a new fifty-foot-wide street on the north side of the enlarged campus, bisecting the block on which Yale stood along College Street. Adding this new street to those that already bounded the campus on three sides — College to the east, Chapel to the south, and the recently established High Street to the west — they would have made Yale the occupant of its own self-contained block within the city's nine squares.[50] Judging from Trumbull and Hillhouse's measurements and adjustments in build-ing placement, they seemingly intended to make the

college block a near perfect square. Its existing depth was approximately 465 feet, and they measured off 474 feet for its new width.[51]

It was an intriguing proposal in light of Jefferson's Virginia State Capitol and L'Enfant's plan for Wash-ington, D.C., both of which featured freestanding public buildings set on their own city squares. Trum-bull and Hillhouse may have seen an opportunity to underline the college's civic stature with a similar planning strategy. They certainly considered their design an appropriate vehicle for Yale's national prospects. "The proposed plan would be attended with an Air of Elegance and beauty beyond any thing in America," boasted Hillhouse in his letter, "and would give that Seminary a reputation in those respects which might be of great Advantage."[52]

It was undoubtedly Hillhouse who proposed the bold changes to Yale's boundaries. The northward expansion represented by the two additional build-ings was located on property that the college did not yet own, and only he would have known if such an expansion was possible. Since the mid-1780s, he had actively advised both Yale and New Haven on matters of land acquisition and, in the city's case, directed the laying out of new streets that subdivided the original nine blocks. Indeed, it was Hillhouse who in 1796 directed the purchase of the land north of the campus for Yale, making the plan's realization possi-ble. The plan also made clear that he intended to make the campus an integral part of New Haven's civic improvement efforts.[53] It was ultimately this relationship of the campus to the Green, as a unified ensemble, that drove Trumbull and Hillhouse's conception. What so perplexed them about the Corporation's perpendicular placement of the new hall — precluding "any degree of elegance or unifor-mity" — was that it turned away from the public square. Aligning the college halls as a row, looking out onto the Green, would, Trumbull wrote, "unite utility with ornament & would admit of being pur-sued gradually & whether partially or completely executed would be in all its stages handsome." Such a strategy, they felt, was obvious to anyone who appreciated the college's particular location; as Trumbull asserted, "the very nature & form of the ground seems to point it out," adding that it would be difficult to find "in America or in Europe a situ-ation where such an extent of public buildings can be seen to such advantage." It was this situation that the New Haven trustees had established in 1717, when the "fair Aspect" of the first College House was viewed before the Market-place. Trumbull and Hill-house's plan intended to fulfill the promise of that "eminent place" and ordain the campus's evolution into the full Brick Row of the nineteenth century.

———

While the plan has been recognized for its contribution to Yale's architectural development, no less powerful was its design of the campus landscape. It exploited the emphatic division between front and rear yards made by the wall of alternating halls to create two distinct worlds within Yale's precinct, one formal and open to the city, the other private and sheltered. Almost certainly, the elm-lined college yard in front was Hillhouse's contribution, conforming as it did to his ongoing efforts on the adjoining Green. The design divided the yard into three lawns, the whole bounded by the college fence and a gravel walk at its perimeter. Two wider walks led on axis to the academic buildings. A double row of trees—shown as circles on the plan—lined all the walks except the one fronting the halls, where the brick building walls gave enclosure. The spaces thus formed by the pillars of trees echoed the rhythm of hall and chapel: grass-floored "outdoor rooms" corresponded to the dormitories, and embowered "naves" led to the chapels.

Behind the Row, a naturalistic composition of meandering walks defined islands of trees—"elms, acacias, poplars"—and small shrubs, including "laburnums, lilacs, roses, snowballs, laurels." Clearly influenced by the eighteenth-century English picturesque garden, this design was most likely a result of Trumbull's experience. Despite the contrast in style, he used its winding paths, "corresponding to the two broad ones in their front," to draw the axes of the academic buildings into the rear garden. Thus they acted as gates to the rear yard, an effect reinforced by Trumbull's strategic placement of planting groups to close the view through the gaps in the Row. The design clearly alluded to the ideal of the classical academy, with its sacred grove and garden walks forming an open classroom in nature.

Such lofty ideals were served alongside more prosaic functional needs, for the landscape design also helped to screen the various service buildings located in the rear yard. These included the commons hall of 1782 and three new "necessary houses," or privies, proposed by Trumbull and Hillhouse; they dubbed these last, with due classical decorum, "The Temples of Cloacina." The plan thus preserved the traditional use of the rear campus as a repository for the unsightly but necessary functions of collegiate life.

Interestingly, the layered treatment of the campus block from front to back—fenced forecourt, lateral building line, and garden beyond—echoed the com-

mon arrangement of domestic house lots about New Haven's nine squares at the time. A New England *Gazetteer* from 1819 commented on the particular disposition of the city's houses, "many of them being set back, leaving open fronts, which are neatly fenced, and ornamented with evergreens and flowering shrubs…with a piece of ground in the rear, sufficiently large for a good garden and supply of fruit trees."[54] The resemblance underlined the school's inherently domestic character, originally derived from the Puritan cultivation of college life as a type of family institution, whereby the young flock is shepherded within the confines of house and yard.[55]

It was in this guise, the college as a sheltering retreat, that the plan's landscape design resonated with the larger theological meaning implicit in the sacred square. Set off from the world on its own "island," the campus was recreated as a type of Edenic garden, a cultivated pastoral sanctuary that harbored its inhabitants in their Christian mission. In this regard, Hillhouse's efforts to connect the campus and Green took on a deeper meaning. Although the new college square was self-contained, its landscape visibly united it with New Haven's great common; the towering elms knit them together as a continuous embowered garden. While the proposed landscape design was not to be realized in full, the character it imbued to the campus, as a sanctuary both separate from and connected to the city around it, remained in place as an integral part of Yale and New Haven's shared communal life through the coming century.

———

John Trumbull did not lay aside his painterly instincts when asked to set out a vision for Yale's college square. With a practiced eye, he applied the principles of order and composition that he relied upon in painting his Revolutionary War series. "I pay great deference to the opinion of Mr. Trumbull, who appears to be a perfect master of the subject," Hillhouse wrote in his letter to Stiles. Beginning with the campus block, Trumbull used the geometry of the square to organize and idealize the plan's elements (FIG. 42). He laid out the college yard in the proportion of one to three, with the three-square divisions marked by the inside edges of the chapel steeple and hall portico. He centered the chapel types in smaller squares that, in their vertical dimension, helped to compose the building facades. Taking Connecticut Hall as his datum, he extended its eave line to mark stringcourses on the new dormitory halls to the north and south. These in turn marked the edges of squares that organized the halls' overall facade

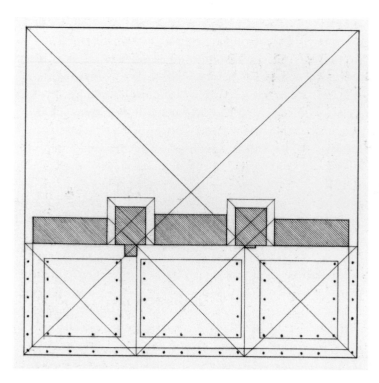

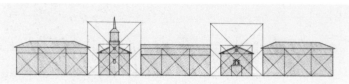

FIG. 42 *Plan and elevation showing geometrical basis of the Trumbull and Hillhouse plan. Drawings by Erik Vogt.*

proportions. Although Trumbull certainly knew that he was idealizing many of the existing building and campus proportions, the harmony of the whole took precedence. To that end, he even recommended that "the uniformity of the two buildings [Connecticut Hall and the new college] may be completed by taking off the roof from the present College & carrying up the walls."

Although Trumbull's work on the plan differed greatly in its aims from his contemporaneous Revolutionary War paintings, the two endeavors nevertheless share a similar compositional motif. This is seen best in his depictions of the great battles, composed in the years immediately preceding the plan. He designed each as a highly theatrical set piece, with an array of soldiers and officers balanced symmetrically about a central heroic figure. These were strung along a middle horizon, which in turn divided the scene emphatically between an upper background of sky and landscape and a lower foreground of open field, with the space before the figures dramatically highlighted (FIG. 43). The campus plan, seen as a layered three-dimensional space, constituted a similar tableau: the symmetrical row

of halls was centered on Connecticut Hall—the "founding father," as it were, of Yale's campus—and divided the space between the landscaped garden beyond and the open "stage" of the college yard in front (FIG. 44). Whether Trumbull was conscious of the compositional parallel or even intended it to have some meaning is unknown. But it certainly served to monumentalize the design, and by extension Yale's stature, in the same way that his historical tableaux aggrandized their subjects. Much as he intended his paintings to convey the values of the Revolution to future generations, the plan for Yale was designed to ensure that the college's traditions could be carried forward in a setting that befitted its mission.

Trumbull's hand was most evident in the architectural character of the proposed buildings. He married a refined style—the light elegance of English Adamesque classicism, to be adopted in America as the Federal style—with the Puritan simplicity of Yale's colonial halls. While retaining the latter's austerity, he gave the new buildings a tauter, more upright appearance. His most significant change was to substitute a low-pitched hip roof for the gambrel roof of Connecticut Hall, which he derided as an "inconvenient & expensive Gothicism." The hipped roof permitted the new hall's fourth floor to emerge from its attic space and form part of the building's vertical mass, thus improving the overall proportions. Trumbull also incorporated wall niches and plaques in the central bay of the dormitory halls, giving a focus and symmetry to their otherwise undifferentiated expanse of wall and windows. Trumbull deviated from the existing types, however, in one significant way. For the proposed second "chapel" or academic hall, he eliminated the attached steeple in front, substituting instead an engaged portico entry beneath an arched Palladian window. Propriety, no doubt, governed his design; the new hall was to be secular in use and thus had no practical need for a steeple. Indeed, Trumbull based the facade design on a precedent closer to his own predilections, Robert Adam's Art Society Building in London. It was a subtle and clever reference, reflecting his lifelong interest in promoting the arts in America.

Although Trumbull and Hillhouse focused on Yale's long-range growth and its physical relationship to the city, they did not neglect the particulars of the new hall's design. In fact, they devoted half their notes to critiquing the deficiencies of Connecticut Hall's layout and suggesting improvements in the new building. Trumbull drew the floor plans of each side by side and wrote below Connecticut Hall:

FIG. 43 *John Trumbull, "The Surrender of Lord Cornwallis at Yorktown, 19 October 1781," 1787–ca. 1828.*

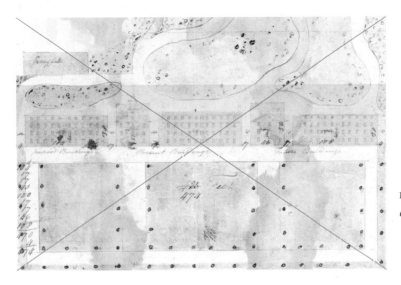

FIG. 44 *Composite of the Trumbull elevation and landscape plan.*

"Several inconveniences are obvious in this plan at first sight: all the rooms are impaired by the studies [along the outer walls], which either lessen the light or incommode the size…they are necessarily untenable a great part of the year, those in front from the heat of summer, the others from the winter's cold." His alternative suite plan was a remarkably simple and elegant solution to these problems. By eliminating the central partition that ran down the middle of the hall, he permitted each suite to span the entire building width. The rooms, "consisting of a large common parlor & two bedrooms, serving as studies also," became far more generous in size, capable of housing four students rather than the two in Connecticut Hall's plan. Although he halved the number of apartments, the increased occupancy in each suite kept the total number of students in the hall the same. Not only was the new arrangement more efficient in terms of construction but, with the larger rooms, Hillhouse felt confident that in times of need six students could be housed in each suite, an advantage not to be overlooked in light of Yale's chronic overcrowding.

The suite plan alleviated the problems of heating, cooling, and ventilation as well. Because they spanned the width of the building, the rooms could be cross-ventilated, moderating the extremes of seasonal temperature on either side. Heating was made more efficient by locating a central chimneystack in each suite, which placed a hearth in every room but reduced by half the total number of chimneys. (Trumbull even went so far as to draw a detail plan of this to ensure that the chimneys were oriented to "show narrow in front," thus balancing aesthetics and function as they overlapped from interior plan

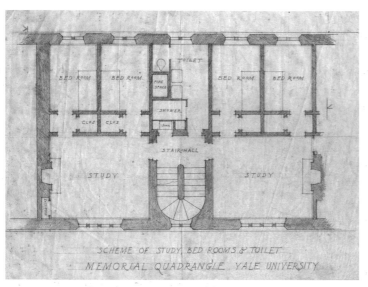

FIG. 45 *Memorial Quadrangle: suite plan by James Gamble Rogers, 1917.*

to exterior elevation.) With the windows set within longer outer walls, natural light was distributed more evenly. Even the rooms' harmonious proportions gave them a heightened sense of spaciousness. The logic, pragmatism, and, not least, economy of the proposed changes more than convinced the Corporation. The suite plan not only superseded Connecticut Hall's layout but also became a model for collegiate dormitories throughout the nineteenth century. It even found its way into Yale's twentieth-century campus as the planning module for James Gamble Rogers's Memorial Quadrangle (FIG. 45). Thus, Trumbull and Hillhouse's plan proved influential in American campus planning at two scales: the larger vision of alternating hall and chapel types, which organized the college as a whole, and the more intimate arrangements of daily student life.[56]

Simple on its face, the campus that the plan envisioned nevertheless held a remarkable range of readings, many of them seemingly paradoxical. The line of buildings, while monumental in their physical breadth and unified front, still retained a modest demeanor, with the increments of hall, window, and brick holding them to a humane scale. Their inherently domestic character reinforced the intimate bond created between the campus and the town around it. That bond was felt most strongly in the college yard; its dual function as both Clap's sanctified garden and Hillhouse's open face to the city was to make it symbolic of Yale's close, and sometimes conflicted, relationship with New Haven in the nineteenth century.

The architectural types of sacred chapel and secular dormitory suggested a much stronger division between public and private realms within the college itself. They embodied both the daily round of collegiate life and a firmly established communal order. By choosing to repeat these original forms, Trumbull and Hillhouse's plan validated that order and projected it into the future. Its basis was fundamentally typological, understanding the reincarnation of types—in this case architectural—as a means of both reconnecting with the community's origins and ensuring its progress forward. Yale was to continue to operate on that basis into the next century, converting the plan into an open-ended system of recapitulating, and reaffirming, types. In so doing, it extended and reinforced the campus's connection with the city, uniting Yale and New Haven in a way not experienced since the school had first moved into its original College House, pressed close beside the Green.

PREDESTINATION

Stiles's diary and the Corporation records preserve the administration's only known responses to the plan. Both accounts were characteristically dry, recording only the particulars of the matter at hand. Nevertheless, the Corporation's immediate vote to proceed signaled their approval. Their motion was limited to the new hall's design and placement, however, and did not pass on the plan in its entirety. Its implementation over the next ten years would serve as the Corporation's ultimate vote of confidence.

The minutes of their meeting on January 1, 1793, described the new hall as Trumbull had drawn it and, essentially, came back full circle to the rejected scheme first outlined on October 23:

Voted that the new College Edifice proposed be erected South of the College Chapel, the Front of the new Edifice to range in a direct Line with the present College…the Edifice in exterior Appearance [is] to be conformed to the present College as nearly as the Alterations will conveniently admit, [and is] to be about 100 feet long and 40 feet broad, the internal Alterations to be left to the Discretion of the Committee appointed to build the College.[57]

Anxious to begin construction, the college immediately sent out a request for builder proposals through the local newspapers.[58] Three months later, President Stiles formally laid the cornerstone before an audience of Yale and New Haven luminaries. He spoke at length of the goodwill redeemed between college and state and looked forward to the fulfillment of his "Plan of a University:"

We rejoice in seeing the foundation of this 7th edifice appertaining to College…especially in the Auxiliary

Glory of the amicable union of Civilians in the Govern-
ment of the College & in the Provision of Funds for the
Establishment of ample Professorships; all these give us
reason with pleasure to anticipate the future distinguished
figure & increasing Utility of this Institution among the
Sister Universities of these States and of the World.[59]

Yale christened the building Union Hall in honor of its reconciliation with the state (FIG. 46), and Stiles joyfully recorded its speedy completion on July 17, 1794, "just one year from laying the first Brick in the Brickwork."[60]

With this important milestone passed, the college directed its sights to other capital improvements. Mischievous students had torn down the college yard fence in 1793, so the Corporation ordered the erection of a new one during the summer recess of 1794. They replaced the previous paneled board construction with a more economical fence of open "wooden palings," or rough-hewn pickets.[61] Repairs to the long-neglected Connecticut Hall were even more pressing. In assessing the work, the Corporation entertained Trumbull's suggestion of changing the roof, asking the Standing Committee to "ascertain... the necessary expense for thorough repair of the old College, and for raising the old College another Story."[62] They ultimately deferred the change, but just considering it was an early sign of their confidence in Trumbull and Hillhouse's overall vision.

In procuring a design for the campus and building Union Hall, Stiles had made an auspicious start on his university plan. But fulfilling its promise was not to come under his stewardship. In the fall and winter of 1794, just after Yale had completed its new hall, devastating plagues of yellow and scarlet fever swept through New Haven. Although Stiles managed to escape infection during the height of the epidemic, he was struck by a "bilious fever" on May 9, 1795, and died three days later.[63]

———

In September 1795, the Corporation selected Timothy Dwight (1752–1817) to succeed Stiles. They had little hesitation in their choice; Dwight, a distinguished Connecticut minister and Yale graduate (B.A. 1769), was highly regarded in New England as both a persuasive preacher and leading intellectual. The selection, and its timing, were propitious for Yale. During the 1790s, deism and secularism had been rising, exacerbated by the recent French Revolution. Yale students were caught up in the fervor as well, to the Corporation's dismay. By enlisting Dwight they were getting a man of unwavering Puritan principles, with a firmly held sense of worldly and divine order. He had inherited the convictions of his grandfather, the brilliant theologian Jonathan Edwards (B.A. 1720), and was eager to engage those who questioned religious faith with highly reasoned arguments. Many of his contemporaries credited him with holding secularism at bay, not only at Yale but also throughout the state.[64]

Dwight had wanted to be president of Yale since his tutoring years at the college. After leaving New Haven, he practiced as a minister and founded two

FIG. 46 *Union Hall in 1874: east (College Street) facade, with the College Chapel on the right.*

schools. It was from his church and academy at Greenfield Hill in Fairfield, Connecticut, that he returned to Yale. Because he had coveted the office for so long, he arrived, in the words of his biographer, with "a clear vision of the place he wanted Yale College to occupy in the life of the nation, and a definite understanding of what his own administration might accomplish toward that goal." Like Stiles, he planned to expand Yale into a university by adding new schools; and by the turn of the century he had established professorships in law, languages, ecclesiastical history, and chemistry.[65] His vision and administrative skills also proved invaluable in carrying out Trumbull and Hillhouse's plan. Although he had had philosophical differences with Stiles, he must have seen clearly the opportunity that his predecessor's efforts afforded him. Lending support was Hillhouse, who continued to guide Yale's finances and campus building. Within a year of his appointment, Dwight began laying the groundwork to implement the plan in full.

Money was the immediate need; despite the windfall of 1792, Yale needed more for both professorships and buildings. In May 1796, Dwight and Hillhouse petitioned the Connecticut General Assembly to modify the agreement of 1792. By its terms, the state was sharing income from tax arrears with the college. Yale now asked that it be given the whole amount. Although the request was unpopular with some Assembly members, who resented subsidizing a Congregational institution, it was approved, yielding an additional $20,000 for Yale. The victory had its price, however, for the college received no more state money for the next twenty years.[66]

In September 1796, the Corporation authorized the Building Committee, led by Hillhouse, to purchase the property north of campus, on which stood the notorious barn, taverns, and boarding house. The purchase signaled Dwight's commitment to an ambitious program of expansion. Only after this strategic move did Yale undertake the long-deferred repairs to Connecticut Hall, which included replacing its gambrel roof with a low hip and raising the walls to meet the higher eave. With Trumbull's desire for architectural uniformity thus met, they then attended to baser needs, constructing in 1800 the Temples of Cloacina—that is, three sturdy brick "necessary houses"—in the rear yard. Meanwhile, in 1799 and 1800 Yale acquired the remaining lots along College Street, containing the jail and poorhouse, and so consolidated the entire street frontage facing the Green. All told, Dwight, in his first five years in office, not only took the steps necessary to complete Trumbull and Hillhouse's plan,

but also cleared the way for a much longer-term vision of the campus.[67]

———

During this time, Yale undertook one building that the campus plan had not anticipated: a new president's house. In 1798, Dwight and the Corporation decided to replace the first president's house of 1722, located on College Street just south of the campus block (see FIG. 37). It had fallen into disrepair, and Yale used the proceeds from its sale for a new one, to be located on the land acquired in 1796 north of the college yard. The Corporation records authorizing construction do not indicate how the site was chosen. It was an unfortunate omission since the location seems related to two campus planning strategies that the college may have been entertaining at the time. The first featured a new street bisecting the College Street frontage, as Trumbull and Hillhouse had proposed. This street appears on the so-called Anonymous Map of New Haven of 1802, which, with the exception of the bisecting street, depicts the campus as it would be built by 1803 (FIG. 47). It shows the new president's house on its own block north of the campus, facing College Street and set forward of the Brick Row. Just to the south of it, the map noted a "Lot for professor of Philosophy." The indication that a second house was planned suggests that Yale may have thought to divide the college land, by way of the new street, into two blocks, with the larger one devoted to academic and dormitory halls and the smaller reserved for faculty residences. Thus the map of 1802 may have been depicting an extended planning strategy, which incorporated Trumbull and Hillhouse's plan of 1792 but also set out a use for the additional land to the north.

That the map may be a clue to Yale's intentions is suggested by a number of other anomalies as well, all of which represent deviations from New Haven's actual layout in 1802. These anomalies include newly extended streets running parallel to New Haven's nine-square grid, elm trees planted uniformly throughout, and the Grove Street Cemetery and Hartford Turnpike rendered in significantly altered form. The common thread linking these elements was James Hillhouse, who was closely involved in all of these undertakings. He may have had a direct hand in producing the map of 1802, not just recording existing conditions but including his own projected civic and campus improvements as well. This would explain why the map contains the only known depiction of the campus as Trumbull and Hillhouse had designed it in 1792: a symmetrical row of halls, composed within its own self-contained square.[68]

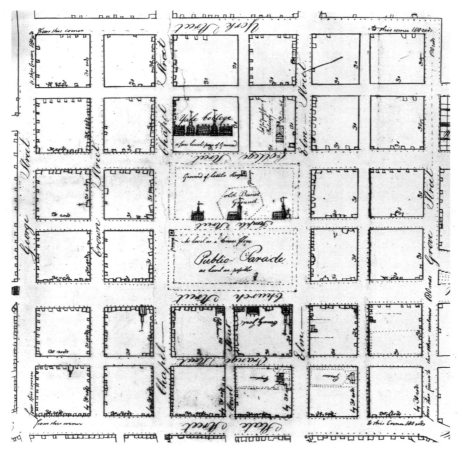

FIG. 47 *"Anonymous Map of New Haven,"* 1802: detail showing the nine squares.

As it was, Hillhouse had just completed his most ambitious civic improvement effort to date, begun in 1799 and financed once again by private citizens. The letter of subscription proposed that "the Green or public square of the City should be leveled, and the upper and lower section railed in and suitable fences erected to preserve the same from the passing of Carriages and Trams, [all of which] would add to the ornament of the City."[69] By raising, grading, and leveling the ground surface, it made possible the first uniform planting of grass on the Green. The enclosing fence was augmented by a double row of elms, which introduced a defining edge not only at the level of the strolling citizen but, with the trees' maturity, at the scale of the enormous Green itself. Thus Hillhouse comprehensively formalized the space in its horizontal and vertical dimensions and transformed its character as a public square.

The bisecting street that would have formed the campus as a square block never came to pass, no doubt a victim of the Corporation's parsimony. Yale had to plan for its growth within the bounds of a single long block and, as such, the president's house hinted at another long-range building strategy, one that Yale ultimately adopted. Although it was hardly apparent at the time, those who projected the Brick Row northward in its alternation of halls

and chapels would have realized that the house was placed squarely in front of the site for a future chapel type. Either by chance or premeditation, its location anticipated the pattern and extent of the Brick Row as it was to be built in coming years. It also signaled an important conceptual change that Yale was to make to Trumbull and Hillhouse's plan. Rather than holding to its symmetrical and self-contained composition, the college chose to convert the strategy of repeating types into an open-ended system, using the increments of hall and chapel to expand its campus as the need arose. The president's house marked the northerly limits of this system, standing in for the last chapel and awaiting the steady progression of halls to take their place in the long Brick Row.

As built in 1799, the house's form echoed the chapel type (FIG. 48). Its designer and builder was Peter Banner, an English contractor and self-styled architect who had recently moved to New Haven from New York. His design differed from the norm for the eighteenth-century New England house, which typically aligned the roof ridge parallel to the street. Instead, Banner turned the house's gable end to the street, presenting as its public face a temple front, like that of the first chapel. At forty feet, it was also the same width as the chapel and was even to be built of brick at first, although this later changed

FIG. 48 *Second President's House: east (College Street) facade.*

to wood. Given the resemblance and the building's placement, the house could be read as a form of domesticated chapel, conflating the types of temple and home.[70]

This conflation of sacred and secular was reflected as well in the duties of the president, which included serving as the college minister. The house's position embodied these responsibilities; by forming the northern edge of the college yard, it reinforced the president's role as community guardian, giving him a constant watchful presence in the daily campus rituals. It also reflected Dwight's particular leadership style. "A real and efficient sway is exerted, where there is scarcely an appearance of it," wrote Benjamin Silliman, Yale's professor of chemistry, in his eulogy to Dwight in 1817. "A great institution, every one of whose members is the subject of a particular and almost parental vigilance, proceeds like some well constructed and well managed machine."[71]

Student enrollment steadily climbed during Dwight's early years as president, helped in part by a strengthening local economy. At the turn of the nineteenth century, Yale once again faced its recurring problem: a shortage of student housing.[72] Fortunately, the State Assembly, in its revised agreement of 1796, had earmarked a part of the funds to "effect another Collegiate Building." At its meeting in November 1800, the Corporation decided to build not one but two new buildings: the much needed dormitory as well as an additional academic hall, adhering to Trumbull and Hillhouse's prescribed repetition of building types:

It was unanimously voted that a brick House be built at the North end of Connecticut Hall, corresponding both as to the site and external appearance especially to the chapel, of about 44 feet wide in front and about 56 feet long and three Stories high, with a projection in front elevated above the ridge and terminating in a cupola…a Brick House [to] be built still further North, leaving room for the Library, corresponding especially both as to Site, and external appearance to Union Hall, and of about 108 feet in length by 40 [feet] in Breadth.[73]

The gap left for the academic hall, or "Library," suggested that they intended to build the dormitory first. The Corporation confirmed this a year later, in September 1801, when they authorized construction of the library only after the dormitory was nearly complete.[74] Building the dormitory first allowed Yale to accommodate a larger student body and take in more tuition, which in turn helped to finance the academic hall. This economic strategy proved ingenious enough that the administration was to follow it in subsequent extensions of the Brick Row.[75]

According to the Corporation's order, the new halls — both of which were designed and built by Peter Banner — were not only to "correspond especially" to the earlier buildings, but also "be done in a Style which shall combine Strength with Simplicity." Their words echoed those that Hillhouse and Trumbull used in their plan description and reflected both old-fashioned Puritan restraint and an awareness of the campus's evolving aesthetic character. The dormitory, named Berkeley Hall for the Anglican bishop and Yale benefactor, was therefore identical to Union Hall in exterior appearance, although its interior plan was modified somewhat (FIG. 49). Having so often confronted the dilemma of student overenrollment, the Corporation specified that three, rather than two, study rooms be accommodated where possible and that an extra bedstead, stored upright in the partition wall, be included as well.[76]

The new academic hall, eventually named the Lyceum, was Yale's first building wholly devoted to secular functions (FIGS. 50 & 51). Its program (which followed closely Trumbull and Hillhouse's prescription) included the library on the third floor, relocated from the chapel, and study and recitation rooms on the first and second floors. To accommodate a large lecture room, Banner introduced a cross-gable at the rear, the span of which permitted the room to be clear of supports. Banner was also called upon to design a space for which no precedent yet existed in America: a teaching laboratory. In 1802, as the hall was being built, President Dwight appointed Benjamin Silliman Yale's first professor of chemistry and ordered Banner to create a laboratory space for him in the rear basement.[77] Initially

FIG. 49 *Berkeley Hall (North Middle College) in 1874: east (College Street) facade, with the Cabinet on the left and the New Chapel on the right.*

FIG. 50 *The Lyceum in the 1870s: east (College Street) facade.*

FIG. 51 *The Lyceum in the late 1890s: north facade.*

FIG. 52 *Moses Bradford, "Yale College," 1803: from the left, Union Hall, College Chapel, Connecticut Hall, Lyceum, and Berkeley Hall.*

Banner installed a low vault, sealing up the chamber's few exterior openings. Silliman later speculated that the odd design must have been inspired by the builder's "vague impressions of chemistry — perhaps a confused and terrific dream of alchemy, with its black arts, its explosions, and its weird-like mysteries." He had the vault removed but was still consigned, for "fifteen of the best years of my life," to the cavern-like room where he began to lay the foundation for Yale's preeminence in the natural sciences during the nineteenth century.[78] The location of the laboratory reflected Yale's mixed feelings about the role of science at the time. Although the school was to become a leader in the field — helped by Dwight's broadminded and unequivocal support — some on the Corporation and faculty still harbored misgivings about the place such studies should have in a Christian institution. The laboratory symbolized both sentiments. Its very existence, unprecedented as it was, demonstrated Yale's commitment. But relegated to near invisibility beneath the Row, it also represented the field's lowly status within the curriculum.

The most telling change to Trumbull's original design for the new academic hall, the addition of a steeple and spire, reasserted in no uncertain terms the place of religion at Yale. Unlike the chapel, the hall had no religious program. Nevertheless, the steeple's iconic significance apparently superseded functional requirements in the eyes of Dwight and the Corporation. A powerful religious revival had swept through the campus in 1801–2, coming on the heels of a so-called second Great Awakening in Connecticut. Many credited Dwight for the newfound spirit. "Yale College is a little temple," wrote Benjamin Silliman at the time. "Prayer and praise seem to be the delight of the greater part of the students, while those who are still unfeeling are awed into respectful silence." From 1801 to 1804, the steady rise of new college halls must have seemed a visible manifestation of the revival, with the library's brick steeple a reassuring icon of restored Puritan order and faith (FIG. 52).[79]

The final element of Trumbull and Hillhouse's plan to be implemented was to prove as important to the life of the campus in the nineteenth century as the buildings themselves. In September 1803, the Corporation ordered the Building Committee to "set out proper trees in both fronts of the Collegiate Buildings, the next spring season, in such order as shall best conduce to convenience and beauty."[80] Hillhouse, a member of the committee, most likely took personal charge of this task, planting elms like those that he had used to transform the Green four years earlier. The planting marked an appropriate end to the intensive building campaign. With construction winding down, the saplings were safe from incidental harm, and their placement could be coordinated with the walks and entries of the expanded row and yard. The order called for trees "in both fronts" of the Brick Row, extending a grid not only over the college yard but into the rear campus as well, as indicated by rows of dots on a New Haven map of 1812 (FIG. 53). Trumbull's picturesque garden

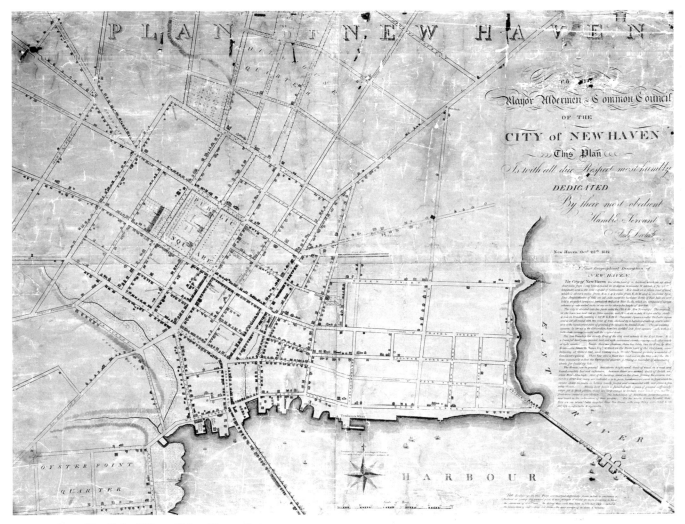

FIG. 53 *Amos Doolittle, "Plan of New Haven," 1812.*

was thus replaced by a rank and file of elms. The effect, nonetheless, was of a cultivated grove surrounding the red-brick buildings. The allusion, intended or not, to the academies of Plato and Aristotle may not have gone unnoticed; six months after the tree planting, the Corporation decided to rechristen its new academic hall the Lyceum.[81]

The situation of the academical buildings is uncommonly pleasant, fronting the green on the northwestern side, upon a handsome elevation, with a spacious yard before them. The buildings are plain, but so arranged as to strike the eye with pleasure.
Timothy Dwight, *Travels in New England and New York,* 1817[82]

After eight years—far short of the twenty that Hillhouse had predicted in his letter—Dwight had implemented the campus plan of 1792 in full (see FIG. 3). Building Berkeley Hall and the Lyceum ratified the use of repeating types as a strategy for expansion, while the acquisition of the entire College Street front gave direction and space for the

Brick Row's future expansion. It is hardly surprising that Dwight had set in place such a clear and far-sighted program. His strong Puritan faith committed him to cultivating a visible order in the world and promoting its progress and improvement through time. He set forth his views on such matters in his famous journal, *Travels in New England and New York,* written between 1790 and his death in 1817. It presented his observations on "the New England Way:" its people, history, culture and, most pointedly, the transformation of its natural landscape into a cultivated pattern emblematic of Puritan ideals. Along the way, it also gives insight into what the building and improvement of Yale's campus must have meant to him as an embodiment of those ideals.

Dwight extolled the virtues of New England's unique township system, which not only "converted the wilderness into fruitful fields" but also imparted to its inhabitants a strong social cohesion. "Almost the whole country is covered with villages, and every village has its church and its suite of schools," he wrote. "All the people are neighbors: social beings converse, feel, sympathize, mingle minds, cherish sentiments, and are subjects of at least some degree of refinement…Of all these advantages the mode of settlement has been one and, it is believed, a powerful cause."[83] In equating physical propinquity with an active civic life, Dwight was tapping into long-held Puritan beliefs and traditions. The township was a corollary to the congregation, a self-contained body circumscribed in size and arrangement by its central meetinghouse and church. Repeated as a type over time, it propagated a connected web of communities and improved the land toward human and, ultimately, divine ends.

For Dwight, the emblematic form that connected the earthly and spiritual realms was the ubiquitous New England church: "In almost every part of the country they are found at the distances of five, six, and seven miles; and with their handsome spires and cupolas, almost universally white, add an exquisite beauty to the landscape."[84] Their beauty was not just visual but symbolic; each marked the center of a cultivated, and cultivating, township and pointed heavenward as a finger to God. The fruitful fields, orderly houses, and handsome spires of the New England town became, in Dwight's eyes, exhibits of work, family, and God, visibly displayed from distant countryside and town green alike.

New Haven's clarity of form and grace of setting constituted, for Dwight, a model of the type.[85] The straight broad streets, shaded by Hillhouse's elms—"a species of ornament in which this town is unrivaled"—organized rows of "neat and tidy" houses, ornamented by tree-filled "courtyards in front and gardens in the rear." At its center was the Green, "the handsomest ground of this nature which I have seen." Here Dwight's ideal of natural, social, and spiritual harmony was distilled into its most resonant image, readily visible from his house in the college yard: "Rarely is a more beautiful object presented to the eye—I have never met with one—than the multitudes crossing the green in different directions to the house of God…Few places in the world present a fairer example of peace and good order."[86]

Trumbull and Hillhouse's plan thus offered the perfect means by which he could contribute, as president of Yale and citizen of New Haven, to the order and beauty of his town. The campus that it projected and he built was a microcosm of the many villages he had admired and described in his *Travels*, forming with its "neat and tidy" houses, spired chapels, and common yard a fundamental pattern of communal order. For Yale, it reaffirmed not only a continuity with the college's own origins—the propagation of Clap's types into a community whole unto itself—but also an affinity with New Haven's nine-square plan itself, the most explicit exemplar of New England's congregational ideal.

———

In January 1817, following a yearlong struggle with cancer, Dwight died while still in office. Shortly before his death he chose Jeremiah Day, professor of mathematics and natural philosophy, as his successor. Day had graduated from Yale in 1795 (and, incidentally, as a student had assisted Hillhouse with his elm planting) but left before Dwight's appointment to the presidency. He returned as a tutor in 1798, and Dwight promoted him to professor three years later. He was one of a triumvirate of Dwight appointments—Day, Benjamin Silliman, and James Luce Kingsley (B.A. 1799), professor of languages and ecclesiastical history—who were to lead Yale's academic and administrative development through the first half of the nineteenth century. Continuity was the hallmark of Day's presidency, which at twenty-nine years was the longest of any in the college's history. He built effectively upon the foundation that Dwight had laid, pursuing a steady course that nonetheless often required bold decision-making in the face of financial hardship.

The college that Day inherited was much expanded from what it had been when Dwight assumed the presidency in 1795. It was, indeed, the largest in the country, with a student population of 275 housed in three dormitories, instructed in two classroom buildings, and served by a commons hall in the rear yard. His administration quickly replaced the latter with a new dining hall in response to overwhelming student complaint. Yale's first new building since 1802, it went up in 1819 directly behind the Lyceum. The old Commons of 1782 was converted to a chemical laboratory, allowing Silliman to emerge finally from his basement quarters.

In Day's first few years, Yale once again found itself short of money despite greater revenue from tuition. Dwight had seen the crisis coming and secured another Connecticut General Assembly grant of $8,000 in 1816, but it was not enough to meet expenses. In 1818, Professor Kingsley penned a pamphlet, *Remarks on the Present Situation of Yale College, for its Friends and Patrons,* to inaugurate the college's first fundraising effort among alumni and the general public. He listed a number of deficiencies, including a pressing need for additional buildings, and couched his plea in a familiar Yale refrain:

FIG. 54 *North College in 1901: east (College Street) facade.*

FIG. 55 *New (Second) Chapel: east (College Street) facade, with Berkeley Hall on the left and North College on the right.*

The College is subjected to very serious evils for want of adequate buildings. Long experience has shown that good order, industry, and morals, cannot be effectively secured while a great proportion of the students are dispersed, in different parts of the town. That watchful guardianship requires that they be under the immediate notice of their instructors, within the walls of College.[87]

Kingsley noted that only three-fourths of the students could be housed on campus and thus that a fourth hall would neatly bridge the gap. Although patron and alumni pledges proved meager, Day nonetheless moved forward with the construction of a new dormitory, North College, in 1820 (FIG. 54). As anticipated, it followed the established type, identical in all essential features to its predecessor, Berkeley Hall. Aligned with the Row, it also adumbrated the college's next building, leaving a space between itself and Berkeley sufficient for a new chapel type. That building was not long in coming. A dramatic increase in enrollment—370 students admitted in 1823— followed the construction of the new dormitory, and Kingsley reissued his pamphlet plea, again lamenting the lack of housing but adding that "the evils proceeding from the want of a suitable house of worship are still more alarming." The overriding need to accommodate its enlarged congregation pushed Yale once more into construction before it had raised the necessary funds. In January 1824 they broke ground for the New (or Second) Chapel and, with remarkable speed, completed it eleven months later (FIG. 55).[88]

FIG. 56 *John Warner Barber, "A View of the Public Square or Green in New Haven, Con.," 1835.*

FIG. 57 *New Haven Centennial Medal, 1838. Designed by Ithiel Town. New Haven Colony Historical Society.*

It took its place between Berkeley Hall and North College, conforming to the steepled box type but incrementally larger than the Lyceum—fifty-six by seventy-two feet rather than forty-four by fifty-six feet—just as that hall had been slightly larger than the first chapel, which measured forty by fifty feet. Significantly, the design for the New Chapel (the builder and architect are unknown) included a columned front portico and ornamented pediment and eave.[89] These features, together with the Chapel's larger size, gave it a close resemblance to the recently rebuilt Congregational churches on the New Haven Green. Both the First and Third Churches had replaced their earlier meetinghouses between 1812 and 1815; the Gothic Episcopal Church was added at this time as well, taking the place of the old State House. All three adopted the frontally oriented type that Clap had used for the first chapel in 1760 and which Dwight had repeated for the Lyceum in 1803 (FIG. 56). Thus the temples of town and college came into line with each other, ranged across the Green and yard with their spires piercing Hillhouse's continuous canopy of elms (FIG. 57).

The New Chapel filled a mix of needs that had spilled over from the crowded halls. The main galleried assembly space was a place of worship

FIG. 58 *B. F. Nutting, "Yale College, New Haven," 1829–33.*

for the expanding college congregation. It housed student sleeping quarters on the third floor and the college library in the attic, relocated once again after its brief sojourn in the Lyceum. By this time, the library had become a reliable metaphor for campus expansion, leapfrogging to the front of the line as the Brick Row expanded along College Street. It was to continue to play this role into the mid-nineteenth and early twentieth centuries, anticipating with its various relocations the direction of campus growth.[90]

Meanwhile, the first chapel of 1761–63, its function rendered obsolete, was secularized into an academic hall and renamed the Athenaeum. The assembly space was carved up into recitation rooms and libraries for the student societies, and in 1829

FIG. 59 *Divinity College in the 1860s: east (College Street) facade.*

its spire and belfry were replaced with a cylindrical observatory housing a newly acquired telescope (FIG. 58). In the spirit of the hall's new name and partaking of the current taste for ancient Greek architecture, the observatory was modeled on the Athenian Tower of the Winds. Displacing God for science was a telling symbol of change on the campus, signaling the growing importance of the new field to Yale's academic mission. As it was, the shift from the sacred to secular heavens was blessed with good fortune shortly thereafter, when Yale was the first in America to sight the return of Halley's comet in 1835.[91]

Theological concerns remained a primary focus of scholarship at Yale, however, as the Brick Row's last addition made clear. In 1835, the new Divinity College rose at the end of the line, next to Elm Street, and left the requisite (although ultimately unfilled) gap for a chapel type (FIG. 59). The Divinity School had been founded in 1822 as the Theological Department, independent of Yale College. It had raised its own funds, to which New Haven citizens had contributed generously. Thus Divinity College, although visibly indistinguishable from the other Brick Row halls, was nonetheless administratively and socially distinct. Reinforcing the distance physically was both the gap between North and Divinity Colleges and that gap's placeholder, the president's house, which stood forward of the Row's line and separated the divinity students from the all-important college yard. So, with some irony, Yale's first Divinity School found itself somewhat removed from its parent, an institution that had been founded for

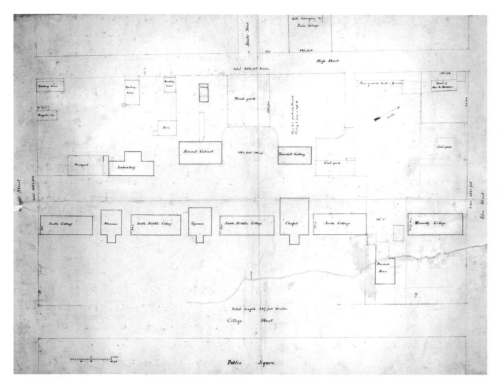

FIG. 60 *Plan of the College, ca. 1841.*

FIG. 61 *E. Valois, "Yale College," ca. 1860.*

FIG. 62 *Trumbull Gallery in 1865: east facade.*

divine ends but was increasingly concerned with more secular pursuits.[92]

The natural sciences were foremost among these. Their growth in particular denoted an increasingly complex and specialized academic program, which strained the functional limits of the Row. To accommodate unorthodox additions to its curriculum, Yale turned to its rear yard, which had traditionally been dedicated to back-of-house services—coal yards, commons, privies, and the like (FIG. 60). There the sciences, still not quite legitimate in all eyes, had to content themselves with quarters in the original Commons building of 1782 (renamed the Laboratory in 1820) or, in the case of the geological collection known as the Cabinet, piggybacked onto the second floor of the new Commons of 1819 (FIG. 61).

An even more radical addition came in 1830 when John Trumbull proposed to the Corporation via his nephew, Benjamin Silliman, that he bequeath his collection of historical paintings to Yale in exchange for an annuity and the construction of a picture gallery on the campus grounds to house the collection. To their credit, Day and the Corporation agreed immediately. The Trumbull Gallery, designed by the artist and funded by a state grant, became the first art museum to be associated with a college in the United States and, indeed, one of the first established in the English-speaking world (FIG. 62).[93] It was built behind the New Chapel and aligned precisely with its center axis, establishing a formal relationship with the front Row. The alignment also reflected a programmatic connection; a theological lecture room occupied the gallery's first floor, with the skylit *pinacotheca* raised above. The building thus had, in part, a devout purpose, tempering

somewhat the incursion of art into an institution founded by iconoclastic Puritans. The artwork also served a didactic role, with Trumbull's historical tableaux intended to instill a patriotic sentiment in students. He clearly designed the soberly neoclassical gallery as a monument, honoring love for God and country. It had one other purpose as well, betrayed by its tomblike character. Upon his death in 1843, his body was placed, alongside his deceased wife, beneath its stone flooring and, as requested, under his own portrait of General Washington. All rested behind the stately Brick Row he had helped to design fifty years before.

MOSES AND AARON

In 1833, two years before Divinity College was built, Yale replaced the wooden paling fence enclosing the yard with a post-and-rail fence. Physically and symbolically, it consolidated the enlarged campus, presaging the Row's imminent completion and reaffirming the sanctity of the college yard. The fence of 1833 quickly came to play a significant role in college and city life. It not only marked the boundary between the campus and surrounding city but, in the particular use that students made of it, also acted as a mediator between the two communities. By now, the Brick Row was a formidable presence in the city; at over 850 feet, its breadth equaled that of the Green, no mean feat given the common's extraordinary size (FIG. 63). In its proximity to the Green, it also embodied the ambiguous relationship of the college to the city, alternately cooperative and competitive. By 1830 New Haven had completed its new State House, an imposing Greek temple sited at midpoint along the top of the Green, opposite the Brick Row and yard. In its own way, the building was an act of confirmation for the city, visibly establishing its political and cultural position alongside its burgeoning commercial and industrial importance. Alexander Jackson Davis's famous and oft-copied view of 1832 captured best the tension in the space between college Row and city temple (FIG. 64). The evocative image vacillates from a tableau of unified civic purpose—the "Moses and Aaron" of Stiles's day—to one more confrontational, with each community asserting autonomy within its respective fenced realm.[94]

In the day-to-day life of college and town, the Yale fence came to symbolize that ambiguity. This had much to do with its construction. In contrast with the earlier, distinctly urban fence types made with boards and palings, the new fence was rural in origin; its horizontal rails were intended to enclose

FIG. 63   *The Brick Row and New Haven around 1860. Drawing by Erik Vogt.*

large agricultural fields and control the movements of livestock. One fateful consequence of this design, unforeseen by the administration, was the suitability of the rounded top rail for sitting. The fence—or "The Fence," as it was soon called—became famous for such accommodation during the nineteenth century, as class after class discovered the joys of seeing, and being seen on, the literal boundary between town and gown (see FIG. 31). Their use of it in this way resonated with the biblical meaning of the bounding fence as an allegory of moral law. Perched on the pastoral boundary between enclosed academical garden and the encompassing wilderness of the "outside" world, students could claim to be within the limits of the college's legal and moral authority while still in contact with the temptations of city life. It was a habit that President Clap and his early successors would have certainly frowned upon or perhaps banned outright; but now, ironically, it became a beloved Yale tradition. An eminently civic institution, the Fence—and the college yard behind it—created a mediating social realm between college

and town, Yale's front porch to the city. It also reflected and amplified the campus's inherently domestic character, defining the yard as a tree-filled garden court before the private "houses" of the college. Altogether, the elements composing the enclosed yard gave the nineteenth-century campus the character of a pastoral retreat, a hushed oasis embedded in yet removed from the urban life just outside its gates (FIG. 65).

That distinctive character was to have a mixed effect on Yale and New Haven's relationship in the ensuing decades. By appropriating the Fence, the students reinforced its implied territoriality. At its best, this provided them with a constructive experience of communal life, but at its worst it exacerbated already existing tensions between the student body and the surrounding townspeople. Most significantly, it laid bare the underlying contradiction between the ideal of an academic sanctuary and its enactment in the midst of a thriving city. Although the Brick Row masterfully negotiated this paradox, Yale's confidence in the campus model was eventually to erode in the

FIG. 64 *Alexander Jackson Davis, "Yale College and the State House, New Haven, Connecticut," 1832.*

FIG. 65 *The Fence and the college yard, looking north from Chapel Street with the Brick Row on the left, ca. 1875.*

FIG. 66 *Students in Connecticut Hall in 1862.*

face of its many conflicts. When that confidence finally gave way, the sanctuary ideal was to prevail with a vengeance, upsetting the delicate balance achieved between the life of the college and the larger community in which it resided.

———

The Brick Row's completion in the early 1830s marked the beginning of a distinct era in Yale's history: a close-knit community was formed, compact and whole, separate from the city beyond yet undeniably part of it. The stark brick halls stood aloof in simple dignity and gathered strength in their numbers. Yet their fundamentally urban order, making a space before them which was joined with the great Green beyond, engaged them fully with the city, sharing the responsibility of forming a public realm. At the time, observers appreciated the virtue of their Puritan simplicity and the priorities they invoked. Ebenezer Baldwin (B.A. 1808), describing the campus in his *Annals of Yale College* of 1838, wrote: "The buildings are constructed in a plain substantial manner, and with a view throughout to convenience and economy, rather than architectural embellishment…the simplicity of the buildings comports with their object and their extent gives enough of magnificence."[95] The Brick Row's sober forms set into high relief the colorful student life within and created a crucible of sorts for the formation of student character. It impressed itself deeply on the experiences and memories of Yale

men. "The Row and what we may call its personality, had their acute relations to scholarship, to discipline, to undergraduate purpose, to student morals, to the day's walk and the day's work," wrote Clarence Deming (B.A. 1872) in his memoir of student days. "A student life that converged on a single Campus and four dormitories was necessarily intense. Men rubbed each other hard and the attrition spelled character." It was "an inner and intense life…and if it had fewer things to think about, it thought harder about the things it had."[96] The close quarters of each college house promoted a powerfully communal existence and forced the students to adopt a public and private face, a paradoxical mix that the campus as a whole embodied. While promoting an inward-focused intensity, it also forged civic awareness, dictating "a life which had to be lived openly and in the sight of one's fellows" and encouraging "straightforward conduct and reputable habits."[97]

Within the four identical dormitories—which students dubbed straightforwardly South, South Middle, North Middle, and North Colleges—the undergraduates managed to construct an intricate matrix of subcommunities (FIG. 66). They dispersed by class, with seniors getting the most prized rooms: in South College, officially Union Hall, favored for its proximity to Chapel Street and the adjoining Fence (with "south entry, second floor, front corner" being the top choice); and in North College, the newest of the four and thus equipped with more modern conveniences. Each hall had a vertical hierarchy: seniors claimed the second floor and juniors the third, leaving to freshmen and sophomores either the weary ascent to the top floor or the damp and noise of the first floor. Finally, they grouped themselves by entry, with the occupants of rooms letting out onto each of the stair halls forming their own student clubs.[98]

Thus occupied, the Row acquired a varied personality across its breadth. Campus life centered on South College, with its segment of the Fence along Chapel Street a point of congregation for students (see FIG. 31). Deming remembered the hall as "the chief font of undergraduate trickery... Standing at the end of the Brick Row it projected as a kind of prow into the currents of the town. The fugitive from the street rush found it a quick asylum from city authority, while conversely, the student chased by the tutor passed easily to the street."[99] As one moved from the southern prow to the northern stern at Elm Street, campus life steadily calmed. Divinity College, buffered by the president's house, was an oasis of relative tranquility.

What most characterized the Brick Row campus, however, was its permeability. If the appearance of the Fence and the Row's monumental wall of buildings obscured this fact somewhat, day-to-day reality revealed it clearly. Student life flowed out, town life ebbed in, and the crosscurrents swirled around the college yard and Fence. Deming recalled that:

the Row smiled open-faced on the city with a sort of democratic greeting. "Jump the fence," [it] said. "Come in where you please and go where you please"...The Campus, in fact, became well nigh as open as a village green. Tramps, beggars, organ grinders, agents, peddlers went in and out at will. As a short cut to the corners of a large city square, [it] thus became a kind of thoroughfare.[100]

The gaps between the Brick Row buildings alternated with the stair hall passages to filter people through in the daily ritual of campus life, some passing to the grounds beyond and some absorbed into the buildings themselves.

The open-railed Fence operated in much the same way. One could easily pass through its many openings or, more likely, occupy its space for a while before moving on. As the favorite meeting place for students, it had its own patterns of use as well. Only seniors and juniors were allowed to sit facing Chapel Street, while sophomores occupied a stretch around the corner on College Street and freshmen were barred altogether, except when they had achieved some athletic victory.[101] Despite these class distinctions, students viewed the Fence as symbolic of Yale's open character and spirit of camaraderie. "They believed that it formed at once the opportunity for and inspiration of the democratic community life of the place," wrote Lewis Welch (B.A. 1889) and Walter Camp (B.A. 1880) in their book on Yale life in the late nineteenth century. It reinforced Yale's "character as a social institution. Men of all tastes and modes of life were there together...on the common rail."[102] No other structure or institution on the Yale campus gathered such intense sentiment among students and alumni in the nineteenth century.

———

"Tres faciunt Collegium" each jurist now agrees,
Which means, in the vernacular, a College made of trees.
William Croswell, B.A. 1822[103]

By the mid-nineteenth century, Hillhouse's elms had risen to prominence, both on campus and in the city streets. Charles Dickens, who passed through New Haven on his famous trip to America in 1841–42, noted their effect, especially in uniting the Green and college yard: "Many of [New Haven's] streets are planted with rows of grand old elms; and the same natural ornaments surround Yale College, an establishment of considerable eminence and reputation. The various departments of this Institution are erected in a kind of park or common in the middle of the town, where they are dimly visible among the shadowing trees."[104] Indeed, visitors and residents alike often remarked on New Haven's forest or gardenlike appearance and dubbed it "The Elm City" and "The City of Gardens" (FIG. 67). Nathaniel Parker Willis (B.A. 1827) wrote in his well-known *American Scenery* of 1840:

[New Haven] has the appearance of a town roofed in with leaves; and it is commonly said, that, but for the spires, a bird flying over would scarce be aware of its existence. Nothing could be more beautiful than the effect of this in the streets; for, standing where any of the principal avenues cross at right angles, four embowered aisles extend away as far as the eye can follow. The roads below are kept moist and cool with the roof overhead, the sidewalks, between the trees and the rural dwellings, are broad and shady; the small gardens in front of most of the houses are bright with flowering shrubs; and the whole scene, though in the midst of a city, breathes of nature.[105]

Narratives of Yale life echoed these observations, sounding a note of gratitude for the benefits bestowed on the college by Hillhouse's work. Ezekiel Porter Belden (B.A. 1844), in his *Sketches of Yale College* of 1843, wrote:

FIG. 67 *Temple Street, looking north from Chapel Street, ca. 1875.*

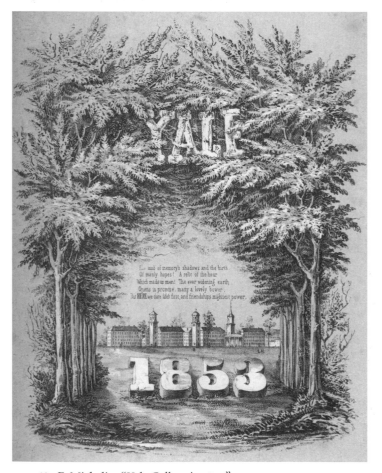

FIG. 68 *F. Michelin, "Yale College in 1853."*

It is not our purpose to establish for New Haven the reputation of a Paradise, were that possible; but no one can have failed to hear of the beauties of our forest city…the College is nearly the centre, and the beautiful parks in front afford a glimpse almost of woodland scenery. These separate us entirely from the noise and bustle of trade, and furnish coolness and delightful shade to our classic retreat.[106]

New Haven's *rus in urbes* offered a balance between urban and rural life particularly suited to the needs of the young student. "The situation of Yale College is peculiarly fortunate," wrote Belden. "Such an institution can hardly flourish in the seclusion of a country village where the manners and habits are necessarily framed on the model of rural life; while, on the other hand, the numerous temptations…which abound in a metropolis, render such a location extremely dangerous to the interests of the young."[107] Indeed, the setting itself could contribute to their education; Ebenezer Baldwin, echoing the earlier words of Timothy Dwight, suggested as much in his *Annals of Yale College:*

The scenery of New Haven should not be disregarded in estimating its advantages as a place of education. It is not a fanciful idea merely, that external objects operate on the mind, and quicken or deaden its impulses, by their silent influence…New Haven, spread out amidst gardens and shady walks, in simplicity, perfect neatness, and unostentatious elegance…realizes to the student all the quiet beauties and charming retirement which the school of Plato enjoyed: "In sacred Academus' shady walks."[108]

The reference to Plato's Academy revealed not only the contemporary concern with the ideals of a classical education (as reflected in the famous "Yale Report" of 1828) but also the campus's physical ethos.[109] Bounded by its enclosing fence and looking out at the Greek temple of the State House, the college yard took on the qualities of a sacred *temenos,* sheltered under the enormous grove of elms (FIG. 68). The three rows of trees sprang into "two vast arches, high, symmetrical, a great nave of bough and leaf," Deming recalled. Their high canopy "left the Campus open to summer breeze, intercepted blazing sunlight and made [it] at once a studio and a lounging place; and they transmuted for a large fraction of the day the indoor to an outdoor life."[110] That outdoor life more often than not included the Green across the street. Students used its upper half as a football field, to the irritation of the townspeople, and adopted the State House's imposing portico as the site for their various rituals (FIG. 69). The Green, in fact, was inseparable from both the life and appearance of the Brick Row campus. Its buildings,

Willis observed in *American Scenery*, "buried in trees and standing on the ridge of a sloping green, have altogether a beautiful effect, and an air of elegant and studious repose." The view he described was the same that had so impressed Timothy Dwight. A favorite of engravers as well, it never failed to include, in image or word, the Green's presence as a proper foreground to the stately alignment of halls and chapels.[111]

———

However, the idyllic tableaux rendered by writers and artists alike rarely included the encroachments of an expanding industrial city. That reality pressed in, as the Row's "inner and intense life" often spilled out, with sometimes tragic results. The pressures of urban life combined with a volatile student body—which directed its outbursts both inward at unpopular college policies and outward at an increasingly wary citizenry—to produce a number of skirmishes on and around the open campus. The period of greatest unrest began soon after the Brick Row campus's consolidation in the mid-1830s and did not subside until the onset of the Civil War. The first serious clash occurred in 1841 when students playing football on the Green interfered with the exercises of town firemen and were subsequently detained by city police. In retaliation, they attacked the newly built firehouse on High Street, behind the campus, destroying one engine and inciting a near riot. The

next and most notorious incident occurred in 1854. Students attending the theater on Church Street engaged in a taunting match with locals that lasted over two nights, culminating in a brick, knife, and gun fight along Chapel Street. One townsperson was killed as the students retreated to the safety of South College. That safety turned out to be shortlived, as the mob of citizens hauled in two cannon to bombard the building. The faculty, including President Theodore Dwight Woolsey, were among those who had to barricade themselves in the hall. Fortunately, a constable sabotaged the weapons before they could be fired, and the crowd eventually dispersed. The third and final major conflict, in 1858, again involved the fire company of High Street, and the brief run-in resulted in the death of a fireman. In the aftermath of each incident, the students suffered only light punishment despite the fatalities and their obvious complicity in instigating the violence. The final episode persuaded town and college authorities to share the cost of relocating the firehouse away from campus grounds.

Historians have attributed the rise of conflict in this period to several factors: the frictions inherent to a growing city, the constraints of a highly structured academic life on an energetic student body, and, more generally, the charged national context preceding the Civil War.[112] In addition, a territorial instinct may have also played a role. From the 1830s

FIG. 69 *"State-House and Public Square, New Haven, with College Buildings in the Back-Ground,"* 1856.

FIG. 70 *Yale College Library (now Dwight Hall) in the 1860s: east (Old Campus) facade.*

on, the students possessed a physically unified campus to which they could attach an insurgent sense of collegial pride. The Fence, determining "the limit of direct municipal authority," was a real and symbolic marker of that pride.[113] It delineated the students' own "College Green," which became, like its public counterpart across the street, the repository of communal solidarity. New Haven's citizenry seemed to respond in kind, growing increasingly resentful of student incursions on their own territory. Perceived boundaries probably underlay student hostility toward the firemen on High Street as well. The students no doubt felt that the firehouse's eventual removal represented a victory in their long-fought turf battle. As it was, it marked the close of a particularly volatile era in the relationship of Yale and New Haven, one that was to have repercussions in the redesign of the college campus in the post-Civil War years.

The first sign of a new campus planning strategy came in the final years of President Day's long stewardship. In the late 1830s the administration began raising funds for a library building, needed to consolidate and house the growing collections of the college and student societies. Tradition would have

dictated that it occupy the Brick Row's last chapel space, between North and Divinity Colleges. But the administration instead chose to place the library behind the Brick Row, roughly centered on the block and pushed up against High Street. A stone building in the Gothic Revival style designed by the New Haven architect Henry Austin, it was completed in 1846, the year of Day's retirement (FIG. 70).[114] Corporation meeting minutes do not reveal the reasons for the location, stating only that the Prudential Committee charged with the construction shall "proceed and erect a suitable building on such place of the College grounds as they judge most proper for the purpose."[115] The latter qualification hints at one of two probable reasons for the break with tradition. Because the building was to contain books, fire safety was a matter of overriding importance. Given a recent history of disastrous fires both in the city of New Haven and, more ominously, at Harvard's library, Yale would have been ill advised to place its priceless collection in the Row's last gap, between two coal-heated, student-tended dormitories. Instead, they located it not only away from the residential halls but also across the street from a city firehouse (the same one that attracted student ire in the 1840s and 1850s).[116]

The second reason related to the larger issue of campus planning. With Divinity College closing out the Row and the last chapel space disqualified as a site for the new library, the administration found itself without a definite strategy for future growth. It is uncertain whether the library's siting was provisional or part of a larger plan—no record written between 1835 and 1850 has yet surfaced referring to any such thought—but its design and placement hinted at a general direction that the college was to take in coming years. Most telling was the building's orientation. Although placed along High Street, it turned its back on the street—as well as on the new Library Street that aligned with its high nave—and faced the rear yard of the Row. Given the library's functional and symbolic importance, the move seemed to signal that the administration considered the interior of the college square, rather than the yard on College Street, to be a future focal point for the campus as a whole. Ezekiel Porter Belden, writing while the library was being built, said as much when he observed that its placement at midblock made it "the central thing in the whole establishment." The orientation of subsequent buildings—Alumni Hall in 1851 and Street Hall in 1864—was to confirm this presumption.[117]

The change of focus also signaled a shift away from Yale's desire for public display. Much of the Brick Row's power, and by extension Yale's visible stature, derived from its "eminent place" at the top of the Green; each new building along that elevation was a benchmark of institutional growth and prosperity.

Placing the library away from such a vantage was a turning inward of another sort. It foreshadowed an attitudinal change, a diminished regard for the connection to New Haven that had always been embodied in the Row's public face. The college now valued more dearly its autonomy and internal cohesion. Standing as the "central thing" in a new campus yet to be formed, the library was a building for Yale alone.

————

The first official recognition that a dramatically new campus plan was in order came in 1850, in President Theodore Dwight Woolsey's "Historical Discourse," delivered in honor of Yale's one hundred and fiftieth anniversary.[118] Woolsey (B.A. 1820) had succeeded Day in 1846 and was also to have a long presidency, stepping down only in 1871. Concluding his address with a description of Yale's future needs, he judged that "the present ugly row of colleges cannot remain for more than twenty-five years: that is to say one or two of them will probably need to be pulled down within a quarter of a century for very age."[119] Their austerity, once considered a virtue, was now deemed an ugly vice. This was the first recorded mention of a desire to demolish the existing buildings, couched in an argument that the administration would return to over and over again in coming years. The halls had outgrown their usefulness, and removing them seemed to be the only option.

In this respect, they also fell victim to an unfortunate circumstance of the changing times. New industrial buildings, built of brick and characterized by plain, regimented facades, were springing up in many northeastern cities, including New Haven (FIG. 71). Observers began to associate the Row's spare appearance with factories. As early as 1842, Benjamin Silliman somewhat apologetically characterized the campus as being in "a very humble style of architecture, a long and solemn array of plain brick walls, like manufactories."[120] In 1858, an article in *Harper's New Monthly* described the Brick Row as "the factory-like façade of 'old Yale,' certainly more venerable than beautiful."[121] Their once "plain substantial manner" now struck critics as belonging more properly to the world of industry than to an institution embodying Puritan virtues.

The belief that the Row still retained a didactic influence seemed to be waning as well. Woolsey implied as much in his "Discourse" when he proposed a new plan for the campus: "If new buildings should be found to be desirable, it would then be of the greatest importance to form a new plan, which should give to the College grounds their greatest capacity of embellishment, and which by imposing

FIG. 71 *"Whitney Arms Company, New Haven, Connecticut," ca. 1860.*

FIG. 72 *The Brick Row from Chapel and College Streets in the 1860s.*

architecture, should have a healthy effect on the taste and morals of the students."[122] Thus the colonial halls, once a formidable presence in a town of two-story wooden houses, had outlived their symbolic usefulness. Nevertheless, they imparted one last important lesson to Yale's leadership: the need to form a new campus within the framework of a larger plan. The Brick Row, however modest in its individual parts, had collected them into a whole much greater than their sum (FIG. 72).

SANCTUARY

Despite Woolsey's call for a plan in 1850, Yale took no action on a new campus building strategy for the next eighteen years. Only one building, Alumni Hall (1851), went up on the college square in the 1850s (see FIG. 81). Nevertheless, its orientation and placement at the corner of Elm and High Streets reinforced the library's precedent and further implied an intention to build along the campus edge and face inward. The onset of the Civil War postponed any other plans, but in 1864, Yale received or was promised four substantial private donations dedicated to new buildings: one for an art school (Street Hall, begun that same year), one for a new chapel, and two for additional dormitories. The college's

good fortune precipitated a crisis of sorts: the promise of new buildings could not be fulfilled without rethinking the future of the college square.[123]

The Corporation waited until 1868 before they addressed the issue decisively. Their initial consideration was to abandon the original campus altogether. "The prospect of [new buildings] has given interest and earnestness to a question sometimes raised before – whether the College should leave its old site, to gain a more spacious one in some other part of New Haven," wrote the Society of the Alumni in their annual report on Yale College for 1869, documenting the previous year's progress. "The present site, indeed, is not without its advantages: it has the old traditions of the institutions; it looks out pleasantly on the public square; it is within easy access of the railroads; it feels the influence, at once enlivening and restraining, of the city life around it. The only strong objection to it is its smallness." The nine acres of the college square would be "barely sufficient…in the present and the immediate future," requiring buildings "to be placed near each other, without much regard to the best architectural effects." Equally onerous, they would "stand inconveniently near to city streets, which with the growth of the town will become more and more crowded and noisy. The retirement and quiet desirable for academic pursuits will to considerable extent be lost."[124]

Although the Corporation identified a suitable new site—a fifty-acre plot behind the Hillhouse estate to the north of the nine squares—they concluded that such a move would be too costly. Costly as well was their other considered option, the purchase of a substantial amount of land near the existing campus. Although they might be able to raise the money, the administration felt that the outlay would threaten the economic viability of the academic program. They concluded that a solution must be found on the original college square.[125] "It became an important practical question, how the present ground could be used in the most economical and effective way for the accommodation of buildings now or hereafter to be erected," the alumni report in 1870 recounted:

From this point of view, it seemed most expedient to arrange the new buildings around the sides of the College Square in a form, so far as may be practicable, of an enclosed quadrangle. The plan contemplates a continuous line of buildings on the College Street side, with arched entrances at convenient points. This line is to be terminated at the north end by the new chapel, which is to stand lengthwise on Elm Street, and the remaining space on that street will be occupied by Durfee Hall.[126]

Under their criteria of economy and practicality, the plan made sense on several counts. By lining the perimeter of the campus block, it used the land efficiently, gaining the maximum exterior wall surface for light and ventilation while occupying the least amount of buildable land. It also allowed new buildings to go up while the Brick Row remained in use. By now, the Row was perceived as essentially obsolete, held over only by necessity.[127] And finally, it could accommodate the new mode of construction financing that had arisen after the war. No longer dependent solely on tuition, public grants, or piecemeal fundraising, Yale could now look to individual private donors to fund its new buildings. These were most often alumni who had profited in the great industrial expansion of the mid- to late nineteenth century and who had amassed enough wealth to endow entire projects singlehandedly. The quadrangle plan would set in place a comprehensible framework for this new scale and pace of construction. Beginning with the gifts of 1864, it did just that. Over the next forty years, donors who had more likely than not spent their college years in the Brick Row now lent their names to buildings that were to wall it off from the surrounding city and ensure its eventual destruction.

In 1869 Yale began dismantling the Brick Row and enclosing the college yard (FIG. 73). The first of the new dormitories, Farnam Hall, occupied the northern yard where the president's house had stood.[128] To make way for Durfee Hall along Elm Street, Yale took down the newest Brick Row building, Divinity College, which was replaced the next year by East Divinity Hall across the street (FIG. 74). Farnam and Durfee were Woolsey's contributions to the quadrangle before his retirement in 1871, and they were not an auspicious beginning to the campus's new relationship with the surrounding city. Their fortresslike character, exacerbated by low retaining walls that took up the yard's slight rise, perhaps had something to do with Woolsey's experience of the town and college riots; he had been among those barricaded in South College during the "siege" of 1854.

Noah Porter (B.A. 1831), professor of moral philosophy and metaphysics, succeeded Woolsey in 1871 and remained in office until 1886. Conservative-minded, he advocated the ethos of "old Yale," centered on "the common life of the college." He too favored the quadrangle plan, for it properly reflected the inward focus of a college community, "more completely separated and farther removed than almost any other from the ordinary influences of family and social life."[129] Nevertheless, he accomplished relatively little new construction during his term. In 1874, Battell Chapel went up at the corner of College and Elm Streets as planned; and in 1885 Lawrance Hall was added to the College Street wall beside Farnam. Neither building required the demolition of any Row halls. Although Porter shared his colleagues' disdain for the antiquated buildings, he must have felt some relief from that fact. For a president who so dearly cherished the college tradition, the Row was a forceful reminder of its history at Yale, rivaled but not yet overshadowed by the new halls at the campus's edge.[130]

In 1886, the quadrangle's slow, fitful progress quickened with the election of its greatest champion, Timothy Dwight (B.A. 1849), to the Yale presidency. Grandson of Yale's ninth president and a professor of sacred literature in the Theological Department, Dwight had long seen the need for dramatic change at Yale. In 1870–71, he had passionately endorsed the quadrangle plan in a series of articles written for the journal *The New Englander*. For him, it was a momentous undertaking that signaled the beginning of a new era for Yale. "We speak of the plan as a great one," he wrote, "it has reference to nothing less than the rebuilding of the whole College. Of the vast

FIG. 73 *North College, with construction materials for Farnam Hall in the foreground, in 1869.*

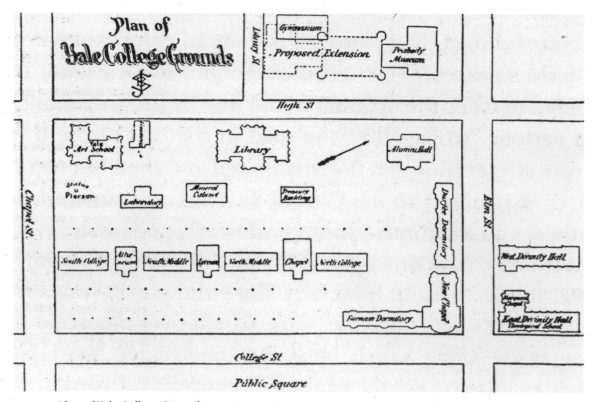

FIG. 74 *Plan of Yale College Grounds, ca. 1877.*

importance of this work there can scarcely be any doubt. For this reason, it appears to us that it should *be most carefully studied, in all its parts, at the outset.*" While he supported the enclosure of the college square—"the beauty of this arrangement will readily be appreciated by any person…the great quadrangle must look inward, not outward, and College life must find its center within its own borders"—he had cautioned against a campus that *only* looked inward. This would ill serve the college's responsibility to the surrounding city. The campus, he reminded his readers, "[is] in the central part of one of the most beautiful of our American cities. The ground is contiguous to and faces the large public square, which is so well-known an ornament of New Haven. Under these circumstances, whatever is done in the matter of laying out and erecting the College buildings must have a most important bearing on the appearance of the city." To that end he urged the administration to consult New Haven's citizens on the building plans. As a general principle, he felt that "all new buildings ought to be designed with [a] double frontage or with the appearance of a handsome front toward the town." He regretted the closed and fortified character of Farnam and Durfee Halls and argued that future halls be designed to acknowledge the city around them, "because it is right, because it is respectful to the citizens, [and] because it will tend greatly to the adorning of New Haven." In the long run, this would serve Yale's interests as well: "If the permanent growth and welfare of the institution are to be secured, New Haven must not fail to cherish and support it…It certainly ought not to be repressed by adopting the disapprobation of those who feel a pride in the beauty of the city."[131]

Dwight turned from the quadrangle's outward obligations to its inward appearance, offering a consideration of its aesthetic and even moral implications. He regretted the use of brick in the just completed halls, arguing that "the glory of architecture lies in stone, and the cherished hope of those who have looked forward to the coming age of architecture in the College [is] that the old line of unsightly brick buildings might give way, not only to beautiful ones, but to those made of stone." His view was essentially Ruskinian, echoing the English critic and artist's stance on the proper use of building materials.[132] For Dwight, a quadrangle enclosed by an architecture of stone would create a morally and spiritually uplifting environment. "These new buildings and the re-arrangement of the College Square are not things belonging *only* to the outward life of the institution," he wrote: "the student will not go away from his College life with only those influences which come from the books he has studied, or the minds he has been brought in contact with. The very buildings which have met his vision from day to day will have taught him other and valued lessons. They will have entered, by their insensible yet constant influence, into his inward life."[133]

To that end, he had recommended—unsuccessfully—that the new college chapel be placed at the center of the quadrangle. The chapel, in type and function, held the greatest symbolic and moral force and represented Yale's preeminent mission as a college of Christian learning and faith. "The location or the architecture of a building may seem a small thing in itself, but it may prove to be of more force than labored argument," he contended. "The placing of the house of religious worship for the university at the central point of all the other edifices will be one means of defending and preserving the true faith here…the turning and pointing of all things will be *visibly* toward religion."[134]

An awareness of his grandfather's legacy pervaded Dwight's thoughts and actions. He looked back often on the elder Dwight's accomplishments, not least the construction of the Brick Row plan, and considered it his self-appointed mission to continue in that tradition, to remake Yale for the next century as his grandfather had remade it for the present one.[135] Nowhere was the affinity more evident than in their shared faith in the power of the physical realm to shape the character of a community. Dwight, trained as a minister, inherited as well the Puritan belief in a larger divine plan that patterned human progress and disclosed itself in time. Such a belief influenced greatly the actions of both Dwights. It gave meaning to the plans each had inherited, so that their fulfillment became part of a larger mission. The plans set forth a visible order for the Christian sanctuary and projected its future, a reflection of the underlying pattern that God had ordained for the world. Although it seems antithetical that the younger Dwight would want to abolish the Yale his grandfather had built, it was, nevertheless, his belief in the continuity of that underlying pattern which sanctioned the break. For him, the quadrangle plan would at once supersede and redeem the Brick Row, returning Yale to the ideal of the enclosed sanctuary even as it carried it forward into a new era.

Reversing Porter's conservative stewardship, the younger Dwight immediately set to work effecting the changes he had called for in his articles of 1870–71. Above all, he wanted Yale to recognize officially its status as a university. In October 1886, he succeeded

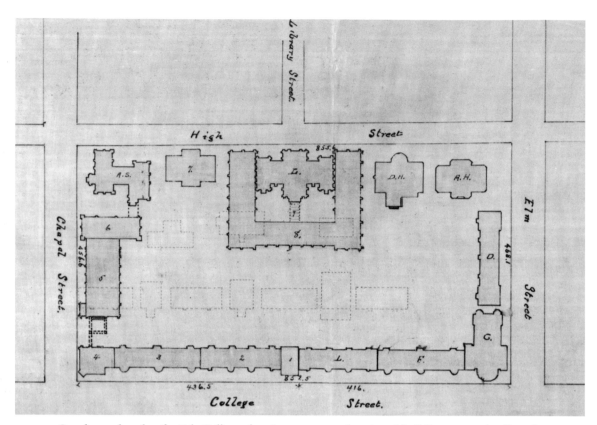

FIG. 75 *Quadrangular plan for Yale College, showing present and projected buildings, 1887. Attributed to William W. Farnam.*

in changing its name to Yale University, a deliberate and symbolic act that set the tone for his administrative policies.[136] Turning next to completion of the quadrangle, he used his yearly reports to the Corporation, faculty, and alumni as a platform to push for its speedy construction. Although the need for new buildings was real enough — Yale's combined enrollment in all departments surpassed 1,000 students by 1886[137] — it was their symbolic and didactic meaning that energized him. Pleading for donations to effect "the consummation of the plan," he wrote in his first report of 1887 that "the silent power of architectural taste and beauty…upon manners and even morals cannot be easily estimated…The benefactor who gives to the University a building may, therefore, be providing not only a temporary dwelling place or place of instruction for the students, but also an educating force which will bear upon their subsequent life."[138] That same year, Dwight had drawn up a speculative plan for the new quadrangle (FIG. 75). The drawing is attributed to Yale's treasurer, William W. Farnam, but was almost certainly produced under the president's direction.[139] It depicted mirrored plans of Farnam and Lawrance Halls on the south side of a central gate building, along with a large U-shaped hall surrounding the library, a

surrogate perhaps for Dwight's lost chapel. The Brick Row, its destruction a foregone conclusion, was rendered as a ghostly outline, floating in the midst of the newly formed interior yard.

Dwight launched his building campaign boldly, to say the least. During his first year in office, an anonymous donor offered to finance a much needed new recitation hall, with the condition that it be located on the campus's most conspicuous site, the corner of College and Chapel Streets. Aware of the implications for this hallowed stretch of the college Fence, Dwight accepted the offer nonetheless. The need for a new hall notwithstanding, he saw that it would serve a larger end: the stipulated site pinned down the final corner of the future quadrangle (Street Hall, Alumni Hall, and Battell Chapel already occupied the other corners).[140] Yale alumni, incensed that their cherished Fence was threatened (along with, not inconsequentially, a number of elms in the yard), signed a petition of protest and submitted it to the Corporation in the spring of 1888.[141] But it was to no avail; by summer the administration had uprooted the Fence and trees and begun construction on Osborn Hall (FIG. 76). Dwight had to weather the wrath of generations of Yale men, some of whom never forgave him. But, ironically, by tearing out

FIG. 76 *Osborn Hall from the north, with the Brick Row (Athenaeum [First College Chapel], Connecticut Hall, and Lyceum) on the right, in 1890.*

the Fence—the heart of collegiate life—he eased his longer-term task of destroying the Brick Row. After the events of 1888, many in the Yale community came to share, for very different reasons, Dwight's view that its fate was sealed.

Over the next ten years, Dwight's administration repeated the cycle of destruction and construction set in motion by Osborn Hall; a piece of the old campus fell as new buildings were added to the quadrangle's wall. In 1888, the chemical laboratory (originally the first Commons) came down for Chittenden Library; in 1890, the Cabinet (the second Commons) was torn down to make way for Welch Hall; and, in 1893, the first chapel (or Athenaeum) and South College (Union Hall) were razed to make way for Vanderbilt Hall. Phelps Hall and Gate filled the last gap in 1896, following the destruction of North Middle College (Berkeley Hall) and the New Chapel of 1824. All that remained standing of the Row by 1897 were Connecticut Hall, the Lyceum, and a lonely North College at the end of the line.

Throughout, Dwight remained loyal to his dictum of 1871: Yale's new buildings must open in some way to the city around them. His first effort, Osborn Hall, did so dramatically, with a screen of arches

looming over steps that spilled onto College and Chapel Streets. Welch Hall was pierced by a large archway leading from College Street to the interior yard (it has since been filled in). Vanderbilt Hall's three-sided court opened onto Chapel Street, with a carriage drive and center passageway connecting the busy commercial street to the campus. Finally, Phelps Hall, centered on the quadrangle and the Green, formed the ceremonial gateway between city and college, through which the Commencement procession, Yale's most enduring link with New Haven, would pass.

Dwight vigorously defended the building campaign in his yearly reports, hammering away at his themes of progress and renewal. He responded to grumbling over the Row's loss by disparaging its timeworn appearance and functional obsolescence. He even went so far as to remind disgruntled alumni that their "sentimental concern" would pass away as surely as they would.[142] Believing firmly that the splendor of the new campus, once completed, would put an end to all argument, he declared in 1890: "Let the quadrangle be once seen in its true beauty, and there will be no desire to have the old buildings restored, or to have new ones put in their places."[143] All of his utterances on the subject were suffused with this revolutionary zeal. Institutional progress could only be made by destroying the old to usher in the new; Yale would be frozen in the past if it did not complete its appointed task. "The removal of [the Row] is a marked event in the history and progress of the passing years," he wrote in 1893. "It indicates in a very impressive way the change from the old to the new era, and constitutes a sign of what must soon follow."[144]

The final years of Dwight's building campaign brought a wave of public lament from alumni. In 1896, when he released his report with yet another plea for the quadrangle's completion, the *Yale Alumni Weekly* published a scathing response. "The purpose of those who guide the destinies of this ancient and honorable university is to remove at the earliest date possible all conspicuous evidence that Yale has a past," the author remarked sarcastically. "It would have been folly ten years ago to doubt that Yale's 'past at least' was secure. But Yale's past, as a valuable asset of a Yale education, is not as secure as a great many less valuable things." The editorial turned Dwight's argument for the didactic value of new buildings on its head, holding up Connecticut Hall as a worthy lesson from that past, and asserting that "it makes more of an impression on a sensitive student's mind than any other structure."[145] Lewis Welch and Walter Camp, joining a growing number of Yale men seeking to save Connecticut Hall, echoed the same sentiment three years later: "Those who believe that the past of an institution—its old life and achievements, and heroes—are a tangible part of its assets as an educator…count it a remarkable waste of the resources of Yale to remove [Connecticut Hall]." They saw in the administration's actions a self-destructive impulse, fueled by a genuine disdain for its own history. "What a rough and ready way Yale has of using her historical relics, not to mention the disposing of them!…But it is one of the many signs of the present disposition of Yale towards the visible things of the past."[146]

Yet to the end Dwight remained defiant, always confident that Yale's "spirit," its underlying pattern, would endure beyond the loss of "the visible things of the past." "The fears which some men of our University brotherhood seem to have as to the danger that what is good in the Yale spirit may pass away, or be lost, are certainly astonishing," he wrote in one of his last reports. "The Yale democratic spirit is no such weak, sickly, worthless, impracticable thing as this. If it is in these closing years of the nineteenth century taking to itself such a character, the sooner it [should] die absolutely, and give way to something

nobler and more worthy of the name of an intelligent, scholarly, Christian democracy."[147]

———

The work that he had meant to do, Dwight said, was now about completed: the century of the two Dwights was rounded out…So in 1899, having brought his University to the border of the Promised Land, Yale's Moses took an almost puckish pleasure in stopping resolutely on the threshold…Dwight had such faith in the divine plan that he seemed invariably serene.
George W. Pierson, *Yale College: An Educational History, 1871–1921*[148]

Confident that his vision of the great open quadrangle would soon be consummated, Dwight stepped down as president in 1899, on the eve of Yale's third century. He left to his successor, Arthur Twining Hadley (B.A. 1876), the task of destroying the remaining Brick Row buildings and thus sweeping away the last vestiges of the old era. In the summer of 1901, the year of Yale's Bicentennial, President Hadley oversaw the final cycle of demolition and construction. The Lyceum, North College, and the Trumbull Gallery were torn down on what was now called the Old Campus (FIG. 77), as the buildings of Yale's new University Quadrangle (renamed Hewitt University Quadrangle in 1914) rose to the north, all in time for the celebration of Yale's founding (see FIGS. 158–163). As a culminating symbolic gesture it could not have been better staged. Hadley noted in his first president's report that the plan's completion, with the removal of the last Brick Row halls, marked another anniversary as well; it came fifty years after Woolsey had first "obscurely hinted at" a new campus plan in his "Discourse" for Yale's one hundred and fiftieth anniversary celebration.[149]

The new University Quadrangle was intended in part to fill a need left by the destruction of the college Fence. Dwight had proposed the buildings as early as 1890 as a place for the students of Yale's separate departments to congregate.[150] It was telling, however, that the desire for communal unity no longer included the greater life of the surrounding town; the Yale Bicentennial Buildings, like those of the Old Campus quadrangle, turned decidedly inward. The plans for both left behind something fundamental to Yale's history and purpose: a place of meeting and common faith shared with the city of New Haven.

In the Bicentennial's wake all that remained of the Brick Row was Connecticut Hall. As Yale's oldest building it had become the focus of alumni preservation efforts during the height of demolition in the 1890s. Begrudgingly, Dwight came to accept that its destruction was not, like that of its brethren, foreordained; by 1900, the president's report allowed

FIG. 77 *"The Passing of Old Yale," 1901, showing the demolition of the Lyceum, North College, and the Trumbull Gallery.*

that it could remain "for the sake of its historic interest and of the associations of what Yale was in the times gone by." A renewed effort by the administration to remove it in 1902–3 met with another wave of protest. In 1903, an alumni group raised money to renovate it, not only preserving but also restoring it to the original gambrel-roofed design of 1752 (see FIG. 34).[151] Thus rescued from near certain demise, Connecticut Hall stands as the first built and last remaining incarnation of its type, no longer prophesying the Row's fulfillment but memorializing its abolition. Cut off from the worldly wilderness of the surrounding city, it floats in the enclosed garden of the Old Campus, redeemed from the spiral of time (FIG. 78).

A COMMON LIFE

The past in its ordering has reason in itself.
Timothy Dwight, *Memories of Yale Life and Men,* 1903[152]

The wholesale sacrifice of the Brick Row may seem, in retrospect, rash or even incomprehensible. Nevertheless, the pragmatic reasons for its replacement were numerous and compelling, all of them driven by a growing campus and the constraints imposed by its urban setting. Perhaps equally powerful as an impetus for change was the administration's desire

to symbolize through architecture Yale's progress in the nineteenth century and its advance into the twentieth; "modern" buildings meant a modern Yale. Students and alumni responded as well to such a call. Stylish new living quarters drew back classmen who, if they could afford it, had been opting for better accommodations in town. Alumni donors, meanwhile, seized a conspicuous opportunity to display their wealth and generosity. The perceived role of the new campus as a didactic force also played its part. It could exercise its influence not only in its parts — sober and edifying buildings — but most powerfully as a whole, in the open sweep of green solemnly bounded by an architecture of stone. The Brick Row had long since lost favor in this regard, at once a remnant of the provincial colonial past and an unfortunate invocation of the industrial present.

However, the quadrangle's most powerful symbolic gesture was directed toward its larger context, New Haven. Deliberately and emphatically, it turned away from the city, fortifying Yale's edge and recentering its life inward. The administration was aware that the quadrangle's insular character could bode ill for Yale's relationship with New Haven, as Dwight's thoughts on the matter in 1871 demonstrated. Yet that relationship was already changing in ways that

FIG. 78 *Connecticut Hall within the Old Campus quadrangle in 1902–3.*

relieved the pressure on Yale's college square as the symbolic link between college and city. Student philanthropic organizations, which often directed their efforts at New Haven, became more active after the Civil War. With the establishment of Dwight Hall in the 1880s, their missionary work took on a fevered pitch that lasted through the turn of the century. Social engagement with the city was matched by physical engagement in places other than the Old Campus. University expansion in the mid-1800s, most prominently along the Scientific School's Sheffield Row on Prospect Street, linked the institution with New Haven's urban life in a manner far more forthright than the quadrangle plan proposed. The administration may have seen all these changes, which represented an openness to the city in other quarters, as compensating somewhat for the enclosure of the Old Campus.

Nonetheless, all practical, symbolic, and social justifications for that enclosure were subsumed to a large extent under the force of a more deep-seated and persistent ideal, one that had governed Yale's self-conception from its beginning: the Christian college as sanctuary. The enclosed quadrangle was only the latest and most explicit physical form of this ideal. As a recurring type in Christian tradition,

the sanctuary was first identified with the paradisiacal Garden of Eden, sheltered by the Tree of Life and Tree of Knowledge. The original elements of the type coalesced with particular power in the institutions entrusted with safeguarding Christian knowledge: the monastery at first and then its successor, the college. As George Hunston Williams identified them in *Wilderness and Paradise in Christian Thought,* "it is within the Paradise Cycle that the college or university has at its center a green, symbol of Paradise restored amidst the wilderness; its campus for the training of the spiritual militia of Christ; and its *wall,* library, and commons the practical means and the symbols too of the autonomy of the university in the transfer of its law, its learning, and its lore."[153]

The sanctuary ideal was one that Yale shared with the city in which it resided. New Haven's nine-square plan, recreating the biblical type of the sanctified temple city, made visible that ideal. Protected at its center was the sanctuary of the Green, a place of meeting and communion, a symbol of the congregation's covenanted bond.

The religious schism of the 1750s and the construction of the first chapel by Clap signaled Yale's first retreat from that common bond. Nevertheless,

Yale still shared with New Haven the great space of the Green, joined with the college yard beside it. The Brick Row's recapitulation of the original house and chapel types extended and strengthened the common edge of town and college, where Hillhouse's elms joined the dual sanctuaries of yard and Green in a single embowered garden. By the 1860s, however, the city was overgrown with new commerce, industry, and people, and Yale felt again the need to withdraw, to reconstitute itself as a "Paradise restored amidst the wilderness."

The Old Campus quadrangle was to prove a durable invocation of the type, repeated as a system in the famous residential college plan of the 1930s. The growing university used that plan as a means of returning to its communal ideal, hiving off its classes into autonomous collegiate communities. Each college, formed around a courtyard, was an island unto itself. It carried within a fragment of the original garden, a *paradeisos* captured and contained in its enclosing walls. Thus removed from the city, these sanctuaries harbored the memory and reenacted the type on which New Haven had been founded three centuries before. And yet the garden restored was to belong to Yale alone. In the creation of the quadrangle plan, Yale foreclosed on a greater communal vision and sacrificed the visible expression of the bond that for almost two centuries had joined its fate to that of New Haven.

George Dudley Seymour, New Haven's tireless civic activist in the early twentieth century, saw clearly what had been lost with the Brick Row's destruction, even though he himself had never experienced it in its full incarnation. Writing of the lost campus in his memoir, *New Haven* (1942), Seymour moved beyond issues of style and progress to convey the deeper meaning of the Row's life in the city as a whole:

These buildings had the supreme merit of being just right in pitch—they exactly suited their purpose and the genius of the place. Their correctness of pitch, their nice adjust-ment to the situation, their felicity of expression, their relation to the common life of the day but lifted just above it, all combined to give them a charm and a sense of belonging to the scene such as none of their successors has had.[154]

Those who had lived a part of their lives on the campus remembered it most vividly and mourned its loss most keenly. Donald Grant Mitchell (B.A. 1841), like Seymour a citizen and true champion of New Haven, was a student at Yale during the heyday of the Brick Row. He stayed on in New Haven, becoming a writer and involving himself in the enlargement and design of the city's urban parks. In a memoir of his college days, *Dream Life* (1851), he looked back on life in the Brick Row as a dream indeed, capturing in one elegiac passage both the haunting beauty of its setting and the sadness of its eventual demise, for Yale and New Haven alike:

As the night wanes, you wander, for a last look, toward the dingy walls, that have made for you so long a home… You step upon the Chapel-porch, in the quiet of the night, as you would step on the graves of friends. You pace back and forth in the wan moonlight, dreaming of that dim life which opens wide and long, from the morrow… With one more yearning look at the gray hulks of building, you loiter away under the trees. The monster elms which have bowered your proud steps through four years of proudest life, lift up to the night their rounded canopy of leaves, with a quiet majesty that mocks you. They kiss the same calm sky, which they wooed four years ago; and they droop their trailing limbs lovingly to the same earth, which has steadily, and quietly, wrought in them their stature, and their strength. Only here and there, you catch the loitering foot-fall of some other benighted dreamer, strolling around the vast quadrangle of level green, which lies like a prairie-child, under the edging shadows of the town. The lights glimmer one by one; and one by one—like breaking hopes—they fade away from the houses. The full risen moon that dapples the ground beneath the trees, touches the tall church spires with silver; and slants their loftiness—as memory slants grief—in long, dark, tapering lines, upon the silvered Green.[155]

Building Yale & Razing It from the Civil War to the Great Depression

CATHERINE LYNN

As the twentieth century dawned on New Haven, many of its citizens found their houses dwarfed by new neighbors: the solid, stolid, five- and six-story masonry structures of a Yale that had breached the boundaries of its old "Campus Green" (FIG. 79). Since the Civil War, ten new buildings had nearly enclosed that central quadrangle, displacing all but three seemingly doomed remnants of the Brick Row.[1] Four new memorial gateways now dignified the campus.[2] But more significantly for the citizenry who lived west and north of the old college, sixteen other Yale buildings had risen on High, York, Prospect, and Elm Streets.[3] Many of these, including three blocky brick halls that Yale's Sheffield Scientific School had recently finished on Prospect Street facing the Grove Street Cemetery, reached heights more familiar on the streets of New York. To the south, near the neighborhood called Sodom Hill on old New Haven maps, Yale's medical faculty had been closely involved in building what is now Yale-New Haven Hospital. Between 1873 and 1900 a total of at least ten new structures were added to and around the original Greek-temple-fronted hospital designed by Ithiel Town (1784–1844) and begun in 1830.[4] Although the university's building ventures to the east had been limited, town and gown alike took pride in the fact that Hendrie Hall, the Law School's new quarters, was nearing completion on Elm Street, facing the New Haven Green (FIG. 80). In 1909 it would be characterized as "a decorous, even an 'elegant,' edifice" by Montgomery Schuyler (1843–1914), the best-known and most influential American architectural critic at the turn of the twentieth century. However, he also dismissed Hendrie Hall as "simply a municipal erection, which might very

well belong to the city of New Haven" because it did "not in the least convey the sense of belonging to Yale."[5] That is, it was not Gothic, as was the array of buildings for which Henry Austin's Library of 1842 had set a mode which was subsequently interpreted in several varieties on and around the Old Campus (FIG. 81). On that central plot stood, in Schuyler's opinion, all the "Architecture" Yale had: "The architecture of the University is confined to the single quadrangle west of the Green," he wrote, because "the remaining buildings being scattered...cannot conduce to a general impression."[6]

Not only were they scattered, but too many still appear to have been experiments in untried styles, demonstrations of their architects' novel theories about the nature of Art in Architecture. Some were parts of things meant to be larger, whether they were wings of unfinished structures or oddly isolated buildings that had been conceived as parts of larger complexes yet, or never, to be completed. There was a great deal of stopping before a project was finished when Yale built during the late nineteenth and early twentieth centuries, so much of it that unfinished projects become a minor theme in the pages that follow. They will deal almost exclusively with structures built for the institution itself, not those of the student societies and fraternities that grew up around it. Nor do they often touch on the structures Yale bought and adapted. The chief concerns here are with Yale's own shaping of its buildings and campus, as well as with how and why it made choices that affected their design. As university presidents came and went—there were five between 1850 and 1937—and as power within the Corporation changed hands, a succession of conflicting opinions and

FIG. 79 *"Bird's-eye View of the Principal Buildings of Yale University,"* 1895.

FIG. 80 *Hendrie Hall: south (Elm Street) facade from the New Haven Green.*

tastes, supported by elaborately argued architectural theories, found and subsequently lost favor along with the architects who espoused them.

Soon to be critically dismissed or not, Hendrie Hall, which its architect described as "Early Italian Renaissance,"[7] still fronts the New Haven Green. The former law school's staying power perhaps owes something to its congeniality with civic and commercial structures that were soon built across that great public space. Like them it aspires to be monumentally classical. On the other hand, Hendrie Hall's scale is monstrous compared with that of the eighteenth-century houses that flank it, and the severe classicism of its masonry presents a glaring contrast to the gentle vernacular of their wooden detailing. The blankness of Hendrie Hall's side walls, which seems to anticipate large adjoining buildings, suggests a hope of extending Yale's frontage on the Green. But the rising prices of real estate there put

any such ambition out of reach. Yale may also have underestimated the growing force of the Colonial Revival, whose enthusiasts succeeded in preserving something of the domestic scale that had prevailed around the Green from the seventeenth century through the nineteenth. Whatever might have been anticipated, Yale has never, as Schuyler suggested it ought to have done, extended its campus eastward to embrace the New Haven Green.

Hendrie Hall, and classicizing architecture in general, soon fell out of favor at Yale. When desertion by its tenants, who moved to a much grander law school in 1931, was added to scorn for the building's appearance, many assumed it would be razed. But logical thinking could rarely have predicted the survival of a Yale asset like Hendrie Hall. Nor did architectural merit assure that the university would keep one building rather than another. Some exploration of the circumstances that doomed or spared

FIG. 81 *"Yale College: Library and Alumni Hall," after 1853.*

FIG. 82 *Berkeley Oval (right) and the University Gymnasium (far left) in 1920: south (Elm Street) facades.*

random specimens of the university's Victorian and early-twentieth-century buildings will follow.

Unless it happened to be on the Old Campus, most of Yale's late-nineteenth-century architecture was fated to meet the wrecker's ball. Of twenty-nine buildings that Yale constructed beyond the Old Campus during the period from the Civil War until the turn of the century, Hendrie Hall is one of only four that are still standing.[8] Josiah Cleveland Cady (1837–1919), its architect, was the man who designed for Yale most often during this period, employing a variety of styles. Between 1900 and 1903, he added three more buildings for a total of fourteen. Cady was also responsible for the addition of 1893 to Battell Chapel, some fencing, some renovations, and the home of the renowned professor, Othniel C. Marsh (B.A. 1860). That house—now part of the School of Forestry & Environmental Studies—the chapel addition, a gate to the Old Campus (which has long been erroneously attributed to another designer), along with Hendrie Hall and only three other buildings— two of which are hidden or defaced—are all that survive on the campus by this architect whose work was briefly the pride of Yale.[9]

The ten late Victorian "Halls" on the Old Campus itself enjoyed a happier survival rate, although two of them were demolished during the 1920s: most famously Bruce Price's Osborn Hall of 1888, as well as Cady's Dwight Hall of 1885–86. A slightly earlier example of Yale's experimentation with Gothic architecture on the Old Campus, Alumni Hall, designed by Alexander Jackson Davis in 1851, had been taken down in 1911 (see FIG. 81).

Most of the late Victorian buildings fell before the massive construction projects lavishly financed by the Harkness family[10] and by John W. Sterling (B.A. 1864), that began in 1917 and continued through the Great Depression. Yale's demolition reached a peak between 1931 and 1933, when it took down not only most of what it had built during the late nineteenth century but also some substantial buildings in which it had invested since the turn of the twentieth century. The shortest-lived of all the major buildings that went before the tide of destruction ridden so gloriously by James Gamble Rogers was Delano and Aldrich's Day Missions Library, only twenty years old when it was razed in 1931.[11] It was built to complete a nineteenth-century group, in this case the Divinity School, about which Yale had changed its mind. In the same category were two dormitories and a lecture hall of the first decade of the twentieth century that were added to two dormitories of the 1890s, forming what was almost a quadrangle—a cramped and narrow one—called the Berkeley Oval, which stood across Elm Street north of the Old Campus. From the sidewalks along High and Elm Streets, its dormitories rose to five and six stories. In old photographs they look like apartments for moderately prosperous Manhattanites (FIG. 82).

What a contrast the Berkeley Oval's sharp-edged urban bulk must have presented to the silhouette of the great Memorial Quadrangle. This, begun in 1917 as a complex of dormitories surrounding interior courtyards, was the first of James Gamble Rogers's masterpieces at Yale. It rose catercorner to the Berkeley Oval like a naturalistic rock formation receding in successive stages to the culmination of Harkness Tower (FIG. 83). The Corporation and administration discussed for more than a decade what to do with their new Berkeley Oval as Rogers's vision, realized now as a working model of a yet newer Yale, took form. In the end, Rogers's image was the compelling one, and the Berkeley Oval fell before it.

But for the most part, what Yale built during the opening third of the twentieth century is still with us. Although the two dormitories in the Oval did not survive, three built on the Old Campus—Wright of 1911, and McClellan and Bingham, built during the 1920s—are still there, housing freshmen. All the other early-twentieth-century dormitories were soon to be incorporated into residential colleges. The Corporation's formal vote in December 1928 to plan "small units housing from 150 to 250 students each, with Common Rooms and other facilities designed to foster a spirit of social intimacy and companionship" was a milestone on the path along which James Rowland Angell had been steadily

FIG. 83 *Yale and New Haven from the southwest in 1920.*

moving since 1921, when he arrived from the University of Chicago to become Yale's president.[12] As early as January 1925, Angell had proposed adopting a system of this kind, one that would create collegiate communities of a scale comparable to the old college, which was fast being overwhelmed by sheer numbers within the burgeoning university. Even the Memorial Quadrangle, whose completion in 1921 had set a new standard for Yale dormitories, was renovated in the early 1930s to adapt to the residential college system. Rogers inserted dining halls, common rooms, classrooms, and other facilities to create two colleges, Branford and Saybrook.

However, despite the importance of the Memorial Quadrangle, student housing was not the major building program of the first third of the century. During this period Yale's officials focused first on buildings that commemorated the founding of the institution two hundred years earlier and also celebrated its relatively new status as a university. ("University" had been substituted for "College" on the title page of Yale's annual catalogue for the first time in 1886). The Bicentennial Buildings of 1901 — Commons, Woolsey Hall, and the Memorial Hall that gave entrance to these great spaces — accommodated

alumni and students in numbers larger than any earlier Yale building could have done. Together with Woodbridge Hall, built at the same time to house the administration, they formed only two sides of a projected group. Though incomplete, it was labeled the "University Quadrangle" on maps of the early twentieth century, and its classical forms added to its distinction from the Gothic of Yale College.

During the decades before the First World War, alumni had their own pet projects for Yale. The sports enthusiasts formed Yale-affiliated organizations that acquired large acreage on which they built improved athletic facilities, most memorably the Yale Bowl of 1911 to 1913. Then, for the war effort, alumni rallied to build a Yale Armory, which survives, and an Artillery Hall, which was demolished only a decade later. After the war many of them chipped in to enhance the playing fields still further, building field houses, baseball stands, a golf course, and a boathouse.

Meanwhile, in the years shortly before Harkness and Sterling money transformed New Haven's skyline, the administration was attending to building projects that moved steadily north from the old core campus: to the block north of Elm, to Hillhouse

Avenue, as well as to the acreage that is still being developed as "Science Hill" (FIG. 84). Most of those early-twentieth-century classroom and laboratory buildings continue to serve the university in roughly the same ways they were originally intended to do. And although many of them have gone through repeated and intense interior renovations and have received additions, they still can be recognized as discrete buildings whose public facades are for the most part intact. The same cannot be said for all the buildings—about sixteen—associated with the medical school and Yale-New Haven Hospital that went up between 1900 and 1930 (FIG. 85). Five were demolished and one was sold, and so much has been built around several of the rest that it is difficult to identify them today except in plan after careful study.

The puzzle of reconstructing a vision of turn-of-the-century Yale is intriguing not only because so much of it has vanished but also because so many images of the lost buildings are preserved in Sterling Library's collections of architectural drawings and photographs. These provide a startling record of just how many buildings Yale put up in the late nineteenth century, shortly regretted, and promptly took down. The speed with which the fortunes of an architect riding high with one administration would plummet as soon as another took office is impressive. Late Victorian architecture at Yale, most of it either long demolished or altered beyond recognition, is very little known either to the Yale community or to architectural historians. Therefore the pages that follow give more space to descriptions and illustrations of the lost buildings than to those which survive.

A wealth of material in the archives documents as well the complex of pressures that shaped—or in the eyes of many at the turn of the century mis-shaped—the public face of Yale. The pressure the administration felt most acutely before the full beneficence of Sterling and Harkness revealed itself was, of course, financial. Part of the reason several buildings were designed all too individualistically for the liking of some Yale administrators was that certain donors wanted their buildings to stand out from all others. Constrained by poverty, Yale often yielded to donors' unwelcome notions about architecture simply to ensure that cash would be forthcoming to erect some sort of shell for classrooms or dormitories.

And Yale was, and felt, land poor. That became a pressure acutely decisive in its architectural history as enrollment mushroomed from 682 students in 1865 to 5,915 in 1930.[13] That pressure pushed buildings up to five and six stories along relatively narrow walkways and streets. The pictorial archive, which records not only facades and interiors of discrete structures but also their contexts along the streets, clearly shows that Yale blasted away the domestic scale of New Haven north and west of the Old Campus during the late nineteenth century. Photographs illustrate just how uncomfortable the juxtaposition was of a two-story house with, for instance, the enormous gymnasium built in 1890–92, an alley-width away, looming more than twice as high, with windows, doors, and details of grand institutional scale.[14] Elm Street, where it passed the old Divinity School, the Berkeley Oval, and the University Gymnasium, looked very citified indeed at the turn of the century (see FIG. 82).

FIG. 84 *Sterling Chemistry Laboratory in 1923: east (Whitney Avenue) facade.*

FIG. 85 *Yale and New Haven from the south in 1930–31.*

Such vertical growth followed the Corporation's rejection in 1868 of a possible move north when "a hundred thousand dollars would secure a lot of fifty acres, extending from Prospect Street to Whitney Avenue, about half a mile north of the residence of the late James Hillhouse, Esq…on the ridge between East and West Rocks, and commanding the finest views of both." After wrestling with and dismissing that tempting proposal, Yale had to return through the closing years of the century to its long-established procedures for acquiring, piece by piece, parcels of real estate around its existing buildings. As the executive committee of the Society of the Alumni gloomily predicted while the Corporation pondered whether or not to buy the fifty acres, failure to do so would mean that "the College buildings hereafter to be erected will have to be placed near each other, without much regard to the best architectural effects."[15]

New Haven was not a sleepy college town. The *City Year Book* of 1888 made much of that point:

Unlike many university seats, New Haven the third city in size and wealth in New England is not satisfied to be known merely as a college town, but is one of the largest manufacturing centers in the country. Nearly a thousand manufactories are now located in New Haven, representing a capital of 25 million dollars actively employed, while the valuation of dwelling houses in 1888 was 13 million dollars, of unoccupied land, five million, and of railroad property…one million dollars.

In one decade the volume of business has more than doubled…Today there are upwards of 700 manufacturing institutions and 3,300 business and mechanical establishments.[16]

As land prices in New Haven rose through the late Victorian period and past the turn of the century, successive generations of university officials built as far up and out as they could on the plots already owned or painfully acquired, bit by bit. Yale built in the blocky vernacular manner of New York real estate development, and used New York architects to do it. Then, although Harkness and Sterling money brought appreciable relief, space restrictions continued to shape Yale's buildings. James Gamble Rogers's skill in manipulating elevations and setbacks brought perhaps even more crucial visual relief from the vertical walls that were crowding the streets and walkways through the undergraduate center.

There were other pressures molding those buildings, pressures whose strengths were not always so clearly pictured or written about, although, as the documents reveal, they were strong indeed. These include the pressures of architectural theory, of educational theory, and of personalities. Individuals—a particular Yale president, secretary, treasurer, or Corporation member of strong conviction and persuasive power—figured decisively in determining the forms Yale buildings took and the places they were sited. Some of those who assumed the role of client for the university crucially affected designs by architects who are sometimes blamed, sometimes credited, for formal moves that were in fact forced upon them. And unpredictably, the whims of donors, or the accidents of their kin or relationship by marriage to designers, steered Yale's architectural course.

Additional pressure came from a widely held faith in a Yale spirit which could and should be preserved and strengthened by the buildings that gave it shelter. Preservation of the special character of "America's University," of strengths that were regarded as constituting the "real" Yale, took precedence over maintaining the mere materiality of the old Brick Row. Gamble Rogers, as everybody apparently called him, was a Yale graduate (B.A. 1889) who understood all this with an exquisite subtlety unmatched by his predecessors, who worked out only parts. Long before his time, the university had wanted to reestablish the collegiate model of shared communal life for a student body it never seemed able to fit into the campus. By the late nineteenth century Yale needed modern dormitories that were not only big enough to house all the students but also attractive enough to entice the rich boys to return from fraternities and the luxurious private dormitories that had sprung up in New Haven. The college's efforts to do this in the Berkeley Oval

as well as in the Old Campus's Vanderbilt Hall furnished important object lessons for Rogers.

For us, some knowledge of the lost nineteenth-century buildings provides a useful benchmark against which to measure his later accomplishments and those of his colleagues who so decisively fixed a longer-lived image of Yale. The lost Yale of 1900 has become a little-known place that is nonetheless of great interest, deserving of study in its own right. But Yale's architecture from the Civil War to the Great Depression presents the student with much the same problem that confronted Arthur Twining Hadley in 1895, writing about the institution over which he would soon preside: "It is hard to give a systematic account of Yale University, past or present," he began a long essay, published with articles about Harvard, Princeton, and Columbia in *Four American Universities,* "because Yale itself is not systematically arranged, and never has been. At no time in its history have its methods and traditions borne the impress of a consistent plan."[17] Yale's fine architectural plan of the late eighteenth century had not only been forgotten and abandoned by Hadley's time, but nearly all trace of it had been demolished, and the college had spilled haphazardly over the bounds of the Victorian plan that replaced it.[18]

The Yale of 1899, when Hadley took over, was becoming increasingly embarrassed by its neglect of architectural planning during the period when other American universities led the world in shaping vast new campuses. Hadley's Yale made determined starts, several of them false, to correct that perceived weakness. Then under Angell, who was president from 1921 to 1937, Yale was blessed with alumni architects of great skill, and with alumni donors of great wealth who made possible the implementation of their plans at a grand scale.

In 1929, just as that greatest era of building was beginning, one of the architects then working at Yale characterized its recent construction: "Yale has sought to disentangle itself from the city of New Haven and to become a visual entity."[19] Through the period of America's penury, Yale was to build lavishly. As it did so, it intensified its physical disentanglement from New Haven, to the regret of architects before and since, who have tried in vain to dissuade it from that course. But it was a course upon which Corporation members and administrators had found their way through fits and starts of building since the Civil War. The successive phases of their experiments with a variety of visual entities for the quadrangles into which Yale would withdraw are the subject of the present essay.

"Our Architectural Incongruities" of the Late Nineteenth Century

In 1865 the unity of the Brick Row and the simplicity of the two building types that alternated along it were qualities that no one in power at Yale valued or counted as "architectural." Fifteen years earlier, the president himself, Theodore Dwight Woolsey (B.A. 1820), had called it "the present ugly row of colleges."[20] Peter Bonnett Wight (1838–1925), the architect who was working on Yale's only major building of the Civil War period, described it as the work of an "intelligent bricklayer" who "here had full swing and sway without the interference of impertinent and intermeddling architects."[21] But now Wight was "the young architect, filled with the Gothic enthusiasm"[22] who had come to Yale to demonstrate what "Architecture" should be, a work of "True Art" in terms defined by John Ruskin (1819–1900). Those terms, as Erik Vogt has suggested in his essay on the Brick Row, struck resonant chords in the souls of the Congregational ministers who were directing Yale's building activities.

Wight's design for Street Hall (FIG. 87) had been rising slowly, stone by stone, since the laying of the cornerstone in November 1864. That was hailed as a relatively momentous event in educational history, for Street Hall would not only serve as Yale's new art museum, into which John Trumbull's collection would be moved, but it would also house the first art school in an American college, and women were to be admitted.

George C. Holt (B.A. 1866), a Yale undergraduate and one of the editors of the *Yale Literary Magazine* for 1865, took exception to Street Hall's introduction of an alien architectural style to the campus green (FIGS. 88 & 89). While admitting that "It is too early to pronounce an opinion upon the Art Building," he saw that "it manifestly will be totally different in style from anything else about the College," and he thought that "The presumption in this case is against a change. Architectural unity in general is desirable in the College buildings." It was already clear that Wight's design was unlike either of two earlier Gothic essays on the Old Campus, the Library of 1842 by Henry Austin, and the Tudorish Alumni Hall of 1851 by Alexander Jackson Davis (see FIG. 81).[23] Holt wrote about Austin's library: "While, considered by itself, it is certainly a very beautiful building, it is, plainly, in extremely bad taste with the rest of the College. Minarets and turrets and gingerbread

embellishments, do not accord with the genius of Yale. The architecture of Yale should be like its character; strong, durable, imposing. Yale is no Gothic College, and it wants no Gothic buildings."[24]

Young Holt may not have wanted them, but subsequent history has shown that he was in the minority. By the time Holt was in a position to influence Yale's architectural history—almost forty years later he would sit on the building committee that directed Yale architecture on its most radical stylistic aberration before the High Modern era, its plunge into the grandeur of Beaux-Arts Classicism for the Bicentennial Buildings—that history had taken a decidedly Gothic course. Harvard had provided the model for a Gothic library based on King's College Chapel, Cambridge, when it completed its own Gore Hall in 1841; but after brief flirtations with stone and Gothicisms, Harvard reverted to its long-accustomed use of brick and classical details for most buildings.[25] As the critic Montgomery Schuyler pointed out in 1909, Harvard came through the nineteenth century with greater unity in the style and material of its buildings, while Yale, at least at its core on the Old Campus, adhered to a more coherent plan. While young Holt would have had Yale stick to a course more like Harvard's, Schuyler argued that Yale would have done better had it built more Gothic structures in the "architecturesque" manner of the "pioneering" Old Library: "If Yale had continued in the direction thus laid down for it, the architecture of Yale would have been purer and more peaceable than it is."[26]

Taking a longer view, one might stretch a point to suggest that Yale's architectural peace had been broken in 1832 when the artist John Trumbull built his Art Gallery (see FIG. 62). For the familiar local brick vernacular of the Row, with its gentle classical details mellowed through generations of workmen's adaptations, Trumbull substituted a new academic classicism. It came in a modest dose and was soon to look rather unschooled itself. But from its relatively obscure position back of the Row, it spoke an unfamiliar formal language in its taut little tomb surfaced with stucco imitating stone, in the rustication of its ground floor, and in the prominence of the Doric order, right from the drawing books, that marched as pilasters around its second story.[27]

When Holt dwelled upon the new buildings, he apparently felt no pressure to cast his architectural evaluations in moral terms of the type that avant-garde architects and their critics had adopted from John Ruskin. Responding more directly to what he

FIG. 86 *Osborn Hall: central portal.*

FIG. 87 *Street Hall: presentation drawing by P. B. Wight, ca. 1864.*

FIG. 88 *Street Hall in the 1860s: south (Chapel Street) facade.*

saw than to theoretical ideas about what he should see, George Holt insisted that "we have a right to find fault with the architecture of the modern College edifices," predicting that "unless more unity is maintained in their style in future, the College architecture will be piebald and ridiculous."[28]

"Piebald and ridiculous" is not far from the judgment that was to be rendered at the close of the period just beginning, a judgment not always so directly put, and one made not only about Yale's buildings, but also about much of the architectural experimentation of late Victorians everywhere. At the century's close, when new administrators assumed office at Yale, they seem to have shared their period's general revulsion against the eclecticism that had so recently gripped the architectural imagination.[29] Anson Phelps Stokes (B.A. 1896), who

became secretary of the university in 1899, oversaw construction of Yale's Bicentennial Buildings, whose classicism in part stands as a reaction against their immediate predecessors. "Our architectural incongruities" he called the Gothic buildings that had broken all earlier patterns.[30]

But in that Civil War era, something different was wanted at Yale, and Wight was an architect who was eager to change the world. He was later to write: "The college seems to have been in danger of falling into an architectural rut, until the Art Building was erected in 1864."[31] In fact, Yale had built nothing on the Old Campus since Alumni Hall in 1851, and five years had passed since it had put up a building of stuccoed brick with a vaguely Italianate flavor for the medical school on York Street as well as the most basic of brick boxes for a gymnasium on Library Street.[32] (The walkway between Jonathan Edwards and Branford Colleges now replaces that street.)

Surviving monuments of American architecture from the war years are rare because few were built. But Yale was blessed during this lean period with a devoted donor, a Yale alumnus (B.A. 1812) and citizen of New Haven, Augustus Russell Street (1792–1866). Street was the son of "a man of wealth." He was "already a confirmed invalid" during his undergraduate days, whose "habits and tastes were of the most quiet character,"[33] and he also studied law at Yale, but never practiced. With his wife and several children he traveled for five years in Europe, including Greece, and in Egypt. He survived all his children, but did not live to see his building completed.

"The gift of Mr. Street was a surprise and an innovation," according to Wight.[34] To bestow upon Yale its largest gift from a single donor up to that time, Augustus Street simply wrote to "The President and Fellows of Yale College"on March 24, 1864, beginning: "Gentlemen: I hereby propose to cause the erection, at my sole expense, of a building on the College grounds, to be used for a School of the Fine Arts. The building to be erected on the corner of Chapel and High Streets…The building is to have one front with entrance on Chapel Street and another on the College Grounds."[35] P. B. Wight was twenty-six when he was asked to design it. Street and his wife "manifested the deepest interest in the prosecution of the work,"[36] rather more than sometimes suited Wight, as his letters to H. C. Kingsley (B.A. 1834), treasurer of the university, reveal.[37] It was the young architect's second important commission and, as he later wrote, "It was not only a new building but a new department of study. It was natural, therefore, that it should result in a

FIG. 89 *Chapel Street looking west, with Union Hall (South College) on the far right and Street Hall beyond, ca. 1874–78.*

new architecture."[38] Wight had only recently come to prominence in New York, after his late entry took the commission for the National Academy of Design away from the three invited competitors of 1861, who were among the city's best-known architects.[39] He was able to do this, it seems, because he emphasized that his work adhered to the principles of John Ruskin, and seated on the jury were some convinced fellow Ruskinians.

Wight had excelled in drawing classes at New York's Free Academy (later City College) where, according to Sarah Landau, he formed a lifelong friendship with Russell Sturgis, Jr. (1836–1909), who would later design four Yale buildings on the Old Campus. In the era before there were architecture schools in this country, they read "together...Ruskin and everything they could find on architecture."[40] They also followed Ruskin in admiring early Italian paintings above all others, and Sturgis accumulated enough expertise about them to be able to catalogue James Jackson Jarves's collection, most of which was hung at Yale in 1868. He also acted as a none-too-competent agent for Jarves in the eventual transfer of his Italian pictures to Yale. These two young architects, dedicated to the proposition that architecture was an art, one they envisioned through a Ruskinian

lens, shared an office during the years Wight was building in New Haven.

It was undoubtedly Wight's much publicized devotion to the English critic that brought him to the attention of Yale's budding art circle, within which *The Seven Lamps of Architecture* burned brightly for a generation. As a professor in the Divinity School since 1858, Timothy Dwight (B.A. 1849) — the future president of Yale — had made known his Ruskinian beliefs about architecture in writing and in lectures, and he was instrumental in bringing like-minded scholars to the school. Among them was the Reverend James Mason Hoppin (B.A. 1840), "one of the more vocal but now forgotten disciples of Ruskin in America,"[41] who in 1864 returned to his alma mater to take up a chair in the Divinity School. A year later, this professor of homiletics and pastoral charge published "Principles of Art" in *The New Englander*, a Yale-dominated journal in which Ruskinian editorial leanings accorded with his own. The Divinity School became a stronghold of Ruskin's conviction that Truth in Art, based on direct observation of God's work in nature, was a valuable tool of moral influence.

In 1866 the Reverend Hoppin delivered the dedicatory speech at the opening of Street Hall, and in

1879 he resigned from the Divinity School to become professor of the history of art there.[42] Such a shift seemed logical enough for a reader of the critic who spelled out how to make aesthetic judgments in moral terms and encouraged the more arcane practice of reading through works of art to discover the truth of Christian faith in the soul of the artist. And true architects, Ruskin's devotees were convinced, must first be artists. "Art-Architecture" could be nothing other than True Christian, Pointed – that is Gothic – Architecture.

Ruskin's devotees in New Haven surely knew about Wight's role in founding an "Association for the Advancement of Truth in Art" and his efforts to render the National Academy's building an agent of that advancement. Following Ruskin's famous example at the Oxford Museum of 1855–60, Wight gave carvers working on the Academy the freedom to devise their own ornaments for capitals, based on direct observation of nature. While Wight did not send his stonecarvers to the fields around New Haven to gather flowers as models for the capitals on Street Hall, he used the building in every way he could to "advance the cause of Art."[43] He tried earnestly to render it a model of Gothic correctness and "honest" stone construction. To him, Austin's Library and Davis's Alumni Hall seemed of a lesser order on both counts. Although Austin had used brown sandstone for the lower parts of the library's walls, the upper parts were less noble: they were wooden, and the library had "stucco masks and wooden cornices or pinnacles."[44] Each was only loosely based on English Gothic models, while Wight had benefited from broader study of the Continental Gothic as published by Ruskin, the English Ecclesiologists, and Viollet-le-Duc.

Wight had derived from these readings a great interest in what the era called polychromy in architecture, the use of stones of different colors, both for sheer decorative effect and to express their specific functions within a building, so that for instance the stones that carried weight might be of one color, while those that filled space in a wall might be of a contrasting color. The polychromy of Street Hall attracted much comment during its early decades. In the monumental two-volume *Yale College: A Sketch of Its History*, published in 1879, John Ferguson Weir, who had been professor of painting and director of the School of the Fine Arts since 1869, contributed an essay that specifically mentioned the building's "Portland and Jersey stone, with yellow Ohio-stone ornaments," noting that "The arches are of alternate Belleville and Cleveland stone.

The columns on the front porch are of Gloucester polished granite, and the capitals are carved with original designs, after natural foliage, in Cleveland stone."[45] Contrasts between the stones, particularly the alternation of dark and light in the voussoirs, are distinct in early photographs, but after years of dirt accumulation and the growth and removal of vines, the contrasts are somewhat subdued.

Street Hall was, in its architect's eyes, something of a failure from the day the art school occupied it in 1866. By then, the bills neared $200,000, Mr. Street had died, his widow disagreed with Wight about details, and Yale's treasurer was more than reluctant to add costly finishing touches. Wight complained that he had devoted his "best energies not only to making, but to preserving it from mutilation…I have never lost sight of the great object to be advanced by this undertaking, the part that the building itself is to take in the advancement of Art. And now I am obliged to see my work bereft of many of its most expressive features, for all of which my reputation must suffer. I have seen numbers of persons who assume that the design is now carried out as intended to be." Wight was so crushed by the omission of his finials, ridge crestings, and especially the stone pinnacles – the faceted conical roofs that should have topped the turrets – that he himself offered "to expend money for the decoration and adornment of the building."[46] By October 1866 the offer had been declined, but thirty-three years later, Wight was still making a drawing of a tower as he felt it should be completed.[47] He tried always to have his renderings published, rather than photographs of the building as it stood, and as late as 1909 it was one of his drawings that appeared among all the photographs of other buildings in an article about Yale architecture by Montgomery Schuyler. But the critic found Street Hall "as nearly as possible unnoticeable." He supposed that Wight must have thought that the "gay and festive effect" of his National Academy "needed to be sobered and made more austere for collegiate uses," but that the architect had "gone so far in the direction of austerity as to…go near depriving it of any effect at all."[48]

Yale has continued to render Wight's Ruskinian essay ever more unnoticeable, indeed to hide it. In 1894, construction of Vanderbilt Hall obscured the principal view of Street Hall's Old Campus facade from Chapel Street; and in 1925 McClellan Hall, built as a "match" for Connecticut Hall, blocked nearly all sight of it from the Old Campus itself. Meanwhile, Virginia Creeper was encouraged to grow, so that

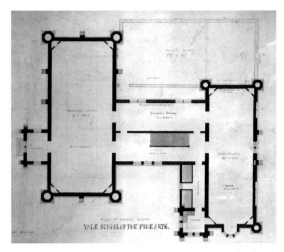

FIG. 90 *Street Hall: plan of the second floor by P. B. Wight, ca. 1864, with penciled notation of J. F. Weir's addition of 1911.*

FIG. 91 *Street Hall: west (High Street) façade, showing the addition by J. F. Weir and, on the left, the Whitman Memorial Gateway.*

FIG. 92 *Street Hall: main gallery.*

seasonally the Chapel Street façade was simply a green mass.

Wight's plan, two parallel bars shifted along their east/west axes and joined by a central bar, was an articulate one in which the major rooms were clearly expressed on the exterior (FIG. 90). It had two entrances, as Street had directed. The one on Chapel Street (on far left in the plan) was a significant doorway to Yale for New Haven citizens, especially for the many young women who enrolled in art classes. Studios, classrooms, and a library on the first floor had tall windows, while two great long galleries in the bars above were windowless but skylighted. In 1909 John Ferguson Weir, still director of the school after forty years, made a large addition that significantly obscured Wight's plan. Collaborating with the New Haven architect Leoni W. Robinson, he brought the exterior wall out to the west, to the sidewalk along High Street (FIG. 91). This made room on the second floor for two new galleries and the enlargement of a hallway for another gallery, and below for five additional classrooms. Weir wrote that he was being careful to conform his "exterior architectural arrangement...strictly with that of the Street building, in every detail," including taking down the "two corner shafts at the west end" and resetting them with "the necessary architectural distinctions in the exterior arrangements...especially as to the roof divisions."[49] In 1928 Egerton Swartwout, architect of the Yale University Art Gallery, showed little of Weir's deference to Wight's design when he butted his bridge across High Street squarely into the western façade and beneath it opened a new entrance. At the same time, over the Chapel Street entrance a new wrought iron railing of C-scrolls centered on a roundel replaced the Gothic stone parapet of Wight's balcony.[50] Then the remains of Wight's elaborate interior finishes— his "wainscotting and wood-work of chestnut" (FIG. 92)—were obliterated in drastic and spectacularly inept renovations of 1963. Whatever the eventual plight of Street Hall, its architect, who largely abandoned architecture for criticism, immodestly if anonymously wrote that "With the erection of this building the record of Yale's architectural progress begins."[51] That progress was to be less than steady.

———

As the Civil War drew to a close, alumni of Yale and Harvard alike formed committees to erect buildings "in memory and honor of the graduates and students who fell in the cause of the country during the late rebellion."[52] At Yale, another committee had previously been appointed by the Corporation to oversee construction of a new chapel toward which Joseph Battell, a New York merchant, had already given $30,000. Drawings made in 1864 by Russell Sturgis, Jr., for a Yale chapel are likely preliminary studies for it. This early work must have been set aside when the Corporation's older committee persuaded the alumni committee, which was formed in July 1865, that Yale's Civil War memorial should be a chapel. They held a competition for its design, inviting submissions from several New York architects, including Emlen T. Littell, designer of many churches, and the better known Leopold Eidlitz (1823–1908), who had emigrated to this country after studying construction and maintenance of farm buildings at the Vienna Polytechnic.[53] Projects by these two have not survived in Yale's archives, but proposals by Jacob Wrey Mould (1825–1886) and Russell Sturgis as well as the competition's winning project by Vaux and Withers are there.[54] Mould, Calvert Vaux (1824–1895), and Frederick Clarke Withers (1828–1901) were all emigrants from England who had been influenced by the writings of Ruskin and other Gothic Revivalists.

Mould described his design as "Anglo Italian Gothic" in a letter of 1866 to Professor Noah Porter (B.A. 1831), assuring him that he would do his "best in a work which if it be not a piece of *Art-Architecture* had better never be built."[55] The devotion to polychromy that he had demonstrated during the 1850s in New York's rather notoriously striped All Souls Unitarian Church (dubbed "the Holy Zebra"), is apparent in four drawings for his Yale project. They show startlingly red walls, which he specified were to be of brown stone, with strongly contrasting stone courses and bold gray and white voussoirs in the pointed arches of doors and windows. Topping it all is a steeply pitched, conspicuously patterned roof.

The Committee of Yale College Memorial Chapel passed over Mould's proposal, and that by Sturgis as well. It chose instead a design by Vaux, Withers and Co. that also displayed the virtues of Art-Architecture. This project, like Mould's, was for a freestanding building, not demonstrably intended for the corner site on which a chapel eventually rose.[56] The committee printed up a handsome "General View" and "Ground Plan" framed in a bright red ornamental border (also designed by the architects), for circulation in what proved to be an unsuccessful effort to extract $150,000 from alumni (FIG. 93). The much admired New Haven citizens and Yale professors on the committee fell short of their goal, even though the circular reported that Battell's gift in hand had increased in value to $36,000.[57]

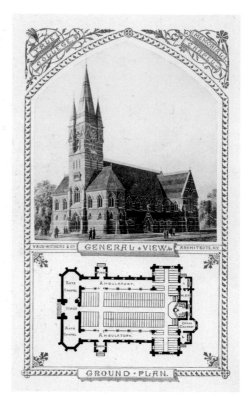

FIG. 93 *Proposed Civil War Memorial Chapel: general view and ground plan by Vaux, Withers and Co., 1866.*

Their campaign could not have been helped by the faint praise Charles Eliot Norton gave the premiated design in *The Nation* of July 1867. Norton, who taught the history of art at Harvard, was John Ruskin's closest personal friend, his voice in America. Neither the design by Ware and Van Brunt for Harvard nor that by Vaux and Withers for Yale was, Norton wrote, an "entire work of art." If either was "to be erected precisely in accordance with the designs now adopted…it would be better that they should not be built at all." While Norton found the Yale memorial the "happier" of the two, he concluded that "the design lacks in variety and abundance of thought and imagination. There is little to distinguish it as a work of original creative power. It is a careful and elaborate construction—a work of intelligence rather than of genius. It has no place in history, as showing the development of the art of architecture."[58] Despite Norton's criticisms, Harvard raised enough money to complete Ware and Van Brunt's Memorial Hall by 1876, although it was slow-going through the financial panic of 1873. Yale, however, never rallied support for a Civil War Memorial Chapel. When construction finally began on Yale's present chapel, in 1874, Battell and his family had assumed the major expense of building it, not as a

FIG. 94 *Battell Chapel between Durfee (left) and Farnam Halls, 1887: south (Old Campus) facade.*

war memorial, but to honor Joseph Battell. The design by Vaux and Withers was dropped in favor of a comparatively subdued one by Russell Sturgis, Jr., situated on a corner that Sturgis himself had hemmed in with his designs for Farnam and Durfee Halls (FIG. 94).

P. B. Wight called those two dormitories the "good fruit…brought forth" by his "seed" planted in the form of Street Hall.[59] In 1864, Henry Farnam, who had come to New Haven as an engineer for the Farmington Canal and gone on to make a fortune as an entrepreneur, offered Yale $40,000: enough, he thought, to build a new dormitory of stone. The earliest date on a surviving drawing for Farnam Hall is 1868, but ground was not broken until August 2, 1869. By the time the dormitory was ready for students in the fall of 1870, Farnam had contributed $70,000, Sturgis had resorted to brick, cheaper than stone, and the cost had exceeded $126,000 (FIG. 95).[60] Nonetheless, Henry Farnam had Sturgis design for him the gabled and turreted mansion on Hillhouse Avenue that was remodeled almost beyond recognition with classical details in 1937 to become Yale's official President's House.

The gift for Durfee Hall was also announced in 1864, but construction did not begin until spring of the year that Farnam Hall was completed. For his second dormitory Sturgis had a budget that allowed him to build in stone—Newark sandstone, North River bluestone, and Ohio sandstone (FIG. 96). This was made possible by a donor whose story is very different from that of the non-alumnus entrepreneur. Yale, as the grateful recipient of the beneficence of Bradford Matthew Chaloner Durfee, included a sad chronicle of his short life in Kingsley's history of the college. Durfee was born in 1843, heir to a textile fortune, in Fall River, Massachusetts. Though "delicate habit forbade regular attendance upon schools," the boy spent six years preparing for Yale, not an easy task since "he was never a ready learner, and his progress, repeatedly interrupted by serious illness, was slow enough to have deterred a boy of less resolute purpose: But while his perceptions were not quick, his memory was accurate and tenacious, and his grasp of a subject was always strong." When he was only nineteen, traveling in Europe, Durfee determined "to devote a portion of his inheritance to the promotion of learning in his own land." He entered Yale in 1863, completed his freshman year, but was so ill he had to "retire" as a sophomore. "With no suggestion from any quarter, and without consulting any person but his mother…he proposed to erect the noble structure which now perpetuates his name." Before he died in September 1872, "it was a source of great gratification to him to see the results of his munificence."[61]

That munificence was a little much for some Yale alumni who considered Durfee Hall's "accommodations…too luxurious for college students" when "it was opened to Seniors and Juniors in September 1871." "Students who received abatement of tuition were not allowed to room in either Durfee or Farnam,"[62] an ironic twist for buildings so largely inspired by Ruskin, a Socialist who volunteered to teach workingmen. In 1882, a guidebook to New Haven informed visitors that Durfee "is generally conceded to be one of the finest, if not the finest, college dormitories in the country," commanding "the best location on the college square, at the north end, facing south and looking down the whole length of the campus." Within, "all studies face on campus and all the bed-rooms on Elm Street."[63]

By 1874, when Sturgis was finally overseeing construction of Battell Chapel, his site was crowded by these two dormitories of his own design. As Wight lamented, it "is pushed off to the corner and suffocated before it is born," especially regrettable because

he judged Battell "best in detail of all that the college has erected, and that whose object claims for it the grandest site."[64] Among exterior details, Sturgis's fellow Ruskinian was surely thinking here of the blind arcade of pointed arches surrounding the base of the chapel, based on Ruskin's favorite Venetian buildings. The Ohio sandstone of the arcade contrasted with the walls' duller tones of rough brown sandstone from New Jersey. As originally built, Sturgis's design made a great deal more sense from the Old Campus side than what is now left of it does, hidden behind later additions. Two low towers with conical roofs terminated the western walls of the chapel, facing the end of Durfee. The tower on the campus side stood tall enough above the dormitory to identify the church as such, and to mark it off clearly from the secular building, while gracefully terminating the wall containing the sanctuary. There, above the blind arcade, rose five tall arched windows. In 1893 the firm of Cady, Berg and See complicated the campus facade with an addition to increase seating capacity by about a third so that all the students could fit in for compulsory daily chapel services. They brought a new wall out to the south, replicated the blind arcade upon it, and inserted a

FIG. 95 *Farnam Hall in 1876: west (Old Campus) facade.*

FIG. 96 *Durfee Hall in the early 1870s: south (Old Campus) facade.*

row of flat-headed windows under a parapet that stopped short of the sanctuary's original height—just short enough to show the tops of the pointed windows peeking awkwardly over the top. They also introduced a new entry porch in front of the corner tower.

When Battell Chapel opened in 1876, the interior attracted the broadest critical and popular approval. Wight made an interesting attribution for that interior work: "the detail and part renderings are such as only could have proceeded from the hand of Mr. Babb, Mr. Sturgis's accomplished assistant in the work. The bad location could not prevent Mr. Babb from making one of the most beautiful interiors to be found in the whole range of modern American church architecture."[65] George Fletcher Babb (1836–1915) was to move on from Sturgis's office to execute classical work for Charles McKim before establishing the solid and successful New York firm of Babb, Cook and Willard. In 1879 Kingsley, the Yale historian, described Babb's interior:

The painting is exceedingly rich, and in its character is somewhat unusual. The walls are divided by bands of elaborate designs, and the surfaces into which the walls are thus separated are diapered in several patterns. The surfaces nearest the eye and immediately above the wainscoting are the most elaborate, and the work grows more simple as it ascends. But what is remarkable about the system of decoration employed is that while very elaborate it is unusually unobtrusive. The object of this seems to have been to allow their proper effect to the brilliant windows.

Kingsley noted the stained glass, enumerated the seating (1,100), and estimated the building's cost ("nearly $200,000"), before continuing: "There is a striking harmony to be observed throughout all parts of it, which is tranquilizing and restful to the eye, and in marked contrast to what is to be observed in some of the churches of modern times, which glow with all the colors of the rainbow."[66] By 1927 these decorations were deemed "inartistic and glaring" in the words of the *Yale Alumni Weekly,* an opinion that must have been widely shared, for the magazine reported that "The interior walls of the Chapel have been given a coat of gray paint, blocked off to imitate stone in such a successful way that the whole impression is now one of dignity."[67] Whether glaring or not, certainly "tranquilizing and restful to the eye" were not the words that first came to mind when the strong polychromy of Battell's interior, after years of having been dully monochromatic, was restored in the late 1980s to its original brilliance.[68]

After the dedication of Battell Chapel in 1876, a decade passed before Sturgis completed Lawrance Hall, the fourth of his buildings that established the quadrangular rim around Yale's Old Campus. Shortly after the death in October 1883 of Thomas Lawrance, the popular junior prom committee chairman of the Class of 1884, his mother made a gift to build Lawrance Hall in his memory. In Sturgis's final building for Yale, he gave especially clear evidence of a habit he shared with other Gothic enthusiasts: while he took much theory from Ruskin, he took many of his forms and images from Viollet-le-Duc. The towers and turrets that Sturgis marshaled along the College Street facades of both Lawrance and Farnam Halls conjure up Carcassonne as Viollet-le-Duc recreated it (see FIG. 7). The French architect, critic, and scholar reconstructed that fortified town beautifully, if too creatively by English preservation standards; and in 1869 Sturgis had published an admiring review of his *Dictionnaire raisonné de l'architecture française du xɪᴇ au xvɪᴇ siècle* in *The Nation*.

Although Ruskinians aspired to build in stone always, Sturgis had to use cheaper brick in Farnam and Lawrance, and he did so with great skill. Stone appears sparingly in the trim, and there are wooden details, including dormer windows. As a result, Sturgis's two brick dormitories are more colorful and lively than his stone dormitory and chapel. Wight admired his friend's handling of brick, writing that Farnam was "a building which shows what can be done with common brick and blue stone…Moulded bricks are here used, the first employed to any great extent since the decadence of brick architecture in America." But Wight nevertheless deemed Farnam "a gloomy building."[69] Perhaps he was betraying a bit of envy after his friend had received so many Yale commissions and been allowed to crown his work with pinnacles like those denied Wight for Street Hall. Their omission so embittered Wight that he categorized his own building as exemplary of a "truncated style" peculiar to Yale.

Sturgis's dormitories invited comparison with one another from the beginning, and their rankings have undergone something of a reversal since they were new. Modern architectural historians have preferred Farnam Hall, to which Henry-Russell Hitchcock called flattering attention when he illustrated it in 1958 in his major survey, *Architecture: Nineteenth and Twentieth Centuries*.[70] Patrick Pinnell in his guide to Yale architecture, published in 1999, registers the preference for Farnam that now prevails when he finds it a tectonically didactic building, of greater interest than Durfee.[71] The exterior clarity of structural expression, emphasized by polychromy, renders it a favorite with modernists. Nineteenth-century students preferred Durfee because it was luxurious, and the public pronounced it better than Farnam, perhaps because it had cost more — the guidebook said "about $130,000," though that does not seem so much more than the "nearly $127,000" reported for Farnam. P. B. Wight also thought Durfee was the better of the two: "There seems hardly to be a foothold for adverse criticism of this building. It will be a long time before the quiet dignity of its roof and chimneys will be surpassed anywhere."[72] And Schuyler, still harboring Ruskinian beliefs in 1909, also preferred Durfee among Sturgis's works at Yale:

That it was well designed there can be little question. The animation and variety it derives from the introduction of the red brick tympana of the entrance arches in the expanses of brown rubble of the walls are not obtained at the sacrifice of repose. The "lay out" is eminently

rational and the architectural treatment its elucidation. Nothing better could have happened to Yale just then than to have this building and its successors of that same authorship…fix the style of the university.[73]

But Sturgis did not "fix the style" at Yale.

———

At the same time that Sturgis was transforming the Old Campus with Gothic buildings, pointed arches were also taking shape across Elm Street (FIG. 97). However, they were not designed by a Ruskinian, nor were they modeled on the Northern Italian Gothic that Ruskinians admired. This is surprising, given that the Divinity School, for which they were being built, was the young Timothy Dwight's personal cause, and that within it Professor Hoppin dwelt upon art and paraphrased John Ruskin even as he taught religion. Both these men, along with Divinity Professor George P. Fisher, University Treasurer Henry C. Kingsley, and President Theodore Dwight Woolsey, were on the school's building committee.

Dwight had come to the Divinity School in 1858 during a low point in its history. Only twenty-two students were enrolled, a quarter of the average number counted annually through the 1830s and 1840s. By 1861 Dwight found himself the only full-time professor in Divinity's northernmost building on the Brick Row. According to Brooks Kelley, "Things were so bad that some at Yale suggested that the school should be closed."[74] A bit of hope arrived in 1864 when the Corporation allotted $25,000 "from the general Theological Fund for the purpose of building a new Divinity College," but the sum was far from sufficient for the task.[75] In 1866 a bequest for a professorship of ecclesiastical history came from the same Augustus Street who was the art school's benefactor. But what really saved the Divinity School was Timothy Dwight. Kelley describes how "Dwight and Leonard Bacon [(B.A. 1820), an acting professor in the Divinity School and pastor of Center Church on the New Haven Green] walked New York City and, without receiving any really large gifts, raised enough to increase the endowment…and then to pay for building East Divinity Hall."[76] Yale's divinity professors contributed, as did other faculty members and a great many clergymen.[77] Samuel F. B. Morse, the painter, inventor, and graduate of Yale (B.A. 1810), was one of six men who each donated $10,000.[78]

In 1864 the Corporation appointed professors Fisher, Hoppin, and Dwight to a building committee. All three were editors of *The New Englander*, in which Ruskinian sentiments were copiously set

FIG. 97 *Divinity School in the 1880s: south (Elm Street) facades. From the left: West Divinity Hall, Trowbridge Library, Marquand Chapel, and East Divinity Hall, with New Haven's First Methodist Church beyond.*

forth.[79] But in 1868 the committee chose an architect who was no Ruskinian: Richard Morris Hunt (1827–1895), a man in the vanguard of those who would professionalize the practice of architecture in America, the first American graduate of the Ecole des Beaux-Arts. It is not entirely clear just how or why he got the commission. Perhaps it was simply a case of American academicians responding to the distinction of his Parisian degree. Immediately upon his return to this country in 1855, Hunt had positioned himself at the center of New York's architectural community, becoming a founding trustee of the American Institute of Architects in 1857. Before he was thirty years old, after only a year and a half in the city, he had been "accepted as a leader among New York architects," according to Paul R. Baker, his biographer.[80] Perhaps family friendships, formed when Hunt's widowed mother brought her young children to reside briefly in New Haven, lay behind the Yale commission. The first major acclaim to be accorded Hunt—for the Lenox Library in New York—lay in the future, and his great success in designing the world's first skyscraper, New York's Tribune Tower, and palatial mansions, including Biltmore for George Washington Vanderbilt, were even farther ahead.

By 1864, for Scroll and Key, Yale's second-oldest senior society, Hunt had made preliminary designs for the "tomb," a meeting hall not built until 1869, that still stands on the corner of College and Wall Streets. It was commissioned by a group whose founding members had "dedicated themselves to 'the study of literature and taste,' and vowed to make their meeting place 'the home of friendship, the hall of literature, and the studio of fine arts.'"[81] A surviving presentation drawing of ca. 1867–69 shows that the tomb as built, with its exotic details alluding to the Moorish world, was less than a third of the proposed scheme, which included a low wing to the north, penetrated by a central pass-through, to join a projected three-story pavilion with eight bedrooms under a pitched roof (FIG. 98).[82] New York-based links to the artistically inclined members of Scroll and Key may have been the source of Hunt's Divinity School commission, but by 1868 none of his built work so distinguished his talent as to explain why Yale's most ardent admirers of John Ruskin chose Hunt to be their architect.[83] The polychromy of Scroll and Key might have appealed to them, but the pointedly non-Christian, even anti-Christian imagery of the world of Araby was anathema to Ruskin and his adherents.

FIG. 98 *Scroll and Key: presentation drawing of front elevation by Richard Morris Hunt, ca. 1867–69. Prints & Drawings Collection, The Octagon, The Museum of the American Architectural Foundation, Washington, D.C.*

The "mediaeval style," as Hunt called it, that he utilized for the Divinity School was not his specialty. Baker writes that "at Yale he tried out what were for him new styles of design."[84] They were new for Yale as well, and the two he tried in New Haven were very different one from another. To the simplicity, symmetry, and compactness of the tomb's overall form, to the severity of its striping and its intense concentrations of ornament, Hunt countered at East Divinity Hall with asymmetrical complexity of overall form and a relaxed spreading of decoration over the facades and roofs (FIG. 99). He embellished the corner of Elm and College with busy profiles and highly patterned brick trimmed with olive-colored Nova Scotia sandstone, topped by tall slate roofs that were interrupted by a profusion of dormers and by still taller chimneys.[85] Perhaps the decorative effusions and busy silhouettes, recalling Hunt's early houses, seemed to him appropriate for this institutional building that was to be home for about sixty students. It all looks a good deal more tough and jagged, indeed more French in derivation, with its incised ornaments drawn from the Neo-Grec, than the work of Sturgis and Wight just to the south.

East Divinity Hall's frontage on Elm was narrow, only about forty-five feet, the dimension of the square mansard-roofed pavilion that Hunt placed on the corner and raised a full story above the bar of the building that extended back 164 feet along College Street. The face of its roof was so high and steep that a second slope forming the mansard shape is

hidden in most old photographs. Hunt sliced off the prominent corner and upon the angle set an even taller, projecting, flat-fronted semi-tower crowned by the narrowest and tallest of roofs, sprouting with finials. Chamfering the corner of the building recalled the cuts across many Parisian corners pictured in one of the albums of photographs that Hunt compiled during his extensive residence and travel abroad.[86] But Hunt elaborated on the theme not only by beveling his corner, but also by making the projected surface of the bevel the major feature, and by extending it above the roofs as a little tower. Further, he undercut it with a complexly ornamented brick and stone support where, he wrote, "provision is…made for a statue, which it is hoped will be given to the college," but apparently never was. While East Divinity Hall was under construction, he described the "balcony, running crosswise at the angle," which "projects boldly, and extends above the roof, thus forming a tourelle directly in the axis of the one of the diagonal paths of the green or common opposite, and which is one of the principal approaches."[87] Hunt's "tourelle" seemed to be calling—in a sharp, shrill, rather cracked voice—to the northwest corner of the New Haven Green, from which it was most frequently photographed, and toward which its architect had consciously oriented it.

A library filled a square of thirty-three feet on the ground floor of the corner pavilion. Along College Street, where the lower bar of the building stepped back a little, there were three lecture rooms, each

FIG. 99 *East Divinity Hall from the New Haven Green in 1870.*

FIG. 100 *East Divinity Hall: corridor from the Elm Street entrance.*

thirty feet square, on the ground floor, along with a janitor's residence in a taller rear pavilion. Hunt noted that "the interior sub-divisions" were "distinctly marked by architectural lines: thus buttresses separate the class-rooms." All these rooms opened to a wonderfully photogenic corridor, ten feet wide, into which the main entrance from Elm Street led (FIG. 100). The corridor ran the full length of the western facade, past a staircase at its southern end and under pointed arches that rested on the buttresses Hunt mentioned, to another generous stair at the north. Flat-arched windows flooded its patterned English floor tiles with light from the west. For the four floors above, Hunt broke with the multiple-entry arrangement that was becoming standard in Yale's dormitories. Instead, his suites opened off double-loaded corridors, with bathrooms at their northern ends. The guidebook of 1882 characterized "every room in the building" as "very high-posted, light and pleasant."

In 1871, a year after completing East Divinity Hall, Hunt again used brick elaborately trimmed with the olive-colored Nova Scotia stone for Marquand Chapel just to its west (FIG. 101). The chapel was connected to the earlier building through the stair hall, and both were planned as elements in a projected quadrangle, for which Hunt's early perspective drawing and plans survive.[88] Hunt shaped the chapel's cruciform plan by cutting square corners out of a rectangle, so that the major entrance on Elm Street extended only a few feet south of the sanctuary. He kept the entrance facade several feet behind the building line of his earlier structure to create a shallow yard edged by an ornamental fence of stone and iron. This helped set off the special intensity of a piquant little chapel—it seated only 250—that bristled with finials and pinnacles. In size, detail, and massing it recalled the chapels of French chateaux and village churches pictured in Hunt's albums, but it duplicated no single one among them.

The chapel presented to the street a big, sharply pointed gable carrying a central six-lobed window within a circle. Beneath it, the major entrance was through a trefoil-headed door under a smaller gable whose roof echoed the angles of the big one above, which rose in a great expanse of slate. Its steep pitch and height were dramatized by elaborate metal crestings that topped a narrow ridge. At either end of that ridge, slender metal finials shot up, framing against the sky the heavier vegetation of a metal finial crowning the central gable. Stone finials fixed smaller, quieter points atop two smaller flanking

FIG. 101 *Marquand Chapel in the 1870s.*

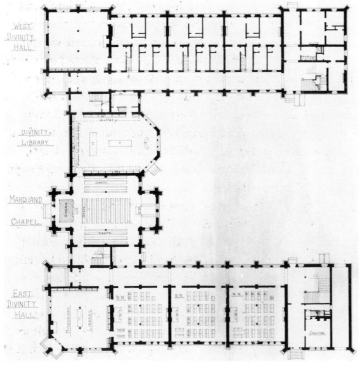

FIG. 102 *Divinity School: plan of the ground floor drawn by Harrison W. Lindsley, 1893.*

gables. These many gables and finials repeated the diagonal lines of the roof slopes and of stone pinnacles that topped buttresses marking each corner across the front elevation. The exaggerated height of the roof allowed Hunt to create a dramatic space within it, a single high volume, "finished in Southern pine, beautifully carved and decorated" according to the guidebook of 1882. The chapel was lighted by narrow trefoil-headed windows with lead mullions forming diamond grids that, along with the diagonal boards on the wooden doors, multiplied a play of diagonal lines across the facade.

Frederick Marquand of Southport, Connecticut, paid the full bill of about $27,000 for this gemlike structure "In memory of Hetty Perry Marquand, Wife of Frederick Marquand, of Southport, Connecticut, died 1859," as an inscription on the chapel's west wall recorded. Though Marquand was not a Yale graduate, his faith led him to make "many munificent bequests to religious and educational institutions, mostly of the Presbyterian denomination" in the words of his obituary in the *New York Times*. Frederick Marquand's link to Richard Morris Hunt was a direct one, through his nephew, Henry G. Marquand, a lifelong friend of Hunt. The younger Marquand was a railroad financier and a founder and president of the Metropolitan Museum of Art in New York. The nephew paid for another Marquand Chapel at Princeton, which Hunt designed in 1880, and also commissioned Hunt's designs of his houses in New York and in Newport, as well as his family's tomb in Newport along with work on his New York office buildings.[89] His uncle, Frederick Marquand, was eighty-four when he died in 1882, having retired more than thirty years earlier from Marquand and Co., "the leading jewelry house of New York."[90] The elder Marquand's generosity to Yale continued posthumously through directives and bequests to Elbert B. Monroe, the husband of his niece, Mary Virginia Marquand Tompkins Monroe, whom Frederick Marquand had adopted. Following Marquand's wishes, Monroe paid for the original Dwight Hall, built on the Old Campus in 1885–86, as the home of the Yale University Christian Association, the center of religious and charitable life among students.

Two years after completing Marquand Chapel, Yale constructed a near mirror image of East Divinity Hall, omitting the elaborated corner. Leaving a gap of about forty feet west of the chapel, West Divinity Hall was a repetition of the formula: two taller pavilions connected by a lower bar (see FIG. 97). Again, the narrow end of the building faced Elm Street, and a long ground-floor corridor appears on the plan,

FIG. 103 *Trowbridge Library in the 1880s.*

this time set on the eastern side, giving access not to classrooms but to student suites and stair entries. The space across which the corridors of the two divinity halls faced one another was partially closed to the south by the chapel. The series of arched windows along the opposed corridors created arcades, and the courtyard reminded at least one writer of a cloister.[91]

The program for the second divinity hall was simpler than that for its match to the east. This was to be a dormitory of suites, each with a study and two bedrooms, and it was to have only one public room, for "the valuable and extensive Musical Library of the late Lowell Mason."[92] Although a plan of only the first floor survives, it suggests clearly enough that for the upper floors, Yale chose not to duplicate Hunt's double-loaded corridors across the courtyard (FIG. 102). Instead it reverted to the college's more usual arrangement of suites around entryways, substituting entry from the corridor and thereby interiorizing the more usual outdoor entry to stairways.[93]

Frederick Marquand was again the major donor, giving half of the $160,000 it cost to build West Divinity Hall. Rufus G. Russell of New Haven is recorded as its architect, but it is clear enough that the concept was Hunt's: P. B. Wight referred in 1878

to "The new divinity school, by R. M. Hunt," and the guidebook of 1882 attributes it to him. Russell probably developed Hunt's concept and was supervising architect for construction, completed in 1874, during a period when Hunt was not only busy with the Tribune Building, but also fell ill.[94] Russell's fee was only $1,000 for West Divinity Hall, while Hunt was paid $7,500 at the time he designed East Divinity Hall and $1,000 for Marquand Chapel, further indicating that Hunt's was the larger design for the complex.[95]

The gap between West Divinity Hall and Marquand Chapel was filled in 1881 by the Trowbridge Library (FIG. 103), the last of the Divinity School buildings financed by Marquand. Edward E. Raht, who was almost certainly introduced to Yale as Hunt's employee, is credited in Yale's records as the architect. Raht had supervised construction of Hunt's Tribune Tower in 1873, proving himself so adept on the job that it was to Raht rather than Hunt that the Tribune's owners turned for the design of an addition in 1881,[96] the same year Yale hired Raht to work on the Trowbridge Library. However, the hand of Richard Morris Hunt, or of someone in his office, had set its mark on this last element of the proposed Divinity School quadrangle to be built in the nineteenth century. The materials were the same, the inspiration still French, and the details continued and embellished upon themes from the earlier buildings.

A reference collection established by Henry Trowbridge of New Haven as a memorial to Henry Stuart Trowbridge and Virginia Hull Trowbridge was housed in the single great room that filled the building. The facade continued straight along the Elm Street frontage, following the setback line that had been established for the body of the chapel, a few feet back from its projecting entry. There was no entrance on Elm Street, and with doors to both the chapel and the newer dormitory, the front portion of the library served as a corridor between the two. Trowbridge Library linked all earlier pieces of the Divinity School, so it became one U-shaped building (see FIG. 102), with the bottom of the U resting on Elm, the right vertical stroke fronting College Street, and the left stroke fronting on a walkway across which the dormitories of the Berkeley Oval would soon be sited.

To the street, the Trowbridge Library presented bands of windows under a wide three-part dormer projecting from the most prominent feature, a full-blown, visibly double-angled mansard roof. That voluminous structure sprang from a cornice about the height of the chapel's cornice, and it was nearly as high as the chapel's roof, making space for a forty-foot-high ceiling in the library below, which had a gallery along three walls. Its rear wall pushed out into the courtyard as a bay. The interior received an enthusiastic description in a guidebook: "The woodwork is mostly of oak, finished in oil, though the ceiling, which is arched, is worked in white pine and matched panels, and is finished in Shellac and varnish…A handsome carpet and costly furniture complete the equipage of the edifice, which is the most elegant theological library building in the United States."[97] While the writer of this little publication of the eighties admired the Divinity School without reservation, in 1909 Montgomery Schuyler, still harboring English Gothic prejudices, published only a few words of praise for it, sprinkled with some caustic derision. "In its distinguished author's own particular and personal variety of French Gothic," he found that Hunt's Divinity School was marked by "sprightliness and animation, and something of…restlessness." Schuyler thought that "the architecture has this mark of good Gothic, that it is the straightforward expression of the actual facts of construction, emphasized by the coloring," but then professed to see "evidence that the buildings have

not been studied in perspective, only in elevation." The chapel he branded "humble," quipping, "it is not altogether clear at the first glance whether it is a chapel or a highly ornate stable." Looking at the old photographs of what appears to have been a beguiling little landmark, it is hard not to take offense on Hunt's behalf. Schuyler concluded that Hunt's Divinity School "'belongs,' as well as one could expect from so strong and aggressive an individuality as that of its author."[98]

Twenty years later, in 1911, the quadrangle Hunt had planned was finally closed not with the dining hall that he had drawn in 1869, but with another library. The Reverend George Edward Day, Holmes Professor of the Hebrew Language and Literature and of Biblical Theology, who in 1888 became the Divinity School's first dean, and his wife Olivia Hotchkiss Day, made it possible through a bequest. It specified their wish "to have somewhere a complete collection of books relating to the missions of all Christian denominations and peoples…housed in a theological school," and to "stimulate candidates for the ministry to consider a vocation of missionary work."[99] Perhaps Day's interest in missions dated back to 1839 when he tutored the Africans taken from the ship *Amistad,* who were in the New Haven jail awaiting the trials that led in 1841 to their exoneration by the U.S. Supreme Court from charges of murder and piracy.

Delano and Aldrich, whose later, important work for Yale will be discussed below (see especially pp. 224–26), designed the Day Missions Library to close off the U formed by the existing buildings (FIG. 104), neatly fitting it between the northern ends of East and West Divinity Halls, which had been renamed Edwards and Taylor Halls in 1909. Centered in the space, the library was linked to the older buildings by one-story wings. It was a Collegiate Gothic building for which no one could have accused Delano or Aldrich of strong or aggressive individuality, certainly not on the exterior. Its forms were much like others Yale was building in stone at the time, though here the architects used brick, and set into its walls a band of patterning — diamonds at the ceiling level of the ground floor, in the manner of a stringcourse — thereby giving a nod to the patterned surfaces of a High Victorian context. The plan was compact and efficient on the ground floor, where a long rectangle was portioned out as classrooms and offices whose many partitions supported a single lofty space, a high-windowed reading room open-trussed to the roof, contained within five bays that were marked on the exterior by buttresses

FIG. 104 *Day Missions Library: south (interior) facade.*

READING ROOM

FIRST FLOOR PLAN   SECOND FLOOR PLAN

FIG. 105 *Day Missions Library: interior and plan.*

(FIG. 105). Although it was not really an enormous room—it measured just under fifty-nine feet by thirty-three and a half—photographs show that it was an impressive one dominated by a great vertical window with a pointed arch that nearly filled the gable end. Dark wooden bookcases lined the walls to the bases of the windows, and the four corners of the room were partitioned off by dark wooden panels to form three little studies and to mask the top of the staircase that gave entry. On the facade, the buttresses stepped back to a crenellated parapet edging a slate roof.

The glory days of the Divinity School's second home at Yale were few in number. In 1922 the faculty of the school complained to the Corporation that "the school is greatly cramped for room. Its buildings are old and ill adapted for modern instruction. Its chapel is dingy and inadequate in size." This kind of complaint seems to have sounded the death knell of virtually every one of Yale's late-nineteenth-century buildings, whether they housed the scientists or the divines, and it was to echo again through the halls of the third Divinity School at the end of the twentieth century.[100] The addition only eleven years earlier of the Day Missions Library had apparently done little to counter the early-twentieth-century perception that the Victorian buildings, the oldest of which was little more than fifty, were hopelessly out of date. Charles R. Brown, dean of the school, wrote that same year to John V. Farwell, chairman of the Corporation's Committee on Architectural Plan, that the chapel was too small, adding "We need therefore a tasteful and appropriate chapel which Marquand is not." By April 1930 the decision to do away with the nineteenth-century Divinity School had clearly been reached when Farwell wrote to the secretary of the university, Anson Phelps Stokes, that "The old Divinity building…is getting to be so old that the repairs are very large each year. One of the new Quadrangles designed by John Russell Pope will eventually go up on that site."[101] In the summer of 1931, the wrecking crew had at it so that construction could begin on Pope's Calhoun College.

Well before that summer, two of Yale's most beloved Victorian structures, a boathouse near New Haven harbor, and a grandstand at Yale field, had been razed. Although the students illustrated these jaunty wooden buildings in their own publications more often than they did any others at Yale, they were not, strictly speaking, Yale buildings, for throughout the nineteenth century the Corporation distanced itself from direct underwriting and management of sports. It left it to students and alumni to pay quite independently for such early facilities, and they did so with delight. As early as 1863, alumni had contracted with William P. Dickerman to build a boathouse "just north of the steamboat storehouse."[102] A little more than a decade later, rowing enthusiasts commissioned Cummings and Sears, one of the leading firms in post–Civil War Boston, to design a more substantial boathouse, built in 1875 on the Mill River off Chapel Street (FIG. 106).[103] Judging from many illustrations in Yale's archive, had it survived, it would have stood up well in a comparison with the beloved collegiate boathouses of the era that still edge the Charles in Cambridge and the Schuylkill in Philadelphia. Square in plan, Yale's boathouse was surrounded by broad porches under shingled roofs whose gentle slopes met steep slopes over the core of the building to lift a central spire above large dormer windows on each roof face. This boathouse lasted until 1910.

In 1881, an association of students and alumni bought thirty acres of the city's old Hamilton Park and had Frederick Law Olmsted draw up plans for three baseball diamonds, a cricket field, and an archery field, as well as for six tennis courts enclosed within a running track (FIG. 107).[104] A guidebook to New Haven, published in the 1880s, reported that "horse-cars, passing the College every twelve minutes, go within a short walk of the field."[105] Olmsted's plan clearly locates the "Grand Stand at Yale Field" above the baseball diamond numbered one. Not content with simply roofing over the open-sided bleachers set upon a plan that brings two banks of seats forward from the central group at a gentle

angle, the grandstand's unknown designer crowned it all with an elaborate centerpiece: behind a central pediment, a large cupola raises an open viewing platform above the roofs, with another stage above supporting a large flagpole (FIG. 108). The field was conveyed to Yale in 1902, and the old wooden grandstand was gone by the time new concrete stands went up in 1927.[106]

———

The old wooden relics of Yale men's enthusiasm for baseball and rowing in the nineteenth century must have yielded relatively easily to wreckers of the early twentieth century. But when in the 1930s workmen set about destroying the more formidable constructions that the Corporation itself had erected not so many years previously, they had tougher jobs. At about the same time that they were demolishing Hunt's and Raht's divinity school, workmen were also destroying two other buildings that Raht had designed for Yale after leaving Hunt's office. While supervising construction of the Trowbridge Library, Raht must have been planning the Sloane Physical Laboratory, the first of his two Yale College laboratories built west of the Old Campus on Library Street during the 1880s (FIG. 109). It was the gift of Henry T. Sloane (B.A. 1866) and Thomas Chalmers Sloane (B.A. 1868), in memory of their father William C. Sloane, founder of W. and J. Sloane, the carpet and department store.[107]

The beginning of Sloane Laboratory's construction in 1882 marked a milestone for Yale, after painful and prolonged delay, in introducing the study of modern science into the curriculum of the college. That curriculum became notoriously conservative

FIG. 106 *"The Yale Boat-House," ca. 1875.*

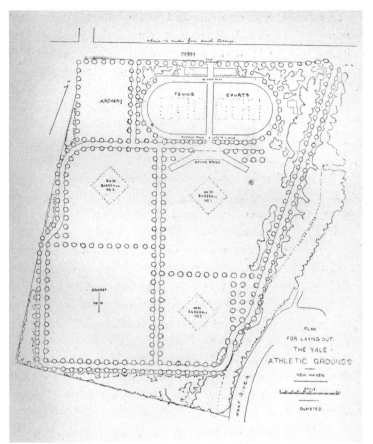

FIG. 107 *Frederick Law Olmsted, "Plan for Laying Out the Yale Athletic Grounds, New Haven," 1881.*

FIG. 108 *Grand Stand at Yale Field in the 1890s.*

FIG. 109 *Kent Chemical Laboratory (left) and Sloane Physical Laboratory (right) from across High Street, before 1907, with the Old Library (now Dwight Hall) on the far left and the Old Gymnasium on the far right.*

during the administrations of Theodore Dwight Woolsey and Noah Porter, presidents from 1846 to 1886. Earlier in the century Benjamin Silliman's eminence as professor of chemistry, mineralogy, pharmacy, and geology had placed Yale in the forefront of centers for scientific study among American colleges. But it lost that status as science became more specialized, and as Woolsey and Porter defended and emphasized the rigid classical curriculum at the very time Harvard was launching its innovative elective system of course selection.

Since 1858 Yale had managed to sidestep the problem of assigning science its proper place in the college by accepting at something of an arm's length extremely generous donations from Joseph Earl Sheffield. He made a fortune in the railroads, and he used it to build and personally to nourish a Scientific School "of this College," in the terms of its incorporating documents, but not fully of it in the eyes of other undergraduates. It grew up around his own home, on Hillhouse Avenue north of the Old Campus. Here students who had not studied Greek and Latin could pursue a course very different from the classical curriculum in which their counterparts to the south were drilled, and they could receive a degree after three years, advancing to the status of Junior after only one year of study. During President

Porter's reign, neglect of the Scientific School became so pointed that in 1871 its distinction from Yale College was made more formal by its incorporation with a separate board of trustees.[108] The separateness was also recognized in less formal ways. Writing about "Odd Corners of the Campus," an undergraduate in the college's Class of 1876 suggested just how peripheral it seemed: "Our knowledge of the Scientific School, outside of a few personal friends, is confined to the fact that each year brings forth a swarm of young men who do not come on the campus, but remain with us for a season and never become Sophomores."[109] A decade before Raht was hired to design a "Physical Laboratory" for use by "Academic" students in the college, the Sheffield Scientific School hired Josiah Cleveland Cady to design the first of three major classroom and laboratory buildings he was to execute by 1894 for the "Sheff" students. The resultant duplication of science buildings was not eliminated until 1912.

For the college's Sloane Physical Laboratory, Raht was not given a site on the Old Campus, though there were several. President Porter's dim view of the sciences perhaps precluded placing it within that venerated precinct. Raht's site was just to the west, on the south side of Library Street. As if he wanted to attract attention from the Old Campus, half a block away, he gave his building a tall tower with some of the most elaborate ornament in town. Sloane Lab was a High Victorian concoction of brick with stone trim that had two principal stories under steep slate roofs, over a high stone basement. Although it was in the middle of the block where Jonathan Edwards College now stands, Raht treated the building as if it commanded a corner. He set its two wings at right angles to one another, forming an L-shaped plan, and faced the high, ornate "Flemish" gable of the narrower wing toward Library Street (FIG. 110, top). Inside the right angle where the wings met, Raht jammed a slender octagonal tower that had the proportions of a NASA rocket. He shot it well above the principal roofs, crowned it with a dome over a tiny open arcade, gave its lower elements elaborately curved and faceted roofs, encircled it with a balcony, and pierced it with four stages of variously shaped windows. It housed stairs rising from the principal entry, whose arched opening was partially blocked by a central column that stood atop an exterior staircase aligned on a forty-five degree angle to the wings. A vestibule gave entry on the left to a large lecture room with a sloped floor — "beautiful…high, light, and commodious, and capable of accommodating a large class"[110] — which filled two full stories of the eastern wing. To the right, a big recitation room occupied most of the ground floor of the wing facing the street. Straight ahead, a stair hall led to what the guidebook deemed "undoubtedly the most elegant and thoroughly appointed physical laboratory in the United States," intricately divided for specific functions "in complete accord with the suggestions of Professor A. W. Wright."[111] Such suggestions by Yale's scientists figured largely in all their dealings with architects.

For a second science building for the college, Kent Chemical Laboratory of 1887, Raht was given the southwest corner of Library and High Streets just east of Sloane, right across the street from the Old Campus (see FIG. 109). This time, when he really did have a corner to turn, Raht did it with a curve that smoothed off the outside angle of the intersection of two wings of another L-shaped plan. He centered the entrance in the curve, again squarely aligned on a miter of the corner, and cut the curve with a door that was a play on a three-part Palladian window. Over the curving outer angle Raht raised the roofs through two stages to a low cone that seemed to crown a circular tower absorbed within the larger mass, a tower a little larger in diameter than the one so obtrusively pulled forward from the inner angle of Sloane Laboratory next door. Like Sloane, Kent was a building of two stories over a

raised basement, but it was all of rough-finished stone, the choice of which, along with the round-headed windows, was probably influenced by H. H. Richardson's masterpieces of the 1880s.[112] Kent was much calmer in tone than Sloane, in part because it presented relatively flat masonry walls along its two principal facades, while Sloane displayed its two wings and almost freestanding tower to the street, creating a public face that was more agitated and articulate of interior spaces. Kent's roofs were also calmer in silhouette, and behind a parapet of stone and iron finials, were less dominant than the steep roofs over Sloane.

A measured drawing shows the two laboratory plans side by side and suggests that Kent's plan was consciously drawn in response to Sloane's (see FIG. 110). The parallel alignment of their entries and the stairs leading up to them is striking, as is the flipping of the L shape. Kent's ground floor plan was simpler, and here again Raht had to follow the dictates of a scientist, one who was concerned above all with the functional efficiency of laboratories. By one account

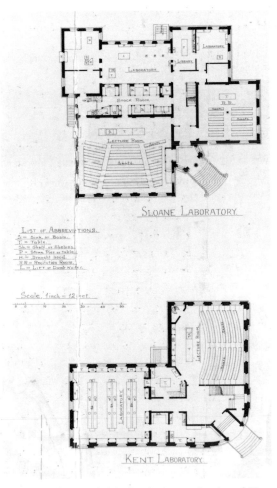

FIG. 110 *Sloane Physical Laboratory (top) and Kent Chemical Laboratory (bottom): plan of the ground floors drawn by Harrison W. Lindsley, 1893.*

Kent was built "according to plans elaborated by Mr. E. E. Raht, architect, from sketches by Mr. F. A. Gooch, Professor of Chemistry." This statement comes from an article, "Construction of Chemical Laboratories," in a pamphlet from the Paris Exposition of 1889, in which W. H. Chandler, Ph.D., emphasized that because the Kent Laboratory was "located centrally in the city upon valuable land, the building was planned with a view to securing the greatest possible compactness consistent with suitable provision for apartments abundantly lighted, adequately ventilated, easily accessible, properly connected, and of size and shape adapted to the special purposes for which they were intended."[113] Chandler also stressed the importance within work spaces of light on three sides in "rooms not too wide to permit the perfect illumination of central spaces, and abundant wall surface for the proper distribution of draft chambers and ventilating flues." The language of the scientist giving precedence to function is very different from that of the Ruskinians who had articulated concern for the moral influence of architecture twenty years earlier. Functional priorities, especially the need for fireproofing where volatile chemicals were to be put in the hands of undergraduates,

yielded in the Kent laboratories rooms pleasing to twentieth-century modernists with their exposed brick walls and metal girders: I beams decorated only with rivets. Striking photographs of the great laboratory on the ground floor (FIG. 111) appeared in the Paris Exposition article of 1889, along with a picture of the large lecture room.

Albert E. Kent (B.A. 1853) and his son William Kent (B.A. 1887) paid for the building. The father was "a merchant, banker, and founder of the packing industry in Chicago" who purchased a large estate in San Rafael, California, in 1871. His only son was still an undergraduate editor of the *Yale Literary Magazine* and a member of Skull and Bones while the building was in the works.[114] Albert Kent left a bequest for enlargement of the building, which was carried out in 1901 by Ernest Flagg (1857[?]–1947) and Walter B. Chambers (B.A. 1887). They slightly extended the wing on High Street southward, to add another wing to the west, making the L shape into a short U. They also added a story, so that the corner tower roof disappeared. From 1922 until it was demolished in 1931, the building was called Kent Hall.

Before Sloane Physical Laboratory also came down in 1931, it had been improved in 1906–7 with

FIG. 111 *Kent Chemical Laboratory: ground-floor laboratory in 1889.*

FIG. 112 *Sheffield Scientific School in the late 1890s: west (Prospect Street) facades. From the right: west wing of South Sheffield Hall, Winchester Hall, North Sheffield Hall, and Sheffield Chemical Laboratory.*

funds from its original donors.[115] In 1912 when the Sloane Physics Laboratory, still standing on Science Hill, opened to serve the whole university, Raht's building was renamed Sloane Lecture Hall, and its old labs became psychology, economics, and sociology classrooms.

Later halls of science for the greater university of the early twentieth century also usurped many of the functions of three late-nineteenth-century buildings that Josiah Cleveland Cady designed for the Sheffield Scientific School along Prospect Street, facing west, across the street from the long, high wall of Grove Street Cemetery (FIG. 112). The rear facades of Cady's buildings loomed rather conspicuously over the houses on Hillhouse Avenue that were gradually taken over by Sheffield's school (FIGS. 113 & 114).

In 1872 Joseph E. Sheffield was prepared to pay $100,000 for the first of Cady's Yale buildings, North Sheffield Hall (FIGS. 115 & 116). It seems to have given space to every homeless interest of his school, accommodating "the departments of Civil and Dynamical Engineering, Physics, Botany, and drawing…the apparatus, instruments, and collections pertaining to them, a large examination room, shop, etc." and at the rear a "small and unobtrusive, but very useful little observatory, containing an astronomical clock and a transit instrument…Here time

observations are made for the school and the city." By 1879, when this information appeared in Kingsley's history of Yale, the Sheffield School needed more room, but had been in financial straits since the depression of 1873–78, when professors' salaries had been cut and the school had been forced to ask the university to cover deficits.[116] More than a decade was to pass before funding from Mrs. Oliver F. Winchester made it possible to build Cady's Hall of Mechanical Engineering in 1892, and before the trustees were able to begin Cady's Sheffield Chemical Laboratory in 1894, using the school's own resources. In the interim they adapted and enlarged various houses on Hillhouse Avenue and Prospect Street for the school; and in 1876, its departments of geology, mineralogy, zoology, and physiology moved into Cady's newly erected Peabody Museum on the southwest corner of High and Elm Streets.

Precisely why the professors of the Scientific School approached Josiah Cleveland Cady to design for them is no clearer than why their colleagues in the Divinity School chose Hunt, but their choice proved to be an important one for all of Yale University. Cady was about thirty-five when they fixed upon him in 1872, and for the next thirty years he was the architect Yale administrators relied upon

FIGS. 113 & 114 *Hillhouse Avenue (west side) in 1895. Contiguous views showing, from the left: Sheffield Mansion and rear views of Winchester Hall, North Sheffield Hall, and Sheffield Chemical Laboratory.*

FIG. 115 *North Sheffield Hall in the early 1870s.*

most often for major and minor additions and adaptations of structures, as well as for the design of fourteen good-sized buildings along with some smaller ones. His importance was not limited to Yale, as Kathleen A. Curran recognized in her monograph on Cady, *A Forgotten Architect of the Gilded Age*, published in 1993.[117] Cady was born in Providence and studied for one year at Trinity College in Hartford, which later gave him two honorary degrees. Montgomery Schuyler recorded that "He received his technical training from the professor of architecture of a German university, who, exiled for political reasons, was spending some time in this country."[118] Curran found that Cady was paid as a draftsman for the New York firm of Town and Davis between 1864 and 1868, before opening his own office in 1868. In 1873 Cady took two teenagers into that office, Milton See (1854–1920) and Louis DeCoppet Berg (1856–1913), who became partners in 1881. Berg had studied at the Royal Polytechnicum in Stuttgart, which perhaps reinforced Germanic stylistic leanings that Cady could have absorbed from his teacher, and that Curran emphasizes in her study.

In the course of a prolific practice Cady's firm built a great many institutional buildings in New York, among which the south-facing wing of the Natural History Museum on Central Park is the best-known surviving example. His firm designed two buildings for Williams College and three for Wesleyan. In 1897 "The Works of Cady, Berg & See" were the subject of a thirty-six-page article by Montgomery Schuyler in the *Architectural Record*.

Cady opened his practice in Richard Upjohn's Trinity Building, overlooking Trinity Churchyard, where the fledgling American Institute of Architects had its headquarters. Curran found that he signed the original constitution of the organization, founded in 1857, and that he served on its board between 1878 and 1882. Several neighbors within the building were also architects, including Richard Morris Hunt, who took an office there in 1869—the year his East Divinity Hall was under construction—and stayed for four years.[119] In 1869 Cady won his first major commission for a public building, the Brooklyn Art Association, to which he gave a Modern Gothic interpretation. It was just being completed when he won the Yale job.[120] Cady produced his crucial first design in New Haven under peculiar circumstances. By Montgomery Schuyler's account, not only were there "stringent limitations of cost," but, "so careful, indeed, was the committee…lest the appropriation should be exceeded that they directed the preparation of a design without informing the architect where, or for what institution it was to be built."[121] Whether or not the process was veiled in quite so much secrecy, the design development of North Sheffield Hall was heavily influenced by Cady's clients, the Sheffield School's faculty. The official Yale history of 1879 recorded that the building "was planned by a committee chosen by Mr. Sheffield from the professors of the school. The architectural designs and details are by Mr. J. C. Cady, of New York."[122] As Edward Raht was to find a decade later working for the college's physicists, scientists in New Haven actively assisted their architects. Curran notes *Rundbogenstil* influence in North Sheffield Hall, citing Friedrich von Gartner's State Library in Munich as a probable model for the building.[123] She also found that a member of the committee that hired Cady, George J. Brush (PH.B. 1852), had studied in a building designed by Gartner and was but one of several of the school's scientists who had trained in Germany.

"The glory of architecture lies in stone," Timothy Dwight once wrote,[124] echoing John Ruskin, and stone had been the material of choice at Yale since the mid-nineteenth century. If brick had to be substituted because it was cheaper, it was made to look as much like stone as possible: dark-colored brick walls were given stone trimmings as well as stone foundations, and wooden trim was painted the colors of stone. But the Sheffield Scientific School was a different world. Although it was being partially supported between 1863 and 1893 by its status as Connecticut's land grant agricultural college, Sheff's resources were more limited than those of the college. Economic necessity forced the scientists to build in brick, and to build simple boxes rather than complex forms like those of other Yale buildings in which pavilions stepped in and out and walls were broken into picturesque compositions, sometimes expressing the individuality of rooms under many-gabled and multi-sloped roofs. Cady calculated that North Sheffield Hall cost only about fifteen cents per square foot.[125] This building and his two others for Sheffield were decorated sheds par excellence, to borrow Robert Venturi's useful term.

North Sheffield Hall was the first of the three emphatically *brick* facades Cady lined up along Prospect Street. On the flat surfaces of its walls he emphasized the brickness and redness of the material, decorating it with darker- and lighter-colored bricks. And although he did use some blue stone, he kept the material two-dimensional in the watertables and sills, using it to create flat lines of lighter color, so that it hardly looks weight-bearing. The plan measured seventy-six feet across the street facade and had a depth of eighty-four feet. Over a raised brownstone basement, its three full stories plus an attic looked a little like a palazzo stripped of its usual stone clothing. The fourth—attic—story, which Schuyler thought must have been a later addition, was there from the start, somewhat hidden behind a boldly projected "machicolated cornice," as he learnedly described the feature that broke the monotony of the building's vertical silhouettes. Cady drew crenellation to finish the top of the walls, which would have enlivened the skyline, and although it appears on a published perspective rendering, early photographs show that it was not executed.

The building was set on a slope that dropped off to the rear. Its raised stone foundation stood several feet back from the sidewalk, partially hidden in a light well rather like the dry moats of Rogers's later colleges. An iron fence edged the well and a stone entry porch bridged it to meet seven steps that descended to the sidewalk (FIG. 117). Before North Sheffield was flanked by Cady's two brick buildings of the 1890s, high walls of brick fronted their sites and further masked much of the stone base, which was more apparent along the sides. More of the stone base was exposed by the 1890s, as the slope

from Prospect Street was cut away along the sidewalk to create a sheer drop that was faced with a masonry wall, so that although the buildings fronted on Prospect, the yards at their bases were about on a level with Hillhouse Avenue. The rear facade of North Sheffield had great visual prominence from Hillhouse Avenue, where it formed part of the background just to the north of Joseph E. Sheffield's own mansion (on the left in FIG. 113). Sheffield's home was the Italianate villa that Henry Austin designed in 1859 as an enlargement and remodeling of Ithiel Town's home, a Greek Revival house of 1836; it was razed in 1957.

All four facades of North Sheffield Hall were polychromed with bold patterns that set up strong horizontal rhythms of insistently repeated round-headed windows with voussoirs of alternating blue and light-colored bricks. The third-floor windows were half the width of those on the first and second floors, and at each level the voussoirs were connected by bands of diamond and zigzag patterns, so that it looked as if two arcades encompassed the building, the upper with narrower, shorter openings, the lower with wider, taller ones. Cady made the lower arcade appear to be especially tall by recessing the glass of the first and second floors well behind a couple of courses of brick contained within long

FIG. 116 *North Sheffield Hall: drawing room for Mechanical Engineering.*

FIG. 117 *North Sheffield Hall: students posed on the steps of the entry porch.*

vertical recesses, which created the effect of double-height openings. The horizontal bands of windows and boldly patterned stripes marched right around the five bays of the street facade, interrupted only by the entry porch, then continued through six bays on each side, and onto the rear facade, until they were stopped by a protruding single-story wing that displayed a central triptych of small, round-headed windows. But above that little wing, the horizontal bands of zigzags continued to meet as a banded ring, like a clasp binding the decorative straps together. In his description of North Sheffield Hall, Montgomery Schuyler commented: "The Architecture...is really in the treatment of the walls and is as satisfactory a solution as could have been expected of so vague a problem."[126]

When Cady again worked for the Sheffield School, the program was not so vague, and in the long interim he had completed four more buildings for Yale. In 1892 he was asked to design Sheff's new hall of mechanical engineering (FIG. 118) for a site just south of North Sheffield Hall. It was named Winchester Hall to honor Oliver F. Winchester, whose widow gave most of the $120,000 it cost to build it. Monies generated by the dramatic expansion of New Haven's post-Civil War armaments industry, especially the Winchester Repeating Arms Company, funded not only this Yale building but also important structures in the medical area.

Behind frontage of 115 feet on Prospect Street, Winchester Hall was wider than it was deep, extending back only eighty-four feet as a simple rectangle with a low wing appended to the rear, on the north side, for a steam engine laboratory. The plan within the main rectangle depended on a T-shaped hall, centered on the front door, which confronted stairs. The hall gave entry to rectangular rooms of various sizes, one a library, the others for drawing classes and lectures. Cady fit mechanical and hydraulic laboratories into the basement and placed a physics laboratory, "the optic room," and "several large drawing rooms" on the second and third floors. Two large examination rooms filled the fourth floor.

The architect attached slender round towers to the four corners of Winchester Hall, where they raised four small domes, supported on miniature Doric colonnades, above the gentle slope of its hipped roof. The brick facade had trim of terra cotta and pressed brick, so it was monochromatic in contrast to the colorful variety of North Sheffield Hall. Round-headed windows again dominated the composition, but they were much wider, three-part windows. From the curves above the third floor, their terra-cotta trim extended down to frame the windows of the second floor, again visually suggesting double-height arched openings. The generosity of H. H. Richardson's fenestration of the Marshall Field

FIG. 118 *Winchester Hall in 1928.*

FIG. 119 *Sheffield Chemical Laboratory (now Arthur K. Watson Hall), ca. 1900.*

Warehouse of 1886–87 very probably affected Cady's treatment of the elevations. While patterned brick surfaces dominated North Sheffield's walls, Winchester's bloomed with glass—expanses of glazing, set close to the outer surfaces. Again there were five bays, but much wider, and again a dense line of smaller windows finished the top of the facade. Winchester's first floor was treated like a rusticated basement, and below it, small windows pierced the smoother masonry surface of a raised basement. The rear facade, looking much like the front facade, loomed a full five stories behind Sheffield's mansion on Hillhouse Avenue.

On Prospect Street, a granite entry porch that, viewed in elevation, had very little relationship to anything else about the building, protruded in a half-round plan from the center. A single story tall, it seemed too small for the building, its Ionic columns and balustrade stuck on. However, in the old photographs looking north along Prospect Street, across the facades of Cady's three Sheff buildings, the curve of this porch is seen to be one in a series of protruding curves. It calls to the rounded corner towers that flank it, setting up a rhythmic beat that breaks the monotony of the street wall and suggests what the architect was after (see FIG. 112). Winchester Hall opened for classes in January 1893, and two years later the *Yale Alumni Weekly* published its photograph on the front page, hailing it "as a type of the best of the new University buildings."[127]

By that time, the Sheffield Chemical Laboratory, the last of Cady's brick trio for the scientific school, was already in the works (FIG. 119). Less than a year after finishing Winchester, Sheff's trustees felt that increased activity and "significant success" in chemistry was work that "needed support; it was neither for the interest of the school, nor for the credit of the alumni and friends…to allow such work to lag through lack of space and the proper facilities." So although no major donors were forthcoming, they found the $100,000 required, piecing together a few gifts, and "compelled to draw upon" their own funds. Again Cady's firm was presented with "the plans for the interior arrangements," this time "having been prepared by Professors Mixter and Wells."[128] This third Sheff building by Cady was sited farthest north in the row, with a facade of seventy-two feet, only three feet narrower than North Sheffield Hall, but extending much farther back toward Hillhouse Avenue: 130 feet. The full width of the facade was carried back only about forty feet before angling in ten feet for a rear wing.

Although Cady had by now abandoned polychromy for terra-cotta trim that was close in color

FIG. 120 *Demolition of North Sheffield and Winchester Halls in 1967.*

to his brick, and although no entry porch protruded in front, the new facade repeated many themes sounded on North Sheffield Hall. The two buildings were about the same height, and each had five bays and round-headed windows. The double-height window-framing effect was repeated across two principal floors over a raised basement, and there were twice as many round-headed windows in the topmost row as in the row of larger windows immediately below. Although there were notable variations from the earlier building, including roundels recessed in the brick panels between the glazing of the first two floors, and an arcaded parapet along the rear roof line, Cady quite evidently planned his third Sheff building as a complement to his first. This last is the only one of his buildings for the Sheffield Scientific School that survives.

By 1928 Cady's work had fallen into disrepute: in his *History of the Sheffield Scientific School,* Russell H. Chittenden (PH.B. 1875), the school's director from 1898 to 1922, wrote: "Today, North Sheffield Hall is justly looked on as a type of architecture woefully deficient in that grace and beauty which usually pertain to a modern college building."[129] By the 1960s the scientists had long since deserted it for newer quarters on Science Hill, and North Sheffield was largely occupied by the Naval Reserve Officers

Training Corps. Both North Sheffield and Winchester Halls were demolished in 1967 to clear the site for Marcel Breuer's Becton Engineering and Applied Science Center of 1970 (FIG. 120).

The interior of the sole survivor, the Sheffield Chemical Laboratory, is now much altered from the simple line-up of rooms on either side of a long hall that ran from the front door straight through the depth of the building. It was renovated in 1922 and renamed Sheffield Laboratory of Engineering and Mechanics, then again, more drastically, in 1984, when it was renamed Arthur K. Watson Hall. In the most recent work, the New Haven architectural firm of Roth and Moore not only completely redesigned the interior plan and installed new mechanical systems, but also made changes in the facade.[130] These included accommodation for handicapped entry and "corrections" of the original asymmetry. Cady's facade was nearly a full bay wider to the south than to the north of the entrance, but he treated it as if he had placed the door in its center: at the south end, rather than introducing windows in an extra bay, thereby calling attention to the imbalance, he built a quiet corner pier of brick, a plain enough trimming for the full height of the building. In his presentation rendering, a tree partially masked the absence of a balancing pier. Roth and Moore added a narrow bay to the north, fronted by a brick pier, so now the front door really is central.

In addition to these halls of science by Cady for the Sheffield School, and those by Raht for Yale College, Winchester Observatory by Rufus G. Russell (1823–1896), a New Haven architect, was a more distant outpost for Yale's scientists of the late nineteenth century. In 1871 Russell drew an elegant elevation for it as a two-story building of eleven bays under a tall roof boasting three gables, the whole adorned with impressive scrolls and flourishes. This was to be the central structure, joined by relatively long, one-story wings to flanking pavilions that were circular in plan, and were topped by the domes of the functioning observatories. The financial panic of 1873 and the subsequent recession delayed construction of any observatory until 1882–83, when the Honorable Oliver F. Winchester paid for only partial realization of Russell's plans (FIG. 121). His eleven bays were reduced to four, the roof became a flat one; no scrolls and few details relieved its plain brick walls, and although two little observing pavilions were constructed, only one of them was ever connected by its wing to the central block. Sold in 1956, the central block has survived at 485 Prospect Street. Long obscured by additions to the school building that surrounded a remnant of the old building, it is at this writing being partially restored within the new Celantano School.

———

If the late-nineteenth-century work by Russell at the Observatory and by Cady for the Sheffield Scientific School has fared badly over the years, the closely contemporary work by Frederick Clarke Withers for the state hospital in New Haven, a Yale affiliate that was farther distanced both geographically and organizationally, has done even worse. Only an obsessive search can discover one battered, well-disguised fragment of the big Gothic wards built to Withers's High Victorian designs in 1873 and 1874, now enclosed within the tangled masses of Yale-New Haven Hospital.

Withers was an English architect recruited by A. J. Downing to work in Newburgh, New York. He arrived in 1852, the year Downing died in a steamboat accident. Withers, who was twenty-four, stayed on in partnership with Calvert Vaux, another English architect Downing brought to this country, where Withers met him only after immigrating. In 1866 they won the competition for Yale's unbuilt Civil War memorial chapel. After moving to New York, Withers's "professional reputation came to maturity when he received the commission to design the Hudson River State Hospital for the Insane at Poughkeepsie," according to Francis R. Kowsky.[131] This commission of 1867 resulted in an enormous building, "from one end to the other more than half a mile." Its construction began in 1868 and took a decade. Withers repeated much of its planning and detail in New Haven when the General Hospital Society of Connecticut hired him in 1872.

The history of the General Hospital Society of Connecticut, which has evolved to become Yale-New Haven Hospital, was closely intertwined with that of Yale College from the time the society was founded in 1826. Yale's Professor Benjamin Silliman and four members of the Medical Institution of Yale College were among its ten original incorporators. Four of the others were doctors in New Haven, and one was a generous citizen.[132] After receiving funds from the state in 1828, the directors hired Ithiel Town to design the first hospital and administrative building, completed in 1832. It had a Doric temple front of red sandstone finished with stucco (FIG. 122; see also FIG. 125, to the left of center). It was sited about half a mile south and a little west of the center of the Old Campus, in the middle of a block bounded by Cedar Street and Congress, Howard, and Davenport Avenues. Its central pedimented pavilion was forty-six feet wide and was placed well back from Cedar Street, which it faced with two great fluted columns set between square pillars, its elevation looking like a temple front *in antis*. This formidably Greek entrance piece projected forward of two flanking wings to terminate the vista for those approaching from the New Haven Green along the irregular angle of Broad Street, which no longer exists. As the hospital's "Main Building," the original structure survived until 1930.[133] Between the autumn of 1862 and August 1867 it was leased to the U.S. government as a military hospital and called Knight General Hospital in honor of Dr. Jonathan Knight, a Yale faculty member and a founder of the hospital.

Yale's medical faculty used Town's building as a teaching facility and, just before the Civil War,

FIG. 121 *Winchester Observatory from the north.*

FIG. 122 *Main Building of the General Hospital Society of New Haven in the 1890s: east (Cedar Street) facade.*

moved from Prospect Street into a building on York Street that was the first designed specifically for it. Sidney M. Stone (1808–1888) of New Haven is named as architect in contracts of 1858 for this three-story masonry building with sparse classical detailing.[134] It stood about a quarter mile southwest of the Old Campus just off the direct route to the hospital.

In 1871 the General Hospital Society officially began to plan new buildings. Dr. Pliny A. Jewett, who served on the building committee, recorded the selection of Withers in his *Semi-Centennial History of the General Hospital Society of Connecticut,* published in 1876: "The plans submitted by him were adopted by the committee, after having been examined and altered in some important points by Mr. Russell, an architect of this city. We are under great obligations to Governor English for many valuable suggestions with reference to the plan and construction of the building."[135] "Mr. Russell" was Rufus G. Russell, who had just completed Calvary Baptist Church (1871), now the home of the Yale Repertory Theatre, and who was to begin work on West Divinity Hall (built in 1873 and 1874) about the same time he designed Winchester Observatory. The financial recession that delayed construction of the observatory for a decade also made it difficult to fund hospital structures, which were badly needed, "especially in winter," when its officers were "forced to refuse admission to many deserving patients for want of

room."[136] But faced with such pressing necessity as well as with the fledgling medical school's need for a better-equipped hospital in which to teach, and given the active support of rich and influential New Haven citizens like James E. English, governor of Connecticut twice between 1867 and 1871, money was pieced together to execute Withers's designs for new wards. Fundraising was supplemented by back rent for wartime use of the hospital due from the federal government.[137] In 1873 the directors authorized construction that by 1876 had cost over $92,000.

Withers designed agitated High Victorian Gothic forms in pointed, even hostile, contrast to the quiet, heavy classicism of Town's Greek temple front with its low-angled gable, calm symmetry, simple silhouette, and monochromatic stone-colored stucco. The new wards had busy asymmetrical silhouettes, towers, multi-angled polychromed brick walls, steep-pitched pediments, and very tall roofs pierced by a great many dormer windows and high chimneys. East Ward, the first built, was a long narrow bar which Withers set at a right angle to the temple front, about fifty feet to its south (FIG. 123; also on the far left in FIG. 125 and in the center of FIG. 126). His new wing pushed its way out, well past the older building, to present a narrow apsidal end toward Cedar Street. Across two stories, long rows of round-headed windows, topped by voussoirs of alternating dark and light bricks, and joined by bandings of

FIG. 123 *Farnam Operating Amphitheatre (left) and East Ward (right) from the southeast.*

FIG. 124 *Farnam Operating Amphitheatre: south (Congress Avenue) facade.*

colored bricks, demonstrated Withers's enthusiasm for polychromy in patterns that looked much like those Cady was creating at about the same time for North Sheffield Hall.

The wards filled three stories, including one under the tall mansard roof. Each ward accommodated twenty-two beds in one continuous open space that was ninety feet long by twenty-six feet wide, with what a historian described in 1926 as "an objectionable row of iron pillars along the middle... [that] interfered with the free movement of attendants."[138] A corridor connected the ward with the original Greek Revival building through a "central building" housing a dining room, a nurses' room for each ward, and closets. Within a year or so this central building also gave entry to a slightly smaller West Ward, sixty-five feet long by twenty-six feet wide with sixteen beds on each of its three floors. It was another long, apsidal-ended bar, but Withers sent it out behind Town's Greek Revival building, facing west, toward Howard Avenue.

While two small isolation pavilions and a morgue were built in 1877, a nurses' dormitory in 1881, and a superintendent's house in 1886, there were no further major additions to the main hospital building until 1888, when Mrs. Henry Farnam gave the Farnam Operating Amphitheatre in memory of her son, George Bronson Farnam (M.D. 1869).[139] Extending southwest of the East Ward, this third apse-ended form (FIGS. 123 & 124; also on the far left in FIG. 126) faced Congress Avenue. Now the hospital's plan took on the appearance of a pinwheel, with its center shifted south of the Greek Revival building to Withers's "central building" (FIG. 127). As a building paid for by one individual, Mrs. Farnam's gift marked an important first for the hospital. The record does not specify who designed the amphitheater. Perhaps it was Russell who shortened and embellished the apse-ended wing type established by Withers. Old photographs show an exterior with great charm of scale and ornament, and an interior that was a wonderfully high, bright space. It was, like Withers's wards, topped by a steep roof, but this time the roof was of glass. It lighted a two-story space that had banks of seats for students along the semicircular wall. Just under the cornice line was a continuous row of windows, and beneath them, three round windows that not only amplified the copious day-lighting for the surgeons' work but also served on the exterior as distinctive decorative elements. Surrounded by contrasting bands of brick, their glazing was set like jewels within rings set in bands of decorative brickwork. The device was much like Cady's on the rear facade of North Sheffield.

Before the turn of the century, three more wings with apsidal ends were added at right angles to a corridor extending along the north south axis centered through Ithiel Town's first hospital building. Within Ellen M. Gifford's Home for Incurables of 1889, a tablet described the donor as "The Only Child of Philip Marrett of New Haven," acknowledging that the building was "supported by funds bequeathed in part by each." Simeon E. Baldwin (B.A. 1861), her executor, was cited as "the means of securing" the bequest in histories of the hospital. After graduating from Yale College, Baldwin taught in the Law School through the 1870s and was a "historian, president of the American Bar Association, chief justice of the Supreme Court of Connecticut, and twice governor," who served on the hospital's board for fifty-six years.[140] His role here forms part of a tradition of alumni lawyers directing major gifts from families with no other connection to the college, a tradition that was to become important in Yale history.

Leoni W. Robinson (1852–1923) designed the Gifford Ward and Gifford Chapel of 1892 (on the right and far right, respectively, in FIG. 125). Robinson's office was in New Haven, and from the time he was hired to work on these buildings until the First World War he served virtually as the architect for the hospital. He received sole design responsibility first for these buildings, then for five others, including the William Wirt Winchester Hospital built in 1918 for tuberculosis patients on the site of the present Veterans' Administration Hospital in West Haven. Robinson was associated with Day and Klauder in designing the Brady Memorial Laboratory of 1917. Yale also called upon him for lesser work: a boiler house and chimney in 1893, repairs to the gym's leaky glass roof in 1902, and design work on the Heliostat Building on the grounds of Winchester Observatory in 1915.[141]

Robinson designed the Gifford buildings to correspond more or less to the pattern established by Withers for the wards to the south. He sent out a long, narrow corridor to the north, aligned with Town's Greek Revival building, so that the oldest part of the hospital again became the center of the extremely long facade of the whole complex. He terminated the axis with yet another half-round shape, this one facing Davenport Avenue. Its semicircular wall enclosed an apse in a more traditional ecclesiastical context, that of Gifford Chapel. At right angles to the long connecting corridor between the Greek temple and the chapel, the length of Gifford Ward extended to the west, to yet another apse-shaped end. Again long, open wards on three floors filled

FIG. 125 *Hospital buildings from the northeast in 1898.*

FIG. 126 *Hospital buildings from the southeast in 1899.*

most of its interior, including the space under the steep roof. But this time, "the objectionable pillars in the middle of the East and West Wards were omitted."[142] The elevations repeated the brick polychroming, round-headed windows, steep roof lines, towers, and dormers of Withers's buildings, though they had grown a little higher and bulkier in silhouette. One of the apse-ended wings set west of the long corridor between Gifford Ward and the chapel was shorter than the wards. Built around 1890, probably as an isolation ward, it was reconfigured in 1900 as a medical clinic, using university funds.[143]

A maternity ward was so badly needed that by 1899 the hospital used its own funds to build a freestanding one of two stories in the angle formed by West Ward and the Farnam Amphitheatre. The design, following Withers's precedents, is attributed to Robinson. It had polychromed brick walls with round-headed, banded windows and a high, dormered roof.

In 1913 the slow process began of enclosing this nineteenth-century hospital complex within a peripheral quadrangle of new buildings lined up along Cedar Street and Davenport, Howard, and Congress Avenues (see FIG. 210). The first of these was an Isolation Pavilion, at the corner of Howard and Davenport.[144] Rather than clearing out the center of a new quadrangle, as Yale had done on the Old Campus, the hospital hung on to some of its old buildings, renovating and enlarging them, or it replaced old buildings with new and larger ones built over the old footprints. Consequently, the interior of the medical quadrangle has come down to the turn of the twenty-first century not as a grassy

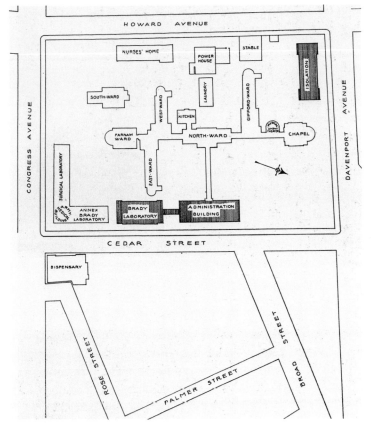

FIG. 127 *Map of the hospital buildings, 1922.*

found favor in 1922, but six years later it was gone. By then, pretty much everything else built before 1913 was already scheduled for drastic remodeling or demolition. Both the East and West Wards were catastrophically remodeled during the summer of 1921, just after which a report assessed them: "these have been entirely wrecked and only the outer shell of the building left. The mansard roof was removed, the walls were continued to make a complete third story, reinforced concrete floors replaced the old wooden ones, modern sanitary equipment was installed, and large piazzas placed on the south side; in fact these wards have been restored to meet the most modern ideas in hospital construction."[147] Only a decade after all this work, West Ward was leveled. But a diminished remnant of the East Ward, renamed Tompkins East, still stands, immured within the quadrangle, sheathed in polychromed bricks, with Withers's round-headed windows, distinctly different from those on a floor added above them in 1921 (see FIG. 211, in the lower left quadrant). Clinging to it, looking like two nightmarish oversized cages for unimaginable animals, are what must be "the large piazzas [porches] placed on the south side" in 1921. Withers's stone base has literally been bashed and battered by service vehicles that must make their way along an extremely narrow driveway past the half-round curve at the end of the old ward.

———

After working for the hospital, Frederick Clarke Withers designed no more buildings for Yale or its affiliates. In contrast, Josiah Cady had just been getting started with his contemporaneous work for the Sheffield Scientific School. During the two decades between Cady's commissions on Prospect Street, he was busy designing elsewhere for Yale: or, to be strictly correct, first for the Yale-affiliated board of trustees of an institution that contracted to give its completed building, on land donated by Yale, to the college. This second project of Cady's was the Peabody Museum, whose development was intimately involved with that of the Sheffield Scientific School. While North Sheffield Hall was still under construction, Cady set to work on a very grand project for this natural science museum, made possible by "the munificent gift of the late George Peabody" of London, a financier and philanthropist. Peabody also gave Harvard its natural history museum, among many major gifts to educational institutions. He endowed Danvers, Massachusetts, the place of his birth in 1795, with its Peabody Institute, and also gave Peabody Institutes to Salem, Massachusetts, and Baltimore, Maryland. As early as

campus but as a crowded, confusing jumble of survivors, useless remnants, remodelings, and replacements of a confusing sequence of structures.

The demise of landmarks at the hospital inevitably followed reports that they could not be adapted to serve vastly increased numbers of patients or accommodate technological innovations in medicine. But vituperative comment on their architectural merit also inevitably preceded demolition. In 1922 a publication of the School of Medicine described Ithiel Town's Greek Revival building as "an old ramshackle structure, and although somewhat improved by paint and decoration within the last two years, it is entirely unsatisfactory from every standpoint."[145] The centenary history of 1926 characterized it as "the present central stucco building with its composite front of Doric columns and ungainly square pillars."[146] Four years later, a year before its hundredth anniversary, it was demolished to make way for the present Clinic Building.

Withers's buildings also became objects of scorn. "Large, unsanitary, unhygienic halls, poorly adapted to the medicine of to-day," they were labeled in 1922. Gifford Ward was similarly dismissed: it came down in 1929. The Farnam Operating Amphitheatre of 1888 had been remodeled in 1913 as a ward which still

1863, Peabody had decided to leave $100,000 to Yale; but in 1866, when his nephew Othniel C. Marsh was appointed professor of paleontology, he immediately gave an even larger sum, $150,000, directing that $100,000 was to be used for a museum building "planned with especial reference to its subsequent development." Then he provided in advance for that development by specifying that "$20,000 was to be invested and to accumulate as a building fund until it should amount to at least $100,000, when it was to be employed in the erection of one or two more additions to the building." Peabody wanted the remaining $30,000 invested for the care and increase of the collections. And he gave these sums not to the college itself, but "in connection with Yale College," to a board of seven trustees he named. Among them was his nephew, America's first professor of paleontology and Yale's most renowned dinosaur man.[148]

Before making his gift, Peabody traveled to New Haven and chose a site for his museum on the Old Campus where, fronting Chapel Street, next to the picture galleries in Street Hall, it would have fallen into a proto-museum row. Othniel Marsh wrote that only when construction was about to begin in 1874 did Peabody agree to exchange this site for "what was then considered a more suitable location" west of the Old Campus, across High Street between Elm and Library Streets. Science on this occasion had come about as close as it ever would to winning that forever elusive foothold on the Old Campus. Just south of the Peabody, across Library Street, Sloane

and Kent Laboratories were soon built, so the area became the college's science district.

Scientists again took an active role in shaping the design of the Peabody Museum. Marsh wrote that "The interior arrangements...were planned by the Yale members of the board. The ground plans, thus prepared by those who knew what was needed, were then given to the architect...with the request that he give them an exterior."[149] Cady's exterior for those plans emerged as a building intended to stretch 350 feet along High Street. For many years Yale published his perspective drawing of the whole expanse as a scheme it meant to complete (FIG. 128).[150] Cady's perspective showed a building of five parts, arranged symmetrically. At its center was a large block of four full stories over a raised basement, joined by hyphens — recessed, lower-roofed, three-story links — to high-roofed, three-story flanking wings. This grand design employed the vocabulary of High Victorian Gothic, despite its symmetry, which did not conform to the era's usual preference for asymmetry. It was to be executed in polychromed brick much like that of Withers's hospital buildings and Cady's own North Sheffield Hall. However, where those earlier buildings had round-headed windows, here pointed arches appeared over windows on three levels, with voussoirs of alternating dark and light masonry. And unlike the low and flat-roofed boxes for Sheffield, steep hipped roofs, conical tower roofs, tall complex chimneys, many dormers all around, and iron finials and crestings gave the proposed nat-

FIG. 128 *Peabody Museum: perspective drawing by J. C. Cady, ca. 1872–73.*

FIG. 129 *Peabody Museum in 1880: High and Elm Street facades.*

ural history museum a highly agitated silhouette more like those of Withers's wards.

By 1876 Cady was to see constructed only a subordinate part of his design, the northernmost pavilion, along with a wing intended to be the link to the central block (FIGS. 129 & 130).[151] In this incomplete form Yale's first Peabody Museum was a decidedly asymmetrical building with its entrance on High Street, four bays in from the corner of Elm. P. B. Wight recorded his impressions of it in 1879, describing details that are not apparent in the images that survive:

There is the Peabody Museum, fresh with its finishing touches, or at least so much of it as we will see for the next twenty years or so;…What appears to be a wing to this structure is only the connecting portion which is to join it to the great central building which is to be. Already the wing just built overtops all the other college buildings. The style, as in all the other new college buildings, is in the advanced Gothic, the materials brick and stone. The architect has introduced considerable buff brick, and the polychromatic treatment prevails throughout the exterior to a greater degree than in any of the other college buildings…Cady…has given this building a grand entrance, which is the most elaborate piece of work done for the college.

Wight went on to give us some sense of what it was like inside:

The interior is plainly treated throughout, except the entrance hall and grand stairway, which are faced throughout with brick of various colors arranged as a wainscot following the line of the stairs. The stairway is of cast-iron and about as good as it could well be in that material. There is some excellent painted glass, especially about the main entrance, and in the traceried heads of the first story windows.[152]

Montgomery Schuyler, writing about the building in the mid-1890s, was especially impressed by its height, and his comments suggest how the client's participation in the design had again shaped Cady's forms:

It is noteworthy for its unusual scale among the college buildings, which have otherwise become so heterogeneous. This is fixed by the height of the stories, something over twenty feet, which in turn is the result of a requirement for galleries in the principal exhibition rooms. Provision for the cases and the need of abundant light determined the size of the openings and the intervals between them, and this requirement operated unfavorably on the architecture, huddling the openings much closer than a consideration of the best architectural effect would have admitted.

Schuyler regretted that this "attenuates the piers, especially and painfully on one front…and leaves the architect to seek at the top of the building for the expanses of wall surface that are so much more effectual at the base." The second-floor galleries had to be so tall to accommodate the "Fossil Vertebrates from the Rocky Mountain region" — Othniel Marsh's famous dinosaurs. In the end Schuyler praised Cady's building more than he criticized it: "The effect of the combination of material, red pressed

FIG. 130 *Peabody Museum: plan of the ground floor drawn by Harrison W. Lindsley, 1893.*

FIG. 131 *Peabody Museum: lecture room, ca. 1890.*

brick and Nova Scotia stone, is very good; the detail of the doorway, the cornice and the crocketed gables scholarly in design and effective in scale, and the fragment, in spite of its fragmentariness and of its drawbacks, an impressive piece of work."[153] In an old photograph, even the Peabody's classrooms with their intricate woodwork and decorative stained glass are impressive (FIG. 131).

In the late 1870s Yale boasted a dazzling array of brick polychroming. The contrasts between very dark and very light bricks called attention to geometric patterns and prominent horizontal bands on the walls of the High Victorian Gothic buildings by Withers at the hospital, Hunt at the Divinity School, and Cady at the Peabody Museum, as well as on Cady's decorated box at the Scientific School. It was enough to justify describing Yale's newest buildings as "piebald" in a sense young George Holt probably could not have imagined as he worried over the novelty Street Hall presented to Yale. But the taste for colorful brickwork was soon to wane, and the one poor sample surviving at the hospital hardly suggests its original effect. The Peabody Museum proved the shortest-lived of the group. It was demolished in 1917 to clear the site for the Memorial Quadrangle by James Gamble Rogers. Its demolition

left the natural history collections homeless until the present museum, by Charles Z. Klauder, was completed in 1924 (see FIG. 206).

After finishing one wing of the Peabody scheme in 1876, Yale was not to build another of Cady's designs until 1885. In the meantime, Professor Marsh had Cady design a quite wonderful High Victorian mansion for him, built in 1878 near the crest of Prospect Street (FIG. 132). It is a high-roofed, high-chimneyed, many-gabled-and-dormered stone and shingle house with elaborate porches and a tower, from which Marsh could survey Yale to his south. West Rock, though a little distant, was well framed in his view, and he could see East Rock as well. Marsh's home is now one of six buildings occupied by the School of Forestry & Environmental Studies, and because of Marsh's importance to the history of science, it is a National Historic Landmark.

In 1885 Yale began to build the first of two projects that Cady designed for the Old Campus. Montgomery Schuyler characterized them as Cady's "contributions…to the Richardsonian phase of Yale architecture."[154] The first, Dwight Hall, was for the University Christian Association. President Noah Porter, a notoriously conservative man, always doubtful of the sciences and focused on the moral and spiritual training of his students, presided over its construction a year before he retired. The second was Chittenden Memorial Library of 1888, a wing of a larger library that was planned, but never completed.[155] The Old Campus had room, it seems, for buildings serving religion and traditional scholarship, if not for science.

The site of Cady's Dwight Hall is now a grassy plot fronting High Street, just south of Wright Hall. An entirely different building, Austin's Library of 1842, is now called Dwight Hall and houses activities relocated from Cady's building. The first Dwight Hall was named to honor Timothy Dwight, president of Yale College from 1795 to 1817, grandfather of the Timothy Dwight who became president a year after the building was completed. Although Elbert Brinckerhoff Monroe is the acknowledged donor, funding for the original Dwight Hall ultimately came from the same Frederick Marquand who paid for much of Hunt's Divinity School. Monroe was married to Marquand's niece, adopted daughter, and principal heir, Mary Virginia Marquand Tompkins Monroe. Before his death in 1882, Marquand instructed Monroe to fund and to name the building for Dwight.[156]

Dwight Hall was perhaps Cady's best building at Yale. Its asymmetrical stone facade faced the campus with two big frontal gables behind the generous arches of a low, flat-roofed porch (FIG. 133). The porch was a favorite subject of photographers, and they often brought their cameras within it to frame pictures of the Old Campus in its arches. The irregu-

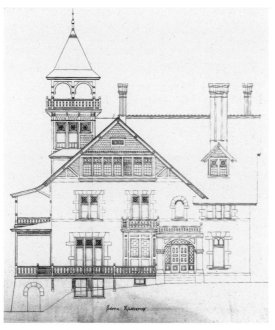

FIG. 132 *Othniel C. Marsh House (now Marsh Hall): south elevation by J. C. Cady, 1878.*

larity of the campus elevation suggested not at all the balanced plan behind, a rectangle symmetrically partitioned. Four nearly square rooms, each with a corner fireplace, were aligned, two to a side, flanking a broad hall that ran straight through the center, its front third partitioned off as a stair hall. Beyond the stained glass and paneling of the partition was a great comfortable "Lounge," with a fireplace dominating its north wall and the rear wall pushed out into a half-round apse. The curved wall of the apse rose tower-like through two stories under a big conical roof and was the most prominent feature of the High Street facade (FIG. 134). Although we have no plan of the second floor, surviving photographs of Dwight Hall's large assembly room with sloping ceilings suggest that it must have filled the space under that roof. Schuyler judged this building "very simple, very massive, very rugged," one "which aims to make its effect merely by the force of its masses crowned with large expanses of unbroken roof."[157] Dwight Hall was demolished in 1926, in compliance with the wishes of Mrs. William L. Harkness, whose late husband had left money for a classroom building on the Old Campus. Though Mrs. Harkness was persuaded to locate William L. Harkness Hall on the Cross Campus, she presided over the removal of Cady's Dwight Hall because she wanted an unobstructed view of Harkness Tower from the Old Campus.

Cady's Chittenden Library (FIG. 135) does survive, though it has been repeatedly and extensively altered. Like Dwight Hall, it faces the Old Campus and backs onto High Street. Its round-headed arches with rough-finished stone voussoirs recall Romanesque precedents. Schuyler, having first categorized the library as part of Yale's Richardsonian phase, then wrote that it was: "a work entirely free and eclectic, without being outrageous. One would have to classify it as Romanesque, perhaps, if he undertook to classify it at all, though by no means Romanesque of the Richardsonian variety. But, in fact, it seems intentionally to elude classification and to aim at inclusion in the category of buildings which are of no style and which yet have style."[158] This library was the gift of Simeon B. Chittenden, a New York merchant who, according to Brooks Kelley, had been "an apprentice in a New Haven store at the time he might have been in college." Cady recorded that "Mr. Chittenden near the close of his life, was seized with the desire to build a Library for Yale, and to make it in a measure a Memorial to a beloved daughter."[159] He gave Yale $125,000 to realize that desire.

Cady was again to see executed only one wing of a larger proposed building, about a quarter of his

FIG. 133 *Dwight Hall after 1894: east (Old Campus) facade, with Alumni Hall on the right.*

FIG. 134 *Dwight Hall after 1912: west (High Street) facade, with Wright Hall on the left.*

design (FIG. 136). His project would have stretched from Chittenden north across the site of the present Linsly Hall and right through the site of Austin's Library (the building now called Dwight Hall)— necessitating its demolition—to a point thirty-eight feet south of Cady's Dwight Hall. Had this scheme been fully executed, J. Cleveland Cady's would have been the hand that shaped much of the face Yale presented to New Haven along High Street, between Street Hall and Alumni Hall. More importantly to the Yale community, the facades of harmoniously related buildings by Cady would have dominated the western edge of the Old Campus yard.

The existing Chittenden Hall differs only a little from the portion of the facade that represents it in the full library project. Cady's proposed forms began with its relatively low mass at the southern end, polygonal in plan, dominated by a great broad cone of a roof that rose to a point. This was built as the main reading room for the whole university, a room that is now a lecture room and seems remarkably small compared to the vast spaces within Sterling Library. The lecture room still boasts the old reading room's elaborate fireplace and its allegorical stained glass windows by Louis C. Tiffany (FIG. 137).[160] North of this, Cady's three-bay pavilion was also

FIG. 135 *Chittenden Library in the 1890s: east and south (Old Campus) facades, with the Old Library (now Dwight Hall) just visible at the far right.*

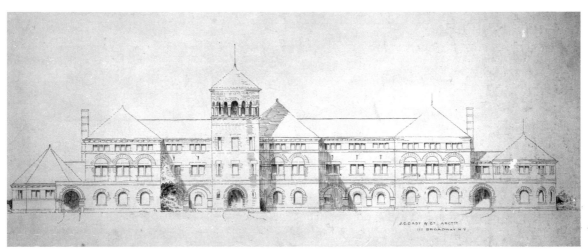

FIG. 136 *Chittenden Library: presentation drawing by J. C. Cady, ca. 1889.*

built, much of it given over to book stacks. It was intended to be one of three hipped-roof pavilions that appear in the full scheme, where they step forward at regular intervals across the great length of the three-story bulk of the building. Cady terminated the northern end of his proposed library with another polygonal pavilion with a conical roof, but he drew it a story taller than the built one. In fact Cady's whole ambitious scheme was nearly symmetrical, with the major exception of a round tower that he placed just off-center, well forward of the mass of the building, and raised a full story above its roofs. With this gesture he undercut most sense of the regularity that underlay his design.

While Chittenden Library was under construction, the *Mail and Express* of March 21, 1888, quoted the architect's remarks emphasizing the importance of fireproofing this repository for valuable books. This concern, it said, guided choices of materials, including "brown stone of two shades" and "iron beams and brick arches with finished floors of rock asphalt and tile…Nothing is combustible except the wooden window frames, a few of the doors, the most of which are to be of iron."[161] On May 16, 1889, Cady wrote a letter to Yale's treasurer, William W. Farnam (B.A. 1866), trying to get another job, and expounding on his practical and thrifty approach to designing the library:

it was first thoroughly considered with reference to the needs—not the exterior—then the exterior was taken up and is I think a well studied development of the interior—…

The aim was to get a dignified sensible exterior, with enough ornament to relieve it of baldness—but there was

FIG. 138 *Osborn Hall at the corner of Chapel and College Streets, ca. 1890, with Union Hall (South College) on the left.*

YALE UNIVERSITY. Osborn Hall.

FIG. 139 *Osborn Hall after 1894, with Vanderbilt Hall on the left.*

first, dated April 15, 1887, from President Timothy Dwight to Sterling, recalled "the pleasant conversation which I had with you the other evening," that "quite carried my mind back to the old College days, when we used to meet so often." Then, apparently responding to Sterling's questions, Dwight wrote: "Of all the matters *of building*, our great want now is a building for lecture rooms and for the direct influence, in teaching, of the minds of the teachers upon the students...The finest site on our college grounds is open for such a building. It could be built in stone, I think, and could be made a very handsome and imposing building, for a sum not exceeding one hundred and twenty five thousand dollars."

Sterling formally offered the gift on May 24, 1887, in a letter that begins: "On behalf of a friend whose name is to remain unknown until after the completion of the work, I am authorized to propose the erection, upon the College Campus, of a Memorial edifice...[for] lectures and recitations." The identity of the donor became known to Dwight and his wife when Sterling brought her to visit New Haven, but it was carefully guarded from the press. To alumni assembled in 1887 at the banquet that was the annual highlight of commencement activities, Dwight announced that $125,000 was in hand for "a palatial recitation and lecture room given by a gentleman not a graduate of the college who did not care to be known." One reporter, frustrated in his attempts to learn the secret, told readers of the *New Haven Union* for September 21 that same year, "No one seems to know anything about it, and if anyone knows anything definite, he seems determined that no one else shall."

Through the winter and spring of 1888–89, the New York press repeatedly revealed the identities, on the best authority, of supposed donors. Papers published the names of two rich New York ladies, one a widow, the other the bereaved mother of a son who died a few weeks after entering Yale, neither of whom proved to be the one who did not care to be known. Speculations about the mysterious nongraduate also appeared in the newspapers of New Haven and Hartford, and even in the *Cincinnati Commercial Gazette*. Miriam A. Osborn's lawyer carefully clipped all the newspaper coverage and pasted it in a scrapbook.[171] That fact, and the documentation he assembled covering the whole process of building Osborn Hall, would be interesting enough, whoever that lawyer might have been. But it becomes of even greater interest because he was the same John W. Sterling whose own stupendous bequest of 1918 was to fund the great Sterling Memo-

rial Library, the Law School, the Hall of Graduate Studies, the Sterling Hall of Medicine, the Medical Library, the Sterling Chemistry Laboratory, the Sterling Divinity Quadrangle, Trumbull College, the Sterling Power Plant, and Sterling Tower at the corner of Grove and College Streets, among other benefactions to Yale. Bringing Mrs. Osborn's gift to the university, and representing her through the construction of Osborn Hall, marked his first involvement with the physical development of the campus.

Sterling's letters to President Dwight and to Mrs. Osborn suggest how he interested her in the college. She was the widow of Charles J. Osborn, a New York stockbroker who, "although he was not a graduate of the college, was always a true friend of the young," as Sterling wrote Dwight when offering the gift. In a letter of May 28, 1887, to the widow, Sterling characterized her husband, who was only forty-six when he died: "There probably has never been a better broker, who was a better banker, nor one who has done a larger commission business in the purchase and sale of stocks since the foundation of the New York Stock Exchange." Sterling also rehearsed points he must have made in persuading Miriam A. Osborn to support Yale, including "the fact that your own ancestors came from New Haven" which "would of itself be sufficient reason why you should personally select the City of Elms." He boasted that, "There is no educational institution upon this continent which stands higher than Yale," and that "The sons of New Yorkers prefer Yale to her rival and the children of the countless friends of Mr. Osborn will naturally tend to New Haven."

The formal letter of gift specified that "a sum not less than" $125,000 would be provided for construction, that the building would be sited on the corner of Chapel and College, and that "enough ground will at all times be reserved around the building to keep it entirely separate and distinct from any other buildings which may hereafter be erected near it." As Dwight noted in his first presidential report, "The Corporation, in accepting the offer, are prepared to meet the donor's wishes and the conditions of the gift."[172]

An uproar that far exceeded the administration's fears exploded when old Yalies learned that their alma mater intended to tear down the Yale Fence. A remarkable 2,100 graduates signed a letter of protest. They objected to just about everything Yale was planning for the new recitation hall on the most prominent—and the noisiest, as they were quick to point out—corner of the Old Campus. They said that trolleys rounded the corner so loudly that lectures would be inaudible. They were still saying it was too noisy a corner for classrooms when Osborn was torn down after only thirty-five years of occupation. Their fury over the loss of the Fence surely prejudiced their initial viewing of Price's plans, and it was not quelled by the persistence of the donor in claiming the most prominent spot in New Haven for a memorial to a non-alumnus. Then there was another protest, copiously reported in the papers, over "our beautiful elms" that would have to be taken down to make way for the new hall. Timothy Dwight and especially his wife joined the general objection to destruction of the trees, and wrote to Price about them. The students also protested the loss of a favorite football playing field.

Before choosing an architect, Sterling sought Dwight's suggestions, writing on May 25, 1887: "The donor will select an architect as soon as possible; although perhaps it might be better, in the first instance, to make the selection by a limited competition. If you have a preference for any architect, I should be glad to have you put me in communication with him at once." Yale's president replied the next day: "I have only to suggest that I would rather not have Russell Sturgis, unless the donor is earnest to have him, as I presume may not be the case. I have a very favorable opinion of Cady, and I think he has more genius than Raht. But you know more of the architects than I do—and I only suggest the exclusion of Sturgis."[173] Only a year earlier, Sturgis had completed Lawrance Hall, the dormitory that was the last of his four buildings for Yale. We might speculate that Dwight had had enough of the architect who executed so much work during the presidency of his predecessor, Noah Porter, and had received an honorary master's degree in 1872 during Porter's presidency.[174] However, exactly why Dwight so emphatically rejected Sturgis for this first building project of his presidency remains undocumented, as is evidence that any formal competition was conducted.

Bruce Price's name—unlike those of many who worked for Yale during the late nineteenth and early twentieth centuries—is well known to students of modern American architecture. Major figures in its history, especially Frank Lloyd Wright, were influenced by Price's open plans and skillful adaptations to specific sites of some of his best known buildings.[175] The most spectacular among those, Chateau Frontenac in Quebec City, established a style for Canadian national architecture, but it was not built until 1892. In 1887, when Price was chosen

to design Osborn Hall, his reputation was growing among architects, who had seen his published drawings for houses at Tuxedo Park in the professional journals. Price's selection by Pierre Lorillard, a cigarette magnate, to design that country retreat for New Yorkers also signaled that by the mid-1880s he had come to the attention of the rich and powerful. Further, he was a lawyer's son who had briefly attended the College of New Jersey (which became Princeton), and he belonged to the Century, Union, Player's, and Racquet Clubs in New York.[176] Price's name would readily enough have come to the attention of a New York financier and lawyer like Sterling or the widow of a leading stockbroker. He seems to have been just the kind of architect Dwight expected Sterling to know about.

By the autumn of 1887 Price had produced plans which the president of Yale had reviewed and returned. Dwight wrote to Sterling on September 19: "Mrs. Dwight and I both like the plans very much, both outside and inside—except so far as the matter of the trees is concerned. I think Mr. Price will have to give his mind further to the solution of this problem."[177] The Fence's survival through the autumn was noted in the press, as was its removal, by "unknown parties," reported in the New Haven Morning News for June 22, 1888. It had been secreted away the previous night, apparently for souvenirs. On August 7, 1888, the New York Times lamented the destruction of some elms, noting "four of the trees are now kindling wood." By August 20 the elm toll stood at seven according to the Suffield Republican. It called them "stately," and recorded that their removal, "required four pairs of oxen and twenty men." The same day the Hartford Courant added to the tree story: "the worst part of the job was the removal of the stumps after the trees were felled… Some of the stumps weighed six tons. They were carted off and dumped into Beaver ponds."

In December 1887 Price's plans were out for bids, which came in about $25,000 over the gift in hand. Only after the widely reported site preparation of the following summer could building begin. It was, inevitably, a messy process that did not calm student or alumni objections. An undergraduate returning after summer break described the construction site in the Yale Record of September 29, 1888: "The scene at the south end of campus is…suggestive of the ruins of Sardis." He resented the Corporation's having made the students "look upon the 'abomination of desolation.'"[178] On September 26 the New York Evening Post described the "first sight of Yale to an expectant student…The fence and its beautiful environments have gone. A medley of sand, dirt, huge stones, timber, and engines infest the place where once stood lofty elms." The *New York Times* published an account, remarkably distasteful to our contemporary sensibilities, of the actual physical labor of digging out the deep basements and foundations:

The rivalry between the Italian and Irish laborers is very strong, and their bosses utilize race prejudice in a curious manner. In digging it is often necessary to dig so deeply that the men are placed in layers. At the bottom the overseer places two stout, strapping young Irishmen; just above them a couple of Italians who are good workers, then two more Irishmen, and so on until the surface of the ground is reached. The two Irishmen at the bottom, feeling a contempt for the inhabitants of Italy above them, shovel like Trojans, in order to load up the Italians with more work than they can do. The Italians, between two layers of Irishmen, have every incentive to shovel in order to knock out the Celts. The overseer stands above and keeps order. The only difficulty is that the side which is getting worsted usually makes pretense for getting up a quarrel, and the workers come to blows. A continual war of words is waged, and the Italian and Celtic gibberish that is flying around loose under the old Yale Elms is a poor substitute for the Greek and Latin roots that the staid old trees have been wont to hear.[179]

Before the walls went up, Timothy Dwight seems to have anticipated that the very stones from which they were to be built would further irritate Osborn's critics. Price chose Stony Creek granite, which looked nearly white and had a reddish tinge in contrast to the darker browns and duller reds of all the other buildings on the Old Campus. And it contrasted sharply with the very red tile Price chose for Osborn's roofs as well as the red stone he chose for the trim, a brownstone—Ribbe—from East Longmeadow, Massachusetts. Dwight's letters of the spring of 1888 virtually begged the architect to rethink his choices. "The grey or white granite I most earnestly hope will not be pressed by the donor. My mind turns against it more and more, and I am sure it will not suit the taste of the Faculty," he wrote on May 20. "I think the success of the building in every way is largely dependent on the selection of a different stone." Dwight's account in the same letter of his trip to Newport to assess the appearance in a completed building of "McCurdy Stone," the material he preferred, suggests just how involved the president had become in the project. In urging the specific alternate, he described it: "The McCurdy has, I should think, a sufficiently *light* character to suit the donor, while it is free from all

that is objectionable in the Worcester Norcross and grey granite. It will also tone in well with our buildings, while unlike them and having nothing of the ordinary brown stones."[180] But in the end, perhaps inspired by H. H. Richardson's success in using light-colored stone with boldly contrasting red trim and roofs for Trinity Church of the mid-1870s in Boston, or perhaps egged on by Mrs. Osborn, Price used materials that made the building boldly distinct. The *Sun* for January 13, 1889, reported: "Architect Price considers the granite used in this building about as fine stone as can be found. He himself discovered it in the abandoned Redpath quarries on Stony Creek, ten miles north of New Haven, and persuaded the builder to buy 200 acres of land containing the rock."

Price had discovered granite of a type admired by some of his leading colleagues, including Richard Morris Hunt, who had used similar stone from the nearby Leetes Island quarries to face the concrete base for the Statue of Liberty in 1884–86.[181] The *Cincinnati Gazette* on January 12, 1889, published its opinion that "the granite will make a rather violent contrast to the brick and red sandstone which have been used in all the other buildings." Such opinions were to prevail. Montgomery Schuyler described the building itself as "aggressive bichromate."[182] The color clash is not so apparent in most of the photographs that survive, which are sepia-toned, but a few colored postcards and the unanimity of descriptions leave little doubt about the visual impact of its color scheme.

Osborn Hall turned the corner of Chapel and College with an L-shaped plan hinged on a big, nearly round polygon with a relatively low, conical roof. This dominant central element was bracketed by taller, round towers with conical roofs. Price formed a visually powerful curve of seven steps as the podium for the building's great feature: a grand entranceway that spanned 125 feet from tower to tower and was penetrated by five imposing arched portals. In Mrs. Osborn's memorandum of November 1888, which was deposited in the cornerstone, she wrote that "the reason why such pains have been taken to have such an extensive entrance as the steps and podium will afford" was her hope that "the students will tend to congregate there, as they have for generations on the old fence." Elaborate ornamentation in carved relief bordered the arches of its portals, and the central one bore the deeply incised words "Osborn Hall" (see FIG. 86). The five arches rested on entablatures with relief-carving of intertwined foliage encircling animal and human heads.

Each section of entablature was carried by three columns, each capped with more heads and foliate carving. One writer traced the decoration to twelfth-century sources, commenting that grotesque forms were here "replaced with designs from American animals, modeled by the sculptor Kenneys."[183] A writer for the *New Haven Evening Register* was more impressed by the bill for these "costly ornamentations...some $20,000 in carvings alone."[184]

Those who counted the twelve sides of the principal form with which Osborn Hall faced the corner knew that it was a dodecagon in its highest stage where it rose free of the lower walls and supported twelve roof segments that reached a height of seventy-five feet at the central apex, just lower than the two towers on either side. One tower rose eighty feet above Chapel Street, while the other, on College Street, was ten feet taller. On the ground floor the plan was complex, and much of it was given up to hallways (FIG. 140). The three central portals gave entrance via additional steps to a wedge-shaped hall that narrowed to several more steps mounting to a small central hallway, a rectangle directly under the apex of the roof. This little hall opened, past yet more steps, into another wedge-shaped hall that broadened again. In plan, these hallways, their

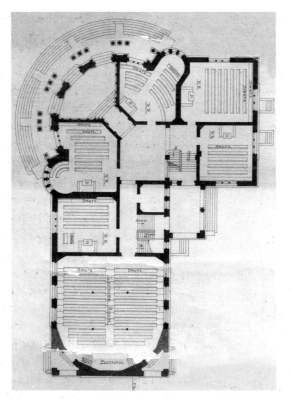

FIG. 140 *Osborn Hall: plan of the ground floor drawn by Harrison W. Lindsley, 1893 (Chapel Street at top).*

length centered on a straight line that miters the street corner, appear cinched in the middle. Their walls form an irregular figure that looks like two straight-sided funnels joined at their narrow ends, as if to squeeze in the flow of foot traffic from the town's busiest intersection before releasing it to the southeast corner of the Old Campus (FIG. 141; see also FIG. 76). By some reports, students usually avoided this route over many stairs and took paths on either side of the building. The portals beside the two towers each gave direct entry through exterior doors into oddly-shaped recitation rooms whose spaces occupied wedges of the central dodecagon and extended into the bases of the towers. A door north of the tower led directly into an auditorium, seating 400 and filling most of the ell on College Street.

The shape of a dodecagon is not immediately apparent on the ground floor plan because so many walls of the geometric figure were omitted at this level. That central figure merged into the shorter leg of the L along Chapel Street, which had frontage there of 102 feet, and into rooms along College Street, where the frontage was 155 feet. There were five other rooms on the ground floor and six recitation rooms above. Plans of the upper two floors have not come to light. In fact none of Price's own drawings for Osborn Hall have been located in Yale archives, or in other indexed sources. The only plan of Osborn Hall known to survive at Yale is shown here. It was measured and drawn in 1893 by Harrison Wheeler Lindsley (1853–1893), an architect who was teaching in the School of the Fine Arts when he included it on his great campus map, which detailed ground-floor plans of Yale buildings on the Old Campus and on Elm and High Streets.[185]

Newspaper reporters and architectural critics struggled to describe and characterize Bruce Price's design from the time it was first revealed. In September 1888, as construction began, the *New Haven Register* tried "Arabesque and Romanesque: The Style of the Magnificent New Recitation Building" over a story about plans the writer had seen "in the office of Engineer Cole, just south of the foundations," where "they have been inspected by a large number of students."[186] The *New Haven Palladium* for November 23 repeated the opinion of "a gentlemen who has traveled considerable on the continent" that "the new building has a very foreign aspect, although it is in accordance with no special school of architecture. It resembles somewhat the gallery at

FIG. 141 *Osborn Hall: north and west (Old Campus) facades, with the Ninety-Six Memorial Gateway on the left.*

Amsterdam and some of the buildings in Belgium." Mr. Sterling must have enjoyed such erudition. For the *Sun* of January 13, 1889, a reporter seems to have tapped more learned sources who thought "the architecture…may be termed Italian-Romanesque of the twelfth century." A line drawing of Osborn Hall appeared in the *New Haven Evening Register* of December 1, 1888, with text that admitted:

the style of the building is hard to describe by any of the terms applied to architecture of to-day and attempts made by some in this direction have resulted in all but failure. The style is one which shows great study and one which it is safe to say is a combination and develop-ment from the brain of the architect…While the building seems to be designed to bring out especially the solidity and durability of the structure, yet the aesthetic part has by no means been neglected. When this building is completed it will be a satisfaction to the mind and a pleasure to the eye.

Later in 1889, a reporter who asked Price about charges that the building was functionally deficient, said that he replied: "Why, the purpose for which the building was erected was secondary to the architecture."[187] While it was under construction some writers predicted that Osborn would be "one of the finest in the country," "the handsomest

one on the campus," and "the most magnificent of Yale's buildings."

But harshly negative critics also weighed in at an early date. "The building has been the object of such a storm of adverse criticism" according to the *New York Tribune* of December 23, 1889, that when a faculty committee inspected the building, its positive findings were news, headlined: "Yale's New Lecture Hall: The Building is a Success." Several berated the administration, as that undergraduate George Holt had done in the 1860s, for not demand-ing more consistency with the older buildings. The *New York Evening Post* of May 2, 1889, was among them, expressing "sincere regret that some uniform style of architecture has not been followed by the University…the [Old Campus] quadrangle when completed will be a medley, indeed a patchwork in architecture." It focused on Osborn: "In its design the new recitation building is radically different from any structure yet erected here. It is very elabo-rate and thousands of dollars have been spent in the carving." It deemed the red tile roof "grotesque" in a context where "seven of the eight buildings already erected…have slated roofs." The *Post* also faulted Osborn for being "too plain on the interior side of the campus. As it is, it will be the least impressive

FIG. 142 *Demolition of Osborn Hall in 1926.*

of all the college buildings." Along College Street, it found "a gross violation of symmetry...Instead of making a sharp angle to correspond with that of Battell Chapel, the architect has projected a cumbersome porch right in the L. The effect is uncomfortable."

Through that "cumbersome porch," students entering from the town side first filed into classes after a formal "occupation" on January 7, 1890. Mrs. Osborn's name had been announced to alumni at the commencement banquet the previous spring. Months earlier the press had finally ferreted it out. A month after classes began, the *New York Tribune* calculated Osborn Hall's total cost at $200,000.[188] In an example of the sincerest form of flattery, William A. Potter took Osborn as his model for Alexander Hall at Princeton two years later.

But well after Osborn Hall ceased to be news, the critics could not let it alone. In 1909 Montgomery Schuyler, in his piece on Yale's architecture, called it a "barbarian invasion" of the campus, and an "insubordinate edifice." He reprinted a blast at Osborn's "unneighborliness" that he had published earlier, concluding: "It contradicts all the other buildings with more violence than any two of them contradict

each other, and it is so aggressive that it is no wonder Yale should forget there was any quarrelling before it arrived, and should hold it exclusively responsible for the disturbance of the peace."[189]

On October 5, 1911, Yale's Secretary Stokes registered his opinion of Osborn in a letter to the new chairman of the architectural planning committee, doubtless helping to seal its fate: "Osborn Hall stands in a class by itself as an architectural monstrosity. It can be slightly improved by substituting slate for red tile and perhaps by adding slightly overhanging eaves, but nothing but dynamite can really remove the bad effect and bad influence of this building."[190] In the early 1920s Mrs. William L. Harkness briefly fixed on Osborn's site for her proposed gift of a classroom building, before finding another place for it on the Cross Campus. But Osborn's reprieve was brief. In October 1924 the Corporation had Walter B. Chambers (B.A. 1887) draw up plans for remodeling it as a dormitory, but in the spring of the following year its Committee on Architectural Plan, faced with the loss of Osborn's classrooms, considered having Chambers "prepare sketches for an entirely new building" that would include some classrooms.[191] Yale easily found excuses for removing the controversial structure that had been a constant irritant during all the thirty five years of its occupancy.

But taking Osborn down was no easy matter (FIG. 142). Miriam Osborn had written in 1888: "I fondly and sincerely hope that the edifice, which it affords me so much pleasure to erect, may for ages stand." It became abundantly clear that Price had designed it and Norcross had built it to do just that when workmen finally were able to remove the cornerstone in which she had sealed her statement. A prolonged struggle to undo the work of 1888 and 1889 again disrupted the southeastern end of the campus through much of 1926, and Yale publications marveled over its unyielding solidity. Osborn Hall, with its arched portals opening to the town and a plan largely given up to hallways funneling people through to the Old Campus, was replaced in 1928 by Bingham Hall, designed by Chambers to block all such access with a sharp-edged corner tower. Devoid of doors on the street side, it rises more than ten stories, signaling Yale's lofty presence up and down Chapel Street and out across New Haven's Green.

After Bruce Price completed Yale's most obstreperous building of the late nineteenth century, he soon designed one of its least obtrusive, Welch Hall of 1891 (FIG. 143; see also FIG. 14). Sited just north of Osborn on College Street, it originally mediated, across a gap on either side, between his own earlier building and Sturgis's Lawrance Hall. Welch has a row of dormer windows apparently responding to those of Lawrance, and its brownstone façades were related to Osborn in scale, if not in color, and in some details.

Like Osborn it has round-headed windows and an arched entrance, now sealed, from College Street. That original entry to the town was of importance to the donor, Pierce N. Welch (B.A. 1862), who gave the dormitory as a memorial to his father, the Honorable Harmanus M. Welch, a mayor of New Haven. The son was one of several individuals who came forward in the 1890s to fund dormitories that honored their family members by meeting Yale's pressing need to house a burgeoning student population.

———

While Welch Hall was nearing completion, Josiah Cleveland Cady was suffering through the ordeal of designing an infirmary to suit the tastes of ladies of New York and New Haven who formed two committees to pay for it (FIG. 144). In an entertaining series of long letters to William W. Farnam, he described meetings in one city or the other to review the architect's plans. Through March and April 1892, Cady documented the ladies' consideration of cutting plumbing to stay within the budget of $20,000, their fears of drafty halls, and their hopes for further economy by using wood rather than brick. By his account, every detail was scrutinized at successive gatherings in the homes of various committee members. Those in attendance at one inevitably came to conclusions different from those who met in others. By April 21, a letter marked "confidential" detailed his most recent meeting with the New York committee. He confessed to Farnam: "I don't think I ever felt quite as powerless to further anything! The (feminine) human nature in such a committee is a curious study—I could analyze it very well, but not influence it to any extent." The stinginess of the

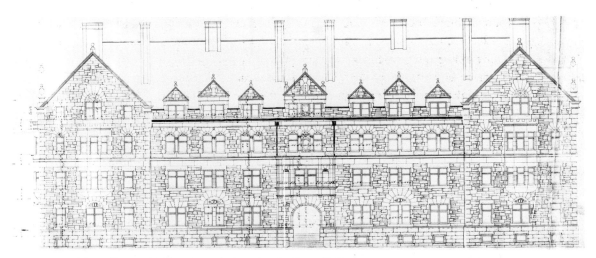

FIG. 143 *Welch Hall: east (College Street) elevation by Bruce Price, 1890.*

FIG. 144 *Yale Infirmary in the early 1900s.*

wives of some very rich men impressed him: "Some (whose sons will be in the senior year next season) — did not care for it at all unless it was to be in operation during their stay in college — so it was now or never with them." He continued: "I have sometimes noticed that the richer the person the more remarkably economical experiences they have had in building!" Cady seems not to have harbored disdain for women's capacities, but for the dynamic of the committee: "Of course a *large* committee is unfortunate — there were ladies on it that could have formed an excellent committee of three — it could have been sensibly and reasonably discussed — but a large committee — —."[192]

An infirmary, "The Yale Home," was completed in November 1892 as a rectangular block of pressed brick and sandstone with simple classical details and a slate roof. The *Yale Alumni Weekly* found that its "small porches on three sides" lent "a pleasing and homelike appearance." In three floors and a basement it had thirty-two rooms, twenty-three of them bedrooms. The ladies, it was felt, provided well for sick boys: "The location is high and airy and commands a delightful view. The rooms each contain an open fireplace and are fitted up in a comfortable and home-like manner."[193] Cady made additions in 1905, and his building was the center of student health services until 1929, when they were brought closer to the heart of the campus in a Collegiate Gothic building at 435 College Street. Cady's infirmary still stands on Prospect Street, near the summit on the west side. He compromised the ladies' wishes with the university's needs in a simple vernacular box, handsome enough and unobtrusive in scale and detail on its residential street. It is now a very sad sight:

stripped of its blinds, bereft of trees, with an asphalt parking lot for a front yard.

Despite Cady's difficulties with committees, the infirmary had been planned and built within a year. In contrast, Cady's work and the phased construction of a new home for the Yale Law School began in 1893, then dragged on for much of the last decade of the nineteenth century and past its turning (see FIG. 80). The Law School had lodged on the third floor of the courthouse annex to New Haven's City Hall since 1873 (see FIG. 6). Early in 1894, Cady's firm drew up plans to house the school in greater dignity on a prominent site facing the Green. They showed a "rear building" and a "front building" which together would form an H shape, with one of the long strokes of the H paralleling Elm Street. But that bar along the street was omitted in the initial building phase. In 1894 funding was available only for the rear part of the building, which was put up as a T-shaped brick building, with the end of a narrow central bar reaching toward the street from the center of the lot. A space was left for the wing along the street frontage, and Cady made a handsome perspective drawing of the Elm Street facade that the lawyers used to pursue additional building funds (FIG. 145). The facade as finally realized differs in detail, but not in overall form, from the drawing circulated in 1894.

Lawyers' names dominate the list of contributors, but a non-lawyer, John William Hendrie (B.A. 1851), made the largest gift, and the Law School's former home still bears his name. He worked hard as a schoolteacher in Greenwich, trapping and selling lobsters during spare time to pay his own way through Yale College. He was thirty when he graduated, according to the biography in his class history.

He returned to teaching for three years, at Stamford Academy, before he caught the "spirit of adventure that was wafted to us from the West" and "took ship" to San Francisco. There Hendrie and a partner opened a store in 1854, and "advertised largely," while he "taught school at night for a time." They soon opened four more stores in California, where Hendrie also invested in real estate. It was all so phenomenally successful that after he sold out to his partner in 1863, he was "able to permanently retire," visit Europe, farm, and buy and sell real estate. His class's historian wrote: "Hendrie is certainly one of the richest men in the class, and what is more, he is known to make a generous use of his wealth…He has never married."

As the "rear building" of the Law School that bore Hendrie's name was nearing completion, the *Yale Alumni Weekly* reported: "It contains recitation rooms, professors' rooms, library, a large study and a comfortable lounging room in the basement where the students can meet socially, and where lockers and other conveniences are provided. The work throughout is thoroughly fire-proof, even to the book-shelves in the library, which are made of iron, handsomely polished."[194] Classes met in the new building as spring term began in 1895, although it was not formally opened until April 26. Cady's new staircase, which is still there, dazzled the *Yale Alumni Weekly:*

An architect may be pardoned for an extravagance once in a while, especially if he err in favor of the aesthetic. This is what Messrs. Cady, Berg & See must plead guilty to in the Law School staircase. Architecturally it is a masterpiece. Imposing, graceful, and yet in perfect taste… its bronze and gold balustrades, vaulting and tracery, its Romanesque windows hexagonal-paned and massive,

and its dark substantial stone steps, suggest the luxuriousness of a metropolitan business block.[195]

Not until the end of June 1899 did Sperry and Treat, the New Haven builders who worked so often for Yale, sign contracts for the "New Front Portion of the Yale Law School Building on Elm Street." It was to be of steel construction with a limestone facade derived from the palazzos of Italian cities, and ultimately from classical sources. It introduced an unprecedented urban scale among the houses fronting the New Haven Green along Elm Street, and it had the biggest auditorium on campus. Cady had pleaded in letters of 1898 for the retention of the limestone he had specified for the facade, arguing against the substitution of granite in a redesigned Romanesque scheme. He wrote with some emotion and perception: "the design of the Law School is of the early Italian Renaissance period, extremely delicate and pretty in its detail; it is dependent, besides the detail and ornamental work, upon two principal things for its beauty: first, plain, simple and smooth masses of wall surface; and, secondly, the 'play' of the light and shade in the delicate mouldings and details of the work."[196]

Although money ran short and finishing touches awaited fundraising, Hendrie Hall was nearly complete before the turn of the century. However, there remained a few kinks to work out: a message taken down in May 1900 and preserved in the archives records Dean Wayland's telephoned surprise "that there was no provision for electric lighting" in the building and wondering if something shouldn't be done about that. In November both gas and electric lighting were installed. Final payment to the contractors was not made until February 1901. The Law

School abandoned Hendrie Hall in 1931 to move into the lavish expanses of the Sterling Law Quadrangle designed by James Gamble Rogers. By then the chairman of the Committee on Architectural Plan was referring to it as "the horrible old Law School," writing that "of course" it "will be torn down, and I trust some old Colonial house…can be placed on the front part of the lot." But Cady's old law school has endured to serve a succession of tenants.[197]

———

Through the 1890s and past the century's turning, Cady was but one of several architects who continued to use classical detailing when building beyond Yale's Gothic core. One of the more obscure of those architects was E. E. Gandolfo, an "Engineer-Architect," who designed a gymnasium on Elm Street of a grandiosity worthy of Yale's preeminence in collegiate sports, not to mention its obsession with them.[198] In 1892, when the University Gymnasium was completed, Timothy Dwight could say in his annual report that "For the building of the new gymnasium more than seven hundred graduates and undergraduates contributed. The cost…was nearly two hundred and twenty-five thousand dollars." In rallying to support this project, the sons of Yale were carrying on a long-standing tradition: students and graduates not only supported intercollegiate sports, they also initiated and organized Yale's participation and competition in them.

Just after the building committee handed over Gandolfo's gym to the Corporation in formal ceremonies of January 1893, the *Yale Alumni Weekly* printed a "History of the New Gymnasium" tracing its origins to the launching of a building campaign eight years earlier by Professor Eugene Lamb Richards (B.A. 1860). Richards, who taught mathematics, had rallied "the most prominent Yale Alumni of the country" to build a new gymnasium. They formed a Gymnasium Corporation, with Arthur M. Dodge (B.A. 1874) of New York as its president and William L. McLane (B.A. 1869) as its treasurer. McLane was to bequeath funds for a dormitory of 1909. George A. Adee (B.A. 1867), for whom the boathouse of 1909 was later named, was one of three members of a building committee, on which he served with Professor Richards and the same William W. Farnam, Yale treasurer, whose mother donated Whitman Gate. Augmented by four other distinguished graduates on a "Gymnasium Committee," this was a powerful Yale group. Among the Yale College students whose help they enlisted was Grosvenor Atterbury (B.A. 1891). The future architect published a drawing in the *Yale Record* of 7 June 1890

depicting the dingiest basement corner of the old gymnasium and captioned it: "A Bitter Reality: The above is not a joke. It is the most eloquent appeal that we can make for subscriptions to the New Gymnasium."

Gandolfo's perspective was used on a fundraising brochure and reproduced in several Yale publications of the 1890s. It was even appropriated as the background for an illustration by another future architect, Donn Barber, produced while he was a student in the Sheffield Scientific School's Class of 1891 (FIG. 146). Gandolfo's drawing shows a hipped roof overhanging a flat facade with classical ornamentation. Four tall, broad arches set on pilasters dominate the facade. This composition appears to have borrowed its most prominent themes from H. H. Richardson, although the borrowings did not include Romanesque stylization. Rustication of the ground floor gave way at the eastern end to a pedestrian entrance under an arch and to a driveway that, as the plans show, passed through to the rear. One arrived at the principal door only by following the driveway back to the middle of the building and stepping up to the left. Photographs of the gymnasium as executed with a terra-cotta facade show that Gandolfo made changes to the published design (FIG. 147). Most significantly, he replaced the hipped roof with one that had a ridge running parallel to the street and stopping in the stepped gable ends of party walls, apparently anticipating future construction right up against them.

Gandolfo's big, lavish gymnasium took up 138 feet along Elm Street between High and York Streets, and extended back ninety feet. It loomed over the adjacent house to the east and the shop to the west with a height "from ground to top of roof" of 100 feet. A feature of the building that is not apparent in the photographs was the glazing of the roof (see FIG. 158, upper right). But correspondence through 1892 and 1893 with the Plenty Horticultural and Skylight Works of Jersey City, New Jersey, makes it clear that, from the first, a glass roof was there, and it leaked. The most detailed old photographs do show elaborate figural reliefs in the lunettes under the arches: athletic nudes recline among crossed oars, bats, and balls of various shapes.

Gandolfo's original plans situate a pair of rowing tanks, a swimming tank, and a complex of little rooms on the ground floor around a circular Turkish bath. Because that plan is fine-lined and reproduces poorly, Harrison Lindsley's more summary plan of 1893 is illustrated here (FIG. 148). There are five sets of stairs. The most important, which rose toward the

FIG. 146 *Donn Barber, "Here's to Good Old Yale," with Gandolfo's perspective of the University Gymnasium, 1891.*

FIG. 147 *University Gymnasium, ca. 1894: south (Elm Street) facade.*

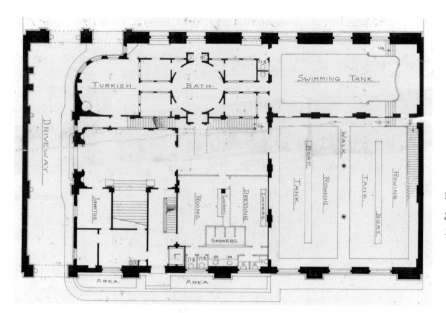

FIG. 148 *University Gymnasium: plan of the ground floor drawn by Harrison W. Lindsley, 1893 (Elm Street at top).*

back from the entrance hall, dazzled at least one visitor of 1895: "The Gymnasium staircase, with its white marble banisters, steps and posts, always impresses one with a certain degree of something akin to awe. In the presence of that structure one always takes off his hat, makes sure that his shoes are not muddy, and feels like begging the pardon of each separate step for setting his foot upon it."[199] These intimidating steps led to a trophy room on the second floor where photographs record elegantly detailed classical trim, painted white, and an impressive array of flags (FIG. 149). Gandolfo's own plans detail the arrangement of many lockers, baths, and specialized rooms on the same floor and a track on the floor above, around the major space, a general exercise hall under the leaky skylight (FIG. 150). This main exercise room offered "clear floor-space of 10,000 square feet" and was "from twenty-two to fifty-six feet in height" according to the *Yale University Catalogue* for 1899–1900, which specified that the Turkish bath was "complete," and the swimming pool and tubs were marble. It also listed bowling alleys and free showers, as well as "separate rooms for boxing, fencing, wrestling, and manly sports" among the amenities.

In 1931 the *Yale Record,* which had taken such an interest in the gym completed only thirty-eight years earlier, published a full-page cartoon showing a tiny wrecking crew, dwarfed before that same gym, its great size exaggerated. The caption is the foreman's line as he faces the building with his hand on his chin: "Gee, I just don't know where to start!" But the demolition team successfully cleared it away to prepare the site for Trumbull College.

If during the mid-1890s the commission for the gym went to someone who was never again to design a building for Yale, a commission of about the same time went to an architect who would subsequently add eleven more to the list of his Yale buildings.[200] When Cornelius Vanderbilt with his wife Alice decided to give a dormitory as a memorial to their son, William Henry Vanderbilt, who died of typhoid fever in 1892, the year before he would have graduated, they chose Charles Coolidge Haight to design it. A later Yale treasurer recorded, "Vanderbilt Hall was given us by the family, as a building; not in the form of a building fund. We paid none of the bills and have not even an approximate idea of the actual cost."[201] At least not for publication. In 1893 Haight began to work out its design for a site fronting College Street, between Osborn Hall and Street Hall (see FIG. 175), necessitating the removal of the Brick Row's South College (Union Hall) and Athenaeum.[202] Since it was on the Old Campus, the Gothic context had to be acknowledged, and the style Haight chose was characterized in the *Yale Alumni Weekly* as "of a late Gothic type, with a suggestion of Renaissance, and based upon the English collegiate type of architecture of Oxford and Cambridge."[203] He specified Massachusetts sandstone, which pleased President Dwight, who wanted all of Yale built in stone. Indeed everything about the building seems to have suited Dwight, who wrote in his annual report of 1899: "The educating influence of a building like Vanderbilt Hall, which comes from its architectural character, as compared with that which pertains to one like the old North Middle College, or the Lyceum, is no insignificant force in making the students of a university what educated men ought to be."[204] On the strength of such success, Haight became a fixture on the Yale scene before the

First World War. All of his buildings survive, and he and his work will be discussed at greater length below. His dormitories served as experiments in residential accommodation and were important precedents for James Gamble Rogers's colleges.

The buildings of the Berkeley Oval, which do not survive, also served Rogers and Yale as case studies for dormitories.[205] Their overall scheme was the work of Cady's firm, drawn in 1893 in response to Yale administrators' request for proposals for a largely residential group. The architects showed contiguous structures arranged in a U-shape with the narrow open end of the U fronting Elm Street (FIG. 151). Along the street, the central courtyard was to be bounded only by fences with gates that met in the center at a small entry lodge, round in plan.[206] While the fences as built guarded access from the street, they allowed the passerby to look into the courtyard, so that its central grassy oval was

open to the gaze of the town. This late-nineteenth-century project was not completed until 1908.

In June 1893, Cady was rushing to finish designs for the first building of the group, a dormitory that Andrew J. White (M.D. 1846) of New York had come forward to fund (FIG. 152). White, whose son was an undergraduate at Yale, had written to Treasurer Farnam on February 18:

If you will intimate that such a proposal mite [sic] be acceptable, I will send my architect to examine the grounds, and consult you concerning plans & c. When this shall have been done I will have plans and estimates made and if they come within the sum I have decided to donate, I will have detailed drawings made and submit them with a formal offer. It is my wish that no publicity whatever *shall be given to this matter* [White's emphasis].[207]

Just how the architect who had built more for Yale than any other during the previous two decades had a month later become Dr. White's architect is unclear, but Dr. White was soon writing to Farnam that he had "called upon Mr. Cady and examined the plans. He is progressing quite rapidly and making a fine looking building…The style is such that it will look well for all time." But by the end of March, White's enthusiasm for the design had been somewhat deflated by his son, who had "written me of his disappointment on seeing the plans of the Dormitory—First because the rooms do not run through like the Durfee and Lawrance." Dr. White asked "Why not let me modify my offer so as to provide for two dormitories" and for the "handsome fences…connecting the two buildings…I am aware that the expense will be a little more, but I will not object." Dr. White subsequently had the original plan for White Hall lengthened, and spent more than first estimated on the interior finishes, especially on mantelpieces to make the student rooms more attractive. Perhaps he was trying to compete with Vanderbilt Hall, which was under construction just as he was building. Dr. White also took on an additional expense of about $3,500 to provide offices for student newspapers in the basement. Cady reported to Farnam:

He now has quite a desire to have the four college papers, or journals, have their rooms in the basement of his building. He seems to have a great regard for these journals, says they have been of great value to his son, and that the quarters they now occupy, are mean, and it has occurred to him that it would be nice, to give each one of them good accommodations in the basement of this dormitory, and he had been inclined to fit up the rooms nicely for them with suitable furnishings, etc. This would be extra—beyond what he intended to do for the building proper.

Whether it was because these added expenses precluded his grander ideas or for some other reason, Dr. White in the end paid only for one dormitory, a sum that came to $167,270.83,[208] and in 1894 agreed to pay about $7,000 for the fences and "Lodge."[209] By April 19, 1893, the *Brooklyn Eagle* had revealed Dr. White's identity, and although he had said he wanted no publicity, he seemed happy enough about it all when he sent the clipping to Farnam.[210]

Correspondence between Cady and Farnam suggests the extent to which the architect had fallen into the role of virtual agent for Yale. Cady's letters detail White's several visits to his New York office and the architect's encouragement of the client's mounting ambitions for the building. Cady's inquiry of June 13, 1893, conveys a sense of his involvement in the greater project:

Can you not get a name for this quadrangle? It is quite a place, and ought, it seems to me, to have a good name. It should not all pass under the name of "White Dormitory" for the lack of any other designation, but have a name as a quadrangle, so that other possible donors would feel no disinclination to having their buildings located there; and if a name could be decided upon before commencement time, it would also seem wise, would it not?[211]

Other donors proved slow to fund the needed dormitories, so Yale reached into its own coffers to begin building Berkeley Hall along with White Hall. In choosing to name this dormitory for the college's great eighteenth-century benefactor, Bishop George Berkeley, it was reusing the name of a dormitory,

better known as North Middle College, built in 1801 along the Brick Row. Berkeley, Dean of Derry and Bishop of Cloyne, gave land and books to the college in 1732 after returning to Ireland when his expedition of 1728 to found a college in Bermuda failed. It is possible that Yale's administration responded in a formal way to Cady's suggestion and chose the name Berkeley to designate the whole open-ended quadrangle. However, Thomas Bergin recorded in his book of 1983 about Yale's residential colleges that undergraduates of the 1890s coined the name because "the driveway within the courtyard suggested Berkeley Oval at Morris Dock, New York, where the intercollegiate track meets were held."[212] Certainly the oval path laid out in front of Berkeley and White Halls would have identified the place much more readily than a reference to Cady's still nonexistent quadrangle, which remained only an ambitious scheme on paper past the turn of the century.

Dr. White's dormitory did not match the grandeur of the Vanderbilts', which was also in construction during the school year that began in the autumn of 1893. Vanderbilt Hall's Massachusetts sandstone was more expensive than the pressed red brick with terra-cotta trimmings that was forming the walls of White Hall.[213] Through the winter of 1894, the *Yale Alumni Weekly* grouped its reports of progress on the three dormitories—Vanderbilt, White, and Berkeley. In his correspondence with Farnam, Cady, who was also designing Berkeley Hall, called it the "Low Rent Dormitory," a characterization borne out by the calculation in the *Yale Alumni Weekly* for average rentals for suites when the three new dormitories opened the next fall: for Vanderbilt, about $293 ($157.30 per man); for White,

FIG. 151 *Berkeley Oval: south (Elm Street) facade, after a presentation drawing by J. C. Cady, 1893.*

FIG. 152 *White Hall (left) and Berkeley Hall beyond, with gate lodge on the right, ca. 1895.*

about $185 ($100 per man); for Berkeley about $85 ($68.40 per man).[214]

White Hall was a relatively plain building, a long rectangle on the northeast corner of High and Elm Streets with its narrow end fronting Elm. The principal eastern facade, 190 feet long, faced the courtyard of the planned quadrangle, its monotony broken by three entries and by a slight projection of the center, where five bays came forward just enough to create shadow lines. Above this center-piece Cady raised the four-story facade in a low, dormer-like fifth story that had a row of seven oval windows. The ridge of the low-hipped tile roof supported six tall chimneys. The entrances had extremely plain vestigial porches formed by shelf-like projections supported by brackets. Detailed pictures evoke the most unobtrusive entrances to city apartments.

White Hall's restrained classical details included dentils and brackets under broad projecting eaves, stringcourses, and light-colored corner quoins. The most arresting motif was a white Doric half-column, which Cady used again and again to separate the big sheets of glass in the many pairs of double-hung windows. There was no entrance from Elm Street, where the narrow facade had a decorative central relief on its third floor—winged, leopard-like creatures confronting a roundel. On its second floor a central balcony was recessed behind the facade, its opening split by a Doric column. White Hall was "fire-proof throughout, the floor being supported by iron beams." It had fifty-two suites accommodating ninety-six men, with sitting rooms "larger than any on the campus, being fourteen feet wide and nineteen feet long."[215]

Berkeley Hall, also of brick, was attached to White Hall's northern end, but came forward a few feet into the courtyard (see FIG. 152). A wall set at an odd angle awkwardly spanned the gap to its narrow facade. Under a low-hipped roof, there were round-headed windows on its four principal stories, with flat-headed windows across the full story above its cornice. The double-hung windows had, like White's, large sheets of glass without mullions. For its forty-six students there was a single entrance on the courtyard, protected by a round-headed hood. Iron balconies extended across the three central windows of the third and forth floors. The contracted price of May 1893 was $48,398.

Within two years of completing White and Berkeley Halls, Cady was asked to design another dormitory for which the college itself was prepared to pay—as little as possible for as many students as possible, to be built as quickly as possible. Rather than placing Pierson Hall within the projected quadrangle, however, Yale chose to situate it on the east side of York Street, between Elm and Library Streets on a site now occupied by Saybrook College (see FIG. 249). A rush to demolish existing buildings on this recently acquired land was delayed by the presence of their occupants as late as March 17, 1896. For a story published on March 18, Cady told the *Yale Alumni Weekly,* "Plans and specifications have been devised, completed and placed under contract in a little less than two weeks—a force working on them day and night. The builders are under a heavy penalty to have the work completed in time."[216] Those builders, Smith, Sperry and Treat, contracted to do the work for about $80,000, and they met their deadline. On September 18, five and a half months after demolition began, Cady's office could "recommend that the building be accepted as completed under the terms of the contract," and Pierson Hall was ready for occupancy by 100 students when school began.

Pierson Hall was more like a developer-built urban apartment building than any of Yale's earlier dormitories. Over a raised stone basement, the first floor was faced with stone, the four floors above with brick. The end bays were pulled forward only enough to accent corner quoining and lend a touch of interest to a very pedestrian facade. An iron balcony spanned the full width of 122 feet across the eleven windows on the top floor, and the building was fifty-five feet deep. Although no plans have come to light, the presence of a single central entrance makes it clear that Yale's preferred plan for suites off multiple entries was not the model followed. The *Yale Alumni Weekly* described a hall leading from the entrance to meet, at right angles, at the building's center, a double-loaded corridor paralleling York Street, with stairs at either end and toilet rooms stacked above the entry hall. This hurriedly constructed Pierson Hall, a dreary enough thing, lasted only twenty-one years before being demolished for the Memorial Quadrangle by Rogers.

No matter how cheaply Cady could turn them out, nor how badly Yale needed new dormitories, the scheme of 1893 to build out the Berkeley Oval remained a proposal on paper through the 1890s. Progress was slow, but Yale's new president, Arthur Twining Hadley, was determined — for many reasons — to complete this quadrangle. As he noted in a speech to Chicago alumni in January 1900: "We are working for interior quadrangles. Student life on the interior is a good deal healthier and better — and provokes less conflict with the police — than student life on the exterior.[217] Money was not available until 1900, when the college withdrew $156,438.88 from its own funds to build most of the eastern range of Cady's group as Fayerweather Hall. The name was bestowed "in view of the very considerable gift of the late Mr. [Daniel B.] Fayerweather," who died in 1890.[218]

The narrow end of the long bar of Fayerweather, like that of White Hall, fronted Elm Street, and its massing corresponded to White's, echoing the earlier building's taller, projecting central block between longer, lower, recessed blocks (FIG. 153). Cady's firm aligned three entries on the west-facing facade with those on White's east-facing facade. Six chimneys mirrored those of White. Fayerweather was taller by half a story, rising a full five stories to the roof line. Its double-hung windows were again made up of single panes of glass top and bottom, and there were a great many of them, their repetition interrupted by entrances and by quoins emphasizing the projection of the taller blocks. Marking each entrance, ornamented stone work in vertical panels extended from the ground to the cornice. A Yale publicist wrote in the summer of 1900: "Fayerweather Hall is to be a companion building to White, but will be by no means its exact counterpart. There will be much more stone in its construction…the face will be largely stone with brick panels."[219]

Unlike White Hall, it had a major entrance at the center of its Elm Street facade, set at the base of one of the ornamental stone panels.[220] The door gave entry to the post office — Yale Station — and to four recitation rooms in the raised basement. On the very public eastern facade, along the walkway that separated the Berkeley Oval from Hunt's Divinity School, there were two doors. The walkway, then known as "Grub Street," was in the process of becoming much more important. While Fayerweather was being built in 1900 and 1901, Commons was also under construction, terminating the northern end of the walkway. As the pedestrian thoroughfare from the Old Campus to the new Bicentennial Buildings, which were generally called the "University Buildings" at the turn of the century, the walkway was formally named University Avenue about this time (FIG. 154).[221]

North of Fayerweather Hall, the site for another dormitory in the Berkeley Oval remained open until 1909. In the meantime, a bequest from William Lampson (B.A. 1862) made it possible in 1902 to spend $163,371.85 to build a new "Lyceum" in the quadrangle, and Cady's firm, at this time called Cady, Berg and See, was entrusted with its design.[222] The program included classrooms and an auditorium that became the setting for major public performances, musical and theatrical.

Lampson Lyceum crossed the northern end of the planned quadrangle as a building lower than the dormitories flanking it: the ridge ends of its tiled roof just about met their cornice lines (see FIG. 153). Its centerpiece was a wide bay projecting slightly forward and above the three-story brick facade. The bay rose to a half-round cresting over a clock to which two stone lions turned their backs, brandishing shields. Below, a round-arched passage opened from the courtyard through to Wall Street, less than half a block beyond. West of the arch, a large auditorium filled the first two stories, its presence expressed on the facade by three tall windows. Above them were heraldic reliefs and a row of square windows. As the firm had done in other buildings within the Berkeley Oval, they gave this one classicizing details: half-columns flanking the arch and a great deal of quoining. But there was also some post-medieval stylization in stained glass shields and diamond-gridded mullions in many of the windows, and the suggestion of a Tudor porch in the central bay. The facade east of that bay was nearly square, a shape emphasized by the placement of nine square windows in rows of three across its three stories and by the division of each window into nine square panes. Breaking down the glazed surfaces in this way helped differentiate an academic building from the earlier dormitories, with their mullionless windows.

When Cady, Berg and See completed their work on Lampson Lyceum, they had designed their last building for Yale. By 1903 when students first attended classes there, Cady was sixty-six years old.

FIG. 153 *Berkeley Oval before the addition of Haughton Hall in 1909, with Fayerweather Hall on the right and Lampson Lyceum in the rear.*

FIG. 154 *University (Blount) Avenue, betweeen Fayerweather and Haughton Halls (left) and West Divinity Hall (right), before 1912.*

In the summer of 1902, President Hadley, who was about twenty years younger, had written about Cady in a series of letters to the vacationing secretary of the university. Hadley's comments leave little doubt that he considered it a difficult task "to try to instill some notions of architectural beauty conforming to those of the corporation into the minds of the architects." He met weekly with Cady in New York, and by August 5 Hadley sounded like a man who had won a struggle: "You will be glad to know that I have at last come to substantial agreement with Mr. Cady regarding a good front for Lampson. He has a design which is certainly much better than any of those which you have seen."[223] The architect who had practically been a staff member, whose letters to the previous treasurer of the university are those of a friend who gossiped about mutual acquaintances at the Century Club, had lost his special status at Yale. In 1911, Anson Phelps Stokes, the recipient of Hadley's letters about Cady's last building, lambasted the architect in a letter to a Corporation member: "Probably the most unfortunate thing that ever happened to Yale architecturally was getting tied up during the Dwight administration with the firm of Cady, Berg & See, a firm of good contractors with little architectural taste or ability."[224]

Cady's great and particular usefulness to Yale had lost its value. At the century's turning, a new generation of administrators replaced those who had for two decades relied upon Cady for solid, efficient work, confident that he would make the successful effort to save them time and money. Hendrie Hall is probably Cady's strongest contribution to Yale's classicizing phase. In some of his other late work at Yale, the regularity of his simplified classical forms became pedestrian, betraying perhaps the tight budgets he was inevitably given. His later buildings may be duller simply because they had become the routine productions of a large staff. Cady himself could rarely work on them, and he was no longer an ambitious young man with a make-or-break incentive to display, within restraints, the inventiveness that he had lavished on the ornament of North Sheffield Hall. His High Victorian and Richardsonian-influenced buildings at Yale were more interesting than most of his classical designs.

In 1908 Yale passed over Cady's firm when it hired a designer for a dormitory to fill the one remaining gap in the quadrangle he had planned fifteen years earlier. Robert Henderson Robertson (1849–1919) was the choice of the executors or heirs of William L. McLane (B.A. 1869), whose bequest funded the building. In the strictest sense, this was Robertson's only contribution to Yale's architecture, although he had designed a "tomb" for the Sheffield student society, Book and Snake, built in 1900 at the corner of Grove and High Streets.[225] He has been described by Sarah Landau as "a successful and prolific New York architect" whose "skyscrapers contribute to the variety of lower Manhattan's skyline."[226] The dormitory was named in honor of Ann Haughton, McLane's widow. Haughton Hall not only provided rooms for sixty students, but also for a mixed bag of occupants on its first floor: the Bursar's Office, the *Yale Record,* and El Centro Español de Yale. By July 1, 1908, the bill for Haughton stood at $122,245.00 plus architect's fees of $6,000.[227]

On a site that abutted both the northern wall of Fayerweather Hall and the eastern end of Lampson Lyceum, Robertson had been left with room on the courtyard of the Berkeley Oval for only a short length of Haughton Hall's facade (FIG. 155). Here he brought just forward of Fayerweather a four-bay pavilion a story taller than the adjacent bar of the earlier building, and gave it a hipped tile roof.[228] Robertson's tall pavilion echoed the raised mass of Cady's central pavilion to the south. North of his first pavilion, Robertson stepped the building back and lowered it to four stories over the raised basement. Here he squeezed in two entrances from the courtyard, one on either side. Continuing north he introduced a light well for rooms abutting the eastern end of Lampson Lyceum, then continued for a single bay beyond the older building.

Haughton Hall's east-facing elevation along University Avenue was nearly twice as long as the courtyard elevation, and more of its basement was revealed above grade (see FIG. 154). Here Robertson could expose a greater length of the recessed bar before again pulling the facade out and raising it higher to form a square terminating pavilion that matched his other pavilion to the south, as well as Cady's in the center of Fayerweather. In some photographs Cady's and Robertson's buildings appear to be one building that has three square-roofed pavilions, nearly six stories tall, that step out just a little and rise at regular intervals above a long bar. Robertson's fenestration, materials, and classicizing details were much like Cady's, though he introduced dormer windows and elaborated a little on Cady's precedents for stone ornamentation of the entryways, which were more elaborate on the courtyard than on the eastern facade.

Robertson's quite handsome drawings for these details survive in the Yale archives, along with his

FIG. 155 *Haughton Hall (right of center) between Lampson Lyceum (left) and Fayerweather Hall (far right): preparatory drawing by Robertson and Potter, 1908.*

plans for the building, showing its suites grouped around entryways. Others illustrate his "Suggestions for Extension of Dormitories and Additional Lecture Rooms." In a plan and perspective, Robertson proposed a continuation of the bar and pavilion sequence of the Berkeley Oval to form a second courtyard north of Lampson Lyceum, culminating in a great north-facing block, entered through an archway much like that of Phelps Gate on the Old Campus. Crenellated corner towers are shown rising above its seven or eight stories. It is a dull proposal attempting to relieve the boredom with an agglomeration of medievalizing details. It repeats elements that had, by the time it was drawn, become all-too-familiar not only at Yale, but also on many American college campuses. Comparing such proposals to the residential colleges Rogers created in the 1930s enhances appreciation for Rogers's accomplishment, as does a comparison of the photographs of the Berkeley Oval with the college by Rogers that replaced it. While Cady and his colleagues designed dormitories that looked like stodgy apartment buildings of the sort developers put up in the Bronx, Rogers created residential groups whose aspect removed the viewer from the ordinary. They conjured up the peace of ancient academic towns in the center of the busy manufacturing city that New Haven had become. Cady's were competent background buildings. Rogers's are far greater works of the creative art of architecture. Unfortunately for Cady, his latest and weakest work at Yale was mildly classical, for which Yale's taste was shortlived, and his quadrangle was set squarely in the foreground of a new image the university's rising architectural star was creating. As early as 1917, the Berkeley Oval's "dull drabness" was the object of scorn in an anonymous letter to the *Yale Alumni Weekly.*[229]

It is true that the Corporation that had so recently paid for much of the Berkeley Oval did not rush to tear it down. In 1919, John Russell Pope proposed to retain the Berkeley Oval in his plan for Yale, using the northern facade of Lampson Lyceum to help define the line of a central east west axis along Wall Street, which he terminated with a big gymnasium (see FIG. 234). Two years later, James Gamble Rogers took over what, in the official language of the university, "would be in its broad principles the Pope Plan, brought down to various limitations of property and changes required by such further study of specific conditions, limitations, and the necessities that such a working plan would involve."[230]

Among his fundamental changes, Rogers shifted the major east-west axis southward, so it became a cleared Cross Campus well south of Wall Street. Lampson Lyceum, which occupied part of the green space that now lies between the two halves of Berkeley College, stood in the way of his proposal to give an unobstructed view of the terminating structure—Sterling Memorial Library—that would dominate his new vista from College Street.

Architects, Corporation members, and James Rowland Angell, Yale's new president, considered from every angle the serious proposal to cut off the end of the Oval and move it north. On December 13, 1922, Farwell sent Rogers "photos of moving of the large recitation building, four or five stories high, at Andover," suggesting, "When the time came, if we desired to, we could move our buildings—Lampson Hall, way up at the south side of Wall Street. It may be a portion of the dormitory space and wings could

<small>FIG. 156</small> *Sterling Memorial Library with the buildings of Berkeley Oval split in parts and flanking the open space of Cross Campus: proposal by J. G. Rogers.*

be taken along with it." Early in 1923 the legality of moving or destroying the buildings under terms of the relevant gifts and bequests was cleared by F. H. Wiggin, Yale's lawyer.[231] In mid-April Farwell got estimates from Thompson-Starrett Company for the "cost of cutting off, moving toward Wall Street and building up the ends of Haughton, Lampson, and Berkeley Halls, placing same on new foundations @ the sum of $302,926.00." When Yale first published Rogers's campus plan in January 1924, the Berkeley Oval's preservation was featured: the *New Haven Register* reported that it "will be made into two residential quadrangles by the erection of additional dormitories on each side of the cross-campus and on Elm street."

Plans for saving at least parts of the Berkeley Oval were kept alive through the decade. The many letters about it that Angell, Farwell, and Rogers exchanged during this period convey a sense of the seriousness with which Yale's leadership and its architect weighed their aesthetic aspirations against their abhorrence of wasting built assets. President Angell was the first of the three to make it clear that he wanted to abandon all schemes for retaining any of the Berkeley Oval. Early in 1928 he wrote that he had

always been skeptical of the wisdom of…the moving of Lampson…skeptical of the possibility of making it architecturally a satisfactory plan. Two elements…have disturbed me; first, the great height of the building on Wall Street, which is a very narrow street and which

would certainly be unfavorably affected if Lampson were to be put flush with the sidewalk…second the appearance of the building facing the new cross campus. How these could possibly be treated to make even a moderately satisfactory architectural neighbor for the new Library has always passed my comprehension. Mr. Rogers' drawings…fail, of course, to give the color effects and… they would involve a large amount of stone work on the cross campus fronting the Library, were they to be at all acceptable.[232]

In response to Angell's concern, the Corporation had Rogers restudy the plan and draw fragments of the Berkeley Oval in place across the new Cross Campus. One of Rogers's many drawings that propose relocations and refacings for parts of the Oval is shown here (FIG. 156). On May 11, 1928, Rogers reported his investigations of the costs of moving Lampson, Berkeley, and Haughton Halls to the Corporation. The minutes record his opinion that "it would be cheaper to move these buildings than to rebuild them. He felt that it would cost roughly twice as much to rebuild as to move and modify the exposed ends."

By the summer of 1928, the economic arguments seemed to be losing ground to an aesthetic one. Rogers and Farwell were closer to Angell's position. John Farwell, abandoning his initial interest in repositioning the existing structures, wrote to Rogers: "I would be favorable towards expending considerable extra money for a new building rather than move this old one, especially as Lamson [*sic*]

Hall is not very good any way."[233] A few days later Rogers replied, recalculating relative costs in favor of new buildings. He now figured that housing the same number of students in an entirely new building would come to no more than the cost of moving and rehabilitating the old ones, a proposition that, he cautioned, held only if some office space in the old buildings really was expendable. The architect betrayed little of his profession's usual ardor to design from scratch, except perhaps when he commented that "a new group of dormitories would certainly be a much greater improvement than the results obtained by moving the old buildings because in their palmiest days these old buildings were never very beautiful." But a month later Rogers was still worrying about throwing away assets: "At the same time we are practically destroying buildings that would cost to replace them somewhere in the neighborhood of $500,000."[234] Some Corporation members were even more worried about that, and into the fall insisted on

trying to save at least parts of White and Fayerweather Halls, the buildings that fronted Elm Street. In November they asked Rogers to make yet more studies, preserving parts of those two buildings in some, doing away with them in others. Their indecision reigned into 1931. But that year, as difficult as it must have been for businessmen on the Corporation to swallow the loss of so recent an investment, they finally agreed to demolish the Berkeley Oval in time to begin building Berkeley College in 1933 (FIG. 157).

The style, "such that it will look well for all time," that had so delighted Dr. White as he planned his dormitory in 1893 had long since fallen out of favor in New Haven. Cady had not lived to see the destruction of that object of so much devoted care on the part of donor and architect alike. But before he died in 1919, one of his most important buildings for Yale, the first Peabody Museum, and one of his least, Pierson Hall, had been razed to clear the site for the Memorial Quadrangle.

FIG. 157 *Demolition of the Berkeley Oval in 1933.*

"An Harmonious Building Plan" for the Twentieth Century

Yale could hardly have ignored America's enthusiasm for planning its towns, cities, and campuses during the decade following the World's Fair of 1893.[235] Chicago's Columbian Exposition bedazzled the whole nation with its Great White City, and the year it opened, Yale bestowed honorary degrees upon Daniel Hudson Burnham (1846–1912) and Frederick Law Olmsted (1822–1903), the fair's chief planners.[236] Their work inspired the belief that architecture could transform the setting for life in any place and make it better. At the turn of the twentieth century, an emerging architectural profession was capitalizing on that belief. The American Institute of Architects focused on creating a model for the country with the MacMillan Plan for Washington, D.C., which evolved after the profession's leaders met there in 1900. Building on this momentum, architects and landscape architects shaped the planning movement of the first two decades of the century more crucially than did engineers and technicians, the professionals who later came to dominate planning. They were joined by an array of dedicated lay activists—lawyers, journalists, and others—some of whom worked full-time while many more took on supportive volunteer roles. Together they succeeded in exciting individuals in hundreds of towns to assume responsibility for building beautiful public places in every one of them. Among them were Yale alumni who brought their interest in planning to the campus when they assumed leadership roles within the university.

Just at the outbreak of the First World War, the city planners created their own professional organization.[237] Campuses were especially interesting for its members because institutional hierarchies could shape them more rationally and immediately, and could control them more fully, than civic officials could their towns and cities. The campus as special neighborhood, town, and community emerged within this context as a central subject of study and action.[238]

Yale's own neglect of the subject, however, drew mounting criticism. The university was faulted for the dissonance of architectural styles and materials in the new buildings that enclosed the Old Campus, and for a lack of planning beyond it. Montgomery Schuyler in particular aimed his barbs to this point, writing in 1899:

An unusual number of the college buildings of Yale, so far as they made any architectural pretensions at all, had been done by designers who were evidently anxious about the separate success of their own works, and desired that attention should be attracted to them, without the least regard to the effect of them upon the works of their disesteemed predecessors or their disesteemed contemporaries or their disesteemed successors, all of whom they seemed openly to flout.[239]

The kind of thinking that lay behind the great American planning triumphs of the era should ideally have preceded Yale's building activity in the first decades of the twentieth century (FIG. 158). Although many actions of the Yale Corporation make it clear that such planning was a serious concern, neither its members nor Yale's administrators pushed for a far-reaching illustrated plan, for grand drawings that would not only locate the footprints of buildings but also guide their appearance in three dimensions. While other universities were commissioning such images, Yale at the turn of the century was land-poor and cash-strapped. It had no expectation that the Sterling and Harkness gifts would soon make possible physical expansion of unprecedented dimensions. In the meantime, its leaders did try to plan in terms as large as it must have seemed reasonable to think for the future development of the real estate that Yale already owned, as well as for adjacent plots whose acquisition seemed feasible.

These men faced immediate pressures piecemeal as they got on with commissioning commemorative buildings by a crucial, immovable date, or quickly accepted a donor's offer before any suggestion of hesitancy provoked its impatient withdrawal. They sometimes acquiesced to the benefactor's insistence on design control of a proposed gift. Lacking larger plans and guidelines, after a brief foray into classicism the Corporation fell back on old preoccupations with the Gothic style in attempting to bring coherence to the campus. Not until 1919 did an alumnus, Francis Patrick Garvan (B.A. 1897), force Yale to consider comprehensive proposals that were specific and concrete by commissioning John Russell Pope to draw a two-dimensional plan for a greatly expanded university and to render it realistically in bird's-eye images of the whole gloriously Gothic ensemble, along with carefully detailed perspectives of major new buildings.[240]

FIG. 158 *Yale from the sky, flying south, in 1925, with the Bicentennial Buildings in the foreground, the Berkeley Oval in the middle, and the Memorial Quadrangle beyond.*

Arthur Twining Hadley (B.A. 1876) was inaugurated president of Yale just in time to preside over a building project of unprecedented scale, commemorating the two hundredth anniversary of the founding of Yale. As soon as he came into office in 1899 he appointed a new secretary of the university, Anson Phelps Stokes, who was only twenty-five and had not quite completed his studies to become an Episcopal minister.[241] The appointment was significant for the immediate history of architecture at Yale. Hadley and Stokes inherited an old building program from President Timothy Dwight and a commitment to seek alumni support to build it as the symbol of the greater university, distinct from the college—comprehending it and the growing professional schools.[242] Hadley and Stokes saw Dwight's Bicentennial Buildings through to near completion, but the buildings' Beaux-Arts classicism departed radically from the Gothic halls that Dwight had envisioned. Their new monumental classicism was something from which Yale's Corporation and administration would then almost immediately and decisively turn away, although some donors, among them powerful alumni, continued to bestow gifts of classical architecture.

Indeed, experimentation with classical forms continued into the 1910s at Yale. In some lights, it appears to have been a rather naively superficial grasp for the look of the White City, of Washington as the MacMillan Plan was expanding it, and of the magnificent vision for rebuilding Chicago that Daniel Burnham published in 1909. Donors and architects seem to have wanted the City Beautiful's image, but the university had not adopted its underlying and all-important planning concepts. By these lights, the Bicentennial Buildings themselves figure as the university's emblem of progressive aspiration, an emblem Yale presented to the world before it could possibly work out fundamental plans for the expansion so soon to come but at the time so totally unforeseen (FIGS. 159 & 160). I can only speculate that the presence of Secretary Stokes near the height of the administration might have influenced the university's own initial decision to build in the manner of the City Beautiful, and that his brother, Isaac Newton Phelps Stokes (1867–1944), a Harvard graduate who had studied at Columbia's architecture school and at the Ecole des Beaux-Arts, probably shaped his tastes.

The three major Bicentennial Buildings of 1901–2 include Woolsey Hall, an auditorium; Commons, a dining hall; and Memorial Hall, a vestibule in the form of an enlarged tempietto between the two

other buildings, giving entry to each. The walls of the rotunda in Memorial Hall are inscribed with the names of Yale's dead in many wars. The three buildings were sheathed in gleaming light-colored limestone and were of grand dimensions that introduced rooms of a size and scale approached in no other buildings at Yale. The formal terraced courtyard on which they fronted was also unmatched at Yale. Together the buildings were known during the early twentieth century as the Memorial Group—not to be confused with James Gamble Rogers's Memorial Quadrangle—and were often called the University Buildings (as opposed to Yale College buildings). The courtyard was called University Quadrangle or Court until 1914, when its name was changed to Hewitt University Quadrangle, in recognition of a bequest from Frederick C. Hewitt (B.A. 1858).

John M. Carrère (1858–1911) and Thomas Hastings (1860–1929), both of whom had studied at the Ecole des Beaux-Arts, made the preliminary designs for a competition held in 1899. They won it with their classical scheme over two Gothic proposals and two others that relied, like theirs, on Renaissance models and ultimately on classical sources. Of the competition's six invited architectural firms, two had worked extensively for Yale: Cady, Berg and See; and Charles Coolidge Haight. Robert Henderson Robertson, after losing this contest, was to do so again when he submitted a Gothic design for a library in 1905. But in 1908 he would finally be selected to work at Yale on Haughton Hall, filling the last gap in the Berkeley Oval. Another competitor, Cyrus L. W. Eidlitz (1853–1921), was a successful New York architect who had been one of six finalists in the competition of 1897 for the New York Public Library, another occasion on which he lost to Carrère and Hastings. McKim, Mead and White (active 1879–1909) withdrew from the Yale competition without producing a submission. The university enlisted the professional advice of George B. Post (1837–1913) to assess the entries. Post's New York Stock Exchange of 1903 is today the most familiar example of his work. In 1899 he was a long-established figure on the New York architectural scene, widely known for his early tall buildings, the Equitable Building of 1870, the Western Union Telegraph Building of 1873–75, and a succession of more recent ones.

George C. Holt was one of the five members of the Building Committee for the Bicentennial Buildings, which was chaired by William W. Farnam, former Yale treasurer. Holt, now a judge and an important figure in New York's legal world, had maintained his concern with Yale's architectural

FIG. 159 *R. Rummell, "Yale University," 1905.*

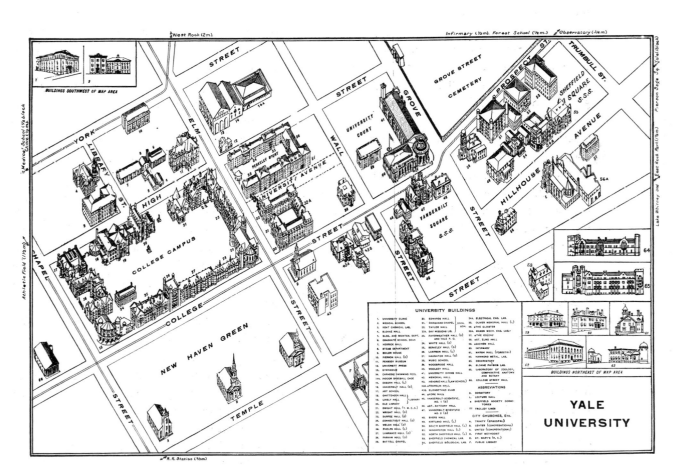

FIG. 160 *Map of Yale University, 1912–13.*

FIG. 161 *Bicentennial Buildings: presentation drawing by Carrère and Hastings, 1899.*

FIG. 162 *Bicentennial Buildings: presentation drawing of the interior view by Carrère and Hastings, 1899.*

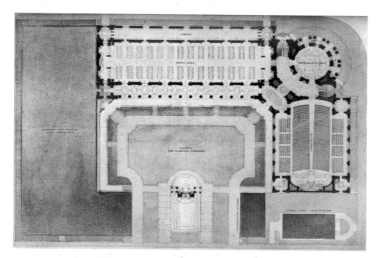

FIG. 163 *Bicentennial Buildings: plan by Carrère and Hastings, 1899.*

development during the thirty-five years since, as an undergraduate in 1865, he had grumbled in the *Yale Literary Magazine* about Street Hall breaking the architectural unity of the college buildings.[243] Now he participated in the choice of a design that deviated more spectacularly from Yale precedent than anything in its history.

Yale's concern to plan not just for the Bicentennial group but also for the whole block on which they were to be built is reflected in Post's seven-page report of November 24, 1899. He advised careful consideration of "the block plan and the style of architecture," because these buildings would "fix beyond the possibility of change the character of the future development of the property." In his opinion:

The authors of the Renaissance designs have arranged the buildings to secure grandeur of effect by long open vistas through continuous and symmetrically arranged parks. The authors of the Gothic designs have closed the vistas at the south end of the lot by the position of the Administration building, and have paid little attention as far as the block plan is concerned to secure other qualities than light, air, and picturesque individual masses. The several designs are a good illustration of the fact that very much the same relation exists in art between grandeur and picturesqueness as in mechanics between speed and power—what you gain in one you almost necessarily lose in the other.[244]

For Post, Carrère and Hastings's design had "a marked superiority in its disposition on the block of both the buildings at present contemplated and those that may be subsequently built…The buildings as designed are very monumental and eminently suitable for memorial structures." Robertson's Gothic design was "next in merit," Post thought, despite some conspicuous flaws, which he enumerated. His conclusion posed the choice between Renaissance and Gothic: "If you desire…the greatest dignity and grandeur, award the competition to Carrère and Hastings…If you desire…stately picturesqueness and a separate treatment for each group of buildings on the block, award the competition to R. H. Robertson."

Dignity and grandeur carried the day, and Carrère and Hastings's winning scheme was published as "The new Yale" in a special "Bi-Centennial Building Issue" of the *Yale Alumni Weekly* for January 31, 1900, under President Hadley's headlining exhortation: "We must do one of two things: Either not build, or build for the future." A perspective view of the corner of College and Grove Streets showed the "Memorial Vestibule" pushing the grand half-round of its entry out toward the town (FIG. 161). It was topped by a low dome, like that of the Pantheon,

FIG. 164 *University Commons set for a dinner, ca. 1906.*

barely rising above the roofs of the "Auditorium" – Woolsey Hall – on its south and the "Dining Hall" – Commons – to the west. A second view across the grassy sunken courtyard focused on a colossal colonnade fronting Commons, and had an entrance on angle at its western end, corresponding to the one that now leads to the rotunda on the east (FIG. 162). That second entrance led to a building that was only sketchily suggested, facing Woolsey and closing the courtyard off from High Street. The published plan (FIG. 163) detailed only the three buildings Yale hoped to complete for the anniversary celebration in the fall of 1901, the only ones of the proposed group that were ever constructed. Across the courtyard from Commons, at the head of University Avenue, it showed an elaborate central entry structure to the courtyard: double flights of stairs down to a grassy lawn.

With the drawings came a plea for contributions: "these are first and foremost alumni buildings, to be built for the alumni if the alumni want them, and primarily needed because the Yale life which comes surging back year by year needs a local habitation such as it does not now possess." Although the competition's budget was set at $400,000, the sum already raised in "the preliminary canvas," Post wrote in 1899 that he doubted "any one of the

designs can be completed…for less than about one million dollars." By January 1900, President Hadley was estimating the cost of Carrère and Hastings's scheme at $750,000. In the end, construction bills of 1900–1903 added up to $1,047,386.[245] The *Yale Alumni Weekly* carried enthusiastic reactions to these plans, but one letter in March 1900 picked up on a criticism of Yale's architecture that had been recurring in some printed form or another since Street Hall's construction in the 1860s. This time Henry Selden Bacon (B.A. 1893) of Rochester, New York, filled a long sarcastic column, complaining: "The custom which these most costly buildings will beautifully illustrate is of course that unique practice which reached an almost perfect recognition under the last administration, of making in every new building not merely a complete departure from all precedents established for academic structures, but a striking contrast with every other building of the University."[246] Criticism aside, as funds came in, Yale built out most of the plan: Commons came first, after contracts with Norcross Brothers were signed in July 1900. The enormous dining hall was needed not only annually for reunion festivities, but also daily for the student body (FIG. 164). Since an earlier commons behind the Brick Row had been closed in 1842, there had been none at Yale until early in the

FIG. 165 *University Commons in 1909.*

1890s, when the new gym was built on Elm Street and an older gym on Library Street was converted into a temporary dining hall. But nothing before had approached the size and scale of the Carrère and Hastings building, most of which was finished by January 1902. Contracts for the "Auditorium and Vestibule Buildings Complete" were signed in July 1901, and by this time the dome over the rotunda of the vestibule had been raised in the drawings to its present height, a design change that yielded a rather cumbersome exterior profile, while accommodating (as the lower Pantheon-dome profile would not have done) the useful space now known as the Presidents' Room.

But over a quarter century would pass before Yale built the colonnade that Carrère and Hastings characterized in their competition entry as "an integral and the most important part of the design, without which the building loses much of its dignity and character." The university neither owned one little piece of land on which the western end would stand, nor had in hand the money necessary to start the eastern part. It asked the architects "to devise an inexpensive means of temporarily giving the building a finished appearance for the dedication services, and with this end in view the…cornice…of tin and

plaster was erected" (FIG. 165).[247] However, the contract of 1900 did include foundations—but only the foundations—for those columns destined for land the university already owned.[248] Through years of debate about where and how to expand the campus, the administration put off Carrère and Hastings's pleas to finish their building. The architects, neither of whom were Yale graduates, were so anxious to execute the centerpiece of their design that they "made a small donation to the college and requested that it be applied to the beginning of a fund for the building of the colonnade" but "were urged by President Hadley to donate the fund for some other purpose, and it was finally handed over to the library for the architectural department."[249] In 1907, as the tin and plaster cornice seemed on its way to becoming a permanent fixture, the architects suggested soliciting each of fourteen Yale classes to pay for a single column. The administration did not take up their scheme.

Although Woodbridge Hall fronts the courtyard alongside the Bicentennial Buildings and was built at the same time as they, it was a separate project (FIG. 166).[250] It is Yale's major administrative building, the little palace of Yale's presidents and the meeting place of the Corporation. The name honors Timothy

FIG. 166 *Woodbridge Hall: presentation drawing of the west facade by J.K.J. for Howells and Stokes, 1900.*

Woodbridge, an ancestor of its donors, the remarkable Misses Olivia and Caroline Phelps Stokes of New York. Woodbridge was one of Yale's founding trustees, a minister in Hartford who opposed the move to New Haven and fought to have the college built in or near Hartford. However, after the decision went against him, he continued to serve on the board and sent his sons to New Haven. To make clear that the building's classicism was appropriate to Yale because it was somehow related to the Connecticut of Timothy Woodbridge's day, it was described at the time of its dedication as "Georgian, the style from which the colonial architecture of New England was derived,"[251] although the roots of its planning and formal character lay in France, at the Ecole des Beaux-Arts. The descendants of Woodbridge who honored him in this precise and elegant building inherited the family's devotion to Christianity. Such an exquisite contribution to an elite institution was unusual among their philanthropic activities. They used their ample inheritance more frequently to better the lot of women and oppressed people of all races, especially Native Americans and black people, in this country and in Africa.

Another Woodbridge descendant, Isaac Newton Phelps Stokes, designed the building for his aunts in partnership with John Mead Howells (1868–1959), who, like Stokes, had attended Harvard and studied in Paris at the Ecole. A letter of 1900 from the architect to his brother Anson, Yale's secretary, reveals the family's understanding of the nature of their gift and their role in its design, as well as their attempt to shape the larger grouping of Yale buildings. It pins down information of a kind that seldom survives in writing, documenting some of the ways the usual client-architect relationships became more complicated at Yale. Here ideas had to be negotiated through layers of university administrators, the Corporation, building (and later planning) committees, and donors. Newton wrote, in part:

Of course the Aunts are giving a building and not the money to pay for a building and yet you may think it unwise to bring up the subject so pointedly. I did it because Mr. Winthrop [Buchanan Winthrop, B.A. 1862, a member of the Corporation's Prudential Committee] seemed so anxious to impress us with the fact that we must at every step in the development of the plans consult the Building Committee.

To me it seems far better to get from the officers of the University and from the Building Committee the requirements and needs—and then to draw preliminary drawings and get them approved by the Aunts before submitting them to the Committee...

This letter is meant to explain to you the last line in our formal letter—about the approval of the Aunts.— Please do not show it—One other point—the Aunts are most anxious that the building shall in some way mark the entrance to the new quadrangle—that it shall in some sense be a gate. This I think can be accomplished...by putting it on one side of the entrance, with a corresponding building on the other side and gates—perhaps something like those at Harvard—between. I think these gates should be included in this gift and should be built at the same time as Woodbridge Hall. Mr. Winthrop did not seem favorably impressed by this idea and said the question of gates had not yet been considered—Didn't you speak of this at the time the offer was made?[252]

Woodbridge Hall's buff Indiana limestone is a little darker than the whiter limestone used by

Carrère and Hastings, and the building is more modest in size and scale. Positioned to front on the court of the Memorial Group, it does suggest half a gateway to the classical court, but despite the hopes of the Stokes family, no building was ever constructed to "match" and face Woodbridge Hall across the courtyard to the west, nor were operative gates of the sort envisioned by I. N. Stokes ever to be built, unless one counts the Noah Porter Gateway on Elm Street, well removed from the Bicentennial group (FIG. 167). Howells and Stokes won a competition of 1912 with their design for this gateway. Its monumental red-brick pillars with light-stone trim stand high over pedestrians and flank elegantly ornamented ironwork. When it was built, it fronted the space between the Berkeley Oval and the old Divinity School: now that space is flanked by their replacements, Berkeley and Calhoun Colleges. With its grand scale and classicism, Noah Porter Gateway serves as an outpost of the classical enclave memorializing Yale's bicentennial and marks with ceremony the entrance to the walkway then known as University Avenue, leading from the Old Campus to the center of Commons.

In 1914 that walkway was renamed Blount Avenue in honor of Archibald Henry Blount, Esquire, of Orleton Manor, Herefordshire, England, whose reasons for making Yale his residuary legatee shortly before his death in 1907 remain conjectural. It was thought that this reclusive man disliked monarchy and nurtured an enthusiasm for America, but investigations by a delegation in England failed to reveal just why he attached that enthusiasm to Yale. When Blount's complex estate was settled, Yale received a bequest of more than $300,000.[253]

For more than a decade after acquiring that new name, Blount Avenue's vista was to be culminated only by the temporary facade of Commons, still awaiting its colossal colonnade. In the meantime, the very existence of the whole Bicentennial group was threatened. In 1919 the Corporation briefly entertained John Russell Pope's proposal (his one really outrageous proposal) to erect a Gothic library comparable to the present Sterling Memorial Library squarely in the space of the University Quadrangle and eventually to demolish the Bicentennial Buildings. This idea did not fail to alarm some members of the Corporation, though they found much else to admire in Pope's magnificent plan for the university.[254] To advise their deliberations, the Corporation engaged a panel of well respected architects, Bertram Grosvenor Goodhue (1869–1924), William Adams Delano (1874–1960), and Paul Philippe Cret

(1876–1945), who wrote a formal report on the Pope Plan. The three agreed that plunking the library down where Pope proposed was not a good idea; and, while "regretting the scale of this classical court," they wrote "we feel that with restudy in completing it, it can be made a dignified and adequate place of outdoor assembly for the students and alumni, and a fitting termination of the north and south axis."[255] Corporation fellows also discussed and dismissed a suggestion to hide the classical group from the principal views by building a Gothic "screen" in the form of a building, dropping the idea only after having Goodhue make sketch plans for it in 1920.[256]

During the subsequent decade, the Corporation seems to have come to terms with the Bicentennial Buildings as an asset to be embraced more positively. Goodhue, Delano, and Cret had also recommended in their report that the colonnade be finished, and after the First World War, the project was revived as appropriately monumental for a war memorial. Alumni contributions were forthcoming to build the massive Corinthian columns much as they had first been envisioned. On May 7, 1926, the Corporation voted to let contracts for their construction. The colonnade, its entablature, and a cenotaph were dedicated to Yale's dead of 1914–18 on June 19, 1927 (FIG. 168). The battles in which they fell—Cambrai, Argonne, Somme, Chateau-Thierry, Ypres, St. Mihiel, Marne—were incised across the face of the entablature.

Meanwhile, the Corporation had not forgotten another bit of advice that Goodhue, Delano, and Cret had offered in 1920: that "the classical court started by Carrère and Hastings be completed by the erection of a new wing balancing Woolsey Hall, to be used for administrative purposes or for lecture rooms, or both."[257] Drawings that Carrère and Hastings published in 1902 show a classical facade completing the western edge of their grand courtyard, opposite—"balancing"—the facade of Woolsey Hall, fronting the site now partially occupied by the Beinecke Rare Book and Manuscript Library. In November 1925, it was not, however, Carrère and Hastings, but Clarence C. Zantzinger, a graduate of the Sheffield Scientific School (PH.B. 1892), who "had started work on sketches for the new Administration Building"—intended to house the university's treasurer, bursar, secretary, post office, and Bureau of Appointments—as Thomas W. Farnam (B.A. 1899), the associate treasurer and comptroller, reported to a meeting of the Corporation's Committee on Architectural Plan.[258] Three years later, a push to complete Yale's major classical group brought forth elaborate,

FIG. 167 *Noah Porter Gateway: competition-winning drawing by Howells and Stokes, 1912.*

FIG. 168 *University Commons after completion of the Yale Alumni War Memorial colonnade, ca. 1928.*

apparently competing, drawings from the firms of both Zantzinger and Carrère and Hastings, but no building. Zantzinger and Medary's scheme expressed the presence of three full stories in its fenestration. The windows of the ground floor, like the doors, were all round-headed, and all opened to the ground, creating the image of an arcade. The plans and elevations by Carrère and Hastings retained their original scheme's angled entrance through a round-headed opening that corresponded to the existing entrance from the courtyard to the rotunda. But they refined the fenestration of the longest facade, the one balancing Woolsey, by alternating round-headed and triangular pediments over the rusticated windows of the second floor. They also projected a pedimented pavilion forward to complement Woodbridge Hall across the courtyard.

Although Carrère and Hastings received a fee of $20,000 for plans and specifications, their work of 1928 was never executed.[259] Perhaps the project fell by the wayside for simple lack of money as the Depression cut into alumni giving from sources other than Harkness and Sterling. These large, classically detailed proposals accommodated services very different from those with which Edward Harkness was currently preoccupied as his dream of residential colleges became more absorbing and ambitious. And just then, funds available from the Sterling trustees were being diverted to another Yale administration building, the tower that crowned the enormous Sheffield-Sterling-Strathcona Hall (see FIG. 119), soon to be built—by Zantzinger's firm—as the administration building and crowning jewel of the Sheffield Scientific School. In June 1927, the Architectural Plan Committee had begun discussions with Sheffield's dean, Charles Hyde Warren (PH.B. 1896, PH.D. 1899), that would soon give Yale's administrators new offices in a building that had room to spare.

Although there was to be no more raising of classical buildings around Hewitt University Quadrangle, the university did pursue the further elaboration of its courtyard. With their winning submission of 1899 for the Bicentennial Buildings, Carrère and Hastings had included a memorandum which began: "The fundamental idea of the accompanying design is the great central court, around which the future buildings are to be erected. This court, which will contain some 36,000 square feet, will furnish a retired and agreeable place for academic gatherings." Their design development of a "memorial campus" in the measured plans of an elegant rectilinear landscape was delayed until 1903. Then, as most of the initial construction was being completed, the architects developed the terracing, planting, and paving around the central lawn, along with balustrades and flagpoles, in a simplification of the scheme suggested in their competition drawings. In 1908 they designed the Ledyard Memorial Flagstaff honoring a member of the Class of 1897 who had been killed in the Philippines. In 1917 Frank Miles Day drew up elaborately patterned paving, which was never executed. In 1928, just after the colonnade was built, with the memorial cenotaph centrally placed in front, the landscaping of the courtyard was redone under the supervision of Beatrix Farrand (1872–1959; M.A.H. 1925), again quite formally, with cobblestones paving the center and a good deal of green edging them (see FIG. 168). By this time, the facade of Woolsey was almost completely covered with vines that effectively screened it from Blount Avenue, though not so totally as some had hoped a Gothic building might do. With the construction of Beinecke Library in the early 1960s, the courtyard was ruthlessly paved over, and the balustrade in front of Commons was hidden behind a grim wall of solid gray blocks that masked the bases of the great columns, so that as one walks north from Phelps Gate on Blount Avenue, they appear to sit not on their proper bases, but gracelessly on that wall. The cobblestones that had covered the central area were carted off to be laid along the waterfront at Mystic Seaport.[260]

The Bicentennial group was to remain Yale's single most ambitious essay in monumental classicism. Cady's work of the 1890s had reintroduced simple and restrained classical forms to Yale, first for White Hall and more imposingly for the facade of Hendrie Hall. Before the First World War, the college completed the Berkeley Oval with comparatively simple buildings, rather sparingly detailed in the language of classicism. A mile and a half away, on the playing fields west of the central campus, the alumni-sponsored project of 1911 to build a Yale Coliseum was an exuberant expression of classical tastes in quite another voice. And across town, in the medical area, classical forms also fronted the only two buildings that went up between 1900 and the war: the simplest vernacular expression of classicism shaped an isolation ward by the local architect, Leoni W. Robinson, and classicism was more elegantly

expressed in the Brady Memorial Laboratory on which Robinson also worked in association with Day and Klauder. Meanwhile, near the Bicentennial Buildings, Yale added a few other classical structures to its inventory. Their styles were sometimes dictated by donors who, like the Misses Stokes, specified the hiring of their chosen architects in the terms of their gifts.

One of the more imposing of these was the Sheffield Scientific School's new social center, Byers Memorial Hall (FIG. 169), built across College Street from the Bicentennial Buildings while they were under construction. Byers Hall was intended, in the words of the annual report of 1901, "In material and design…to be in harmony with the Bicentennial buildings…of which group, in fact, it may almost be said to form a part."[261] Hiss and Weekes, another New York architectural firm (Philip Hiss, 1857–1940; H. Hobart Weekes, 1867[?]–1950), based it on the Petit Trianon at Versailles, but gave its College Street facade monumental stairs that rose the height of its raised basement. They led to the major entrance, recessed behind four colossal fluted columns with Ionic capitals. Mrs. Alexander MacBurney Byers, of Allegheny, Pennsylvania, gave the building in honor of her husband and their son, Alexander MacBurney Byers, Jr., a Sheffield Scientific School graduate (PH.B. 1894). Sheff's Young Men's Christian Association occupied one of its three floors. In a history of

FIG. 169 *Byers Memorial Hall in the early 1930s, with the second Vanderbilt-Scientific Hall on the right: west (College Street) facades.*

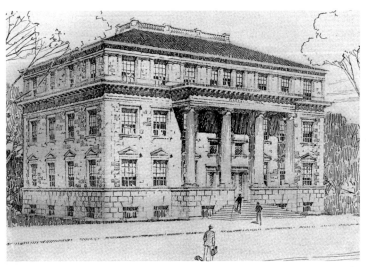

FIG. 170 *Kirtland Hall: presentation drawing of the east (Hillhouse Avenue) facade by Kirtland Kelsey Cutter, 1902–3.*

undergraduate life at Sheffield, Loomis Havemeyer (PH.B. 1910) wrote in the 1950s that this building "gave to the entire student body…a social and religious center—a sort of general clubhouse—for the first time in the history of the School…and one which surpassed anything else of the kind in the University, in attractiveness as well as in the facilities it provided."[262] Yale College students, on the other hand, had had Dwight Hall since the late 1880s. In 1940 Byers was shorn of its stairs, and the doorway from College Street became a window when the building became part of Silliman College. Reoriented away from the public street and toward the private courtyard, it now provided the college with a lounge, a library, and fellows' suites.

The Scientific School's first laboratories of the twentieth century, Kirtland and Hammond, were also given classical forms, though they were very different one from another, as well as from the monumental structures of the new university center. Kirtland Kelsey Cutter (1860–1939), who designed Kirtland Hall of 1902–4 (FIG. 170), was a successful architect in Spokane, Washington, and a great-grandson of the man for whom the building was named, Jared Potter Kirtland (M.D. 1815). Although Dr. Kirtland lived in Cleveland, Ohio, where he was a founder of the medical college and died in 1877, his niece—Mrs. Lucy Hall Boardman—lived on Hillhouse Avenue. In 1902, when she decided to give this geology laboratory in his memory, she had her nephew duplicate the size, spacing, and detailing of the portico on her house, designed by Ithiel Town in 1839, as the frontispiece for Kirtland Hall on the southwest corner of Hillhouse and Grove.[263] Although its interior has been much changed, its

exterior remains much the same: behind the portico, it is a dark, ponderous rectangular box constructed of East Haven brownstone in three stories over a raised basement.

Hammond Hall of 1904 (FIG. 171) is the work of another architect otherwise foreign to Yale, W. Gedney Beatty (1869–1941[?]). It is named for John Hays Hammond, a Sheffield graduate (PH.B. 1876) who had a colorful, and profitable, career in gold mining as an associate of Cecil Rhodes in South Africa. His Yale class historian reported in 1921 that Hammond "was one of the four leaders in the reform movement in the Transvaal in 1895–6; After the Jameson Raid (with which he was not in sympathy) [he] was arrested and sentenced to death; sentence was afterward commuted to 15 years' imprisonment; and later [he] was released on payment of a fine of $125,000."[264] By 1902, Hammond was safely back at Yale, as Professor of Mining Engineering, a post he held until 1909. His classes must have been considerably enhanced after he used some of the profits of his African ventures to underwrite the new facility for instruction in his specialty. Well away from the center of either the Sheffield School or Yale College, Hammond Hall (originally Hammond Metallurgical Laboratory) presents an orderly classical facade to Mansfield Street, two brick stories over a raised stone basement, fronting classrooms and offices. Behind them, next to a rail line, Beatty placed a vast shed with a single high space to house formidable-looking apparatus. A photograph of the interior in 1918 shows a gargantuan "experimental concentrator plant" installed under its exposed metal trusses (FIG. 172).[265]

Back across College Street from Byers Hall, just south of the Bicentennial Buildings on the far corner of Wall Street, a headquarters building for the School of Music was added to the classical district in 1916–17 (FIG. 173).[266] This memorial to Colonel Albert Arnold Sprague (B.A. 1894) of Chicago was described as "Colonial Style" in Yale's first publications that pictured its red-brick facades with their crisp white Tennessee Marble trim. Its major space is a sparkling white auditorium for chamber music recitals and small concerts, where great clear windows fill it with light. An important architect from Boston—not, as usual, one from New York—designed Sprague Hall. He was Charles Coolidge, who was responsible for Harvard's medical school as well as Harvard's formidable range of red-brick freshman dormitories, the River Houses along the Charles, three of which had been built by 1913. His sister-in-law, Elizabeth Sprague Coolidge,

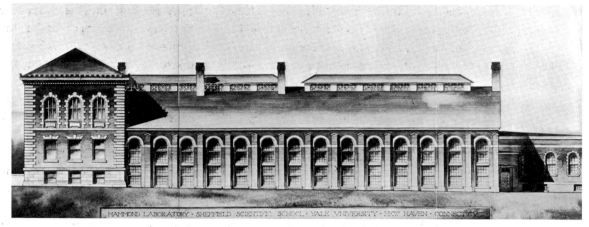

FIG. 171 *Hammond Hall: side elevation by W. Gedney Beatty, 1904.*

FIG. 172 *Hammond Hall in 1918: interior with concentrator plant.*

who with her mother, Mrs. Albert Arnold Sprague, gave the building, specified in the letter formally offering the gift that Coolidge was "my mother's choice of architects."[267]

———

In the years leading up to the establishment in 1911 of a committee to guide the university's architectural planning, key decisions about Yale's expansion within New Haven were sometimes dominated not only by individuals willing to pay for construction, but also by the boards of organizations—the Sheffield Scientific School, the hospital, and alumni groups—that had power the Corporation could not always control. For properties over which the Corporation had more control, most of which were closer to the old heart of Yale, its members and the

administration tried hard to put in place effective mechanisms to guide a mounting number of building projects during the opening years of the twentieth century.

Most far-reaching among these was the development of the thirty-acre Hillhouse property, located at an awkward remove north of the campus, on the far side of the Grove Street Cemetery: the future Science Hill, bounded by Whitney Avenue and Sachem, Prospect, and Edwards Streets. In September 1905 its purchase was front-page news in the *Yale Alumni Weekly,* where Anson Phelps Stokes, "speaking for the trustees of the Hillhouse property," among whom he was the major one, announced: "The three graduates of Yale University who recently purchased the major part of the Hillhouse estate...for the University and park purposes have decided not to hand the property over to the University [which would have avoided property taxes] until they have raised sufficient money to leave it clear of encumbrance," adding that they would pay property taxes for the coming year, as they held themselves personally liable for the mortgage.[268] The tract surrounded the Hillhouse mansion, which was its centerpiece, but the land immediately around the mansion itself remained in the hands of the Hillhouse family.

Also in 1905, five years before Yale became the outright owner of the tract, the Corporation commissioned the leading American planning and landscape architecture firm, Olmsted Brothers of Brookline, Massachusetts,[269] to draw up a "Plan for the Developement [sic] of the Hillhouse Property" (FIG. 174). The Olmsted plan bracketed the face of the hill along Sachem Street with a pair of L-shaped buildings, one addressing the corner of Whitney Avenue and Sachem, the other the corner of Prospect and Sachem, as Osborn Memorial Laboratories now does: each arm of each L shape paralleled an adjacent street, and each plan showed a diagonal cut across the corner fronting the angle of the streets' crossing. These two buildings framed a central opening along Sachem Street that gave a vista up the hill that was stopped just shy of the crest, at the site of the Hillhouse mansion. On that site their plan called for a building with a relatively small footprint paralleling Sachem Street, a building that would front an irregular string of buildings extending northward up the hill, all the way to Edwards Street, where it would join another extensive complex of structures fronting Edwards, forming a narrow line running west, and then turning the Prospect Street corner to form another long edge of buildings along that street.

At the same time, the university tried to appease New Haven's concern about the removal of this former Hillhouse land, which was conspicuously ripe for residential development, from the city's tax list. Yale published its "desire…that not only the section in front of the manor house, which is permanently set aside for a public park, but most of the property to be owned by the University, shall be thrown open as far as practicable, and under proper restrictions, to the enjoyment of the people of New Haven."[270] Yale was finally able to buy the property, excluding still the mansion itself, in 1910 with funds given by Mrs. Russell Sage. In her honor, and that of her ancestor Abraham Pierson (Yale's first rector), the property was named Pierson-Sage Square. That same year, the Corporation adopted "Long Meadow brown stone, smooth finish, as the main material of construction for all buildings in the Laboratory Quadrangle of the Pierson-Sage Square."[271] This attempt to impose some sort of unity on future construction in at least one sector of the university gave priority to materials over style. And the recorded commitment to a particular material was to haunt the Corporation within a few years, when a donor who had used the prescribed Long Meadow brown stone objected to the proposed use of brick to save money in a building to be sited next to his.

In the aggregate, Yale's buildings, few of which looked much like many of the others, were embarrassing the key administrators of the institution during the first decade of the twentieth century. Secretary Stokes bemoaned the situation in 1908: "We are one of the only universities of note in America that has no architectural scheme."[272] Three years later, he suggested a leafy solution to the problem:

FIG. 173 *Sprague Hall: presentation drawing of the east (College Street) facade by Coolidge and Shattuck, 1916.*

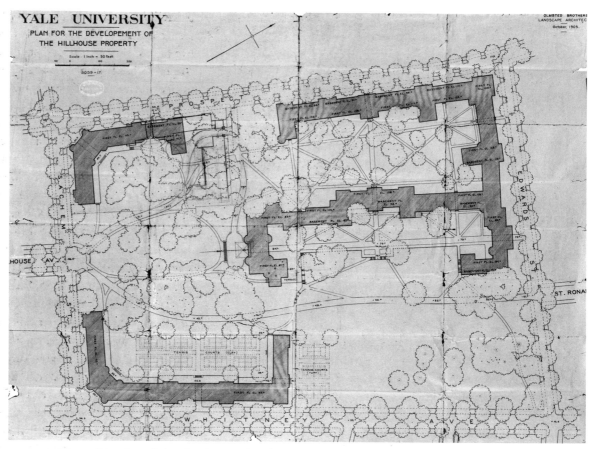

FIG. 174 *Olmsted Brothers, "Plan for the Developement* [sic] *of the Hillhouse Property," 1905.*

"In my judgment planting of shrubs and vines will do much to hide our architectural incongruities."[273] Meanwhile, for most architects and architectural critics who weighed in on the subject, adherence to some expression of Gothic forms in stone seemed an effective strategy for pulling a campus together, especially since at the center of Yale the Gothic precedent had been set more than half a century earlier. Turning a blind eye to the burst of classicism at the corner of College and Grove Streets, variations on the Gothic theme were to dominate most of the new structures that took shape to the north and west of the Old Campus in the first quarter of the twentieth century.

The architect responsible for bringing to Yale the Collegiate Gothic style that became nearly generic on American campuses of the early twentieth century was Charles Coolidge Haight (1841–1917). His name is hardly a familiar one at Yale today, nor are his buildings the focus of standard works on American architectural history; but in 1899 he was the subject of one of the six monographs on "Great American Architects" that the magazine *Architectural Record* published as special issues. Montgomery Schuyler wrote there that Mr. Haight "was distinctly the most successful designer of college buildings in this

country, the man who had more than any other succeeded in making a college building look like a college building."[274] His best known were for the old Columbia College campus of 1880 at 49th Street and Madison Avenue in New York and the General Theological Seminary of 1887, also in New York.[275] Haight was "not only a conservative, but it is scarcely unfair to describe him as a reactionary." These are again the opinions of Montgomery Schuyler, who went on to write of Haight:

His business has been, not to fit new requirements with new forms…It has been to cull, from assemblages of forms long ago settled and harmonized, what may best suit modern requirements, to do this with strict observance of the particular environment, and to do it with the very minimum of pretension and self assertion.[276]

The old Ruskinian Gothic buildings that P. B. Wight and Russell Sturgis built for Yale from the 1860s to the 1880s were different in scale, detail, and spirit from the Collegiate Gothic structures of the twentieth century. Wight and Sturgis had turned to the densely ornamented palaces of Venice and to French chateaux and cathedrals for inspiration, while this later generation found their models in the medieval college buildings of England, where

FIG. 175 *Vanderbilt Hall: presentation drawing of the south (Chapel Street) elevation by J. K. James for Charles C. Haight, 1894.*

the detailing was simpler and cheaper to execute. Wight and Sturgis had been concerned to build "honestly," stone by stone, with "true" load-bearing masonry walls. The evolution of their Ruskinian Gothic into Haight's Collegiate Gothic resulted in part from abandonment of their preoccupation with "structural honesty" and its forthright expression in the face of early-twentieth-century demands for much bigger structures within which vast rooms were required, with floor space cleared of supporting columns. The later generation also had to accommodate more technologically complex systems of plumbing, lighting, and heating, and it was asked to do all this more economically and more quickly. To meet these requirements, architects turned to steel frame construction over which masonry became only a thin facade. At the same time, many practitioners who used Gothic details found that increased demands for more and more square footage of usable space were not matched by proportionate increases in budgets for detailing. When the details became spare, sparse, or repetitious, it was not necessarily in response to modernist leanings toward simplicity.

In the 1890s, Haight had designed two much admired buildings for Yale. The first was the dormitory that Cornelius and Alice G. Vanderbilt gave as a memorial to their son, William Henry Vanderbilt. It was built in a U-shaped plan on the Old Campus, with a courtyard facing Chapel Street (FIG. 175). At the center of Vanderbilt Hall's campus facade, Haight set an entrance tower-block like ones he had been using on campuses since the mid-1880s.[277] It became a characteristic set piece of the architect, who reused it several times at Yale. At the base of a square tower-

block that rises above the mass of a building, a big arched opening is flanked by still taller turrets—two of four slender turrets that are attached at each corner of the tower-block and rise above it. Crenellation tops it all. In Vanderbilt Hall, the four turrets are hexagonal, and the arch at the base of the tower-block was intended to open a pathway between the town and the Old Campus, but the courtyard was promptly fenced and its gates closed.

The second of Haight's contributions to Yale's architecture of the 1890s was Phelps Hall of 1896, the Tudorish gateway to the Old Campus, facing the New Haven Green (FIG. 176). It is named in honor of William Walter Phelps (B.A. 1860) and is the gift of his family. Phelps, the son-in-law of Joseph Earl Sheffield, took an active part in successful efforts made by alumni during the 1870s to liberalize the college curriculum and the membership of the Yale Corporation. As Brooks Kelley relates, from 1874 until his death in 1894, Phelps "contributed annually one-half of the entire funds used for the purchase of books. On his death, however, the fund from which this income came was donated to the university to build Phelps Hall."[278] Fortunately for Yale, other sources were soon found for library purchases.

Haight garnered a great deal of published praise for skillfully using Phelps Hall to close a gap between two dormitories, Lawrance and Welch Halls, which were not closely related to one another in either

FIG. 176 *Phelps Hall: sketch by Charles C. Haight on a letter to William W. Farnam, 1895.*

FIG. 177 *First Vanderbilt-Scientific Hall: presentation drawing of the south (Wall Street) facade by Hughson Hawley for Charles C. Haight, 1902.*

detailing or materials. Montgomery Schuyler thought Haight had been correct when he recognized that "to unite these two something different from either was distinctly 'indicated,'" and that Haight had "gotten very well out of his dilemma" of inserting four floors of lecture rooms above the more "monumental effect" of the lower stage of the tower, without spoiling the monumentality of the arch. This building is another of Haight's square towers—indeed, it is all tower—taller than the flanking buildings, crowned with complex stepped and curved battlements, and with a taller hexagonal turret attached to each corner, each of which is capped with a domed roof. Similar towers rising above their surroundings to mark arched entries to Collegiate Gothic buildings became familiar sights at American colleges during the first two decades of the twentieth century, most notably when Cope and Stewardson utilized them repeatedly at Bryn Mawr, Princeton, and Washington University in St. Louis.[279]

Just after the turn of the century Frederick W. Vanderbilt, a Sheffield graduate (PH.B. 1876) and trustee, decided to give the Scientific School its first two dormitories, each named Vanderbilt-Scientific Hall, in honor of his brother Cornelius, who died in 1899. He followed his brother's lead and chose Haight to be his architect.[280] Construction on the first, in light-colored granite and Indiana limestone, began on Wall Street in 1903 (FIG. 177), soon to be followed by the second on College Street, a little smaller but, as the president's annual report for 1906 put it, "having

the same general appearance as the first Vanderbilt-Scientific, though necessarily not so large" (see FIG. 169). Haight gave a more imposing entrance tower to the second dormitory, on the more important street, which was described in the same report: "in the center over the archway rises a large and lofty tower, with rooms on six floors and with ornate battlements above."[281] These dormitories, with Byers Hall, created the principal boundaries of a new quadrangular campus for the Scientific School: Vanderbilt Square, bounded by College, Grove, Temple, and Wall Streets (FIG. 178). According to a letter written by Yale treasurer George Parmly Day (B.A. 1897) in 1912,

Insofar as Vanderbilt Square is concerned it would probably be impossible, without offending Mr. Vanderbilt, to do anything at all in regard to the architecture as he has been accustomed to employ his own architect and to send up the plans only when completed. This square will really have to be left to him for development, and I think we can all trust to his continuing to plan wisely in regard to the architecture thereof.[282]

Twenty-eight years later, Vanderbilt's bequest to the university would fund the construction of Silliman College, within which Byers and the two Vanderbilt-Scientific Halls were incorporated.[283]

In 1906, Yale bestowed an honorary degree (M.A.) upon Haight; and between 1908 and 1913, he was chosen as architect for four of the nine laboratories and halls of science built during the first quarter of the century on Hillhouse Avenue and on the former Hillhouse property. The two on Hillhouse Avenue are Collegiate Gothic structures in limestone, built for the Sheffield School. Leet Oliver Memorial Hall, given by Mrs. James Brown Oliver of Pittsburgh in memory of her son, Daniel Leet Oliver, a member of Sheffield's Class of 1908, was finished first, in 1908. It is a classroom building that looks rather like a large, post-medieval, many-gabled manor house. Although it has no tower, Haight did give it an arched entrance at the base of its central bay, which he set between buttresses under a small frontal gable.

The second, of 1910–11, the Mason Laboratory of Mechanical Engineering (FIG. 179, on the left), was the gift of William S. Mason with his brother George Grant Mason, both graduates of Sheffield's Class of 1888. G. G. Mason, an industrialist, was an influential leader of the Alumni Committee on a Plan for University Development, formed after the First World War. His group pushed Yale to improve the quality of liberal education at Sheff, which eventually led to the merging of the Scientific School with Yale College.[284] For the small street frontage of Mason, a building that is larger than it appears to be when seen from Hillhouse Avenue, Haight designed a relatively simple facade of four repetitive bays, filled with groupings of large vertical windows separated

by buttresses. Originally this was a screen for one great, high space housing large engineering apparatus, an unlikely neighbor for St. Mary's Church to its south, and a Sheffield fraternity, now home to the Collection of Musical Instruments, to its north.

Across Hillhouse Avenue another Collegiate Gothic laboratory went up in 1912, for electrical engineering (FIG. 179, on the right), given by the president of the Hartford Electric Light Company, Austin C. Dunham (B.A. 1854). The Sheffield Trustees did not choose Mr. Haight to design it, but rather Henry G. Morse (1884–1934), "an architect who is very highly recommended by Professor [Charles F.] Scott of the Electrical Engineering Department because of his practical knowledge" according to a letter of 1912 in which George Parmly Day also registered some concern about the choice: "in endeavouring to plan a building to harmonize with Leet Oliver Memorial Hall, he is probably going to find himself engaged upon a style of architecture with which he has had little experience."[285] Morse, however, produced in Dunham Laboratory a competent enough Collegiate Gothic hall, giving it some delicate ornaments.[286] In 1922 his building was illustrated in the *Yale Alumni Weekly* as only "the right wing" of a

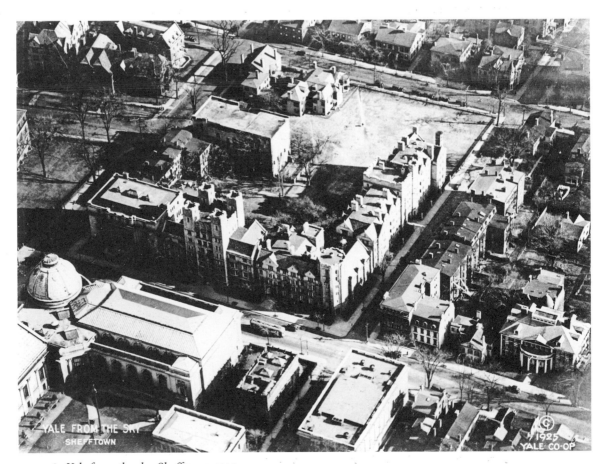

FIG. 178 *Yale from the sky, Shefftown, 1925.*

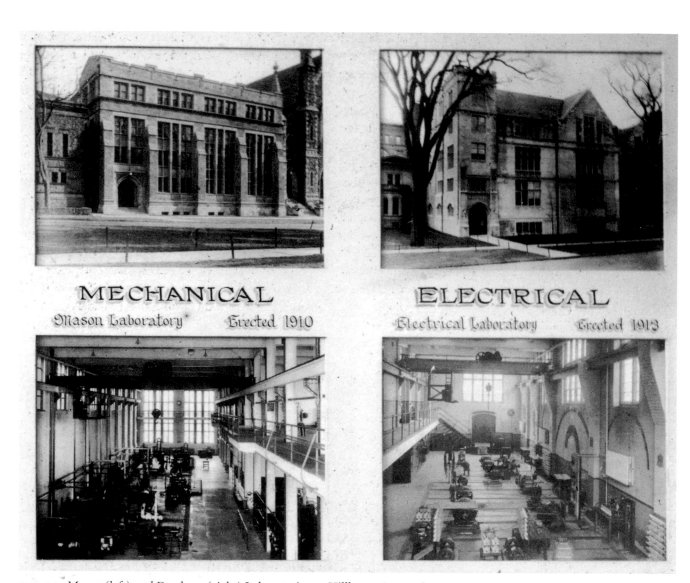

MECHANICAL
Mason Laboratory   Erected 1910

ELECTRICAL
Electrical Laboratory   Erected 1913

FIG. 179 *Mason (left) and Dunham (right) Laboratories on Hillhouse Avenue in 1918.*

much larger proposal for the laboratory "designed to effect architectural unity with the groups on the west side of Hillhouse Avenue." In the drawing, the facade of the building completed in 1913 made up only a third of the one envisioned, but never executed, and the existing tower was subsumed within a central tower seven stories tall.[287] Dunham Laboratory is the only Yale building on which Morse is known to have worked.

Haight's two buildings on Science Hill, Sloane Physics Laboratory and Osborn Memorial Laboratories, are brownstone Collegiate Gothic structures. Haight's placement of them on the western side of the former Hillhouse property bears an interesting relationship to the scheme the Olmsteds had laid out for the area in 1905. For the Sloane Physics Laboratory of 1911–12 (FIG. 180), given by the same

family that had given the college its Sloane Physical Laboratory of the 1880s,[288] Haight deviated from the Olmsted Plan, which had suggested that a continuous narrow building should edge Prospect Street for the northern half of the long block that climbs the hill from Sachem to Edwards (see FIG. 174). Instead, Haight presented only a narrow facade to the street and ran the length of the lab across the hill to the east. Above it he raised only one crenellated tower, a small hexagon in plan. But Haight followed the Olmsteds' site plan fairly closely when he designed Osborn Memorial Laboratories of Zoology, Comparative Anatomy, and Botany of 1913–14 (FIG. 181), working into the Olmsteds' scheme a close variant of the now established set piece for Haight-designed entries. He positioned two wings at right angles to one another, on either side of the southwest corner of the site, where each paralleled a street. He joined them with an entry placed on angle, squarely facing the angle of the northeast corner of Prospect and Sachem Streets with two tall crenellated towers on either side of an arch. This arch formed a major way through the building to the future Science Hill. Ironically, money bequeathed by the same Miriam A. Osborn who had insisted that Bruce Price's Osborn Hall be so distinctive from its neighbors paid for this building, which was part of a prolonged effort to unify the university's new structures with brown masonry and the Gothic. In 1913 Haight also designed the Pierson-Sage Heating Plant adjacent to Osborn's northernmost wall, blending an essential working facility with its neighbors as inconspicuously as possible.

All of these very institutional-looking specimens of Collegiate Gothic moved Yale's physical presence still farther north in New Haven. Back on the Old Campus, Haight had won the competition of 1905 for a new library with another Gothic design (FIG. 182). In his project, two frontal-gabled pavilions bracketed the long bar of a lower building that had its roof ridge running parallel to its facade. Each pavilion had much in common with the formula Haight so often repeated for entrances. The single pavilion that was constructed has an arched entry like his taller towers—set off-center this time, with polygonal corner turrets—but it does not rise to the height of a true tower; and here a frontal gable replaces the battlements with which Haight more often adorned the skylines of his buildings at Yale.

FIG. 180 *Sloane Physics Laboratory in 1912: north facade.*

FIG. 181 *Osborn Memorial Laboratories from the corner of Prospect and Sachem Streets.*

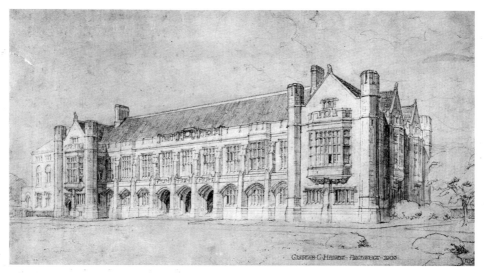

FIG. 182 *Linsly Hall: competition drawing by A. M. Githens for Charles C. Haight, 1905.*

That pavilion, called Linsly Hall, was built in fulfillment of the bequest of William B. Ross (B.A. 1852) for "an imperishable monument to his patron Jared Linsly [B.A. 1826],"[289] who had been a doctor in New York. Attached to the north wall of Cady's Chittenden Hall, the earlier fragment of another large library project that was never completed, this fragment of Haight's unfinished library now houses part of the English department.

For the Old Campus, Haight also designed two gates giving entry from Elm Street.[290] The earlier is Miller Memorial Gateway, between Durfee Hall and Battell Chapel, a Gothic archway honoring Theodore Westwood Miller (B.A. 1897), "Who fell mortally wounded in the charge on San Juan Hill at Santiago de Cuba 1st July 1898," as its inscription records. It was erected in 1899 by his Yale College classmates, led by a committee that included two important future shapers of the architecture of their university: Edward S. Harkness and Francis P. Garvan.[291] The second of Haight's gates — an arch between buttresses under a battlemented parapet, is on the opposite side of Durfee, spanning the gap between Durfee and Wright, and was built in 1911–12 (FIG. 183). It is Daniels Memorial Gateway, given by Mr. and Mrs. John W. Daniels to commemorate their son Forrest Leonard Daniels (B.A. 1907), who died less than a year after his graduation from Yale College.

Haight's contributions to Yale, unlike the great majority of Cady's, remain important functioning parts of the university complex, even if they are now little noticed by students of architecture. Their present usefulness is perhaps comparable to Haight's personal usefulness to Yale administrators in the years before the First World War. Haight was experienced in academic design and planning, and he not only drew buildings for Yale that pleased university administrators, but he also enjoyed broader influence there, according to a letter that Anson Phelps Stokes wrote in 1911:

He has done more to redeem Yale architecture than anyone else. He has never been appointed our consulting architect but we would certainly not do anything on the old Campus or on the Hillhouse property without consulting him and he does all of the work for the Sheffield Trustees. There is probably more chance of the University and the Sheffield Trustees agreeing on Mr. Haight as consulting architect than on any one else of high standard.[292]

But by then he was, as Stokes put it, "pretty well along in life, probably seventy."

A man who was twenty years younger, Frank Miles Day (1861–1918), became the first "Supervising Architect to Yale University" at the close of 1913. This was a full five years after key members of the administration and Corporation had taken positive steps to persuade their colleagues to finance such a post and to find a man to fill it. By 1908, as correspondence in the archives makes clear, the administration perceived that the architectural quality of Yale's campus had fallen below current standards, and it was anxious to catch up. One of the first acts in this direction was to ask other major universities whether they had architectural plans or a system for coordinating future building, and who was supervising designs by architects working on individual structures.

In January and February 1908, Stokes received at least six letters in response to these inquiries. Harvard's, dated January 13 and signed by an assistant secretary, came first:

FIG. 183 *Daniels Memorial Gateway: drawing by A. M. Githens for Charles C. Haight, 1911.*

Mr. Eliot [Charles W. Eliot, president of Harvard] directs me to tell you that there is no architectural plan here at Harvard for the development of the University. When a new building is planned, the question of site and design is referred to a committee of architects who have already designed buildings for the University to consult with the architect who has charge of the proposed structure. The work of this committee, however, has not hitherto been regarded as entirely successful.[293]

Especially after such an uninspiring report, one written the same day from Princeton was a good deal more promising, and it came from the president, Woodrow Wilson, himself. But it too reveals that America's most prestigious old universities had only very recently begun to make self-conscious and self-critical assessments of the ways they were going about shaping their campuses:

Our method of architectural management here is very simple indeed. We have employed, during the last year, (before that we had no system at all) Mr. Ralph Adams Cram…as our Advising Architect. He has submitted to us a general and comprehensive plan for the development of our property, and we are working on the basis of that plan. For each building projected an architect is selected, and the plans which he submits are accepted only after they

have been passed upon and approved by Mr. Cram. Of course, Mr. Cram does not impose his own tastes and judgment upon the architect engaged, but seeks only to bring about such uniformity in standards of taste and style as can be brought about by frank and friendly consultation.

We have worked for so short a time upon this system that I can hardly yet judge whether it is entirely satisfactory or not. I can only say that up to this time we think we have derived great benefit from it and have been prevented from making further mistakes.[294]

Letters from Stanford and the University of Chicago also came later in January, followed in February by one from the University of California describing the much publicized international competition for a campus design at Berkeley that produced an extravagant, grandiose winner by a Parisian architect, H. J. E. Benard. However, the situations at those three newly founded institutions, where elaborate campus planning preceded initial building campaigns on clear sites, bore little comparison with Yale's. The University of Pennsylvania's circumstances were more relevant. From Philadelphia, the response to Stokes's inquiries came from the professor in charge of its architecture department, Warren Powers Laird. Although he regretted that "no report is in existence," he offered to have photographed for Stokes's use his perspective drawings "for the development of property contiguous to that of the University" as well as "a large plan of civic improvement prepared by Professor Cret…with…Zantzinger and Borie of Philadelphia."[295] Both Paul Cret (1876–1945) and Clarence C. Zantzinger (PH.B. 1892) were later to advise or design for Yale.[296]

No immediate action at Yale was forthcoming, however, and three years later, in the fall of 1911, George Parmly Day, Yale's treasurer, sent out another battery of letters asking colleges and universities how they were managing their building and planning programs and who was doing the designing. If we can assume that those who responded represent the list to whom the inquiries were addressed, then this go-round seems to have involved a larger mailing, though apparently only to colleges and universities that had existing campuses in need of improvement and expansion. The responses described systems, if they had any, for guiding the architectural design as well as the engineering of new heating, lighting, and plumbing. Finally, Day elicited a great many opinions about the past performances of specific architects and engineers. Amherst, Williams, Harvard, Dartmouth, Penn, Brown, Columbia, Cornell, Princeton, and Bryn Mawr all wrote about what they were doing, and how, and whether they deemed it successful. Harvard's comptroller was perhaps most discouraged of all who responded, concluding "I do not believe that the policy we have followed is the correct one. I think it would be much better if we had always employed the same firm of architects, or at least had had a single consulting architect."[297] In contrast came a cheery letter from Princeton, which was way ahead of its two traditional rivals. Three years after Woodrow Wilson had written optimistically about the system so recently put in place, Andrew C. Imbrie, Princeton's financial secretary, wrote a favorable report of progress there. It was being guided by "Mr. Ralph Adams Cram, of Boston" who six years earlier had been appointed "Supervising Architect of the University." Imbrie wrote:

He drew up a comprehensive plan for the architectural and topographical development of the University… several buildings have been built in accordance with it— that is to say, that their location and general outline conform with the plan as originally drawn, though, naturally many changes in detail were introduced when each particular building came to be studied…several firms of Architects have been employed to design buildings, though our plan is to have every building approved, as to location and design, by the Supervising Architect before the contracts for it are let.[298]

Although Princeton's enthusiasm for these new planning practices encouraged Yale to adopt similar ones within a few years, the Corporation delayed the appointment of a consulting architect and the hiring of designers for specific buildings until it had made a great many more inquiries of other institutions, its own alumni, Corporation members, and their friends. The responses to Yale's subsequent questions constitute virtual performance reports by their academic clients for some of the leading American architects of the first decade of the last century. In addition to their formal inter-university correspondence, there is an especially interesting exchange of personal, confidential notes between the two chief financial officers of Yale and Princeton, Day and his friend Imbrie. It would appear that Imbrie's favorable opinion influenced the eventual choice of Frank Miles Day as Yale's first supervising architect, a position he accepted in 1913.[299]

The year 1911 emerges as pivotal in Yale's architectural history. In that year the university established a committee "to consider a plan for supervising the designing, locating, and constructing of University Buildings" and "the advisability of employing regularly a consulting architect and consulting engineer."[300] John Villiers Farwell (B.A. 1879) of Chicago

was appointed its chairman. He was a new member of the Corporation who formally represented the alumni and, less formally, the Middle West, a region that had never before had a voice in Yale's governance. Corporation members could not have appreciated just how much power, or future power, to remake the campus they were bestowing upon him with this appointment, for no one had reason in 1911 to expect that the university would soon have undreamed of resources for an enormous building campaign, or that Farwell would so decisively seize the opportunity to influence the shaping of the campus. When Harkness and Sterling made possible the transformation of Yale, Farwell came into his own. A merchant and civic leader, he brought to Yale the valuable experience he had acquired as a director of the World's Fair of 1893 and as an executive committee member for the commission that sponsored Burnham's Plan of 1909 for Chicago. Farwell devoted enormous energy and formidable intelligence to the planning of Yale. He had strong opinions on questions of design, large and small, and his surviving correspondence gives evidence that he worked diligently to convince others to see things his way. President Hadley came to nearly every meeting of Farwell's committee, as did his successor, James Rowland Angell. Their near perfect attendance records during the 1920s attest to the centrality of the committee's task in the eyes of the administration, as does its elevation to the status of a Standing Committee of the Corporation, first listed as the "Committee on Architectural Plan" in the *Catalogue of Yale University* for 1920–21.

From one point of view, it is surprising that Farwell does not seem to have pushed immediately to commission the drawing of actual plans for a Yale of the future, with specific suggestions for the three-dimensional shapes buildings should take, because such plans were so fundamentally important to other universities and were crucial in galvanizing support for the civic improvement of Chicago in which Farwell had participated.[301] But from the vantage point of the Corporation's new meeting room in Woodbridge Hall, a grand plan probably looked either superfluous or likely to provoke a bad situation for Yale within New Haven. By 1911 the Corporation had had in hand for a decade Carrère and Hastings's plan for the larger city block in which they sat, but had not yet been able to acquire all of the real estate that plan encompassed. They also had the Olmsted Brothers' plan of 1905 for the Hillhouse property, Pierson-Sage Square, but so far had realized only a fraction of its proposals and had encountered citizen displeasure over the removal of that formerly private property from the tax rolls. There might have been more opposition of that sort had Yale drawn up any larger plans, but even more painfully, to do so might well have provoked inflation of the prices for property Yale would need to realize them.

During the second decade of the century, the newly formed committee on architectural planning did, however, issue some directives aimed at coordinating the design of new buildings, and these did have an immediate effect in shaping several. As Farwell later wrote: "When the Architectural Plan Committee was first formed…the Committee recommended to the Corporation, which…adopted the recommendation, that the style of architecture in what might be called the University Center—that is the block bounded by Grove, College, Elm and York Streets and nearby—should be what is called 'Collegiate Gothic' on all new buildings."[302] Farwell tried in vain to persuade James Gamble Rogers (B.A. 1889) to become Yale's consulting architect in 1913, and his committee was then instrumental in choosing Frank Miles Day, who did accept Yale's offer to fill the newly created post. Day's best known collegiate works, in a Philadelphia-based partnership with Charles Zeller Klauder (1872–1938), were Gothic quadrangles begun in 1910 for dormitories and dining halls at Princeton: Holder, Hamilton, and Madison Halls.[303] To this experience he had added planning for Cornell, Delaware College, Penn State, and Wellesley, as well as, "in conjunction with Mr. Olmsted," for New York University.[304] He also designed buildings at many of those institutions as well as at the University of Pennsylvania, his alma mater, where he had also studied architecture. Only after protracted negotiations and the drafting and discarding of several contracts did Frank Miles Day finally accept the supervisory appointment, signing the contract on December 26, 1913. At that point, fewer than five years remained to him before an untimely death in 1918 at age fifty-seven. The contract called for no "Plan for the University." Rather, Day agreed to advise "as to the general architectural development…relating to the location, style and character…and to the selection of architects for any new buildings…and to furnish an opinion as to the suitability of sketches or plan submitted."[305] He was also to give advice about plans that had been further developed for particular buildings, and to prepare the programs for any competitions the university might decide to conduct as well as act as adviser for competitions. Day consulted on the early planning

of the Memorial Quadrangle and lived long enough to make consultative visits with Farwell to the office of James Gamble Rogers to review the project for dormitories in this quadrangle that later became Branford and Saybrook Colleges. After three years of service to Yale, Day had garnered admiration enough to be given an honorary degree. Concurrently, he held the position of supervising architect for the hospital and produced a "Proposed Lay-out of New Haven Hospital and Yale University Medical School" for a site off Cedar Street. That plan appears to have had little effect on the medical area's future growth, though Day probably helped fix the preference for the Georgian style which was later to dominate the medical neighborhood with red brick and light-colored stone trim.

Previous to Day's appointment, the administration and Corporation seriously debated the policy of allowing any supervising architect to design buildings for the university, but Day's firm designed three at Yale during his tenure. Had it not come to such an unexpectedly early end, perhaps the residential colleges built during the 1930s would have looked more like the quadrangles at Princeton. The first Day and Klauder design for Yale during this period was a relatively minor one of 1915 for the Heliostat Building, which housed the instrument for astronomical photography and printing that gave the building this peculiar name.[306] For this job, the Philadelphia firm was associated with Leoni W. Robinson, the local architect who executed so much work at the hospital. Most of the building was a tower about fifty feet tall. It lasted until 1957 on the site near Winchester Observatory later occupied by Divinity School dormitories.

At another geographical extreme of Yale's New Haven outposts, Day and Klauder's Brady Memorial Laboratory of 1917 was the first of what Reuben Holden (B.A. 1940, PH.D. 1951), writing in the 1960s, considered "the more modern buildings" of the medical school (FIG. 184).[307] For Holden, "modern" seems to have meant the Georgian buildings. The Philadelphia firm again worked in association with Robinson. They placed the laboratory right up against the sidewalk on the east side of Cedar Street, where it fell in line to help form the new quadrangular perimeter around the older hospital buildings. They left an open site on the corner of Congress Avenue, which was filled ten years later by the Brady Laboratory Annex, designed by Henry C. Pelton (1868–1935).

Day and Klauder reduced the apparent height of Brady Memorial Laboratory by placing a prominent

FIG. 184 *Brady Memorial Laboratory in the 1920s: east (Cedar Street) facade.*

parlance), his firm was also designing the Central Power Plant, just west of the Grove Street Cemetery (FIG. 185). Housing huge steam engines, the building presented a big, dark, blank brick box to Grove Street. The facade was relieved only by a raised parapet over the central, arch-topped entrance and, high above, by two relatively small window-like vents. Its sparse stone details were Gothic, and the pair of tall chimneys that rose above it were thinly trimmed as Gothic towers. From the corner of York Street, they seemed to call across Grove Street and over the site of the future Law School to Harkness Tower, which was already in the works.

———

The year 1911 not only introduced the oversight of a committee on architectural planning, but also marked the first year Yale commissioned its own graduates to design major new structures for their university.[308] One was a Yale College and School of the Fine Arts graduate, William Adams Delano (1874–1960; B.A. 1895, B.F.A. 1907), who designed the very short-lived Day Missions Library for the Divinity School (see FIG. 104) and Wright Hall on the Old Campus. Three were Sheffield Scientific School graduates: Charles Addison Ferry (1852–1924; PH.B. 1871), the engineer who designed the Yale Bowl; Donn Barber (1871–1925; PH.B. 1893), the architect for the Bowl; and Edward G. Williams (PH.B. 1887), advisory engineer for the Bowl. While at the time it may have been mere coincidence that four graduates won these important Yale commissions in the same year, in hindsight the date emerges as a watershed: thereafter not only did Yale's own win more and more design jobs at their university, but in 1923 the

cornice below the top story, partially masking it. They used stone for the raised basement to produce another strong horizontal line low on the facade where the stone met the brick of the two principal stories. Other architects who added to the row on the east side of Cedar Street followed the precedent, aligning their cornices and raised basements with those of Brady Laboratory, to make a harmonious street facade, along which there was a steady rhythm set up by the repetition of the windows' rectangles at a relatively small scale, and where the perceived height of buildings that were actually much higher was visually concentrated within a more human two stories.

In 1918, before Day's sudden death on June 15 of apoplexy (probably a stroke in modern medical

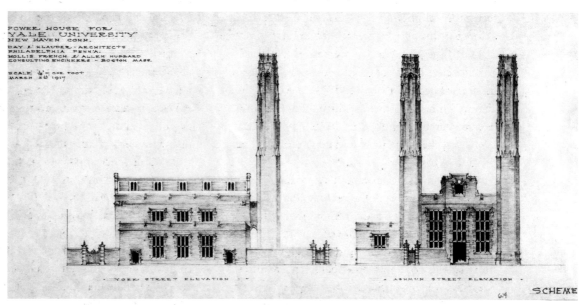

FIG. 185 *Central Power Plant: preliminary design for the York and Ashmun Street elevations by Day and Klauder, 1917. As built, fenestration was greatly reduced.*

FIG. 186 *Yale-in-China College and Hospital, Changsha, China: bird's-eye presentation drawing by T.F.H. for Murphy and Dana, 1916.*

Corporation formally established a policy giving them preference. The list of other Yale College men who became architects and designed buildings that significantly shaped the campus shortly after this date includes not only James Gamble Rogers (B.A. 1889) but also Grosvenor Atterbury (B.A. 1891), Walter B. Chambers (B.A. 1887), John W. Cross (B.A. 1900), Everett V. Meeks (B.A. 1901, B.F.A. 1917), and Egerton Swartwout (B.A. 1891). Three other Sheffield graduates who designed for Yale were Harrison Wheeler Lindsley (PH.B. 1872), Duane S. Lyman (PH.B. 1908), and Clarence C. Zantzinger (PH.B. 1892). Henry Killam Murphy (B.A. 1899, B.F.A. 1913) did important, if distant, work for Yale as well when he designed the campus for Yale in China at Changsha in 1916 (FIG. 186), in partnership with Richard Henry Dana (1879–1933; B.F.A. 1910). Dana was a graduate of Harvard who had studied architecture at Columbia and at the Ecole des Beaux-Arts before earning a degree in architecture from the Yale School of the Fine Arts. He commuted from his New York practice to teach at Yale from 1908 to 1916. Only three years before Murphy and Dana received the Yale-in-China commission, Murphy too earned a degree in architecture from Yale. In 1928 he executed a building closer to his alma mater, the Yale Hope Mission at 305 Crown Street.[309]

Architecture became a popular calling for Yale men around the turn of the century, and their individual achievements made them major figures with national reputations. All that was new in this era. Architecture was now emerging as a learned profession that was not only a potentially remunerative one, involving big business with a large office staff, but also a highly glamorous one, involving enormous, even inflated, social prestige. Delano's fame,

for instance, was to extend well beyond the profession: his face filled the cover of *Time* magazine on June 2, 1930. Nine years later his alma mater awarded him an honorary degree (M.A.).

With the exception of Lindsley, all of these architects had been students at Yale during Timothy Dwight's presidency. They must have been exposed to his sermonizing about the powerful role architecture could play in influencing the very souls of men. A new recognition that architecture was important in the nation's life and could fulfill Yale's often-repeated mission to train the country's leaders could well have been inspired by Dwight's ideas, even before an architecture program was formally established. Living near the construction sites on the Yale campus must surely have played some role in interesting these future architects in their profession. So too did the presence of the School of the Fine Arts, which introduced some undergraduates to the study of architecture. There both Yale College and Sheffield students could attend the lectures of Professor James M. Hoppin after 1879, when he left the Divinity School to occupy an office in Street Hall. For twenty years Hoppin brought Ruskinian passion and belief in the moral purpose of art to his courses in architectural history and to his books about the early Renaissance and Greek architecture.[310] He accepted emeritus status in 1899; and when he died in 1906 he left $60,000, "pending the life use on the part of a son...with which to establish a Chair of Architecture in the Art School."[311]

Hoppin's bequest, although it did not actually come to Yale until 1923, was a major boost toward a goal that had eluded John Ferguson Weir since 1869, when he became the first director of the Yale School of the Fine Arts. Its mission statement of 1872–73 specified that the school "embraces in its object the cultivation and promotion of the Plastic Arts, viz, Painting, Sculpture, and Architecture, both in their artistic and aesthetic aims, through practice and criticism."[312] During the 1870s some courses, including those in perspective drawing, were useful to future architects. Mechanical drawing was also briefly taught in Street Hall by instructors enlisted from the Scientific School's engineering program, and reciprocally, for many more years the art school offered freehand drawing classes that every freshman entering Sheffield was required to take.

The art school's first major attempt to establish a real course in architecture was short-lived and relied on technical courses in the Scientific School. In 1878 Harrison Wheeler Lindsley, who had graduated with Sheff's Class of 1872 and stayed on to earn a postgraduate degree in engineering, returned to New Haven after three years in Paris at the Ecole des Beaux-Arts. He set up an architectural practice and was listed as an instructor in architecture in the Yale School of the Fine Arts from 1879 to 1886. Only one report of Lindsley's efforts to launch architectural education in the school survives in minutes of faculty meetings:

This department commenced January first, 1879 with a class of two students—Howard Sibley and William Jewett…The course of study laid out has consisted chiefly in making the students copy the most characteristic examples of the more important styles of Architecture and read the history of those styles.

Sibley has also done some work in sketching Architectural details out of doors—and has made good progress in all his studies—Jewett on account of frequent absence has not done nearly as well as he should have done.[313]

In 1886 Harrison Lindsley opened a practice in New York, but "after five years in that city of close and severe application, his health became impaired, and he returned again to his native place in 1891." His name again appeared in the college catalogues, this time as an instructor in perspective, but only briefly, for he died of "pulmonary trouble" in late December 1893, when he was only forty-one.[314] During the two previous years, he had also done architectural work for Yale, converting the old Library Street gymnasium for use as a dining hall and designing a laboratory addition to the old Yale Medical School building on York Street.[315] Although these two minor bits of his architectural work have not survived, oversized maps of the campus that Lindsley made in the year of his death have been preserved. On them he carefully drew measured floor plans of every building

then standing (see FIGS. 102, 110, 130, 140, & 148); in some cases these are the only plans of long-demolished buildings that Yale now has in its archive.

Through the 1890s, as larger numbers of Yale College undergraduates took courses in the art school, Weir was working to expand the architectural curriculum. Late in 1893, "Professor Weir had two meetings with a committee of the Scientific School and laid before them a definite plan for instruction in Architecture," but "No action could be taken as no agreement could be reached." Weir, Hoppin, and John Henry Niemeyer (1839–1932) discussed "the question of a chair in Architecture" in a faculty meeting, but to no positive conclusion. Meeting with his faculty at the end of the school year in 1894, Weir had to report that: "The special effort made to establish a course in Architecture failed from inability to secure the necessary funds and a proper co-operation on the part of the Scientific School, but the subject now stands in a better light before the college from the Agitation in this direction—as shown in the report of the President."[316] Niemeyer, who had taught drawing in the art school since 1871, apparently tried to fill the gap left by Lindsley's death. The college catalogue for 1896–97 records his first offering of a course entitled "Architecture…adapted to students who wish to prepare themselves to enter a school of architecture or an architect's office." Niemeyer taught the course for nearly a decade, after which junior instructors took it over. The art school kept trying to set up an architecture program and annually published in the *University Catalogue* variations of the statement of 1906–7: "Until the organization of a department of Architecture shall have been completed, provisional instruction only is now given in this art, intended chiefly as an elective for undergraduates, and for those who wish some preparation for entering an architect's office…What is now provided may be considered as a course preparatory to a course in architecture."

The award to William Adams Delano in 1907 of a degree designated in the registrar's records as B.F.A.A.—the last A standing for architecture—is the earliest award of any Yale degree in architecture for which record has come to light.[317] Beginning in 1908, Richard Henry Dana commuted from New York to offer graduate students a "Technical course in Architectural Design and the fundamental principles and historic development of architecture." With an assistant instructor, he also taught undergraduates in an elective course entitled "Architecture," that met weekly for four hours in the art school and included, in 1909–10, "study of styles and orders, of the details of architectural construction, and of the rendering of original projects, supplemented by readings in the History of Art."

In 1912, John Ferguson Weir ended his forty-four year term as head of the art school. Throughout it, with little support from Yale presidents, he had nursed his early hope to establish an architecture program. Richard Henry Dana continued to teach in a three-year "regular" architecture program under the new director of the School of the Fine Arts, William Sergeant Kendall, through the academic year 1915–16. By then the "Department of Architecture" was offering a four-year program. In the annual catalogue for 1916–17, Dana's name was replaced by that of Everett V. Meeks (B.A. 1901, B.F.A. 1917), instructor in architecture. The school's architecture faculty also included two of Meeks's classmates: Arthur Kingsley Porter (B.A. 1904, B.F.A. 1917), a lecturer on the history of medieval and renaissance architecture, and Franklin Jasper Walls (B.F.A. 1917) an instructor in architecture. A succession of pairs of teachers of architecture retained the lower ranks as Meeks quickly took over not only the architecture department but also the entire art school. He became an assistant professor the year following his initial appointment, was made a full professor a year later, given an honorary degree in 1919, and designated dean elect in the catalogue for 1921–22.

Under Meeks, graduate instruction was emphasized. For 1918–19, the catalogue urged aspiring students "to obtain…a general college or science school education before entering the course in Architecture for the reason that there is much general knowledge necessary to the successful career of a fully equipped architect which cannot be included in a strictly technical course of four years duration." The next year it laid out undergraduate elective courses as well as a combined PH.B. and B.F.A. program that could be completed in seven years. By 1929 the principal architecture program leading to a B.F.A. was a five-year one, though "for those who have a bachelor's degree or who have had two years of college work, four years only" were required.

Earlier, throughout the undergraduate years of the men who would become the architects who changed the face of Yale, some architectural history was available in academic courses in the Department of Ancient Languages and Literature and the Department of History. Classical scholars, especially the archaeologists, lectured on the history of architecture at least as early as 1889–90, when an undergraduate elective course in "Topography and Monuments of Athens," taught by assistant professor of Greek Thomas T. Goodell (B.A. 1877, PH.D. 1884), first appeared in the catalogue. As Professor Goodell by 1893, he specified in his course listing that architecture figured largely in his syllabus for Greek archaeology, as it did in listings of the archaeology courses taught by Theodore Woolsey Heermance (B.A. 1893, PH.D. 1898), who joined the department just before the turn of the century. In 1900 Heermance introduced a course in Greek and Roman architecture. In the same department, Latin professor Tracy Peck's (B.A. 1861, M.A. 1864) course descriptions also mention Roman architecture; and during the first decade of the twentieth century, Paul Victor Christopher Baur lectured on Greek, Roman, and Etruscan art and architecture. Beginning in 1903, Daniel Cady Eaton (B.A. 1860, M.A. 1865), professor of the history and criticism of art, taught a graduate course in art history within the Department of History until he received emeritus status in 1907.[318] He admitted juniors and seniors if they also took drawing courses. Of his three prescribed texts, one was "Hamlin's History of Architecture."

Although, as this summary recapitulation of early architectural courses at Yale has suggested, Yale students who wanted to study architecture had to piece together formal instruction during most of the late nineteenth century and the first decade of the twentieth, the college produced during these years a remarkable slate of influential architects who served it well. Informal discussion of architecture within the walls of the Scroll and Key "tomb" must also have played some part in nourishing an interest in design that later flourished in some of the most distinguished architectural careers of Yale College graduates. It probably encouraged the decisions to study architecture in Paris that were made by the most important architects who shaped their university during the first third of the twentieth century. They were all—Atterbury, Delano, and Rogers, as well as Chambers—members of this senior society.[319] After graduating from Yale, all of these Scroll and Key architects studied at the Ecole des Beaux-Arts (as did Harrison W. Lindsley, Clarence C. Zantzinger, and Donn Barber, all Sheffield graduates). In addition, Scroll and Key numbered among its members George Parmly Day, who was treasurer of Yale from 1910 to 1942 and oversaw the financing of construction for the buildings his fellow alumni designed for Yale. John V. Farwell, chairman of the planning committee, also belonged to Scroll and Key, along with a few donors of buildings, including Edwin McClellan (B.A. 1884) and William H. Sage (B.A. 1865).

William Adams Delano—or "Billy" Delano, as he was often called in correspondence with his alma mater—had decided to become an architect when he was a child. In 1950 he recalled: "During my junior and senior years, I was thought a bit 'cracked' by my classmates because I elected courses in drawing with Professor Niemeyer, and in painting with Professor John Weir—one of the most delightful gentlemen I have ever known. (Yale men were not interested in the arts in those days.)"[320] Beginning with the Day Missions Library in 1911 and culminating in the Sterling Divinity Quadrangle over twenty years later, he would have a substantial role in New Haven. Delano's partner, Chester Holmes Aldrich (1871–1940) was a graduate of Columbia who went to the Ecole des Beaux-Arts in 1895. Delano, after graduating from Yale that same year, was a special student at Columbia's architecture school for two years, then worked for Carrère and Hastings, where he met Aldrich as a fellow employee. In 1900 Delano began his own studies at the Beaux-Arts, crediting Hastings's persuasive powers with getting him there: "At the end of nearly a year in this office, Tommy Hastings, who was a charmer, persuaded my reluctant Presbyterian family to let me go [to Paris]... The family thought it was a little short of sending me to hell."

This recollection comes from a transcript of oral reminiscences, recorded in 1950, that forms part of Delano's papers in Yale's archives. It includes his account of the formation in 1930 of the partnership of Delano and Aldrich, which soon won a remarkably important commission for a fledgling firm: the design of the Walters Art Gallery in Baltimore. He credits it to the chance of having met Henry Walters in Venice, when Walters docked alongside Cornelius Vanderbilt's (B.A. 1895) yacht while Delano was aboard, visiting his old classmate. In 1905 the young firm unsuccessfully entered a competition for work at Yale, that for the library on the Old Campus that produced Haight's Linsly Hall. And they lobbied for upcoming Yale work about which they learned from old school chums, when their friend William Sloane (B.A. 1895) told them over lunch in September 1909 that his uncles were about to build a new laboratory building. That job also went to Mr. Haight. In 1911 they entered and lost another Yale competition, for the Noah Porter Gateway, in which Howells and Stokes were victorious.

The loss of that little job was probably not so hard to take, for in addition to the Day Missions Library commission, they had just triumphed in the competition for a new dormitory on the Old Campus. It was to be named for Henry P. Wright (B.A. 1868), dean of Yale College from 1888 to 1909, a man who had so endeared himself to students that they responded by the hundreds to an appeal to honor him by building a dormitory.[321] The fundraising campaign seems to have begun with a letter from William Kent, written on letterhead that styled him "President of the Golconda Cattle Company, Nevada." It was addressed to Yale's treasurer:

My dear Mr. McClung,

You can get a big dormitory for under classmen by having a subscription list started among the alumni for a testimonial to good old Baldy Wright. It is a cinch. I'm pretty well drained of currency but will make a $1000 start.

Kent, who during his senior year had been the donor, with his father, of Kent Laboratory (see FIG. 109), went on to suggest "a plain clean brick building." His letter also assured McClung (B.A. 1892) that "the dormitory whatever its conventional name would be either Dean Wright or Baldy Wright," and had a postscript: "Baldy has been the good friend of thousands of students who would like to show appreciation of him while living."[322] A great many did. A Wright Memorial Committee was formally established at the alumni's annual Commencement meeting in June 1909. It held an architectural competition and proposed not only to build the winning scheme but also to use part of the income from room rentals to pay an annuity of $3,000 to Dean Wright and his wife. Cornelius Vanderbilt was the committee's treasurer, according to the printed appeal on which forty prominent names appeared, including that of William Kent, who used his Chicago address, rather than his more colorful Nevada one.[323]

The appeal featured a plan, an elevation, and two perspectives by Delano and Aldrich, the drawings with which they had won the competition. One was a handsome bird's-eye view of the whole campus with their proposed Wright Memorial Hall in the foreground on its corner at Elm and High. Another view, drawn as from the Old Campus, showed a many-gabled masonry building, an enlargement of a post-medieval manor house (FIG. 187). It was planned around a raised courtyard and set between Old Dwight and Durfee Halls. Early photographs taken from High Street suggest that Delano and Aldrich worked out the western and southern facades of Wright Hall in response to a context that no longer exists: Old Dwight Hall stood but a few feet south of their building until 1926. The contrac-

FIG. 187 *Wright Hall from the Old Campus: perspective view by Delano and Aldrich, with Old Dwight Hall on the left and Durfee Hall on the right, 1911.*

tor's estimate, based on the competition drawings, was $224,950.[324] Records of contributions to the building fund go on for forty pages—gifts ranged from $1 to $25,000. However, it was February 1911 before the committee's chairman, George E. Ide (B.A. 1881), was confident that enough money was on hand to authorize more substantial work by the architects.[325] Wright Hall was nearly complete and opened for inspection by its alumni donors at Commencement 1912. Following this, Delano was one of the three architects to whom Yale turned for a professional assessment of the Pope Plan of 1919, but it was not until June 1920 that he received his next commission for a major building at Yale, a chemistry laboratory. In the meantime, the First World War intervened.

In 1911, while Delano and Aldrich were at work on Day Missions Library and Wright Hall, all of Yale turned its focus to construction of the "Yale Coliseum" that we know as the Yale Bowl. Charles Addison Ferry, a Sheffield-trained engineer, had the basic idea of digging out a playing field below the natural grade and piling up the dirt from the recessed area around it to support the concrete viewing stands (FIG. 188). Donn Barber, who had worked in the office of Carrère and Hastings and studied architecture at the Ecole des Beaux-Arts after graduating from Sheffield, was responsible for the architectural design of the Bowl. They found their model in the construction of water reservoirs.[326] The Bowl was ready for a grand opening game with Harvard on November 21, 1914, when Harvard beat the home team, 36 to 0. In 1987 the Bowl was officially recognized by the National Park Service as a National Historic Landmark.[327]

The Yale Bowl was the centerpiece of an athletic complex that had been growing on thirty acres a mile and a half west of the Old Campus since 1881 (FIG. 189). In 1902 a group of alumni gave the university eighty-seven additional acres nearby.[328] These acquisitions of green space came during the period between 1870 and 1910 that was "the great athletic age at Yale," when it "became *the* power in college sports."[329]

A governing corporation of alumni initiated and guided development of these early twentieth-century athletic facilities, with a committee of twenty-one graduates who began in 1908 to plan for the property, as well as for projects farther afield.[330] In 1910, on the opposite side of town, near the mouth of the Quinnipiac River and New Haven's harbor, they built a new boathouse for the crew (FIG. 190), whose fortunes remained of consuming interest to Yale men of the period. They named it for George A. Adee (B.A. 1867), an active fundraiser who had overseen construction of the gymnasium on Elm Street in 1893 and had been a director of the "Yale Field Corporation" during the 1880s.[331] The old Yalies hired Boston architects, Peabody and Stearns, rather than any of the New York firms who more often worked in New Haven.[332] Peabody and Stearns were the designers of two Harvard boathouses that still survive as powerful landmarks on the Charles River. The charm of their beloved rivals' buildings, added to the fact that Robert Swain Peabody (1845–1917, Harvard Class of 1866), had been captain of Harvard's crew and was a lifelong sailor, doubtless recommended his work to these Yale alumni, even more than his past presidency of the American Institute of Architects.[333] Peabody and Stearns's Tudorish Adee

FIG. 188 *Construction of the Yale Bowl, October 17, 1913.*

FIG. 189 *Playing fields and the Yale Bowl after 1928.*

Boat House is rather less memorable than their designs for Harvard crews or than the firm's many Shingle Style houses of the 1880s. Though out of Yale hands, Adee Boat House still raises its scrolled gables and looks rather stiff at the water's edge, near the Quinnipiac Bridge, which carries the roaring traffic of I-95 very nearly overhead.[334]

From 1914 to 1916, while construction began on a few projects — most notably Sprague Hall for the Music School — Yale's attentions were largely diverted from campus building. In March 1917, one month before the United States finally declared war, the Corporation announced the gift of Mrs. Stephen V. Harkness to build a dormitory quadrangle in memory of her son, Charles W. Harkness (B.A. 1883), but construction on the Memorial Quadrangle and Harkness Tower was delayed by the war. It was other construction, directly supportive of Yale's war effort, that was of much greater interest to many alumni until the signing of the armistice on November 11, 1918. And more excitement was generated by such events as the arrival in September 1917 of a battery of 75mm guns loaned by the French government. (Four great-wheeled weapons, the beloved "*soixante-quinze*" still in use for military training at the time of the Second World War.) In 1915 the country's first Army Reserve Officers' Training Corps program was begun at Yale, and the following year the Yale Artillery Battalion was formed.[335] Much later George Pierson would say that the ROTC had been established at Yale "because of President Hadley's enthusiasm for light artillery maneuvers."[336]

Two war-related structures were hurriedly put up on Yale property in 1917. University funds paid for one of those, Artillery Hall, built downtown,

behind the gymnasium on Elm Street, as a "completely furnished and equipped school for artillery officers" in the Reserve Officers' Training Corps.[337] It lasted only ten years, until its site was cleared in 1927 to make way for construction of Sterling Memorial Library. But the other building, the Yale Armory and Stables, is still standing on Central Avenue near the Yale Bowl (FIG. 191), home to the Polo and Equestrian Center and the Yale Rifle Club.[338] Alumni paid for it, and a Sheffield graduate, Duane S. Lyman (PH.B. 1908), designed it, volunteering the professional services of his Buffalo firm, Lansing, Bley and Lyman. However, the appearance of the stucco-covered brick building has been much compromised since its dedication on June 19, 1917, less than two months after Congress had declared war on April 6. A. Conger Goodyear (B.A. 1899) had launched an appeal "somewhat more than a year before the United States declared war against Germany, when the University had already been committed to training future field artillery officers."[339] He wanted to build the armory as "an earnest of what the University may accomplish hereafter in service to the country." Goodyear personally guaranteed payment of any shortfall that might arise between money raised and payments needed to begin construction promptly. It was under way by November 1916. His letters about it to George Parmly Day were written in 1916 on stationery of the Goodyear Lumber Company of Buffalo. In 1918 they came from "Battery A, 307th Field Artillery, Camp Dix," where the writer was now "Captain Goodyear." When the total costs of $115,622.69 were calculated in January 1918, there remained a balance due of $14,307, which Goodyear made up through the intermediary of his wife in Buffalo. The building was "placed in temporary custody of the military authorities for the use of the second regiment...a regiment [of] which we, as citizens of New Haven, are justly proud" the secretary of the university wrote to its Colonel Isbell on June 5, 1917.

The broad frontal gable of the armory's drill hall, 100 by 220 feet, faced Central Avenue, flanked by aisles on either side, the gun sheds that were each thirty feet wide. Under its roof of asbestos-covered steel, the main hall itself, where the horse artillery drilled, was flooded by light from windows on all four sides. Windows filled all of the gable above the rear entry and, on the street facade, they surrounded a projecting two-story entry piece, which was crowned by battlements. According to the *Yale Alumni Weekly,* "Varying in size, the many windows at the sides and ends give the idea of hugeness."[340]

FIG. 190 *Adee Boat House on the Quinnipiac River, New Haven, in 1910.*

FIG. 191 *Yale Armory and Stables in 1917.*

A great many of them, including windows on the facade, are now covered over with unsightly metal plates. Twenty feet behind this building were stables "accommodating 120 horses or more" with a second floor that included "comfortably appointed living apartments for the stable men...stable sergeant... and caretaker."

Aside from the Armory, construction on the playing fields was in abeyance through the war and until 1924 when the Lapham Field House, designed by Charles Klauder, was built (FIG. 192). The Board of Control of the Yale University Athletic Association, made up of alumni, named it for Henry G. Lapham (B.A. 1897), who in 1917 made the first gift toward its construction. Klauder clad the structural steel and concrete building in red brick and stretched a white two-story porch across most of its facade, so that it looked rather like a remote, and magnified, descendent of Mount Vernon with that house's small flanking structures, there attached by gracefully curving covered walkways, here jammed against the building. In the end, it looks much like a country club in the South.[341]

The year 1927 brought three additional major structures to the athletic complex: the baseball stands, the Charles E. Coxe Memorial Gymnasium, and the Walter Camp Gateway. Both the gymnasium and the gateway reinforced the themes sounded at Lapham Field House: red brick and classicism. Lockwood, Greene and Company designed the gymnasium, 330 feet long and 159 feet wide, as one vast room with a thin veneer of classically detailed red brick stretched over a steel frame, its gable end displaying an overscaled play on a Palladian window (FIG. 193). The walls interrupt as little as possible the glass surfaces of outsized windows and support

the trusses that raise the glass roof to a ridge high above an uninterrupted volume of space designed for indoor track and baseball. From the very beginning, its users called it Coxe Cage. The gateway (see FIG. 189) honors the Yale man beatified across the land as the Father of American Football, Walter Camp (B.A. 1880). It is the design of another Yale College man, John W. Cross (B.A. 1900). On the north side of Derby Avenue it lifts four colossal white columns flanked by brick walls bearing commemorative tablets.

The gateway is a grand and imposing entrance to the walkway linking the Bowl, which is so largely invisible from its exterior and which is set at an odd angle to the street, with the baseball field on the south side of Derby Avenue, set at yet another odd angle. Wrapped around home plate with a plan in the shape of a boomerang, the concrete and steel wall backing the baseball viewing stands raised a thin, attenuated arcade above the spectators, and was perhaps also classicizing in its distant recall of a Roman aqueduct. But more immediately its designer, Charles A. Duke — an engineer registered in the state of New York — "deliberately invoked the arcaded look of the original Yankee Stadium, erected four years earlier."[342]

———

After the war, as much as William Adams Delano was valued at Yale, it was clear that James Gamble Rogers, who began work on the Memorial Quadrangle in 1917, was the university's coming architect. Previously, he had worked only for Yale-associated groups rather than the university itself, and had built well away from the Old Campus: as far away as Changsha, China, where Rogers designed, in a convincingly Chinese idiom, the Yale-in-China Hospital

FIG. 192 *Lapham Field House: drawing by D. O. Stebbins for Charles Klauder, 1923.*

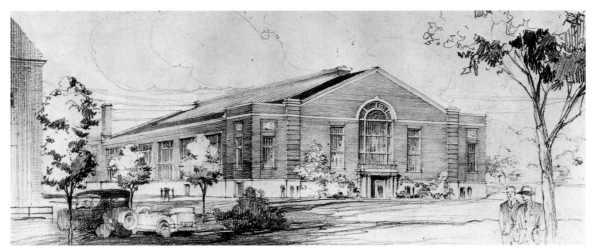

FIG. 193 *Charles E. Coxe Memorial Gymnasium (Coxe Cage): drawing by O.R.F. for Lockwood, Greene and Company, 1926–27.*

of 1915. That same year he also built a Yale boathouse at Gales Ferry, Connecticut, as well as the Yale Club in New York. As the Memorial Quadrangle took shape, Rogers secured the nearly universal confidence of the administrators and Corporation members who made the key decisions about building policy. While the dormitory group was still under construction, Yale's President Hadley wrote: "Its chief significance for Yale as a whole lies in its wonderful architectural charm. There is no group of collegiate buildings of America on anything like similar scale which equals it in beauty of design; and apart from the touch which is added by the lapse of centuries, there is nothing in Oxford or Cambridge that surpasses it." He added, recalling Timothy Dwight's words: "To those of us who believe…that the intangible influences of a university are of even greater importance than the tangible assets, the completion

of this quadrangle marks an epoch in Yale's history."[343] When the Memorial Quadrangle was completed in 1921, Hadley's final president's report included a testimonial: "The charm of design and execution have become more apparent each month. It is a work of inspired beauty. Like the best of the English colleges, it is more than an example of art; it represents the kind of art which takes hold on the lives of generations of students, and will make Yale a better place for the teaching of ideals."[344] In the ultimate undergraduate signal of approval, the senior class established priority of claim to rooms in the Quadrangle dormitories, which now eclipsed Vanderbilt as the most desirable on campus. The seniors' activities soon took root there, as Hadley's successor, James Rowland Angell, would attest in a letter of 1928 to a Corporation member: "Harvard has no such class-conscious, chauvinistic attitude in its college group as exists in the Yale College of the present generation, much less is there any such concentration of their upperclass undergraduate life as now centers in the Harkness Memorial."[345]

Despite this great success at his old college, where he had first come as a scholarship boy from Chicago, Rogers remained uncertain that Yale would ever give him another important commission. He was leery of accepting the post left vacant by the death of Frank Miles Day, though John Farwell, a home-town friend to whom Rogers was related by marriage, finally persuaded him to accept the appointment.[346] Rogers agreed to become architect of the university in November 1920. By this time Farwell was well entrenched as a powerful member of the Yale Corporation: not only did he retain the leadership he had held since 1911 of the committee that supervised architectural planning, but he also chaired the search committee that found Yale's new president at the University of Chicago. With such a friend in a strategic place, it might be supposed that Rogers would not have been so doubtful that important Yale work would come his way. But Farwell had difficulty overcoming Rogers's perception that Yale's supervising architect would be ineligible to design buildings for the university; and designing buildings, not planning for others to design them, was Rogers's real passion.[347] The terms of Rogers's appointment as supervising architect, spelled out in the annual report, included his acknowledgment that he would "not be chosen by the Corporation as architect... except where it might happen that it is the expressed wish of the donor that I be the architect."[348] That exception proved to be a large loophole, one that had been knowingly inserted into the agreement.

Rogers immediately began to attend all meetings of Farwell's planning committee and to discuss with its members every aspect of Yale's architectural development. In the new position he influenced the work of other architects who were employed by Yale, locating and guiding their production of classroom buildings and laboratories, a new theater, a natural history museum, and an art gallery.

Under a separate contract of 1921 Rogers was also hired to develop a long-postponed comprehensive plan for Yale's architectural development, prompted by the presentation to the Corporation of John Russell Pope's "Plan for the University" two years earlier. But not until 1924 was he given the kind of design job on the campus that he really most enjoyed, when he was asked to design the Wheelock-Dickinson College Dormitories on Library Street, which he later incorporated into Jonathan Edwards College.

The same year brought construction of the starkly simple and flat-roofed Bob Cook Boat House, paid for by alumni, which Rogers designed for a site on the Housatonic River in Derby, Connecticut (FIGS. 194 & 195).[349] And, with the death of Bertram Goodhue in 1924, Rogers inherited—Goodhue's successors in his office thought illegitimately— by far the largest design job at the very heart of it all: Sterling Memorial Library. His worries about getting a chance to build buildings at his old college were over.

When Rogers assumed the supervisory role in 1920, he was immediately drawn in on planning the chemistry laboratory for which Delano had been given the commission a few months earlier (FIG. 196; see also FIG. 84). The Sterling Trustees had agreed to pay for it, and Farwell's architectural planning committee had decided to place it on Pierson-Sage Square (FIG. 197), just north of Haight's Sloane Physics Laboratory (see FIG. 180). When budget restrictions pushed them to adopt brick, Henry T. Sloane, one of the donors of the neighboring physics laboratory, objected, citing the Corporation's resolutions of 1910 that dictated the use of brownstone for all new buildings on the Pierson-Sage Square. Farwell wrote to Delano on May 18, 1921: "It seemed to the Committee, and in this Mr. Rogers concurred, that we should meet Mr. Sloane's ideas, by having some mixture of the brown stone with the brick, rather than having all brick."[350] He had Delano make drawings for Mr. Sloane, illustrating "the exact relations between the Sloane Laboratory and the Chemical Laboratory." On the facade of Sterling Chemistry Laboratory, opposite Sloane Laboratory, the use of brownstone is lavish in comparison to the other facades: here it dominates the entrance surround, the buttresses, and the base below the water table, testimony in stone to Sloane's pushing Yale to conform to an earlier policy statement.

Yale scientists as future users of the laboratory also had a great deal of input, and Delano—in the tradition of his nineteenth-century predecessors Cady and Raht—had to juggle their very specific demands within his plan. Professor John Johnston, chairman of the chemistry department, and Professor Treat B. Johnson (PH.B. 1898, PH.D. 1901) were appointed to a special committee to confer with the architect and with the architectural planning committee. The chemists chose a site and drew a rough plan for a four- or five-story building. Delano recalled that at a meeting at which President Hadley presided, things came to a real impasse after Hadley told the chemists that the trustees had slated the chemists'

FIG. 194 *Bob Cook Boat House: watercolor of the original proposal by James Gamble Rogers, 1924.*

FIG. 195 *Bob Cook Boat House as built on the Housatonic River, Derby.*

preferred site for something else. Professors Johnston and Johnson "said they had no further interest in a new laboratory." When Delano then "asked what they would like, if they could have anything,"

they said a piece of ground where they could build temporary buildings, to be torn down and replaced—as need demanded. Hadley said he was afraid that that would not please the Sterling Trustees and told one of his fund of stories about visiting a lumber camp in Maine, where he was offered a drink. It was in the days of Prohibition. He asked his hosts what it was. A lumberman replied, "It's made out of molasses: we guess it's rum, but we wait until it's cool before we drink it." That put everybody in a good humor and then and there I drew out on the back of an envelope a sudden inspiration: it was a large one-story laboratory, with a sawtooth roof, which could be divided into classrooms by movable partitions; everything—

water, gas, electricity, etc., I proposed should be laid out on a unit basis and the whole area surrounded by a facade housing private laboratories for the professors… The proposal met with enthusiastic approval.[351]

In quantities of ensuing correspondence Delano repeatedly assured everybody concerned that the sawtooth roof would not be visible. And indeed it is not behind its Gothic facades, except in aerial photographs which reveal the great expanse of the building under a roof that might well have topped a large factory (FIG. 198). After the Chemistry Laboratory was dedicated on April 4, 1923, at the Annual Meeting of the American Chemical Society, the *Yale Alumni Weekly* reported that it was "the largest single unit devoted to chemical purposes that has ever been constructed," recording the maximum length at 328 feet and maximum width at 256 feet, yielding

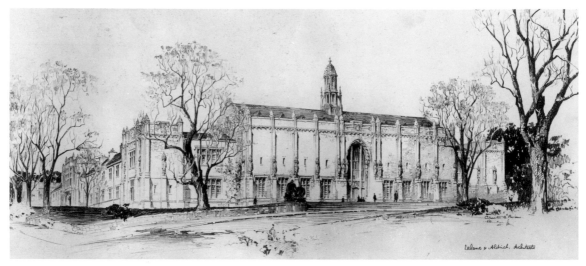

FIG. 196 *Sterling Chemistry Laboratory: south elevation by Chester B. Price for Delano and Aldrich, ca. 1920. The small tower was not executed.*

FIG. 197 *Excavation of the Sterling Chemistry Laboratory site from the south, September 7, 1921.*

FIG. 198 *Sterling Chemistry Laboratory from the east in an aerial view of Pierson-Sage Square in 1954, with Sloane Physics Laboratory on the far left.*

FIG. 199 *Sage Hall: perspective drawing by Chester B. Price for William Adams Delano, 1922.*

a total finished floor area of 167,580 square feet.[352] For all that, Yale's architectural planners took into account the probability of its future expansion when they positioned its neighbors.

Chief among them was the School of Forestry, founded in 1900 by the Pinchot family and housed in Marsh Hall (see FIG. 132), the former residence of Professor Othniel C. Marsh. William Henry Sage (B.A. 1865) chose Delano as the school's architect, designating his choice as a provision of the $300,000 gift he offered on May 7, 1920, to build and maintain Sage Hall (FIG. 199).[353] Doubtless, Sage's choice of the forestry school as beneficiary of this largess owed something to the fact that his fortune was based on one his father had made in the lumber business in Ithaca, New York. Sage gave the building in memory of his youngest son DeWitt Linn Sage (B.A. 1897), who had died in 1901.[354] Dean James W. Toumey of the School of Forestry wanted to stake out space for enlargement of his domain, which he expected to be rapid because Yale had inherited Cornell's forestry students and leadership in the field when New York State cut off funding for Cornell's school. And Toumey felt some real priority of claim in the parceling out of the thirty-acre Pierson-Sage tract. His interests were defended by Anson Phelps Stokes, who reminded John V. Farwell in May 1921 that he was "personally very much interested in this matter because, as you know, I was mainly responsible for securing the Pierson-Sage Square." When there was talk of siting the Forest School off near the Observatory, Stokes weighed in — effectively in the end — favoring its placement in the square that was fast being claimed by the sciences. He cautioned Farwell against putting "the Forestry School into a small corner," and sited a clause in the property's purchase

agreement stipulating that it "is to be mainly used for the Forest School, the Botanical Gardens, the proposed School of Irrigation of Yale University, or for similar purposes, and for no other purposes unless approved by the Corporation." While conceding that this wording was open to broad interpretation, Stokes wrote: "I feel under moral obligation to try to see that the Forestry School is amply provided for on the property, and feel that it is the part of tact in dealing with Mr. Hillhouse to do so." Yale still did not own the small acreage immediately surrounding the Hillhouse mansion. "We want his central property very badly, and we should not give him any reasonable ground for criticism."[355] In the mix of pressures that always shaped Yale buildings, Yale's hunger for a key piece of a neighbor's real estate came to the fore in determining the eventual placement and shaping of Sage Hall. But so did the involvement of a powerful member of the administration. Stokes concluded his letter: "Of all buildings, a building devoted to Forestry, which should suggest out-of-door life and interests, should not be put in a little corner with buildings on two, and probably ultimately on three sides."

Rogers played his official supervisory role through the complicated process of siting Sage Hall and shepherding the architect through design development. Its program, devised by the school's professors, was first sent to Rogers, who was to deliver it to Delano. By early 1922 all those with conflicting interests had settled on the present site, on the western slope of Science Hill, fronting Prospect Street. The *Yale Alumni Weekly* for February 24 published a perspective drawing and a plan. The architectural planning committee had prescribed Sage Hall's brownstone and its Gothic stylization, which Delano

had used to design tall, flat, four-story facades coming down the hillside, looking soberly post-medieval, derived from domestic models rather than the ecclesiastical forms of the full-blown Gothic. Above the flat-headed windows, some of his facades have steep gables; others are topped by parapets that hint of battlements over suggestions of towers where he pushed halls and elevators forward to express them as distinct elements. In the article accompanying his illustrations, Delano wrote proudly about the design, admitting "it is quite as unreasonable to expect an unprejudiced description of a building about to be erected, from the architect, as it is to look for an unbiased description of a new-born baby from the mother." By April 1930 Delano's sketch plans for adding " two units" to the north of this building were under review by Yale planning committees, and the addition—Bowers Hall—was built in 1931. It includes a high, pleasant auditorium filling a two-story space.

The wishes of a donor determined the siting of another of Delano's contributions to Yale's Collegiate Gothic, William L. Harkness Hall, completed in 1927 (FIG. 200). This classroom building found its place between Wall Street and the Cross Campus only after Mr. Harkness's widow had been persuaded with difficulty to give up the idea of building on the Old Campus, where her husband had intended to place his building. After she relinquished the site of Cady's Dwight Hall, and had that building demolished to clear the view of Harkness Tower from the Old Campus, and after she gave thought to replacing Osborn Hall with her classroom building, she was finally induced to accept one of the few sites available near the heart of Yale, next to Sprague Hall.

Rogers used the Gothic stone mass of William L. Harkness Hall to hide the red brick and classical details of Sprague Hall from his new Cross Campus. He was able to integrate Delano's building into the new Gothic vista from College Street, past new Gothic colleges, focused on Sterling Library, which was completed in 1930. Here, he gave the citizenry a clear view of the building that housed the symbolic core of the university—the books whose giving marked, at least in myth, the foundation of the school—when he laid out a broad grassy lawn before it, inviting unobstructed entry from College Street to its front door. The library, with its treasure room enshrining the Gutenberg Bible, was a place of public pilgrimage, and Rogers announced the way to it in this formal and emphatic way from the streets of the city.

Strengthening the Gothic presence in this vicinity, and intended to be "an important factor in the development of the Pope Cross-Campus plan,"[356] much of which Rogers was implementing, a new infirmary rose in 1929 across College Street, south of William L. Harkness Hall. The New York firm of Cross and Cross, headed by John W. Cross (B.A. 1900), who had designed the Walter Camp Gateway two years earlier, was responsible for this Department of University Health (FIG. 201).[357] Cross was another Yale graduate who went on to earn a diploma from the Ecole des Beaux-Arts (1906) and attained national importance during the early twentieth century. In 1918 he became chief architect for the U.S. Housing Corporation of the Department of Labor,[358] whose Wartime Emergency Housing—largely forgotten by modern architectural historians—remained the greatest accomplishment of the federal government in the planning and design of public housing until the coming of the Hope VI program at the end of the century.

A decade after World War I, Cross and Cross clad the Department of University Health in Indiana limestone, by then customary for Yale's Collegiate Gothic buildings. They called on another alumnus, Charles F. Neergaard (B.A. 1897) "as Hospital Consultant" for the job. Rogers intended the infirmary to define the southern edge of an extended Cross Campus, continued across College Street, following Pope's scheme. Because its principal entry—centered beneath three gabled pavilions topping the four stories of the infirmary's most important elevation—was meant to address the lawn of this elongated Cross Campus, the building was given relatively narrow frontage on College Street, with a lesser entrance there under the steep gable of the roof. The Cross Campus extension was never realized however, its axis still blocked by the red-brick bulk of a former Sheffield student society building, Franklin Hall of 1910, with its showy white classicizing trim (see FIGS. 160 and 178). The School of Music now inhabits the former infirmary at 435 College Street, which was renamed Leigh Hall in 2001 to honor Abby and

Mitch Leigh (B.MUS. 1951, M.MUS. 1952), long-term supporters of the school. Yale has used Franklin Hall for a variety of offices since buying it in 1935.

At the same time that Rogers was orchestrating framed views of the Gothic heart of the university north of the Old Campus, Yale was extending the Gothic facade she presented to New Haven on its southern edge by building along Chapel, the city's busiest commercial street. The university's boldest move was to throw a bridge across High Street just back from Chapel Street (FIG. 202). This formed the most impressive entrance anywhere from the city to the campus. Beyond it, Harkness Tower dominated the view along High Street, which gave automobile access to the library until the block between Elm and Wall Streets was closed to traffic in 1992. The idea of a bridge linking Street Hall with a new gallery for the art school across High Street had been kicking around at least since 1898, when Timothy Dwight suggested this in his annual report, noting that "If the two buildings were to be connected by a bridge or covered passageway, constructed after some fine architectural design, the whole combined edifice belonging to the school would be an ornament to the city as well as a useful and beautiful home of the

FIG. 201 *Department of University Health: west (College Street) facade.*

FIG. 202 *High Street Bridge: south (College Street) facade.*

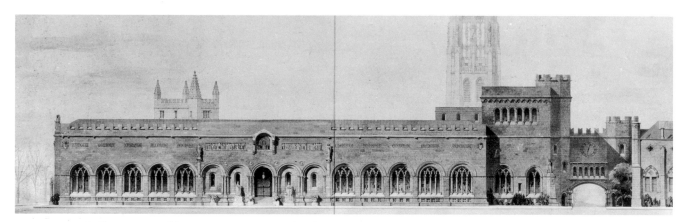

FIG. 203 *Art Gallery: proposal by Egerton Swartwout for the complete Chapel Street facade, 1926.*

FIG. 204 *Art Gallery: plan of the ground floor by Egerton Swartwout, 1926.*

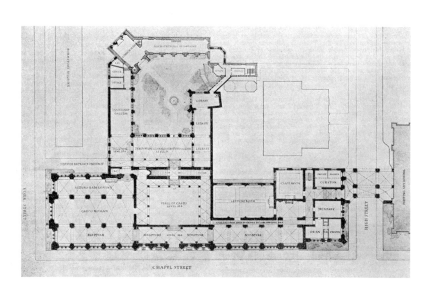

FIG. 205 *Art Gallery: proposal by Egerton Swartwout for the Chapel Street facade as built, 1926.*

Fine Arts in the University." Neither Pope nor Rogers showed a bridge across High Street in their plans for Yale. But the idea had not been lost, and in November 1924 Yale appointed another Yale graduate, Egerton Swartwout (B.A. 1891), architect for a new museum, connected by a bridge to Wight's old art building. When Swartwout's drawings were first published, along with the announcement that two anonymous donors had given a million dollars to erect the first half of a university art museum, Yale predicted that the bridge would "add to New Haven an architectural detail second to none for its beauty and old-world feeling." Its erection over a public street was of course subject to approvals from relevant authorities, and Yale assured them that "such an arch would not interfere with traffic, but would add greatly to the beauty of the City."[359]

The ambitious scheme published in the *Yale Alumni Weekly* at the time of the gift's announcement in 1926 showed more towers than were executed, in an asymmetrical grouping on the west side of High Street, and a much longer facade on Chapel Street (FIG. 203). Swartwout's museum would have filled the length of the block between High and York Streets. The facade had a total of seventeen round-headed arches arrayed along Chapel Street. They were Romanesque in inspiration, and twelve were filled with Gothic tracery. Swartwout's plan (FIG. 204) showed a great length of vaulted galleries behind the long facade, paralleling it. A door centered in the principal fifteen-bay frontispiece of that facade opened through the vaulted gallery to a great "hall of casts," a cloister around a two-story space. Behind this, the plans melded into the complex of buildings around an open courtyard that still another

alumnus architect, Everett Meeks, was developing as Weir Hall for the architectural program.

The same issue of the *Yale Alumni Weekly* also illustrated the portion of Swartwout's facade for which the million-dollar gift could pay, the part that would therefore be built immediately (FIG. 205). Only the bridge, anchored by a reduced clustering of towers, and five of the fifteen bays that fronted the principal low mass along Chapel Street were built. Because construction stopped short of the proposed principal entry, a door was introduced in a truncated tower near the bridge, with a balconied window above it. Ultimately, that was all of Swartwout's scheme that Yale would ever build. The site of its proposed western wing is now occupied by Louis I. Kahn's Art Gallery of 1953.

As plans for the art museum were taking shape, Rogers oversaw the building of several other, less memorable Collegiate Gothic buildings. Worries about severe limitations imposed by the budget plagued one of these, the University Theatre at the head of Library Street, from the very inception of its planning in 1924. Gothic and stone masonry were mandated because of its proximity to the Harkness group, but working within their budget, Blackall, Clapp and Whitemore produced a facade that was soon deemed too severe. Rogers improved it in 1931.

Rogers campaigned actively at Yale for the assignment of architectural work to fellow alumni, and Blackall, Clapp and Whittemore were one of the few non-alumnus firms to be awarded commissions in the 1920s and 1930s. In 1923, Rogers went so far as to give notice of his resignation as consulting architect, which he afterwards retracted, specifically in protest to the award of a design commission to a non-Yale

135 degrees. Klauder turned that corner by drawing his entry piece back as a concave curve, nearly a quarter round, in the middle of which he set the front door. And here he concentrated most of the building's ornament—abstracted, modernized classical motifs, among which a few finicky traditional ornaments were plastered. This concave entrance facade was the building's centerpiece, four stories high, and was surmounted by a parapet that stepped up above it. The three bays of that centerpiece had themselves already stepped awkwardly up from the three-story bulk of the two long wings on either side.

Klauder's entrance piece and the wings along Cedar and Broad Streets were constructed during 1923 and 1924 (FIG. 210), but his principal facade did not last very long. It disappeared when Grosvenor Atterbury subsumed Klauder's building within his much larger Sterling Hall of Medicine of 1929 and faced it with more regularly classical facades. Behind them he integrated a "psycho-biological unit" for which, according to minutes of the Architectural Plan Committee, he was asked in February 1926 to "prepare a sketch plan."

By 1926 Atterbury was another Yale College graduate who had achieved fame as a major architect, one in the forefront of the planning movement. Atterbury not only designed mansions for the very rich but also housing for the middle class, most famously in his Forest Hills Gardens, the planned community in Queens, New York, begun in 1909 and under construction into the 1920s. In this precedent-setting project of the Russell Sage Foundation, Atterbury had experimented with the use of precast concrete sections to lower housing costs. He clad them in picturesque forms derived from Tudor precedents. Though his technological experiment was not an economic success, as a real-estate development the beautiful neighborhood he designed with Frederick Law Olmsted, Jr., continues to flourish, and the strong community that has evolved in the setting he created has never ceased to engage the admiration of progressive planners.

For Yale, he undertook no such bold experiment. To enlarge the Sterling Hall of Medicine, Broad Street was closed (FIG. 211; see also FIG. 85), and across its site Atterbury added to Klauder's building another curved facade to form a half-round recess for a central, pedimented portico that now serves as the main entrance to the medical school, fronting Cedar Street. It links the Sterling Hall of Medicine with Atterbury's building for the Institute of Human Relations—that "psycho-biological unit" on which

he had begun work in 1926 (FIG. 212). The Institute of Human Relations building, funded by the Rockefeller Foundation, was constructed to house a new entity, one for which hopes and ambitions were high, but one that came to very little in the end. Its program was to foster integrated research leading to a holistic understanding of human behavior. Such work could potentially transform understanding of the physical and mental being entire, so its founders wanted it built, as it was, in the medical center. But many of them contended that the Law School and even the Divinity School belonged nearby as well. President Angell, who wanted graduate study positioned more coherently within the physical plant of the university, was among those who leaned toward grouping it all near the hospitals. Indeed, there was discussion, and a lot of letter writing between President Angell and members of the Corporation, about placing all graduate study near the medical center, especially graduate work in the social sciences.

Taking graduate study and especially the Law School away from the heart of Yale seemed a bad idea to John V. Farwell, whose power as chairman of the Corporation's Committee on Architectural Plan was by then well entrenched. In 1928 he argued against the removal of the Law School to the medical area in a series of letters to members of the Corporation. In one of them he cautioned:

Personally, I cannot see how the location will necessarily affect the type of law school which we wish to conduct in New Haven, nor can I see the intimate relations between the Law School and the School of Human Relations. It does not seem to me to be as directly connected with it as, for instance, the Department of Industrial Engineering, including the personnel department...History is simply the story of Human Relations, while everything we have, except astronomy, has some bearing on the Human Relations element.[361]

As Farwell later recorded, "though Dean Winternitz [of the School of Medicine] and later on Robert M. Hutchins [dean of the Law School] had also favored it...the plan was prevented...When this move finally came up in the Corporation there was only one man voted for it."[362]

The grand vision of an Institute of Human Relations at the heart of graduate education at Yale flourished under Angell's administration. Gaddis Smith has written about it in a forthcoming book, *Yale and the Exterior World: The Shaping of the University in the Twentieth Century*.[363] He has found that Angell was approached by leaders of the eugenics movement about the possibility that they might endow

FIG. 210 *School of Medicine and hospital buildings from the southeast in 1926, showing what was built of Klauder's Sterling Hall of Medicine (center right).*

FIG. 211 *School of Medicine and hospital buildings from the southeast in the early 1930s, showing Atterbury's additions to the Sterling Hall of Medicine and Pelton's Clinic Building.*

professorships of eugenics. According to Smith, Angell agreed that the key to understanding human behavior was eugenics, but the existing faculty did not support such a professorship. Given the direction which study of hereditary improvement of the race by genetic control was soon to take in Germany, the faculty's shying away from eugenics when they did so seems wise and fortunate. The stock market crash and the Depression dried up the promised support from the proponents of eugenics, while the Rockefeller Foundation ended its funding of an institution that had disappointed its grand promise by using its splendid building for an assortment of traditional projects. It is interesting that the building Atterbury designed for an institute that was supposed to be so bold and experimental was very traditional in its outward appearance. It was much more

conservative and correct in its classicism than the short-lived modern classical facades on Klauder's Hall of Medicine.

Red-brick Georgian facades rose over ever-increasing square footage in the hospital area during the period leading into the Depression, enclosing and replacing most of the High Victorian Gothic of the late nineteenth century. The largest classical hospital structure of them all was Henry C. Pelton's Clinic Building of 1929–31 (FIG. 213; see also FIGS. 85 & 211). Pelton was a New York architect who, with James Gamble Rogers, beginning in 1926 designed a series of rural health centers for the Commonwealth Fund, a Harkness family charity. His best known work is the Memorial Sloan-Kettering Hospital of 1937–38 in New York, which again was designed with Rogers. In New Haven, Pelton's Clinic Building

FIG. 214 *Sheffield-Sterling-Strathcona:*
presentation drawing by Schell Lewis
for Zantzinger, Borie and Medary, 1929.

FIG. 215 *Construction of Sheffield-Sterling-Strathcona, September 24, 1931.*

questions arising from the application of scientific knowledge to the Industrial, Social and Economical problems of the time...with special reference to the construction, equipment and operation of transportation of passengers and freight."

Strathcona Hall is the wing of the building that faces Grove Street, where modest reliefs — an anchor, a biplane, a steamship — stand out against the smooth stone skin of the building.[365] On the facade fronting Hillhouse Avenue is a stone inscribed: "This stone is from/Mt. Sir Donald in the Selkirk Mountains/British Columbia/named to honor/Sir Donald Smith/Lord Strathcona." The Strathcona wing houses offices and classrooms and originally had a library devoted to work in transportation. Its grandest room is a large lecture hall that has its own entrance, through a lobby, from the street. The lecture hall's exposed-beam ceiling is painted, in the spirit of medieval heraldry, with motifs adapted from Lord Strathcona's coat of arms, including a maple tree with a beaver working at its base, a lion rampant, a railroad spike crossed with a hammer, codfish, thistles, and fleurs-de-lis. Leaded medallions in the center of its windows depict an array of vehicles, from a quaint old locomotive to a newer steam-powered one, from a full-rigged sailing ship to a pontoon boat and an ocean liner, and on through an intriguing display of transportation's variety: a dirigible, a monoplane, an aerial tramway, a trolley.

The Sheffield Hall wing, along Prospect Street, preserves the name of the donor of the old South Sheffield Hall, which was demolished in 1931 to make way for Sheffield-Sterling-Strathcona. At its core was a building that James Hillhouse (B.A. 1773) had begun constructing in 1812 for a hotel but sold to Yale two years later for its "Medical Institution" before opening it for business. Joseph E. Sheffield bought it in 1858 when the medical school moved to new quarters, added two wings, and gave it to Yale for the Scientific School; further enlargement in 1865 included a central tower that faced Grove Street and housed an equatorial telescope (see FIGS. 112, far right, and 158, lower right). Displacing that quirky Italianate Victorian landmark, the Sheffield wing of Sheffield-Sterling-Strathcona originally housed administrative offices of the Scientific School, offices of the Department of Industrial Administration, classrooms, and accounting laboratories. Although numerous modest reliefs of scientific apparatuses — rock hammers, a microscope, a light bulb, a vacuum tube — decorate its rear facades, the great feature of the Sheffield Hall wing is its covered portico with a wooden ceiling elabo-

rately painted, gilded, and inscribed "Sheffield Scientific School," and decorated with evocative mathematical symbols — for plus, minus, multiplication, infinity, pi, and the like. The portico serves as something of a reliquary, sheltering a large chunk of pink sandstone conglomerate inscribed: "This stone was part of/Sheffield Hall/which stood on this site/the earliest building of/the Sheffield Scientific School/1860–1931."

Sheffield-Sterling-Strathcona was planned, according to an anonymous writer in the *Yale Alumni Weekly* of February 12, 1928, to be the "handsomest building of the new Sheff Square" that had been rising north and west of the Bicentennial Buildings since the construction of the Vanderbilt-Scientific dormitories just after the turn of the century. That writer could predict that "when the Hillhouse property begins to be used for future University purposes," the new building "will be at the exact geographical center of the future Yale University." Could he also have suspected that administrators of the greater university would so soon displace the Sheffield School's officers in that strategic location? Considerable space within Sheffield-Sterling-Strathcona that remained officially unassigned well into the design detailing phase might already have been unofficially assigned to the business of the greater university. In 1933, as Sheffield's administrators occupied their new offices, Yale was implementing major changes in the character of its undergraduates' education. When the first colleges had opened two years earlier, they welcomed not only Yale College undergraduates, but also those enrolled at the Sheffield School, erasing much of the school's separateness. Soon Yale would further restructure the curriculum and totally absorb the Scientific School within the greater university. In the fall of 1945, as the Sheffield School became the university's division of science, the Dean of Yale College, William C. Devane, moved into offices in "SSS," and the building became the permanent seat of the Registrar of Yale College.

In the early 1930s, as Yale was planning and building these tallest and most elaborate of its Gothic structures, the Architectural Plan Committee's members were also awakening to the several appeals of red-brick Georgian for major building projects. None of their favored alumni architects used the Georgian with quite the finesse of William Adams Delano. As well designed as his Gothic essays for Yale were, it was in classical forms, usually softened as expressions of the Georgian mode, that his office came into its own at the university as well as in a wider world.

FIG. 221 *Weir Hall, ca. 1924: south (Chapel Street) facade, with Skull and Bones on the far right.*

of his concern is preserved in a letter Rogers wrote in 1928 to Thomas Farnam (B.A. 1899), who was secretary of the university at the time:

When I was up in New Haven, I noticed that the model for the pinnacles of the old Library show that these were to be restored with caps that were not like the original caps on the old building. I was very much disturbed by this because it seems to me to be a great mistake. We are keeping the old Library, not because it is a great piece of Gothic Architecture, but because it is one of the older buildings and certainly has a charm from its naive manner. I think we should do everything to keep the spirit of the building. Do you not think so?[382]

Rogers's efforts to save the Berkeley Oval have already been discussed, and the many drawings he made in planning for the building campaigns of the 1920s and 1930s reveal his diligent attempts to accommodate existing structures, while fitting in the enormous new graduate and professional schools, the library, and all the new colleges. Some were eventually razed, but there is ample evidence in the Yale archive that Rogers's concern for the work of his predecessors was genuine. It is also clear from the records of the Corporation and of its Committee on Architectural Plan that crucial decisions on demolition were not in the end left to his discretion.

After giving so much attention to the history of Yale's architecture between the Civil War and the Depression, it is clear that many devoted individuals produced a number of interesting buildings—and some rather fine ones—during the period, and that Yale soon demolished many of those buildings. It would indeed be fascinating to see the Yale of 1910 that has so largely disappeared. However, James Gamble Rogers's Yale of 1945, to which so much of that was sacrificed, was an architectural achievement of much greater magnitude. If money had been available, it might have been better to buy alternative sites for some of the new colleges so that Hunt's Divinity School, for instance, could have been saved and adapted to some other use. It would have been wonderful if someone had arisen with the foresight and eloquence to save Osborn Hall, both for itself and to have kept that strategic corner porous, open to easy communication with the town. Yet it was probably easier in the 1920s for someone with an informed concern for architecture to sanction the destruction of so many buildings that were pretty good than it would be today. Then, one could have confidence that something good was being sacrificed for something better. (Osborn for Bingham always excepted). The preservation movement of our own generation has flourished because so many people recognized that something good was all too often being sacrificed for something very bad indeed, and that too few of modern architecture's bold experiments were creating places where anyone wanted to be. In the 1920s, a walk through the Memorial Quadrangle would have given anyone confidence that Rogers had the power to create a place that was better than the old places, and one that students infinitely preferred. And Rogers's beautiful drawings of things to come, which promised more of the same, did not lie. In fact, the new reality was often even better than they were.

The drawings could hardly have conveyed what Rogers was actually able to accomplish with something so seemingly minor as a ten-foot increase in the distance between the facades of the buildings on either side of Blount Avenue. The space between the five- and six-story facades of the Berkeley Oval and the equally tall walls of West Divinity Hall was seventy-five feet. Blount Avenue looked like a rather ordinary city street in the Bronx (see FIG. 154). Rogers increased by only ten feet the distance between his new Berkeley College and Pope's Calhoun College, and they rose just as many stories. But he and Pope shaped the rise, sloping setbacks and roofs away from the verticals almost naturalistically in comparison with the plumb lines from cornice to ground of the older buildings. The two architects also stepped the walls in and out enough to relieve the former monotony of the place and to enrich its space. They chose the materials carefully, using stone with a warm honeyish glow, consciously intended to brighten the grimness of the bleak Connecticut winter. Blount Avenue received just enough extra light and air and so much loving detail as to become a graceful way through a collegiate precinct not quite garden, but special indeed, distinguished from the ordinariness of city streets.

Rogers, who is so much criticized for closing Yale's residential colleges off from the life of the street, was given no choice but to do so. It was a directive worked out in the Committee on Architectural Plan and ratified by the Corporation, consciously reacting against the openness to New Haven that Pope had proposed. Nevertheless, while guarding his domestic enclaves from public trespass and largely from public view as well, Rogers was skillful in shaping and opening out the approaches to those places where Yale wished to receive a broader public— Sterling Library most of all (see FIG. 285). And while the public was not welcomed to the residential colleges, it was meant to be beguiled by the carefully modulated elevations and beautiful details of their facades on the street, all of which were softened by the exquisite plantings of Beatrix Farrand. Comparing these facades with the monotonous residential blocks offered by Cady's firm a generation earlier leaves little doubt that Yale's sacrifice of capital investment was wisely made. And was the sacrifice of other individual buildings justified by a more coherent vision of the university as a whole? The generation of John Farwell thought that it was. The surviving evidence suggests they were usually right.

He saw the plan's purpose as twofold: to rationalize the chaotic development of the past and to guide orderly growth in the future. He couched his idealism in pragmatic terms, however, noting that a plan is primarily a "business proposition:" "A city developed on a well-considered plan based on an organic design founded on a principle clearly seen, has its valuations raised, its grand list greatly increased, and attracts a higher class of citizens. This is now so well recognized that the leading American cities have invited experts from the outside to study and report a plan."[6] Seymour's formulation hit upon most of the Progressive Era's principles of urban planning and reform. The rational order of a plan had to supplant the laissez-faire, makeshift arrangements of the recent past. This would bring not only physical but also moral order, creating an environment conducive to a "higher class of citizens." The plan's success was contingent on its "organic" character, that is, arising from the city's own history and traditions and not imposed as a generic solution. Nevertheless, it should be in the hands of newly minted outside experts, insulated from "local prejudices." And, most of all, it had to be attended to with businesslike efficiency, the model of success being the modern commercial enterprise that had emerged so vigorously in the Gilded Age.

Seymour had another rationale for emphasizing efficiency and professionalism. Although the City Beautiful Movement had reached its zenith at the time of his "Open Letter," it had also gained a reputation among urban leaders and citizens as an undertaking primarily concerned with aesthetics rather than practical benefits. This view was to haunt New Haven's improvement efforts in the coming years, despite Seymour's pointed efforts to disavow it. "In an undertaking of this sort, beauty is secondary; utility is and must be the first consideration," he argued in his letter. "To make our City more convenient, easier to live in, easier to do business in, easier to keep clean, and in every way a better and more wholesome place—these are the primary objects."[7]

With insight born of his historical perspective, Seymour saw a direct line from New Haven's past to its future. The starting point for a twentieth-century plan was to be found in the city's original frame, the famous nine-square plan laid out by the Puritan colonists in 1638. "The plan of New Haven with its central square suggests the principle on which the City should be developed," he wrote. "When we better realize what a heritage we have in the Green we shall carry on in a larger spirit and with a clearer

vision the improvement of a plan so happily begun for us by the founders of the City."[8]

New Haven had had a long and fitful development since its founding. For the first hundred and fifty years, it grew slowly, filling out its nine-square grid but retaining the modest scale of a well-ordered colonial town (see FIG. 2). Only after the Revolutionary War and the town's incorporation as a city in 1784 did it begin to expand beyond the original limits and consciously cultivate its physical character. Much of this transformation was instigated by James Hillhouse (B.A. 1773), whose own campaign for civic improvement included subdividing the original nine blocks, extending new streets and highways (including his eponymous avenue to the north), establishing a public cemetery, transforming the Green into an ordered civic square, and planting the row upon row of elm trees for which New Haven became so famous. Following on the heels of these improvements, new outlying neighborhoods were settled in the 1820s and 1830s, often centered, like the nine-square plan itself, on a public square (see FIG. 5). These included the "New Township" around Wooster Square to the east; and York, Jocelyn, and Spireworth (later renamed Trowbridge) Squares to the north, east, and south.[9]

Urban expansion from the 1790s to 1830s provided the physical framework for the enormous growth of the late nineteenth century. Like many cities along the northeastern seaboard, New Haven was intensively urbanized from the 1860s onward, with new industries and successive waves of European immigration transforming the scale and face of the city (FIG. 223). From 1870 to 1900, New Haven's population more than doubled, from 40,000 to 108,000. After the turn of the century, growth from immigration increased sharply; and by 1910, the immigrant population exceeded 50 percent in every ward except the First, a stronghold of Yale and Yankee elites.[10] It was the thriving, industrial New Haven of 1907, a city that had become a stranger to itself in the last forty years, that Seymour was addressing in his call for civic reform.[11] His was not a reactionary plea for "native" control, however, decrying social dislocations or industrial ills. He focused instead on the city's lack of managed change and made optimistic and practical-minded proposals for meeting the opportunities that lay ahead. First among them, as previously noted, was to recognize the inherent value of the Green, an asset "we should seek in every way possible to preserve as a center for the civic and social life of the people of the City." Seymour associated it with the City Beautiful planning ideal of the

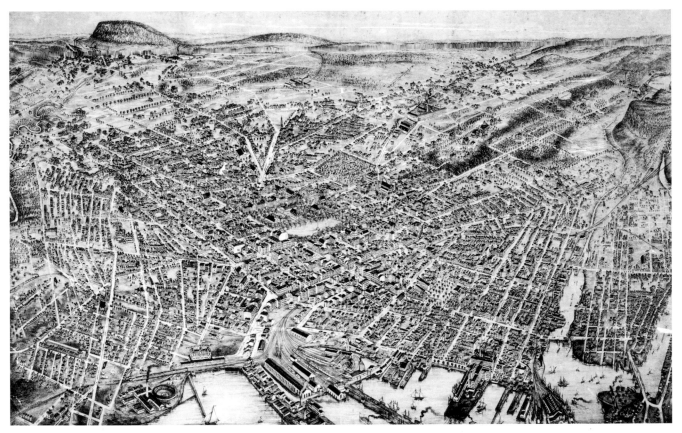

FIG. 223 *"The City of New Haven, Connecticut," 1879.*

civic center, arguing that its re-creation as such, with new public buildings, was "in line with its original purpose and actual historical function…for nearly two hundred and seventy-five years." He saw another planning opportunity in the design of a grand avenue linking a new Union Station to downtown. "It requires but little imagination to picture a fine street leading from the new railway station to the Green," Seymour noted, "forming a stately approach to the largest open square in the heart of any city that I recall."[12]

He reserved his final thoughts for two of the most pressing urban issues of the day: the need for public parks and improved streets. New Haven's collection of nineteenth-century squares and parks required a coordinated master plan. So too did its network of streets (FIG. 224). Although the extent of the automobile's impact was barely foreseeable at this point, population growth made the prospect of an urban grid throttled by traffic seem imminent. Seymour's answer to both challenges typified his era's approach: "Impatience will not solve it. But experts can do it, and will do it, if we will be reasonable and progressive and give them a chance."[13]

Seymour's letter catalyzed New Haven's citizenry. Rapturous headlines met its publication: "All Praise

Mr. Seymour's Plan," "They All Want a City Beautiful," and "Seymour's Plan Called Invigorating."[14] To build on the momentum, Seymour quickly enlisted Cass Gilbert, the prominent New York architect who had been commissioned in 1907 to design the city's new Union Station, to follow up with a letter to the New Haven papers. "[Mr. Seymour's] recommendations are of such self-evident merit that they need no argument to sustain them," Gilbert wrote on June 5. "What can be done elsewhere can be done in New Haven, and the advantages that New Haven now possesses should be utilized to maintain the reputation which it formerly had as one of the most beautiful places in this country."[15] New Haven's mayor, John Studley, called for an open meeting of citizens on June 19 to discuss Seymour's proposition, and they resolved to form a Civic Improvement Committee to commission a master plan. The committee included, among others, Seymour, the mayor, Yale secretary Anson Phelps Stokes, Jr. (B.A. 1896), and Connecticut governor Rollin Woodruff as chairman. The balance of members came from the city's social and business elite, many of whom belonged to New Haven's oldest families. In a reflection of changed times, the committee broadened its make-up, if only slightly, by including Sylvester

FIG. 224 *New Haven in 1907: looking west from Chapel and State Streets. New Haven Colony Historical Society.*

Poli, a prominent businessman, "in order that our Italo-American citizens might be represented."[16]

The committee's first tasks were to take up a private subscription to underwrite the cost of the plan and to hire the experts who would produce it. Seymour lobbied successfully for Cass Gilbert (1859–1934), who was retained shortly thereafter as the architect of the new public library as well.[17] To complement Gilbert's skills, the committee also hired the landscape architect Frederick Law Olmsted, Jr. (1870–1957), of Brookline, Massachusetts. A leading figure in the City Beautiful Movement and the nascent city planning profession, Olmsted was also the son of the great Frederick Law Olmsted, creator of Central Park and founding father of the nineteenth-century Park Movement. Like Gilbert, he had extensive experience designing and implementing city, campus, and park improvement plans across the country.[18]

Another important figure in the City Beautiful Movement became briefly involved with New Haven's improvement effort in these first few weeks. Charles Mulford Robinson, a journalist who had published two influential books synthesizing and popularizing the varied activities of the urban reform movement, wrote to Seymour offering his services as a "civic advisor":

You have two good men on your commission in Messrs. Gilbert and Olmsted but my work supplements that of these other men. There is the profession of architect, the profession of landscape architect, and the profession which I seem to have succeeded in creating, of civic advisor, or specialist in municipal improvement…who looks at matters neither from the standpoint of the architect nor of the landscape man, but from that of the city as a living organism.[19]

Although Robinson lobbied further in a letter to the *New Haven Register*, recalling his own childhood memories of New Haven's "elm-shaded streets, broad green, and…the wonderful Rocks,"[20] the committee did not take up his offer. Gilbert apparently thought little of his expertise, considering him to be "something of a Beaux-Arts man," that is, more concerned with municipal art than serious city planning.[21] Yet Robinson's proven skills as a spokesman and advocate for city planning were quite formidable.[22] In the years to come, Seymour may have regretted not retaining such an adviser, whose public relations skills would have served the master plan well in the face of increasing citizen apathy and political opposition.

———

In all this we are participating in a national impulse for civic improvement. My own feeling about the movement

here in New Haven is far more serious than is expressed by the term "City Beautiful." The fruits of the movement here will be found, not alone in a city better adapted to the requirements of modern life, but in a city in which there will be as near as humanly possible an equal opportunity for every citizen to enjoy such privileges as the city affords.
George Dudley Seymour, "Looking Forward: An Address," 1908[23]

The changing fortune of New Haven's Civic Improvement Plan from its inception to its demise can be traced to changes taking place within the City Beautiful Movement as a whole in those same years. Although many of the movement's motifs were first demonstrated in the famous White City of the Chicago Fair in 1893, its planning ideals gained widespread attention almost ten years later with the MacMillan Plan of 1901–2 for Washington, D.C. (in which both Gilbert and the younger Olmsted participated). Adding momentum was the publication in 1901 of Charles Mulford Robinson's *The Improvement of Towns and Cities*, which was to become the bible of the movement.[24] While the MacMillan Plan highlighted the efforts of America's foremost architects, Robinson's book called attention to the many lay organizations — street cleaning committees, civic improvement associations, municipal art commissions, and the like — that had sprung up across the country in the previous decade. It was these volunteer societies, along with the work of the professionals, which Robinson tied together under the rubric of the "City Beautiful." From 1901 to 1909, the movement came into its own, with grassroots organizers and professional experts joining together in a unified national effort. New Haven's participation in this effort was typical in many ways, as was Seymour's civic activism.[25]

Much as 1901 constituted a breakthrough year for the movement, 1909 marked another turning point in its evolution, with the publication of Daniel Burnham's monumental *Plan of Chicago*, the most ambitious attempt at city planning ever undertaken. Although universally admired for its breadth of vision and technical virtuosity, the plan also drew criticism for its perceived formal and stylistic rigidity.[26] The critique fixed upon the widely held but generally mistaken view that the City Beautiful Movement was more concerned with aesthetics than with the practical problems of urban life. Leaders in the movement sought to rectify this misperception when they organized their first National Conference on City Planning in Washington, D.C., held the same year that the *Plan of Chicago* was released. They distanced themselves from the "City Beautiful" label and emphasized the pragmatic benefits of their

work. "If I were disposed to delay, interrupt, or confuse the progress of city development," Cass Gilbert himself declared in a speech, "I would publish the phrase 'city beautiful' in big headlines in every newspaper. Let us have the city useful, the city practical, the city livable, the city sensible, the city anything but the city beautiful."[27] His remark reflected the true nature of the problem, which was one of semantics rather than substance. Although most of the City Beautiful plans produced before 1909 were directly concerned with utility and practicality, this fact was often overshadowed by the more accessible imagery accompanying their prodigious written reports (the *Plan of Chicago* being the most notable example of this phenomenon).

The planners' disavowal of the City Beautiful in favor of the City Practical was also driven by a general trend in the Progressive Era toward professionalization. Their attempts to legitimize the status of their calling required a decisive break with the lay improvement organizations, which were often perceived to be motivated by mere beautification.[28] Ironically, the change of emphasis only compounded the public misperception. With both politicians and professional planners decrying the pursuit of city beautification, many citizens began to lose confidence in the efficacy of comprehensive planning. For the implementation of a master plan, which required a long-term commitment, such a loss could prove fatal. The fact that New Haven's plan emerged in the midst of this transitional period spelled trouble from the start.

————

Gilbert and Olmsted's fee for the plan, which they considered to be preliminary to a more in-depth study, was $10,000. The committee was able to raise $8,000 through private subscription, enough to retain the architects and set them to work.[29] In a letter to Seymour shortly after they were hired, Gilbert and Olmsted set the tone for the task ahead. They stressed their desire "to proceed in a tentative and conservative way, especially at the outset." And while they understood that the aim was to "preserve and perpetuate the beauty of the city and suggest lines of further development," they realized "that such a plan must be *practicable* as well as *beautiful,* or it will fail to commend itself to the community."[30]

As the experts worked, Seymour hardly kept still, initiating a new campaign to strengthen the ties between New Haven and Yale. Seymour firmly believed that the university had a solemn responsibility to support the city in which it resided. Well aware from his historical studies that New Haven's citizens had more than once rescued Yale from

your beloved city. I know of no other way than the one you have followed to redeem our cities and make them worthy. Incidentally, the raising of the standard of citizenship—practical, effective, city building citizenship—is going to be the best achievement of all."[35]

THE PLAN

As our interest in human life is in the distinctly personal, so is it in towns and cities. We need a local concept, a love and pride in local traditions and local ideas. Civic art furnishes the most available means to express these local customs and local aspirations, and it should be remembered that only in expression do we truly possess them.

John Nolen, "Address to the First National Conference on City Planning," 1909[36]

Gilbert and Olmsted commenced their *Report* with a chapter on "Present Conditions and Tendencies," which laid out the physical, social, and economic parameters of the master plan. New Haven, whose population numbered 133,605 in 1910, was "being transformed into the widespread urban metropolis of the twentieth century," they declared, and its "citizens will be wholly dependent upon joint action for a very large proportion of the good things of civic life." They underlined the moral and social dimensions of civic improvement in rather patronizing terms, typical of the Protestant urban reform movement:

People of the old New England stock still to a large extent control the city, and if they want New Haven to be a fit and worthy place for their descendants it behooves them to establish conditions about the lives of all the people that will make the best fellow-citizens of them and of their children…a laissez faire *policy applicable to New England Yankees is not going to suffice for [the newer elements of the population].*[37]

Despite this note of condescension, the authors focused almost wholly on the more normative purposes of early city planning: improved commercial efficiency, residential livability, and the creation of a coherent visual and spatial order for the city's public realm. Toward these ends, the *Report* was divided into a summary of "most needed improvements"—including streets and traffic, preservation of street trees, burial of telephone wires, sewer system installation, and upgrading squares, parks, and playgrounds—and a second, larger section devoted to detailed recommendations for various areas in and around the city. In both scope and approach, New Haven's Civic Improvement Plan was an exemplary synthesis of City Beautiful and City Practical planning ideas, balancing the pragmatic

and utilitarian needs of urban life with a proper concern for the beauty and character of the civic realm (FIGS. 225 & 226). The balance, it turned out, was to be short-lived.

———

Early planners considered the design of the public street system to be the most important aspect of their work; as Olmsted declared in 1910, "the success of a city is more dependent upon good means of circulation than upon any physical factor under its control."[38] Its commercial viability depended on an efficient network: a view shared, not coincidentally, by the planners' major patrons, the business community. New Haven was no exception to this, and the *Report* lavished attention on recommended street improvements. Gilbert and Olmsted proposed two strategies to address what they perceived to be a system inadequate for present and future traffic needs. Both were widely accepted practices of City Beautiful planning. The first was to impose "build-to" right-of-way lines along major traffic streets to prevent building encroachment and to allow for future street widening. Since zoning laws did not exist at the time, the *Report* detailed possible legal and design mechanisms to implement such setbacks. The second strategy was to organize New Haven's existing streets by type, analyzing and categorizing them by use and location and establishing a hierarchy.[39] While local streets "may profitably be made a good deal narrower," it maintained, "main thoroughfares need to be very much more capacious than the average street. [They] may vary in type from the ordinary city street of respectable width to the broadest layout having shaded promenades for people on foot and other special features, with perhaps a more or less park-like character."[40] Using a technique borrowed from German city planning, Gilbert and Olmsted offered a series of "street sections," drawings that defined each type's constituent elements such as travel lanes, sidewalks, tree planting, and spatial proportions. These treated the street as a contained space with a multitude of functions, regulated by design standards but retaining its traditional role as a place of public use and gathering.

Gilbert and Olmsted suggested one specific—and radical—solution to the problem of traffic congestion in New Haven's downtown commercial district. To segregate traffic moving north-south from that moving east-west, they proposed not only rerouting certain thoroughfares at key points but also, more dramatically, constructing a "subway," or submerged roadway, through the center of town. Collecting traffic at an enlarged intersection north of the nine

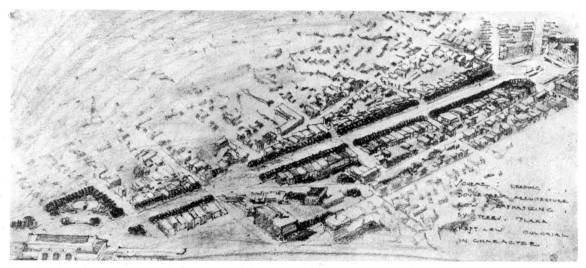

FIG. 227 *Cass Gilbert and Frederick Law Olmsted, Jr., "Sketch view…showing how the Avenue would connect the Station with the City," 1910.*

squares, the subway would run below a widened Temple Street across the Green and emerge at a new public plaza to the south (see FIG. 226, middle right). The heavily traveled east-west streets of the nine-square grid would then run unimpeded over it, relieving gridlock at downtown intersections. As it was an ambitious and costly undertaking, Gilbert and Olmsted did not discuss the subway in depth, treating it as a suggestion to be taken up or discarded in the plan's future development. Easily overlooked in the text and accompanying drawings, it remains one of the least known elements of their plan.

On the other hand, the best known and most striking aspect of Gilbert and Olmsted's plan was a proposed grand avenue connecting the new railroad station to the center of the city. Inspired by Seymour's suggestion in his "Open Letter," the avenue received relatively little textual attention in the *Report*—half a page describing its purpose and character—but was featured prominently in the accompanying drawings and sketches (FIG. 227). City Beautiful planners had eagerly adopted the monumental Baroque avenue or boulevard, as exemplified in the plans of Paris and Washington, D.C., for the new American city. Although subsequent critics and historians have fixed on the spatial and stylistic grandeur of their proposals, visual effect was only one of the advantages that the early planners exploited. Equally important was its ability to cut through the existing street network, imparting to it the efficiency deemed necessary for the scale and speed of the new metropolis. Capacity as well as character were the watchwords, adhering to the planners' oft-repeated dictum of the "useful made beautiful."

In contemplating a connecting avenue to the new railroad station, New Haven was following a course common in American cities at the time. With the consolidation of the nineteenth-century railway industry, many urban centers were sponsoring the construction of new, larger stations. Coinciding with the emergence of city planning, these stations often precipitated large-scale city master plans, becoming the tail wagging the dog of civic improvement. In New Haven's case, the new railroad line, or "cut," laid out in 1905–6, mandated the placement of the station to the south, isolated from the downtown by an intervening section of densely built, irregular city blocks. Connecting it more directly with the city center thus became a priority.

Gilbert and Olmsted's proposal included not only the avenue, cutting a 120-foot-wide swath through the tangled blocks, but also two anchor spaces at its ends: a plaza fronting the station and a public square, or "secondary civic center," deflecting the axis of the avenue onto Temple Street as it led to the Green. The processional sequence thus formed would provide a new and important entry to the city. "The first impression of most visitors will be gained on emerging from the station," Gilbert and Olmsted wrote. "An ample and agreeable vestibule to the city should be provided and be properly connected with the business section of the city beyond."[41] Welcomed into the "vestibule" of station and plaza, visitors were led up the spacious "hall" of the avenue and swept into the broad expanse of the Green, the grand living room of the city. The avenue itself was lined with large swales of grass planted with rows of trees on both sides, which gave it the aspect of a long park and connected it with the pastoral character of the Green.

As always, the planners ascribed practical benefits to the ambitious undertaking, arguing not only for its convenience, civic character, and aesthetic beauty but also for its economic advantages: "An avenue through this part of the city, cutting through cheap lands and opening up the property for development, although it will mean a considerable initial outlay, would justify itself upon a purely economic basis through the increase in land values along the route."[42] It was an early argument for the area's urban renewal, but in this instance it followed a time-tested model used in many European cities, where the broad *percée* of the newly opened avenue brought a welcome contrast in scale to the fine grain of older, flanking neighborhoods.[43]

Gilbert and Olmsted's proposal, although scaled to the requirements of the twentieth-century city, shared a common purpose and heritage with New Haven's most famous street, Hillhouse Avenue, to the north of the nine squares. James Hillhouse, in laying the avenue out in 1792, intended it to open up his land to residential development. A broad promenade, it established a model of the urban street as linear park, replete with overarching elms and flanking gardens. Both Hillhouse's design and Gilbert and Olmsted's avenue, despite their separation in time, may even have found a common inspiration in L'Enfant's plan of 1790–91 for Washington, D.C. The nation's capital, a touchstone for City Beautiful planners since the MacMillan Commission of 1901, made use of wide, tree-shaded avenues, bordered by grand houses on spacious garden lots and terminating on public squares and elevated civic buildings.[44] Hillhouse, a U.S. Senator in Philadelphia at the time and closely involved with urban planning in his own New Haven, would have likely followed the progress

of L'Enfant's plan with intense interest. Indeed, his original conception for Hillhouse Avenue, as depicted in the Doolittle Map of 1812, hewed closely to the model of Washington avenues. It included both an elevated public square at its northern end (where Hillhouse's son was to build Sachem's Wood, the family estate) and an axial geometry that, if extended south, would have connected the avenue back to the Green, landing precisely at the intersection of Temple and Elm Streets (see FIG. 53). That Hillhouse may have intended such an eventual link is suggested not only by the avenue's axis but also by its original name, Temple Avenue.

Although the northern square was not laid out and the axis never extended, Hillhouse Avenue nevertheless retained a measure of rustic monumentality, due in no small part to the long line of elms closed by Sachem's Wood's imposing portico (FIG. 228). This same combination of urban and pastoral grandeur characterized L'Enfant's avenues and underlay Gilbert and Olmsted's conception as well. Consciously or not, they built on Hillhouse's legacy in much the same way that Seymour had taken up the senator's mantle as civic reformer.

———

The planners concurred with Seymour that the New Haven Green was indeed "the Heart of the City." They seconded his recommendation that new public buildings should be located about the square's perimeter, ensuring that its traditional civic function continue into the twentieth century. Unlike the new City Beautiful civic centers being proposed for other cities however, the Green had an established character born of its long history. This made attempts to

FIG. 228 *Hillhouse Avenue looking north toward Sachem's Wood, ca. 1868.*

dictate its form and development more difficult. The *Report* grappled with this as best it could with the limited regulatory means at its disposal. "The question of control over the character of the buildings surrounding the Green is a serious and perplexing one," it declared. "Unreasonable restrictions should not be attempted, but the common interest of all citizens requires that the city's historic center should not be defaced." The planners settled on a maximum height limit of 100 feet for future construction at its perimeter. This restriction had legal precedent in other American cities, and it dealt effectively with the important issue of scale. As Gilbert and Olmsted explained, it was "not a question of light and air" — a common rationale for limits at the time due to dramatic increases in building heights — but "a purely aesthetic matter...where a certain uniformity of height is greatly to be desired in order to preserve an already established character."[45] Foreseeing the introduction of tall buildings, they only sought to reconcile the new scale of the twentieth-century city with the underlying principles of urban form that had shaped the space of the Green up to their time.

The character of the Green itself also came under scrutiny. It was not, of course, the ornate and ceremonial plaza so often favored by City Beautiful planners. Rather, it embodied a unique combination of types, conflating the function of a civic center with the qualities of an urban park. Recognizing this special synthesis, Gilbert and Olmsted recommended the restoration of James Hillhouse's century-old plan. The double row of elm trees at the Green's edges, already sickened by disease, should be "completely restored and permanently maintained," and the "simple, dignified character of the Green itself" kept intact by excluding any built structures and decorative planting.[46] Enclosed by the mall of trees, the expanse of open and unadorned lawn would constitute not only the heart of the city but its lungs as well, a pastoral retreat gathering about it the daily round of public life.

Gilbert and Olmsted recommended rescuing not only the elms around the Green but also those that lined the city streets (see FIG. 67). Most were nearly a hundred years old and they had begun to die off, afflicted by Dutch Elm disease and neglected by the city. Seymour had initiated yet another of his campaigns in 1909 to save them: "New Haven enjoys a great reputation throughout the country on account of her elms," he wrote in another "Open Letter," "a reputation she does not now deserve and cannot keep unless she bestirs herself and begins the work of redemption. Mr. Hillhouse and his associates con-

ferred great benefits upon the city, but those benefits were not everlasting. They were in the nature of a trust; in that trusteeship the citizens have been found wanting...The trees can be reclaimed only by the united efforts of the community."[47]

Urban tree planting was already a mainstay of civic improvement efforts, recognized as a practice that not only enhanced a street's aesthetic and spatial quality but also added economic value to the city as a whole. "Trees are among the first things which impress a stranger in forming a judgment as to whether a city is, or is not, a good place to live in," Seymour argued. "Healthy trees in front of or about any dwelling make the place more livable, as well as more beautiful, and increase the value of property in consequence."[48] Gilbert and Olmsted put the argument in terms that New Haven's business community could understand, helping them to see this civic amenity as an investment in its future:

One of New Haven's assets as a pleasant place to live in is the comeliness of its shade trees. On any reasonable basis of valuation, tree for tree, it has a large amount of capital so invested. It is not a negotiable asset...but it is none the less a valuable asset and one which can be to a great extent preserved and increased, or which can by neglect be completely lost.[49]

Seymour had urged the hiring of an "urban forester" and the *Report* seconded this recommendation. In 1911, the city's Department of Public Works, with the help of the Yale Forestry School, appointed a trained superintendent to run its newly created Bureau of Trees. The work of reclamation began immediately, starting on the Green and moving outward through the nine squares.

———

The *Report* addressed as well the issue of local parks and playgrounds. Progressive Era urban reformers devoted a great deal of attention to such spaces, seeing in them a positive force for the moral and physical development of neighborhood children.[50] New Haven's planners treated them more as a matter of social equity. They admonished the city that "any plan that deliberately...leaves any considerable neighborhoods permanently without the benefit of accessible parks and playgrounds for local use...is as so far illogical, unjust, undemocratic and unwise."[51] They called for the creation of a variety of small parks throughout the city, so placed as to be within a half-mile of every home (FIG. 229). In addition to providing play space for city children (especially in rapidly expanding immigrant communities), the parks would also form the nuclei of new and existing neighborhoods.

The local park was not new to New Haven, with its central Green and stock of nineteenth-century public squares already organizing many of its outlying neighborhoods. First- and second-generation American city planners developed first the small park and later the prototypical "neighborhood unit" around it as a coherent increment of urban growth. The neighborhood unit design, as proposed by Clarence Perry in 1929, even shared the nine-square plan's half-mile radius and 160-acre size. This congruency is made clear in Gilbert and Olmsted's "Small Parks" diagram, where the half-mile radius perfectly circumscribes the colonial grid that New Haven's founders had laid down nearly three hundred years before.

The planners paid even more attention to the larger outlying parks that ringed the city, devoting a full third of the *Report* to recommendations for improving their design and management. The extensive treatment reflected the close alliance between city planning and landscape architecture at the time, with Olmsted taking the lead in developing the proposed improvements. These were organized into two geographical sections, an "Inner Circuit" and "Outer Circuit" of parks, parkways, and reservations (FIG. 230). The "Inner Circuit" focused on devising a coherent physical and managerial framework for New Haven's existing parks, including Edgewood, East Rock, and West Rock. The city had created these in the late nineteenth century, prompted by the efforts of Donald Grant Mitchell (B.A. 1841), a renowned writer and amateur landscape designer who had made his home in Edgewood.[52] For a city of New Haven's size, it was an impressive system, bounding it on three sides and forming an effective limit to urban growth along much of its perimeter. Olmsted praised the foresight and efforts of the local park administration and suggested only minor adjustments and connections.

He was much more urgent about the need for the city to secure additional land, especially along the urban edges not yet given over to private development. This included the waterfront around the harbor, where, Olmsted recognized rightly, the last opportunity was at hand to acquire it for public use. In addition, he urged that stretches along the neighboring Quinnipiac and West Rivers be purchased to preserve their function as watersheds. Aware of

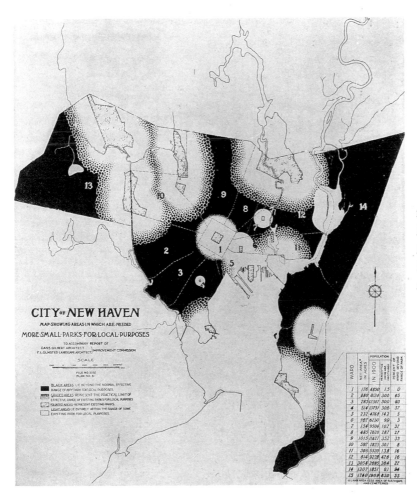

FIG. 229 *Cass Gilbert and Frederick Law Olmsted, Jr., "City of New Haven: Map showing areas [in black] in which are needed more small parks for local purposes," 1910.*

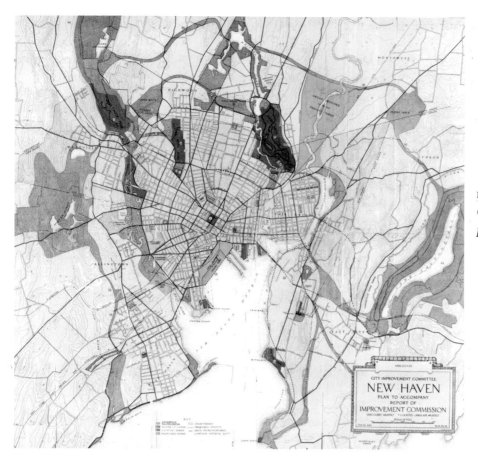

FIG. 230 *Cass Gilbert and Frederick Law Olmsted, Jr., "New Haven [Regional park plan]," 1909.*

the potential long-term negative effects of urban development on the surrounding ecosystem, he begged the city to adopt a farsighted policy of resource management. His proposed acquisitions, in concert with the existing parks, would have made the "Inner Circuit" a greenbelt around the city, buffering growth and protecting the environment upon which it depended.

The "Outer Circuit," as the name implied, formed a second concentric ring of parklands around the city, thinner and more tenuous than the "Inner Circuit." Its purpose was to connect existing or proposed watersheds and reservations with parkways, or landscaped drives, which would encircle the city as an "emerald necklace." These greenways, although Olmsted did not characterize them as such, were the armature of a proto-regional plan. They divided the surrounding territory into manageable parcels and directed, in some measure, future growth. If adequately maintained, they would have contained city extensions as discrete, organically whole neighborhoods, radiating out from the center. Unfortunately, this much needed framework, as well as Olmsted's program of property acquisition, was not implemented in the years to come, sharing the same fate as those proposals directed at the heart of the city itself.

VALEDICTORY

Outside experts and special commissions may be valuable to arouse or educate public opinion, or to stimulate and inform local officials...but the real work of getting the results, toward which any paper plan is but a step, depends mainly upon the right sort of unremitting, never-ending work by the proper administrative officials.
Frederick Law Olmsted, Jr., "Address to the Second National Conference on City Planning," 1910[53]

Despite the long delay in the *Report*'s release, New Haven's drive for civic improvement retained its momentum, and the city opened a number of fronts based on the planners' recommendations.[54] Of first importance was creating a municipal commission to oversee the improvements. This was a legal and political undertaking that revealed at the outset the "unremitting, never-ending work" required to implement the plan. It took two and a half years but finally, in May 1913, the Connecticut State Assembly passed the City Plan Commission Act for New Haven. The commission's founding members included Mayor Frank Rice, the presidents of the Board of Aldermen and the Chamber of Commerce, the city engineer, and George Dudley Seymour as secretary.[55]

Politics did not delay all action, however. The city moved promptly on one of the *Report*'s more pressing recommendations, burying the web of overhead wires that engulfed the center of town.[56] More significantly, it hired Frederick L. Ford, a Sheffield Scientific School-trained architect and engineer (PH.B. 1893), to develop the avenue connecting the train station to the Green. Ford was based in Hartford, where he had the distinction of being the first permanent municipal engineer and planner in the United States, a position created in 1907. Subsequent to his consulting work on the avenue, New Haven hired him away from Hartford and made him its first city engineer, as authorized by the Commission Act.[57]

In September 1912, Ford released his report on the avenue or, as it was commonly called, the railroad approach.[58] Following Gilbert and Olmsted's plan, he used the axis of Commerce Street to connect the station plaza with downtown George Street, but he reduced significantly the size of the civic plaza at the avenue's north end, where it intersected with Congress Avenue (FIG. 231). He also introduced another public square at the avenue's midpoint, to be used as a market garden for New Haven County farmers. Like the civic plaza, the new square deflected the avenue's axis, a move motivated in part by the need to find the most economically feasible route. Indeed, his elaboration of Gilbert and Olmsted's schematic design typified the process of translating the broad gestures of City Beautiful planning into physical reality. The result, far from compromising their plan's intent and principle, was a richer, more complex scheme. It provided a succession of civic spaces, varied in shape and function, which inflected the approach to the Green.

Progress continued after the Commission Act of 1913, beginning with improvements to the Green. The New Haven Park Commission retained Olmsted in 1914 to design a landscape plan for the civic square. Following his recommendations, they planted a double row of elms around the perimeter of the lower Green, outlining a mall walk.[59] Less fruitful was an effort in 1916, led by Seymour, to pass state legislation limiting the height of buildings around the Green. "As these sites are very valuable we must then look forward to having some very high buildings and an incongruous effect," Seymour warned. "If we are ever going to establish a height limit, now is the time to do it."[60] Unfortunately, his call went unheeded and, in the coming decades, the loss of scale and harmony at the Green's edge became an all-too-predictable reality.

The lack of will was a harbinger of things to come. In the years after 1916, city planning activity slowed to a trickle in New Haven, with no discernible action taken on any front. Ford's "railroad approach" plan languished for several years after its release. It resurfaced briefly in 1917 as a modest extension to Orange Street, but the city failed to implement even this reduced version.[61] The City Plan Commission, which met every month for the first two years, gradually ground to a halt, meeting on average four times a year and, after 1920, once or twice a year.[62] Even the ambitious campus master plan being developed by Yale from 1919 to 1924 failed to stir renewed interest. In 1920, James Gamble Rogers (B.A. 1889), prior to becoming the architect of Yale's "Plan of Architectural Development," consulted with his friend George Dudley Seymour (whom he called his

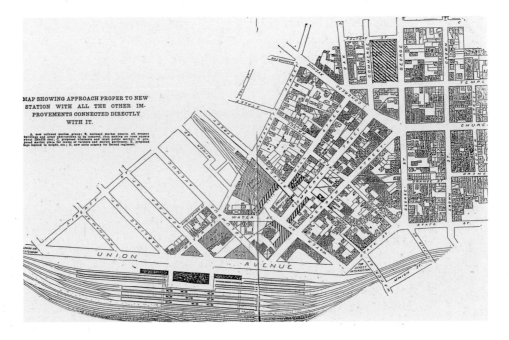

FIG. 231 *Frederick L. Ford, "Map showing approach proper to new station," 1912.*

"classmate," Seymour having received an honorary degree from Yale in 1913 for his public service). Seymour helped Rogers draft his letter to Yale accepting the appointment; and Rogers, an unwavering advocate for the city's involvement with the campus plan, assured him that the university would cooperate with New Haven's improvement efforts.[63] However, those efforts never materialized, and the city could only stand by and watch Yale's remarkable progress in the ensuing years, stalled as it was on its own plan.

In 1924, the same year that Yale unveiled its new master plan, Seymour finally laid down his arms and admitted defeat in his campaign for comprehensive planning. Seventeen years after his first "Open Letter," he wrote a public "Valedictory," published in the New Haven newspapers on July 17.[64] In it, he took leave of his role as an advocate for civic improvement and gave notice of his resignation from the City Plan Commission. The letter was also an apologia for the commission's record of inactivity, recounting the years of effort made in vain. In his opinion, lack of political will was the ultimate reason for the plan's failure, beginning with the commission's first meetings under Mayor Rice (who had been elected in 1909, prior to the plan's release). Although the mayor's background as a business-minded Yankee Republican fit the profile of a planning supporter, he saw the surface of the City Beautiful Movement and not the substance. "He failed rightly to understand the significance of the movement," Seymour recalled, "which he seemed to think was based upon aesthetics, rather than upon fundamental social and economic conditions, transportation, traffic, sanitary engineering, street and building lines, parks, recreation grounds, etc."[65]

Rice compounded his lack of understanding with a failure of political nerve. "I often think how much would have accrued if our plans had received attention from the community," Seymour lamented to Gilbert many years later. "But the Mayor at the time was very timid, knew nothing about city planning, and would not act, and proved what Olmsted said, that 'however earnest the effort, city planning cannot be carried on without the cooperation of City Hall,' which I never had."[66] Both as mayor and chairman of the City Plan Commission, Rice effectively curbed its ability to act, refusing to appropriate funds to hire consultants or staff and slowly reducing the frequency of meetings. David Fitzgerald, a Democrat of Irish descent elected mayor in 1918, undermined the commission as well, starving it of money and meetings throughout Seymour's remaining years as secretary.[67] Meanwhile, the Board of Aldermen, responsible to their local wards, provided no sustained or significant support; indeed, their parochial needs served to frustrate any attempt at citywide consensus.

That the commission met with resistance from both political parties and from mayors representing old Yankee and new immigrant power bases demonstrated that city planning was not a partisan issue. Rather, it was a cause that required a level of political maturity and broadmindedness not yet present among the city's leadership. Achieving a consensus that saw past local or bureaucratic concerns, as well as beyond the timeframe of the next election, came at too high a cost for elected officials; as Robert Dahl surmised in his study of New Haven politics in the twentieth century, they "saw no particular political gain and much political loss if they were to push hard on city planning."[68] It was only after World War II that community leaders perceived and exploited the political benefits of urban development, but by then the ideal of the "City Functional" had fully eclipsed the "City Beautiful." Seymour knew well the kiss of death that the earlier misnomer had planted on his city's plan, allowing narrow-minded officials to summon easy public sentiment against its broad aims. "I never urged anything but a 'City Practical'—the great aim of city-planning," he wrote plaintively in his "Valedictory."

It was my misfortune and I think the City's misfortune, to have the sensational slogan "City Beautiful" fastened upon the project by the newspapers, by ultra-conservatives and by those whose chief pleasure resides in deriding progress and who delighted to dub my project "the dream of a dreamer." My conception of a "City Beautiful" will be realized by a city which has addressed itself manfully to these practical problems and other problems of a kindred nature. Fine architecture is and has been the least of my concerns in this enterprise.[69]

Nevertheless, and with some irony, fine architecture was one of the conspicuous successes of New Haven's drive for a City Beautiful. The new Federal Post Office, anticipated by Seymour in his first "Open Letter," broke ground in 1913 beside the City Hall, taking its place as a twentieth-century addition to the Green's civic ensemble (FIG. 232; see also FIG. 11).[70] Designed by James Gamble Rogers, who was soon to build much of the "new Yale," it embodied perfectly the era's ideals of beauty and utility. Its simple boxlike volume evinced modern efficiency while the monumental portico, scaled to the distant view across the square, symbolized its public role. The public library (see FIG. 10), completed in 1910, and Union Station, finished in 1918, constitute Cass

FIG. 232 *New Haven Green from the colonnade of the United States Post Office and Courthouse, with the United Congregational Church in the middle-ground and the New Haven Free Public Library on the right, ca. 1918.*

Gilbert's architectural legacy in New Haven. Each blended classical ideals with local building tradition, the library echoing the colonial churches on the Green and the noble station bringing order to the city's industrial edge.

Not only did the library and station bookend the most fruitful years of the civic improvement era but they also constitute a fitting reminder of its vision. The residue of the plan's urbane character and ambitious scale can be felt in these two buildings, which mark the endpoints of the great avenue that would have spanned the breadth of the city. They are, however, the closest that New Haven ever came to realizing that vision. As the era's sense of civic idealism and practical foresight shrank in coming years,

its emphasis on utility and efficiency grew in inverse proportion. In the postwar period of the "Model City" and urban renewal, the City Plan Commission was revived, but only as an instrument of a larger technocratic mechanism, which possessed all the administrative and legal recourses that the early reformers lacked but little of their ethics or skill. Dependent on wholesale destruction and displacement, the scheme of Redevelopment in the 1950s and 1960s was, ironically, far more removed from the realities of urban life than Seymour's "dream of a dreamer." Indeed, the Plan of 1910 was the first and last true city plan that New Haven had in the twentieth century, one well worth remembering for the scope of its vision and the wisdom of its convictions.

A New Yale: The Pope Plan of 1919

ERIK VOGT

In 1917, thirty years after President Timothy Dwight (B.A. 1849) formalized Yale's status as a university and ten years after George Dudley Seymour rallied New Haven to the cause of city planning, Yale University took its first step toward a comprehensive campus master plan. Significantly, the impetus came not from within the administration but from an alumnus, Francis Patrick Garvan (B.A. 1897), who commissioned the architect John Russell Pope to project a framework for the university's future development. Released in 1919, the Pope Plan helped to instigate a complex and ambitious program of construction, resulting in the campus's complete transformation by the late 1930s.

Although more circumscribed in its evolution and scope, the Pope Plan shared with New Haven's Civic Improvement Plan a common purpose. Both were embedded in the Progressive Era urban reform movement and motivated by its preoccupations: rational order, efficiency, and the perceived need for a long-range vision to meet the demands of modern growth. Governing these aims was the theme of unity and its expression through architecture and public space. Pope, in presenting his design, declared that "the principle on which the plan has been developed is that of unification — the unification of present buildings among themselves and of present buildings with those of the future."[1] This principle reflected a much larger institutional goal that Yale had set for itself. Much as Seymour and his fellow New Haven citizens saw a "unity of civic spirit" as both a precursor and product of their Plan of 1910, the Pope Plan gave physical shape to Yale's quest to reform and reunite itself as a community in the twentieth century (FIG. 233). To that end, it

was an auspicious beginning to a mission that was to culminate, twenty years later, in the construction of a new Yale.

———

Despite President Dwight's prodigious efforts in the last decade of the nineteenth century, the buildings and grounds of Yale fell far short of the harmonious whole that he had achieved on the Old Campus quadrangle. The university that Arthur Twining Hadley (B.A. 1876) inherited from him in 1899 extended beyond that square to the adjoining blocks north and west. Yale had acquired most of the land on these blocks in the latter half of the nineteenth century and built an *ad hoc* assortment of academic, residential, and support facilities, with no general plan guiding their placement. The same held true for the campus of the Sheffield Scientific School, strung out along Grove Street and Hillhouse Avenue.

Indeed, the only buildings constructed in the late nineteenth and early twentieth centuries that attempted to organize and connect with the sprawling campus were the Bicentennial Buildings, built in 1901–2 (see FIGS. 158–163). Designed around a spacious court (christened Hewitt University Quadrangle in 1914) as the first phase of a larger group that was never realized, they were assigned two highly charged tasks: to embody the authority and centrality of the new university structure and to help bind the separate communities of Yale College and the Sheffield Scientific School. The architects — Carrère and Hastings designed University Commons, Woolsey Hall, and Memorial Hall; Howells and Stokes designed Woodbridge Hall — accomplished the former through the use of a monumental Beaux-Arts classical style, the sobriety of which distinguished their buildings from the eclectic mix of late-nineteenth-century structures. To connect the quadrangle with the Old Campus, they designed an enormous colonnade (which would not be added until 1927) along the Commons's south facade, giving a clearly visible landmark to the swarm of students marching northward at mealtime. On the corner of the site, they reinforced the tenuous joint between College and Grove Streets with a grandly overscaled *tempietto*; its high rounded form not only collected and terminated the row of Sheffield buildings along Grove Street but also complemented the sweeping corner of Osborn Hall three blocks to the south.

While the university did little to build upon the quadrangle's unifying gestures in the years following, it was thinking of the future. In 1905, Anson Phelps Stokes, Jr. (B.A. 1896), Yale's recently appointed secretary and a prime mover in later campus planning efforts, purchased property around the Hillhouse estate at the north end of Hillhouse Avenue for future expansion.[2] But it was not until 1913 that the administration sought guidance in its architectural development, retaining Frank Miles Day of the firm Day and Klauder as "Consulting Architect to the University." His untimely death in 1918 cut short his tenure, however, and he had little effect on campus planning. One of the projects he did initiate was the design of a new dormitory on the block northwest of the Old Campus, a building that would eventually become the Memorial Quadrangle. Designed by James Gamble Rogers and built between 1917 and 1921, the Memorial Quadrangle was Yale's most ambitious undertaking since the Bicentennial Buildings, and it profoundly influenced the future direction of Yale's campus (see FIG. 14). It was during the years of the Quadrangle's construction that Yale began to take decisive steps toward planning its growth. Prompting those steps, and precipitating the Pope Plan, were the events leading up to the university's great reorganization of 1919.

In the years before World War I, President Hadley did much to consolidate the university administration and streamline its operation. However, many influential Yale alumni called for more sweeping changes, including the adoption of long-range planning for the university's future needs. In these goals they found two powerful allies within the administration: Secretary Anson Phelps Stokes and Treasurer George Parmly Day (B.A. 1897). In early 1917, Stokes and Day convinced the Corporation to create an Alumni Committee on a Plan for University Development to advise on a course of academic and organizational reform. Comprised of prominent

graduates, the committee would prove to be a powerful force for change in the ensuing two years.[3]

One of the alumni concerned with his alma mater's lack of direction was Francis Patrick Garvan (1875–1937). Trained as a lawyer and an expert on the U.S. chemical industry, Garvan was also a wealthy patron of the arts, specializing in colonial American decorative arts and nineteenth-century sporting art. He amassed leading collections in both, which he subsequently donated to Yale. His circle of friends included Payne Whitney (B.A. 1898), whose family later helped finance the construction of Yale's new gymnasium.[4]

In the spring of 1917, soon after the formation of the Alumni Committee, Garvan offered an unusual gift to Yale: a master plan for campus development, to be designed by John Russell Pope (1874–1937). Pope, a prominent Beaux-Arts architect who was later responsible for Payne Whitney Gymnasium (1926–32) and Calhoun College (1929–33) at Yale, is perhaps best known today for the Jefferson Memorial (1937) in Washington, D.C. He was already working for Garvan on several residential projects in New York and was Garvan's personal choice for the campus plan proposal.[5]

President Hadley and the Corporation, assured that they would not be bound by the plan, accepted the offer. There is little doubt that Stokes and Day actively supported it, seeing it as a catalyst for the long-range planning that they felt was essential to the campus's orderly growth. Most important to Garvan, it would also prompt the administration to begin acquiring the land necessary for that growth.[6] What was exceptional about the proposal, however, was the indirect relationship of architect and ostensible client. Pope would produce the plan outside the channels of university administration, with little input or oversight by Yale officials. In its way, the arrangement was not unlike the one that New Haven had undertaken in its Civic Improvement Plan: private funding sponsored the work of an outside expert, intended for the benefit of the community at large.

It was perhaps for the best that the university had little involvement, as America's entry into World War I, coincident with Garvan's offer, wholly consumed Yale's attention and resources. When the war ended in 1918 and collegiate life returned to normal, Yale was forced to confront wrenching changes. The Alumni Committee had continued its work apace, energized in its reform mission by the organizational changes already wrought by wartime mobilization. Its leverage against the more conservative

Corporation and administration was strengthened by the considerable financial support that alumni had provided to cover Yale's deficits during the war. In early 1919, the committee presented its plan for reorganization, a list of reforms designed to rationalize the university's academic and administrative structure. Faced with little choice, the Corporation capitulated and, on March 17, adopted the committee's sweeping platform.[7]

One of the reorganization's mandates was the creation of several new standing Committees of the Corporation, including a Committee on Architectural Plan. Formed in anticipation of Pope's plan, it was given added urgency by the enormous bequest of John W. Sterling (B.A. 1864) in 1918 for, among other things, a new library. Pope had completed his work by late 1918, but he and Garvan delayed its presentation until the Alumni Committee had achieved its mission and the Committee on Architectural Plan was in place to receive and act upon it.

In July 1919, Pope released the plan to the Corporation and Yale officials.[8] Entitled *Yale University: A Plan for its Future Building,* it took the form of a series of thirty-five engraved prints, bound in a large, folio-sized book and printed as a limited edition of 250 copies. The beautiful plates, after drawings by Otto R. Eggers, Pope's assistant and lead draftsman, consisted entirely of plans and perspectives illustrating both the spatial organization of the proposed campus and the character of its significant buildings and public spaces. The elaborate presentation was not only in keeping with Pope's taste for ceremony but also reflected Garvan's keen interest in prints.[9] The plan that the plates depicted, however, was more striking still. It envisioned a building framework that would take the university far into the future, more than matching the ambitions of a newly reorganized Yale to both expand its campus and unify its community.

PAST, PRESENT, AND FUTURE

Pope organized his plan according to three geographic areas, corresponding with the past, present, and future development of the campus. The Old Campus quadrangle represented the most established and least modified section. The six blocks bounded by York, Grove, Temple, and Elm Streets, already occupied by a loose assortment of Yale buildings, became the focus for a "New Campus" to be built in the near term. And, finally, the axis of Hillhouse Avenue leading up to the Hillhouse estate was designated for future expansion as the need arose (FIGS. 234 & 235).

To unify these far-flung sites, Pope created a grand deflecting axis, which started at the long centerline of the Old Campus, crossed north to the New Campus, turned east to a new public square at Temple Street, and cut back up north again along an extended Hillhouse Avenue to a sprawling academic quadrangle at the top of Sachem's Wood. The deflections were necessitated by the presence of the New Haven Green and Grove Street Cemetery, which pinched the spine of the campus to the east and west.

The planning strategy that Pope employed was typical for its day, used for campus and city master plans alike. It relied on Beaux-Arts principles, as filtered through the City Beautiful Movement: grand axes defined by continuous building walls and terminated on open public spaces and monumental buildings. Although contemporary architects and planners often applied this technique perfunctorily, Pope's use of it for Yale's campus was appropriate and effective, given the attenuated area he was called upon to organize. Just as important, it permitted him to weave the university into the existing fabric of city streets, opening it up to New Haven through overlapping vistas and spaces.

In addition to the larger shared public spaces, the plan created a number of enclosed courtyards and semi-enclosed quadrangles, both within proposed buildings and between existing and new ones. The use of such spatial types was almost mandated; overwhelmingly preferred by campus architects and university officials at the time (including Yale, which looked to its transformed Old Campus as a model), they provided a level of privacy and flexibility that was indispensable given the constraints of the school's urban setting.

Pope chose the Collegiate Gothic as the uniform style for the plan's buildings. Popular at the time, the Gothic style was also in keeping with the sentiments of the Yale administration, which had earlier sanctioned it for Rogers's Memorial Quadrangle. Pope proposed its general use as a way to gain a measure of visual harmony for the otherwise architecturally eclectic campus. Although combining it with classical Beaux-Arts planning principles struck some purists as antithetical, Pope was one of many architects of the period who detached style from plan type, understanding each as serving its own pragmatic ends. A formal order gave the campus an immediate spatial legibility, while the more picturesque massing of the Gothic style lent it a character long associated with the traditions of the Anglo-American university.[10]

Pope recommended only one change to the Old Campus quadrangle: the removal of Durfee Hall on Elm Street in order to open up one of his organizing vistas. This long axis had been hinted at previously in the plan of Vanderbilt Hall (1894) at the south end of the Old Campus and would be reinforced later by the placement of McClellan Hall (1925), mirroring Connecticut Hall. Pope saw two advantages in Durfee's removal: the Old Campus would be visually linked to the new university center across Elm Street, and the space between the existing Fayerweather Hall and Taylor Hall (West Divinity Hall) on the northern block could be transformed, in his words, into an "interesting avenue, connecting these areas in an imposing monumental fashion."[11]

That "avenue," for pedestrian use only, led into the heart of Pope's plan, the New Campus (see FIG. 233). For this, he designed what was in essence a City Beautiful civic center, substituting a campus green for the urban plaza. Just as city planners advocated the grouping of public buildings to aggrandize their visual and spatial effect, Pope collected the most symbolically important elements of the university program—library, gymnasium, chapel, and administration—around this space. Its long axis, perpendicular to the one from the Old Campus, was aligned with a widened and repositioned Wall Street (FIG. 236). The space itself measured 180 feet across

FIG. 236 *Pope Plan: "The New Campus," looking west along the Wall Street axis toward the gymnasium, 1919.*

(building face to building face) and spanned two city blocks, from High Street to a new public square and gateway at the intersection with Temple Street.[12]

Pope considered the court of Hewitt Quadrangle, terminating as it did the Old Campus axis within his New Campus, to be "the centre of gravity, architecturally and mentally, of the University." Here he placed the new library, "the intellectual centre of an educational institution"[13] (FIG. 237). Because it effectively blocked the Bicentennial Buildings and required the relocation of Woodbridge Hall, this placement was to prove his most controversial proposal. Pope rationalized the move on several counts. First, the site's visual importance, reinforced by the new axis, dictated that the vista be terminated not by the broad flank of Commons but by a vertical spire, which he duly provided in the library's soaring tower. Second, by blocking the classical facades of the Bicentennial Buildings with a Gothic library, he could achieve a uniformity of style in the major buildings facing the New Campus green. Finally, Pope felt that the size of Hewitt Quadrangle was "totally inadequate for the open space suitable for the central group of buildings in the plan."[14] Thus he filled it in and, in effect, replaced it with his much larger New Campus, a space that he considered more properly scaled to the enlarged university campus.

The new gymnasium was given a prominent site as well, at the western head of the long green (FIG. 238). Unlike the library, it was a low broad mass, flanked by enormous gate buildings that enclosed a raised forecourt. Pope intended this court to be the formal ceremonial space of the university, replacing Hewitt Quadrangle.[15] The importance given to the building by its site was to be a source of consternation to Yale officials. The chairman of the Architectural Plan Committee expressed his concern to Stokes that "the first impression at the gateway [at the eastern end of the New Campus] would...be that Yale was a college to develop athletics."[16] This effect was by no means accidental, however; the plan's sponsor considered sportsmanship to be an essential component of collegiate life. "Sport...is the proving ground for the development and exemplification of the laws of right living and fair play," Francis Patrick Garvan declared to President Angell, upon donating his collection of sporting art to Yale in 1932. "I believe that in the comprehension of all her facilities Yale has the opportunity to become a great model research laboratory or institute of sport for the improvement and culture of the body and of the spirit of every boy and girl in the country."[17] Athletics had been central to his own life as a Yale

FIG. 237 *Pope Plan: "The Campus," looking north from the Old Campus toward the library, 1919.*

FIG. 238 *Pope Plan: "The Gymnasium," 1919.*

FIG. 239 *Pope Plan: "The Square," looking east toward the gateway at Temple and Wall Streets, 1919.*

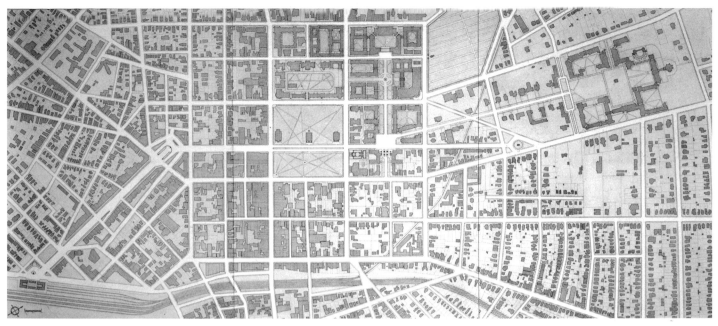

FIG. 240 *Synthesis of the New Haven Civic Improvement Plan of 1910 and the Pope Plan of 1919. Drawing by Erik Vogt.*

student and, given the opportunity provided by his gift, he sought to ensure that they would occupy a central place in Yale's future development.

Opposite the gymnasium, at the eastern end of the New Campus, Pope proposed a "monumental Square" carved from the adjoining blocks and flanking Temple Street. It occupied a crucial position in the overall design, acting as a knot that tied together not only two separate parts of the campus but also connected the new university center clearly and directly with the city (FIG. 239). A twin-towered entry arch, resembling Phelps Hall on the Old Campus, spanned Wall Street on the east side of the square and established a new gateway to the university from Church Street. By treating both Church and Temple Streets as the main approaches from the city, Pope may have been building on the prescriptions set down in New Haven's Civic Improvement Plan of 1910. That earlier plan had recognized Church Street as a main north-south thoroughfare and incorporated Temple Street as part of a grand avenue running from Whitney Avenue to the new train station south of downtown (see FIG. 226). Had both the Plan of 1910 and Pope's square been implemented, the relationship of Yale and New Haven urbanistically would have been close indeed (FIG. 240). Pope's placement of the new university chapel on the shared public square thus became a poignant reminder of Yale and New Haven's common bond in the college's first half-century, when students and townspeople gathered as one congregation in the meetinghouse on the Green.[18]

The freestanding block on which the chapel stood, between Wall and Grove Streets, was created by Pope's extension of Hillhouse Avenue to the new square. This transformed the avenue into the third and final leg of the plan's long deflecting procession. "Hillhouse Avenue, with its termination on a fine plateau," Pope wrote in his preface, "offers an obvious opportunity for the great future development of the University."[19] Yale had long seen this possibility and had been acquiring property in the area. It had built several laboratories on the western side of the Hillhouse estate, intending them to be used by the university at large (and so help close the divide that still existed between Yale College and the Sheffield Scientific School). It hoped to consolidate its various holdings in the Hillhouse area as part of a long-range building strategy; in a letter to Pope, Stokes predicted that "Hillhouse Avenue—in half a century—will be devoted to University buildings."[20]

Pope's initial move in this direction, extending the avenue, was perhaps the boldest. It was the first attempt in the city's history to connect one of New Haven's many radiating streets back into its colonial nine-square grid. Although motivated by the desire to unite Yale's campus, the proposal also followed through on what may have been the original intent of the avenue's planner. James Hillhouse had aligned its axis precisely with the intersection

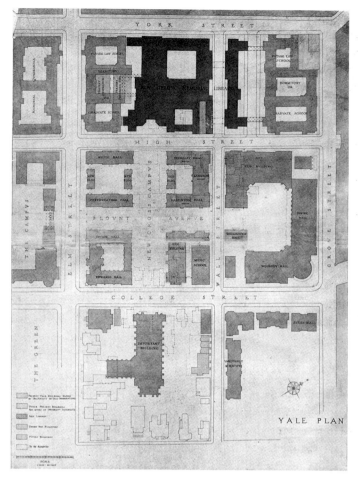

FIG. 244 *James Gamble Rogers, "The Corporation's Plan,...showing the definite location of the Sterling Memorial Library, the proposed sites of other buildings..., and the creation of the 'cross-campus' motif achieved by moving Berkeley, Lampson, and Haughton Halls and by the destruction of some old buildings on College Street," 1924.*

FIG. 245 *James Gamble Rogers, "Bird's Eye View of New Cross Campus," 1924.*

feature of the original design was not simply its unification of Yale's campus but the synthesis of the campus with the urban structure of New Haven. By opening up the communal spaces of the university to the city, Pope wove together the public realms of each, uniting the civic life of the street with the collegiate world of the quadrangle.

In Rogers's plan, especially as it was expressed in the college system of the 1920s and 1930s, that synthesis and unity were abandoned. Indeed, the spatial distinction between city and university, public and private, was sharply drawn and firmly held. There can be no doubt that the Yale administration was the motivating force in this; their reaction to the Pope Plan from the outset signaled their dismay over a campus "opened up" to the city. Ever pragmatic, Rogers tailored his planning strategy to their concerns. Instead of Pope's bold integration, he consciously polarized the spaces of the university into two realms: the court and the street. He looked to Oxford for his model in this respect. "Oxford is made up of a number of 'intime' colleges," he wrote in 1920, describing his ideas for Yale. "At the same time there are the vistas through the streets…Vistas should be long, but courts should be as short as the requirements will permit." He was to achieve the vista by "designing" the city streets between the university blocks, "co-ordinating the buildings on the two sides into a harmonious grouping."[39] While the long street view organized the outer public realm of the university, the intimate garden court characterized its inner private life. Rogers's buildings thus became highly articulated walls, both enclosing the garden and shaping the street as the demands of harmony required.

In its way, Yale's conscious retreat from the city reenacted its earlier turn inward, at the end of the nineteenth century. The Pope Plan, like the Brick Row campus before it, opened Yale to New Haven, knitting them together in a shared communal life. In Rogers's hand, the fortifying wall of the Old Campus quadrangle would be wrapped around block after college block, enclosing each as an island unto itself. Even as they flowed around these stone-clad sanctuaries, the streets of New Haven remained a world apart, separate from a new Yale that seemed, in its withdrawal, not so new at all.

HALF PLAN AT "A"

OPENING

TILE ROOF COPPER FLASHING

DRAIN

PLAN AT "B"

OPENING NOTE

COPPER LEADER

STAIR WELL

COPPER COVERED CUPOLA

PLAN AT "C"

DRAIN

TILE FLOOR

COPPER LEADER

PERPEND. ANCHORS IN EACH PIER SEE DRG. # 105 T.

STAIR WELL ABOVE

TEMPORARY OPENING 6'-0"x8'-0"

PLAN AT "D"

CONCRETE

COPPER LEADER CONCRETE

STAIR WELL 4'-4"

COPPER COVERED CONCRETE DOME

TEMPORARY OPENING 6'-0"x8'-0"

12"x12" HOLE TO DRAIN SOUTH BALCONY

PLAN AT "E"

DRAIN

TILE FLOOR COPPER LEADER

TILE FLOOR COPPER FLASHING

STAIR WELL BELOW 5'-4"

BRICK WALL ON TOP 4" CONCRETE SLAB COPPER COVERED

SEE DETAILS ON DRAWING # 456 T.

OPENING 2'-6"x7'-0"

COPPER COVERED GLAZED DOOR

STAIR WELL ABOVE

TEMPORARY OPENING 6'-0"x8'-0"

DIAL

PLAN AT "F"

CROWN

LANTERN

r 245'-10½"

r 227'-5½"

r 225'-4"

PERPENDICULAR ANCHOR B IN EACH PIER

r 197'-10"

FOR DETAIL DIAL SEE

OR CLOCK DRG # 207 T.

178'-0½"

James Gamble Rogers & the Shaping of Yale in the Twentieth Century

PAUL GOLDBERGER

It is difficult to imagine an institution whose architectural form revealed deeper contradictions than those embodied by Yale at the beginning of the twentieth century. Yale's campus was at once understated and grandiose; it seemed at once to be connected to New Haven and to stand apart from it. The heart of the university was the Old Campus, whose buildings were mainly examples of very high Victorian Gothic, and which had come with each piece of new construction to feel more firmly set apart from the city. The open space at the center of the Old Campus formed a counterpoint to the New Haven Green, but its grassy interior was private and closed, where the Green was public and open. And yet Yale did not stand entirely apart. The streets surrounding the Old Campus were lined with a mix of smaller university buildings, commercial structures, and residences that served by the very fact of their coexistence to weave the university into the fabric of the city. The newest and largest buildings at Yale, the Bicentennial Buildings of 1901–2 by Carrère and Hastings (with Howells and Stokes as architects of the smaller, adjacent Woodbridge Hall), represented the deepest contradiction of all (see FIG. 158). Their monumental grandeur brought a degree of Beaux-Arts sumptuousness to the campus that it had never before seen, and yet these structures, by virtue of their striking layout around a central rotunda in the form of a *tempietto*, did not turn inward to a private courtyard, but rather addressed the city streets. It was a striking paradox: the most imperial of Yale's buildings were also the most open to the city.

There was great diversity in the university's choices of architectural style in the last half of the nineteenth century and the early years of the twentieth, and the very absence of an official style seemed, if only by accident, to say a great deal about Yale's sense of itself. The university worked with a wide range of architects, most of whom were distinguished if not at the very forefront of the profession, and their work tended to be relatively conservative but typical of the moment in which it was designed. Thus there were Victorian Gothic buildings like Street Hall by Peter B. Wight and Farnam Hall by Russell Sturgis, Jr., Richardsonian Romanesque in Osborn Hall by Bruce Price, and the Beaux-Arts classicism of Carrère and Hastings. With the exception of the Old Campus quadrangle, there was relatively little thought given to the question of how it all came together. What visual power the university had as a totality came from the cumulative effect of its individual buildings, not from any conscious attempt to create a sense of ensemble, and what order there was was conferred by the streets, not by the architecture. At the beginning of the twentieth century, the city streets played a significant role in defining the feel of the campus, and the story of Yale's development over the ensuing decades is, in large part, a tale of the diminishing meaning of the street. Over the course of the twentieth century the streets passing through the campus would never disappear—though a handful would be closed to traffic over the years—but the university's buildings would increasingly turn away from them.

It was this curious mix of monumentality and ordinariness, of separation from the city and integration with it, that faced James Gamble Rogers (B.A. 1889) in 1917 as he began to design the complex that would define not only his own career but the physical form of the university for the rest of the

FIG. 247 *Memorial Quadrangle: presentation drawing, ca. 1918.*

century, the Memorial Quadrangle. Yale before the Memorial Quadrangle was an entirely different place from Yale after it. In this one project, Rogers established a kind of soft, highly picturesque Gothic as Yale's primary architectural style; he gave the university a physical symbol, Harkness Memorial Tower (FIG. 246), that has never been supplanted; and he created a prototype for the completely enclosed quadrangle that was to become the university's main mode of building for the next generation (FIGS. 247 & 248). The Memorial Quadrangle would eliminate the sense of ambiguity that the campus had possessed for so long, both architecturally and urbanistically, in favor of a vision that was consistent and clear, and which represented a brilliant synthesis of visual and urbanistic values. It was an extraordinary achievement for a single project, and it is impossible to overstate its significance. The Memorial Quadrangle was at once masterwork and archetype. No single building project has changed Yale as much, or contributed as much to the creation of its architectural image.

The university was not unaware of the importance of the Memorial Quadrangle. The cornerstone for the project was laid on October 8, 1917, two hundred years to the day after construction began on Yale's first building in New Haven. The symbolism underscored the university's belief that the Quadrangle marked the beginning of a new era. The

Memorial Quadrangle was the gift of the Harkness family, whose vast wealth, derived from Standard Oil, would play a role second only to the bequests of John W. Sterling (B.A. 1864) in shaping the physical form of Yale in the twentieth century. Mrs. Stephen V. Harkness offered the university $1.8 million to erect a dormitory complex in memory of her son, Charles W. Harkness (B.A. 1883), with the understanding that if it cost more than that to erect the first-rate structure that she and her surviving son, Edward S. Harkness (B.A. 1897), had in mind, she was prepared to make her gift — enormous by the standards of the day — larger still. The university at that point was bursting out of the Old Campus, and the hitherto helter-skelter nature of its expansion seemed increasingly at odds with Yale's image of itself as an institution devoted to the education and training of an American elite.

In the early years of the twentieth century Yale had begun to see itself less and less as an institution of New Haven, and more as an institution whose reach extended across the nation, if not the world. The university's administrators and Corporation fellows had for some time been eager for an architectural expression appropriate to that self-image, one that would lend both distinction and a sense of continuity and wholeness to the entire campus. It was an ambitious prescription for a building program, especially given the fact that the fellows were presum-

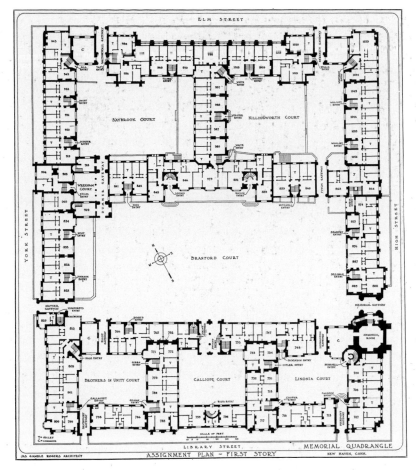

FIG. 248 *Memorial Quadrangle: plan of the ground floor.*

ably motivated not only by a wish to give the campus clarity, but also in part by a desire to give their urban university some of the picturesque ease that is more naturally associated with rural campuses. They were especially fortunate, then, to have put so much of their trust in James Gamble Rogers, for it turned out to be Rogers's particular gift to be able to create buildings that blended the appeal of the rural with the unified strength of a healthy urban fabric. Rogers could design in a manner that simultaneously satisfied the desire for grandeur, the desire for picturesqueness, and the desire for wholeness and consistency.

The Yale Corporation took an early step toward its goal of reshaping the physical form of the university with the appointment, in 1913, of a consulting architect to oversee development of the campus. Rogers, who had graduated from Yale in 1889, was offered the position by his old friend John V. Farwell (B.A. 1879), a powerful and well-connected alumnus, but turned it down, probably in the belief that it would prohibit him from designing any buildings on the campus himself. It went instead to Frank Miles Day of the firm of Day and Klauder, who had designed several Collegiate Gothic buildings at Princeton. A prime order of business for the consulting architect was to work with the university on the

development of Peabody Square, as the site just west of the Old Campus was known. Bounded by York, Elm, High, and Library Streets, it housed the original Peabody Museum of 1873–76 and Pierson Hall of 1896, both designed by J. Cleveland Cady; the Old Gymnasium (Herrick Hall) of 1859, designed by Chauncey A. Dickerman; the university's power plant; and several commercial structures (FIGS. 249–252; see also FIG. 160). The university had targeted it for expansion, and Day, who apparently did not share Rogers's concerns about limits on a consulting architect, had begun working on a design. Two deaths soon changed Yale's history: that of Charles Harkness in 1916, which led to his family's gift for a residential building to occupy the entire Peabody Square site, and that of Frank Day in 1918.

The Harkness family made the right to select its own architect a condition of its gift, and Rogers, who had designed Edward Harkness's house on Fifth Avenue in New York in 1904 and had continued to have close ties both to the Harkness family and to Yale, was invited by the family to design the Memorial Quadrangle in 1917, putting a halt to Day's plans. Day's death the following year cleared the way for Rogers to take an even more active role in the shaping of the growing campus.

FIG. 249 *Peabody Square looking southeast from the corner of Elm and York Streets, with Pierson Hall and the barrel-vaulted D.K.E. on York Street, July 21, 1917.*

FIG. 250 *Construction of the Memorial Quadrangle looking south from the corner of Elm and York Streets, July 16, 1918.*

FIG. 251 *Construction of the Memorial Quadrangle looking southeast from the corner of Elm and York Streets, July 10, 1920.*

Rogers's previous work offered no certainty that he would create a project as powerful as the Quadrangle turned out to be. A native of Chicago, he had begun his architectural career with hesitation. He was an undistinguished student and had not even decided to become an architect at the time of his graduation from Yale. He appears to have accepted his first position, as an apprentice in the office of William LeBaron Jenney, the engineer-architect noted primarily for his early work with Chicago skyscraper construction, almost casually. Rogers began to bloom in 1894, when he left Chicago to enroll at the Ecole des Beaux-Arts in Paris. He spent five years there (February 1894–December 1898), earned the Ecole's highest honors, and returned to Chicago with what was, at that time, the most sophisticated academic training an architect could have. Rogers could charitably be described as having been more ambitious socially than academically at Yale, and when he returned to Chicago in 1898 to open his own architectural office, his social ambitions combined with his Beaux-Arts training to place him comfortably within the city's elite. Among his earliest clients was Mrs. Potter Palmer, the unchallenged queen of Chicago society, for whom Rogers designed decorations for extravagant balls.

Unlike his contemporary in Chicago, Frank Lloyd Wright, Rogers was not an architect who took pleasure in challenging his clients. He was not particularly interested in modern architecture as it had been developing in Chicago in the work of Wright and, before him, Louis Sullivan, although it is not possible to know whether his strong preference for historical styles came out of deep conviction bred in Paris, out of a desire to please conservative clients, or, as Frank Lloyd Wright would assert many years later in *A Testament*, merely out of a timidity toward modernism. Wright and Rogers were both members of a luncheon club of young architects known as the Eighteen, and Wright, writing about the group toward the end of his life, recalled that his fellow architects "often wanted to know how I convinced my clients that the new architecture was the right thing. 'Do you hypnotize them?' was a common question…Almost all admired what I was doing though they were not yet willing to say it was the right thing…All the Eighteen were friendly but not willing to cut their umbilical cord to the Colonial or the French Chateau, the English manor house or the grandomania of Beaux Arts days…Gamble Rogers never left Gothic; Howard Shaw never dared leave colonial English."[1]

However Wright may have remembered it, it seems unlikely that fear kept Rogers from embracing

FIG. 252 *Construction of the Memorial Quadrangle looking west from High Street, with the University Gymnasium on Elm Street on the far right, November 1, 1918.*

modernism. He was by nature conservative; he saw himself less as an artist than as a gentleman in a profession, serving other gentlemen who were his clients. He believed himself to be the social peer of his clients, and he saw his mission as bringing security and delight, not intellectual challenge, to their lives. Rogers and his clients were joined in the belief that traditional architectural styles were conveyors of values. To build a Georgian or a Renaissance house or a classical courthouse or a Gothic dormitory was not, to them, a rejection of the twentieth century, but a means of connecting their time with the past, a way of assuring that what they considered the best aspects of the past would enrich the present. Yet Rogers was no Luddite. He was happy to adopt the technological advances that the modern movement was bringing to architecture. Perhaps as a result of his early training with Jenney, he felt no hesitation in using any of the latest technologies, and many of his buildings used the most up-to-date structural systems. His eclecticism carried with it no dogma. Unlike another Gothicist of his period, Ralph Adams Cram, Rogers had no desire to justify

his choice of Gothic by means of citing the symbolic connections between Gothic architecture and the ecclesiastical mission of the church. To Rogers, styles were visual and emotional, not ideological.

It was probably through his fellow Chicagoan John Farwell that Rogers met Edward S. Harkness, who was to become the most important client of his life. Harkness commissioned Rogers to design a house for him and his wife on Fifth Avenue at 75th Street in 1904, and it is likely that it was because of Harkness that Rogers decided to relocate his practice to New York. By the time the house was finished in 1907, Rogers had begun a short-lived partnership with Herbert D. Hale of Boston, who died in 1907; after Hale's death, Rogers practiced on his own, and New York would remain his base for the rest of his life.

The Harkness house, which still survives — a New York City landmark, it has been the headquarters of the Harkness family foundation, the Commonwealth Fund, for more than half a century — is the project which established Rogers as a peer of such architects as McKim, Mead and White, Richard

FIG. 253 *Memorial Quadrangle: Branford Court looking southeast toward Harkness Memorial Tower in 1921.*

FIG. 254 *Memorial Quadrangle: Branford Court looking northwest toward Wrexham Tower in 1921.*

Morris Hunt, C. P. H. Gilbert, Horace Trumbauer, and Carrère and Hastings, whose work could be seen in direct comparison to his up and down the blocks of Fifth Avenue. Beside most of the other mansions along the avenue, the Harkness house is a model of restraint and dignity. It is Italianate, but with a remarkable balance of spareness and picturesqueness, and unlike many Fifth Avenue mansions, the Harkness house seems comfortable in an urban setting. It is inventive in its detailing, but it never feels extravagant, and while the size of the house is large, the scale is not, as if Rogers were constantly trying to make it seem smaller than it is. While some of this is undoubtedly due to the personality of Rogers's client, a man who so often wished to disappear that it is not surprising he would have wanted his house to do the same, Rogers himself clearly felt more comfortable with buildings that demonstrated a certain understatement. At the same time that he was working on the Harkness house and in the years immediately following it, he designed classical courthouses in New Haven, New Orleans, and Memphis; an exquisite Renaissance museum, the Brooks, in Memphis; and the Yale Club in New York City, among other projects. All are notable for a delicacy of detail, an understated picturesqueness, and a tendency toward modesty of scale, traits that would emerge to become defining characteristics in the design of the Memorial Quadrangle. If Rogers's work has tended to be somewhat overshadowed by that of such competitors as McKim, Mead and White, Cass Gilbert, Thomas Hastings, and Whitney Warren, it is probably because it is less bombastic and more quietly urbane.

Of course, despite the quality of the Harkness house and several of his civic projects, including New Haven's large and distinguished U.S. Post Office and Courthouse of 1914 (see FIG. 11), in 1917, when he received the commission to design the Memorial Quadrangle, Rogers had not yet had the opportunity to design a building that would be as likely to receive national attention as, say, Cass Gilbert's Woolworth Building or Thomas Hastings's New York Public Library. The Memorial Quadrangle was his chance: it was to be large, extravagant, and monumental. Rogers added to his staff for the Quadrangle project two architects who would play major roles in the design and execution not only of this project, but of much of his major work to follow: E. Donald Robb, a designer from the office of the famed (and ideologically inclined) Gothicist Ralph Adams Cram, and Otto Faelten, a Beaux-Arts-trained architect and alumnus of Yale's School of the Fine Arts (B.F.A. 1924) who had come from the office of Herbert Hale.[2] Still, it was Rogers who made the basic design decisions and set the tone of the structure that was to shape Yale's future so definitively. It is Rogers who made the Quadrangle a masterpiece of refinement and understatement. Of all the great eclectic architects of the early twentieth century, he had the greatest gift for making architecture that would simultaneously be both monumental and picturesque.

The Quadrangle, which was built originally to house 630 students, actually comprises six quadrangles: a major central court, handsomely landscaped by Beatrix Jones Farrand (FIG. 253); two medium-sized courts to the north, and three intimate courts on the south. The complex is lower on the south to allow maximum penetration of sunlight into the courtyards, and it is punctuated by two skyline elements, the tall and graceful Harkness Tower in the southeast corner of the large courtyard and the smaller, boxier Wrexham Tower, a replica of the tower of St. Giles in Wrexham, Wales, where Elihu Yale was buried, diagonally across from it (FIG. 254). No small part of the goal of the Memorial Quadrangle was to create a kind of iconography of Yale's history. To that end the three larger courtyards were given names that honored the college's early locations before it settled in New Haven—Branford, Saybrook, and Killingworth—and the smaller ones were

named in honor of three nineteenth-century Yale societies, Linonia, Brothers-in-Unity, and Calliope. The common rooms bore the names of buildings that had been demolished on the Old Campus, and the thirty-seven entries and ten gateways were named for distinguished Yale graduates. The ornamentation of Harkness Tower continues this iconography (FIG. 255). Rogers placed statues of Elihu Yale, Jonathan Edwards (B.A. 1720), Samuel F. B. Morse (B.A. 1810), Eli Whitney (B.A. 1792), James Fenimore Cooper,[3] John Calhoun (B.A. 1804), Noah Webster (B.A. 1778), and Nathan Hale (B.A. 1773) in canopied niches atop the corner buttresses. Notable historical figures who did not attend Yale, but who might be thought nonetheless to exert a positive influence upon students, such as Phidias, Euclid, Aristotle, and Homer, made it into the mullions of the belfry windows, too high to inspire passersby but perhaps able to commune with the four grotesque birds representing the freshman, sophomore, junior, and senior classes which are slightly above them. Higher still are statues symbolizing law, business, medicine, and the ministry, as well as life, progress, war, death, peace, prosperity, effort, order, justice, truth, freedom, and courage, while atop these are gargoyles representing the four types of student: the scholar, the socialite,

FIG. 255 *Harkness Memorial Tower: detail showing the statue of James Fenimore Cooper.*

the literary man, and the athlete. It is perhaps worth noting that the athlete is the only gargoyle with a happy expression. Masks of Homer, Virgil, Shakespeare, and Dante share the top of the tower.

Rogers enjoyed the notion that the iconographic role of the Quadrangle followed Gothic tradition, but he was motivated far more by the earnest desire to create a Yale monument that would inspire loyalty to the university (FIG. 256). Early in the design process, the architect urged Yale secretary Anson Phelps Stokes (B.A. 1896) to suggest some new icons, as he felt that the Yale shield and bulldog had been overused. Rogers noted that the ornaments did "not necessarily have to be good architecturally, for I shall take a poet's license in translating the forms into something that will suit our buildings."[4] His priority was always picturesque composition, in the service of making what he could consider a beautiful building. Save for Wrexham Tower, which is perhaps the least smoothly fitting part of the composition, Rogers had no real precedent for any part of the design. The massing appears to have evolved from a practical plan for the layout of residential suites that would allow a maximum amount of light and ventilation, and from the height limitations worked out to maximize sunlight. The larger tower was based

loosely on the tower of St. Botolph's in Boston, England, but Rogers made it far more lyrical, with a slender, tapered profile and a double crown. The way in which Harkness Tower makes a transition from a solid base to an increasingly light, airy top, almost dematerializing as it rises, is remarkable, and has no precise precedent.

The evolution of the tower design reveals a great deal about Rogers's design methods. In his first studies, he used the tower of Magdalen College, Oxford, as a model, but rejected it as too heavy and instead selected the more delicate St. Botolph's. In his first version, based closely on St. Botolph's, there was a regular octagonal crown with flying buttresses atop a square tower. This produced, Rogers decided, a somewhat disquieting effect: the four faces of the octagon that rose directly above the sides of the square base appeared disproportionately narrow, and the four corner sides of the octagon seemed to recede too sharply from the base, making the crown appear somewhat disjointed from the lower section, as it does at St. Botolph's. The seamless transition from heavy to light that Rogers aspired to was impossible with this model. The logical solution to the problem would have been to make the octagon irregular, lengthening the sides of the faces that rose above the sides of the square, and thus also pushing the other faces closer to the corners. But Rogers also wanted the points of the octagonal crown to form a perfect circle, which would have been impossible with an irregular octagon. The final double-crown solution in which Rogers put an irregular octagon immediately above the base and topped that with a regular octagon satisfied both demands; that it pushed the tower even farther from its prototype clearly did not disturb Rogers at all. Literal replication meant little to him; indeed, the element of the Memorial Quadrangle that seems the least integrated into the whole is the one thing that comes closest to being an exact copy of something else, Wrexham Tower. Rogers was asked to include it as an icon, and it was never a fully comfortable part of his composition. While Rogers was not inclined to disapprove of the kind of superficial connection to history that the copy of Wrexham Tower represented—he liked any effect that would increase the level of emotional connection to Yale—his priority was nonetheless his own composition. Even where Wrexham was concerned he worked only from a photograph rather than from precise drawings of the original tower to assure, he said, that he would not replicate it exactly.[5] Rogers was always willing to forsake stylistic consistency for picturesque effect, and in the Memorial Quadrangle he achieved this to a degree that can only be called extraordinary.

Rogers was a gifted, not to say brilliant, compositionalist. He understood proportion and scale and materials, and he placed his buildings with reference to the sun, if not always with reference to those parts of the urban context that he did not himself create or control, and he remained throughout his career more conscious of scale than any of his contemporaries. His consistent tendency to design details at slightly smaller than normal scale made his best buildings gentle and welcoming. Nowhere in the Memorial Quadrangle is there a detail that does not appear to have been conceived with deep and genuine concern for human use.

That there was nothing truly "Gothic" about the building—that it was essentially a modern building draped in highly picturesque garb—was an essential part of Rogers's way of making architecture. Actually, there was one element of the Memorial Quadrangle that was created in the manner of traditional Gothic architecture, the fan vaulting in the roof of the Memorial Room at the base of Harkness Tower (FIGS. 257 & 258). It is exquisite, but it has the air of an architectural parlor trick, as if Rogers wanted to show that he could do it to amuse and to entertain,

and after all, what better place to be literally Gothic than in the one sacred space of the Quadrangle? Rogers was no ideologue; the act of making a Gothic building had none of the meaning for him that it had had for the architects of the Gothic Revival in the nineteenth century, or for an architect such as Ralph Adams Cram, who sought a kind of spiritual connection with the architects of the great cathedrals, and who saw in his work a kind of moral imperative toward a style. Rogers was far more pragmatic. In what may have been the most revealing of all the comments he made about the Quadrangle, Rogers wrote to Anson Phelps Stokes in 1919 to defend his decision to use tile roofs rather than the slate that might have been more historically authentic because:

As far as traditions go, I hope that the only traditions governing us will be Yale traditions and our country's tradition. Architecturally we will I know keep our effects as essential and not the traditions. Of course we will have to have architectural traditions because in most cases there is no other way of getting the desired effect except by employing the traditions which we use only because in these cases they are necessary to get the effects. It does seem awfully hollow and servilely cringing to use a tradition that means nothing to us.[6]

"We will keep our effects as essential and not the traditions"—Rogers could not have said more clearly that he had no interest in designing authentically Gothic buildings. He would carry the notion of the stage set as far as ordering his craftsmen to build stone steps with slight indentations, to suggest that the granite had been worn by centuries of use, but this was a visual conceit, not an attempt at authenticity. No wonder, then, that the Memorial Quadrangle, for all its lilting, graceful beauty, was sharply attacked by modernists in the years after its completion in 1921. Rogers produced a building that openly spurned the idea of moral truth in architecture at precisely the time that morality was coming to the forefront of architectural ideology. By the 1920s, there was almost no moral force left to any kind of eclectic architecture—that belonged to the nineteenth century, and the moral high ground of the twentieth century had been seized by the modernists. Architects like Rogers who sought to work within the styles of the past in the early decades of the twentieth century tended to rely, as Rogers did, on the appeal of the picturesque. In place of moral force Rogers was offering charm. But he had an ability, almost unmatched, to conjure out of charm the power of the monumental.

That was no incidental point to an institution that wished to view itself as home to cultivated and dignified men. Yale in the first decades of the twentieth century came increasingly to see itself as a preeminent American university whose educational mission consisted not just of imparting information, but of shaping leaders. To the extent that the physical form of the university was a part of this mission, it had to represent something more refined than the somber, almost industrial buildings that architects like Josiah Cleveland Cady had built on the campus in the late nineteenth century (which now appear, in retrospect, far more civilized and urbane than they were thought to be), or the conventional and somewhat dull Collegiate Gothic that Charles Coolidge Haight had added to Yale early in the twentieth century. Rogers's brand of Gothic was warmer, gentler, and richer. His buildings did not offer the same kind of moral authority that Pugin's or Ruskin's Gothic possessed in the nineteenth century, and they did not aspire to it. By Rogers's time, the notion of style as possessing a moral force in and of itself had been taken over by the modernists. Rogers's architecture offered a different kind of ethical lesson. It suggested that architecture could teach by example: gentle buildings for gentle men. It was an architecture of ease and intelligent cultivation, intended as an environment in which to shape a civilized, educated class. It was not designed to teach lessons of cheapness or efficiency, but lessons of graciousness and cultivation. The Memorial Quadrangle provided a variety of exciting and, in some cases, even subtle visual experiences, with exquisite materials and elegant details joined together in what can only be called a masterly composition. Rogers sought to provide pleasure for the eye along with a casual, undemanding association with a noble past.

Rogers was a romantic pragmatist.[7] He embraced the romantic associations of historical styles, but he had no desire to buy their ideologies as part of the package. How it looked — which is to say how much visual pleasure it provided — and how well it worked were the only things that mattered to him once the basics of structural soundness had been achieved. The notion of compositionalism — the belief that picturesqueness or visual pleasure can be principles in the making of architecture — was sufficient not only for Rogers but for many critics of the day, who generally embraced the Quadrangle. Typical of the critical response was that of the magazine *Architecture*, which wrote in 1921 that the Memorial Quadrangle was "a group of Gothic buildings that we believe will bear comparison with any in the world...In many ways, notably in their details and picturesqueness, they are the most distinctive colle-

FIG. 257 *Memorial Quadrangle: preliminary sketch of the Memorial Room, ca. 1918.*

giate buildings in existence...It is in the very absence of stiff and rigid uniformity that we are made to feel a mood of buoyancy, of cheerfulness, of youth. Invention, design, and careful thought for every detail are evident everywhere."[8]

As the 1920s wore on, however, and International Style modernism began slowly to spread through Europe and eventually across the Atlantic, an increasing number of critics took offense at the very idea that charm, even if presented with the formal brilliance of Rogers, might be a valid architectural virtue. Among them was William Harlan Hale (B.A. 1931), who edited a Yale publication called, appropri-

FIG. 258 *Memorial Quadrangle: fan vaulting in the Memorial Room.*

ately enough, *The Harkness Hoot.* In 1930, by which time the buildings were nine years old and modern architecture had become increasingly visible in the urban, if not the academic, realm, Hale was clearly under the spell of Le Corbusier. He wrote of the Memorial Quadrangle: "It seems almost incredible. When the world is witnessing a sweeping rebirth of genuine architecture, and when every clear-headed designer who is not bound to copies and formulas is envisioning a new order of forms and masses and relationships, then the builders of Yale join the tribe of impotent imitators who grind out their lifeless plagiarisms."[9] Hale was not content to challenge Rogers's historicism; he took issue also with the fact that the architect was so free in his interpretations. The Quadrangle, Hale wrote, "violates all canons of taste by deliberately misusing the Gothic details and ornaments with which it abounds. How can students be educated to artistic appreciation under the eaves of an architecture that puts water tanks into church towers, and lavatories into oriels? It seems dubious just what lesson of honesty the young man can derive from such misuses and untruths."[10]

The rising drumbeats of modernism notwithstanding, university officials expressed such pleasure with the Memorial Quadrangle that they decided to confer an honorary degree upon Rogers in June 1921. But his success in perceiving and satisfying Yale's desires as a client had already led to a substantial change in his relationship with the university. In the fall of 1920 Rogers was again offered the position of consulting architect, and this time, after initially saying no, he accepted. By then, two events had changed the climate of building at Yale. The first was the $15-million bequest in 1918 of John W. Sterling, a gift

that ultimately realized more than twice that amount for the university. The second event was the presentation in 1919 of a plan for the development of Yale by John Russell Pope, privately commissioned by Francis P. Garvan (B.A. 1897) and Mabel Brady Garvan and published in an elaborate volume dedicated to the memory of her father, Anthony N. Brady.[11] The unusual gift had been sanctioned by the Yale Corporation but was otherwise unofficial. Pope was an architect whose greatest work, the National Gallery of Art in Washington, D.C., was years away, but his love of bold gestures and vast scale, the opposite of Rogers, was already apparent. He proposed that Yale in effect merge Gothic historicism with City Beautiful planning, and his scheme was based on a trio of grand, Beaux-Arts vistas: one for a widened Wall Street, which would have been closed to traffic; another from the Old Campus across Elm Street through what is now the Cross Campus, which would have necessitated the removal of Durfee Hall; and a third up Hillhouse Avenue to an enormous Renaissance square to be framed in Gothic buildings for the sciences.

Pope was responding in a different way to the impulse to bring order to Yale that had motivated Rogers in his design for the Memorial Quadrangle. But Pope's desire to have a uniformly Gothic campus was so strong that he placed a new library directly in front of Carrère and Hastings's Bicentennial Buildings, culminating his new axis with an appropriately vertical building, but virtually obliterating one of Yale's most ambitious works of architecture in the process. Mindful of the need to plan more rigorously in view of the Sterling bequest, the Yale Corporation named a panel of three architects, Bertram Goodhue, William Adams Delano (B.A. 1895), and Paul Cret, to evaluate the plan. In February 1920, the group made the curious recommendation that the plan be adopted, but with enclosed squares like those of the Memorial Quadrangle rather than Pope's open vistas, and with a relocated library, effectively rejecting Pope's central ideas even as they claimed to be accepting them.

What was clear by then was that Yale could not grow piecemeal, and that Rogers, more than Pope or any of the architects on the panel, had the confidence of the Corporation to direct that growth. It took nearly two years from the initial recommendations of the committee to the decision to ask Rogers, late in 1921, to prepare a formal plan for the growth of the university, and it would be more than two years before Rogers would submit his plan early in 1924. Initially, Rogers began his period as consulting

FIG. 259 *Sterling Memorial Library: preliminary sketch by Hugh Ferriss of Bertram Grosvenor Goodhue's design, ca. 1923.*

architect by working on a revised version of the Pope Plan, emphasizing courtyards rather than monumental axes but still keeping aspects of Pope's vistas. The Rogers plan incorporated an old proposal of Anson Phelps Stokes that one of Pope's axes could be achieved not by removing Durfee Hall but by cutting a low, arched gateway through its ground floor. Rogers's old concern for urbanistic relationships, never as strong as it might have been but never entirely absent, either, showed itself promisingly in his suggestion that university officials and donor Garvan meet with city officials to brief them on the impact of Yale's growth on the city. (If these meetings took place, there is no record of their having any significant effect on the university's plans, or on the city's.) Rogers intended to take on no work at Yale himself while he was consulting architect, and his contract specified that he was not to design any buildings except by specific request of the donor. Another death, as timely for Rogers as that of Charles Harkness had been, changed that situation entirely.

Bertram Grosvenor Goodhue had been named architect of the new Sterling Memorial Library by the trustees of the Sterling estate, and he had been promised the commissions for other Sterling buildings as well. Goodhue had only completed some basic studies for the library, whose site Rogers had moved to the head of the Cross Campus, when he died suddenly in 1924. Goodhue and Rogers had

been not mere competitors in the New York architectural scene, but rivals. Each was the favored architect of one of the university's major donors, and they had strikingly different temperaments. Where Rogers was politically adept, Goodhue was earnest. Goodhue was in many ways the more creative of the two, and spent most of the last decade of his life struggling to reconcile his respect and love of traditional detail with his deep desire to create an architecture that would be visually as well as technologically of the twentieth century. When Goodhue died, his office had expected to continue the library project, but the university instead turned it over to Rogers, who was rapidly consolidating his power over the physical form Yale would take.

While Sterling Library ranks with the Memorial Quadrangle as Rogers's best work at Yale, the basic design of the building is nonetheless not his but Goodhue's. Sketches left by Goodhue, some of them done by the great renderer Hugh Ferriss, indicate that the library's entrance and tall, chunky stack tower were conceived by Goodhue, who also prepared a plan (FIGS. 259 & 260). Rogers altered the plan and at first attempted to make the overall proportions of the mass more slender, though he soon returned to an even stockier version of Goodhue's massing. He retained his own interior layout, however, in effect squeezing it into what was essentially Goodhue's overall composition (FIG. 261). Rogers's plan is more

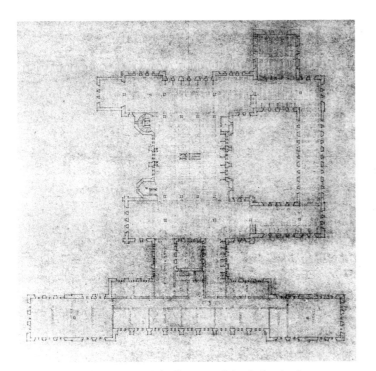

FIG. 260 *Sterling Memorial Library: original plan by Bertram Grosvenor Goodhue, ca. 1923.*

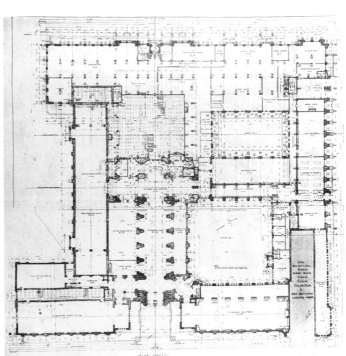

FIG. 261 *Sterling Memorial Library: plan of the ground floor by James Gamble Rogers, ca. 1925.*

graceful, more fully processional, than Goodhue's would have been, but the most memorable aspect of the building—the way in which the sixteen-story stack tower rises with powerful verticality over a handsomely sculpted, arched entry wing—had its origins in Goodhue's early designs.[12] As completed by Rogers, the Sterling Library ended up being squatter than Goodhue appears to have envisioned it, but there can be no question that Rogers's design is based on Goodhue's conception of the building. One detail is particularly telling: at the street level, Rogers's gracefully massed front door (FIG. 262) resembles the entrance to Goodhue's Nebraska State Capitol of 1916–28 far more than the fussier and less fluid entrance shown in Goodhue's early drawings for the library. A curious reversal of influence suggests itself here: did Goodhue's Nebraska entrance, which would have been completed by the time that Sterling was built, provide the inspiration for Rogers's revision of Goodhue's earlier Sterling Library entrance? Or did Goodhue leave another drawing, more Goodhue-esque, so to speak, than the ones that were published, that Rogers followed? It is impossible to know. In any event, the approach to the building from College Street along the axis of the large open space on which it fronts is splendid: the stack tower gradually recedes and the arch of the entrance emerges as the dominant visual element in a complex, active composition, a village

of small masses set along High Street (FIG. 263; see also FIG. 285).

The library was Rogers's first attempt to design in what he later called a "modern" Gothic style, though it is likely that Rogers would have sneered at any suggestion that he shared Goodhue's determination to evolve a new and different form of Gothic architecture. Still, it is difficult not to see how clearly

FIG. 262 *Sterling Memorial Library: High Street elevation by James Gamble Rogers, ca. 1925.*

FIG. 263 *Sterling Memorial Library: east (High Street) facade, June 20, 1930.*

Goodhue's preliminary work seems to have directed him toward a willingness to think more in terms of massing than small-scale, picturesque detail. Although Rogers later wrote that the design was "as near to modern Gothic as we dared to make it," he noted that he had "kept, however, sufficiently close to the sound principles and tried traditions of the old Gothic to be certain that there would be no sense of freakishness and no danger of becoming, in the passing of time, a little out of style."[13] In truth it is only the bookstack tower that seems to represent any real attempt to evolve a modern Gothic scheme, and the stack tower is really a boxy skyscraper clad in Gothic detail, with a strong emphasis on verticality in its fenestration. The major public spaces—the nave-like entry vestibule, the circulation desk that all too closely resembles an altar, and the long, narrow reading room replete with Gothic details and high, traceried windows—do little to acknowledge the decade of their design. And the building's iconographic details, like those of the Memorial Quadrangle, fill every available surface in the lower sections of the building. Outside walls on one side of the building contain a series of tableaux in relief depicting the history of the library; the main entrance is adorned with banal, if thematically appropriate,

phrases like "The library is a summons to scholarship"; and a modest service closet is elevated to aesthetic eminence by the placement of a broom and mop carved in stone above its door.

As for the book tower, its tall lancet windows, on some sides running the full height of the tower, work well to lighten the enormous visual weight of the bulky bookstack, on which ordinary rows of punched windows would have created an inert, dead mass. Rogers's use of verticals here seems to recall not so much other Gothic buildings as the striking and proto-functionalist rear facade of Carrère and Hastings's New York Public Library. But here the bookstack is not an element of a rear facade but the dominant element of the entire building. The book tower is for all practical purposes a modern skyscraper, and it is an ironic twist that here structural steel is used to support decorative stone buttresses. Rogers characteristically took pride in the fact that, as a piece of engineering, it was very much of its time, again seeing no contradiction between the structure and the garb in which he sheathed it. Needless to say, the design of Sterling offended the *Harkness Hoot,* which asked, "Is the Sterling Library beautiful? Is anything admirable in a highly functional building which dresses up like a cathedral, its

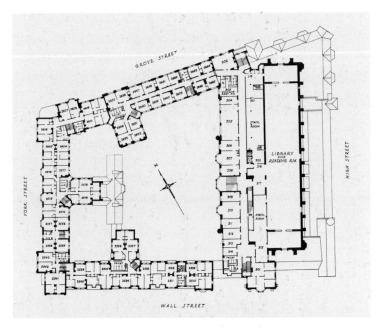

FIG. 264 *Sterling Law Buildings:
plan of the third floor.*

FIG. 265 *Sterling Law Buildings:
High and Grove Street facades.*

entrance hall a nave, its reading rooms a crossing, and its delivery desk a high altar? All this, in the University whose motto is Lux et Veritas. There is not one suggestion of Veritas in the Sterling Library;— and for that matter there is precious little of Lux."[14]

The steel bookstack of the library as it rises over the more overtly Gothicized lower wings, which contain not only the ecclesiastically designed spaces to which the *Hoot* refers, but cloisters and courtyards as well, is the clearest manifestation in Rogers's work of the duality of his approach. But while the juxtaposition is more striking here than in the Memorial Quadrangle, it is essentially the same. The primary concerns in both cases are practical ones: the plan is foremost, followed by the organization of the mass to allow for light in the Quadrangle and function in the bookstack. The romanticism, however

essential it was to Rogers's concept of the building, is applied later.

In 1926, as construction on the library was about to begin, Rogers received the commission for two other major Sterling-funded buildings, the law school and the graduate school. Each would represent a further leap forward in complexity, particularly in terms of the way in which Rogers was able to achieve a notable degree of cohesion and urbanistic success with a highly active series of masses. Beside both of these buildings the Memorial Quadrangle, for all its grace, seems static. The Sterling Law Buildings, completed in 1931, contain dormitory space, dining halls, classrooms, offices, and a library, organized around three courtyards (FIGS. 264–266). The mass is an irregular agglomeration of Gothic, Norman, and even occasional early Renaissance forms, combining

FIG. 266 *Sterling Law Library: east (High Street) facade in 1931.*

to make a lively if not always fully resolved composition. Dominating the overall mass, appearing from some angles to rise out of the uneven lower wings as the Gothic bulk of St. John the Divine rises out of Harlem, is a block-long reproduction of Kings College Chapel, Cambridge, which serves as the library (FIG. 266). The interpretation is typical of Rogers: brick, a material not used at all in the real Kings College Chapel, is here mixed freely with a grayish limestone, and Rogers has given his chapel thirteen bays, one more than at Cambridge, to stretch the mass the length of the block. The end bays, however, are false and contain no windows. The Law School library is another prime example of Rogers's romantic pragmatism: a European prototype with no direct relation to the program at hand is adopted to satisfy romantic yearnings and then is changed, in an utterly businesslike way, to satisfy a new program and fit into a new picturesque whole. The irregular form of the block on which the Law School sits breaks the order of the interior courts and enlivens the compositional mass considerably: when viewed from Grove Street, which is set at a diagonal to the New Haven street grid, the library appears to rise from the whole grouping at an angle, adding a welcome tension to the overall composition (see FIG. 265). While there are a few striking details, such as a triple window that, with its combination of arches, flamboyant tracery, and square panes, is a kind of Palladian Gothic, most of the

exterior details are dull, and lack the delicacy of detail of the Memorial Quadrangle. And the combination of mottled brick and limestone gives the facade an almost freckled appearance, neither as warm nor as subtle as the golden granite of the Quadrangle.

The Hall of Graduate Studies of 1930–32, just across York Street, accommodates an equally diverse program (FIGS. 267 & 268). Here Rogers again separated the functions, relegating dormitory space and dining facilities to the rear of the two irregularly shaped courts (which deftly respond to an oddly shaped site) and stretching offices and classrooms across the front of the building. Lacking a function such as the Law School library to give the composition a symbolic anchor, he thrust several of the dormitory rooms up into a fourteen-story tower that straddles the two courts. The tower exaggerates the qualities present in the building as a whole. It is of brick with limestone ornament in geometric patterns such as a checkerboard arrangement, an attempt to create a modern Gothic expression somewhat different from any Rogers had used before. The tower's windows are set back from the facade in sheer vertical recesses, and it is topped with a bright metallic pyramid. It is now Jazz-Age Gothic, Art Moderne, or Art Deco more than anything else Rogers had done, and in its massing even calls to mind some of the better skyscrapers of the period, like Clinton and Russell's Sixty Wall Tower in Lower

FIG. 267 *Hall of Graduate Studies: east (York Street) elevation.*

FIG. 268 *Looking west on Wall Street toward the Hall of Graduate Studies, with the Sterling Memorial Library on the left and the Sterling Law Buildings on the right, ca. 1935.*

Manhattan of 1932, which has a similar Deco-Gothic crown, this time sixty-six floors above Wall Street. Rogers was hardly trying to replicate this kind of architecture in miniature—his tower is really a campanile punctuating his Gothic courtyards, not a freestanding skyscraper—but he was clearly paying attention to it, and showed enormous imagination in the way in which he was able to integrate its themes into his eclectic composition.

The tower functions best, however, in an urbanistic sense. In its position at the head of Wall Street, it anchors a vista with considerable finesse, and its scale is perfect—big enough to be a magnet, small enough to seem at home amid its lower surroundings. The triple entrance to the building beneath the tower spans the street like a great gateway and serves as a reminder that this structure is not simply a tower, but a complicated arrangement of buildings out of which the tower rises. While the courtyards of the Hall of Graduate Studies are not themselves as distinguished as those of the Memorial Quadrangle, and the attempts to create a slightly more modernistic air with such details as patterned brick are only moderately successful, the tower is one of Rogers's finest gestures, neither a pure symbol like Harkness Tower nor a dominating mass like the Sterling Library bookstack, but a graceful element of punctuation.

————

James Gamble Rogers's hegemony over the shaping of Yale in the first half of the twentieth century was ultimately realized, however, not through the Sterling buildings, immense though they were, but through a project of his original patron and continued close friend, Edward Harkness. Harkness, like many alumni of his generation—he was born in 1875—took pleasure in the extent to which Yale was solidifying its position as a university of international renown. At the same time, however, he was disturbed by the lack of intimacy in the new Yale. The goal of making Yale a place to mold an elite class was succeeding, but at a price. Harkness wondered if average Yale men—having been shy as an undergraduate, he could think of himself as average, no irony intended—would get lost at the larger, more institutional Yale that he had helped to bring forth. The solution, he came increasingly to believe, was to divide the undergraduate college into smaller units. Rogers, shocked when he discovered that freshmen didn't know their classmates and were often housed inadequately, came to agree. Samuel H. Fisher (B.A. 1889), a member of the Corporation who was close to both Rogers and Harkness, thought the answer

lay in following the model of Oxford and Cambridge, and in 1927 Harkness invited Rogers, President James Rowland Angell, and Fisher to England on a secret mission to study the Oxbridge college system. The men came back convinced that the best solution to Yale's increasing depersonalization was to break the undergraduate body up into a series of residential colleges. They were only loosely based on those of Oxford and Cambridge, of course, since they were created by fiat out of a larger unit, not truly individual academic institutions that had grown up on their own, and they were conceived primarily as residential units with only minimal academic roles. Rogers was certain that creating the colleges was the best route to preserving the network of Yale-inspired connections that had been so important in his own life. "The loss of these cherished advantages may be the penalty that we have to pay for the great expansion in the size of our classes of the last few years," he wrote in a memorandum entitled "The Future of Yale College," which concluded that "More and more of us, I believe, are now becoming of the opinion that [Yale's traditions] can be secured only by some kind of division into smaller units."[15]

Rogers prepared a preliminary plan to divide the undergraduate body into ten colleges, and Harkness agreed to underwrite the cost anonymously. A series of misunderstandings between Harkness and Angell, who believed the offer to be secret rather than anonymous and thus did not direct the faculty to come up with a system for implementation before the deadline Harkness had set, led to the withdrawal of the offer in July 1928 and to Harkness's presentation of a similar plan to Harvard. Yale's embarrassment over the loss of this gift to its greatest rival, by a man with no ties of his own to Harvard, was immense. Rogers was deeply involved in the negotiations that persuaded Harkness to agree, later that year, to renew his offer. In 1929, after the faculty had finally developed a plan, the offer was accepted. Harkness ended up donating nearly $16 million to Yale to implement the residential college system, and Rogers received his largest Yale commission of all.

Four of the original seven colleges that opened in the fall of 1933 were reconstructed from existing Rogers buildings (FIG. 269). Rogers reworked the Memorial Quadrangle to form Branford and Saybrook Colleges, inserting dining halls, faculty suites, and master's houses into the original structure, but making only minor changes in the exterior elevations. Perhaps the most unusual was the insertion of automobile garages into several of the street facades, a function for which there was scant Gothic

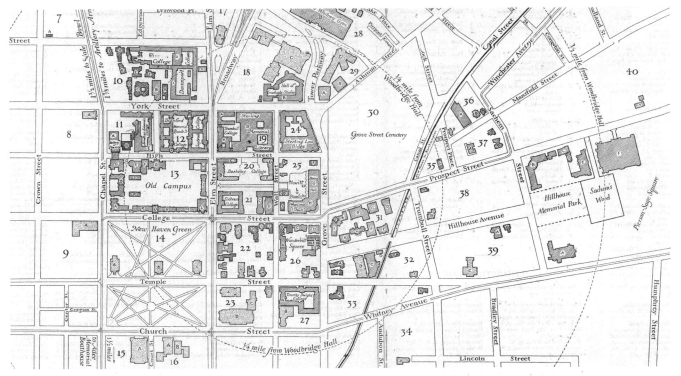

FIG. 269 *Map of Yale University, 1935: detail showing the central campus and Pierson-Sage Square.*

precedent. (Rogers actually disturbed these facades more by his use of Georgian paneled doors for the main entrances to both master's houses, a decision apparently based on the belief that such doors were an instant signal of comfortable domesticity.) The necessity of working within the limitations set by the structure and plan of the original Memorial Quadrangle restricted Rogers considerably, and the new interior spaces are not among his best.

The third reconstruction was of Sterling Quadrangle, a dormitory unit built in 1929–30 adjoining the then-unfinished library (FIG. 270). A dining hall (on the site of the University Gymnasium), library, and common rooms were added to make the quadrangle into Trumbull College, which faced the north facade of the Memorial Quadrangle, now Saybrook College, across Elm Street. Rogers designed a facade with high corner wings and a continuous midblock arcade in literal echo of his earlier facade, establishing a pattern of urbanism by imitation that he was to follow with varying degrees of success for some years (FIG. 271). The overall style of Trumbull, however, is closer to the attempt to create a "modern Gothic" idiom that Rogers had begun with Sterling Library, though it is not nearly as successful. The facades of Trumbull are flat and severe, and the overall massing is somewhat heavy-handed and stocky. The best aspect of Trumbull is a sense of tightly compressed energy; the college is squeezed between the enor-

mous bulk of the library and Elm Street (see FIG. 16), and you can feel the pressure acting upon its form. If the details are not particularly sharp, the sense of compression gives Trumbull a quality unlike any of Rogers's other buildings. It makes Trumbull less picturesque but, perhaps inadvertently, more modern, than any of Rogers's other buildings at Yale.

Rogers was far more successful, at least by his usual standard of gentle visual pleasure, in Jonathan Edwards College, where he incorporated two of his earlier dormitory buildings, Dickinson and Wheelock Halls (1925–26), into a new composition. Here, one large, L-shaped court provides an excellent processional sequence (FIG. 272). The elevations of the buildings themselves are less sophisticated than at the Memorial Quadrangle, but they at least lack the heaviness of Trumbull, and the movement from open to closed spaces in the court and the spatial definition provided by the heavy landscaping are the equal of any open space at Yale. Rogers's achievement in the Jonathan Edwards court is all the more notable for the successful integration into the composition of a number of small elements such as the tiny gardener's cottage, and a well-executed relationship to adjacent Weir Hall, a castle-like building completed in 1924 by Everett V. Meeks (B.A. 1901, B.F.A. 1917) from designs from Tracy and Swartwout (see FIG. 221). Rogers also managed a particularly successful transition from stone to brick on the York Street side

FIG. 270 *Construction of the York Street section of the Sterling Quadrangle (Trumbull College) looking northeast from the corner of York and Elm Streets, with the Sterling Memorial Library in the background and the University Gymnasium on the right, February 22, 1930.*

FIG. 271 *Trumbull College: south (Elm Street) elevation.*

of Jonathan Edwards, where the two materials seem almost woven into each other at a corner.

Both Rogers and Harkness foresaw the space between High and York Streets becoming a "Gothic corridor," in effect a district of Gothic-style build ings stretching across the entire campus, taking in the Memorial Quadrangle, Jonathan Edwards College, Sterling Library, and any future construction along either street. Indeed, in 1931 Harkness asked Rogers to add a Gothic facade to the University Theatre of 1926 by Blackall, Clapp and Whittemore, so as to render that building more compatible with the Memorial Quadrangle and Jonathan Edwards College across the street and, not incidentally, to culminate a short Gothic vista looking west along Library Street (FIG. 273). Thus it is perhaps not all that surprising that Rogers decided to design the York Street wing of Davenport College in a manner that Russell Lynes was later to call "a quick transition from the age of the moat to the age of the minuet,"[16] giving the building a Gothic facade facing York Street and a Georgian facade toward the courtyard (FIGS. 274 & 275; see also FIG. 17). He felt compelled to preserve the identity of the "Gothic corridor" of York Street even though he had decided to design Davenport and its neighbor, Pierson College, in Georgian rather than Gothic style.

This may be the ultimate piece of romantic prag- matism, a single building in which one side is Gothic and the other side is Georgian. It is not possible to stray farther than this from the belief that architec- tural style implies some moral imperative, or to suggest more definitively that the architect is, at the end of the day, a set designer. Yet for all that Rogers's design here appears facile, even glib, it has profound implications. For the set he is designing is the streetscape, and Rogers was making a clear state- ment that the integrity of the streetscape was more important than the integrity of the building as an object. He may have expressed this idea in a primi- tive, not to say almost vulgar, fashion, but it is worth noting that his view of urbanistic relationships, if oddly literal-minded, was also highly successful. It was motivated by an awareness that buildings do not stand alone as islands in the city, that they must establish urbanistic relationships among themselves, and that their civic responsibility, so to speak, is to the streetscape. Rogers's buildings strove to reach out to each other, and to create some sort of whole that was larger, if not necessarily any more diverse, than the individual parts.

The switch to Georgian in Pierson and Daven- port Colleges of 1933, later continued in Timothy Dwight College of 1934–35, remains surprising, yet

FIG. 273 *Library Street looking west toward the University Theatre, with Jonathan Edwards College on the left and Branford College on the right.*

FIG. 274 *Davenport College: east (York Street) facade, ca. 1933.*

FIG. 275 *Davenport College: east facade from the courtyard, ca. 1933.*

it was carefully considered. Rogers was on record as stating that he did not believe that buildings away from the central core of the campus had to be designed in the Gothic style, but he was not specific about an alternative. Why, then, should they be Georgian? One of his associates said many years ago that Rogers was sensitive to criticism about the small windows of the bedrooms in the Memorial Quadrangle and felt that Georgian architecture provided an easy excuse for more glass. It was certainly more domestic in feeling than Gothic, and a more natural style for buildings that, despite the broader programs of the colleges, were still primarily residential. Significantly, the Corporation's Committee on Architectural Plan announced the embrace of the Georgian as, in part, an effort to reintroduce some of the feeling of the architecture of colonial New England and the Brick Row to the campus.[17] It is also true that brick was less expensive than stone, and for all the extravagance with which Yale appeared to build, not since the Memorial Quadrangle had the university been able to order its architect to design literally without regard to cost. And Rogers certainly had plenty of experience designing Georgian buildings; at the time the Yale colleges were under way he was also at work on several Georgian-style hospitals for the Commonwealth Fund, the Harkness family foundation, and he was also building a Georgian monolith for the Aetna Life Insurance Company in Hartford. Rogers may also have felt that as Yale continued to expand, it needed some visual relief; that block after block after block of Gothic buildings, however well-designed, could be monotonous, and visual monotony was what he as an architect always seemed to fear most. Indeed, one might argue that at the scale of an entire campus, stylistic change was the only way that Rogers could achieve the sense of variety and visual pleasure that he always sought.

In one sense, though, it hardly matters why Rogers and the Yale Corporation made the change, since Rogers's Gothic and Georgian buildings were essentially the same under the skin. Style, at least in the case of Rogers's work, was a matter of surface appearance, not deep structure. It is worth noting, however, that the Georgian buildings Rogers designed at Yale were quite different from the Georgian houses that were going up with Harkness's money at the same time at Harvard. Rogers's Georgian architecture was far more picturesque than Harvard's, just as the Gothic architecture Rogers produced for Yale was more picturesque than the Gothic of Princeton or of the University of Pennsylvania. The Harvard buildings, most of which were designed

FIG. 276 *Pierson College courtyard.*

FIG. 277 *Timothy Dwight College courtyard looking south toward the dining hall, September 3, 1935.*

by Shepley, Rutan and Coolidge, are of deep-red brick, and they are austere, tight, and almost puritanical in the manner of New England colonial houses. For Yale, Rogers used a warmer, lighter-red brick, and his buildings seem softer, more textured, their masses sprawling across their sites, not huddled tall and taut like their Harvard counterparts. Yale's Georgian was Southern, and Southern imagery so seemed to pervade the buildings that a small, informal wing of white-painted brick that Rogers inserted into a corner of Pierson College became known as the "Slave Quarters," a nickname whose unfortunate symbolism undercut its visual quality (see FIG. 18). The courtyards of both Pierson and Davenport are generous spaces, expansive yet defined, and Pierson should rank with those of Jonathan Edwards and the Memorial Quadrangle as among Rogers's finest (FIG. 276). In his final Georgian college, Timothy Dwight, Rogers attempted to move somewhat closer to New England—and to old Yale—, inserting a dining hall wing in the form of a New England meetinghouse (FIG. 277). This forms another L-shaped court, not as successful spatially as that of Jonathan Edwards, since there is no complex processional sequence. The only major route across the space is a short, direct line from the main gateway to the dining hall.

FIG. 281 *Calhoun College: north (Cross Campus) facade, after 1949.*

FIG. 282 *Construction of Silliman College, July 2, 1940.*

FIG. 283 *Payne Whitney Gymnasium: presentation drawing by Otto R. Eggers for John Russell Pope, 1930.*

without either the inventiveness of most of Rogers's work or, more tellingly, the bombastic grandeur of so much of Pope's. Silliman is a series of Georgian wings connected to three preexisting buildings: Byers Hall, a French Renaissance chateau of 1903 by Hiss and Weekes, and the two Vanderbilt-Scientific Halls, Collegiate Gothic dormitories of 1903–6 by Charles C. Haight. The architecture of the new sections by Eggers and Higgins is loosely inspired by Colonial Williamsburg, and it is dutiful more than lively.

Payne Whitney Gymnasium is a far more characteristic Pope building by virtue of its sheer size and enormous scale, though it, too, is hardly typical of his work (FIG. 283; see also FIG. 19). Payne Whitney is a wildly overscaled Gothic cathedral whose exterior is a strange combination of institutional blandness and Art Moderne fervor, as if Pope were trying to make a modernistic factory. (It foreshadows, in a sense, Giles Gilbert Scott's great power stations in London.) In the end the gymnasium is more grandiose than banal, and while it could certainly be described as being both romantic and pragmatic, it isn't Rogers's brand of romantic pragmatism at all. Rogers's architecture always emanates a certain degree of modesty, even sweetness. His buildings are not unselfconscious, but they bespeak a kind of sincerity. Payne Whitney, by comparison, is a bit overblown, even pompous, and it takes itself far more seriously than Rogers's buildings. Rogers prances, where Pope—at least at Yale—seems to plod.

It is lightness, in the end, that distinguishes Rogers, that renders his work graceful and confers upon it such continual freshness. Rogers's view of himself as a gentleman extended into his architecture: it is always deferential, always designed to make one feel a sense of delight and ease. One senses that Rogers would have explained his architecture to a doubter by smiling gently and saying that this is what I am doing, and I know you may find it silly, but no matter, just relax and let this architecture weave its spell. Pope, by contrast, would have tried to awe this skeptic, not to enchant him, but enchantment is an essential element of Rogers's work. It is not surprising, then, that the Rogers buildings tended to be more fanciful in their decoration, even humorous. Indeed, there was something of a minor scandal when it was discovered that one of the quotations carved into the exterior of the Hall of Graduate Studies was not from Shakespeare or Dante but was a line from *Scaramouche,* a popular novel by Rafael Sabatini: "He was born with a gift for laughter, and a sense that the world was mad."

For most of his career, Rogers's work at Yale benefited from his association with Beatrix Jones Farrand

(M.A.H. 1925), a landscape architect of extraordinary gifts, who had been designing gardens for Princeton since 1912 and was invited to landscape the Memorial Quadrangle in 1922. Like Rogers, Farrand's route to Yale commissions came through personal work for Edward Harkness. She had met Harkness through her husband Max, a Yale history professor, and was asked to take charge of the gardens at Eolia, Harkness's country house near New London. Harkness was apparently pleased with the result, since shortly thereafter, Farrand was doing work at Yale. She began with the Memorial Quadrangle (see FIGS. 253 & 254) and came eventually to be in charge of landscape design throughout the campus, including the creation of courtyard gardens for all of the residential colleges and landscape plans for the Divinity School by Delano and Aldrich, the School of Medicine, and the gardens of the President's House on Hillhouse Avenue, as well as a private nursery to supply and replenish the Yale landscapes.

Farrand and Rogers may not have had the personal relationship of Edwin Lutyens and Gertrude Jekyll, but they appeared to collaborate nearly as well, and a remarkable body of work bears their joint stamp. Farrand remained active at Yale until 1945, and at one point, as consulting landscape gardener, she supervised a staff of sixty Yale employees. Farrand seemed to understand the strengths of Rogers's architecture, and she was able to play to them with varied, inventive, and gentle plantings. She was particularly attuned to seasonal plantings, and to finding plant material that would flourish during the academic year rather than in midsummer. Her most notable landscape concept, and surely the one that responded most directly to Rogers's architecture, was her decision to landscape the moat-like spaces that Rogers often placed between the sidewalk and the bases of his buildings (FIG. 284). Rogers saw these moats as a means of assuring that light could enter the basements, and he probably liked the way that the moat walls set his buildings off slightly from the sidewalk, separating them subtly from the pedestrian walking along the street. Farrand created the idea of the "garden moat" by filling Rogers's voids with magnolias, crabapples, viburnum, dogwood, and wisteria vines, landscapes as lavish as any she created in the residential college courtyards. She referred to the garden moat as a place for "a kind of planting that was protected from being trodden on and, at the same time, created a canopy for the sidewalk."[18]

Farrand's garden moats softened a hard edge that Rogers's architecture, usually so soft-edged, could sometimes display toward the sidewalk. Indeed,

FIG. 284 *Davenport College: moat along the east (York Street) facade.*

paradoxically it is Farrand's landscape rather than Rogers's buildings that sometimes contributed more to the urbanistic success of the Yale campus. Where Rogers succeeded in establishing an architectural tone that was enticing, and at its best even enthralling, his achievement is less certain in an area of urbanism—an area in which he appears, superficially at least, to have succeeded so well. As an urbanist, Rogers's instincts were sound, but fatally limited. He clearly believed in the notion of context, and in creating a common fabric for the university he was building. He never made the mistake of seeing his buildings as isolated objects, distinct from their surroundings, and every Rogers building at Yale is inflected to some degree toward its neighbors. At Davenport College, he carried this to a striking extreme. Yet the building type that Rogers—and Yale—liked best was still, at bottom, anti-urban. The courtyard organization of the colleges was almost entirely inward-looking; the finest aspects of the intricate and subtle composition of the Memorial Quadrangle, save for Harkness Tower, are within the courtyards. They do not face the street. Indeed, what faces the street could almost be considered a series of backs, not a front. The real facades, the ones that convey the building's most important message, are the private ones that face the courtyards. It is in the

nature of the residential colleges that the public realm they create is really a kind of expanded private realm, turned inward, away from the city.

James Gamble Rogers crafted an urbanism for Yale that is neither truly urban, in the sense of being open and public and committed to the life of the street, nor truly rural, in the sense of being made of buildings that exist in isolation from one another. Yet this in-between condition is, in a way, a great accomplishment, for Rogers created at Yale a unique balance between the idea of the city and the idea of the non-urban campus. His goal was to unify these opposites—to make a picturesque campus that was knitted together on city streets.

Rogers tolerated the street more than he loved it, which is why his streets are corridors, not places. Elm Street, in the heart of the campus, where the back of Trumbull College faces the back of Saybrook College, for example, is a corridor if there ever was one, and it probably seemed truly inviting only in the days when Beatrix Farrand's moat gardens flourished there. (Most of Farrand's landscape designs, unlike Rogers's architecture, have not been well-maintained, and some have not been maintained at all.) A somewhat more sophisticated urbanism is present at the Sterling Memorial Library and the other Sterling buildings, however, where

FIG. 285 *Looking west along Cross Campus toward Berkeley College and the Sterling Memorial Library, October 1, 1934.*

there are gestures toward the street, or at least toward the grandeur of an open axial vista, that render the architecture a bit more public, and more visually alive from the exterior (FIG. 285). Still, Rogers had little interest in enlivening the street as an experience. When siting meant that passersby could be enveloped in his stage set, Rogers was happy to oblige, but he never engaged the street except to the extent that it supported his own picturesque and compositional goals. The service of Yale's image, and the support of Yale's mystique as a special and private place, were always the most important thing. The city and its streets were something to be coped with because they were there, and Rogers accommodated his designs to them. And yet Yale, left to its own devices, would not have been as beautiful as it is, or as civilized, without him, and it would in all likelihood have had a relationship with the cityscape that was less benign than the one Rogers established. Surely it would have been more arrogant. Without Rogers, Yale might well have developed more as John Russell Pope would have had it — grand, formal, dry, and distinctly overbearing. It was James Gamble Rogers's particular skill to be able to design in a manner that supported the institutional ambitions of Yale in the early years of the twentieth century while keeping them lyrical

and not letting them become overblown. Rogers may not have connected his buildings to the larger city around Yale, or even have done much to acknowledge that city. But neither did he allow Yale to become pompous and to express its aloofness through an architecture of total separation. The urbanism he created for Yale brilliantly navigated an architectural compromise between the relentless sameness of the typical cityscape of the time, and the architectural free-for-all of the non-urban campus. Yale as designed by James Gamble Rogers was not the Bronx, and it was not Princeton. It established a strong, even sublime, balance between private and public realms, and it established a sense of place that remains powerful more than three-quarters of a century after Rogers began his work. Rogers's architecture conferred a lightness on an institution that did not take naturally to it and, indeed, might almost be said to have been seeking something entirely different: a sense of gravitas. That Rogers could create an architecture that supplied this gravitas and possessed an exquisite lightness at the same time was, in the end, his greatest gift, and it conferred upon Yale a genuine grace.

Modern Architecture at Yale: A Memoir

VINCENT SCULLY

Looking back from the icy pinnacle of the twenty-first century, it seems obvious that Yale University created an architectural wonder for itself in the years between the last century's world wars; but in 1950, when A. Whitney Griswold (B.A. 1929, PH.D. 1933) took office as Yale's sixteenth president, almost nobody thought so. Our objections to the architecture of James Gamble Rogers (B.A. 1889), John Russell Pope, and Delano and Aldrich (Delano, B.A. 1895, B.F.A. 1907) were not based on the grounds one might expect. We did not object to the fact, which indeed rarely crossed our minds, that the residential colleges especially were designed to cut Yale off from New Haven. Their quadrangles created small, closed communities of considerable quality, as they were intended to do, but by the same token they fragmented Yale as a campus into separate, almost unconnected pieces, and they were, where possible, moated against the encroachments of the town. For most New Haveners they were alien fortresses, inconceivably rich and exotic, literally beautiful beyond description and concealing secret gardens and other mysterious places that nobody but the elect had ever seen. Pope's proposed plan for Yale, of 1919, and Olmsted's for New Haven, of 1910, which would have gone far toward unifying the two in a common urban grandeur, were long forgotten. Yale's physical autonomy, its separation from New Haven, was taken by most of us to be a natural condition. We hardly recognized the long-range problems involved; indeed at that time they were not as serious as they were soon to become. Later, when the situation was fully faced only by Saarinen's Morse and Stiles Colleges, the remedies came too late, and perhaps by that time were the wrong ones anyway.

No, in 1950 our criticisms of Yale's buildings of the Golden Age of the thirties were founded not on broadly urbanistic but on narrowly stylistic grounds. We despised them because they were not "Modern." They were "Eclectic"; they employed familiar forms deriving from several styles of historical architecture and so were outside our range of perception at that time. It would be difficult to imagine a critical doctrine more hermetic and, indeed, more childish than that. It is of course still passionately espoused by a large part of the architectural and critical community — especially by its most conservative, neo-modernist, members. In 1950, by way of contrast, the modernist view was held by almost everybody *except* the most conservative conservatives, and, whether we recognized the fact or not, it was derived from a revolutionary cast of thought. Like most modern revolutions since the French it preferred ideological purism and conformity over sensory experience; or, rather, it subjected sensory experience, no less than reason itself, to ideological tyranny. A good many

FIG. 286 *Looking west on Chapel Street, ca. 1965. From the right: Old Art Gallery (Egerton Swartwout),
Yale University Art Gallery (Louis I. Kahn), and Art and Architecture Building (Paul Rudolph).*

architects, especially, say, in England, are still doing so, and they are trashing their old world in spectacular fashion. James Gamble Rogers and the other architects of his generation had been almost the opposite. With the exception of Ralph Adams Cram and the really die-hard Gothicists, they had little that could be called an ideology, perhaps less than any other architects in history have ever had, and the Modernists despised them for that most of all. The Eclectics simply adored architecture and were supremely skilled at putting it together. They knew how to build—for rich and poor alike, we should remember—and they knew how to ornament, to adorn. Those last words are still capable of driving the modernist avant-garde (now rear-guard) crazy. In 1950 it mattered not at all to most of us that the grassy courtyards of the colleges were shaded and beautiful, and their masonry walls lovingly detailed, and their high roofs and monumental chimneys splendidly marshaled in the sky. Few of us saw those things. Or, put more truly and madly, we all saw them and profited from them in our souls every day and in our hearts loved them, but our ideologies rarely allowed our minds to register any of that. We professed to find them gloomy. We regretted that they had not been built by Walter Gropius or Frank Lloyd Wright. (If they had been, one thing at least is likely, that they would be piles of rubble today.) In 1950 we thought that Harkness Tower was silly. We wanted Modern Architecture.

What did we mean by that? On the whole we meant that we wanted forms nobody had ever seen before. Sometimes we said that we wanted flat roofs and white walls and factory windows like the Bauhaus, or that we wanted everything arranged in weightless planes emphasizing volume rather than mass, as Hitchcock and Johnson had said the new architecture had to do,[1] and sometimes we wanted those planes to be arranged in floating pictorial patterns as de Stijl had once done, or set up on thin columns like Le Corbusier's pilotis. Others might have preferred the deep cantilevers of Wright's work, shadowing long bands of horizontal windows. Note should be taken that all these forms had been characteristic of early modern architecture, at a period when modern buildings, as distinct from modern urbanistic theory, were hardly destructive at all of the traditional city. Though simplified and in a sense reduced from the more traditional forms of architecture, they were still civilized. But by 1950, after World War II, we had become restless; we wanted stronger meat, and our late modern architecture was becoming structurally and sculpturally aggressive, curiously primitive in form and supremely destructive of the city. We were no longer designing buildings to get along with each other. Each one had to be unique; we were no longer working with types or with the repetitive and complementary kinds of forms that a city needs. We were no longer decorating construction—we were refusing to do so—but were constructing decoration. Anyway, in 1950 we had lost our tradition; we wanted anything that was new. We tried, like Gropius before us, to believe that the forms we wanted derived from function, which few of them did. If pressed, we would say that "Our Time," the implacably German *zeitgeist* that we wanted to rule us, demanded special new forms for all its functions, as historians like Sigfried Giedion were saying it did. That could be carried to absurd lengths as when, as late as 1996, a member of the Divinity School faculty, approving the university's scheme to butcher his quadrangle, declared "You can't teach 1990s theology in a 1920s building." Few except the most deluded would voice such a sentiment today, but in 1950 almost all of us pretended to be stifled by the old forms. Few of us, and nobody at Yale that I knew of, were conscious revolutionaries, but, as I have noted, we had their purist aesthetic. Somehow we wanted to wipe the present clean of the past, to sweep it pure of contaminating objects. Everything had to begin anew and be clothed anew. We would brook no compromise.

That point of view was not new in 1950. It had been publicly voiced at Yale in the early thirties, just at the moment when the major programs of eclectic building were reaching their climax. The vehicle of publication was a newly founded undergraduate magazine of opinion called *The Harkness Hoot* with which, in modern myth, a student named A.Whitney Griswold was closely associated but with which he had in fact nothing to do. He graduated in 1929 and was in graduate school at Yale during the years of the *Hoot*'s publication. As an undergraduate he was an occasional columnist for the *Yale Daily News,* writing short humorous pieces under the name of Sancho Panza. A cursory scanning of them suggests a studious avoidance of serious topics. It was young Griswold the jokester (dialect stories and comic verse) that the future president chose to reveal to his peers. The *Harkness Hoot* was a different matter entirely. It was founded in October 1930 by two Yale seniors, William Harlan Hale (B.A. 1931) and Selden Rodman (B.A. 1931), and it ran a lively course through the spring term of 1934. In its second number it published an all-out attack by Hale on James Gamble Rogers and his Collegiate Gothic ("Girder Gothic," Hale called it), employing all the catchwords of the modern movement of that time: function, truth to materials, and so on. If naive and sometimes rather brutally categorical in the Bauhaus manner, it is still delightful reading, because, like almost everything else in the *Hoot,* it was very well written, and it might have been speaking for the Griswold of the 1950s who brought modern architecture to Yale. In the next issue the *Hoot* proudly published letters by Frank Lloyd Wright and Henry-Russell Hitchcock applauding the *Hoot*'s stand and calling for the destruction of the eclectic architectural enemy in roundly revolutionary terms. The *Hoot* also attacked Yale's senior societies as part of "an Outworn, Unwanted, Social System." Indeed Yale's whole educational system was denounced by the *Hoot* in splendidly intellectual terms, decrying alike its lack of scholarly rigor and the meager opportunities it offered for independent work. It all sounds much like Griswold proposing his plans A and B in the early fifties: revolutionary restructurings of the curriculum shot down by the faculty but forming the basis for Directed Studies and the Scholar of the House program. Of it or not, Griswold the graduate student would seem to have read the *Hoot* and remembered it. In 1950 he became president of Yale, and Yale's modern era began.

It was Griswold who in general shepherded the university into the new postwar world. He did not rebuild it from the ground up but augmented its structure incrementally, and the character of his architecture reflects that goal. His accession perfectly coincided with the first years after the war when it again became possible to build. There had been a long hiatus in construction since the thirties, a period of time longer conceptually than as measured in actual years. Modernism, as we have said, now reigned, alike in the Departments of Architecture and History of Art as in Griswold's

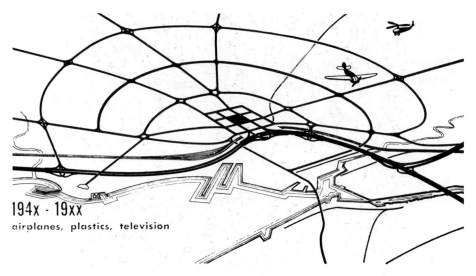

194x · 19xx
airplanes, plastics, television

FIG. 287 *Maurice Rotival, Aerial perspective of the nine squares of New Haven with proposed road network.*

heart. More than that, it now seems that the architects, planners, and critics of that period, and, most important, the public itself, had forgotten a good deal that was fundamental about architecture: about how, for example, its major mission was to build the human settlement entire, shaping towns with coherent plans in which the most important thing about each building was that it got along with the buildings around it. American planners had known all that from the seventeenth century onward. Their work culminated in the City Beautiful Movement of the early twentieth century, augmented in the United States by the influence of the English Garden City program. In its last great decade, that of the 1920s, its last great masters, such as John Nolen, produced hundreds of fine new towns and neighborhoods all over the United States. Then, during the 1930s and afterward, the whole tradition disappeared before the advance of modernism, fueled by depression and war, and it was almost forgotten by the postwar period. It was replaced literally by nothing. Modernist planning was cataclysmic, almost wholly destructive. It was contemptuous of the traditional fabric of cities and was out to obliterate it, largely in order to encourage the free passage of the automobile at the expense of all other urban values. Robert Moses (B.A. 1909) was already running wild in New York.

At that very moment, toward 1950 — exactly when Yale established its Master of City Planning degree — the French planner Maurice Rotival returned to New Haven from Caracas, upon which he had just inflicted almost mortal wounds, and picked up where he had left off in 1941 with a plan for New Haven involving the intersection of two vast superhighways just east of the nine squares (FIG. 287).[2] From this interchange a band of devastation was to stretch to the Green. Downtown New Haven disappeared. Rotival's aerial perspectives of New Haven as so rearranged might have served as illustrations for Aristophanes' *The Birds,* in which the dramatist burlesques Hippodamos of Miletus, the first hero planner of Greek history, in the person of a character named Meton, who flies with the birds and looks down upon the surface of the earth, which he redraws into abstract patterns of his own. Rotival was just like that. He and I were fellows of Jonathan Edwards College at the time, and he would often reappear in the common room after a long absence, rotund, genial, and well turned out, with the Legion of Honor in his buttonhole. I would normally say something like "Ah, Maurice, where have you been?" and he would reply "I have been planning — [pause] — Madagascar." It was all very impressive and utterly destructive of places, and it achieved its full scope in the Redevelopment of New Haven.

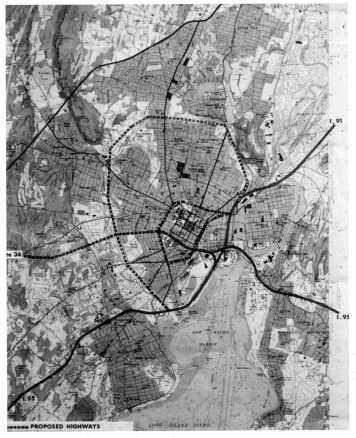

FIG. 288 *Map of New Haven showing the planned intersection of I-95 and I-91, with additional proposals for a network of highways, limited-access connectors, and enlarged streets, 1954.*

That cataclysmic epoch in New Haven's history was initiated, here as in hundreds of other American cities, by the coming of the interstate highways. When Congress voted them into being in 1956 it was decided, at the national level, that they should be encouraged to run right through the center of cities. Decisions regarding the precise route that swathe of destruction would take were to be made by the Departments of Transportation of each state in conjunction with whatever local planning agencies were able to cooperate with them. In New Haven, Rotival's scheme was trotted out, and I-95 and I-91 met at Water Street, and the Redevelopment Agency and the D.O.T. worked out an elaborate scheme of ring roads and connectors that were intended to cut the city to ribbons to permit the car to run free (FIG. 288). No thought was given to supplemental public transportation of any kind. The Oak Street Connector was the first one in place, aimed at wiping out an area described by the mayor as consisting primarily of "whore houses and gin mills," but which was in fact a highly integrated neighborhood, one of the few integrated enclaves in New Haven (FIGS. 289 & 290). It was home to Jews, African Americans, Italians, and even some White Russians. It would have been recognized as a viable community by Jane Jacobs, who wrote her splendid revisionist work, *The Death and Life of Great American Cities,* in 1961, and by Herbert Gans, who wrote his fundamental book, *The Urban Villagers,* just a year later.[3] But since it was all too obviously not WASP or suburban or middle-class, it was not recognized as a community by the political powers of the period, nor apparently by Yale's sociologists either. Its inhabitants were scattered, pushed into other neighborhoods where they didn't want to be, and a process of disintegration—more truly a "domino effect" than the fanciful phenomenon which the Johnson administration was projecting upon Southeast Asia in those very years—began to work its way through the less affluent neighborhoods of the town. Once started, that

FIG. 289 *Construction of the Oak Street Connector, with Mayor Richard C. Lee and Norris C. Andrews, Director of New Haven's City Plan Commission, Fall 1959.*

FIG. 290 *Looking southeast over the New Haven Green toward the Oak Street Connector in 1978.*
© Alex S. MacLean/Landslides.

process — or metastasis — has never really ceased, though it has been kept at bay and even reversed in some specially favored areas, such as that along the banks of the Quinnipiac in Fair Haven and perhaps now in the area adjacent to Dixwell Avenue.

Even so, the potential for disaster was recognized at the very beginning by such people as Margaret Flint, director of the New Haven Preservation Trust, and so partially averted. The so-called Outer Circumferential Ring Road, which would have eaten up Mill River and gone on out Armory Street, was stopped by neighborhood action led by Paul Mitarachi, an architect who never got another job from the City. The Inner Circumferential Ring Road (these names) was to have taken off from the Armory Street exit of I-91 and gone below ground in a cut at Hillhouse Avenue, emerging behind the Payne Whitney Gymnasium to protect Yale from Dixwell Avenue and Newhallville, although a couple of beautiful Yale buildings were also to be destroyed along the way. All these were four- to six-lane, limited access thruways, remember, not boulevards. In 1968 the Connecticut Department of Transportation told us that New Haven would be in complete gridlock within three years if the Inner Circumferential Ring Road did not go through. Now, almost thirty-five years and millions more automobiles later, there is no sign of that at all, even in the rush-hour traffic along Trumbull Street. The terrible jams take place on I-91 and I-95 themselves and especially near their intersection. Thus, "gridlock" is a typical misnomer of the D.O.T. The town grid is the very last urban street type to jam up because drivers can choose various routes and filter through it.[4] Indeed, the experience of the past thirty years has shown that everything the D.O.T. and New Haven Redevelopment wanted to do was utterly wrong in every way. This was true in all urban categories. For example, thousands of low-income housing units, many of them perfectly sound, and in New Haven's durable frontal-gabled style, were torn down and, as of 1968, only six new units had been built. New housing proposals, such as that for the Hill neighborhood in 1968, were for middle-income housing and wholly ignored New Haven's wonderful two- and three-family vernacular house types and their powerful urban relationship to its pattern of streets. And if it had not been for the heroic resistance of Margaret Flint, assisted, however ineptly, by those of us she rallied around her, New Haven would have been hurt even more seriously than it was. What if all those connectors had gone through? The wounds were grievous enough in any case and have never entirely healed. All the federal money ran out, along with Johnson's sad war, and, in a truly Greek irony, there is, except for H.U.D.'s wholly commendable programs, very little federal money available now when the planning and architecture professions are much better equipped to deal with the realities of city making.

But New Haven came to occupy a special position in that tragic history. Everything was learned in New Haven fighting Redevelopment during the sixties: the respect for the structure of the traditional city and for its vernacular architecture, the necessity to discipline the automobile, the concept of contextual design, indeed the revival of the splendid tradition of premodern American town making as a whole. Over the next thirty years, this knowledge was transmitted from New Haven to American culture in general. The new towns that are now being built around the country, the Main Streets that have been rescued from the malls, the neighborhoods revived, can be attributed directly to architects and planners trained at Yale during and shortly after the Redevelopment era. One thinks especially of Andres Duany (M.ARCH. 1974) and Elizabeth Plater-Zyberk (M.ARCH. 1974) and their New Urbanism; and of Robert A. M. Stern (M.ARCH. 1965), now dean of the School of Architecture; Jaquelin Robertson (B.A. 1955, M.ARCH. 1961); Alexander Cooper (B.A. 1958, M.ARCH. 1962); Peter Calthorpe, who studied at Yale in the late 1970s; Ray Gindroz, who taught at Yale; and Allan Greenberg (M.ARCH. 1965), himself a combat veteran of the struggle here as a student architect and an employee of the Redevelopment Agency. Therefore, New Haven's sorrow should also be its pride, and the point that emerges is of New Haven and Yale affecting each other, learning together, and working in a kind of partnership to shape an urban future better than might have been hoped for otherwise. Here one thinks especially of historic preservation, now a mighty popular force, and once again of Margaret Flint, who in many ways initiated its modern phase in New Haven. Not an architect or planner, but a citizen of New Haven, the wife of Richard Flint, professor of geology, Peggy separated us from our ivory towers and forced us to put what we knew at the service of our city. I am proud to have been drafted into her army; as an art historian, I owe her a moral debt I have never ceased trying to repay.

One historical fact to keep in mind is that during those decades of the fifties, sixties, and seventies when some of the proudest examples of Yale's modern architecture were rising from the ground, New Haven as a city was largely falling apart, a victim not only of the cruel economics that stripped her of her industries after World War II, but also of faulty architectural and planning practices of which Yale itself may be felt to have set an example. Other than the hellish Utopian visions that laid New Haven waste, there were few physically specific plans involved in the modernism of 1950. They were normally vast diagrams with blobs indicating "areas" set off by different colored pencils as if seen by Meton from the sky. The physical structure of buildings, streets, and squares had somehow slipped out of mind. There were no axes, no real architectural decisions, no places. And there was no modern plan for Yale as a whole until Eero Saarinen (B.A. 1934) put a sketchy one together in the late 1950s. It resulted in a model containing some proposals for special building groups (FIG. 291), but in the end nothing comprehensive was done and any general suggestions Saarinen may have made to the Corporation were without results. That lack was especially serious if we consider Yale's great urban structures of the past, involving much more than one building: the old Brick Row itself, so integral to New Haven, and, whatever their limitations, the colleges as well. In fact, all campus planning in America had been marked by its special capacity to put buildings together to shape an environment. Still, with some justice, Griswold saw Yale's problem in those years as one of infill, of scattering new buildings among the old. His program for their architecture was bold and simple. He was determined to employ the best modern architects he could find and to give each one of them absolute freedom to produce the best building he could imagine, which at that time usually meant the most inventive, the most unlike anything else. The architects of course loved all that, because those were their fundamental objectives as well. Each was free to outdo the other in

FIG. 291 *Eero Saarinen with scale model of the Yale campus, 1959.*

reinventing the wheel in every building, often no more confined by urban responsibilities than a painter might have been. Indeed, that was probably what Griswold had in mind, a collection of new buildings infinitely varied in design and meant to be viewed like paintings in an exhibition. There were few worries about contextual problems, just a kind of delight in innovation and a curious faith that it would all come out all right in the end. Curiously, it almost did so, and at least one overwhelmingly great building, and a couple of pretty good ones, emerged from the process.

More than that, the architects so utterly trusted, who might have been expected to do their worst, normally did their best instead. Most of them seem to have looked hard at the character of the sites where their buildings were to be placed, and with only a few exceptions they did what they could to bring the principle of contextuality into play. The result was a diversity of modern buildings that did much less damage to the fabric of the university than buildings of that period did elsewhere — and which were on the whole much livelier and more delightful besides. Looking at other campuses we also realize that because of Griswold, Yale escaped late modernism's most atrocious horrors, a negative accomplishment of no mean importance. In the end, Griswold turned out to be one of the greatest of architectural patrons, among the university presidents of his era (1950–63) the most successful of all. This was probably so because he built out of his own integral and long-standing passion to be modern, whatever that meant to him: I suppose to be daring, courageous, and free.

It is true that the very first buildings designed just before Griswold's presidency and during its early years may be felt to have slipped through his net. Many of these were the work of the local firm of Douglas Orr (B.F.A. 1919, M.F.A. 1927) and tended to represent late modernist design at its most banal. This was especially disappointing because Orr and his colleagues had done splendid

FIG. 292 *Dunham Laboratory (Office of Douglas Orr), with the original Dunham Laboratory of Electrical Engineering on the right: east (Hillhouse Avenue) facade.*

work during the thirties in more or less traditional, or popular, architecture. His Art Deco Telephone Company of that decade is still by far the handsomest skyscraper in New Haven and contrasts tragically with his appalling postwar building for the same company on the Oak Street Connector. It was as if modernism had swept Orr clean of any capacity to design the basic elements that buildings had always been made of: doors, windows, walls, roofs, cornices, everything that he had once handled so well. Louis I. Kahn was soon to make a virtue of those very deprivations, but for many fine traditional architects such as Orr they were deeply destructive. A number of buildings of the fifties from Orr's office therefore exhibit a skinned and vacant look: a surprising number at Yale-New Haven Hospital, as well as Dunham Laboratory (FIG. 292), the Dean's House (now gone) and student housing at the Divinity School, Bingham Oceanographic Laboratory (also gone), and so on. Helen Hadley Hall was one of the latest of the group. Touchingly, Orr's first proposal had adorned it with white classical pilasters. These received a chilling reception from Griswold, perhaps like that of a statue of Priapus proffered to the reformed St. Augustine, and after a further series of proposals and studies that reflected no credit on anyone, the building achieved its present blank appearance.

Nevertheless, the Office of Douglas Orr continued to offer sympathetic and efficient associational services to other architects, and the first of these in the fifties was Louis I. Kahn. Kahn had been educated under Paul Cret at the University of Pennsylvania in the twenties and had worked as a young draftsman on some of Cret's strongest "Modern Classic" buildings in Washington, such as the Folger Library and the splendid Federal Reserve. Modernism and the Depression then hit, and Kahn was not only deprived of the traditional order of design he had learned from Cret but lacked commissions as well. He was for a time in partnership with the elegant Boston Brahmin George Howe, with whom he did some good wartime housing.[5] In 1947 Kahn was hired by Yale's Department of Architecture and was soon loved by everyone, if not, I think, properly appreciated by them. He was obviously a great teacher and was instrumental in bringing Howe to the department as chairman in January 1950. That same year Kahn returned to Rome as a fellow of the American Academy. There he came in contact with Yale's incomparable archaeologist Frank E. Brown (PH.D. 1938) and, in large part through him, with the Roman ruins in brick and concrete which were to be so central an influence on his later work. He also traveled to Greece and, most important to him, to Egypt. While drawing his beautiful pastels of the pyramids at Gizeh he learned that Howe had managed to secure him the commission to design a new art gallery for Yale, which he was to do in association with Douglas Orr (FIGS. 293–295). In practice that meant with Orr's structural engineer, Henry Pfisterer, who was another much appreciated teacher in the Department of Architecture. Howe had already decided that the building should be a simple rectangular loft structure entirely open around a central service core. That configuration was in accord with the ideas of Lamont Moore, then associate director, later director, of the Art Gallery, who wanted the full volume of the galleries to be visible, with sculpture standing free and paintings hung on movable screens — he called them "pogo panels" — that would also stand free in the space. To span those vast exhibition areas Kahn finally came up with the grand tetrahedronal braced-beam system that is the building's glory. Though, as constructed by Pfisterer, it is not a true space-frame, its tetrahedrons had surely been inspired in part by the tetrahedronal "geodesic" domes that were being designed by Buckminster Fuller at that time. One was built of cardboard by Fuller and his students after a series of his lectures at Yale in 1952, while Kahn's building was in construction. It was placed on the roof of Weir Hall, where it slowly rotted away. But the pyramids of Egypt represented, I think, an even more cogent force for Kahn, who was wary of acknowledging influence from other architects anyway. His drawings of the pyramids, of spring 1951, indeed show them as tetrahedronal vessels of light, like his slab, and in a poem he called them, again suggesting his Art Gallery: "The sanctuary of Art, of Silence and Light." Whatever the case, the great concrete frame looms over the gallery spaces, enforcing a sense of heavy physical pressure which had generally been absent from earlier modern architecture but which was coming into its own at that time in Le Corbusier's late work. Kahn's slab has therefore been described in part in terms of Le Corbusier's "Brutalism," which had a savagely primitivizing effect on buildings in cities during the following years. Boston City Hall is a prime example. But Kahn's slab was not really that; it was more mathematical than animal, structural rather than sculptural: not figural, not Neanderthalic but the insistent, if archaic, embodiment of a supremely architectural order, having something to do with the lost classical geometry in which Kahn had been trained no less than with the solemn masses of the ruins he had just experienced. That somber presence is contained inside the building, concealed by a severe skin which, on Chapel Street especially, clearly wants to be civilized and urbane. In fact, it suggests a primitive version of the Italian palazzo, heightened by the horizontal stringcourses Kahn finally employed. On Chapel Street, too, even Kahn's modernist unwillingness, or inability, to design a traditional doorway works to the building's advantage in the powerful placement of the brick wall planes framing the glass curtain of the entrance. Setting back the new wall adjacent to Swartwout's noble Art Gallery of 1928 was surely the best way to make that transition, and the stringcourses intensify and quicken the westward movement of Swartwout's slowly wheeling, magisterial arches (see FIG. 286).

FIG. 293 *Yale University Art Gallery (Louis I. Kahn) in 1953: stairwell ceiling.*

Might it have been better, however, if Swartwout's building had been completed to York Street, with its great entrance in the middle of the block on Chapel Street and its grand cross-vaulted spaces inside (see FIG. 203)? There are many people today who think so. Kahn's building is surely less well developed than Swartwout's in many ways. It requires more maintenance. But it is another voice, a fresh voice, that responds creatively to Swartwout's and so affirms the dialogue across the generations which is the only way that cities can grow and remain alive. Here one awaited a building across York Street to conclude that conversation in a splendid chorus, and it was eventually to come. Kahn's facade on York Street also seems to need to be completed by something beyond it. It simply stops, as if incomplete. Indeed, the whole building is designed as a simple volume, chopped off on the west, leaving a surface of glass with concrete piers and steel mullions all in the same plane, like the result of an amputation. Behind the Art Gallery, in Weir Court, Kahn surely created one of the most beautiful spaces at Yale, defined by cliffs of masonry and glass and conveying a sense of elevation, as of a high plateau broadly planted with trees. Here, too, is the only facade of the gallery which shows us what it is made of inside, with glass walls revealing the insistent tetrahedrons of the major spaces and brick planes sheathing the central service core (see FIG. 295).

A good many of us will claim that this, the first of Yale's modern buildings, is the best of them all. No other moves most of us so much. It is surely sad that a later director of the Art Gallery, imbued with the more conventionally modern aesthetic of the Museum of Modern Art, was able to induce Paul Rudolph (who had barely arrived at Yale) to redesign the interiors in the late 1950s. In that process the piers supporting the slabs were concealed behind planes of wall, and the open volumes of the galleries, defined as they had been by walls of concrete block and populated by movable panels on which the paintings were hung, were transformed into fluid continuities defined by fixed white planes. If the director could have gotten away with covering the slab—which in any case he had already made to look linear, abstract, and rather weightless—he would have done so.

Kahn, who was at first bitterly upset by all this, finally said that it had taught him how to design in future so that his buildings could not be so easily transformed, as he was later to do in the British Art Center across the street. Today, his original work in the Art Gallery is being stripped back to what he intended. The concrete core is reemerging; the piers are standing clear; and that incredible slab, the most awesome embodiment of architectural presence that Yale has yet seen, is free once again to work its whole will upon us, while the pogo panels set up a gentle flow of Miesian space below it.[6]

FIG. 294 *Yale University Art Gallery in 1957: ground floor east, with the exhibition "Form in Art."*

FIG. 295 *Yale University Art Gallery: north facade from Weir Court.*

Surely the Art Gallery is an imperfect building. Kahn thought it was; he had felt his way through it, working toward the mature design that was soon to do nothing less than astound the architectural world. But not at Yale. The administration found Kahn hard to work with. He was always changing things. Despite his aspirations, even Griswold had his limits here. He never gave Kahn another building, and Kahn got one at Yale only when Paul Mellon (B.A. 1929), close to two decades later, made his wishes known. True enough, like all the major monuments of modernist mythology, the Art Gallery was probably too good for us and took a while to get used to. As late as 1957, when Kahn finally left Yale, most of us thought that, though the best of teachers, he would probably get very little to build in the years to come. In 1957, as a matter of fact, all of us, including President Griswold, wanted Kahn to become the new chairman of the Department of Architecture, but Kahn refused to consider the appointment unless the university would also promise him a building to design. For various reasons which I will discuss later, Griswold refused to give such a guarantee.[7]

So by the mid-fifties Kahn was gone. It was Eero Saarinen who had Griswold's confidence; he was a graduate of Yale and a truly brilliant architect, beloved and trusted by his clients in ways foreign to Kahn. His tragically short career was therefore unique, advancing rapidly from success to success like Marlowe's Tamburlaine. His designs from Kennedy to Dulles exemplified what he called "the style for the job," and each of them invoked a brand new, knock-your-eye-out form coupled with some equally new and spectacular structural device and functional innovation. At the time I did not like Saarinen's buildings very much, but I respect and admire them now. They have rather surprisingly worn very well. His first work at Yale, David S. Ingalls Rink — the "Whale" — exemplified all his qualities, but it was preceded by another building, Josiah Willard Gibbs Laboratories of 1955, by Paul Schweikher (B.F.A. 1929), with which Saarinen was indirectly involved. He had begun to put together a plan for Yale, clearly with Griswold's full support (see FIG. 291). Like the rest of Griswold's programs the plan dealt largely with infills, but the first part of it that Saarinen worked on, that for Science Hill, was fairly completely elaborated. It featured a long slab running east-west right across the summit of the hill, effectively masking the summit and blocking the axis of view toward East Rock. At that time Gibbs Laboratories came up for design and the job was given to Schweikher, who succeeded George Howe as chairman of the Department of Architecture for a few stormy years. It was certainly suggested to Schweikher that he follow Saarinen's placement of the new building, but to his everlasting credit he refused. Instead he turned his slab north-south and set it on the east slope off the summit, so liberating the high space and the view beyond it and raising the first of the architectural boundaries that came to define it (FIG. 296). (Philip Johnson was later to honor Gibbs's precedent and complete its spatial suggestion.) The sad thing is that nobody liked Gibbs as a building. It is probably superior to Orr's work of the fifties only in proportion. It is banal and rather tacky late modernism clearly enough, but its siting should be honored. It constitutes a civilized contribution to that kind of contextual design, that "dialogue" as I have called it, out of which cities are made. But it was largely because of Gibbs that Griswold refused a guarantee to Kahn.

FIG. 296 *Josiah Willard Gibbs Laboratories (Paul Schweikher, in association with the Office of Douglas Orr) from the east in an aerial view of Pierson-Sage Square in 1955. The quonset huts along Whitney Avenue were erected after World War II to house enrolled veterans and their families; in the far right background are the high-rise public housing buildings (now destroyed) of the Dixwell Neighborhood.*

On the other hand, Saarinen, had he lived, could probably have built almost as many buildings at Yale as Josiah Cleveland Cady or Rogers himself. His first was Ingalls Rink, for hockey (FIGS. 297 & 298). Griswold was its champion. When Saarinen's drawings for it were unveiled, it was immediately apparent that the project was at once smaller than required and potentially expensive beyond even Griswold's most extravagant dreams. It made no sense. Charles Gage (B.A. 1925), the treasurer of the university, began to pass around a photograph of a perfectly unobjectionable hockey rink that had just been constructed at Cornell and was close to twice as large as Saarinen's and surely less than half as expensive. At this threat to his darling, Griswold called upon the history of art department to come to his aid. Flattered by that unwonted attention, its members set to work and produced a letter now mercifully lost.[8] The contents are nevertheless burned into my brain, and I can loosely paraphrase it, noting that our medievalist said that Saarinen's hung cables and suspended roof planes embodied the tensile qualities of Gothic architecture, and the orientalist said that the roof had the fine symbiotic relation to nature of the best Chinese work, and somebody else said that it exemplified the strong geometric order of the Renaissance, and the modernist said, in effect, that it was the hottest thing since button shoes. Heaven forgive us all, because none of it was really true. Nobody said or probably perceived, until later, that the building was sited without regard for its surroundings, that it had no place on a street, that it was in every way a shameless intrusion. On the other hand,

FIG. 297 *David S. Ingalls Rink (Eero Saarinen) from the south, between Mansfield (left) and Prospect (right) Streets, in 1960.*

FIG. 298 *David S. Ingalls Rink: east (Prospect Street) facade.*

nobody could really perceive until later what a wonderful place it was in which to watch hockey; how it swooped with the puck and reverberated with speed and violence and how, with too many people inside it, the better it became. The teams loved it; they said it was like skating outside. Useless to point out that in comparison with, say, Kenzo Tange's similar but enormous suspended structures for the Tokyo Olympics, the conception here, with its one concrete arch, is thinly two-dimensional. No one has ever cared very much. Was it all worth it? I think we have to say that it probably was, just as in relation to the absurd siting it has to be recognized that the thing does come rather splendidly swimming up like, I suppose, a whale. It is embarrassing to be fond of a building which seems so fundamentally flawed. As such, the rink formed a perfect setting for the enormous mass meeting that was held there during the Panther trials in 1970, when, in response to some burning life-or-death issue which I now forget, the vote was tallied at something like one thousand six hundred and eighty-one for, to one thousand six hundred and eighty-one against (FIG. 299). A Yale solution, saving trouble for everyone. And how the building thrummed with the roar of the crowd. If I remember correctly, it was the next day that somebody set off a bomb in front of it.

FIG. 299 *David S. Ingalls Rink, May 1970.*

It seems, anyway, that Griswold felt vindicated by the rink, as perhaps he was, and Saarinen's stock continued to rise. In 1960 he received the commission for Ezra Stiles and Samuel F. B. Morse Colleges, the first colleges to be built since the thirties, and the last so far (FIGS. 300–302; see also FIG. 315). Here again Saarinen outdid himself in formal, structural, and functional innovation and in a spectacular "style for the job." Some of these devices worked and others did not, but probably the most important thing about the buildings is how well they are fitted into their surroundings, how lovingly (and unlike Ingalls Rink) they reflect their urban context and enhance it. It was a question of towers: on one side the tower of the Graduate School, across Broadway that of Christ Church, and across Tower Parkway John Russell Pope's more than Assyrian gymnasium, a towered mass of overwhelming bulk and power. Saarinen decided that those towers should be matched by others on his buildings, carefully adjusted to them in height, color, and placement. In accordance with that intention, he flew balloons on the site to get everything right beforehand, and his towers do indeed mediate beautifully between all the others. Few buildings of that period were so sensitively sited; Saarinen's were ahead of their time in that.

Saarinen used the famous towers of the Tuscan hill town of San Gimignano as distant models for his own. At this very moment, in 1960, Kahn was also appropriating them for his Richards Medical Research Laboratories at the University of Pennsylvania. Kahn had various other functional and structural considerations affecting his forms, but it is fair to say that Saarinen's intentions were purely picturesque. So his towers feel rather less fully thought through than Kahn's, and that seems to show too in the way they are built. Saarinen wanted them to echo preexisting masonry structures, but his modernism would not permit him to employ traditional masonry itself. Here again he felt the need to invent something. He fixed on thick concrete walls laid up in forms with a lot of big, rough

FIG. 300 *York Square and Broadway area from the southeast in 1958, before the construction of Morse and Stiles Colleges. The New Haven high schools originally on the site were (1) Boardman Trade School, (2) Hillhouse High School, and (3) Commercial High School.*

FIG. 301 *Samuel F. B. Morse and Ezra Stiles Colleges (Eero Saarinen): site plan, ca. 1958.*

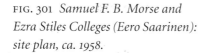

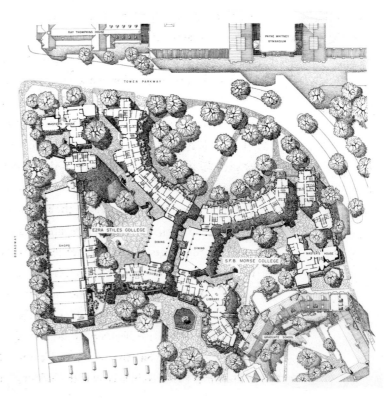

FIG. 302 *Walkway between Morse and Stiles Colleges, with the tower of Payne Whitney Gymnasium in the background.*

stones in the mixture. He had some idea of buffeting the walls before they were completely dry with hydraulic jets of enormous velocity, intended to cut away the concrete under the edges of the stones. This was apparently supposed to make the wall seem more laid up than poured. Naturally, none of that worked. The red stones float flat on the surface of the buff concrete, so resembling Frank Lloyd Wright's concrete walls carrying desert boulders at Taliesin West. But Saarinen's flat, chunky towers are mostly the color of adobe, and that and their grouping suggest the forms of the pueblos of the Southwest more than those of their Gothic neighbors. The effect is a little disorienting; the scale is strange, and in this Saarinen's most important innovation plays a part. Saarinen determined, surely to his credit, that the colleges should not be arranged in a fortified quadrangle, as the old colleges had been. He was the first of the modern Yale architects to worry much about New Haven. He wanted the townspeople to be able to walk diagonally through the block from York Street to Tower Parkway. From that, no less than from his memories of San Gimignano, his irregular plan derived (FIG. 301), and it set up a beautiful, much photographed pathway between the colleges, culminating to the west in the tower of the gymnasium and surely one of the most attractive achievements of Yale's postwar architecture (FIG. 302).

The colleges themselves are more problematic. Their irregular courtyards fail to produce the stable volumes of space that the older quadrangles provided. Their medievalizing irregularities seem a little forced. "Sets for *Ivanhoe*," Rudolph rather unkindly called them. The interior planning also presents problems. Saarinen organized it generally around single rooms off narrow corridors. Their arrangement seemed in accord with student preferences at the time, but it soon proved to be much less satisfying and, most of all, less flexible than Rogers's wonderful system, actually very old at Yale, of four suites off every landing, each consisting of a living room with two attached bedrooms. The living rooms normally had a fireplace as well. In 1960 that had come to seem overly luxurious, but as Yale's truly awful crowding intensified during the sixties it became apparent that while four people could be crammed into the old suites, there was little that could be done with tight single rooms and narrow halls. As a former master of Morse, I remember how hard we all tried to transform the arrangement into suites of some kind, always with limited success. Stiles is now working on the problem once again.

Another problem was the design of the common rooms. These had been major glories of the old colleges, expansive in scale, often with high ceilings and beautiful paneling and usually with vast windows flooding the place with a wonderful light. That was old stuff, and Saarinen would have none of it. He sank his common rooms, low-ceilinged and virtually windowless, in the depths of his adobe masses behind walls of amazing thickness. He called them "butteries," whatever that was supposed to mean: they were nowhere near the kitchens.[9] Every master of both colleges has struggled to find a way to make these appalling basements attractive and to invent a use for them. We tried three or four different arrangements during my six years at Morse, all of them using up money better spent elsewhere and none of them in any way reasonable or satisfactory. One apologizes for the domestic details, but in their own way those butteries were one of modernism's most egregious follies. One can learn from them.

Saarinen's determination to keep the quadrangles open to the public is in another category. It may not even have been a good idea.[10] But Saarinen was deeply sincere in his intentions, which were generously motivated in an urbanistic sense, and he fought with the university over the question of gates. He didn't want any at all. His untimely death then ensued, and his widow, the distinguished critic Aline Saarinen, kept up the fight. By the time the colleges were opened she had agreed to allow gates to be installed, with the university's solemn promise that they would never be locked. That was in 1962. Now, of course, they are locked all the time, like the gates of all the colleges; they have to be. It is one of the saddest stories I know about the economic deterioration of New Haven in the second half of the century and its integral relationship with Yale.

In 1958, the year Ingalls Rink was built, Paul Rudolph was installed as chairman of the Department of Architecture. Gibson Danes was appointed dean of the School of Design (a modernist nomenclatural horror: no more Fine Arts). Rudolph and Josef Albers, who had been at his post since 1949, were with him as chairmen of the Departments of Architecture and of Painting and Sculpture. The manner of Rudolph's appointment deserves some description. In 1956 a palace revolution overthrew Paul Schweikher and his all-powerful lieutenant, Eugene Nalle (B.ARCH. 1948), as well as Charles Sawyer (B.A. 1929), dean of Fine Arts. Griswold replaced Sawyer with Boyd Smith, a splendid administrator from the School of Drama, and in a year or so, Kahn having refused the chairmanship, a committee with no architects on it was appointed to search for a new chairman and dean. It consisted of Boyd Smith and Sumner Crosby (B.A. 1932, PH.D. 1937) — a professor, twice chairman of the history of art — and, presumably as representing callow youth, myself. President Griswold promised to interview every candidate we could produce, and he most thoroughly did so. We produced every-

FIG. 303 *William B. Greeley Memorial Laboratory (Paul Rudolph): south facade.*

body. They came from everywhere, and Griswold would meet with them and us in that wonderful small room on the second floor of Woodbridge Hall where Yale presidents were accustomed to bring the full majesty of the institution to bear on prospective candidates. It was just big enough for a few chairs and one high colonial desk of stupendous quality. The Corinthian columns of the War Memorial loomed just outside the window, enormous in scale, with Old Glory on its monumental flagstaff flapping red, white, and blue before them. That was the room to meet people in and test their mettle; Benno Schmidt (B.A. 1963, LL.B. 1966), Yale's twenty-first president, made a crucial mistake when he moved that function downstairs to the rear of the building into a rambling lounge with homey touches. Anyway, that's where the aspirants came, and Griswold showed himself to be a genius at evaluating them. He seemed to see right into their souls. Of course, the room played a part in softening them up. There was only one occasion when Griswold truly frightened me. The candidate was a very nice man long in the trade but about whom most of us at the time didn't think too highly. He sat forward on the edge of his chair, eyes shining with pure intelligence, and outlined his views about architecture schools, few of them more ridiculous than such things normally are, and Whit kept saying, "Yes, yes, how wonderful, and then what would you do," and the man responded with enthusiasm, hitching forward, all bushy-tailed and glowing, and I thought, My God, he's snowing Whit, we're going to get this guy, and Whit finally said something like "That's splendid! Would you excuse us for a moment?" And the man went out, and Whit said, "I thought he was going to pee on the rug."

In any event, Paul Rudolph impressed us all, Griswold not least. Though trained at Harvard, Rudolph had come up from the South, as brilliant as Tennessee Williams, and had just completed a building, Jewett Arts Center, at Wellesley College. He was a spectacular draftsman, and his lively pencil was leading him toward rather baroque effects, highly articulated, decorative, and complex, that seemed very new at the time. Beyond that he was in those years very much a straight shooter, honest and open, wholly dedicated to architecture and education. For some years he was surely the finest chairman that architecture had ever had at Yale, and he trained a generation of students who revered him.

Almost at once, along with his disastrous remodeling of the Art Gallery, Rudolph was commissioned to design a building. (Poor Kahn.) This was the William B. Greeley Memorial Laboratory for what is now the School of Forestry & Environmental Studies (FIG. 303). I for one found it a

FIG. 304 *Art and Architecture Building (Paul Rudolph) from the corner of Chapel and York Streets in the mid-1960s.*

disappointment. It was sited on the slope of the hill below the school's Marsh Hall, a house designed by Josiah Cleveland Cady for the distinguished paleontologist Othniel C. Marsh (B.A. 1860). Marsh Hall was a powerful Stick Style structure of the 1870s, with strong gables and a heroically detailed tower rising above the slope (see FIG. 132). Seen from there, Rudolph's building down below was all flat tar and gravel roof, which Rudolph patterned as best he could but which was irremediably what it was. The building itself was a forest of concrete piers with capitals branching out (though only fore and aft) to suggest a grove of trees. All of this stood on a platform that rode forward on the slope and was packed with various laboratory facilities having little to do with the structure as a whole. The building is surely one of the very few where Rudolph built his first sketch without his usual sustained attempt to study and restudy and integrate the whole. A good many buildings were being built that way at the time, like thin little pseudo-temples, and Greeley, despite everything, is more appealing than most of them.

The same is true of the Mansfield Street apartments for graduate student housing that Rudolph designed in 1961. Here the big concrete lintels supporting brick walls recall Le Corbusier's Brutalism once again, in this case especially his Maisons Jaoul at Neuilly. Rudolph's design is nevertheless thinner, more linear than Le Corbusier's formidably heavy work, and it suggests an intermediary in the housing group at Ham Common in London, designed by James Stirling in 1955–58.

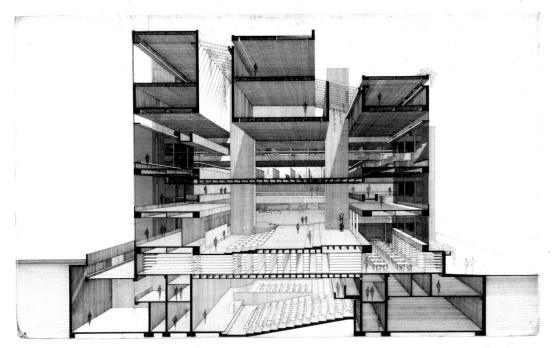

FIG. 305 *Art and Architecture Building: section perspective by Paul Rudolph. Collection Richard Nash Gould, B.A. 1968, M.ARCH. 1972.*

Stirling was one of the first of the young English architects whom Rudolph invited to Yale, Richard Rogers and Norman Foster (now Sir Richard Rogers and Lord Foster) among them, and he returned to the school as a critic for many years. But if Rudolph encountered Le Corbusier only at second hand in the Mansfield apartments, he was soon to confront him *mano a mano* and no-holds-barred in his Art and Architecture Building of 1961–63 (FIG. 304).

This turned out to be one of the great tragic monuments of the modern era. No building was ever conceived and built with more commitment and passion. It was the climax of Rudolph's career, and its completion brought him little but sorrow. To its design Rudolph devoted every ounce of his energy as a draftsman and artist. He must have made a thousand elaborate studies for it, always changing it and, in the process, complicating it step by step, intersecting its floor levels, interweaving its concrete floor slabs, and articulating their structural connections with the giant piers (FIG. 305). Critics of Rudolph's work up to this time had tended to describe it as rather thin—as I have already done—and in this quality it differed, as in his High School for Sarasota, Florida, from the late work of Le Corbusier, which was increasingly becoming its model. Indeed, Rudolph surely felt that he had to challenge Le Corbusier to emerge as the great architect he wanted with all his soul to be. It was that way with all the heroes of the modern movement; they were all after the gold medal. Hemingway, for example, used to talk about how he intended to become "the Champ" and was taking on Mr. Turgenev, Mr. Flaubert, and maybe even Mr. Tolstoy. By 1960 competition was rising to a heroic climax in architecture. It was heroic in many ways: in, for example, the primitive brutality of the rough concrete that had become its favorite building material, and the sculptural aggressiveness of the massive forms, so totally different from those of early modern architecture, into which that harsh and hurtful material could be tortured. "Hurtful" is not an exaggeration. It is exactly what Rudolph caused the surface of the Art and Architecture Building to be. He formed its rough concrete walls into corrugated surfaces which workmen then bashed with hammers, breaking them into splintered projections like shards of broken glass. You could literally hurt yourself if you bumped into them.

FIG. 307 *Beinecke Rare Book and Manuscript Library (Gordon Bunshaft of Skidmore, Owings and Merrill), looking southwest from the roof of Commons in 1963.*

concentration he had pushed it all farther than architecture as an art could sustain. And if there was one building in the world that instigated the revolt against modernism, Rudolph's Art and Architecture was it. Now, however, the building is being brought back to its beginnings as much as it can be. It has also been left to architects alone. All the other arts have moved into an undistinguished loft building down Chapel Street, once the Jewish Community Center—now Holcombe T. Green, Jr., Hall—and the object of a few drawings by Louis I. Kahn early in his career. It has been sensitively renovated by Deborah Berke, in recognition of the fact that painters do not need too much architectural interference and are better off without it, and that they of all people understand and respect "generic" architecture. (Nevertheless, they don't seem to like this example of it too well, objecting especially to the noise of the whole fanned-air system of heating and ventilation, including the air conditioning which Rudolph's building totally lacked.) The architects have been left alone at last in what is in a way their ultimate monument, their shrine, the tomb of their vaster pretensions. And stripped down now to a somewhat more spartan version of the way it used to be, it comes across as surprisingly powerful, grand, and tough.

If the Art and Architecture Building is one that has almost everything wrong with it but still leaves us feeling all right about human beings, even about the city, the Beinecke Rare Book and Manuscript Library has always seemed to me to be just the opposite (FIGS. 307 & 308; see also FIG. 314). It is not enough to say that if the former has too much vitality, the latter has too little, or that one architect tried too hard and the other not hard enough. Because the Beinecke does embody a kind of frigid perfection. There it is on the empty plaza that was sterilized for it by its architect, Gordon Bunshaft of Skidmore, Owings and Merrill, as perfect as a table radio and conveying no more sense of architectural scale. There are several reasons for that. Scale, which is the perceived physical relationship

FIG. 308 *Beinecke Rare Book and Manuscript Library in 1963: bookstack. Ezra Stoller © Esto.*

between a building's size and that of human beings, can be suggested by elements of use with which human beings can identify, such as doors and windows and floor levels. There are none of these here. It can also have a structural basis, as in columns and arches and even cantilevering roof planes. All these elements are related to our sense of body weight and are empathetically experienced by us. There is nothing like that here either. Instead, the vast Vierendeel trusses of which the exterior walls are composed give no sense of structural action, especially as they are held up off the ground at the four corners. The eye does not really help us believe that the beams, which are supported on the little conical piers, are actually spanning those distances, and in fact they are not. But they seem to be supporting the whole building, which in consequence has got to be very small. The effect is disorienting, as in some of Giorgio de Chirico's paintings. This is especially so because the plaza as a whole, once a very nice cobblestoned space in front of the War Memorial, was redesigned by Bunshaft to have no scale either. The landscape is that of dream. Just about this time, in 1963, Norman Mailer wrote that modern architecture is creating "the empty landscapes of psychosis,"[11] and that is pretty much what the Beinecke does. The best comment ever made about it was Claes Oldenburg's when he proposed the fabrication of a long cigarette butt to be balanced on the lip of the sunken terrace in front of the building. And there they were: the ashtray, the radio. It is a sterile setting, but one has to admit that the building is impressive, if heavily theatrical, inside. The books enshrined in the center, the unearthly light, the height to the roof, all create another dream landscape, but here a more richly emotional one. A good many people have thought so, notably Jacqueline Kennedy when she toured the country in search of a model for her husband's memorial. And surely the Beinecke is another if very different kind of tomb.

It was interesting for my generation at least to speculate about what would have constituted a better arrangement of this plaza across from Woodbridge Hall, in the heart of the university. Carrère and Hastings's original proposals were of course never carried out (see FIG. 162). In the 1960s many of us thought that Mies van der Rohe should have gotten the Beinecke job: not the contemporary Mies of the Bacardi Pavilion in Mexico City or the Neue Nationalgalerie in Berlin, who might have inserted into the space a pavilion of about the same proportions as the Beinecke—thus too much like the surrounding buildings in height and bulk—but the young Mies who in 1922 had wanted to set a tall tower all of glass in the center of a preexisting city square defined by solidly traditional buildings of moderate height. Some of us hoped to induce him to build that tower of light for us here, a crystal shaft signaling the center of the university from afar. All the many functions that are stuck underground in the Beinecke might have gone up in the air with it, as they do in Sterling Memorial Library. Alas, those who had the choice, Rudolph among them, decided, for whatever reason, on another architect. Again, though, it was an early modern image that seemed preferable to what the late modernists were doing. It had also begun to seem that the more truly heroic stance, the solid new beginning that Yale had encouraged in Kahn's Art Gallery, had given way to fashion and superficial "style" in no more than ten years. When the drawings of the Beinecke were first exhibited I criticized the building in class along those lines, and it was apparently some of my students who tore down a few of the hoardings around the site of the excavation. It was a symbolic act, I suppose, not suggested by me but reflecting one of my pitiful attempts to influence the university's architectural policies.

The architecture of Philip Johnson has often been criticized for qualities like those of the Beinecke, trendiness and superficiality among them. But Johnson's work never quite fit that description. There was always something more to it than slickness of conception. There was mind in it and a grasp of fundamental issues, even if the finished product, probably because Johnson himself draws very little, often gave some impression of being under-detailed and schematic. In the early sixties, Johnson's Glass House of 1949 was still his finest and most historically important work, and I think it remains so today. Far more completely—if not necessarily more sensitively—than Mies's Farnsworth House, which was one of its models, the Glass House wholly defined one pole of modernist aspiration: the liberation of the individual from community and his release to nature. This was an old romantic dream, deep in the modernist psyche. With heat and electricity and all modern services Johnson was able to set the single individual—hardly the family—out in space with nothing anywhere between him and nature but transparent sheets of glass. Once that had been accomplished, one realized that it was the end. Liberation could go no farther, and the major problem that remained was how to build up community again, how to start moving from the individual to the neighborhood to the town. Most modernists have tried to avoid that problem; it still goes against their romantic grain, but it can be argued that Johnson immediately sensed it, or part of it, in view of the fact that, the Glass House barely finished, he instantly turned to Rome, looking for a more solid architecture of masonry, much as Kahn had done a year or so before. In 1952 Johnson, too, visited Frank Brown at the American Academy in Rome and then Hadrian's Villa and Trajan's Market, but unlike Kahn, who studied them a long time, he instantly began to use versions of Roman walls, vaults, and arches in his own impa-

FIG. 309 *Laboratory of Epidemiology and Public Health (Philip Johnson): detail of the south facade.*

tient way. Le Corbusier had done much the same thing twenty years before, turning almost instantly from the Villa Savoie, all taut and up in the air on its pilotis, to a little "weekend house" beautifully vaulted and set mostly underground, like a Roman ruin not yet excavated.

During all this time Johnson had been close to Yale, gave important lectures there from 1947 onward, and generously held what amounted to a continuous salon and seminar for Yalies in the Glass House. He certainly deserved the commission for Science Hill that he received in the sixties; and, in contrast to his more conventionally modern Laboratory of Epidemiology and Public Health (1964), standing on piers beside the Oak Street Connector (FIG. 309), Johnson did his level best to give his science buildings as much Roman bulk and solidity as he could. The first of them, the Kline Geology Laboratory (1963), is of three chunky stories; the second, the Kline Chemistry Laboratory (1964), is of two. They are both clad in solid brick walls, suggesting those of Roman brick and concrete construction, and endowed with an even more Roman gravity by the cylinders of brick which model them at intervals. These of course are simply housing the thin columns of the actual structure, which is a light steel frame. Outside, therefore, the building is expressed as something it is not, which would have bothered some modernists, especially Kahn, but for which Johnson didn't care a rap. One of the items in his striking lecture entitled "Fallacies of Modern Architecture" was the fallacy of structure. He realized that architecture has a humanistic objective which may or may not be served by the simple expression of the way it is built.

Whatever the case, Johnson carried the illusion of masonry mass even further in the Kline Biology Tower (1965), the last of the series to be constructed and indeed its major monument (FIG. 310). Here Johnson sheathed his slender metal columns in complete cylinders of brick looking like

FIG. 310 *Kline Biology Tower (Philip Johnson), with the Josiah Willard Gibbs Laboratories on the right: south (Sachem Street) facade.*

mighty masonry columns themselves, and he ran them tightly packed all the way up the building with spandrels between them. It all looks a lot like a brick version of Louis Sullivan's Guaranty Building of 1895. But at the top the columns emerge again to shape a kind of classical temple high in the sky. There is a restaurant up there, and a crown of light, and plumes of smoke as of sacrifice emerge from it on occasion. Sometimes it cries out like a wind harp. It is difficult to induce scientists to approve of any laboratory building without reservation, especially towers like this one and Kahn's earlier Richards Medical Research Laboratories (1957–61) at the University of Pennsylvania. Kahn, like Johnson, claimed integral functional justifications for the form of his building, but it was criticized by its occupants even more seriously than Johnson's has been.

It cannot be denied that the Kline Biology Tower is magnificently sited. Here the Gibbs building comes into play. We remember that Schweikher, contrary to Saarinen's wishes, had run it north-south and pushed it far over to the east side of the hill, leaving the summit open. Johnson might then have placed his tower right in the center of the summit on axis with Hillhouse Avenue, if he had chosen to do so; but, like Schweikher, he did the right thing and kept his building, also inflected north-south, well over to the west. Now the two buildings could act together in a fundamentally architectural way. They could shape a place; they frame the height, as Michelangelo had done on the Campidoglio in Rome. This is no Campidoglio, but it is a fine high windy place with a wonderful view southward down the slope of the hill to Hillhouse Avenue and the rest of downtown New Haven, while to the north the red butte of East Rock, Ezekiel's mountain, rises above the city. That climactic view was eventually blocked from the summit by the rather nervous and overarticulated hedge of the Nancy Lee and Perry R. Bass Center for Molecular and Structural Biology, designed by Kallmann,

FIG. 311 *Kline Biology Tower and colonnade from the inner court in 1966.*

McKinnell and Wood, and built in 1990–93 across the northern side of the enclosure. The building was at least in the right place because of the site of Gibbs and Kline, and it respected the massive colonnade that Johnson had persuaded the university to allow him to build to frame and dramatize the square (FIG. 311). That colonnade rather successfully masked Gibbs (admittedly no prize close to) and defined the rectangle of space in a fundamentally classical way, much as Johnson was proposing to do at Lincoln Center about that time.

In both cases the result was a kind of return to traditional place making, which modern civic design, especially that of the Harvard-Bauhaus wing—which was normally preoccupied with buildings as objects in space—seemed to have forgotten. The detailing of Johnson's colonnade is hardly classical, however. The brick columns are perhaps grotesquely chunky, and the concrete slab seems structurally forced, but the effect of walking southward through and down the slope along the west side of the Kline tower is of a more than Egyptian splendor, especially when the wind is blowing with that special velocity which the placement of the buildings encourages here. The composition is an exercise in the sublime worthy of Piranesi, and the group as a whole is, I think, one of the most distinguished that Yale's modern architecture has produced. It deserves to be used more than it seems to be, just as it deserved a stronger building than the Bass Center to complete it.

That feeling of letdown was, however, more general in the late 1960s when Yale's newest architecture appeared to be declining even further from the standard set by Kahn. Becton Engineering and Applied Science Center by Marcel Breuer and Associates was one of the prime disappointments (FIG. 312). Like the Beinecke it was essentially a late modern abstraction, a chilling demonstration of that design in folded paper at which the Harvard Bauhaus excelled. The pilotis are flatly frontal, while

FIG. 312 *Becton Engineering and Applied Science Center (Marcel Breuer and Associates) in 1970: west (Prospect Street) facade, from above the Grove Street Cemetery, with the Sheffield Chemical Laboratory (now Arthur K. Watson Hall; Cady, Berg and See) on the left. The Health Services Center (Westerman and Miller) on Hillhouse Avenue is at the upper left.*

the densely crinkled elements of the upper floors of the blinding white facade seem to be derived from the grave slabs of the Grove Street cemetery across the way. The rear wall rises up as a blankly geometric abstraction, especially obtrusive and hard to bear from one's sickbed in the Health Services Center on Hillhouse Avenue.

Becton is also distinguished by the fact that the two buildings torn down in 1967 to make way for it, Cady's Winchester and North Sheffield Halls, were clearly better buildings than it promised to be. This was apparent from the moment the proposal was unveiled; and, wonderfully assisted by Kingman Brewster's new generation of really smart students, I fought as hard as I could to save those buildings, arguing that they could be renovated, enlarged, and joined with new structures behind them in ways that would serve the purpose as well but also save Prospect Street and be much more architectural in the end. Those efforts were, as usual, unavailing (see FIG. 120). The then dean of Yale College was thoughtful enough to send me a snapshot that summer of the wrecker's ball hitting Winchester in the face.

Becton is also connected with another painful memory. It was there that the entries in the enormous competition for an addition to Leet Oliver Memorial Hall, home to the Department of Mathematics, were exhibited in 1970. That competition was organized by Charles Moore, but it had a very heterogeneous jury of twelve, of which I was one and Kevin Roche, Saarinen's distinguished successor, became chairman. The entries were anonymous, and the jury, according to the perhaps rather silly rules of the competition, chose not a single winner but four finalists. One of them was everybody's first choice. It turned out to be by Robert Venturi, as we were informed after the fact, and it might have been better if the competition had been organized so as to allow it to be announced as

FIG. 313 *Proposed Mathematics Building (Venturi and Rauch): perspective view looking south on Hillhouse Avenue, 1970.*

the winner without further deliberation. When, some weeks later, the four finalists were judged, the jury unanimously chose Venturi's design as the winner. Instantly a storm of protest from some members of the architectural profession broke over the university, which was accused of setting the whole thing up so that Venturi would win.[12] Venturi had just published his great *Complexity and Contradiction in Architecture,* of 1966, wherein he deflated the heroic pretensions of late modern architects, and I had written an introduction to it, calling it, correctly as it turned out, "the most important writing on the making of architecture since Le Corbusier's *Vers une Architecture,* of 1923."[13] Anyway, a good many architects felt themselves diminished by it, and they were annoyed at both of us, and, led by a few fanatics and opportunists, they slandered everybody involved, especially Venturi and me, as outrageously as they could in the architectural press and, I regret to say, the *Yale Daily News.* It all eventually died down, but it was a hurtful experience from which I personally, and perhaps other members of the jury, have never quite recovered. It is not possible for a teacher to argue in public with a student who is willing to suggest that he is a rogue.

Perhaps it was all worth it, however, because it is even more obvious today that Venturi's proposal was a truly great one (FIG. 313). It simply swung a majestic arc of wall off the old mathematics building, spanning the adjacent railroad cut and facing up Hillhouse Avenue. It used the recently completed Health Services Center (see FIG. 312) across the street as a foil and a base for that movement. It echoed the center's window placement and proportions but thinned them all out to emphasize the curving tension of its own wall, a clear plane of windows except at the common room, where a monumental cross-mullion burst forth to focus the view up Hillhouse Avenue. It was all a gate for the university, opening right at the spot where the sciences march down Science Hill to confront the humanities below. And it was so simple; the interior plan was exactly in accord with the exterior's urban intentions and indeed created them. It arced out around one wonderfully lively corridor, serving all the offices, that recalled some of the almost forgotten flexible planning of Le Corbusier's earliest work.

It would have been a great building for Yale, I think the best since Kahn's, perhaps naturally enough, considering how much those two architects had learned from each other. In any event, the mathematics department loved it, and the university administration seemed to do so too, and stuck by it despite the controversy, and was about to build it when the alumnus who was its donor died and, for whatever reason, his estate did not honor his commitment. Building prices rose out of sight when Nixon devalued the dollar, and in consequence it never got built. It was for his alma mater, Princeton, that Venturi was eventually to build some of his greatest, most contextual, and historically important designs. The loss of the mathematics building was the most serious I know in Yale's modern history. In the drawings one can see the great calm gate opening to the historic avenue with a grandeur that I think no other Yale building of any period has ever surpassed.

In 1969, by way of contrast, a happy event had occurred. During the troubles of that year, an architecture student named Stuart Wrede (B.A. 1965, M.ARCH. 1970) — a Swedish prince and a reader of Marcuse — conceived the idea that it would be well to challenge the university by offering it a colossal monument by Claes Oldenburg (B.A. 1950). He came to see me with this proposal and, though I never quite understood why it should be construed as a challenge rather than a delight, I thought it would be a fine way to get a splendid work of art for Yale, especially an outstanding piece of monumental sculpture, which I felt we needed. So Wrede organized a group of students and faculty called the Colossal Keepsake Corporation, of which my dear friend Paul Weiss of the philosophy department and my friend and colleague Sheldon Nodelman (B.A. 1957, PH.D. 1965) were members, and for which Philip Johnson put up a lot of money. The idea was to approach Oldenburg with the proposal. At the time Oldenburg had not yet built any colossal monuments, but he had designed some and illustrated them with wonderful drawings, notably for a gigantic golden toilet float floating up and down in the Thames and a collapsible lipstick mounted on caterpillar tracks. He had made a little model of the latter, and it seemed closer to our purposes than the toilet float might be. The sterile expanse of Beinecke Plaza, which remains the more popular name of Hewitt University Quadrangle, surely needed enhancing more than any place else in the university, and that seemed the best site to aim for, especially because it was right outside Kingman Brewster's office in Woodbridge Hall. In a reconnaissance of the area Oldenburg, as I noted earlier, did suggest how well a cigarette butt would look balanced on the parapet of the Beinecke's sunken courtyard with Isamu Noguchi's moon sculpture down below. It would have been wonderful, but I feared that the director of the Beinecke, a choleric gentleman who at that time was calling all of us Maoists anyway, might die of fury. Only a few weeks previously the architecture students had symbolically buried a corpse in his courtyard and, despite my truly horrified protests, driven a heavy hearse all around the plaza with its honeycomb of library spaces just below the surface. Fortunately, nothing gave way, but my classmate Ben Holden (B.A. 1940, PH.D. 1951), who was then secretary of the university, and a bunch of campus cops, massed in front of Woodbridge Hall, had been rightly upset and were doubly alert for further trouble. Eventually *Lipstick (Ascending) on Caterpillar Tracks* was fabricated at its final scale at Lippincott's Foundry in North Haven, and the date of Thursday, May 15, 1969, at high noon, was set as the moment for its erection in the plaza and official presentation to the university. Our job was to engage the interest of the Yale community in this coming event. So for some weeks beforehand I ended my lectures in the Law School, just next door, by saying "Beinecke Plaza, twelve noon, 15 May."

FIG. 314 *Claes Oldenburg, "Lipstick (Ascending) on Caterpillar Tracks": installation in Beinecke Plaza, May 15, 1969.*

On the great day itself the place was jammed with what we happily estimated as thousands of people. Ben and the campus cops were in position, ready to sell their lives dearly. I had been commissioned by my colleagues on the Corporation (the Colossal Keepsake Corporation, that is), to phone Ben that morning to assure him that what was going to happen was going to be very nice, without violence of any kind and entirely sympathetic to everyone. I don't think he believed me. As the time approached the crowd began to surge a bit, everybody in the best of humor, and at last a truck came slowly up Wall Street, pushing through the crowd and packed with architecture students and pieces of the *Lipstick,* with Oldenburg hanging off the running board like a character in an old agitprop movie. The vehicle came to rest and everybody jumped off and began assembling the *Lipstick* in the middle of the plaza (FIG. 314). The crowd looked bemused but kept shouting encouragement. Soon it was all assembled, but the tracks were only plywood because of limitations of time and money, and Oldenburg couldn't get the shaft of the *Lipstick* itself to stand up. It was fabricated of vinyl and was intended to be fitted with a handle whereby speakers who wanted to use its base as a rostrum could pump it up. The pump had never been installed, however, and the vinyl shaft remained limp, inciting ribald comment. When everything was as complete as it was going to be we approached Ben and ceremoniously read the deed of gift to him. President Brewster never appeared; we learned later that he had slipped out the back way. This was too bad, because we meant well, and I kept slapping Ben on the back and telling him what a great thing it was. Again, I'm not sure he believed me, but it was absolutely true. It was a great thing. That was the year when students at other universities, such as Harvard and Cornell, were locking deans up in their own offices and marching out of the gym with guns in their hands and generally trashing their universities. Not at Yale, where the administration got this little gift instead, presented at a delightful meeting of the community, and surely got teased a little bit too and didn't behave too badly, or too well, about it all. Later that evening Sheldon Nodelman and I were sitting on Beinecke's wall kicking our heels and admiring our monument when we saw the very director of the Art Gallery who had mutilated Kahn's design coming in from Cross Campus and moving around the *Lipstick* with a distinct smirk on his face and then veering off toward Woodbridge Hall. He had obviously been called in to advise the administration about whether it was art or not, and it was clear he was going to tell them it wasn't. It was surely too much for him, as it was for a group probably consisting of two or three members and calling itself the Maoist Brotherhood (the Maoists had surfaced at last), or something of the sort, which brought out a pamphlet denouncing the *Lipstick* on the grounds that it was intended by "institutional liberals" like me and "outright reactionaries" like Paul Weiss to bring obscenity to bear to demoralize the masses. Apparently the administration thought so too, because it never acknowledged receipt of the *Lipstick* and let it rot where it was, covered with graffiti and shunted over behind the buildings when alumni meetings were held in the plaza. It had apparently been something of a challenge after all.

After a year or two Oldenburg came and took the thing back to Lippincott's, and a number of universities besought him to give it to them. In 1973, however, Alan Shestack, a new and more sympathetic director of the Art Gallery, began to agitate for its return to Yale and wrote to all the college masters asking if any of them wanted it for their courtyards. Not one of them did. Some of them thought he was kidding. I was in Europe that year, but I hastened to say that I wanted it for Morse, where I was still master and where Brewster maneuvered me into staying for two more years in order to receive the *Lipstick* properly. The fellows agreed to its installation, and Oldenburg gave them a little talk about how to treat it. At its installation the Yale Band played, bless its dear anarchic heart, and we had a reception at which a wine was served which caused the art critic of the *New York Times* to say that one still couldn't get a decent glass of anything at Yale.

The *Lipstick* looked wonderful (FIG. 315). It might have been made for Morse, and had perhaps been a bit too small for Beinecke Plaza. It now had a stiff plexiglass shaft painted International Orange, the complementary color to the blue of the sky. Indeed, the sky seemed to flash down between the towers when the *Lipstick* went up. "Yes," said Oldenburg, "it turns on the sky." He had also redesigned the base with its tracks, now in imperishable Cor-ten steel, making it all more compact, more suitable for its new tighter, towered setting. It now looked a little like an Ionic column turned upside down. And while it has sustained some of the minor damage that is suffered by all outdoor sculptures, it has never been graffitied, and has become what all works of public art ought to be, the emblem of a culture, the symbol of a community. It even seems able to act as works of art have rarely been able to do in these modern centuries: as the icon of a place, an enigmatic presence, beloved and derided by its people as were the ancient gods. That is why Morse should never permit the Art Gallery to take it over and immure it within its own walls. Rumors of such intentions sometimes surface. They are founded upon a profound misunderstanding of what works of art are all about and how

FIG. 315 *Claes Oldenburg, "Lipstick (Ascending) on Caterpillar Tracks": installation in the courtyard of Morse College.*

they can function in human life. The *Lipstick* was commissioned from Oldenburg by students and faculty of the Yale community, conspicuously not by the Art Gallery, as Shestack himself well understood. It was not designed as a museum piece but as an active if ironic warrior in the gentle culture wars.

In 1972 Yale finally commissioned another building from Louis I. Kahn, to be placed directly across Chapel Street from the Art Gallery. It was to house the Center for British Art, and it was Paul Mellon who chose Kahn as its architect. Early on in the search Jules Prown, a professor of the history of art who was already the director of the British Center, became in effect the client for the building. In that capacity he asked me to write a letter for him to show Mellon in which I discussed the various architects who might be considered for the job. I tried to talk about architects who had been important at Yale, Kahn in particular, but in part because Kahn had a lot of work at that time I suggested that consideration also be given to some younger architects, such as Venturi, to whom Yale clearly owed something, and James Stirling from England. Mellon, though, preferred Kahn and that was it. I have always been glad that Kahn got the job, because the building is clearly one of the great ones, and it marked the return of absolute quality to architecture at Yale (FIGS. 316–319).

There were some odd passages in the process of its design. Kahn's earliest proposals were, probably wrongly, not much liked by anyone. He had been working for some years on schemes that derived directly from his love for Roman ruins, and his buildings for the Salk Institute for Biological Studies and for Ahmedabad in India and Dacca in Bangladesh were fundamentally without glass, as if timeless ruins themselves. Their power, their resonance, was enormous, their scale haunting and strange. Kahn's first proposals for the British Art Center were of that kind. The building was going

FIG. 316 *Yale Center for British Art (Louis I. Kahn): perspective view looking west on Chapel Street.*

to be bigger than the one that was finally built, stretching all the way from High Street to the Yale Repertory Theatre. It consisted of two great arched structures facing Chapel Street and divided by an expansion joint running up the middle of a central column. The material was to be brick and concrete like the ruins of Rome, and the long arches of the upper floors shaped the wide gallery spaces with their strange trajectories, lighted by thin ribbons of glass that as it were outlined the arches. It seemed excessive at the time; in retrospect it begins to seem marvelous and would have made a spectacular streetscape along Chapel. But Mellon decided to make the building smaller, pulling it well away from the theater, so that what has turned out to be a dramatic sunken court opened up between them and was reached down a monumental flight of stairs from Chapel Street. As was usual with him, Kahn then wholly rethought the building and came up with something that for the first time in many years had nothing to do with Roman ruins and was in fact brand new in his design. It was based on a comparatively small bay system of concrete piers that may well have been suggested to Kahn by the fate of his original Art Gallery, where the unimpeded open spaces allowed its extensive remodeling. He had sworn that such would never happen to him again, and it cannot happen in the British Art Center. The whole fabric, and the spaces, even the largest, are shaped by the square bay system, held steady by its structural frame. Outside, too, the aspect of the building is determined by the bony concrete skeleton, between which panels of metal and of glass are set in ways that recall the very beginning of modern city architecture in the work of Karl Friedrich Schinkel and Henri Labrouste in the 1830s and 1840s. Mies van der Rohe's buildings at the Illinois Institute of Technology of the 1950s, which were to create a kind of modern classicism out of that system, are also recalled. In general the final design by Kahn seems to leave the rather Piranesian Romantic-Classicism of his Roman work to rejoin the more canonical development of modernism as it had begun to take shape in the realist-materialist period of the mid-nineteenth century. Such academic musings give way, however, before the miracle of incandescence that Kahn works in his panes of glass. Here was an architect who for years had done his best to eliminate glass from his work or at the very least to subordinate its visual effects. Now all of a sudden he turns to it and so fixes it on his facades that it is not only wholly unshaded by reveals but also spectacularly contrasted with absolutely dead, matte, unreflecting panels of stainless steel, looking like deep gray slate, so that when the sun hits the glass it explodes with reflected light and reflects all the fine row of buildings across the street, Kahn's own Art Gallery among them (FIG. 318).

FIG. 317 *Yale Center for British Art from the Art and Architecture Building, with the Yale University Art Gallery on the left, the Yale Repertory Theatre on the right, and the Taft Hotel in the upper left.*

But the interior of the British Art Center creates a magical environment itself. It is true that one misses a little that first mad entrance around the central column. Like Frank Furness of Philadelphia before him, Kahn seemed to love to impede or to threaten his entrances, and, as in the Art Gallery, he consistently refused to design a conventional portal for them. There is none such in the final design of the British Art Center either, but there is something much more powerful. The whole corner at High and Chapel is cut under, though still defined and punctuated by its concrete piers, and one enters under the volume of the building which then, in the entrance hall, suddenly reveals its whole vertical dimension, rising upward to the heavy beams of the skylighted roof. At intermediate levels the various gallery floors open into this central space. Kahn was able to get away with this arrangement, as Rudolph had not been able to do, because he could design metal shutters on each floor that automatically came crashing down like guillotines as soon as their sensors detected smoke. One could in fact lose one's head in the contraption, and we are so warned by a plaque fixed in each opening. But the effect is overwhelming, especially as the high walls are sheathed between the concrete frame with light-stained English oak, which Kahn thought appropriate here. To the right, under a majestic beam, is the auditorium, tough and simple, all concrete seats in a stern concrete box of space, totally different from the Cinema-1-2-3 effect of the carpeted auditorium that was excavated under the Art Gallery at about the same time, though that is not a bad room either.

One floor above, up a stairway enclosed in a freestanding cylinder, the British Art Center again opens to the roof in its most spectacular space, also paneled and hung with appropriately enormous English paintings, including two ferocious scenes of animal carnage by Stubbs (FIG. 319). Kahn thought of it as the Great Hall of an English country house, but it embodies more of that primitive power that Kahn's work always seemed to have, especially as the enormous gray concrete cylinder

FIG. 318 *Yale Center for British Art in 1975: north (Chapel Street) facade.*

of the stair tower stands out in it, not quite touching the roof. So the kind of Sublime that Kahn looked for in his ruins is not absent here, but most of all there is the Silence that he always loved, the Silence and the Light. The British Art Center is somehow the most stable, the most wholly serene, the quietest building one has ever experienced. It is *built*; it feels right, complete, permanent. This is also true of the gallery floors, especially, of course, of the top level where the light is filtered down through the skylights that Kahn loved so well and had studied previously in his design for the Kimbell Museum in Fort Worth. (Edmund Pillsbury [B.A. 1965] succeeded Prown as director of the British Art Center and left it to become director of the Kimbell. Lucky man, to preside in turn over two such transcendent environments.) The most moving space of all on the British Art Center's top floor is the corner bay in front of the great Turner, where one of the big square panes of glass opens onto Chapel Street. From there, somehow magnified and clarified as in an optical lens, the whole range of buildings along the street from Bingham to the Art and Architecture Building is clearly visible: all that spendid action and reaction, all the richly urban rhetoric that the British Art Center completed at last.

Outside, looking west along Chapel Street, we cannot help but be stirred by it all. How perfectly the heavy beam above the ground floor of the British Art Center defines the street. It is in fact the only tangible result of the student activism of 1969–70 and immediately thereafter. The students demanded that the proposed center include shops along the street, as a civilized gesture to New Haven, and Kahn realized how he could use that condition to give his design the kind of traditional urban base that his Art Gallery, in comparison with Swartwout's, tended to lack. It is under that beam one enters at the corner. All the panes of glass above it reflect the preexisting buildings across

FIG. 319 *Yale Center for British Art: Library Court.*

the street. The angle of reflection is the same as the angle of sight, Descartes told us, so there they all are in sequence: Swartwout's arches, Kahn's stern escarpment, Rudolph's towers, framed, set off, completed as on an urban stage by Kahn's last work. Its windows reflect that first building of his, within which his archaic tetrahedrons brood. They recall his contest with the pyramids, his wrestling like Jacob through the night, here with the Pharaoh of Egypt whose great architects had at last reached out to him and set him on his way.

The British Art Center, completed by Marshall D. Meyers (M.ARCH. 1957) after Kahn's death, was Kahn's crowning achievement. It also seemed to mark important developments in his design. I have referred to the articulated wall system, but even more fundamental might have been a renewed sense of responsibility to the street and the city as a whole. The building acts even more than the Art Gallery does to define Chapel Street in a traditional way. Despite all the "design" that went into it, it comes across as a type, like the wonderful buildings of the old Brick Row. Would Kahn have gone on from that to become a contextual architect, as Venturi was and perhaps even in ways that Venturi himself had explored, involving "generic" architecture and a kind of gentle adjustment of his own temperament to the particular character of individual places? If so, it would have required a kind of subordination of Kahn's overwhelmingly modernist intention — which always drove him to invent, to make his buildings different from everyone else's. He had gotten very good at that, but he had also learned how to build solidly and well in ways that seemed to transcend competition or style and to suggest the timelessness of some inviolable, holy place.

There can be little doubt that architecture was nothing less than a religion for the most dedicated modern architects, not least for Kahn. Hence their intolerance. Or it took the place of religion, as art in general seems to have done for a great many people in the modern age. Yet art is like religion anyway and has always been involved with it: always creating sacred objects, or fetishes, inspiring awe, suggesting transcendence. One shades off into the other. But art may grow stronger as faith wanes. So the contemporary museum has in good measure usurped the communal building energies that once went into churches. Nevertheless, most modern architects, however they've tried, have at best only been able to make them seem palatial—which of course they traditionally were—rather than religious. Today Daniel Libeskind may be an exception. So was Kahn. His museums at Yale powerfully embody qualities normally associated with churches or, perhaps better, with temples: monumental permanence; a tense, sacred body; the terror of the sublime; finally the great quiet, waiting to be filled. For a while concerts were given most days at noon in the British Art Center. The music completed the building, drowning its silence as in a sea of golden light. Here, as under the Art Gallery's dark canopy, the objects on display may take on a special sacral aura.

Whatever the case, a good deal of the most useful architectural work at Yale once the heroics initiated by Griswold had begun to die down and Kahn was no more, was of a kind that tended to disappear into the environment as a whole. The Cross Campus Library by Edward Larrabee Barnes, finished in 1971, was an early example of that. Here too the Yale constituency had something to say about the final result, and a campaign led by Robert Grant Irving (B.A. 1962, PH.D. 1978), then a graduate student, resulted in a much less intrusive presence above ground than would have been the case had the original design gone unchallenged. That new relevance of the informed public to the process of design had already begun to show itself in the battle that erupted in 1967–68 to save New Haven from the final horrors of Redevelopment and helped teach the rest of the country how to do so.

The new willingness to build quietly and to blend new structures into the existing environment was reflected in Barnes's and Macomber's parking garage of 1974 on Pierson-Sage Square, which disappears into greenery, as well as in Barnes's unobtrusive unification of a number of existing buildings to house the School of Organization and Management (now School of Management) in 1978. They all turned out green as well, and the new lecture hall by Herbert Newman (M.ARCH. 1959) behind Kahn's Art Gallery, to which I have already referred, was completely underground. More than that, Newman went to great trouble to design it in an irregular shape in order to spare the root systems of the great trees which shade Weir Court above it. One despaired of those trees at first, but pressure was exerted by Theodore Stebbins (B.A. 1960) of the Art Gallery, and others, and Newman valiantly worked it all out to save them. I have come to enjoy lecturing in that auditorium very much. The audience is closer and the slides can be bigger than in the Law School auditorium, and the lecturer doesn't have to break his neck looking back up at them. Newman and other architects have also carried out extensive restorations of the interiors of the buildings around the Old Campus and elsewhere, without affecting the exteriors of those buildings at all. Extensive cleaning of the exteriors was also begun under Benno Schmidt, partly in response to alumni complaints that Yale was falling

FIG. 320 *Seeley G. Mudd Library (Roth and Moore Architects): east (Mansfield Street) facade, with Hammond Hall on the left.* © Steve Rosenthal.

to pieces. It is true that from Griswold onward the administration had concentrated on new construction without much concern for maintenance, which was for much too long "deferred." Some of the early cleaning under Schmidt, especially that of Connecticut Hall, drew a good deal of criticism from preservationists. It is easier than one thinks to ruin masonry with sandblasting and rough solvents, to skin back and cause stone to exfoliate, as it has done on parts of Skull and Bones and elsewhere. It is also an error to let new mortar set harder than its brick, for example, which wreaks all kinds of havoc when expansion takes place. In time the administration seems to have come to care about these and other problems. It finally began to employ people who understood them, and the extensive cleaning and restoration of practically everything which has gone on since the early nineties has seemed to proceed in an increasingly informed manner.

Fewer new buildings have been built in the past twenty-five years, and those of a quality varying from the solid integrity of Roth and Moore Architects' Seeley G. Mudd Library of 1982 (FIG. 320; Harold Roth [M.ARCH. 1957], William F. Moore [B.A. 1963, M.ARCH. 1966]) and their Joseph Slifka Center for Jewish Life at Yale of 1993, which recall Kahn, and the admirable competence of Herbert Newman's New Residence Hall—or "Swing Dormitory"—of 1998 on Tower Parkway (FIG. 321), which perhaps overly simplifies Rogers, to the simple disaster of Henry R. Luce Hall of 1994 (FIG. 322), which misunderstands the role of the ruin in Kahn's design. Newman's dormitory is an example of a new building well designed to serve its commendable purpose: to relieve crowding and to fit into its context, here consisting of Morse College, the Central Power Plant, and the Payne Whitney Gymnasium. Its forms, appropriately enough, recall those of the Gothic colleges, but as is so often the case with contemporary work, they do not enjoy the richness and complexity of the older forms.

FIG. 321 *New Residence Hall (Herbert S. Newman and Partners): south (Tower Parkway) entrance.*

FIG. 322 *Henry R. Luce Hall (Edward Larrabee Barnes and John M. Y. Lee & Partners): east (Hillhouse Avenue) facade.*

FIG. 323 *Class of 1954 Environmental Science Center (David M. Schwarz Architectural Services) from Sachem Street, with the Peabody Museum on the right.*

There is a sense that nothing like the resources that shaped their predecessors was available to them. In consequence they tend to look rather thin and deprived, not nearly as assured and permanent as their ancestors seemed to be. This may also be true of the Class of 1954 Environmental Science Center by David M. Schwarz (M.ARCH. 1974), completed in 2001 (FIG. 323). It is a welcome replacement for an earlier addition to the Peabody Museum.[14] The interior spaces are all clean, open, and sun-filled, while the exterior, designed contextually with the Peabody, is stiff and dry in detail.

But the story of Luce Hall is something else, the history of its commission itself a dreary one. The first architect engaged was Robert Venturi, working with his wife and partner, Denise Scott Brown, who carried out the first phases of analysis and design in consultation with the members of the faculty of International Studies and to their entire satisfaction. The donor's dissatisfaction, however, led to Venturi's voluntary withdrawal from the project—his second disappointment at Yale—and Edward Barnes agreed to take over the commission. For whatever reason, it is surely not his best work: a building reasonably satisfactory inside, but insensitively massed and fenestrated with abject slots and primitively conceived thermal windows suggestive of those in Roman ruins but inadequately restudied to convince us that they belong in a finished building. There is no sense of contained volumes of space; the voids seem hacked out of a solid building block. The scale is strange. That generally awkward quality was intensified by a change in siting. The architect had intended to place the chunky bulk of the building with its narrow side toward Hillhouse Avenue and on the same plane as the preexisting mansions along that incomparable street. That was obviously the way to do it, at once respecting the structure of the avenue and subordinating the mass of the new building to that of its defining mansions. But the administration seems to have suggested turning the building to face Hillhouse Avenue with its broad side, and setting it well back behind the present houses to create a kind of courtyard in front of its staring facade. The result was the instant destruction of two great streets: Hillhouse most of all because a great hole was cut in it with the building crouching behind it like a frightened animal, but Prospect as well, because the unscaled mass, blind on that side, occupies an uneasy position in relation to it, neither close up nor far away, making no urban sense whatever. It is a sad story, not reflecting much credit on anyone except Venturi, who was called upon to play the unattractive role of martyr once again.

All that is now in the past, however, except that the yellow brick body (yellow brick!) of Luce Hall is still conspicuously where it is and will outlast its critics and will make an acceptable ruin in a thousand years. The firm of Venturi, Scott Brown at last secured a building at Yale, a big one at the School of Medicine, completed in 2003. But first a word should be said about the architecture of the medical complex as a whole. It has tended to be mentioned all too little by me or anyone else (except now by Catherine Lynn), but it has probably occasioned a larger expenditure of funds than all of the other buildings in the university combined. Few students and not many faculty give it much thought unless they are unfortunate enough to become too sick for treatment at the Health Center, but its isolation is also part of Yale's major planning problem as a whole. It is physically cut off from the rest of the university, now especially by the Oak Street Connector. In part for that reason, but even more

FIG. 324 *Boyer Center for Molecular Medicine (Cesar Pelli and Associates): south (Congress Avenue) facade.*

because of the enormous explosion of its function in recent years, it has built up a dense and complicated community of its own, a true warren into which new facilities (a horrid word) have been forcibly inserted almost every year. Some of them, like the Brady Memorial Laboratory and the Sterling Hall of Medicine, were built during the eclectic era and were embellished with whatever classical grace notes their architects felt they could afford (see FIGS. 184 & 207). Since 1950, at least a score of buildings must have been added to the group; many of them, like the Memorial Unit, were designed by the office of Douglas Orr and his successors deCossey, Winder and Associates. In terms of modernist design, little could be done to afford each building much special architectural distinction. The demands of medical equipment and services and the restrictions of the space acted to dominate their forms. But as their numbers grew and they were more and more crowded together, something rather challenging and vital came into being. A sense of urgency and concentrated power began to be felt. Elevated walkways proliferated, fulfilling the old urbanistic fantasies of earlier days. Nothing ever seemed finished. The whole was a megastructure and a town. A kind of brutal urbanism, always beloved by modern architects, seemed all unselfconsciously to be taking shape. Perhaps in part because it remains a distinctly frightening place for many of us whom it serves, the whole complex has taken on a special dramatic resonance. It is disquietingly dynamic. Everything about it tells us that it can hurt us. All in all it is probably more like those medieval towns that architects used to dream about than Stiles and Morse can ever be. The feeling is that, like those towns, the medical area creates its own laws, which are, however, intricately involved with Nature's implacable requirements. Some of our most conspicuous architects have done buildings for it in recent years: Cesar Pelli, the Boyer Center for Molecular Medicine (1991; FIG. 324), a powerful definition of Congress Avenue; Frank Gehry, the Yale Psychiatric Institute across the street (1989; FIG. 325), a rather diffident little building for that architect. "There wasn't enough money to let me twist it," Gehry says. In 2001,

FIG. 325   *Yale Psychiatric Institute (Frank O. Gehry and Allan Dehar): southwest (Cedar Street) facade.*

Venturi, Scott Brown's Anlyan Center for Medical Research and Education was ready for construction. It has turned out to be four-square and upstanding, clear-cut in mass, smooth in surface, and burgeoning in volume, crowned with its high, shiny air vents like the stacks of one of the great old ocean liners (FIGS. 326 & 327). It recalls some of Venturi, Scott Brown's fine buildings for science at Princeton, but it is much bigger — 450,000 square feet — and even more powerfully monumental than they are. It is truly "generic" architecture, a strongly detailed, big-windowed shell able to contain many different uses. Its bulk and its surface have power, its interior is free; and it does indeed rise in the center of that whole daunting city of pain like a great ship, the culminating mass, the dominating symbol of its awful physical command.

———————

But the medical school as a whole makes us think primarily of Yale's relationship to the outside world, especially to the city of New Haven, and that topic surely has to be central to our thinking about Yale's architecture in the twenty-first century. The unification of New Haven and Yale suggested by the plans of Gilbert and Olmsted in 1910 and Pope in 1919 never happened, and right up into the Depression its lack may not have seemed too serious. The Elm City was still beautiful, and a great many of its citizens, whatever their ethnic roots or economic status, still identified with Yale and loved it. The open trolley cars of the summer season were still brought back into service for all the football games, and Yale and New Haven rode them out to the Bowl together, with packs of children running alongside. New Haven loved even the raccoon coats and the banjos and all the crazy costumes at reunion time. Yale was its mascot and its joy. Perhaps only a few New Haveners understood what Yale really meant as an institution of teaching and learning, but all of them knew enough to value it. They were borne up as well by the fact that one of the New Haven scholarships created out of Sterling funds might well send one of their children to Yale if he (unfortunately, only he, until 1969) was lucky

FIG. 331 *Gilder Boathouse (Turner Brooks).*

Community Center for the School of Art, completed in 2000; and Turner Brooks's (B.A. 1965, M.ARCH. 1970) for the new Gilder Boathouse on the Housatonic, finished in the same year (FIG. 331). But there were plenty of non-Yale architects as well. Joan Goody's remodeling of Linsley-Chittenden Hall delightfully enhances the character of the existing building, as does Michael McKinnell's of the Sterling Law Buildings. One can only be entranced by the ebullient new Gilmore Music Library (FIG. 332), which has been inserted into a rather dreary back courtyard of Sterling Memorial Library by the Boston firm of Shepley Bulfinch Richardson and Abbott, Harvard's architects since the 1870s. It is interesting that only two architects were defensive about their work, and both presentations were coldly received by the professional audience. Stephen Kieran's work in Berkeley College, which guts the basements for various activities and enlarges the kitchens, certainly has things wrong with it, among them a clunky balcony inserted between two existing arches and the reduction of the great spaces of common room and dining hall alike into simple corridors by the closing of the great central doors that linked them as complementary volumes. The doors can be opened, if not much can be done with the balcony. The limitations of R. M. Kliment and Frances Halsband's renovation of Sterling Divinity Quadrangle have already been addressed.

By the end of the millennium, Yale was giving more thought to its whole physical structure than it had ever done before during the modern period. President Griswold had modernized, enlarged, and strengthened the university with ambitious buildings of opportunity, without much consideration for the form of the university as a whole. Edward Larrabee Barnes took over as university planner in the mid-1960s, ably assisted in New Haven by Herbert Newman, but there was little funding for general studies of the university's plan and its future. Much the same program continued under Kingman Brewster, whose unrivaled contribution to the structure of the university was not in

FIG. 332 *Irving S. Gilmore Music Library (Shepley Bulfinch Richardson and Abbott).*

buildings but in his heroic remaking of the student body, which during his presidency became, in my opinion, perhaps the most intellectually distinguished and surely the most humanely intentioned in the United States. It was a unique achievement, carried out at great human cost, and it changed Yale for the better forever. Those of us who teach undergraduates and who came to know Brewster and his dean of admissions Inslie Clark (B.A. 1957), and to appreciate, as essential to a university, the bravery and compassion of his great chaplain William Sloane Coffin (B.A. 1949, B.D. 1956), can still recognize their work in the intelligence, sweetness, and openness of heart that characterize Yale College today.

Under Presidents Giamatti and Schmidt attention began to turn, as we have seen, toward the stabilization of Yale's infrastructure and the maintenance of its buildings, clearly too long deferred. Under President Levin, the planning and architectural firm of Alexander Cooper and Jaquelin Robertson was engaged to carry out a thorough study of the university and to make recommendations for its future development.[19] The relationship of Yale's plan to that of New Haven as a whole was of prime consideration, for the first time since Pope's proposal. The architects, both graduates of Yale College as well as the School of Architecture, consulted as directly with John DeStefano, mayor of New Haven, as with President Levin himself.

One of the first things of importance that emerged from that intensive, three-year study was a fresh view of the basic physical structure of Yale itself. I have made numerous references to the east down, west up, orientation that has dominated plans of New Haven and Yale since it first appeared in the Wadsworth plan (see FIG. 2), surveyed by a Yale student in 1748 and reflecting Villalpando's similar orientation in his plan of Ezekiel's New Jerusalem, published in 1604. We became accustomed, generation after generation, to seeing the university stretched out laterally in that way, and it conveyed no particular sense of urban stability or its lack. But Cooper and Robertson turned

FIG. 335 *Broadway, looking north from its intersection with Elm Street.*

steel clapboarding, neat and alert and lively on its site, and beautifully equipped within. It seems to break all the rules of contextuality but comes across as a real joy, a credit to the administration and especially to its architects, Mark Simon (M.ARCH. 1972) with Susan E. Wyeth, of Centerbrook Architects, Charles Moore's old firm.

Larger issues remain, always involving the relationship between the life of Yale and the life of the city. Yale's quadrangles, for example, are still the ideal home for small college communities. They need to be related to larger community spaces that serve the university as a whole and are at the same time open to the town in reasonable ways. Yale's relative homogeneity, spared by Redevelopment, has to be rewoven into the more heterogeneous structure of the city and, at always increasing scale, into that of the state, the nation, the world. The larger relationships are easier for Yale insofar as it is a great international university: they are conceptual relationships. The more difficult problem is the physical and emotional link between Yale and its own city, an infinitely more intricate problem than it was two hundred years ago.

During the nineteenth century Yale was regarded as a desirable place to go to college precisely because it was situated in New Haven, the city of the elms. Life was much the same in both. But in the first half of the twentieth century Yale created a paradise for itself, and something approaching hell soon began to threaten the town. That is and remains an unstable situation. A more reasonably interactive environment has to be achieved, and Yale has pledged itself to help bring that about. It is true that some recent events still give us pause: among them Yale's gentrification of Broadway, however well intended, which included the introduction of Barnes & Noble at the expense of the century-old Co-op, and the elimination of some long-standing, locally owned enterprises (FIG. 335). But, to be fair, the departure of the Co-op had a good deal to do with its unwillingness to remain open in the evening. The decision to house student activities in the upper floors of the buildings along Broadway was also a good one in this regard, ensuring an urban mix of activities throughout the day and into the evening hours. Similarly, Mayor DeStefano's decision to abandon his attempt to build an elaborate shopping mall at Long Wharf ought to help all of downtown New Haven to develop in the right direction. With the mall, the old nine squares were envisioned as becoming a kind of genteel college town (like Hanover? Princeton?), a provincial cultural enclave full of what were unhappily referred to as "boutiques." All this was highly questionable. Malls are deadly to their adjacent Main Streets, and they are failing in many places as well, with disastrous results for everyone. Nor is New Haven Hanover. Though wounded by the times, it still cherishes its history as a proud old manufacturing city, with a downtown that deserves better than reduction to an arts and crafts center, the appendage to a mall. With that threat gone, Yale and the city can now work to revive the old center, including the so-called Ninth Square, in many more integral ways, especially by encouraging the kind of shopping facilities that can compete with the malls, as has been done with great success in Pasadena and many other places. Certainly the future of Yale in New Haven, and of the city as a whole, seems more hopeful now than it did a few years ago. At least more people than ever before are informed about the problems involved and are working to resolve them. We can hope that Yale and New Haven will have another three hundred years to do so.

The issues seem wonderfully important, at least to us. They are, if not timeless, at least very old. Over five millennia ago Gilgamesh, King of Uruk, came to realize that his city offered a kind of immortality to him, perhaps to all human beings. The buildings they built in it lasted far beyond the span of their individual human lives and helped shape the world for generations to come. University buildings are especially like that; they should be among the city's most enduring. It is, after all, something like immortality they deal in, offering an escape from the restrictions to life that ignorance imposes, and a promise to lives unborn. This should be especially true of Yale in New Haven, God's city under the mountain: haven of exiles, heaven on earth for all mankind to see.

Notes

YALE IN NEW HAVEN: AN INTRODUCTION
(pp. 11–35)

1 Brooks Mather Kelley, *Yale: A History* (New Haven: Yale University Press, 1974); Rollin G. Osterweis, *Three Centuries of New Haven, 1638–1938* (New Haven: Yale University Press, 1953); Reuben A. Holden, *Yale: A Pictorial History* (New Haven: Yale University Press, 1967); Elizabeth Mills Brown, *New Haven: A Guide to Architecture and Urban Design* (New Haven: Yale University Press, 1976); and Patrick L. Pinnell, *The Campus Guide: Yale University* (New York: Princeton Architectural Press, 1999).

Douglas Rae's well documented study of New Haven with special reference to Mayor Richard C. Lee and Urban Redevelopment had not been published when this text was written: Douglas W. Rae, *City: Urbanism and Its End* (New Haven and London: Yale University Press, 2003).

2 *Buildings and Grounds of Yale University*, 4th ed., ed. Pasquale Marino (New Haven: Yale University, forthcoming). The 3rd edition of the book, edited by Richard C. Carroll, was published in 1979.

3 Paul Goldberger, "Romantic Pragmatism: The Work of James Gamble Rogers at Yale University" (Senior paper, Yale University, 1972).

4 John Archer, "Puritan Town Planning in New Haven," *Journal of the Society of Architectural Historians* 34 (May 1975): 140–49. Juan Bautista Villalpando was a Spanish Jesuit, self-styled Villalpandus in his Latin commentary. Though his reconstruction was of Ezekiel's description, he soon came to call it the Temple of Solomon, for which he was criticized in his own time, there being no description of the layout of that temple to be found anywhere in the Bible.

5 Jaime Salcedo, *Urbanismo Hispano-Americano, Siglos XVI al XVIII* (Santefé de Bogota: Pontificia Universidad Javeriana, 1994; 2nd ed., 1996).

6 John Winthrop, "A Modell of Christian Charity" (1630).

7 Cited from the Authorized (King James) Version.

8 Naphtali Daggett (B.A. 1748), the first Yale graduate to serve as its head, was president *pro tempore* from 1766 to 1777.

9 Ezek. 43:2,4.

10 Originally called Highwood and then Sachem's Wood, the house was acquired and torn down by Yale in 1942.

11 Timothy Dwight (B.A. 1849) served as Yale's president from 1886 to 1899.

12 Albert J. Booth, Jr., was born and raised in New Haven and earned a B.S. from Yale in 1932. In 1929, weighing about 148 pounds, he scored three touchdowns in Yale's come-from-behind defeat of Army, 21 to 13. In 1930 he was severely injured by Army in a play for which Army was penalized half the length of the field: for piling on—all of them—after the whistle.

13 Established as the Yale Scientific School in 1854 and renamed in honor of donor Joseph E. Sheffield in 1861, the Sheffield Scientific School offered instruction in the natural, physical, and mathematical sciences. Its program remained independent of Yale College's through the early twentieth century, but the two gradually merged after World War I, and Sheffield ceased operations in 1956.

14 Samuel Yellin (1885–1940), the most celebrated and prolific artist-craftsman blacksmith in America during the first half of the twentieth century, was born in Galicia, Poland, and founded the Arch Street Metalworker's Studio in Philadelphia in 1910. By the 1920s he had more than 200 craftsmen fulfilling commissions from leading American architects for custom work, and was receiving honors from his adopted city, the American Institute of Architects, and London's Royal Society of Art. See Jack Andrews, *Samuel Yellin, Metalworker* (Ocean City, Md.: Skipjack Press, ca. 1992), and Yale University School of Architecture, *Samuel Yellin: Metalwork at Yale*, exh. cat. (29 October–16 November 1990). This catalogue lists thirteen buildings as those that incorporate Yellin's major work at Yale, beginning with the gates of 1918–22 for J. G. Rogers's Harkness Tower and continuing right through the 1930s. Much of it was for Rogers—for his colleges, his Sterling Law Buildings, his Hall of Graduate Studies, and perhaps most admired, his Sterling Memorial Library, for which Yellin's workers produced not only many gates but also a variety of ornamental metal fittings as door hardware, radiators, balconies, and elevator doors. Yellin's artistry also devised the radiator grilles in Charles Z. Klauder's Peabody Museum (1923–24), the clockface on Egerton Swartwout's bridge over High Street and the hanging lamps in his Art Gallery's sculpture hall (1927–28), as well as the entrance-hall gates in William A. Delano's Sterling Chemistry Laboratory (1922–23), and the ornamental sign brandishing the emblem of the *Yale Daily News* out from the corner of its Briton Hadden Memorial Building (1932) by Adams and Prentice.

15 Vincent Scully, "The Blacksmith," in *Samuel Yellin: Metalwork at Yale*, 9–10; reprinted in *Yale Alumni Magazine* 54, no. 2 (November 1990): 32–33.

A NEW HAVEN & A NEW EARTH: THE ORIGIN AND MEANING OF THE NINE-SQUARE PLAN (pp. 37–51)

1 In Franklin Bowditch Dexter, *Documentary History of Yale University, 1701–1745* (New York: Arno Press and the New York Times, 1969), 27.

2 Ibid., 21. The title "School of the Churches" was given in the "earliest extant document in Yale history," a "proposal for a university" written anonymously in the spring or summer of 1701, apparently in response to inquiries by the Connecticut ministers (Dexter, *Documentary History*, 1–6). Dexter suggests that Increase Mather may have been the author; he sent the ministers a letter on the same subject in September 1701.

3 Cotton Mather, *Magnalia Christi Americana*, vol. 1 (Hartford: Silas Andrus and Son, 1855), 325.

4 Perry Miller, review of *The New Haven Colony* by Isabel Calder, *The New England Quarterly* 8 (1935): 584.

5 There is no primary evidence in the New Haven Colony's records or in the writings of its founders that sheds direct light on the plan's origin or meaning. Late-nineteenth-century historians of New Haven, influenced by the preoccupations of their own age,

cursorily ascribed its "rational" geometry to the mercantile interests of the founders (e.g., Edward E. Atwater, *History of the Colony
of New Haven* [New Haven, 1881]). A longstanding popular tradition, repeated in nineteenth-century histories and continuing to
the present day, credits John Brockett, a surveyor among the original settlers, with laying out the plan. Although he may have per-
formed the technical task (colony records make no mention of it),
it is highly unlikely that he conceived its form. See Elizabeth Mills
Brown, "John Brockett of New Haven: The Man and the Myth,"
New Haven Colony Historical Society Journal 27 (Winter 1980), for
a thorough debunking of the tradition.

The first scholarly work to focus on the plan's origins came
in 1951. In *Architecture and Town Planning in Colonial Connecticut*
(New Haven: Yale University Press, 1951), Anthony N. B. Garvan
theorized that the classical city-planning prescriptions of Vitru-
vius guided the colonists. Somewhat incongruously, he also
proposed that seventeenth-century English bastide towns in
Ireland may have influenced the design. The Vitruvian argument
was, in the words of the urban-planning historian John Reps, "at
best tortured." Reps himself, however, was at a loss to explain its
basis; see his *The Making of Urban America* (Princeton: Princeton
University Press, 1965), 128–30, for a discussion of New Haven's
plan in the context of New England town making. Since the plan's
geometry was not repeated in other settlements, there seemed
to be a presumption by both Reps and Garvan that its origin was
unrelated to the Puritans' religious mission.

Only in 1975 did that relationship begin to be considered. In
his article, "Puritan Town Planning in New Haven," *Journal of
the Society of Architectural Historians* 34 (May 1975), John Archer
broached the thesis that New Haven's founders may have looked
to biblical models for their settlement. Other historians have
followed up on his opening but offered little expansion or new
information; see Sylvia Doughty Fries, *The Urban Idea in Colonial
America* (Philadelphia: Temple University Press, 1977), 64–68,
and Norris Andrews, "Davenport-Eaton and 52 Rods," *New Haven
Colony Historical Society Journal* 33 (Fall 1986).

My study of the nine-square plan owes a great debt to Archer's
lead but departs from it significantly in the discussion of the
influence of Puritan theology on the plan's origin and form.
This emphasis is based entirely on research into seventeenth-
century New England Puritan writings and thought, exploring
the communal ramifications of their New World mission and
the influence of typological doctrine. Other aspects of the plan's
meaning, form, and use that relate to this thesis but remain as yet
unexplored include the possible influence of idealized agricultural
land planning schemes proposed by such English Puritans as
Samuel Hartlib, a close friend of Davenport, and the relationship
of Puritan millennialist thought to the plan's meaning as a biblical
type. Evidence for this latter aspect can be found in the writings
of Davenport and his circle of colleagues and influences, especially John Cotton, John Dury, Johann Amos Comenius, Thomas
Goodwin, and Joseph Mede.

6 Davenport to Lady Vere, 28 September 1639, *Letters of John
Davenport, Puritan Divine*, ed. Isabel Calder (New Haven: Yale
University Press, 1937), 82. Although scholarship on American
and English Puritanism is enormous, the works of Perry Miller
and Edmund Morgan remain masterful treatments of the subject.
Miller's books include *The New England Mind* (1953), *Errand into
the Wilderness* (1956), and *Nature's Nation* (1967), all by Harvard
University Press. Morgan's work includes *The Puritan Family*
(Boston: Trustees of the Public Library, 1944), *The Puritan
Dilemma: The Story of John Winthrop* (Boston: Little, Brown
and Co., 1958), and *Visible Saints: The History of a Puritan Idea*
(New York: New York University Press, 1963).

A full study of the mission to restore the primitive church, and
an important source for the themes of this chapter, can be found
in Theodore Dwight Bozeman, *To Live Ancient Lives: The Primi-
tivist Dimension in Puritanism* (Chapel Hill: University of North

Carolina Press, 1988). As Bozeman notes, one can find numerous
declarations of this mission in the writings of the first generation
of New England Puritan ministers, including John Davenport and
John Cotton.

7 Published in Cambridge, Mass., 1670.

8 John Winthrop, *The History of New England*, ed. James Savage
(Boston: Phelps and Farnham, 1825), 227; Isabel Calder, *The New
Haven Colony* (New Haven: Yale University Press, 1934), 28–31.

9 Mather, *Magnalia*, 152. For biographies of Davenport and
Eaton see Franklin Bowditch Dexter, "Sketch of the Life and
Writings of John Davenport," *New Haven Colony Historical Society
Papers* 2 (1875); Mather, *Magnalia*, 149–55, 321–31; and Calder,
New Haven Colony, 2–34.

10 Cotton's sermon, *God's Promise to His Plantations*, was one of
the earliest declarations of the Puritan mission in the New World.
He repeatedly invoked the example of the Israelites and designated Winthrop's company of exiles "a choice generation,"
destined to have "the Ordinances of God amongst them in a more
glorious manner, as…in *Solomon's* time," planted "in his holy
Sanctuary." He admonished them to heed the model of the
biblical church: "Go forth…with a *publick spirit,* looking not to
your things only, but also on the things of others. This care of
universal helpfulness was the prosperity of the first Plantation of
the Primitive Church" ([London, 1634], 14–15, 17–18).

11 For evidence of the intent to found a single town, see *Records
of the Colony of the Massachusetts Bay in New England*, ed.
Nathaniel Shurtleff (Boston: William White Press, 1853), 1:10; *John
Winthrop's Journal*, ed. James Kendall Hosmer (New York: Barnes
& Noble, 1946), 1:54; and Darrett Rutman, *Winthrop's Boston:
Portrait of a Puritan Town, 1630–1649* (Chapel Hill: University
of North Carolina Press, 1965), 280–84.

12 William Wood, *New England's Prospect* (London, 1634), 60;
G. B. Warden, "Newtowne, 1630–1636," *Cambridge Historical
Society Publications* 44 (1985); Alan Emmet, *Cambridge, Massa-
chusetts: The Changing of a Landscape* (Cambridge: Harvard
University Press, 1978), 3–6.

13 William Haller, *The Puritan Frontier: Town-Planting in New
England Colonial Development, 1630–1660* (New York: Columbia
University Press, 1951), 17; Rutman, *Winthrop's Boston*, 10.

14 "Essay on Ordering of Towns," *Winthrop Papers* 3:181–85. The
letter, the only known Puritan town planning document, was
placed in Winthrop's papers among other documents dating from
1635; hence its assumed date. Internal evidence indicates that it
was written in response to a request, most likely from Winthrop
or the Colony Court. Given its emphasis on agricultural planning,
it may have been instigated by the shortage of farmland. This is
also suggested by a rather cryptic reference to Newtowne, whose
inhabitants were experiencing some of the worst agricultural
overcrowding in the Bay. See Fries, *Urban Idea*, 48–49, for a
discussion of the "Essay" and its possible authorship by Thomas
Graves, an engineer living in Charlestowne.

15 Haller, *Puritan Frontier*, 43; Charles Walcott, *Concord in the
Colonial Period* (Boston: Estes and Lauriat, 1884), 5–22.

16 *Records of Massachusetts Bay* 1:157. The problem of dispersed
homesteads was not new to the plantations, just worsening in
the years of expansion. William Bradford, leader of the Plymouth
Plantation, lamented as early as 1621 that "no man now thought
he could live, except he had catle and a great deale of ground to
keep them; by which means they were scattered all over the bay,
and the town, in which they lived compactly till now, was left very
thin…this, I fear, will be the ruine of New England, at least of the
Churches of God ther" (William Bradford, *Plymouth Plantation,*
ed. Samuel Eliot Morison [New York: Knopf, 1952], 293–94). John
Cotton decried the phenomenon in 1641, admonishing those who
valued land over the good of the church: "But if we could have

large elbow-room enough, and meddow enough, though we had no Ordinances, we can then goe and live like lambs in a large place: what shall I say then? We have not part in resurrection" (John Cotton, *The Churches Resurrection* [London, 1642], 26).

17 Everett Emerson, *John Cotton* (Boston: G. K. Hall & Co., 1990), 103–4; Larzer Ziff, *The Career of John Cotton* (Princeton: Princeton University Press, 1962), 100–102. Hooker's departure was viewed negatively because he had chosen to leave the Colony altogether, not simply "hive out" as a separate township within the Colony. This latter process was often considered a positive sign of communal growth. See also n. 31 below.

18 Morgan, *Puritan Dilemma*, 138–40; Emerson, *Cotton*, 86–89. At the heart of the theological conflict was the relationship of justification and sanctification, two fundamental tenets of the Puritan belief in salvation. Justification was the individual's predestined and unchangeable fate, chosen by God to be either saved or damned. Sanctification was the Christian believer's adherence to God's holy ordinances in his or her daily conduct. Sanctified behavior could not influence one's fate, or justification, but was nevertheless considered essential to the well-being of the community, bound as it was by God's moral law. Hutchinson claimed that since sanctification had no bearing on justification, it was not necessary for the Christian to practice it in his or her worldly life—hence the name "antinomian," meaning "to be against the law."

19 Cotton, in fact, was the one who dubbed the practice "Congregationalism." He did not introduce it to New England, however, as it was already being practiced in the earlier Massachusetts plantations at Plymouth and Salem. See Emerson, *Cotton*, 35–37, 87–88; and Bozeman, *Ancient Lives*, 223.

A partial list of Cotton's Congregational writings from this period, with their approximate dates of composition, includes *A Sermon Delivered at Salem* (1636), *The Way of the Churches of Christ in New England* (1641; published London, 1645), *The Churches Resurrection* (1641; published London, 1642), *The Doctrine of the Church and its Government* (published London, 1642), *A Brief Exposition upon the whole Book of Canticles* (ca. 1641; published London, 1655), *The Keys of the Kingdom of Heaven* (1643; published London, 1644), and *The Way of Congregational Churches Cleared* (1647; published London, 1648). See Emerson, *Cotton*, 138–41, for a complete list of Cotton's writings.

Davenport's Congregational writings include *An Apologie of the Churches in New-England for Church Covenant* (ca. 1638; published London, 1643), *An Answer of the Elders of the Severall Churches in New-England* (1638–39; published London, 1643), and *The Power of Congregational Churches Asserted and Vindicated* (ca. 1648; published London, 1672). See *Letters of Davenport*, 1–12, and Dexter, "Life and Writings of John Davenport," for a list and discussion of Davenport's writings.

20 Published in London, 1643. This work has sometimes been attributed to Richard Mather; Isabel Calder makes a convincing argument for Davenport's authorship in *New Haven Colony*, 38.

21 See Morgan, *Visible Saints*, for a discussion of the development of Puritan church theory and practice in England and New England.

22 Davenport, *Power of Churches Asserted*, 27, 37; "The Profession of Faith," from *Letters of Davenport*, 73–74.

23 Miller, *New England Mind*, 21–24. Miller makes an important distinction between the individual's covenant with God and the church's. The former was unbreakable, but the latter could be severed by God. Thus the congregation was always cognizant of signs of his judgment, lest they risk breaking their covenant.

24 Cotton, *Keys of the Kingdom*, 158.

25 Cotton, *A Brief Exposition of the Whole Book of Canticles* (London, 1642), 225. This first version is presumed to have been written in the 1620s; the second, titled *A Brief Exposition upon the whole Book of Canticles* (London, 1655), was likely written in the early 1640s. See Emerson, *Cotton*, 138, 140; Bozeman, *Ancient Lives*, 250–51. For a discussion of both tracts, see Mason Lowance, *The Language of Canaan* (Cambridge: Harvard University Press, 1980), 41–54; Jeffrey Hammond, "The Bride in Redemptive Time: John Cotton and the Canticles Controversy," *The New England Quarterly* 56 (March 1983); and Bozeman, *Ancient Lives*, 248–62.

26 Cotton, *Canticles* (1655), 104–5, 108–10.

27 Cotton, "How Far Moses His Judicialls Bind Massachusetts" (ca. 1636–40), in *Proceedings of the Massachusetts Historical Society*, 2d ser., 16 (1902): 281–84; Cotton, *An Abstract or the Lawes of New England* (London, 1641); Emerson, *Cotton*, 112–13; Calder, *New Haven Colony*, 40–44. The Bay Colony did not formally adopt Cotton's code, although the code did influence later efforts at formulating a legal ordinance.

28 Cotton, *A Discourse about Civil Government in a New Plantation whose Design is Religion* (Cambridge, Mass., 1663), 5–6, 14–15. Calder and Emerson date the tract from around 1637. Tellingly, Cotton Mather, in his biography of Davenport in *Magnalia*, credits the New Haven minister with writing the *Discourse*. Calder, in "John Cotton and the New Haven Colony," makes a convincing argument that Mather was mistaken and Cotton was indeed the author. But the confusion hints at a possible collaboration between Davenport and Cotton in the *Discourse*'s argument, if not authorship.

Calder argues further that Cotton wrote it specifically to convince Davenport, who was about to embark on such a "new plantation," that restricting civil office to church members was the best course. She provides no primary evidence for this assertion, however, and it seems unlikely that this was the case, given Cotton and Davenport's already close agreement on issues of church and civil government (e.g., see Morgan, *Visible Saints*, 104–9, for a discussion of Cotton's strict test for church membership, which Davenport adopted for his New Haven church). The very point that Cotton argued for in the *Discourse* came up as a matter of contention among New Haven's founders in a meeting in 1638 to decide on the colony's form of government (*Records of the Colony and Plantation of New Haven from 1638 to 1649*, ed. Charles Hoadly [Hartford: Case, Tiffany and Co., 1857], 12–15). Davenport held firm on restricting civil magistracy to church members only, and his fellow founders quickly assented. It seems probable that he had been long decided on the matter and required little if any convincing by Cotton.

29 Cotton, *Lawes of New England*, 6.

30 Cotton, *Keys of the Kingdom*, 111.

31 Historians have often cited the phenomenon of "hiving off" congregations and towns as evidence of religious and social conflict in the Puritan communities. Although such conflict was the cause of many splits (as in the Bay Colony with Roger Williams), this is distinct from the more normative cause of separation, i.e., the desire to retain an organic limit on the size of the congregation. The Puritans generally considered the multiplication of townships to be a positive process, not a sign of communal disintegration. It is also important to distinguish the division *between* townships from the loss of spatial compactness *within* the town. Community leaders always considered the latter to be a threat to social and religious cohesion.

32 Published in London, 1634.

33 Winthrop, *History of New England*, 236–40; Rutman, *Winthrop's Boston*, 118–22; Ziff, *Cotton*, 129–31.

34 Francis Jennings, *The Invasion of America* (New York: W. W. Norton & Co., 1975), 202–27. Jennings's account gives a full airing of the colonists' campaign of deception and punishment among the tribes, along with their motives and rationalizations.

35 Winthrop, *History of New England*, 225, 233.

36 In John Winthrop, *Winthrop Papers* (Boston: Massachusetts Historical Society, 1943), 3:479, 483.

37 Winthrop, *History of New England*, 237.

38 All biblical quotations are from the Puritans' preferred translation, the *Geneva Bible*, 1560 edition (Madison, Wis.: University of Wisconsin Press, 1969 facsimile reprint).

39 John Underhill, *Newes from America* (1638), excerpted in *History of the Pequot War*, comp. Charles Orr (Cleveland: The Helman-Taylor Co., 1897), 63. Although unsubstantiated by any primary evidence, it was believed that Eaton's party left several men behind at Quinnipiack to retain possession of it over the winter of 1637–38. Calder, in *New Haven Colony*, 46, attributes the story to "tradition" and cites Benjamin Trumbull's *A Complete History of Connecticut* (1797) as the source.

40 Rutman, *Winthrop's Boston*, 122–23. Those who did not recant, including Hutchinson, moved to Rhode Island the following spring.

41 Cotton later recalled his thoughts about the matter in a treatise: *I called to mind the intent of my coming hither [to Massachusetts Bay], which was, not to disturb, but to edify the churches here, and therefore began to entertain thoughts rather of peaceable removal than of offensive continuance. At the same time there was brought to me a writing…to encourage me to removal, and offering their readiness to remove with me into some other part of this country…I took advice to see if my continuance here would breed any further offensive agitation and, if those things were found clearly, then to take opportunity to remove to Quinnipyack whereto at that time a door was opened* (Cotton, *Way of Congregational Churches Cleared*, 242–43).

42 Davenport and Eaton to the Governour and General Court of the Massachusetts Bay (12 March 1638), reprinted in Winthrop, *History of New England*, 404–5.

43 Winthrop, *History of New England*, 259.

44 Both the Pequots' defeat and the providential discovery of Quinnipiack would have recalled to them God's promise to the Israelites in Exodus:

Behold, I send an Angel before thee, to keep thee in the way, and so bring thee to the place which I have prepared.

But if thou hearken unto his voice, and do all that I speak, then I will be an enemie unto thine enemies, and will afflict them that afflict thee.

I will send my fear before thee, and will destroy all the people among whom thou shalt go; and I will make all thine enemies turn their backs unto thee (Exodus 23:20, 22, 27).

45 Davenport and Eaton to Governour, in Winthrop, *History of New England*, 404.

46 Published in London, 1643.

47 For the Puritans' self-conception as latter-day Israelites, see Bozeman, *Ancient Lives*, 2–50; Lowance, *Language of Canaan*, 13–27; and Sacvan Bercovitch, "Typology in Puritan New England: The Williams-Cotton Controversy Reassessed," *American Quarterly* 19 (Summer 1967): 183. English and American Puritan writings provide clear evidence of the Israelite model. John Dury, a colleague of Davenport, evoked the parallel for England in *Israel's Call to March Out of Babylon unto Jerusalem, a sermon before Parliament* (London, 1645); and John Cotton's *God's Promise to His Plantations* (1630) comprises an early example of the American strain.

48 Scholarship on both religious typology in general and its use among New England Puritans has come into its own as an area of study only in the last forty years. Perry Miller made one of the first references to it with regard to American Puritanism in 1948 in his introduction to Jonathan Edwards's *Images or Shadows of Divine Things* (1720; New Haven: Yale University Press, 1948). For a general summary of the typological doctrine and its parameters, see Joseph Galdon, *Typology and Seventeenth-Century Literature* (Paris: Mouton & Co., 1975), 11–69; and Ursula Brumm, *American Thought and Religious Typology* (New Brunswick, N.J.: Rutgers University Press, 1970), 7–33. Its historical basis in early Christianity and the medieval and Reformation periods is given in G. W. H. Lampe and K. J. Woollcombe, *Essays on Typology* (Naperville, Ill.: Alec Allenson, Inc., 1957). My historical summary and general discussion of typology rely on these sources.

Typology and Early American Literature, ed. Sacvan Bercovitch (Amherst: University of Massachusetts Press, 1972), presents a varied collection of essays covering the uses of typology in English and American Puritanism. Articles illuminating the impact of typological thought on the persons and events of the early Bay Colony include Jesper Rosenmeier, "The Teacher and the Witness: John Cotton and Roger Williams," *The William and Mary Quarterly* 25 (July 1968); Rosenmeier, "New England's Perfection: The Image of Adam and the Image of Christ in the Antinomian Crisis, 1634 to 1638," *The William and Mary Quarterly* 27 (July 1970); Rosenmeier, "Veritas: The Sealing of the Promise," *Harvard Library Bulletin* (1968); and Bercovitch, "Typology in Puritan New England: The Williams-Cotton Controversy Reassessed." The hold that typological thought had on the Puritan imagination lasted well into the eighteenth and even nineteenth centuries. Much recent scholarship on typology investigates its influence on early-nineteenth-century American literature, including the works of Hawthorne, Melville, Emerson, and Thoreau.

49 Davenport, in *The Knowledge of Christ* (New Haven, 1652), 26–27, drew out the many parallels that established Moses as a type of Christ: they were both "borne of mean parents," "patterns of meaknesse," deliverers of "the perfect rule" of God, and so on. This tract, which explained the figure of Christ in terms of his many "reall" and "personall" types, reflected a common treatment of the subject in Puritan writings from the early and mid-seventeenth century.

50 Davenport, *An Apologie of the Churches*, 26.

51 The works of Mircea Eliade are invaluable to an understanding of these dual conceptions of time; see *The Myth of the Eternal Return* (Princeton: Princeton University Press, 1954), 102–12; *Myths, Dreams, and Mysteries* (New York: Harper & Row, 1957), 28–31; and "The Yearning for Paradise in Primitive Tradition," *Daedalus* 88 (Spring 1959). My summary of the two temporal conceptions also owes a debt to Stephen Jay Gould, *Time's Arrow, Time's Cycle: Myth and Metaphor in the Discovery of Geological Time* (Cambridge: Harvard University Press, 1987), 10–16.

The millennialist strain that pervades the Judeo-Christian tradition is very much related to typology and its synthesis of cyclical and progressive time. For a discussion of Puritan millennialism, including the roles of Cotton and Davenport in its development, see Bozeman, *Ancient Lives*, 193–262, and Lowance, *Language of Canaan*, 115–59.

52 Published in London, 1672.

53 Genesis 2; Exodus 25–26; Numbers 34–35; Ezekiel 40–48; Revelation 11:21–22.

54 Davenport, *Knowledge of Christ*, 13. Other "Reall types" included Passover, the brazen Serpent, and Water out of the Rock. He also enumerated the "Personall types" of Christ, such as Adam, Abraham, Moses, Solomon, etc.

55 Davenport commended Mede's millennial views in his preface to Increase Mather's *The Mystery of Israel's Salvation* (London, 1669), 8. For Mede's influence on the New England ministers, including Davenport and Cotton, see Lowance, *Language of Canaan*, 123–33, and Bozeman, *Ancient Lives*, 210–36.

56 Joseph Mede, *Clavis Apocalyptica, or the Key of Revelation* (Cambridge, England, 1632), Part 1:33–37; Part 2:2–3.

57 John Lightfoote, *The Temple: especially as it Stood in the dayes of our Saviour* (London, 1650), 254–55. Lightfoote, following a common interpretation, conflated Solomon's Temple with the vision of Ezekiel: "the fashion and pattern which [the Israelites] followed in…the house [Solomon's Temple] was the Temple which Ezekiel hath described" (44).

58 Ibid., 269.

59 Davenport, *An Apologie of the Churches*, 8. Cotton in particular put great stock in the continuing moral equity of the biblical types; his dispute with Roger Williams was largely based on differing interpretations of their "perpetual" nature; see Rosenmeier, "The Teacher and the Witness." See also Lowance, *Language of Canaan*, 42–44, 83–87, for Cotton's use of the types as exemplars for contemporary use.

60 Cotton, *Keys of the Kingdom*, 160–61. The excerpted quotations come from a passage that contains several important points regarding Cotton's interpretation of the Temple type and its relevance to New England:

Something might be added…by comparing the dimensions of the new Jerusalem, *which is a perfect platform of a pure church, as it shall be constituted in the Jewish church state, at their last conversion. The dimensions of this church as they are described by Ezekiel, are* twelve furlongs, *which after measure of the sanctuary (which is double to the common) is about three miles in length, and as much in breadth. But the dimensions of the same church of the Jews, in Rev. 21:16, is said to be* twelve thousand furlongs. *Now how can these two dimensions of the same church stand together, which are so far discrepant one from another? The fittest and fairest reconciliation seemeth plainly to be this, that Ezekiel speaketh of the dimensions of any ordinary Jewish church of one particular congregation. But John speaketh of the dimensions of many particular Jewish churches, combining together in some cases, even to the communion of a thousand churches.*

In making the comparison between the Temples of New Jerusalem and Ezekiel, Cotton clearly implied his understanding of them as types conforming to the same pattern, i.e., that of the pure church. Also contained in the passage is his intriguing assertion that the sanctuary "is double to the common." The "common" has no biblical significance but was a term used by the New England Puritans to describe the public land of the township or plantation, held in common by the settlers and used for agricultural and communal purposes. New Haven's Green was just such a space, as was the Boston Common in Massachusetts Bay. If by "double" Cotton meant that the common was a corollary to the Temple sanctuary, then the statement is compelling evidence that the Temple type was indeed the pattern for New Haven's nine-square plan.

Cotton, expanding on the passage above, identified the recurring type as a "parable" and asserted its relevance as an "argument," or moral exemplar:

If any man say that arguments from such parables and mystical resemblances in Scripture are not valid, let him enjoy his own apprehension…Nevertheless, if there were no argumentative power in parables, why did John and Daniel and Ezekiel deliver a great part of their prophecies in parables, if we must take them for riddles, and not for documents nor arguments? Surely if they serve not for argument, they serve not for document.

61 Davenport, *Power of Churches Asserted*, 57.

62 Exodus 19; Deuteronomy 34; Deuteronomy 4; Ezekiel 40:1–2; Revelation 21:10.

63 Miller, introduction to Edwards's *Images or Shadows*, 4.

64 Mede, *Clavis Apocalyptica*, Part 1:26.

65 The dimension of fifty-two rods for the nine-square blocks may also be derived from the Bible. In Ezekiel, God decreed the dimensions of the holy sanctuary to be "five hundred in length with five hundred in breadth, all square round about," with the unit of measure not explicitly stated as either reeds or cubits (Ezekiel 45:1–2). If it was to be in cubits, as the Geneva Bible—the Puritans' preferred version—asserted, the sanctuary's measure would have equaled 875 feet, using the standard long cubit dimension of twenty-one inches. New Haven's "sanctuary," the Green, along with the other eight blocks, differed by less than two percent from this biblical measure. For a more detailed discussion of the correspondence, see Andrews, "Davenport-Eaton and 52 Rods."

66 *Records of the Colony of New Haven from 1638 to 1649*, 26–27.

67 Reps, *Making of Urban America*, 130. See Edward Johnson, *Wonder-Working Providence of Sion's Saviour in New England* (1653), ed. J. Franklin Jameson (New York: Barnes & Noble, Inc., 1910), for a firsthand description of the form and organization of a number of Puritan townships.

68 Numbers 2:1–2; Numbers 3:38.

69 *Records of the Colony of New Haven from 1638 to 1649*, 26–27; Numbers 35:2–5. The distinction between the city and its suburbs was also decreed in Ezekiel's vision (Ezekiel 48:17).

70 Cotton, *An Exposition upon the Thirteenth Chapter of the Revelation* (London, 1656), 252.

71 *Records of the Colony of New Haven from 1638 to 1649*, 25; Exodus 25:8–9; 26:16–30. The fifty-foot-square dimension came very close to the divine measurements given for the tabernacle in Exodus. Built of wooden planks, the tabernacle was to be thirty cubits square, which, in the long cubit measure of twenty-one inches, equaled fifty-two feet. The size and shape of New Haven's meetinghouse was unprecedented in the Puritan colonies at the time; see Marion Donnelly, *The New England Meeting Houses of the Seventeenth Century* (Middletown, Conn.: Wesleyan University Press, 1968), 15.

72 Ezekiel 43:4.

73 Published in London, 1661, 230–31.

74 *Records of the Colony of New Haven from 1638 to 1649*, 21. In "John Cotton and the New Haven Colony," Calder argued that the colony formally adopted Cotton's "Moses his Judicialls" as the basis for their government. However, the primary evidence for this is inconclusive. Nevertheless, it is true that the colony followed many of the code's prescriptions, as well as those contained in Cotton's *A Discourse about Civil Government*. For a discussion of Cotton's church test for visible election and its application in New Haven, see Morgan, *Visible Saints*, 104–9.

75 The naming of the colony as New Haven in 1640 could also be construed as a reference to this self-conception. Although the settlers gave no explanation for their choice of name, several overlapping meanings can be surmised. The first and most immediate referred to its location beside a harbor, or "haven" as it was commonly called in the seventeenth century. The second related to the Puritans' condition of exile, with their New World plantation serving as a haven from persecution in their homeland. Finally, it recalled the well-known passage in Revelation in which the appearance of the city of New Jerusalem signaled "a New Heaven and New Earth" (Revelation 21:1).

76 *Records of the Colony of New Haven from 1638 to 1649*, 376.

77 Harvard's first president, Henry Dunster, was forced to resign in 1654 when he announced his support for Baptist principles.

78 Calder, *New Haven Colony*, 40, 210; *Records of the Colony of New Haven, 1653–64*, ed. Charles Hoadly (Hartford: Case Lockwood & Co., 1858), 141–42; Richard Warch, *School of the Prophets: Yale College 1701–1740* (New Haven: Yale University Press, 1973),

7–8. Hopkins's bequest did help to fund an eponymous preparatory school in New Haven, still in operation as one of the oldest such schools in the country. However valuable this was to the colony, it did not fulfill Davenport's primary aim, which was the establishment of a college for the training of ministers.

79 See Calder, *New Haven Colony,* for an account of the colony's economic misfortunes.

80 Ibid., 218–60.

81 Mather, *Magnalia,* 329.

82 For a full account of the Collegiate School's founding, see Warch, *School of the Prophets;* and Brooks Mather Kelley, *Yale: A History* (New Haven: Yale University Press, 1974), 3–45.

83 Interestingly, the founders of Yale may have also looked to typology when they set about their task. In "Veritas: The Sealing of the Promise" (see n. 48 above), Jesper Rosenmeier argued for the typological basis of Harvard's seal and motto and asserted that Yale's emblem had a similar genesis. "Lux et Veritas," or Light and Truth, signified the antitypical fulfillment of the type's "shadow" and "prophecy."

CULTIVATING TYPES: THE RISE & FALL OF THE BRICK ROW (pp. 53–99)

1 George Santayana, "A Glimpse of Yale," *The Harvard Monthly* 15, no. 8 (December 1892).

2 Brooks Mather Kelley, *Yale: A History* (New Haven: Yale University Press, 1974), 7–23; Franklin Bowditch Dexter, ed., *Documentary History of Yale University: 1701–1745* (New York: Arno Press and The New York Times, 1969), 93, 132–33.

3 Quoted in Dexter, *Documentary History,* 146.

4 The name change honored the school's first major benefactor, Elihu Yale. There was some confusion for a time as to whether the trustees had given his name to the Collegiate House only or to the school as a whole. The latter was obviously the eventual, if not originally intended, choice. See Kelley, *Yale,* 25.

5 The change in elevation measured more than eighteen feet in the late nineteenth century and was certainly more at the time of Yale's move, before the Green had been filled and graded.

6 Norman Isham, "The Original College House at Yale," *Yale Alumni Weekly* 26 (1916): 119.

7 This "Prospect of Yale College," engraved and printed by T. Johnston after a drawing by J. Greenwood, was, according to its inscription, presented by James Buck to the Honorable Jonathan Law, Esq., Governor of Connecticut. An impression is in Manuscripts and Archives, Yale University Library, RU 703, Box 4, Folder 71.

8 Paul Venable Turner, *Campus: An American Planning Tradition* (Cambridge: MIT Presss, 1984), 27–28.

9 Kelley, *Yale,* 21–45.

10 Thomas Clap, *Annals or History of Yale College* (New Haven: Hotchkiss and Mecom, 1766), 54–55.

11 Holyoke to Clap, 18 August 1747, quoted in Louis Leonard Tucker, *Puritan Protagonist: President Thomas Clap of Yale College* (Chapel Hill: University of North Carolina Press, 1962), 75.

12 Clap, *Annals,* 55.

13 Ibid. Although Clap wrote this in 1766, several years after the chapel had been built, it is likely that he did have such a plan in mind at the time Connecticut Hall was built. Deliberately setting it back and purchasing the additional property implied a strategy beyond the task at hand.

14 *Needlework Picture of Connecticut Hall,* 1755–75. Yale University Art Gallery, Gift of Mrs. J. Amory Haskell in memory of her husband and her parents, Mary Jackson and John Lawrence Riker. 1941.310.

15 Kelley, *Yale,* 61–64.

16 Dean Lyman, *Atlas of Old New Haven* (New Haven, 1929), 11.

17 Clap, *Annals,* 77.

18 *Yale Corporation Records,* 22 July 1760, Manuscripts and Archives, Yale University Library. The Brick Row name did not gain currency until the nineteenth century, when Clap's building types had been repeated several times over. Nevertheless, I will refer to the campus as such from this point, as its two essential types were now in place.

19 Clap, *Annals,* 78; Franklin Bowditch Dexter, "New Haven in 1784," *New Haven Colony Historical Society Papers* 4 (1888): 118.

20 See Edmund S. Morgan, *The Gentle Puritan: A Life of Ezra Stiles* (Chapel Hill: University of North Carolina Press, 1962) for a full account of Stiles's life and work. It is the source for much of the following biographical sketch.

21 The plan's ambitious goals required financial support that, most likely, could only come from the Connecticut General Assembly. Yale's relationship with that body had been damaged by Clap's divisive rule, but Stiles hoped to mend it by convincing them that an expanded Yale would be an asset to the state. Kelley, *Yale,* 92; Morgan, *Stiles,* 322–33.

22 "Plan of Yale College," *Ezra Stiles Miscellaneous Papers,* Item 724, Beinecke Rare Book and Manuscript Library, Yale University. Stiles made no mention of the sketch or his thoughts on the campus's physical design in his *Literary Diary* (ed. Franklin Bowditch Dexter [New York: Charles Scribner's Sons, 1901]) or unpublished "Itineraries" around this time. He did have a habit of sketching, however, producing a number of drawings in his daybooks documenting observations or experiments. His best-known drawing is a map of New Haven, dated 1775 (in New Haven Colony Historical Society), showing the town's nine-square plan and existing buildings.

23 A calculation he made on the sketch — "8 x 4 x 2 = 64" — reflected this. Connecticut Hall was four stories with eight rooms per floor, each housing two students. The additional six students were most likely housed in makeshift quarters at the ends of the stair halls, a common expediency at the time.

24 Stiles would indeed demolish the first College House in 1782, due to longstanding disrepair. See Stiles, *Literary Diary* 3:35.

25 Morgan, *Stiles,* 308, 319; Rollin Osterweis, *Three Centuries of New Haven, 1638–1938* (New Haven: Yale University Press, 1953), 170–71; Richard Purcell, *Connecticut in Transition: 1775–1818* (Middletown: Wesleyan University Press, 1963), 9–10.

26 Morgan, *Stiles,* 320–23.

27 Stiles, *Literary Diary* 3:457–58. See also Leonard Bacon, *Sketch of the Life and Public Service of Hon. James Hillhouse* (New Haven, 1860), 39–40. Stiles's comparison of Connecticut and Yale with Moses and Aaron, the lay and religious leaders of the Israelites respectively, is evidence of how persistent the Puritan mindset was, always analogizing New England history with the narrative of the Old Testament.

28 Stiles, *Literary Diary* 3:475.

29 *Yale Corporation Records,* 23 October 1792.

30 Ibid.

31 Stiles's *Diary* entries provide additional evidence that the change was unplanned and may even have occurred subsequent to the meeting. On October 23, he wrote, "Meeting of the Corporation respecting Building a new College. Present 8 Civilians and 7 Ministers" and made no mention of any action taken or the particulars of the new building. On October 25 he recorded,

"Voted a new College Edifice, 130 ft. long & 30 ft. wide, single Rooms — 4 stories — 24 Chambers; to be placed a Wing at the North End of the College." His mention of the vote and description of the building, both of which would have more logically been included in his entry of October 23, points to the possibility that they may have proposed the change subsequent to the meeting, i.e., between October 23 and 25.

32 Quoted in Kelley, *Yale*, 127. With the exception of the poor house, all were present in 1792.

33 *Yale Corporation Records*, 3 December 1792.

34 Stiles, *Literary Diary* 3:480. Adding to the mystery of the public's reaction, both Stiles's *Diary* entry and his letter to the Corporation stated that the public objected to the new college's "dimensions" and "form" as well as its location. Like the original College House, it was extremely long and narrow — 130 feet long by 30 feet wide — a significant departure from the Connecticut Hall model. Perhaps, by associating it with Yale's first building, some considered it to be a step backward architecturally.

35 Bacon, *Life of Hillhouse*, 16–17. Later in life, Hillhouse also took charge of the Connecticut School Fund, putting it on sound financial footing after near bankruptcy.

36 Hillhouse's formidable physical presence also contributed to his stature; strong features, commanding height, and a dark complexion earned him the nickname "Sachem" (ibid., 42).

37 Letter of Subscription, March 1784, *New Haven City and County Documents*, New Haven Colony Historical Society, MSS 28; Osterweis, *New Haven*, 163. Hillhouse and Stiles also collaborated on the design of the city seal at the time of incorporation.

38 Letter of Subscription, 11 April 1786, *New Haven City and County Documents*. According to the letter, the trees were to serve both aesthetic and functional purposes: "It would be very ornamental as well as very beneficial…and would also be a Means of Stopping the Sand from covering the lower part of the Green."

Elm planting, in isolated instances, already had a somewhat ceremonial significance in New Haven. In 1686, a poor citizen had given two elms as a welcoming gift to the Reverend Pierpont, who planted them in front of his house on the north side of the Green. They appear on the Wadsworth map of 1748 and were the source of Elm Street's name. It was a curious coincidence that Hillhouse planted his Temple Street elm row almost in line with Pierpont's house one hundred years after the planting of these two elms.

39 Hillhouse to Stiles, 24 December 1792, in *The Letters and Papers of Ezra Stiles*, ed. Isabel Calder (New Haven: Yale University Press, 1953), 118–20.

40 Theodore Sizer, *The Works of John Trumbull, Artist of the American Revolution* (New Haven: Yale University Press, 1967), 1–3.

41 His commission letter from the Continental Congress had been misdated, and Trumbull construed the delay as an insult and embarrassment. See Helen Cooper, ed., *John Trumbull: The Hand and Spirit of a Painter* (New Haven: Yale University Art Gallery, 1982), 5.

42 *The Autobiography of Col. John Trumbull: Patriot-Artist, 1756–1843*, ed. Theodore Sizer (New York: Kennedy Graphics/DaCapo Press, 1970), 159.

43 Ibid., 84.

44 Yale University Art Gallery, Trumbull Collection. 1832.3.

45 See *Autobiography of Col. John Trumbull*, 92; Cooper, *Trumbull*, 7–8, 33–34; Frederick Doveton Nichols and Ralph Griswold, *Thomas Jefferson, Landscape Architect* (Charlottesville: University Press of Virginia, 1978), 12–15.

46 *Autobiography of Col. John Trumbull*, 169; John Reps, *Monumental Washington: The Planning and Development of the Capitol Center* (Princeton: Princeton University Press, 1967), 9–15.

47 Hillhouse to Stiles, 24 December 1792. Unless otherwise noted, all of Hillhouse's comments about the plan are quoted from this letter.

48 There is a discrepancy in dating Stiles's receipt of the plan and the subsequent Corporation meeting. Stiles noted on Hillhouse's letter that he had received it on January 2, 1793; and Hillhouse, in the body of the letter, mentioned a Corporation meeting on January 3. Nevertheless, both Stiles's diary and the Corporation minutes record the meeting date as January 1, as originally scheduled.

49 "The Trumbull Plan for Yale College," Manuscripts and Archives, Yale University Library. All of Trumbull's comments about the plan are quoted from his notes on the drawing.

50 High Street's inception was recorded in the *New Haven City Aldermen Meeting Records*, 19 July 1790.

51 The measurement of 465 feet is an average of the block's depth at both Chapel and Elm Streets, taken from the Hopkins *Atlas of New Haven* of 1888, one of the earliest surveyed plans of the city (Sterling Memorial Library Map Collection, Yale University). The combined length of enlarged campus and new street was 524 feet, exactly ten feet less than the sum of the existing campus frontage and the smaller parcels of property owned by others to the north. It seems that Hillhouse had knowledge of the surrounding property, its dimensions, and perhaps its availability. In addition, Trumbull made calculations on the site plan that suggested he was working backward from a fixed overall length when laying out the new halls.

There is a "bite" taken out of the site plan drawing on the southwest corner (upper left in the plan). This was property that Yale did not own and would not acquire until the early nineteenth century. Perhaps Hillhouse was less certain that Yale would be able to obtain this in the near future, a judgment borne out by its acquisition much later than the land to the north. See William Kingsley, "Plot of College Square," *Yale College: A Sketch of its History* (New York: Henry Holt & Co., 1879), 1:198, for property ownership on the College Street block.

52 Hillhouse to Stiles, 24 December 1792. Beyond the relationship to current city planning ideas, the square block also had a biblical resonance. Bounding the Congregational college — or "Seminary," as Hillhouse tellingly labeled it — it recalled the sacred geometry of the Temple type, recurring throughout the Old and New Testaments as a four-square enclosure. Although the allusion was perhaps unconscious on the part of Hillhouse and Trumbull, it would have certainly been recognizable to Stiles and the ministers of the Corporation. Indeed, for Stiles the biblical pattern of types continued to play a part in his sense of American destiny. In 1783, flush with patriotic pride after the colonies' victory in the Revolution, he had delivered the election sermon before Connecticut's governor and General Assembly. He recounted the biblical history of the Israelite nation as a model for "the political welfare of God's American Israel, and as allusively prophetick of the future prosperity and splendour of the United States," and saw its pattern recreated in America by "Divine Providence, [ordering] the time and coincidence of the publick national motives." The events of his age were both a return to Puritan origins — as a time when "Christianity [was] to be found in such great purity in this church exiled into the wilderness of America" — and a harbinger of the coming millennium, an event "which will most assuredly take place in America." In Stiles's vision, Yale had a critical role in the country's unfolding destiny. Stiles, "The United States Elevated to Glory and Honour" (1783), reprinted in *God's New Israel: Religious Interpretations of American Destiny*, ed. Conrad Cherry (Englewood Cliffs, N.J.: Prentice-Hall, 1971), 82–83, 88, 92. See also Morgan, *Stiles*, 454–56.

53 See *New Haven City Aldermen Meeting Records*, 7 June 1791, for Hillhouse's involvement with the laying out of High Street. See

Yale Corporation Records, 1782 to 1810 *passim,* and especially 1792 to 1806, for a record of his duties involving Yale's buildings and grounds; the meetings of 14 September 1796 and 4 November 1800 record his work in acquiring the northern parcels along College Street. He was actively involved with the city on several fronts in this period: arranging his own property to the north of the nine squares, conducting the necessary acquisitions for the New Burying Ground — the Grove Street Cemetery — in 1796 and, finally, acting as an agent for the city in miscellaneous dealings involving its holdings.

54 John Pease and John Niles, *Gazetteer of the States of Connecticut and Rhode Island* (Hartford: William Marsh, 1819), 103.

55 The plan's arrangement of forecourt, building line, and rear garden was also to appear later as a pronounced motif in the redesign of the Green. Following Hillhouse's transformation in 1799–1800, the churches on the Green rebuilt their meetinghouses between 1812 and 1815 as a uniform row of steepled, gable-front halls. In 1839, the city planted a number of trees on the Green's western half, filling in the elm-lined expanse behind the churches and distinguishing it from the open, level ground on the eastern half; see Henry Blake, *Chronicles of the New Haven Green, 1638–1862* (New Haven: Tuttle, Morehouse & Taylor Press, 1898), 29. The resulting effect paralleled Trumbull and Hillhouse's design for Yale: a square block, divided by an orderly building row, which in turn was fronted by the public parade of a formal, tree-lined eastern Green and set off by a dense forest of trees behind.

56 Turner, *Campus,* 41.

57 *Yale Corporation Records,* 1 January 1793. Although the "internal alterations" were referred to the Building Committee, of which Hillhouse was the *de facto* chairman, the plan's prescriptions were largely followed. The Corporation approved of the plan's chimney and window configurations in their meeting on January 1 but waited until May to proceed with the hipped roof (*Yale Corporation Records,* 10 May 1793). Stiles's diary entry of the Corporation meeting added little to the record; his own description mistakenly identified Trumbull's arched niches in the center bay of the new college halls as "Venetian windows" (Stiles, *Literary Diary* 3:483).

58 Anne S. Pratt, "John Trumbull and the Brick Row," *Yale University Library Gazette* 9 (1935): 15.

59 Stiles, *Literary Diary* 3:491–92. The previous six college buildings were the first college house, the president's house, Connecticut Hall, the chapel, and the commons hall.

60 Ibid., 527.

61 Ibid., 530.

62 *Yale Corporation Records,* 7 October 1794.

63 Morgan, *Stiles,* 425–26, 461.

64 Kelley, *Yale,* 116–18; Charles Cuningham, *Timothy Dwight* (New York: MacMillan, 1942), 301–14.

65 Cuningham, *Dwight,* 178, 192–95.

66 Kelley, *Yale,* 127.

67 Ibid., 128; Cuningham, *Dwight,* 187. For the property acquisitions, see *Yale Corporation Records,* 14 September 1796 and 4 November 1800.

68 Bacon, *Life of Hillhouse,* 37–38. Interestingly, Bacon noted that he once heard Hillhouse "express a regret that he did not insist on carrying every street through in a straight line to the water, viz: to the harbor in one direction, and from Mill River to West River in the other." The Map of 1802 depicts just such a layout, suggesting that its other deviations may have also been projects that Hillhouse, for some reason, was not able to carry out.

69 *New Haven City Aldermen Meeting Records,* 1 July 1799.

70 Elmer D. Keith and William Warren, "Peter Banner, A Builder for Yale College, Part I," *Old-Time New England* 45 (1955): 93–94, 100. Banner's gable-front design was ahead of its time and one of the earliest examples of the Federal house type, which was to become a popular form early in the nineteenth century. See *Yale Corporation Records,* 12 September 1798 and 10 September 1799, for details of the house's construction.

71 Benjamin Silliman, *A Sketch of the Life and Character of President Dwight, delivered as an eulogium* (New Haven: Maltby, Goldsmith & Co., 1817), 25. The communal ideal set by the arrangement of Brick Row, enclosed yard, and president's house was extended into the twentieth century with the introduction of the residential college system in the 1930s. The master's house lodged in the college's enclosed quadrangle recapitulated its elements in a much modified and more compact form.

72 Kelley, *Yale,* 128.

73 *Yale Corporation Records,* 4 November 1800.

74 *Yale Corporation Records,* 8 September 1801.

75 Patrick L. Pinnell, "Old Campus Building History" (New Haven: unpublished manuscript, 1996).

76 Two hundred seventeen students had enrolled in 1801–2, already more than the three dormitories could normally hold.

77 Keith and Warren, "Peter Banner," 109; Kelley, *Yale,* 129.

78 George P. Fisher, *Life of Benjamin Silliman* (Philadelphia: Porter & Coates, 1866), 123, 125. Banner, Silliman, and the Brick Row were to intersect in another interesting way at this time. In the spring of 1802, the South Carolina College in Charleston announced a design competition for the "best original plan of a College," to which both Banner and Silliman submitted entries. Silliman's design consisted of a schematic floor plan accompanied by extensive programmatic notes. He proposed a single U-shaped building, with a central academic hall connecting two perpendicular dormitories and all enclosing an open-ended quadrangle. Banner's submission, meanwhile, was modeled directly on the Brick Row. He formalized the facade compositions and details but clearly used its alternating frontal and lateral types. He also submitted, as a supporting precedent, his own drawings of Yale's buildings, including the two new halls he was constructing at the time.

Neither won the competition, but the final design used by the college, which was drawn up by the competition committee, was obviously based on the Row model. It took two lateral dormitories and attached them to either side of a square chapel type, forming a single long centralized building. Their dormitory suite plans directly copied Trumbull and Hillhouse's design for Union Hall, which Banner had drawn up and included with his entry. Thus South Carolina had the honor of being the first of many American colleges to use the Brick Row as a model for its own campus, even before Yale itself had completed Trumbull and Hillhouse's plan. See John M. Bryan, *An Architectural History of South Carolina College, 1801–1855* (Columbia: University of South Carolina Press, 1976), 12–22.

79 Fisher, *Silliman,* 83; Edmund S. Morgan, "Ezra Stiles and Timothy Dwight," *Proceedings of the Massachusetts Historical Society* 72 (October 1957–December 1960): 109; Purcell, *Connecticut in Transition,* 21–22.

80 *Yale Corporation Records,* 15 September 1803.

81 *Yale Corporation Records,* 11 September 1804.

82 Timothy Dwight, *Travels in New England and New York* 1, ed. Barbara Solomon (Cambridge, Mass.: Belknap Press of Harvard University Press, 1969), 148.

83 Ibid., 1:122, 246–47.

84 Ibid., 123–24.

85 A counterpoint to Dwight's opinion of New Haven was his assessment of Boston. Although he approved of the city's lively social life and industrious ways, he lamented its physical state, finding it to be cramped and disorderly. Interestingly, he proposed an alternative design, one that offered a "means of future and distant elegance": a grid of broad tree-lined streets, punctuated by public squares, and terminating on views of the surrounding bay. The natural topography of hills would "furnish the most eligible situations for private and especially for public buildings." The example of New Haven, including Yale's buildings sited on their "handsome elevation," seemed to have had a place, intended or not, in Dwight's idealizing vision. Ibid., 355.

86 Ibid., 131–33.

87 James L. Kingsley, *Remarks on the Present Situation of Yale College, for its Friends and Patrons* (New Haven, 1818; reprinted 1823), 12.

88 Kelley, *Yale*, 144–46.

89 The portico was removed sometime in the late 1870s, bringing the appearance of the New Chapel more into line with its brethren on the Row.

90 The library gained its own building behind the Brick Row in 1846. In the enormous building campaign of the 1920s and 1930s, Yale used the library once again as the impetus for planning a new campus center, this time moving it a block north to what was to become the Cross Campus, headed by Sterling Memorial Library.

91 W. E. Decrow, *Yale and "The City of Elms"* (Boston, 1882), 13; Kelley, *Yale*, 166.

92 Kelley, *Yale*, 145–46.

93 Ibid., 151.

94 Osterweis, *New Haven*, 271. By 1831, New Haven's population was 12,000, and it was on the cusp of its nineteenth-century industrial expansion (set back temporarily by the economic crash of 1837). It shared state capital status with Hartford at the time, with the Legislature shuttling between respective state houses each year.

95 Ebenezer Baldwin, *Annals of Yale College* (New Haven: B. & W. Noyes, 1838), 200.

96 Clarence Deming, *Yale Yesterdays* (New Haven: Yale University Press, 1915), 8, 14.

97 George W. Pierson, *Yale College: An Educational History, 1871–1921* (New Haven: Yale University Press, 1952), 27.

98 Deming, *Yale Yesterdays*, 10–11; Decrow, *Yale and "The City of Elms,"* 18–19. *The Yale Banner*, a yearly compendium of student activities, used the subdivisions of entry hall and floor to organize its directory of students.

99 Deming, *Yale Yesterdays*, 12.

100 Ibid., 6, 9.

101 Pierson, *Yale College*, 28.

102 Lewis Welch and Walter Camp, *Yale: Her Campus, Classrooms, and Athletics* (Boston: L. C. Page and Co., 1899), 30–31. The "openness" of Yale's social and academic life in this period extended to its minority of Jewish students as well. In contrast to the virulent anti-Semitism of the late nineteenth and early twentieth century, Yale generally welcomed Jews into all facets of campus life during the early and mid-nineteenth century. Only by the late 1870s did sentiments change there and in American society as a whole. See Dan Oren, *Joining the Club: A History of Jews and Yale* (New Haven: Yale University Press, 1985), 3–37.

103 Quoted in Deming, *Yale Yesterdays*, 4.

104 Charles Dickens, *American Notes* (London: Chapman and Hall, 1842), 183.

105 N. P. Willis, *American Scenery* (1840; reprint, Barre, Mass.: Imprint Society, 1971), 218–19.

106 Ezekiel Porter Belden, *Sketches of Yale College* (New York: Saxton & Miles, 1843), 67–68.

107 Ibid., 65.

108 Baldwin, *Annals of Yale College*, 201–2.

109 The so-called "Yale Report" (*Reports on the Course of Instruction in Yale College*, New Haven: Hezekiah Howe, 1828), produced by President Day, the Corporation, and the faculty, reasserted the importance of the classical curriculum in American liberal education and was immensely influential throughout the nineteenth century. See Louise Stevenson, *Scholarly Means to Evangelical Ends: The New Haven Scholars and the Transformation of Higher Education in America, 1830–1890* (Baltimore: Johns Hopkins University Press, 1986).

110 Deming, *Yale Yesterdays*, 4–5.

111 Willis, *American Scenery*, 110; Kelley, *Yale*, 213; Henry Peck, *The History of the State House* (New Haven, 1889), 96–97.

112 Kelley, *Yale*, 215–19; Belden, *Sketches of Yale College*, 189–91.

113 Welch and Camp, *Yale: Her Campus*, 32.

114 The Beinecke Rare Book and Manuscript Library at Yale recently (1999) acquired architectural plans (a floor plan and a cross section) produced in 1830 by A. J. Davis for a freestanding campus library. Davis was then a partner with Ithiel Town, and their firm was responsible for Sachem's Wood on the Hillhouse estate (1828) and the new State House on the Green (1829). Like those buildings, Davis's library was in the Greek Revival style. Little is known about the circumstances of the design, predating as it did the college's fundraising efforts for such a building.

115 *Yale Corporation Records*, 18 August 1840.

116 Pinnell, "Old Campus Building History."

117 Belden, *Sketches of Yale College*, 98. Street Hall, per the bequest of its donor, Augustus Street, had entries at Chapel Street and the campus interior, fulfilling his desire that the building serve New Haven as well as Yale.

118 At the time, Yale's founding was erroneously dated as 1700.

119 Theodore D. Woolsey, *An Historical Discourse Pronounced before the Graduates of Yale College, August 14, 1850* (New Haven: B. L. Hamlen, 1850), 125.

120 Benjamin Silliman, "An Address delivered before the Association of the Alumni of Yale College, August 17, 1842," Beinecke Rare Book and Manuscript Library.

121 "The City of Elms," *Harper's New Monthly Magazine* 17 (June 1858): 16.

122 Woolsey, *Discourse*, 126.

123 Kelley, *Yale*, 194.

124 *Report of the Executive Committee of the Society of the Alumni of Yale College in 1869*, 5–6, Manuscripts and Archives, Yale University Library (Film HM 214).

125 Interestingly, Trinity College in Hartford, whose campus was based on the Brick Row model, was to undertake such a move several years later. In 1872, they sold their center city campus to the state and relocated outside town. The old campus was torn down to make room for the new State Capitol; and Trinity's new campus design, although not executed in its entirety, took the form of a quadrangle. See Turner, *Campus*, 217.

126 *Report of the Alumni of Yale College in 1870*, 3.

127 The alumni report of 1870 said as much: "For the present, it will be necessary to retain the old dormitory buildings, unsightly as they are in appearance, and indifferent as are the accommodations which some of them offer" (ibid., 5).

128 Upon his election in 1846, President Woolsey had chosen to remain in his own house, and the official residence was converted to a scientific laboratory; in 1860, Yale had it removed from the campus. Kelley, *Yale*, 183.

129 Noah Porter, *The American College and the American Public* (New Haven: C. C. Chatfield & Co., 1870), 167.

130 Why Dwight's center chapel suggestion from 1871 was ignored is unknown. Porter was at philosophical odds with Dwight over Yale's status as a university (with Porter championing the college tradition), and he may have paid him little heed.
    The chapel did take another form, briefly, in the time between Battell's donation in 1864 and the decision to place it at the campus corner in 1870. The Yale administration, at the end of the Civil War, had intended it to be both a replacement for the Brick Row chapel and a memorial to the war dead. A limited competition was held for its design, won by the firm of Vaux, Withers and Co. in 1867. Their design drawings (see FIG. 93) showed a free-standing building, although devoid of context, which makes it impossible to determine its site (or even if a site was selected, not unlikely given the lack of planning direction at the time). Its type—frontally oriented with a projecting center steeple—hinted at it possibly taking the last "chapel" space of the Row, although the Victorian Gothic stone cladding would have made it an ostentatious addition. The competition and design entries were reviewed in "Yale College Memorial Chapel" in *The Builder* 25 (12 October 1867): 747–48. See also, in the present volume, Catherine Lynn, "Building Yale & Razing It from the Civil War to the Great Depression," pp. 113–15.

131 Timothy Dwight, "Yale College," *The New Englander* 30 (1871): 639–41.

132 Ibid., 641. Dwight's thoughts on the matter were probably influenced by his fellow faculty member in the Theological Department, James Mason Hoppin (B.A. 1840). A professor of homiletics, Hoppin began lecturing on art in the 1860s and became a close follower of Ruskin's theories. In 1879, he was appointed Yale's first professor of art history in the School of the Fine Arts. See Stevenson, *Scholarly Means*, 131–32.

133 Dwight, "Yale College," 645.

134 Ibid., 646.

135 Kelley, *Yale*, 274; Pierson, *Yale College*, 95–97. His sense of mission, in its theological implications, was quite explicit; Pierson notes that the younger Dwight believed "Divine Will had called his grandfather to the Yale presidency" (Pierson, *Yale College*, 597).

136 *Report of the President of Yale University* (1887), 6, Manuscripts and Archives, Yale University Library.

137 Kelley, *Yale*, 271.

138 *Report of the President* (1887), 17–18.

139 Richard Carroll, ed., *Buildings and Grounds of Yale University* (New Haven: Yale University Printing Service, 1979), 44.

140 *Report of the President* (1887), 16; Kelley, *Yale*, 277. It was Dwight who originally suggested the site to the donor, Mrs. Miriam Osborn (who insisted on anonymity due to its controversial location). The donation was arranged by her lawyer, John W. Sterling (B.A. 1864), who was to make an enormous bequest himself in 1917.

141 Welch and Camp, *Yale: Her Campus*, 27.

142 *Report of the President* (1896), 8.

143 *Report of the President* (1890), 10.

144 *Report of the President* (1893), 4.

145 Lewis Welch and Walter Camp, ed., "Yale's Past," *Yale Alumni Weekly* (15 April 1896): 4.

146 Welch and Camp, *Yale: Her Campus*, 392–93.

147 *Report of the President* (1898), 15–16.

148 Pierson, *Yale College*, 98.

149 *Report of the President* (1900–1901), 26.

150 *Report of the President* (1890), 9.

151 *Report of the President* (1899–1900), 22; Pierson, *Yale College*, 31.

152 Timothy Dwight, *Memories of Yale Life and Men, 1845–1899* (New York: Dodd, Mead and Company, 1903), 497.

153 George Hunston Williams, *Wilderness and Paradise in Christian Thought* (New York: Harper & Brothers, 1962), 211.

154 George Dudley Seymour, *New Haven* (New Haven, 1942), 283.

155 Donald Grant Mitchell [Ik Marvel, pseud.], *Dream Life: A Fable of the Seasons* (New York: Charles Scribner, 1857; original edition 1851), 148–49.

BUILDING YALE & RAZING IT FROM THE CIVIL WAR TO THE GREAT DEPRESSION (pp. 101–231)

1 The ten new buildings and their architects were: Street Hall (1864–66), P. B. Wight; Farnam Hall (1869–70), Russell Sturgis; Durfee Hall (completed 1871), Russell Sturgis; Battell Chapel (1874–76), Russell Sturgis; Lawrance Hall (1885–86), Russell Sturgis; Dwight Hall (1885–86, demolished 1926), J. C. Cady; Chittenden Library (1888–90), J. C. Cady; Osborn Hall (1888, demolished 1928), Bruce Price; Welch Hall (1891), Bruce Price; Vanderbilt Hall (1894), C. C. Haight. In 1900, the three remaining buildings of the Brick Row were Connecticut Hall, the Lyceum, and North College.

2 The four gates and their architects were: Cornelius Vanderbilt Memorial Gate (1894), C. C. Haight, from Chapel Street to Vanderbilt Hall; Whitman Memorial Gateway (1895), J. C. Cady, on High Street between Street Hall and Chittenden Library (published by Montgomery Schuyler as "Farnam Memorial Gateway," using the name of its donor, in "The Works of Cady, Berg & See," *The Architectural Record* 6 [1897]: 517–53); Phelps Gate (1898), C. C. Haight, from College Street to the Old Campus; and Miller Memorial Gateway (1899), C. C. Haight, on Elm Street between Battell Chapel and Durfee Hall. In 1900, a fifth major gateway was in the works, the Ninety-Six Memorial Gateway (dedicated 1901), H. Davis Ives, on College Street between Welch and Bingham Halls.

3 The sixteen buildings and their architects were: East Divinity Hall (1869–70, demolished 1931), R. M. Hunt; Marquand Chapel (1871, demolished 1931), R. M. Hunt; North Sheffield Hall (1872–73, demolished 1967), J. C. Cady; West Divinity Hall (1873–74, demolished 1931), R. G. Russell (in conformity with R. M. Hunt's plan for the divinity complex); Peabody Museum (1873–76, demolished 1917), J. C. Cady; Trowbridge Library (1881, demolished 1931), E. E. Raht; Sloane Physical Laboratory (1882–83, demolished 1931), E. E. Raht; Winchester Observatory (1882–83), R. G. Russell; Kent Chemical Laboratory (1887–88, demolished 1931), E. E. Raht; University Gymnasium (1890–92, demolished 1932), E. E. Gandolfo; Yale Infirmary (1892), J. C. Cady and Company; Winchester Hall (1892, demolished 1967), J. C. Cady and Company; Berkeley Hall (1893–94, demolished 1933), J. C. Cady and Company; White Hall (1893–94, demolished 1933), Cady, Berg and See; Sheffield Chemical Laboratory (1894–95, now known as A. K. Watson Hall), Cady, Berg and See; Pierson Hall (1896, demolished 1917), Cady, Berg and See; and Round House, Berkeley Oval (1900, demolished 1933), Cady, Berg and See. Less visible than these were facilities like the power house, nearly a quarter century old in 1900, and a "boiler house and steam department" that had been in operation only seven years. On the Mill River, at the foot of Chapel Street, the jaunty wooden boathouse of 1875 designed by Cummings and Sears was to last but another ten years.

4 The ten hospital buildings and their architects were: East Ward (1873, now Tompkins East), F. C. Withers; West Ward (1873, demolished 1931), F. C. Withers; Power House and Laundry (1876, demolished 1929), architect unknown; Two Isolation Pavilions (1877, demolished ca. 1929–31), architect unknown; Morgue (1877, demolished ca. 1929–31), architect unknown; Dormitory for the Connecticut Training School for Nursing (1881, demolished 1931), architect unknown; Superintendent's Quarters (1886, demolished 1923), architect unknown; Farnam Operating Amphitheatre (1888, demolished 1928), architect unknown; Gifford Ward (1889, demolished 1929), L. W. Robinson; and Gifford Chapel (1892, demolished 1929), L. W. Robinson.

The close association of Yale with what is now the Yale-New Haven Hospital dates from 1826, when the General Hospital Society of Connecticut was incorporated to establish the fifth general hospital in the United States. Four of the ten original incorporators were members of the faculty of the Medical Institution of Yale College, and a fifth was Professor Benjamin Silliman, then professor of chemistry in the college, according to Courtney C. Bishop, "The Hospital at New Haven: the first one hundred years, 1826–1926," *Yale Medicine* 11, no. 2 (Spring 1976): 8–14. The original Greek-temple-fronted State Hospital, as it was then called, was designed by Ithiel Town and built in 1830–32. It was known as the Knight United States Army General Hospital during the Civil War, when it was leased from 1862 to 1867 to the Surgeon General of the Army. In 1884 it was renamed New Haven Hospital. Yale's Department of Medicine occupied offices and laboratories in wood-frame buildings on the site in 1907. The term School of Medicine was not used, according to Dr. Bishop, until 1914–15. In 1945 New Haven Hospital merged with Grace Hospital and was renamed Grace-New Haven Hospital. It became Yale-New Haven Hospital in 1965.

5 Montgomery Schuyler, "The Architecture of American Colleges: II Yale," *The Architectural Record,* no. 26 (November 1909): 411. Harvard had been the first in Schuyler's series, which was to continue in more than a dozen installments until 1912, leaving us the most important source of detailed information and opinion about American collegiate architecture at the turn of the twentieth century. Schuyler's criticism, imbued with Ruskinian principles and a growing prejudice against Beaux-Arts Classicism, was characterized by William H. Jordy and Ralph Coe in an introduction to their collection of his writings as "the most perceptive, most revealing, and most urbane commentary on American architecture to emerge from the critical tenets of progressive nineteenth-century theory" (*American Architecture and Other Writings by Montgomery Schuyler* [New York: Atheneum, 1964; original edition 1961], 10). Since he was, among his contemporary critics, the one who focused most intensely and influentially upon Yale's architecture, describing and assessing it thoughtfully, he is quoted often in the present text.

6 Ibid., 401.

7 Cady, Berg and See to W. W. Farnam, 29 July 1898, Treasurer's Records, Manuscripts and Archives, Yale University Library (RU 151). Hereafter Treasurer's Records.

8 In addition to Hendrie Hall, two of these are still Yale-owned: the Yale Infirmary at 276 Prospect Street, now used for student housing, and Sheffield Chemical Laboratory at 51 Prospect Street (now A. K. Watson Hall), both by J. C. Cady. Winchester Observatory at 485 Prospect Street, by Rufus G. Russell, which Yale sold in 1956, is now much altered. The twenty-nine buildings Yale erected between 1865 and 1900 include nineteen listed in note 3, and ten listed in note 4.

9 Cady's surviving buildings are Hendrie Hall, the old Yale Infirmary, Sheffield Chemical Laboratory (now A. K. Watson Hall), and Chittenden Hall (now incorporated in Linsley-Chittenden Hall).

10 Mrs. Stephen V. Harkness (née Anna M. Richardson), whose husband was an early investor in Standard Oil and an associate of John D. Rockefeller, was the first member of the family to pay for a major building project, Memorial Quadrangle, in memory of her son, Charles W. Harkness, a member of the Class of 1883. Another of her sons, Edward S. Harkness (B.A. 1897) was the major donor of the residential colleges of the 1930s. In 1927 Mrs. William L. Harkness had given the hall whose name honors her late husband (B.A. 1881), the older half-brother of Edward S. Harkness.

11 Artillery Hall, put up during World War I, was razed only ten years later, but it represented emergency construction for a temporary situation. J. C. Cady's Pierson Hall on York Street was nearly as short-lived. Built in 1896, it was razed in 1917 to make way for John Gamble Rogers's Memorial Quadrangle. The more routinely ephemeral categories of athletic and minor service buildings have been excluded from this calculation of the shortest life span of an early-twentieth-century Yale building: in fact the Carpentry Department of 1901 lasted a mere sixteen years, the Carnegie Swimming Pool of 1909 only twenty-three, and the Baseball Cage of 1912 but seventeen years. Assorted stables, storage buildings, and workshops were even shorter-lived.

12 Corporation Records, 8 December 1928, as quoted by Brooks Mather Kelley, *Yale: A History* (New Haven: Yale University Press, 1974), 375.

13 George W. Pierson, *A Yale Book of Numbers* (New Haven: Yale University, 1983), A-1.3 and A-1.6. The book is available online at http://www.yale.edu/oir/pierson_original.htm. An updated version is available at http://www.yale.edu/oir/pierson_update.htm.

14 A wealth of published material describes and pictures Yale buildings: campus guides, student yearbooks, magazines, newspapers, official reports of building activities, and books about Yale aimed at alumni and a general readership. In Manuscripts and Archives, Sterling Memorial Library, Yale University, are great quantities of unpublished documents, official records, including the especially relevant ones of building and planning committees, along with building contracts and specifications, bills of sale, and records of payment that are part of the financial records maintained by successive treasurers of the university. These also include correspondence, as do other collections of the papers of key Yale officials and graduates. The letters can be most intriguing when they reveal ideas about architecture and planning as well as critical opinions about architects that Yale's administrators, Corporation members, donors, and architects would not have publicized at the time of writing them confidentially.

15 "Yale College in 1869," by the Executive Committee of the Society of the Alumni, in *Reports of the President of Yale University* (1 June 1869), 5.

16 As quoted by Arnold Guyot Dana, *New Haven's Problems: Whither the City? All Cities?* (New Haven: Tuttle, Morehouse & Taylor, 1937), 13.

17 Arthur Twining Hadley, "Yale," in *Four American Universities: Harvard, Yale, Princeton, Columbia* (New York: Harper and Brothers, 1895), 47.

18 In this volume, see Erik Vogt, "Cultivating Types: The Rise & Fall of the Brick Row," especially pp. 61–68.

19 Charles Z. Klauder and Herbert C. Wise, *College Architecture in America* (New York: Charles Scribner's Sons, 1929), 19.

20 Theodore Dwight Woolsey, *Historical Discourse,* 1850, as quoted by Kelley, *Yale,* 192.

21 [P. B. Wight], "New Haven Revisited," *American Architect and Building News* 4, no. 150 (9 November 1878): 155. "Professor Huxley" is cited as source for the term "intelligent bricklayer."

22 Schuyler, "Yale," 403.

23 Alumni Hall was also called Graduates Hall. Designed in 1851 and completed in 1853, it was a symmetrical two-story box of Portland (Connecticut) stone. A large examination hall filled its first floor, two literary society library rooms the second, reached by a pair of stairs housed in the two picturesque "Gothick" towers flanking its entrance, through a pointed arch. It was crenellated all around, and its origins were vaguely late perpendicular. Edward C. Herrick, Yale treasurer, wrote A. J. Davis on 12 September 1853: "The building is highly satisfactory and will stand as the chief architectural ornament of our grounds;—and in all probability will survive its only rival—the Library [Austin's Old Library, now Dwight Hall]."

24 G.C.H. [George C. Holt], "A General Grumble," *Yale Literary Magazine* 31, no. 2 (November 1865): 72. George C. Holt won writing and debating prizes, was class orator, and a member of Skull and Bones. He remained an active alumnus throughout his life, an incorporator of the Yale Club, and recipient of an honorary LL.D. in 1904. He graduated from Columbia's law school and became a distinguished lawyer in New York, an authority on bankruptcy, and a judge with concurrent jurisdictions on federal and state courts. In 1899 and 1900 he served on the Building Committee for the Bicentennial Buildings. When he died in 1931 one of his two sons, Hamilton Holt, was president of Rollins College.

25 Gore Hall (built by Richard Bond, 1838–41) was razed in 1913 for Widener Library. Bainbridge Bunting and Margaret Henderson Floyd, *Harvard: An Architectural History* (Cambridge, Mass., and London: Belknap Press of Harvard University Press, 1985), 44–46.

26 Schuyler, "Yale," 403.

27 By 1909, when Schuyler wrote his article, the Trumbull Gallery was no longer standing. As the "Treasury Building," it had housed the President's office from 1869, when Trumbull's paintings were moved into Street Hall, until it was razed in 1901, when the administration moved into Woodbridge Hall.

28 [Holt], "Grumble," 72. While the opinion of an undergraduate of 1865 may now seem prescient in its warning against a break with the architectural unity of the Row, it made no difference of course, especially since it was buried in a rather fatuous little article that skipped among topics as unrelated as the rough manners of students and the character of the College Sweep (the janitor).

29 In 1895, Charles Eliot Norton, professor of art history at Harvard, in a virulent reaction against Victorian collegiate architecture, condemned Harvard's "disregard of the influence of architecture as an element in education…If some great benefactor…might arise,…he might require the destruction of all the buildings erected in the last half-century, and their reconstruction with simple and beautiful design, in mutually helpful, harmonious, and effective relation to each other" (Charles Eliot Norton, "Harvard," in *Four American Universities: Harvard, Yale, Princeton, Columbia*, 3).

30 Stokes to John V. Farwell, 5 October 1911, Treasurer's Records.

31 [Wight], "New Haven," 155. To Wight the "rut" was the "Tudor style, supposed to have been coordinate with scholarship, learning, and monastic mystification. With its freedom from precedent, and evident adaptation to a purpose, it seems to have commenced a new era of college architecture at New Haven."

32 Sidney M. Stone (1808–1888) designed both the Medical School building and the gymnasium, which became a dining hall in 1892; after Commons opened in 1902, it became Herrick Psychological Hall, and was razed in 1917 for the Memorial Quadrangle. His Medical School building was rented in 1924 to an independent school of pharmacy and razed in 1957. Stone was, with Henry Austin, one of "the two architects who dominate" the antebellum period in New Haven, and who had "enormous output." Stone "had begun as an itinerant carpenter and worked his way up through the building trades," according to Elizabeth Mills Brown, *New Haven: A Guide to Architecture and Urban Design* (New Haven and London: Yale University Press, 1976), 6. He was also the builder of New Haven's original State Hospital of 1832, designed by Ithiel Town.

33 James M. Hoppin, "Augustus Russell Street," in William L. Kingsley, *Yale College: A Sketch of Its History*, 2 vols. (New York: Holt, 1879), 2:146.

34 [Wight], "New Haven," 155.

35 A. R. Street to President and Fellows, 24 March 1864, Treasurer's Records.

36 John Ferguson Weir, "Yale School of the Fine Arts," in Kingsley, *History* 2:141.

37 Wight's complaints of Street's censorship include, from a letter to H. C. Kingsley, 1 December 1865: "I very much regret that Mr. Street should wait until this late day to make objections, as he has had elevation drawings and perspectives and has seen the working drawings from which they are made. The reason they do not look as well as they should is that the finials and ridge crestings (always part of the original design) have been omitted, according to orders from head-quarters" (Treasurer's Records).

38 [Wight], "New Haven," 155.

39 Sarah Landau, *P. B. Wight: Architect, Contractor, and Critic, 1838–1925* (Chicago: Art Institute of Chicago, 1981), 16–21. The invited contestants, Richard Morris Hunt, Leopold Eidlitz, and Jacob Wrey Mould, protested the selection of Wight's entry.

40 Ibid., 11.

41 Roger B. Stein, *John Ruskin and Aesthetic Thought in America, 1840–1900* (Cambridge, Mass.: Harvard University Press, 1967), 234.

42 Ibid., 234–36. It was James M. Hoppin (1820–1906) who in 1906 bequeathed $60,000 to establish a Chair of Architecture in the School of the Fine Arts. Yale did not receive the bequest, in the sum of $58,562.50, until 1923, after the death of Hoppin's son, Benjamin.

43 Wight referred to the advance of art three times in a letter refusing to accept reduction of his commission: First, "I believe that I can best advance the cause of art by voluntary gifts…than by deductions from amounts justly earned"; then citing "the part the building itself is to take in the advancement of Art"; and finally, "I have always endeavored to keep in view the success of the building and the advancement of art to which I am devoting my best energies" (Wight to H. C. Kingsley, 23 October 1866, Treasurer's Records).

44 Andrew Dickson White, *Yale Literary Magazine* (1853), as quoted by Lila Freedman, unpublished typescript of a lecture, "Dwight Hall: A Tale of Three Buildings, or The Unravellings of a Mystery," 23 February and 26 August 1983, 14. Manuscript in the files of Vincent Scully.

45 Weir, "Yale School of the Fine Arts," 142.

46 Wight to H. C. Kingsley, 23 October 1866, Treasurer's Records.

47 The drawing, signed "Peter B. Wight/Architect." Des. & Pinx. 1899" and stamped "Yale School of the Fine Arts," survives in Architectural Drawings, Manuscripts and Archives, Yale University Library (RU 698).

48 Schuyler, "Yale," 403–4.

49 Weir to the President and Corporation, 17 May 1909, Treasurer's Records.

50 Two drawings for this balcony, one rejected, the other executed, are signed "R. W. Foote, Arch/N.H. CT/MAY 16 – 1928." Yale University Planning Office, Plan Room.

51 [Wight], "New Haven," 156.

52 Charles Eliot Norton "The Harvard and Yale Memorial Buildings," *The Nation* 5 (July 11, 1867): 34.

53 Biographical information about Eidlitz and Littell is derived from Robert A. M. Stern, Thomas Mellins, and David Fishman, *New York 1880* (New York: Monacelli, 1999), 19, and 279, where Littell's practice is characterized as "successful practice specializing in churches in New York, New Jersey, and Pennsylvania." Littell's birth and death dates have not been found. Emlen T. Penchard Littell shared office space during the 1860s with H. H. Richardson in the Trinity Building on Broadway in New York, according to Henry-Russell Hitchcock, *The Architecture of H. H. Richardson and His Times* (Cambridge, Mass., and London: The M.I.T. Press, 1966; original edition 1936), 61. Hitchcock says that Littell was "about two years his [Richardson's] senior," which would put his birth date about 1836. Hitchcock dismisses Littell's ecclesiastical work as "of a colorless Victorian Gothic character not even significantly bad."

54 The sequence of who designed what for which committee is ambiguous. Receipts bearing dates in 1864 for work by Vaux, Withers and Co. and by Russell Sturgis, Jr., suggest that they might have been submitted to the Corporation's committee before the Alumni Committee was formed in July 1865. Designs by Mould bear dates in 1866. A letter of 12 February 1867 from Littell to H. C. Kingsley quotes from a letter "of the Committee" (no date given) specifying that Eidlitz was "employed to furnish a ground plan and perspective view of this building" and that the committee "would be glad to receive similar sketches for the same from J. W. Mould, Vaux Withers & Co, Russell Sturgis, Jr., and E. T. Littell." On learning "that the competition for the memorial chapel has been decided," Littell requested in a letter of 2 February 1867 that his drawings for it be returned to him. A receipt for a "preliminary study" by Vaux, Withers and Co. bears the date 18 May 1868. All these documents are in the Treasurer's Records.

55 Mould to Porter, 20 July 1866, capitalized and underlined "Art-Architecture," assuring him he could execute the design for $100,000. Mould to "The Building Committee of Proposed Memorial College Chapel," undated, described his cruciform plan, its monumental pronaos enclosing a cenotaph "of highly decorative Architecture," and a colorful variety of stones and slates patterning the walls and roofs. Treasurer's Records.

56 Perhaps these proposals were for the center of the Old Campus, within the enclosed quadrangle, as envisioned by Timothy Dwight in 1870–71, a scheme that, by 1868, must have been taking shape in his thinking. Although Dwight would not become president of Yale until 1886, his influence was substantial by the mid-1860s.

57 Edward F. Salisbury, Joshua Coit, Richard S. Fellowes, Daniel C. Gilman, Joseph E. Sheffield, and Benjamin Silliman made up the committee that failed to raise funding for a Civil War memorial chapel. Printed Circular of the Committee of Yale College Memorial Chapel, dated 20 January 1867, Treasurer's Records.

58 Norton, "The Harvard and Yale Memorial Buildings," 34. Though scathing about the design for Memorial Hall in 1867, in 1895 he began an essay on Harvard: "From whatever side one approaches Cambridge, the tower of the Harvard Memorial Hall is conspicuous. It is an appropriate emblem of the university… duty…sacrifice…No other building in the United States is consecrated by more tender and noble personal and patriotic associations" (*Four American Universities,* 3).

59 [Wight], "New Haven," 156.

60 Kelley, *Yale,* 194.

61 Professor J. L. Dinman's biography of Durfee is within Professor Arthur M. Wheeler's essay, "Durfee College," in Kingsley, *History* 1:493–97.

62 *Report of the President* [Hadley] (New Haven: Yale University, 1905), 83.

63 W. E. Decrow, *Yale and "The City of Elms"* (Boston: Decrow, 1882), 23.

64 [Wight], "New Haven," 156.

65 Ibid.

66 William L. Kingsley, "The Battell Chapel," in Kingsley, *History* 1:288. Babb, Cook, and Willard's house for Andrew Carnegie on 91st Street at Fifth Avenue in New York, now the Cooper-Hewitt Museum, is perhaps the firm's most frequently illustrated work.

67 *Yale Alumni Weekly* 37, no. 2 (30 September 1927): 29.

68 Battell was enlarged in 1893 by Cady, Berg and See; renovated in 1927 by Everett V. Meeks; and restored in the late 1980s by Herbert S. Newman. Patrick L. Pinnell remarked on the "astonishingly bright polychrome" of the restored interior (*The Campus Guide: Yale University* [New York: Princeton Architectural Press, 1999], 19).

69 [Wight], "New Haven," 156.

70 Henry-Russell Hitchcock, *Architecture: Nineteenth and Twentieth Centuries* (Baltimore, Md.: Penguin Books, 1958), plate 96A. Hitchcock noted (p. 193) a "simplicity and sophistication of late High Victorian Gothic design, in marked contrast to the stridency of Hunt's precisely contemporary Divinity School there. This, however, is almost unique [in its period]." Even earlier, in his book of 1936 on H. H. Richardson, Hitchcock had singled out Farnam Hall as standing with Richardson's work of the early 1870s as the only exceptions to his statement that in that period "there was nothing new in American architecture which held promise for the future" (Hitchcock, *Richardson,* 104).

71 Pinnell, *Campus Guide,* 19. He says that Farnam has in Louis I. Kahn's Center for British Art of 1977 its "only…rival" for the title "most tectonically didactic building on campus."

72 [Wight], "New Haven," 156.

73 Schuyler, "Yale," 406.

74 Kelley, *Yale,* 199.

75 Record of Meeting of the Corporation, 26 July 1864, typescript copy in Records of Corporation Committee on Architectural Plan, Manuscripts and Archives, Yale University Library (RU 30). Hereafter Plan Committee Records.

76 Kelley, *Yale,* 200.

77 Bound Ledger, "Y.U./Cost of Buildings and Donors of Funds, Nineteenth Century," Treasurer's Records.

78 George E. Day, "The East and West Divinity Halls and the Marquand Chapel," in Kingsley, *History* 2:51. "By the efforts of the theological professors…the amount of $117,000 was obtained in the course of two or three years for the new building."

79 And all were also members of a group called "The New Haven Scholars" by Louise L. Stevenson in *Scholarly Means to Evangelical Ends* (Baltimore and London: The Johns Hopkins University Press, 1986). These were men whose scholarship, as her title suggests, was focused by deep religious commitment. In 1864 the corporation also voted "that the vacant lot on the corner of Elm and High Streets may be taken as the site of said Divinity College," but on 21 July 1868 a "reluctant recommendation" by the Prudential Committee granted the Theology Department use of a nearby site at Elm and College "without charge for ground rent for the term of 8 years."

80 Paul R. Baker, *Richard Morris Hunt* (Cambridge, Mass., and London: MIT Press, 1986; original edition 1980), 111.

81 Pinnell, *Campus Guide,* 124.

82 Hunt's rendered elevation and plan survive in the Hunt Archive of the Prints and Drawings Collection, The Octagon, The Museum of the American Architectural Foundation, Washington, D.C.

83 At the time he won the commission for the Divinity School, Hunt's experience included supervision of construction for Lefuel's pavilion at the Louvre, which distinguished him as an architect well acquainted with grand building of the most advanced French style. His Tenth Street Studio Building had caused a stir in New York's art world a decade earlier with its rather severe brick facade where structurally expressive detailing replaced allusion to historic precedent. Just after its completion in 1858, some of America's leading painters moved in. It is also possible that an acquaintance with Samuel F. B. Morse played some part in Hunt's winning the commission for the Divinity School. Although Morse was more than thirty-five years older than Hunt, both had studios during the 1850s in the University Building on Washington Square in New York where "there was much coming and going and socializing with the painters," according to Baker, *Hunt,* 69. Perhaps Morse, as a major donor to the Divinity School building campaign, put in a good word for a talented younger friend.

84 Baker, *Hunt,* 186, writes that Hunt's Yale work was "the first of a considerable number of [his] collegiate buildings" at Princeton, Harvard, and West Point. He calls East Divinity Hall "one of Hunt's least successful designs" (187). Ruskin's name does not appear in the index of Baker's book.

85 Schuyler, "Yale," 411, describes this Nova Scotia stone as an olive-colored sandstone.

86 These albums were brought to my attention by Sherry C. Birk, Director of Collections, The Octagon, The Museum of the American Architectural Foundation.

87 Hunt was quoted in an articled entitled "The Theological Department," published (largely as a plea for additional funds to complete his building) in the *Memorial of the Class of Yale College, 1830* (Hartford: Case, Lockwood, 1871), supplement, p. 14.

88 Hunt's perspective and plans for a "Theological Hall New Haven" survive in the Hunt Archive of the Prints and Drawings Collection, The Octagon, The Museum of the American Architectural Foundation, Washington, D.C. They show a complex that is more academically Gothic in form and detail than the one executed. Here Hunt drew stone walls, gabled roofs, and windows with pointed arches, and showed buildings a full story lower than those realized. This early scheme for the complex shows a chapel approximately where he soon placed Marquand Chapel, and a dining hall a little south of the eventual site of the Day Missions Library of 1911. The drawings only sketchily suggest the buildings to the west, and there are no plans for them in the Hunt Archive.

89 Baker, *Hunt,* 240, 293. Marquand had not been a major donor to East Divinity Hall, so this link between Hunt and Marquand does not furnish an explanation for Hunt's winning the original commission for the Divinity School.

90 Obituary of Frederick Marquand, died July 14, 1882, *The New York Times,* 15 July 1882. It records that Marquand "made over" his jewelry store "to Ball, Black & Co., who had been clerks in his employ."

91 [Wight], "New Haven," 156, observed that: "The entrances to the stairways are from a cloister which is decidedly original in treatment, running the whole length of the building."

92 George E. Day, "The East and West Divinity Halls and the Marquand Chapel," 51.

93 The Divinity School's need of a new dormitory in 1873 suggests how successful Timothy Dwight's devotion to it had been. The sixty student rooms of East Divinity Hall had not been able "to accommodate the increasing number of theological students," but the school's own enrollment would not quite fill the 150 places in this new dormitory, so the extra rooms were rented to "Academical and Scientific members." Brooks Kelley writes that both Presidents Woolsey and Porter were relatively indifferent to the plights of the Divinity, Medical, and Law Schools during the 1860s and 70s, as they focused on Yale College. He quotes Woolsey: "I do not know that I have done anything for the Theological professors, except to allow them to raise their own salaries" (Kelley, *Yale,* 254).

94 Hunt contracted double pneumonia in the winter of 1874 and went to Europe in May for a curative stay of nearly a year. Baker, *Hunt,* 247, 249.

95 These figures are taken from a small ledger book marked "Yale University/Cost of Buildings and Donors of Funds," 15, 16, 18, and 280. Treasurer's Records.

96 Stern et al., *New York 1880,* 401–6. Raht was first independently listed as an architect in Polk's *New York City Directory* for 1879–80.

97 Decrow, *Yale and City,* 45.

98 Schuyler, "Yale," 412.

99 Paul Stuehrenberg, *A Library Worthy of the School—A History of the Yale Divinity School Library Collections* (New Haven: Yale Divinity School Library Occasional Publication No. 1, 1994), 3. I am in debt to Martha Smalley, research services librarian and curator of the Day Missions Collection, for this quotation.

100 In this volume, see Vincent Scully, "Modern Architecture at Yale: A Memoir," p. 294.

101 Brown to Farwell, 9 December 1922. Farwell to Stokes, 23 April 1930. Both letters, as well as the faculty complaint to the Corporation, are in Plan Committee Records.

102 Lymann H. Bagg, "Boating," in Kingsley, *History* 2:289, 293.

103 On Cummings and Sears, see Cynthia Zaitzevsky in *Macmillan Encyclopedia of Architects,* ed. Adolph K. Placzek, (New York: Free Press; London: Collier Macmillan, 1982), 1:481. On rowing during this period at Yale, see Lymann H. Bagg, "Boating," in Kingsley, *History* 2:289, 293. In the second ediction of *Yale and "The City of Elms"* (1885), W. E. Decrow specified that the boat house was "…on the Chapel Street bridge, a short distance below East Street," commenting that "It resembles closely the boat house of the London Rowing Club" and noting that it was "…built in the spring of 1875, at a cost, including the land, of about $16,500" (pp. 66–67).

104 Decrow describes the site as:

…about thirty acres…west bank of West River, on the southern side of Derby Avenue, a little over a mile from the college campus…The greater portion of the land lies on a bluff, thirty feet above the river, and looks in one direction toward the harbor, and in another toward the city, while on the western side lies Edgewood Hill. In the fourth direction is a excellent view of West Rock. On the whole, it is difficult to see how a more beautiful situation could have been obtained… Although the land was not purchased until the spring of 1881, considerable work had been done before the close of the following summer…plans were obtained before Commencement. These plans contemplate what will be, when completed, altogether the largest, most convenient and beautiful grounds for athletic sports in America, or, in fact, in the world…The cost of the land was about $21,000, and the improvements will cost from $10,000 to $20,000 more. The money is subscribed mostly by graduates and students of Yale (ibid., 63–64).

105 Ibid., 63.

106 The baseball stands of 1927 were renovated in 1994. See Randall Beach, "Play Ball! Yale's venerable baseball stadium is getting a new lease on life as part of an innovative deal with a

professional franchise," *Yale Alumni Magazine* 57 (May 1994): 34–35.

107 The younger brother, Thomas Sloane, was elected to the Yale Corporation in 1889, just a year before he died "of apoplexy," at age forty-three, the result of "poor health induced by too close attention to business," according to Yale's Obituary Records.

108 George Wilson Pierson, *Yale College: An Educational History, 1871–1921* (New Haven: Yale University Press, 1952), 64.

109 John Addison Porter, *Sketches of Yale Life* (Washington, D.C.: Arlington Publishing Co., 1886), 24.

110 The tower was "modeled after that of the Town Hall at Altenberg" and the building "was occupied early in 1884," according to W. E. Decrow, *Yale and "The City of Elms,"* 2nd edition (Boston: Decrow, 1885), 33.

111 Arthur Williams Wright (B.A. 1859, PH.D. 1861), professor of molecular physics and chemistry, "had a bushy black beard and was called 'Buffalo,'" according to Pierson, *Yale College*, 77.

112 Henry Hobson Richardson (1838–1886) was the leading American architect from about 1870 until his death. Great round-arched openings set in massive stonework distinguished some of his most notable achievements, including the Allegheny County Courthouse in Pittsburgh, Sever and Austin Halls at Harvard, and the Marshall Field Warehouse in Chicago.

113 This document is preserved in the collection of Photographs and Pictures of Buildings and Grounds, Yale University, Manuscripts and Archives, Yale University Library (RU 30), and is marked only "Paris Exposition II." The quotation is from p. 679.

114 After his father's death in 1901, he managed his estate, dealt in livestock, grain, and land in Omaha and Genoa, Nebraska, became a congressman from California from 1907 to 1911, and then ran unsuccessfully for the Senate. Yale Obituary Records.

115 For the conversion, Henry T. Sloane was again a major donor, with another brother, William D. Sloane, who had received an honorary M.A. from Yale in 1889.

116 Kelley, *Yale*, 262.

117 Kathleen A. Curran, *A Forgotten Architect of the Gilded Age: Josiah Cleaveland Cady's Legacy* (Hartford, Conn.: Watkinson Library and Department of Fine Arts, Trinity College, 1993). Because Cady spelled his middle name "Cleveland" in documents in the Yale archives, I have not used the spelling Curran chose. Cady left Trinity his library of 400 architectural books.

118 Schuyler, "The Works of Cady, Berg & See," 517 (see n. 2 above). Schuyler did not name that professor, and his identity remains unknown.

119 Baker, *Hunt*, 163. Perhaps an acquaintance with Hunt was instrumental in bringing Cady his first Yale commission.

120 Four years earlier, Wight had been given a Yale commission on the strength of his first major success, a center of artistic life in New York. Now Cady was chosen by Yale's scientists close following his first wave of recognition for another metropolitan center of artistic life.

121 Schuyler, "The Works of Cady, Berg & See," 521.

122 William H. Brewer, "Sheffield and North Sheffield Halls," in Kingsley, *History* 2:117.

123 Curran, *Cady's Legacy*, 11.

124 As quoted by Pierson in *Yale College*, 55, citing Dwight's *Yale College: Some Thoughts Respecting Its Future*, 92.

125 Cady to W. W. Farnam, 9 March 1892, Treasurer's Records.

126 Schuyler, "The Works of Cady, Berg & See," 521.

127 *Yale Alumni Weekly*, 27 February 1895.

128 Russell H. Chittenden, *History of the Sheffield Scientific School of Yale University 1846–1922* (New Haven: Yale University Press, 1928), 2:259.

129 Ibid., 178.

130 This firm, whose principals are Harold Roth (M.ARCH. 1957) and William F. Moore (B.A. 1963, M.ARCH. 1966), also designed Yale's Seeley G. Mudd Library and the Joseph Slifka Center for Jewish Life at Yale. Arthur K. Watson (B.A. 1942), who paid for the renovation, was also a fellow of the Yale Corporation, 1967–73.

131 Francis R. Kowsky, *The Architecture of Frederick Clarke Withers and the Progress of the Gothic* (Middletown, Conn.: Wesleyan University Press, 1980). Kowsky's work has been the source for my quotations and summary statements about Withers; see his pp. 11, 38, 71ff.

132 On the Hospital's founding board, Faculty of the Medical Institution of Yale College included Drs. Thomas Hubbard, Eli Ives, Jonathan Knight, and Nathan Smith. The practicing physicians were Drs. Thomas Minor, John S. Peters, John Skinner, and Eli Todd. William Leffingwell was the generous New Haven citizen. See Courtney C. Bishop, M.D., "The Hospital at New Haven: the first one hundred years, 1826–1926," *Yale Medicine* 11, no. 2 (Spring 1976): 8.

133 A transcription of the very detailed specifications for Town's building, constructed between 1830 and 1832, was published by Pliny A. Jewett, M.D., in his *Semi-Centennial History of the General Hospital Society of Connecticut*, in *Annual Report of the Directors, General Hospital Society of Connecticut* (New Haven: Tuttle, Morehouse & Taylor, 1876), 17–24. It begins:

The Hospital, consisting of a centre and two wings...The centre to be forty-six feet from front of main walls to the rear, and forty-eight feet in width. The pediment to project twelve feet in front of the whole. The height to be forty-three and a half feet from the top of the water table to the top of the walls, in the line of the eaves. It shall be built...throughout of that kind of red stone of which the new State House is constructed, and obtained from the same quarries...to be plastered and finished in the same manner as the new State House, or like Mr. Hillhouse's new house...excepting the first three feet from the surface of the ground...shall be pointed and finished like the north-west side of the basement of Mr. Ralph I. Ingersoll's new house, but instead of Chatham stone, to have a water table formed on the top of the red stone, beveled off and projecting three inches.

On it goes with equal specificity for more than seven pages, after which Jewett states: "The building was erected under the above specifications by Sidney M. Stone, Esq., for less than $13,000."

134 See n. 32 above.

135 Jewett, *Semi-Centennial History*, 61.

136 Ibid., 62.

137 Bishop, "The Hospital at New Haven," 10.

138 The dimensions are from Jewett, *Semi-Centennial History*, 61–62. The description of the pillars is from Dr. William H. Carmalt, "The Second Half Century of the General Hospital Society of Connecticut," in *General Hospital Society of Connecticut Centenary, 1826–1926* (New Haven: General Hospital Society of Connecticut, 1926), 59.

139 George Bronson Farnam (1841–1886) of New Haven was memorialized by a tablet in the amphitheater, recording that he "faithfully served...as attending physician and surgeon from 1873 to 1877 and though cut off from professional activity during the remainder of his life by painful illness never ceased to further its interests and to minister to the suffering of others" (Carmalt, "Second Half Century," 63).

140 Ibid., 57–58.

141 Robinson's work mentioned in the text is documented in the Treasurer's Records, as is that on the Medical School Building of 1892–94, Farnam Hall, the Boiler House, the University Lecture Hall on College Street (old College Street Church), the Clinical Building of 1901, and the Jane Ellen Hope Memorial Building.

142 Carmalt, "Second Half Century," 64.

143 Possibly the clinical amphitheater was new construction, but more probably it was a conversion of a small ward built under the terms of Mrs. Gifford's will for incurable "colored persons" but "never…used for the purpose indicated for the simple reason that no objection has ever been made throughout the hospital to the admission of colored persons to the general wards" (ibid., 63–64).

144 Funding for the Isolation Pavilion (also called the Howard Building) was financed by "Sundry donors and City of New Haven" (Reuben A. Holden, "Chronological List of Buildings," in *Yale: A Pictorial History* (New Haven: Yale University Press, 1967).

145 Yale University School of Medicine, *The Past, Present, and Future of the Yale University School of Medicine and affiliated clinical institutions including the New Haven Hospital, the New Haven Dispensary, the Connecticut Training School for Nurses* (New Haven: Yale University, 1922), 41.

146 Carmalt, "Second Half Century," 58.

147 School of Medicine, *Past, Present, and Future*, 44.

148 O. C. Marsh, "Peabody Museum," in Kingsley, *History* 2:179.

149 Ibid., 180.

150 As late as 1899 Lewis Sheldon Welch and Walter Camp included it in *Yale. Her Campus, Class-Rooms, and Athletics* (Boston: L.C. Page & Co., 1899), 290.

151 The best-known surviving example of Cady's many buildings in New York is also a fragment of a project never fully executed for a natural history museum. In 1888 his firm won the competition for the American Museum of Natural History with a scheme to build the largest museum in the world. Organized around courtyards, it would have filled the blocks from 77th Street to 81st Street between Central Park West and Ninth Avenue. The central dominating pavilion was built first, not, as was the case in New Haven, a subordinate wing. It faces south on 77th Street. Stern et al., *New York 1880*, 186–89.

152 [Wight], "New Haven," 156.

153 Schuyler, "The Works of Cady, Berg & See," 522.

154 Ibid., 523.

155 An elevation and a plan of Cady's project for a long Richardsonian library survive in Yale's collection of architectural drawings. It has been suggested that these might have been made in 1905 as entries for a library competition won by Charles C. Haight, since it is known that Cady's firm entered this competition. However, Cady's elevation of the extensive Richardsonian building is clearly from the period of the 1880s, not only stylistically but also because it is signed "J. C. Cady & Co., Archts / 111 Broadway," the address appropriate for the 1880s. By 1905, the firm was called "Cady, Berg & See, Architects and Engineers" and had offices at 6 West 22nd Street.

156 A copy of Frederick Marquand's will survives in the Treasurer's Records. In the vestibule of the present Dwight Hall (Austin's Library) a metal tablet memorializing Frederick Marquand records, in part, that " His love for young men and his interest in Yale College led to the erection of this building, to be known as Dwight Hall, in honor of one whom he greatly revered, and to be used by the students of the University as a permanent home for their Christian activity in their social religious work; a work to be carried forward in the name of Christ, by young men and for young men." Below this, inscribed in wood paneling: "From the

First / Dwight Hall / 1886–1926 / Erected by / Elbert / Brinckerhoff / Monroe / To carry out / the wish of / Frederick / Marquand."

157 Schuyler, "The Works of Cady, Berg & See," 523.

158 Schuyler, "Yale," 408.

159 Kelley, *Yale*, 291. Cady to Morris F. Tyler, Treasurer, 1 June 1904, wrote that the sum "appropriated" by Mr. Chittenden was "some $125,000," the figure used here rather than $100,000 as in Kelley. Cady seems a reliable source, given his financial accounting of 1904.

160 The windows portray science, religion, music, and art and were installed in 1889. *The New York Times*, 6 January 1889, reported that Tiffany's cartoons for them were "one of the chief decorations of the exhibition…[at the] Architectural League."

161 Osborn Hall Scrapbook [of newspaper clippings on the erection of Osborn Hall and the fight to save the Yale Fence (1887–1890)], John W. Sterling, collector, Manuscripts and Archives, Yale University Library. The *New York Commercial Advertiser* of 20 June 1889 emphasized that the "framework in rolled iron beams and brick arches is as thoroughly fire proof as possible."

162 Cady to W. W. Farnam, 16 May 1889, Treasurer's Records. "I say to you in all confidence that I think we can give you a more *desirable*…building for a given sum of money than most architects" (Cady's emphasis). He did not get the job.

163 Cady to Morris F. Tyler, 1 June 1904, Treasurer's Records.

164 Kelley, *Yale*, 292.

165 "Minutes of the meetings of the Committee of the Corporation of Yale University on Additions to the University Library" include: James Gamble Rogers to President Hadley, 18 March 1905, accepting invitation to enter library competition; J. G. Rogers to Hadley, 12 May 1905, "respectfully" withdrawing: "I am unable to find a solution of the difficulties of the requirements of the proposed new building that would be an honor to Yale and do credit to one of the sons." Yale Architectural Documentation 1853–1986, Manuscripts and Archives, Yale University Library (RU 2).

A Gothic design, with touches of the Tudor, by Robertson and Potter, and a Gothic one by Howells and Stokes, were published in *Architecture* (August 1905) as plates LXVIII and LXIX. Delano and Aldrich's proposal retaining much of Austin's old library at its center, flanked with courtyard cloisters and naves that nearly equaled it in size, survives in Manuscripts and Archives.

166 Through the spring of 1905, the *Yale Alumni Weekly* ran extensive discussion of proposed library sites, of the threat to Austin's Library, of the choice of an architect, etc. See especially *Yale Alumni Weekly* 14, no. 23 (8 March 1905): 447–50; and no. 24 (15 March 1905): 474–76, which includes, apropos of siting the new library, report of a survey locating Yale faculty homes.

167 Clipping, Osborn Hall Scrapbook.

168 Frederick Jones to Robert W. Carle, 18 March 1921, and 23 May 1921, suggesting Chittenden's as the site for Harkness Hall. Plan Committee Records.

169 This gateway has been listed erroneously in recent Yale publications as a work of Charles C. Haight. Cady's contracts for the "foundations and stone work between Art Building and Chittenden Library" with Smith, Sperry and Treat, Contractors, and with W. H. Jackson and Co. of New York for the "iron gates and bronze tablets between the Art School and Chittenden Library" survive in the Treasurer's Records. Montgomery Schuyler pictured the gate in his article of 1897 on Cady's firm, where the caption calls it "Farnham Memorial Gateway, Yale College," misspelling the Donor's name. Plaques on the gate posts are inscribed: "In Memory of / Samuel Whitman / Fellow of Yale College / 1748–1774 / Erected by / Ann Whitman Farnam / 1895" and "In

Memory of / Elnathan Whitman / Fellow of / Yale College 1748–1774 / Erected by / Ann Whitman Farnam / 1895."

170 A deteriorated Memorandum signed Miriam A. Osborn, November 1888, was transcribed and then destroyed. The transcription survives in "Contents of sealed lead case in copper box in Osborn Hall cornerstone," Yale Architectural Documentation 1853–1986.

171 See n. 161 above.

172 *Report of the President of Yale University for the Year Ending July 1, 1887,* p. 16.

173 Dwight to Sterling, 26 May 1887, advising against hiring Russell Sturgis, was included among the "Contents of sealed lead case in copper box in Osborn Hall cornerstone." No mention of Bruce Price appears therein.

174 The honorary degree awarded Sturgis in 1872 was one of the very few honorary degrees Yale bestowed upon architects during the nineteenth century. In its published lists I can find only one other — Daniel Burnham, awarded an honorary M.A. in 1893, the year of Chicago's Columbian Exposition, the architectural planning of which he directed in close association with Frederick Law Olmsted, who designed the landscaping and to whom Yale awarded an honorary LL.D. that same year.

175 On Price's Shingle Style houses and their influence on Frank Lloyd Wright, see Vincent Scully, *The Shingle Style and the Stick Style,* rev. ed. (New Haven and London: Yale University Press, 1971; original edition 1955), 127–28.

176 Kristel R. Smentek, "PRICE, Bruce," *American National Biography,* ed. John A. Garraty and Mark C. Carnes (New York: Oxford University Press, 1999), 17:855. Surprisingly, there is no major published monograph dealing with Price's work. This fine summary biographical sketch with a solid bibliography is the source of information given here.

177 Yale Architectural Documentation 1853–1986.

178 *Yale Record* 16, no. 1 (29 September 1888): 2. The context adds forgiveness: "Yet members of the Corporation, although you have ruined our beloved roost, cut down our beautiful elms, and made us look upon the 'abomination of desolation' — in spite of all this we forgive you, for you have removed the Old Lab. Like Othello, this building's occupations have been gone for many years, and it has of late been nothing but an eye-sore. Peace to its shade." The Old Lab (1782–1888) was Yale's fourth building and originally contained a dining hall and kitchen. In 1820, it became the home of Benjamin Silliman's laboratory.

179 Clipping, *The New York Times,* 7 August 1888, Osborn Hall Scrapbook.

180 The building was the Channing Memorial Church in Newport. Dwight to Price, 20 May 1888, Yale Architectural Documentation 1853–1986.

181 Baker, *Hunt,* 317.

182 Schuyler, "Yale," 408.

183 Clipping, "New Yale Buildings," *New York Commercial Advertiser,* 20 June 1889, Osborn Hall Scrapbook.

184 Clipping, *New Haven Evening Register,* 6 March 1889, Osborn Hall Scrapbook.

185 Architectural Drawings.

186 Clipping, *New Haven Register,* 25 September 1888, Osborn Hall Scrapbook. The reporter expounded: "There is no special type of architecture. It is a mixture of Arabesque and Romanesque, happily blended, producing an agreeable effect."

187 Clipping, *New York Herald,* 7 September 1889, Osborn Hall Scrapbook.

188 Clipping, *New York Tribune,* 3 February 1890, Osborn Hall Scrapbook.

189 Schuyler, "Yale," 407.

190 A. P. Stokes to J. V. Farwell, 5 October 1911, Plan Committee Records.

191 Corporation minutes, 10 October 1924, and minutes of Corporation Committee on Architectural Plan, 17 April 1925. T. W. Farnam to J. V. Farwell, 27 January 1925, Plan Committee Records.

192 Treasurer's Records.

193 "Infirmary," *Yale Alumni Weekly* 2, no. 7 (15 November 1892): cover.

194 *Yale Alumni Weekly* (9 October 1894). Rendered elevation for Elm Street facade, *Yale Alumni Weekly* (16 October 1894): cover.

195 *Yale Alumni Weekly* 4, no. 27 (1 May 1895): cover.

196 Cady, Berg & See to W. W. Farnam, 29 July 1898, Treasurer's Records.

197 J. V. Farwell to A. P. Stokes, 23 April 1930, Plan Committee Records.

198 *Yale Daily News* published "A full description of the building with architect's plans," 27 June 1890. E. E. Gandolfo's letterhead styled him "Engineer-Architect," 31 Union Square, New York. Treasurer's Records.

199 *Yale Alumni Weekly* 4, no. 2 (1 May 1895): cover.

200 Haight's design of Linsly Hall, built in 1906 and 1907, has been discussed above; see p. 151. Vanderbilt Hall was his first commission for a Yale building.

201 Letter from the Acting Treasurer of Yale University to Mr. Stowe Phelps, office of Grosvenor Atterbury, 7 February 1910, Treasurer's Records. Yale gave Cornelius Vanderbilt an honorary M.A. in 1894, the year Vanderbilt Hall was completed.

202 C. C. Haight to W. W. Farnam, 17 February 1893: "plans for the new dormitory building…not quite ready to send." 27 February, Haight presented plans to building committee. Haight to Farnam, 5 February 1894: "advise as soon as possible if you desire to use gas or electric lamps"; question repeated 7 July. Installation of gas fixtures, 20 December 1894. Treasurer's Records.

203 *Yale Alumni Weekly* 2, no. 24 (11 April 1893): cover.

204 *Report of the President,* 1899, p. 14.

205 Only for Fayerweather Hall among Cady's buildings for the Berkeley Oval are the working drawings to be found in Yale Architectural Documentation 1853–1986.

206 That entry lodge eventually served as Yale's telephone exchange. See Holden, *Yale: A Pictorial History,* caption for fig. 84.

207 Treasurer's Records. For White Hall, correspondence of Yale Treasurer W. W. Farnam with both the donor, A. J. White, and the architect, J. C. Cady, is unusually complete.

208 This figure is from a memorandum of about 1910 in the Treasurer's Records listing costs of eight dormitories. A figure of $153,305.26 appears in the architects' "Statement of Cost of the White Dormitory," 30 November 1894, the cost of Newspaper Rooms, an additional $3,531.69. The contract price of May 1893 was $145,000.

209 W. W. Farnam to J. C. Cady, 14 May 1893: "contract for the lodge railings &c was $6953…his 5% commission…$315" (Treasurer's Records). The lodge was not built until 1900.

210 A. J. White to W. W. Farnam, 28 April 1893, "[this] expressed the sentiment I like best of any I have seen," with clipping from *Brooklyn Daily Eagle,* 19 April 1893, headlined "Dr. White & Yale": "Apparently he believes that a firmly founded and well equipped university can do more with money than a freshly founded establishment" (Treasurer's Records).

211 J. C. Cady to W. W. Farnam, 13 June 1893, Treasurer's Records.

212 Thomas Bergin, *Yale's residential colleges; the first fifty years* (New Haven: Yale University, 1983), 126.

213 White Hall's foundations and trim were stone.

214 *Yale Alumni Weekly* 3, no. 32 (5 June 1894).

215 A description of plans for "White Dormitory" in *Yale Alumni Weekly* (2 May 1893) is especially useful, since Cady's plans for the building do not survive in the Yale archive.

216 "The New Dormitory," *Yale Alumni Weekly* 5, no. 22 (18 March 1896): cover, with perspective drawing of the facade.

217 Arthur Twining Hadley, in a speech of 3 January 1900 to Yale Alumni of Chicago, as quoted in *Yale Alumni Weekly* 9, no. 15 (10 January 1900): 149.

218 Memorandum from Treasurer's Office, 22 December 1922, Treasurer's Records. Daniel Burton Fayerweather was a wealthy leather merchant, of the New York City firm of Fayerweather and Ladew. When he died, he left over $2 million to twenty colleges, including Amherst, Bowdoin, Columbia, Cooper-Union, Cornell, Dartmouth, Lafayette, Northwestern, Wesleyan, and Yale.

219 *Yale Alumni Weekly* 9, no. 40 (August 1900): 415.

220 The Elm Street facade of Fayerweather as built was much changed from that of the project of 1893 for the dormitory quadrangle that became Berkeley Oval. It showed a facade in that position with five bays of fenestration, and a central projected block of two stories, each with three round-headed windows. The projection supported a balustraded balcony in front of a porch recessed behind arches.

221 Cornerstone for Commons laid summer, 1900. Work on Fayerweather began "shortly after July 1," 1900, while Hendrie Hall was in construction. The Treasurer's Office closed building accounts for Fayerweather on 11 October 1901. The name "Grub Street" had semi-official status in the early twentieth century in Yale-affiliated publications; see *Yale Alumni Weekly* (15 January 1925).

222 *The Report of the President of Yale University for the Academic Year 1900 to 1901*, p. 27: "the University, after long and difficult negotiations, ably managed by Mr. Wilson S. Bissell, has entered into possession of the Lampson estate, from which it will receive not less than $450,000." Lampson's bequest also funded establishment of the Lampson Professorships in Greek, Latin, and English Literature.

223 A. P. Stokes Papers, Manuscripts and Archives, Yale University Library (Manuscript Group 299).

224 A. P. Stokes to J. V. Farwell, 5 October 1911, Treasurer's Records.

225 Lee McClung, Treasurer, to Evarts Tracy, architect and alumnus, September 1908, when Robertson's Haughton was the only dormitory being built: "Often-times peculiar conditions determine the selection of an architect as for instance with regard to the new dormitory which we are now erecting. It was the desire of the donor that a certain architect should be appointed and, as an investigation on our part convinced us of the worthiness and ability of such architect, we concluded that to comply with the donor's wish was wholly proper" (Treasurer's Records). On the date of Book and Snake, see *Yale Alumni Weekly* 9, no. 38 (20 June 1900): 375.

226 Sarah Landau, "R. H. Robertson," in *Macmillan Encyclopedia of Architects*, 3:591. Drawings for Haughton Hall Dormitory are signed "Robertson and Potter / Architects / 160 5th Ave. New York City." Earlier in his career Robertson was associated with both Edward T. Potter and William A. Potter.

227 Treasurer's Records.

228 From University [Blount] Avenue there was a rise in grade of a half story to grade level on the facade facing the courtyard, so that doors at grade on the west elevation gave entry to a stair landing halfway between the basement floor and the first floor.

229 The anonymous letter, cryptically signed "Macrar," bore the headline "Yale's Gothic Traditions," *Yale Alumni Weekly* 26, no. 30 (13 April 1917): 791.

230 Thomas Farnam, Secretary, to J. G. Rogers, 14 November 1921, Plan Committee Records.

231 J. V. Farwell to F. H. Wiggin, 18 December 1922: inquiry regarding legal obstacles to moving Lampson, White, and Haughton Halls to the east, or northward, or destroying parts of them. Farwell to Wiggin, 29 December 1922: inquiry regarding legality of tearing down Berkeley Oval buildings. Wiggin to Farwell, 8 January 1923: cautious clearing of such action. Plan Committee Records and Treasurer's Records.

232 J. R. Angell to J. V. Farwell, 23 January 1928, Plan Committee Records.

233 J. V. Farwell to J. G. Rogers, 17 July 1928, Plan Committee Records.

234 J. G. Rogers to J. V. Farwell, 2 August 1928, Plan Committee Records.

235 Arthur Twining Hadley, characterizing a major objective of the university in a speech of November 1899 to Pittsburgh's Yale Association dinner, as quoted in *Yale Alumni Weekly* 9, no. 8 (15 November 1899): 81. Hadley toured the country in the fall and winter of 1899–1900, on a fundraising campaign for the Bicentennial Buildings. From the same speech: "…to get some plan for all the buildings of the University, by which, instead of each building being an inharmonious thing without relation to the others, we can have some plan of building development that shall carry us on further."

236 Frederick Law Olmsted had a long relationship with Yale. In 1837, as he was about to enter as an undergraduate, he became ill, then did eventually spend a semester in the college. In 1866 he prepared, with Calvert Vaux, a plan for landscaping around the proposed Chapel Memorial for Civil War Dead by Vaux, Withers and Co. His "Plan for Laying Out The Yale Athletic Grounds" was published in 1885 by W. E. Decrow in his second edition of *Yale and "The City of Elms."*

237 Mel Scott, *American City Planning* (Berkeley: University of California Press, 1969), especially chaps. 1 and 2. The American City Planning Institute, forerunner of the American Institute of Planners, was founded in 1917.

238 Paul Venable Turner, *Campus: An American Planning Tradition* (New York: Architectural History Foundation; Cambridge, Mass: MIT Press, 1984).

239 Montgomery Schuyler, "A Review of the Work of Chas. C. Haight," in *The Architectural Record: Great American Architects Series*, no. 6 (July 1899): 72.

240 In this volume, see Erik Vogt, "A New Yale: The Pope Plan of 1919," pp. 249–61.

241 According to the *Yale Historical Record*, Stokes completed his graduate studies at Episcopal Theological School in Cambridge, Massachusetts.

242 Kelley, *Yale*, 318.

243 See n. 24 above.

244 A copy of Post's dictated report of 24 November 1899 is preserved in the Treasurer's Records.

245 Pierson, *A Yale Book of Numbers*, F-2.4. See n. 13 above.

246 *Yale Alumni Weekly* (7 March 1900): 228.

247 Carrère and Hastings to Lee McClung, 27 November 1907, quoting an earlier document, Treasurer's Records.

248 Contract with Norcross Brothers, 5 July 1900, for dining hall and colonnade foundations. Second contract, 1 July 1901, for auditorium and vestibule buildings complete. Correspondence between Carrère and Hastings and Lee McClung in March and April 1906 mentions Norcross's bid of $9,123 "for extending the colonnade foundations on the new lot acquired, corresponding to the work now existing on the other part of the lot," and refers to ten foundations laid initially, four under discussion. Treasurer's Records.

249 Carrère and Hastings to McClung, 27 November 1907, Treasurer's Records.

250 The competition program of 1899 for the Bicentennial Buildings had included an administrative office until the Misses Stokes made it their separate project.

251 From clipping, "Description of Woodbridge Hall," probably from Yale Alumni Weekly, in Yale Old and New, scrapbooks compiled by Arnold G. Dana, 37 vols., 1933–43, microfilm, reel 1, 710. The transcription of Donald Grant Mitchell's (B.A. 1841) dedication speech (reel 1, 713) from Yale Alumni Weekly, January 1902, gives a history of the Woodbridge family and of Timothy, the early Yale trustee; and lists attendees at the dedication, including the Stokes family, and a literary contingent including the architect John Mead Howells's father William Dean Howells, George W. Cable, and Thomas Nelson Page. Also present was Booker T. Washington, whose Tuskegee Institute was a beneficiary of Stokes's charity; an archbishop; a senator; and "Most of the Yale Corporation."

252 I. N. P. Stokes to A. P. Stokes, 7 January 1900, Anson Phelps Stokes Papers, Family Correspondence, Manuscripts and Archives, Yale University Library, Group 299. Buchanan Winthrop, a Corporation member from 1891 to 1900, served on the Prudential Committee. He died suddenly 25 December 1900, and was active when Stokes's letter was written.

253 Lee McClung, "Archibald Henry Blount," Yale Alumni Weekly (29 May 1914).

254 See Vogt, "A New Yale: The Pope Plan of 1919."

255 See the "Report of Goodhue, Delano, and Cret on the Pope Plan," 4. Copy in James R. Angell Presidential Papers, Manuscripts and Archives, Yale University Library.

256 G. P. Day to J. G. Rogers, 17 February 1922, characterizes "Frank" Garvan's disappointment with "us all" for "not being willing to plan for the Library at this spot [the courtyard of the University Quadrangle], even though this involves the ultimate tearing down of the so-called Bi-Centennial Buildings" (Treasurer's Records). Bertram Grosvenor Goodhue to John Farwell, 20 May 1920: "In the course of a very few days I am going to send you some extremely rough drawings of the Administration Group screening, or as I prefer to regard it, completing the Classic quadrangle of the Bi-centennial group of Carrere & Hastings. I am doing this because I find that apparently both Cret and Delano have certain objections to the project…" (Plan Committee Records). Farwell to George Parmly Day, 18 May 1920: "it might be a good idea for Mr Goodhue in the sketches he is making to present alternative designs, one showing a Gothic screen for the Bicentennial Group, and the other showing the group without any such screen, and with Woodbridge Hall and the Kingsley Trust Association Building [Scroll and Key] remaining in their present locations" (Treasurer's Records). See also Erik Vogt, "A New Yale: The Pope Plan of 1919," pp. 253, 256–58.

257 "Report of Goodhue, Delano, and Cret," 5.

258 Minutes of Meeting of the Architectural Plan Committee, 6 November 1925, James R. Angell Presidential Papers.

259 Invoice, 11 July 1928, Treasurer's Records.

260 George D. Vail, "New Sites For Old Landmarks," Yale Alumni Magazine and Journal 40, no. 2 (October 1976): 32.

261 Yale University President's Report, 1901, p. 11.

262 Loomis Havemeyer, Sheff Days and Ways: Undergraduate Activities in the Sheffield Scientific School, Yale University 1847–1945 (New Haven, 1958), 13.

263 Pinnell, Campus Guide, 144.

264 Class Book 1921, Supplement to the History of the Class of 76, SSS. Yale University, May 1921.

265 R. Britton Gottsberger, "The Course in Mining," Yale Alumni Weekly 32, no. 13 (15 December 1922): 354 56. Since 1970 Hammond Hall has housed Art School students and now continues to provide studios for its sculptors.

266 Prior to construction of Sprague Hall, music school concerts were held in the College Street Church, purchased in 1895, renamed College Street Hall, remodeled by Cady, Berg and See in 1901, destroyed by fire in 1921.

267 Elizabeth Sprague Coolidge (Mrs. Frederic Shurtleff Coolidge of Pittsfield, Massachusetts), to President Hadley, 5 July 1915, Plan Committee Records: "What sort of small building…could be built and for which a maintenance fund could be established for about $200,000…perhaps a little art gallery, music hall, or hospital? I think a visible structure of some kind appeals to her more strongly than an endowment or scholarship fund…Mrs. Sprague will be glad to know how she can best serve the University he loved, and, at the same time, effectually perpetuate his name therein." Coolidge's firm "was to hold a virtual monopoly on Harvard work under President Lowell" (Bunting and Floyd, Harvard: An Architectural History, 124.

The successor firm to Coolidge and Shattuck, architects of record for Sprague Hall, the first hall built for the School of Music, is the same Shepley Bulfinch Richardson and Abbott, of Boston, who designed the Gilmore Music Library of 1998 within a courtyard of Sterling Memorial Library.

268 "Hillhouse Estate Plans," Yale Alumni Weekly 15, no. 1 (September 1905): 1.

269 By 1905, Frederick Law Olmsted, planner of the Chicago World's Fair and recipient of an honorary degree from Yale in 1893, had retired, turning the firm over to his two sons, Frederick Law Olmsted, Jr. (1870–1957), and John Charles Olmsted (1852–1920), who in 1898 renamed the office Olmsted Brothers.

270 Yale Alumni Weekly 15, no. 1 (September 1905): 1.

271 Record of this action by the Corporation taken at the "next meeting" following 26 May 1910 is quoted by A. P. Stokes in a letter to H. T. Sloane, 26 April 1921, Plan Committee Records.

272 Memo, A. P. Stokes to Lee McClung, 30 December 1908, Treasurer's Records.

273 A. P. Stokes to J. V. Farwell, 5 October 1911, Treasurer's Records.

274 Schuyler, "Haight," 71–72. See also A. P. Stokes to J. V. Farwell, 5 October 1911, copy, Treasurer's Records: "President Andrew D. White of Cornell once told me that he thought he [Haight] did the best Collegiate Gothic work in America."

275 Turner, Campus, 177 and 322, n. 32.

276 Schuyler, "Haight," 80–82.

277 Such an entrance tower by Haight for St. Stephen's College of 1884 in Annandale, New York, was illustrated in ibid., 18.

278 Kelley, Yale, 292.

279 Turner, Campus, 222–29.

280 C. C. Haight to W. W. Farnam, 29 May 1896, Treasurer's Records: "I am informed that a new Dormitory is to be erected for the Sheffield Scientific School; would it be possible for me in any way to capture this work and can you make any suggestions how this might be accomplished?" This letter would suggest both that planning for dormitories for the Sheffield Scientific School began well before a donor was found and that Haight actively sought the commission.

281 *Yale University Report of the President,* 1906, p. 95.

282 G. P. Day to J. V. Farwell, 1 August 1912, Treasurer's Records.

283 "In 1902, through the generosity of Mr. Frederick W. Vanderbilt…land was purchased, bounded by College, Wall and Temple Streets, constituting what is known as Vanderbilt Square. Upon this land Mr. Vanderbilt has erected two large dormitories known as Vanderbilt-Scientific…Later, Vanderbilt Square has been enlarged by other purchases of land and buildings made by Mr. Vanderbilt…Sheffield Square, being the land bounded by Prospect Street, Grove Street and Hillhouse Avenue, together with the Sheffield Mansion, after the death of Mrs. Sheffield in 1889, came into the possession of the Sheffield Trustees" (R. H. Chittenden to L. McClung, 17 September 1908, Treasurer's Records).

Silliman College was pieced together in 1940 from existing buildings, the English Gothic Vanderbilt dormitories and classical Byers Hall, all masonry structures, to which Eggers and Higgins added a red-brick dining hall, a master's house, and two ranges of dormitories. The only building on the block that is not a part of Silliman College was also Vanderbilt-funded. In 1913 he hired Haight to design a new home for St. Anthony Hall (Delta Psi), a Sheffield club, on the corner of College and Wall Streets. The north half of the building (493 College Street) was sold to the university in 1945 and is currently occupied by the Department of African American Studies.

284 The Scientific School was terminated as an active school in 1956, although the Board of Trustees continues as a legal entity to oversee property. The Provost of Yale University serves as chair of the board, *ex officio,* and faculty are defined as teachers of science to graduate students under the division of science.

285 G. P. Day to J. V. Farwell, 1 August 1912, Treasurer's Records.

286 Henry G. Morse's obituary is among those transcribed by Earl G. Shettleworth from *American Art Annual* and its successor volume *Who's Who in American Art,* which he posted online (http://www.sah.org/aame/bioint.html). It relates that "for some years he was associated in New York with Hawes & Morse, architects, and more recently had headed his own firm" and mentions among his buildings the Carnegie Institute and Y.M.C.A. in Camden, New Jersey, and Agecroft Hall near Richmond, Virginia.

287 R. G. Warner '14S, "The Dunham Laboratory," *Yale Alumni Weekly* (10 March 1922), cover.

288 The money for the twentieth-century laboratory came from brothers Henry T. Sloane (B.A. 1866) and William D. Sloane (M.A.H. 1889), who had also paid for the 1906–7 renovation of Sloane Physical Laboratory.

289 From a translation of the Latin inscription cut in the stone of the building.

290 In recent inventories of Yale architecture, Haight is mistakenly credited with a third gate to the Old Campus, the classically detailed one on High Street between Chittenden and Street Halls. That gate (see FIG. 91), by the firm of J. C. Cady, was designed in a style quite foreign to Haight's Gothic and Tudor contributions to Yale. See also n. 169 above.

291 *Yale Alumni Weekly* 9, no. 1 (September 1899): 12. Other members of the committee were Robert S. Brewster, Henry L. Deforest, Charles R. Hemenway, and Thatcher M. Brown.

292 A. P. Stokes to J. V. Farwell, 5 October 1911, copy, Treasurer's Records.

293 Joseph Warren, Assistant Secretary, Harvard University, to A. P. Stokes, 13 January 1908, Treasurer's Records.

294 Woodrow Wilson to A. P. Stokes, 13 January 1908, Treasurer's Records.

295 Warren Powers Laird, Professor in Charge, Architecture, University of Pennsylvania, The College, to A. P. Stokes, 3 February 1908, Treasurer's Records.

296 In 1919–20, Paul Cret served with Bertram Goodhue and William Delano on the architectural advisory panel appointed by the Corporation to evaluate John Russell Pope's plan for campus development. In 1928, Clarence Zantzinger's firm submitted a proposal for the site now occupied by the Beinecke Rare Book and Manuscript Library, and in 1932 designed Sheffield-Sterling-Strathcona.

297 J. A. L. Blake to G. P. Day, 5 October 1911, Treasurer's Records.

298 A. C. Imbrie, to G. P. Day, 10 October 1911, Treasurer's Records.

299 A. C. Imbrie to G. P. Day, 27 October 1911, Treasurer's Records: *Mr. Cram has made an extraordinary reputation as the exponent of Gothic architecture in this country. An enormous amount of work crowds his office, so that he has found it difficult to come to Princeton as often as some of us would like him to come; although he has never neglected any particular problem presented for his consideration. This part of my letter is especially to be regarded as confidential. I would even go further and say that it is my opinion, as that of Mr. Thompson, Chairman of our Committee on Grounds and Buildings, that the man who is qualified to act as Supervising Architect, and whom we should be glad to see act in that capacity, should any change be made, is Mr. Frank Miles Day…They [Day Brothers and Klauder] are able business men as well as good architects. I know that if I were in your position and wanted a man to advise me upon the problem which you are studying, I would go straight to Mr. Frank Miles Day without an instant's hesitation. I don't mind your saying that I have suggested Mr. Day's name among others, but I don't want you to let your Committee think that I am finding fault with Mr. Cram.*

300 *Bulletin of Yale University, President's Report 1910–1911,* 7th series, no. 8 (June 1911), Secretary's report, p. 49. Before 1920 when the name of Farwell's committee was regularized as "Architectural Plan Committee," it had a number of predecessors to which reference was made in a variety of ways within Yale publications and manuscript documents, including: "Committee on Architecture" (1911), "Committee on Architectural Development" (1911), "Committee on Architectural Supervision" (1912), and "Architectural Committee" (1919). On the list of six standing committees in 1920, there was also a "Committee on Grounds and Buildings," of which the treasurer of the university, Thomas Wells Farnam, was chairman. During 1922 the Corporation studied and spelled out the distinctions between the two: the Committee on Architectural Plan recorded the responsibilities of each in the minutes of its meeting of 13 January 1922.

301 Farwell would later write: "If I had any criticism to make as to the course of the Corporation in the past I should say, first, it would be lack of a general plan, and, second, haste in deciding locations and architecture of the buildings…The Plan of Chicago we worked on two years before we evolved the plan, and then spent three or four years in changing it before it was finally adopted" (J. V. Farwell to A. P. Stokes, 29 September 1919, Plan Committee Records).

302 Farwell as quoted in "Quadrangle System Plan Outlined by Chairman of the Architecture Committee…article written espe-

cially for the NEWS, John V. Farrel, (sic) '79…" *Yale Daily News*, 7 May 1930, clipping in Plan Committee Records.

303 Turner, *Campus*, 235–36.

304 F. M. Day to G. P. Day, 23 May 1916, Treasurer's Records, named these projects in response to request, 17 May 1916: "put all modesty aside and write me rather fully…about your work… and specifically what you consider the most notable buildings that you have designed." The architect received an honorary degree that spring.

305 Signed agreement between Yale and F. M. Day, 26 December 1913, Secretary's Papers, Manuscripts and Archives, Yale University Library (RU 49).

306 Specifications and drawings for building, "situated on the grounds of the Yale Observatory" by L. W. Robinson, the local associated architect, Treasurer's Records. A crude drawing by "Mr. Mason F. Smith of the Observatory…a building…required for the new Polar Heliostat mounting," with covering letter, M. F. Smith to G. P. Day, 30 April 1914, and Day's covering letter sending both to President Hadley, 5 May 1914, Presidential Papers of Arthur Hadley, Manuscripts and Archives, Yale University Library (RU 25).

307 Holden, *Yale: A Pictorial History*, 235. See also G. P. Day to J. G. Rogers, 24 June 1914, Treasurer's Records: "The new pathological laboratory is to be erected on the Hospital grounds and by the Hospital authorities, and for this I understand they have already had plans made by an architect of their own selection, Frank Miles Day of Philadelphia."

308 Delano's commissions to design a library for a school that still was a major one within the university and a dormitory on the Old Campus are here distinguished from the relatively minor local work of several Yale graduates who were hired by Sheffield's fraternities and the college's Junior and Senior Societies to design "tombs" and fraternity houses, and who designed offices for student publications. A partial list of them follows:

Lewis Greenleaf Adams (1897–1977; B.A. 1920), with T. Merrill Prentice (PH.B. 1921): in 1932, Briton Hadden [B.A. 1920] Memorial Building for *Yale Daily News*, 202 York Street;

Grosvenor Atterbury (B.A. 1891): in 1897, Chi Phi (now Stoeckel Hall), 96 Wall Street;

Roger Baldwin (B.A. 1890), with Egerton Swartwout: in 1895–96, enlarged and renovated older hall of Psi Upsilon (Junior Society), 120 High Street (demolished 1927);

Donn Barber (PH.B. 1891): in 1910, Berzelius, 76 Trumbull Street;

Horace S. Frazer (1862–1931, PH.B. 1883) of Chapman and Frazer (although John H. Chapman [PH.B. 1876] died in 1895, his name was retained in that of the firm): in 1911, Franklin Hall (Theta Xi), a Sheffield fraternity, 119 [now 451] College Street;

Lorenzo Hamilton (B.F.A. 1921): in 1928, Offices of the *Yale Record*, 254 York Street;

J. Frederick Kelly (1888–1947, B.F.A. 1915): in 1916, Beta Theta Pi (Junior Academic Fraternity), 124 High Street (demolished 1927);

Everett V. Meeks (1879–1954; B.A. 1901, B.F.A. 1917): in 1911–12, additions and alterations for Elihu of house built in 1799, 175 Elm Street; in 1929, Zeta Psi House, 212 York Street;

Louis R. Metcalfe (1873–1946; PH.B. 1895): in 1901, Book and Snake, 214 Grove Street;

Stowe Phelps (B.A. 1890): in 1896, D.K.E. (Junior Society), extension (new, wider facade on York Street) (destroyed 1927);

Thurlow Merrill Prentice (1898–1985; PH.B. 1921), with Lewis G. Adams (B.A. 1920): in 1932, Briton Hadden [B.A. 1920] Memorial Building for *Yale Daily News*, 202 York Street;

Clarence H. Stilson (PH.B. 1875): in 1888, Cloister Hall, after designs by H. Edward Flicken, 1 Hillhouse Avenue;

Egerton Swartwout (1870–1943, B.A. 1891), with Roger Baldwin: in 1895–96, enlarged and renovated older hall of Psi Upsilon (Junior Society), 120 High Street (demolished 1927); with Evarts Tracy (Tracy and Swartwout, active 1900–1915): in 1911, plan for Weir Hall.

Evarts Tracy (1868–1929; B.A. 1890), with Egerton Swartwout (Tracy and Swartwout, active 1900–1915): in 1911, plan for Weir Hall.

During the early twentieth century, Yale was more than willing to favor her own graduates in business dealings, which had come to include architecture. In 1908 Evarts Tracy requested that he and other alumni be considered for architectural commissions he expected a Hewitt bequest of $500,000 to generate, and complained: "It seems curious that as there are at least four firms of architects, who were graduated at Yale, and in the estimation of their confreres and that portion of the public interested in art and architecture, are not only 'coming,' but who have 'arrived' they should not be allowed to do some of the work for their University. Any of them would enter on any such commission with a greater enthusiasm and more careful study than they would" (E. Tracy to L. McClung, 5 September 1908, Treasurer's Records). Yale's Treasurer, Lee McClung, responded: "Yale graduates and friends are frequently approaching us with regard to doing work for us, selling us stocks, bonds, mortgages, and real estate, and we naturally, as far as possible and other things being equal, give a preference to such graduates and friends" (Treasurer's Records); see also n. 225 above. Tracy, however, received no commissions from his alma mater. In 1911, in partnership with Egerton Swartwout (Tracy and Swartwout, active 1900–1915), he drew up plans for a second building for Skull and Bones, incorporating the stones from Alumni Hall to recreate that building's towers. George Douglas Miller (B.A. 1870) planned to pay for this project but ran out of money after construction began. Yale purchased the property in 1917, and Everett V. Meeks completed the unfinished building as Weir Hall (see FIG. 221), preserving the original plan.

309 The Yale Hope Mission of 1928, designed by H. K. Murphy, was for a Yale-affiliated organization; see *Yale Alumni Weekly* 37, no. 41 (31 July 1928): 72, illus. No longer serving its original purpose, the building is now owned by Yale.

310 See Stein, *John Ruskin and Aesthetic Thought in America*, 236: "Unlike Ruskin, who wanted men to return to the mediaeval ideal, Hoppin rejoiced in the Renaissance…Though Hoppin's focus had shifted forward to Donatello, Ghiberti, and Massachio and back to classic Greek art, and his interest was in justifying free democratic art, his criteria of judgment remained essentially those of Ruskin."

Beginning in 1879 the *Yale College Catalogue* listed an undergraduate elective in the Fine Arts as a single course in which Hoppin lectured on Art History. It included studio sessions in painting with John Ferguson Weir and in drawing with John Henry Niemeyer. These three professors listed the same course until 1885, when it disappeared from the college catalogue, but was resumed in 1891, though only for two years. Then, in 1892, Professor Hoppin presented the first of his series of lectures "illustrated throughout by the use of the hydro-oxygen lantern," in which he ranged across the history of western art. Niemeyer (1839–1932), Street Professor of Drawing, was born in Bremen; educated in Cincinnati, New York, and Paris; exhibited in Salon of 1869. See "John H. Niemeyer," in Kingsley, *History* 2:162.

311 See n. 42 above.

312 *Catalogue of the Officers and Students in Yale College with a statement of the course of instruction in the various departments in 1872–73* (New Haven: Tuttle, Morehouse & Taylor, 1872), 69.

313 Typed transcription of "Mr. Linsly's Report," Minutes of the Faculty 1878 Yale School of the Fine Arts, Manuscripts and Archives, Yale University Library, Architecture Administrative Records (RU 189). The *Yale University Catalogue* for 1886–1887 published a two-paragraph course description within its category headed "The Technical Course."

314 "Harrison W. Lindsley," *Obituary Record of the Graduates of Yale University Deceased during 1893*, p. 263.

315 His father, Charles A. Lindsley, M.D., served as a professor in the Medical School. Drawings by Lindsley for the laboratory survive in Manuscripts and Archives, Yale University Library. Although Lindsley's commission precedes Delano's for the Divinity School library, Lindsley's was only a rear addition to an existing building, far removed from the college core. Still, it was an early instance of Yale commissioning an architectural design by one of its own graduates. His gym-to-dining hall conversion is also documented in Treasurer's Records.

316 Minutes of the Faculty (see n. 313 above).

317 John Jacobson, associate dean of the School of Architecture, and Grazyna Kirsch, registrar of the School of Architecture, discovered record of Delano's degree in the School of the Fine Art's alumni directory of 1936. Because that directory listed only living alumni, not all who had received degrees, it is possible that someone else who died prior to 1936 may have received a degree in architecture before 1907.

318 Long before this, in 1869, the very first year the Art School offered courses, it had been disappointed that although this same Professor Eaton had been listed on its faculty, he "never took up the appointment."

319 Pinnell, *Campus Guide*, 125.

320 Typescript reminiscences of William Adams Delano, Oral History Project, W. A. Delano Papers. Manuscripts and Archives, Yale University Library (Manuscript Group 178).

321 Dean Wright was "the first to hold that position permanently," according to his obituary, *Yale Alumni Weekly* (22 March 1918). Wright Memorial Hall was renamed Lanman-Wright Hall in 1993, in recognition of a gift from Colonel William K. Lanman, Jr., B.S. 1928, which helped to fund its renovation.

322 W. Kent to L. McClung, 20 December 1907, Treasurer's Records.

323 On Delano and Aldrich, see Peter Pennoyer and Anne Walker, *The Architecture of Delano & Aldrich* (New York: W. W. Norton & Company, 2003), where the importance of old Yale connections to Delano's career is very clear. Not only did Delano's classmate Cornelius Vanderbilt have something of a client role as treasurer for the fundraising committee for Wright Hall, but he had also introduced Delano to Henry Walters, leading to the Walters Art Gallery commission that really launched Delano's career. In addition, Pennoyer and Walker mention that Delano designed houses for three other classmates: Allen Wardwell, Robert S. Brewster, and William Sloane.

324 G. P. Day to Day and Klauder, 21 December 1916, Treasurer's Records, gave the actual cost of the building as $327,958 including architects' and engineers' fees.

325 Correspondence in the Treasurer's Records makes it clear that Delano and Aldrich had not been authorized to develop their competition drawings in 1909 or 1910 when the printed appeal was circulated. Delano and Aldrich to G. P. Day, 4 February 1911: "The only drawings which we have made are the competition drawings which are of course at very small scale and only approximate, and it would take at least 4 or 5 weeks (perhaps a little longer) for us to prepare the working drawings and specifications."

326 Pinnell, *Campus Guide*, 181. Ferry considered and discarded first a scheme based on bridge construction, in which steel struc-

tures on wheels could have been variously configured for viewing football and baseball, and second a proposal to reconstruct Rome's Colosseum in reinforced concrete, before settling on the water reservoir precedent. Ferry himself describes "practically the method employed in reservoir construction from which the idea of the Bowl was obtained" in "The Yale Bowl," (p. 27), a typescript essay in the Charles Ferry Collection in Manuscripts and Archives, Yale University Library.

327 The Statement of Significance in the nomination of the Yale Bowl as a National Historic Landmark by the Secretary of the Interior (as of designation—February 27, 1987) notes: "This is the second oldest active college stadium in the country and the largest stadium when it was constructed (1914). Yale Bowl was emulated because its 'bowl' shape provided fine views for the spectators from all seats. It also commemorates Yale's influence in early college football due to its noted player-coach-official, Walter Camp."

328 All this property formed an important element in "the linked sequence of parks and cemeteries that emerged along West River under the guidance of Donald Grant Mitchell" (Pinnell, *Campus Guide*, 179–80).

329 Kelley, *Yale*, 299.

330 The complexities of management and financial responsibility for Yale's athletic fields had to be made clear to generations of administrators, Yale lawyers, and alumni. Correspondence attempting to do that goes on at length through the early twentieth century. It is summarized, for instance, in the following: "The Yale Field is the property of the Yale Corporation but its management is wholly in the hands of the 'Directors of the Yale Field Corporation'" (Lee McLung to William S. Pardee, 16 June 1908, Treasurer's Records). In a letter of 3 May 1910 to Anson Phelps Stokes, Walter Camp elaborated upon the functions of the Financial Union, whose concern was the athletic fields, noting that taxes and upkeep of the property were "met by the said Financial Union," and adding that:

The proper handling of the finances of the [Financial] Union is in a way controlled by the Corporation through its appointment of the Treasurer of the Financial Union, and also by the fact that as owner of the properties the Corporation could as a last resort forbid the use of its property to organizations that did not meet with the approval of that corporation either in their financial methods or care of that property…Any expenditure of accounts beyond ordinary upkeep is voted upon not only by the Financial Union, which really manages the property, and like an executive committee pays salaries, etc., but also by the general Athletic Committee whose province it is to direct the athletic policy of Yale University. This committee consists of the captains and managers of the four major branches of sport, Football, Base Ball, Boat Club, and Athletic Association, as well as the vice-presidents, three graduates elected by the undergraduate members at their first meeting in the fall, and the Treasurer of the Yale Field appointed by the Corporation" (Treasurer's Records).

331 For plan of the Yale field of 1882 and a list of members of Yale Field Corporation of that date, see *Yale Banner* 41 (1882): 94.

332 Earlier Yale rowers had also used Boston architects, Cummings and Sears, to design a boathouse of 1875 at the eastern end of the bridge that crossed the Mill River at the foot of Chapel Street (see FIG. 106). Lyman H. Bagg, "Boating" in Kingsley, *History* 2:293.

333 *American National Biography* 17 (1999), 190–91.

334 Plans for a new bridge carrying Interstate Highway 95 over the Quinnipiac River show a structural pier on the site of the Adee Boat House. Because the boathouse was determined eligible for the National Register of Historic Places, federal law required the Federal Highway Administration and the Connecticut Department of Transportation to study alternatives to its demolition. Serious proposals to move the structure to the site of a

planned maritime center were studied but abandoned when estimates for the job came in at $90 million. As of the spring of 2003, the Adee Boat House is slated for demolition, but architectural elements will be salvaged and incorporated into the design of New Haven's proposed $50 million "Maritime Center." The Federal Highway Administration recorded the Adee Boat House according to the standards of the Historic American Building Survey, and the documentation was deposited in the Library of Congress and the Dodd Research Center of the University of Connecticut.

335 Holden, *Yale: A Pictorial History*, figs. 178 and 180.

336 Said to Vincent Scully during the debate over ROTC at Yale during the Vietnam War.

337 The name of the designer of Artillery Hall is yet to surface in Yale's archive.

338 The facilities of the Polo and Equestrian Center include a 100-seat indoor ring, an outdoor turnout area, and a 70-stall stable; and the Rifle Club has a small-bore shooting range. The Armory and Stables, as the building is still known, also includes storage and office spaces and a machine shop.

339 The appeal went to "all of the graduates of the university who had sons in the Yale Battalion" (Goodyear to Day, 8 December 1916, Treasurer's Records).

340 See *Yale Alumni Weekly* 27, no. 2 (28 September 1917): 34, for "a full description of the building."

341 Day and Klauder, "Description of the Club House," *Yale Alumni Weekly* (23 March 1923): 777–78, with perspective drawing and plan. After an extensive renovation and expansion of Lapham Field House and the adjacent athletic fields in 1993, funded by Joel E. Smilow (B.A. 1954), the area was named the Joel E. Smilow Field Center.

342 Randall Beach, "Play Ball!" (see n. 106 above).

343 *Yale University President's Report*, 1920, pp. 21–22.

344 *Yale University President's Report*, 1921, p. 8.

345 J. R. Angell to J. V. Farwell, 24 September 1928, Plan Committee Records.

346 Farwell's brother was married to the sister of Rogers's wife. See Aaron Betsky, *James Gamble Rogers and the Architecture of Pragmatism* (New York: The Architectural History Foundation, 1994), 22.

347 Yale had tried without success to persuade Rogers to become its consulting architect in 1913, shortly after he had told John V. Farwell that he "thought…a consulting architect ought not to build any buildings," as Farwell recorded in a letter to A. P. Stokes, 8 November 1912, Secretary's Papers.

348 Secretary's Report in *Yale University Annual Report*, 1921, p. 48.

349 *Yale Alumni Weekly* (30 May 1924) reported dedication of the boathouse, named for Robert Johnson Cook (B.A. 1876), "the man who made rowing at Yale, and indeed throughout the country, what it is to-day." President Angell's dedication remarks: "in this simple but commodious building there is well embodied his disregard of all but the essentials, and his relentless insistence upon the presence of these." The Bob Cook Boat House was torn down in 1999 to make way for the Gilder Boathouse (see FIG. 331).

350 J. V. Farwell to W. A. Delano, 18 May 1921, Plan Committee Records. Eleven years earlier, Sloane had already expressed concern about the Corporation's longterm commitment to stone; on 26 May 1910, he had written: "I hope that at the next meeting some resolution of the Corporation…will be adopted, which will give my brother and myself more positive assurance of the general adoption of Longmeadow stone as the material for all the buildings on this particular quadrangle. We should feel much disap-

pointed after having yielded to the Corporation's preference for stone on this quadrangle, and having consenting [*sic*] to its adoption in our building, to find that in the interest of economy some other Laboratory were put up in the immediate neighborhood of the Sloane Laboratory of brick, or other cheaper material" (quoted in a letter from Anson Phelps Stokes to Henry T. Sloane, 26 April 1921, Plan Committee Records). Although Stokes argued that the Sterling Chemistry Laboratory's proposed site on the "north-west section of the property" was outside the bounds of the "Laboratory Quadrangle of the Pierson-Sage Square, that is, the southwest quadrangle," he nevertheless assured Sloane that the university would "only act in the matter of this building's material after the most careful consulting with you" (ibid.).

351 Delano, *Reminiscences*, 55–56. He adds: "John Johnston, then head of the Chemistry Department, went for vacation to his native Edinburgh; when he returned, he told me that the University there was planning a laboratory on the same lines. Spontaneous combustion, I imagine, for neither architect had ever consulted or corresponded with the other."

352 *Yale Alumni Weekly* (April 1923): "the term 'unit' is used advisedly because most large laboratories are a more or less heterogeneous collection of independent laboratories housed in a single building."

353 A. P. Stokes to J. V. Farwell, 18 May 1921, Plan Committee Records, records that Sage made the gift in a letter to the Corporation, 7 May 1921.

354 Three of Sage's sons followed him to Yale. Sage himself served on the board of Cornell University, of which his father, Henry Williams Sage, had been a founding trustee who served as president of the board. The Sage family gave important buildings to Cornell, including the former residence of Henry Williams Sage. See Whitehead Duyckinck, Class Secretary, *Class of 1865 Yale College* (New York, 1910).

355 A. P. Stokes to J. V. Farwell, 17 May 1921, Plan Committee Records.

356 "The New Health Department," *Yale Alumni Weekly* 39, no. 15 (27 December 1929): 411.

357 Cross and Cross was described by Christopher Gray as "one of New York's most distinctive native firms," in Placzek's *Macmillan Encyclopedia of Architects* 1:477. The principals—John Walter Cross (1878–1951), more often the designer, and Eliot Cross (1883–1949)—were brothers whose work evolved from, in Gray's words, "an urbane, neo-Georgian style" of the teens and twenties through "diffuse, moderne styling, of which their Egyptoid Tiffany and Company Building (1939–1940) is a well-known example."

358 *Obituary Record of Graduates of the Undergraduate Schools Deceased during the year 1951–1952.* (New Haven: Yale University, 1969), 44.

359 *Yale Alumni Weekly* (16 April 1926): 835: "the University has filed a petition with the New Haven Board of Aldermen asking permission to connect the new gallery with the old Art School by an arch across High Street. There has also been begun, with the approval of the City Authorities, a suit seeking a declaratory judgment defining the powers of the City and the University in this matter. By stipulation of counsel for the City and the University, this suit has been reserved for the advice of the Supreme Court of Errors."

360 See also J. V. Farwell to J. H. Desibour, 28 December 1923: "as far as possible it is the desire of the Architectural Plan Committee to recommend to the Corporation architects who are Yale graduates," as quoted by Betsky, *Rogers*, 120.

361 J. V. Farwell to Samuel Fisher, 6 September 1928, Plan Committee Records.

362 Note dated 16 May 1940, Plan Committee Records, which Farwell filed with many letters he had written to members of the Corporation opposing placing the Law School near the hospital.

363 Gaddis Smith, *Yale and the External World: The Shaping of the University in the Twentieth Century* (New Haven: Yale University Press, forthcoming).

364 Donna McDonald, *Lord Strathcona: A Biography of Donald Alexander Smith* (Toronto and Oxford: Dundurn Press, 1996), 496.

365 The author is grateful to John Gambell and Lesley Baier for their descriptions of the decoration of Sheffield-Sterling-Strathcona.

366 *Time* 15, no. 22 (2 June 1930): 26.

367 Delano, *Reminiscences*, 54.

368 Locating the Divinity School had absorbed the Architectural Plan Committee for an even longer time. J. V. Farwell to G. P. Day, 26 June 1922, Plan Committee Records, commented on three possible sites: "frontage which we own on Temple Street between Grove and Wall;…frontage on Wall Street between Temple and Church,…the Judge Wayland property; and a third…the triangle on the East side of Prospect Street, just north of the Railroad. This would be adjacent to the Hammond Laboratory heating plant and would always have good light and air."

369 Minutes of Yale Corporation, 10 November 1928, as transcribed by C. A. Ohman to J. V. Farwell, 13 November 1928, Plan Committee Records.

370 Farwell as quoted in "Quadrangle System Plan Outlined by Chairman of the Architecture Committee" (see n. 302 above).

371 By the time Weigle turned against the original site, another site near the Observatory was under serious consideration. That area had been mentioned as a possible location for a new Divinity School as early as 1922 and apparently abandoned.

372 E. V. Meeks to J. V. Farwell, Plan Committee Records.

373 Delano, *Reminiscences*, 54.

374 Arnold Guyot Dana, *New Haven's Problems*, 38 (see n. 16 above). Dana's year-by-year lists of buildings bought by Yale between late 1915 and 1936, with notation if demolished (though not the year of demolition), fill pages 56c and 56d. I am indebted to Peter Hall for the reference.

375 Welch and Camp, *Yale. Her Campus, Class-Rooms, and Athletics*, 392–93.

376 A vote by the Corporation in 1887 had seemed to seal the fate of Austin's building, for it adopted a general plan to put a new library on the site of the old one. Timothy Dwight's annual report for 1897 confirmed this in print: "After a longer or shorter period, the old Library building will probably be replaced by a larger edifice which will be more adapted to library purposes." It was assumed that this would be so by the university's leaders, who envisioned a new Yale in the early twentieth century. They left ample written evidence of their long-standing mental erasure of the Old Library. As it had been no obstacle to Cady's library design in the 1880s, it was not to Haight's scheme or those of his competitors in 1905.

377 *Yale Alumni Weekly* 14, no. 23 (8 March 1905): 448. See also no. 1 (30 September 1904): "It was feared by many graduates that this beautiful old structure would have to come down to meet the needs of the growing library. It now seems possible to retain intact the wing next to Chittenden Library and possibly more."

378 G. P. Day to F. M. Day, 5 May 1915, Treasurer's Records: regarding "the future of the old Library…There seems to be an idea entertained by many that this should ultimately be moved to the center of the old campus, and that the campus would look better rather than worse with this dignified old building in the middle of it. As you know I have not shared this view." John Russell Pope kept the old library and Linsly Chittenden as they were in his plan of 1919, and by proposing to build a grand new library in front of Commons, perhaps helped save Austin's Old Library.

379 On the Old Campus, only Connecticut Hall and the Old Library were older. And although South Sheffield Hall at the Sheffield Scientific School, constructed in 1812 with additions in 1858 and 1865, was older than all but Connecticut Hall, it had not been built by Yale. It would be razed in 1931 to make way for Sheffield-Sterling-Strathcona.

380 A plaque in Weir Hall reads: "The original part of Weir Hall, purchased by Yale University in 1917, was begun in 1911 by George Douglas Miller, B.A. 1870, in partial fulfillment of his vision 'to build, in the heart of New Haven, a replica of an Oxford Quadrangle.'" See also n. 308 above.

381 *Yale Alumni Weekly* 33, no. 39 (13 June 1924), cover.

382 J. G. Rogers to T. W. Farnam, 28 August 1928, Plan Committee Records.

THE CITY REDEEMED: NEW HAVEN'S CIVIC IMPROVEMENT PLAN OF 1910 (pp. 233–247)

1 Rollin Osterweis, *Three Centuries of New Haven, 1638–1938* (New Haven: Yale University Press, 1953), 390. This essay is based in large part on both a review of the drawings and text of Cass Gilbert and Frederick Law Olmsted, Jr., *Report of the New Haven Civic Improvement Commission* (New Haven: Tuttle, Morehouse & Taylor Co., 1910) and the writings and correspondence of George Dudley Seymour. Seymour collected his most important articles in the book *New Haven*, which he published privately in that city in 1942. It is an invaluable source for the background to the Plan of 1910 as well as an illuminating record of this fruitful period in New Haven's history. Seymour's voluminous papers and correspondence, located in the Manuscripts and Archives collection of the Yale University Library (MS 442), also give insight into Seymour's relationship to the larger national movement of city planning and urban reform.

Little has been written about the plan in subsequent years. Rico Cedro, *Modern Visions: Twentieth Century Urban Design in New Haven* (New Haven: Cityarts Gallery, 1988), and Sherman Hasbrouck, *Evolution of New Haven's Comprehensive Plan* (New Haven, 1963), concentrate on the better known postwar plans and "Model City" Redevelopment of the 1960s. Osterweis's excellent general history, *Three Centuries of New Haven*, sets the plan in the context of New Haven's social, political, and economic development at the time. Additional political background can be found in Robert Dahl, *Who Governs? Democracy and Power in an American City* (New Haven: Yale University Press, 1961).

For the broader context and history of the City Beautiful Movement, see John Reps, *The Making of Urban America* (Princeton: Princeton University Press, 1965), and Vincent Scully, *American Architecture and Urbanism*, rev. ed. (New York: Henry Holt and Co., 1988). Mel Scott, in *American City Planning since 1890* (Berkeley: University of California Press, 1971), gives a more comprehensive but less sympathetic account of early-twentieth-century planning, while William Wilson, in *The City Beautiful Movement* (Baltimore: Johns Hopkins University Press, 1989), attempts to understand the Movement on its own terms, in contrast to the typical critique influenced by modern technocratic planning ideology. As Italian historians with a Marxist perspective, Giorgio Ciucci, Francesco Dal Co, Mario Manieri-Elia, and Manfredo Tafuri provide a different, and insightful, account of planning's early successes and limitations in *The American City: From the Civil War to the New Deal* (Cambridge: MIT Press, 1973).

The primary writings of City Beautiful and City Practical planners relevant to the period of New Haven's plan include Daniel

Burnham and Edward Bennett, *The Plan of Chicago* (Chicago: The Commercial Club, 1909); *Proceedings of the Second National Conference on City Planning* (Boston: The University Press, 1910); *City Planning*, ed. John Nolen (New York: Appleton and Co., 1916); and articles by leading planners and architects in *The American City*, a Progressive Era journal devoted to civic reform.

Finally, for the background of the Progressive Era reform movement in general, I have relied on several standard histories of the period: Richard Hofstadter, *The Age of Reform* (New York: Random House, 1955); Robert Wiebe, *The Search for Order: 1877–1920* (New York: Hill and Wang, 1967); and Paul Boyer, *Urban Masses and Moral Order in America, 1820–1920* (Cambridge: Harvard University Press, 1978). James Machor's *Pastoral Cities* (Madison: University of Wisconsin Press, 1987) gives insight into the tradition of intellectual thought toward the American city from the seventeenth to the nineteenth centuries, which influenced greatly the Progressive Era urban ideal.

2 Elizabeth Stillinger, *The Antiquers* (New York: Alfred A. Knopf, 1980), 89.

3 Seymour's house, a beautifully proportioned Greek Revival house with wraparound porch, still stands on the corner of Bradley and Lincoln Streets.

4 The three papers were the *New Haven Sunday Register, Sunday Leader,* and *Sunday Union.*

5 Seymour, "An Open Letter to the Mayor and Aldermen and Citizens of the City and County of New Haven," June 2, 1907, reprinted in *New Haven*, 45.

6 Ibid., 16.

7 Ibid., 46.

8 Ibid., 37–38.

9 Trowbridge Square actually formed the central square of a miniature nine-square plan laid out in the late 1820s, visible to the south of the original nine squares in the Buckingham Map. York Square exists in name only today, long since replaced by New Haven's Hillhouse High School and, after its demise in the mid-twentieth century, by Yale's Stiles and Morse Colleges. Jocelyn Square does remain to the northeast of downtown but was radically disfigured when Interstate 91 was run through on its western side.

10 The First Ward covered most of the downtown, including the Yale campus, as well as the more well-to-do neighborhoods to the north.

11 Tellingly, the peak of immigration to the U.S. between the Civil War and the First World War came in 1907, the same year that Seymour wrote his letter. See Hofstadter, *Age of Reform*, 176–77; Osterweis, *New Haven*, 191, 374; and Dahl, *Who Governs?*, 32.

12 Seymour, "Open Letter," 31, 38, 41.

13 Ibid., 32.

14 Seymour Scrapbook collection, Seymour Papers.

15 Gilbert to *New Haven Register,* June 5, 1907, Seymour Papers.

16 Seymour, *New Haven*, 48–49.

17 Seymour lobbied hard for Gilbert to be given the library commission in his capacity as a member of its Building Committee. His friendship with the architect rested on a shared love of history, and each had deep family roots in Connecticut. Seymour even claimed that Gilbert might have been descended from Matthew Gilbert, one of New Haven's original founders; see Seymour miscellaneous correspondence, July 1907, Seymour Papers.

18 Seymour does not recount how Olmsted was chosen, but he was certainly a natural choice for any city contemplating an ambitious master plan. In 1900, six years after graduating from Harvard, Olmsted founded its landscape architecture program and taught there until 1914. He was also a member of the Senate Park Commission of 1901, along with Daniel Burnham, Charles McKim, and Augustus Saint-Gaudens. With his brother, he led a planning office responsible for, among other projects, master plans for Detroit (1905), Utica, New York (1907), Pittsburgh (1910), and Newport, Rhode Island (1913). He was also a founding member of the National Planning Conference, acting as its president from 1910 to 1919.

Gilbert, known primarily as an architect (the Woolworth Building of 1913 in New York City and the U.S. Supreme Court Building of 1935 in Washington, D.C., are his most celebrated works), was responsible for several campus master plans, including University of Minnesota at Minneapolis (1908), University of Texas at Austin (1910), and Oberlin College in Ohio (1912). He was also involved in master plan studies for Washington, D.C. (1900) prior to the Senate Park Commission's work.

Seymour also courted Charles McKim, the accomplished planner and partner in the renowned architectural firm of McKim, Mead and White, to be involved in New Haven's Civic Improvement Plan. Unfortunately, he was in poor health and had to refuse, despite Seymour's repeated entreaties; see Seymour miscellaneous correspondence, July 1907, Seymour Papers.

19 Robinson to Seymour, 9 August 1907, Seymour Papers.

20 Robinson to *New Haven Register,* 23 August 1907, Seymour Papers.

21 Gilbert to Seymour, 24 August 1907, Seymour Papers.

22 Robinson had an extensive career as a "civic advisor" at the time; cities that retained his services included Detroit, Denver, Honolulu, Oakland, Des Moines, Pittsburgh, Los Angeles, and his native Rochester, New York. For Columbus, Ohio, he helped to found a Plan Commission in 1907 and produced a report for the city the next year much like the one that Gilbert and Olmsted were to issue for New Haven in 1910.

23 "Looking Forward: An Address before the Women's Civic Club of New Haven on March 25, 1908," reprinted in Seymour, *New Haven*, 59–71.

24 Robinson, *The Improvement of Towns and Cities* (New York: G. P. Putnam's Sons, 1901). His follow-up book, *Modern Civic Art* (New York: G. P. Putnam's Sons, 1903), was enormously popular as well.

25 Jon Peterson, "The City Beautiful Movement: Forgotten Meanings and Lost Origins," in *American Cities, Vol. 2: The Physical City*, ed. Neil Shumsky (New York: Garland Publishing, 1996), 120–22.

26 Scott, *City Planning*, 100, 108–9. Much of the criticism, both at the time and afterward, reacted to the plan's spectacular imagery. However, by fixating on style, critics largely missed the point of the drawings, which was to delineate the hierarchy and relationship of public space—streets, squares, parks, waterfront—to private building fabric, not to impose any uniform style or building volume. Indeed, Burnham did not dictate any building height limits, a widely held but erroneous assumption based on a reading of the drawings rather than the extensive text.

27 Speech by Gilbert at 1909 Annual Meeting of American Institute of Architects, quoted in Wilson, *City Beautiful Movement*, 287.

28 Wilson, 285–86. Gilbert's disdainful remark with regard to Robinson's work can certainly be seen in light of this break.

29 Seymour, *New Haven*, 49. The committee solicited a contribution of $5,000 from the city, which denied the request. Political infighting, much of it unrelated to the issue of planning, doomed the city's financial support of the plan almost from the start (as reported in *New Haven Palladium,* 6 December 1907). Contribu-

tors to the private subscription were comprised mostly of New Haven's social and business elite; indeed, the patrician class typically supported most of the beautification and planning efforts in American cities during this period.

30 Gilbert and Olmsted, Jr., to Seymour, 2 August 1907, Seymour Papers. It was in this letter that Gilbert and Olmsted characterized their Plan of 1910 as a preliminary study. Despite the plan's enthusiastic reception, they never had the opportunity to expand upon it.

31 Seymour to Stokes, 20 April 1910, Seymour Papers.

32 Osterweis, *New Haven*, 395. The Alumni Association, composed primarily of graduates who continued to reside in New Haven, sponsored events that highlighted and celebrated the relationship of the university to the city.

33 Gilbert and Olmsted, Jr., *Report*, 4, 13, 99; Scott, *City Planning*, 118. In projecting New Haven's growth in the twentieth century, the planners made a crucial error of statistical analysis. They correlated population growth with other northeastern cities but fixed the comparison to a common population size among the cities, irrespective of the time at which that size was achieved. Thus, they ended up transferring the explosive growth rate of the previous fifty years into the future, predicting a wildly exaggerated increase in population – 400,000 by 1950 and 1.5 million by 2000. However, Gilbert and Olmsted gave little weight to the projections in the *Report*'s actual recommendations, stressing that their data were "only a very feeble and uncertain illumination on the future" (14).

34 Various correspondence from Olmsted, Jr., to Seymour, 1909–10, Seymour Papers.

35 Nolen to Seymour, 10 March 1911, Seymour Papers.

36 Nolen, "Address to the First National Conference on City Planning" (1909), quoted in Scott, *City Planning*, 98.

37 Gilbert and Olmsted, Jr., *Report*, 15–16.

38 Olmsted, Jr., "Introductory Address," *Proceedings of the Second National Conference on City Planning* (1910).

39 Subsequently discarded by modernist planners, the street type was one of the City Beautiful Movement's great contributions to American urban design. It defined and controlled a thoroughfare's function and character and thus was a powerful tool in shaping a city's public realm.

40 Gilbert and Olmsted, Jr., *Report*, 20.

41 Ibid., 54.

42 Ibid., 56.

43 The idea of urban renewal was to remain tied to this section of the city in the coming decades, finally acted upon in the razing of the Oak Street neighborhood for a highway connector in the 1960s.

44 Elizabeth Kite, *L'Enfant and Washington* (Baltimore: Johns Hopkins Press, 1929), 18, 62–66.

45 Ibid., 51.

46 Ibid., 49–51.

47 Seymour, "The Rise and Fall of the City of Elms," 21 March 1909, reprinted in *New Haven*, 77, 116.

48 Seymour, *New Haven*, 113. Seymour also quoted the famous MacMillan Plan for Washington, D.C., in its recognition of the elm as the best American street tree. It was prized for "the architectural character of its columnar trunk and the delicate traceries formed by its wide-spreading branches" (101).

49 Gilbert and Olmsted, Jr., *Report*, 30–31.

50 Boyer, *Urban Masses and Moral Order*, 234–39.

51 Gilbert and Olmsted, Jr., *Report*, 35.

52 Osterweis, 331–34.

53 Olmsted, Jr., "Address to the Second National Conference on City Planning" (1910), quoted in Seymour, *New Haven*, 603.

54 Seymour made sure the plan received national attention upon its release, distributing it to colleagues around the country and submitting it for exhibition at the Third National Conference on City Planning in May 1911, held in Philadelphia. Miscellaneous correspondence, 1910–11, Seymour Papers.

55 Seymour, *New Haven*, 588–91. Seymour specifically credited the Chamber of Commerce with taking the political action necessary to pass the Act.

56 *New Haven Register*, 11 January 1911.

57 Seymour, *New Haven*, 592; Scott, *City Planning*, 80. New Haven modeled its City Plan Commission Act and city engineer position on Hartford's precedent of 1907.

58 *New Haven Union*, 8 October 1912.

59 Seymour, *New Haven*, 199.

60 Seymour to unidentified recipient, 15 February 1916, Seymour Papers.

61 Seymour, *New Haven*, 594. The railroad approach returned with a vengeance in the Redevelopment years of the 1950s and 1960s, taking form as the Church Street extension. A completely anti-urban scheme, the extension was related to Gilbert and Olmsted's design only in its stated intent of connecting the train station with the city center.

62 Ibid., 604.

63 Copy of Rogers's acceptance letter to Yale, with notes by Seymour, 12 November 1920, Seymour Papers.

64 Seymour, "A Valedictory," 17 July 1924, reprinted in *New Haven*, 590–605.

65 Seymour, *New Haven*, 593. Such an attitude held sway despite Seymour's initial disavowal of "municipal art" in his first "Open Letter" of 1907; despite Gilbert's declaration in his Yale lecture of 1908 that "I dislike the phrase City Beautiful, for it conveys a wrong idea and suggests the romantic, the sentimental, and the superficial" (Text of Gilbert's lecture, *New Haven Register*, 11 December 1908); and despite the planners' conscious striking of any and all references to the "City Beautiful" in their *Report* (Gilbert to Olmsted, Jr., 12 July 1910, Seymour Papers).

66 Seymour to Gilbert, 17 June 1931, Seymour Papers.

67 Seymour, *New Haven*, 593–94.

68 Dahl, *Who Governs?*, 116.

69 Seymour, *New Haven*, 598, 602–3.

70 *New Haven Register*, 4 June 1914.

A NEW YALE: THE POPE PLAN OF 1919 (pp. 249–261)

1 John Russell Pope, *Yale University: A Plan for its Future Building* (New York: The Cheltenham Press, 1919), 9. The book was presented to Yale by Mabel Brady Garvan, Francis Garvan's wife, in memory of her father, but there is no doubt from Yale records that Francis was the driving force behind its production.

2 Brooks Mather Kelley, *Yale: A History* (New Haven: Yale University Press, 1974), 331.

3 Ibid., 348–57; George Wilson Pierson, *Yale College: An Educational History, 1871–1921* (New Haven: Yale University Press, 1952), 477–82.

4 Helen Cooper and Gerald W. R. Ward, *Francis P. Garvan, Collector* (New Haven: Yale University Art Gallery, 1980), 11–14, 45. Garvan's wealth came from his wife's family. In 1930 he donated to Yale his collection of American decorative arts in her name;

two years later, he donated his collection of sporting art in memory of Payne and Harry Payne Whitney.

5 Steven Bedford, *John Russell Pope: Architect of Empire* (New York: Rizzoli, 1998), 164, 227. In 1924 Garvan was to perform a similar service for Johns Hopkins University in Baltimore, bringing in Pope as architect and planner for a proposed campus enlargement.

6 In a letter of 1921 to James Rowland Angell, the newly appointed president, Day recounted the history of the Pope Plan, mentioning that Garvan was originally motivated by "the idea of the University acquiring sufficient real estate to provide for its future expansion" (Day to Angell, July 25, 1921, Records of the Corporation Committee on Architectural Plan, Manuscripts and Archives, Yale University Library, YRG 1-B, RU 30).

7 For an account of the reorganization and its aftermath, see Kelley, *Yale,* 355–66, and Pierson, *Yale College,* 477–92.

8 In a letter to President Hadley in July 1919, Day mentioned that copies of the plan had been distributed to Corporation members and that the administration would discuss it in detail in the fall. Day to Hadley, July 10, 1919, Arthur Twining Hadley Papers, Manuscripts and Archives, Yale University Library, MS 213.

9 Garvan's collection of prints included a number of nineteenth-century views of American college campuses. See Cooper and Ward, *Frances P. Garvan,* 58.

10 For a discussion of American campus planning and architecture around the time of the Pope Plan, see Paul Venable Turner, *Campus: An American Planning Tradition* (Cambridge: MIT Press, 1984), 186–245. A letter of 1911 to Anson Phelps Stokes from John Farwell, an alumnus who headed up Yale's planning efforts in the 1910s and 1920s, gives early evidence of Yale's preference for the Collegiate Gothic: "I have always been very much interested in architecture in colleges, because I am a great believer in the unconscious influence of good architecture and good art on young people. I have been delighted to see that Yale is adopting the Collegiate Gothic, as there is certainly something about it, with its perpendicular lines instead of horizontal lines, to point the mind upward" (Farwell to Stokes, October 9, 1911, Anson Phelps Stokes Papers, Manuscripts and Archives, Yale University Library, YRG 4-A-09).

11 Pope, *Yale University,* 10. The only other change that Pope proposed for the existing campus south of Elm Street was the construction of an "Art School and Museum" on the block bounded by Chapel, York, Library, and High Streets; the arts were already represented in this area by Street Hall (1864). Yale heeded Pope's suggestion in 1927–28 by building an art gallery on this block, connecting it to Street Hall with a bridge over High Street.

Pope included the Memorial Quadrangle in his plan, even though construction had only just begun. The scale of the Memorial Quadrangle is more fine-grained than Pope's architectural proposals (understandable given that Rogers's building was responding to an actual program and had undergone a more lengthy design process), but their work was obviously sympathetic. One can make a more accurate assessment of their relative design strengths by comparing the Memorial Quadrangle with Pope's Calhoun College of 1929–33.

12 Pope, *Yale University,* 10. The north side of Wall Street in its existing location determined the north building line of the New Campus; the north face of the Berkeley Oval's Lampson Lyceum determined the south building line.

13 Ibid., 11.

14 Pope to Stokes, September 30, 1919, Anson Phelps Stokes Papers.

15 Ibid.

16 Farwell to Stokes, November 1, 1919, Anson Phelps Stokes Papers.

17 Garvan to Angell, June 15, 1932, reprinted in Cooper and Ward, *Francis P. Garvan,* 71–72. In a letter to John Farwell in 1923, George Parmly Day expressed his belief that Pope gave the gymnasium such emphasis because of Garvan's particular interest in the building. Day was sensitive to Garvan's feelings because he felt, rightly enough, that he or his friend Payne Whitney might contribute money toward the construction of a new gymnasium. Day to Farwell, January 23, 1923, Records of the Corporation Committee on Architectural Plan.

18 Pope failed to specify the chapel in his preface or drawings but noted its inclusion and location in his reply of September 30, 1919, to Stokes.

19 Pope, *Yale University,* 10.

20 Kelley, *Yale,* 331–33; Stokes to Pope, September 23, 1919, Anson Phelps Stokes Papers.

21 In this volume, see Erik Vogt, "The City Redeemed: New Haven's Civic Improvement Plan of 1910," p. 241, for a discussion of Hillhouse Avenue's original design.

22 Pope, *Yale University,* 11.

23 Stokes to Pope, September 23, 1919.

24 Although later historians have criticized the Pope Plan for its seemingly ruthless treatment of Yale's existing campus, it actually proposed removing or relocating only two buildings, Durfee Hall and Woodbridge Hall. Pope left the fate of a third, the Music School (now Sprague Hall), up to the university.

25 Prompted by Pope's work, Stokes reopened the long-dormant plan to complete the Hewitt Quadrangle. Thomas Hastings, one of the original architects, submitted several design sketches to that end. Needless to say, he deeply resented Pope's placement of the library, which he proposed relocating to the west of the quadrangle, as Stokes had suggested. Questioning the plan's overall strategy, Hastings insisted in a letter to Stokes that "the spirit of the University should be a secluded series of campuses or quadrangles, rather than a city type plan bringing in all the disturbing influences of city life" (Hastings to Stokes, October 24, 1919, Anson Phelps Stokes Papers). The criticism fell on sympathetic ears in the administration. Passing on Hastings's letter and sketches to John Farwell, Stokes wrote that "I personally sympathize with his position and believe that it is essentially sound" (Stokes to Farwell, October 27, 1919, Records of the Corporation Committee on Architectural Plan).

26 Pope to Stokes, September 30, 1919.

27 Mason to George Parmly Day, December 11, 1919, Anson Phelps Stokes Papers.

28 Oviatt to Stokes, December 4, 1919, Records of the Corporation Committee on Architectural Plan.

29 Farwell to Yale Corporation, November 17, 1919, Anson Phelps Stokes Papers; Farwell to Stokes, November 1, 1919. Farwell, an alumnus from Chicago who had been involved in the famous Burnham Plan of 1909 for that city, was a highly influential figure in the planning of a new Yale. Brought in as a Corporation member in 1911, he remained chairman of the Committee on Architectural Plan throughout Yale's building boom of the 1920s, stepping down finally in 1930.

30 Farwell to Yale Corporation, November 17, 1919, and December 13, 1919, Anson Phelps Stokes Papers. How the choice was made is unknown, but Rogers later expressed that he considered it a slight, given his professional standing and able service on the Memorial Quadrangle. Rogers to Fisher, September 20, 1920, Samuel H. Fisher Papers, Manuscripts and Archives, Yale University Library, MS 213.

31 Report of Advisory Committee to Committee on Architectural Plan, February 7, 1920, Records of the Corporation Committee on Architectural Plan.

32 Rogers was to entertain the possibility of extending College Street in this way in several of his master planning schemes; Farwell to Rogers, November 22, 1922, James Rowland Angell Papers, Manuscripts and Archives, Yale University Library, YRG 2-A-14. The idea had added force since Gilbert and Olmsted had introduced it in their Civic Improvement Plan nine years earlier, using the extension to collect traffic north of the nine squares. The university finally decided against it, in part because the land was owned by the trustees of the Sheffield Scientific School and would require demolition of several important buildings.

The more minor changes that the architectural advisers recommended included leaving Durfee Hall in place but opening a large archway in it (as Stokes had already suggested) and arranging the Hillhouse Group more compactly.

33 Report of Architectural Plan Committee to Yale Corporation, May 8, 1920, Records of the Corporation Committee on Architectural Plan.

34 Memorandum of Corporation Committee on the Consulting Architect, February 17, 1913, James Rowland Angell Papers; Aaron Betsky, *James Gamble Rogers and the Architecture of Pragmatism* (Cambridge: MIT Press, 1994), 114.

35 Rogers to Farwell, August 19, 1920, Records of the Corporation Committee on Architectural Plan.

36 Rogers to Fisher, September 20, 1920; Rogers to Stokes, November 12, 1920, James Rowland Angell Papers.

37 Memorandum of the Meeting of the Yale Corporation, November 5, 1921; Meeting Minutes of the Corporation Committee on Architectural Plan, October 7, 1921, James Rowland Angell Papers.

38 "The Plan for the Physical Development of Yale University," *Yale Alumni Weekly* 33 (1 February 1924).

39 Rogers to Fisher, September 20, 1920; Press statement by Rogers and Corporation Committee on Architectural Plan, January 1924, James Rowland Angell Papers; "Yale Consults City on her $20,000,000 Plan for Building," *New Haven Journal-Courier*, 24 January 1922.

JAMES GAMBLE ROGERS & THE SHAPING OF YALE IN THE TWENTIETH CENTURY (pp. 263–291)

1 Frank Lloyd Wright, *A Testament* (New York: Horizon Press, 1957), 34–35. Wright, writing in 1957, was surely reacting against Rogers's work at Yale, since Rogers was not a prolific architect of Gothic buildings at the time he and Wright were acquainted.

2 Otto Faelten taught architectural design in the School of the Fine Arts from 1922 to 1933.

3 Although James Fenimore Cooper attended Yale from 1803 to 1805, he did not graduate.

4 J. G. Rogers to Anson Phelps Stokes, 28 September 1917, Anson Phelps Stokes Family Papers, Manuscripts and Archives, Yale University Library.

5 Robert Dudley French, *The Memorial Quadrangle: A Book about Yale* (New Haven: Yale University Press, 1929), 129.

6 J. G. Rogers to Anson Phelps Stokes, 23 October 1919, Stokes Papers.

7 I first used this phrase, suggesting an eclecticism concerned more with visual effect than with any moralistic or ideological aspects of style, in "Romantic Pragmatism: The Work of James Gamble Rogers at Yale University," an unpublished undergraduate honors thesis written in 1972 under the direction of Professor Vincent Scully. Pragmatism was intended to have something of a double meaning here, in that I believe Rogers was not only pragmatic in terms of his attitude toward romanticism, but toward architecture in general. The phrase was later adapted by Aaron Betsky and inspired the title of his full-length study of Rogers, *James Gamble Rogers and the Architecture of Pragmatism* (New York: The Architectural History Foundation, 1994).

8 "Editorial and Other Comment: The Harkness Memorial Quadrangle and Memorial Tower, Yale University," *Architecture* 44, no. 4 (October 1921): 297.

9 William Harlan Hale, "The Arts vs. Yale University," *The Harkness Hoot* 1, no. 1 (15 November 1930): 21–22.

10 Ibid., 23.

11 See also, in the present volume, Erik Vogt, "A New Yale: The Pope Plan of 1919."

12 Goodhue's drawings were included in *Bertram Grosvenor Goodhue, Architect and Master of Many Arts,* ed. Charles Harris Whitaker (New York: Press of the American Institute of Architects, Inc., 1925), an honorific monograph of his work published the year after his death. The Yale sketches are identified only as "a university library."

13 James Gamble Rogers, "Sterling Memorial Library: Notes by the Architect," *Yale University Library Gazette* 3, no. 1 (July 1920): 3.

14 Hale, *Harkness Hoot*, 21.

15 James Gamble Rogers, "The Future of Yale College," typescript dated 27 March 1928, Commonwealth Fund Archives.

16 Russell Lynes, *The Tastemakers* (New York: Harper & Brothers, 1954), 269.

17 See "Quadrangle System Plan Outlined by Chairman of the Architecture Committee…article written especially for the NEWS, John V. Farrel, (sic) '79…" *Yale Daily News,* 7 May 1930, clipping in Records of Corporation Committee on Architectural Plan, Manuscripts and Archives, Yale University Library (RU 30). For a complete discussion of the Committee's decision to employ the Georgian, see, in this volume, Catherine Lynn, "Building Yale & Razing It from the Civil War to the Great Depression," pp. 223–24.

18 Quoted in Judith Ann Schiff, "Old Yale: Secret Gardens," *Yale Alumni Magazine* 64, no. 7 (May 2001): 80, as quoted in Julie V. Iovine, "University: Pleasures of Landscape," *Yale Alumni Magazine* 49, no. 2 (November 1985): 26.

MODERN ARCHITECTURE AT YALE: A MEMOIR (pp. 293–353)

1 Henry-Russell Hitchcock, Jr., and Philip Johnson, *The International Style: Architecture since 1922* (New York: W. W. Norton and Co., Inc., 1932).

2 Cf. Carola Hein, "Maurice Rotival: French Planning on a World Scale," Parts I and II, *Planning Perspectives* 17 (2002): 247–65, 325–44. A solid and devastating study.

3 Jane Jacobs, *The Death and Life of Great American Cities* (New York: Vintage Books, 1961); and Herbert J. Gans, *The Urban Villagers: Group and Class in the Life of Italian-Americans* (New York: Free Press of Glencoe, 1962).

4 The way the Orange Bowl empties out through Miami's grid is a perfect example of that as against the newer Pro Player Stadium up north connected to the Interstate, where there is normally an interminable delay getting out of the parking lot.

5 See Robert A. M. Stern, *George Howe: Toward a Modern American Architecture* (New Haven: Yale University Press, 1975).

6 The renovation is by Polshek Partnership Architects, whose principals include James S. Polshek (M.ARCH. 1955).

7 In the course of the negotiations I had occasion to phone Kahn to plead with him to come. During the conversation I was foolish enough to say something to the effect that he would in all likelihood get a building anyway but would probably build comparatively little in the long run and was a superlative teacher and should therefore go with that and make us all happy. Kahn instantly shouted that he was going to build more buildings than anybody else in the United States and hung up on me. A minute later he called back to say he was sorry. But he was right all the time.

8 It has since unfortunately surfaced in the Saarinen Papers, recently deposited in Manuscripts and Archives at Sterling Memorial Library. Its contents are as described in the text.

9 Inscrutable Saarinen. Lesley Baier tells me that the text on Connecticut Hall in the 1919–20 issue of the *Catalogue of Yale University* includes the following: "The southeast corner room was known as the butler's room or buttery, where 'Cider, metheglin, strong beer, loaf sugar, pipes, tobacco, and such necessaries of scholars as are not furnished in the common hall' might be secured. This institution, a famous one borrowed from English College custom, was abolished in 1817" (p. 89).

10 The abysmal scheme for two new colleges later proposed by Romaldo Giurgola, supported by scores of deluded faculty advisers, suggests as much. It was for two additional colleges off Grove Street; its plan was arrived at with the advice of an impressive number of faculty and administrators who junketed extensively in Great Britain and on the continent to study famous universities. One wonders what they looked at and how, because the architect's proposal turned out to be for not much more than a mean street defined by profoundly undistinguished buildings. It was killed by the so-called Guida Amendment, named for Mayor Bartholomew F. Guida of New Haven, who is said to have been treated with less than due respect by the chairman of the relevant committee and therefore dug in his heels and, well aware of Yale's unwillingness to pay taxes on anything, fixed it so that the new colleges would be roundly taxed. He thus killed the scheme. We are all in his debt.

11 Reprinted in "Mailer vs. Scully," *Architectural Forum* 120 (April 1964): 96–97.

12 One of Yale's lawyers who looked into the matter later pointed out that if Yale had wanted to give Venturi a commission, it could have done so without all the rigmarole.

13 Vincent Scully, introduction to *Complexity and Contradiction in Architecture,* by Robert Venturi (New York: Museum of Modern Art, in association with the Graham Foundation for Advanced Studies in the Fine Arts, Chicago, 1966), 11.

14 The Environmental Science Center, made possible by gifts from the Class of 1954 and from Edward Bass (B.A. 1967), replaces the Bingham Oceanographic Laboratory, designed as an addition to the Peabody Museum in 1959 by the firm of Douglas Orr.

15 Gaddis Smith, *Yale and the External World: The Shaping of the University in the Twentieth Century* (New Haven: Yale University Press, forthcoming).

16 Lee had attended Yale (Class of 1928) but did not graduate. Yale awarded him an honorary degree in 1961.

17 As of this writing, the Bush Administration seems determined to terminate this most humane and effective of federal housing programs.

18 The renovations were supported by Roland W. Betts II (B.A. 1968), a fellow of the Corporation, and his wife, Lois Phifer Betts.

19 Their study was published by Yale in March 2000 in an extensively illustrated volume, *Yale University: A Framework for Campus Planning.* It is available online in PDF at http://www.yale.edu/about/YALEFRMW.pdf/.

Illustration Credits

NHCHS   New Haven Colony Historical Society, New Haven, Connecticut
YBL   Beinecke Rare Book and Manuscript Library, Yale University
YM&A   Manuscripts and Archives, Yale University Library
YMC   Map Collection, Yale University Library
YNHHA   Yale–New Haven Hospital Archives
YOPA   Office of Public Affairs, Yale University
YUAG   Yale University Art Gallery
YVRC   Visual Resources Collection, Yale University Arts Library

1   Yale and New Haven looking northeast toward East Rock. Photo: Michael Marsland. YOPA.

2   James Wadsworth, B.A. 1748, "Plan of the City of New Haven," 1748. From Dean B. Lyman, Jr., *An Atlas of Old New Haven; or, "The Nine Squares" as shown on various early maps* (New Haven: Chas. W. Scranton & Co., 1929). YMC.

3   A. B. Doolittle, "A View of the Buildings of Yale College at New Haven," 1807. Colored engraving. Gift of James M. Hoppin, B.A. 1840. YM&A. RU 703/Cabinet B/Drawer 21/Folder 70.

4   Whitneyville: detail from "The City of New Haven, Connecticut," 1879. Drawn and published by O. H. Bailey and J. C. Hazen, Boston. YMC.

5   D. W. Buckingham, "Map of the City of New Haven," 1830. YMC.

6   New Haven City Hall and County Courthouse annex, after 1871. YM&A. Image no. 4915.

7   Farnam and Lawrance Halls in 1888. YM&A. Image no. 2249.

8   Woolsey and Memorial Halls, looking north toward the buildings of the Sheffield Scientific School, ca. 1905. YM&A. Image no. 4925.

9   Yale Bowl during the Yale–Harvard game in the 1970s. Yale Sports Publicity.

10   New Haven Free Public Library and New Haven County Courthouse. YVRC.

11   United States Post Office and Courthouse, ca. 1918. Photo: Kenneth Clark, New Rochelle, N.Y. YM&A. Image no. 6654.

12   Looking east from Harkness Memorial Tower toward the New Haven Green in 1942. Photo: John Phillips / Time Life Pictures / Getty Images. YM&A. Image no. 4868.

13   Model of City Government Center Project and speculative office tower designed by I. M. Pei, 1966. YVRC.

14   Looking west over the New Haven Green and the Old Campus toward the Memorial Quadrangle in 1925. Photo: Yale Co-op. YM&A. Image no. 4870.

15   Memorial Quadrangle: Samuel Yellin's gate for the Memorial Gateway. YM&A. Image no. 6650.

16   Looking north from Harkness Memorial Tower over the courtyards of Saybrook and Trumbull Colleges toward Sterling Memorial Library in 1942. Photo: John Phillips / Time Life Pictures / Getty Images. YM&A. Image no. 4867.

17   Looking west from Harkness Memorial Tower over Branford College toward Pierson and Davenport Colleges in 1942. Photo: John Phillips / Time Life Pictures / Getty Images. YM&A. Image no. 4136.

18   Pierson College: "Slave Quarters." YM&A. Image no. 1232.

19   Payne Whitney Gymnasium in the 1930s. YM&A. Image no. 4538.

20   New Haven Colony around 1640. Drawing by Erik Vogt. Ink on vellum, 30 x 30 inches. © Erik Vogt.

21   Plan of New Haven in 1641. Drawn by F. R. Honey, 1880. From Anson Phelps Stokes, *Historical Prints of New Haven, Connecticut* (New Haven: The Tuttle, Morehouse & Taylor Co., 1910). YMC.

22   "Cambridge around 1638, drawn by Erwin Raisz from data compiled by Albert P. Norris." Map reprinted by permission of the publisher from *The Founding of Harvard College* by Samuel Eliot Morison, p. 350, Cambridge, Mass.: Harvard University Press, Copyright © 1935 by the President and Fellows of Harvard College.

23   "The Garden of Canticles (Song of Solomon)," 1633. From Henry Hawkins, *Partheneia Sacra* (Rouen: Printed by Iohn Cousturier, 1633). YBL.

24   "Sacred Theory of the Earth," 1681. From Thomas Burnet, *Telluris Theoria Sacra* 1 (London: Typis R. N., impensis G. Kettilby, 1681). YBL.

25   Juan Bautista Villalpando, "Encampment of the Israelites," 1596. From *El Tratado de la Arquitectura Perfecta en la última visión del profeta Ezequiel* (Madrid: Servicio de Publicaciones, Colegio Oficial de Arquitectos de Madrid, 1990). Courtesy Colegio Oficial de Arquitectos de Madrid (COAM).

26   Juan Bautista Villalpando, "Plan of the Temple of Solomon," 1604. From *El Tratado de la Arquitectura Perfecta en la última visión del profeta Ezequiel* (Madrid: Servicio de Publicaciones, Colegio Oficial de Arquitectos de Madrid, 1990). Courtesy Colegio Oficial de Arquitectos de Madrid (COAM).

27   "Plan of the New Jerusalem of Revelation," 1627. From Joseph Mede, *Clavis Apocalyptica* (Cantabrigiae: Apud Thom. Buck celeberrimae Academiae Typographum, 1632). YBL.

28   "New Haven, View from East Rock," 1872. From William Cullen Bryant, *Picturesque America* 1 (New York: D. Appleton and Co., 1872).

29   "East Rock and Meadows," 1872. From William Cullen Bryant, *Picturesque America* 1 (New York: D. Appleton and Co., 1872).

30   "The Garden of Eden," 1675. From Athanasius Kircher, *El Arca de Noe*, 1675. YMC.

31   Fence-sitting and the Brick Row from Chapel Street in 1872. YM&A. RU 703/Cabinet C/Drawer 23.

32   Yale College House: reconstruction of the plan and elevation. From Norman Isham, "The Original College House at Yale," *Yale Alumni Weekly* 26 (20 October 1916). YM&A. Image no. 5009.

33   Harvard College in 1726. From F. O. Vaille and H. A. Clark, eds., *The Harvard Book. A Series of Historical, Biographical, and Descriptive Sketches* 1 (Cambridge, Mass.: Welch, Bigelow, and Company, 1875).

34   Connecticut Hall in 1906. YM&A. Image no. 5290.

35   Connecticut Hall: plan of the ground floor. From Brooks Mather Kelley, *Yale: A History* (New Haven: Yale University Press, 1974). © 1974 by Yale University.

36   "A Front View of Yale-College, and the College-Chapel, in New-Haven," 1786. Colored woodcut published by Daniel Bowen. YUAG. Gift of Jesse Lathrop Moss, B.A. 1869. 1940.317

37   Ezra Stiles, "Plan for Yale College," 1777. Ezra Stiles Miscellaneous Papers, Reel 18, Item 724. YBL.

38   Perspective of the Stiles plan. Drawing by Erik Vogt.

39   Building placement plans of 1792 as initially rejected and approved by the Corporation. Drawing by Erik Vogt.

40   John Trumbull, "Plan and elevation for the development of Yale College," 1792. Pen and ink and graphite on paper, 13 x 30 inches. YM&A. RU 1/Drawer 1/Folder 3.

41   John Trumbull, "Landscape plan ('The Temples of Cloacina') for the development of Yale College," 1792. Pen and ink and wash on paper, 13 x 16 inches. YM&A. RU 1/Drawer 1/Folder 3.

42   Plan and elevation showing geometrical basis of the Trumbull and Hillhouse plan. Drawing by Erik Vogt.

43   John Trumbull, "The Surrender of Lord Cornwallis at Yorktown, 19 October 1781," 1787–ca. 1828. Oil on canvas, 21 x 30⅝ inches. YUAG. Trumbull Collection. 1832.4

44   Composite of the Trumbull elevation and landscape plan. Conceived by Erik Vogt and executed by Julie Fry.

45   Memorial Quadrangle: suite plan by James Gamble Rogers, 1917. YM&A. Image no. 4530.

46   Union Hall (South College) in 1874. YM&A. Image no. 2172.

47   "Anonymous Map of New Haven," 1802. From Dean B. Lyman, Jr., *An Atlas of Old New Haven; or, "The Nine Squares" as shown on various early maps* (New Haven: Chas. W. Scranton & Co., 1929). YMC.

48   Second President's House. YM&A. Image no. 2091.

49   Berkeley Hall (North Middle College) in 1874. YM&A. Image no. 5283.

50   The Lyceum in the 1870s. YM&A. Image no. 5282.

51   The Lyceum in the late 1890s: north facade. YM&A. Image no. 5281.

52   Moses Bradford, "Yale College," 1803. Pen and ink on paper. From Moses Bradford, "Miscellaneous Observations Made in the Recitation Room." YBL.

53   Amos Doolittle, "Plan of New Haven," 1812. YMC.

54   North College in 1901. YM&A. Image no. 3179.

55   New (Second) Chapel. YM&A. Image no. 5285.

56   John Warner Barber, "A View of the Public Square or Green in New Haven, Con.," 1835. From John Warner Barber, *History and Antiquities of New Haven from Its Earliest Settlement to the Present Time* (New Haven: J. W. Barber, 1831 and 1846). YBL.

57   New Haven Centennial Medal, 1838. Side showing New Haven Green and Yale College, designed by Ithiel Town. Bronze, DIAM. 2³⁄₁₆ inches. NHCHS. Gift of the Connecticut Academy of Arts and Sciences.

58   B. F. Nutting, "Yale College, New Haven," 1829–33. From a Yale University Library facsimile, 1946. YM&A. RU 703/Cabinet B/Drawer 21/Folder 70.

59   Divinity College in the 1860s. YM&A. Image no. 5288.

60   Plan of the College, ca. 1841. YM&A. RU 1/Drawer 60/Folder 306.

61 E. Valois, "Yale College," ca. 1860. Lithograph. YM&A. Image no. 6557.

62 Trumbull Gallery in 1865. YM&A. Image no. 5286.

63 The Brick Row and New Haven around 1860. Drawing by Erik Vogt. Colored pencil on paper, 22 x 28 inches. © Erik Vogt.

64 Alexander Jackson Davis, "Yale College and the State House, New Haven, Connecticut," 1832. From a Yale University Library facsimile, 1946. YM&A. RU 703/Cabinet B/Drawer 21/Folder 70.

65 The Fence and the college yard, looking north from Chapel Street, ca. 1875. Photo: C. A. Gulliver. YM&A. Image no. 5289.

66 Students in Connecticut Hall in 1862. YM&A. Image no. 3178.

67 Temple Street, looking north from Chapel Street, ca. 1875. YM&A. Image no. 991.

68 F. Michelin, "Yale College in 1853." From *Class Album 1853*. YM&A. Image no. 5000.

69 "State-House and Public Square, New Haven, with College Buildings in the Back-Ground," 1856. Wood engraving. YM&A. RU 685/Box 6/Folder 137.

70 Yale College Library (now Dwight Hall) in the 1860s. Image no. 3295.

71 "Whitney Arms Company, New Haven, Connecticut," ca. 1860. Engraving published by Van Slyck & Co., Boston. YM&A. Image no. 4140.

72 The Brick Row in the 1860s. YM&A. Image no. 3160.

73 North College, with construction materials for Farnam Hall in the foreground, in 1869. YM&A. Image no. 5284.

74 Plan of Yale College Grounds, ca. 1877. YM&A. Image no. 5050.

75 Quadrangular plan for Yale College, 1887. Attributed to William W. Farnam. YM&A. Image no. 4533.

76 Osborn Hall from the north, with the Brick Row on the right, in 1890. YM&A. Image no. 5545.

77 "The Passing of Old Yale." From *The Yale Banner,* 1901. YM&A. Image no. 6723.

78 Connecticut Hall within the Old Campus quadrangle in 1902–3. YM&A. Image no. 5001.

79 "Bird's-eye View of the Principal Buildings of Yale University," 1895. From *Four American Universities: Harvard, Yale, Princeton, Columbia* (New York: Harper & Bros., 1895). YM&A.

80 Hendrie Hall. YM&A. Image no. 4881.

81 "Yale College: Library and Alumni Hall," after 1853. Artist unknown. Pen and ink and watercolor, 14¾ x 23½ inches. YM&A. RU 610/Drawer 22/Folder 73.

82 Berkeley Oval and the University Gymnasium in 1920. YM&A. Image no. 4875.

83 Yale and New Haven from the southwest in 1920. Photo: Bell Keogh. YM&A. Image no. 4871.

84 Sterling Chemistry Laboratory in 1923. YM&A. Image no. 5246.

85 Yale and New Haven from the south in 1930–31. Photo: New England Airways, New Haven, Conn. YM&A. Image no. 4872.

86 Osborn Hall: central portal. YM&A. Image no. 4858.

87 Street Hall: presentation drawing by Peter Bonnett Wight, ca. 1864. YM&A. Image no. 2041.

88 Street Hall in the 1860s. YM&A. RU 698/Box 1/Folder 2.

89 Chapel Street looking west, ca. 1874–78. Photo: C. A. Gulliver. YM&A. Image no. 6647.

90 Street Hall: plan of the second floor by Peter Bonnett Wight, ca. 1864, with penciled notation of John Ferguson Weir's addition of 1911. YM&A. Image no. 2036.

91 Street Hall: west facade, showing the addition by John Ferguson Weir. YM&A. Image no. 3162.

92 Street Hall: main gallery. YM&A. Image no. 2032.

93 Proposed Civil War Memorial Chapel: general view and ground plan by Vaux, Withers and Co., 1866. YM&A. Image no. 4865.

94 Battell Chapel, 1887. From *Four American Universities: Harvard, Yale, Princeton, Columbia* (New York: Harper & Bros., 1895). YM&A.

95 Farnam Hall in 1876. YM&A. Image no. 2247.

96 Durfee Hall in the early 1870s. Photo: C. A. Gulliver. YM&A. Image no. 6648.

97 Divinity School in the 1880s. Photo: Pach Bros., New York. YM&A. Image no. 6552.

98 Scroll and Key: presentation drawing by Richard Morris Hunt, ca. 1867–69. Prints & Drawings Collection, The Octagon, The Museum of the American Architectural Foundation, Washington, D.C.

99 East Divinity Hall in 1870. YM&A. Image no. 6556.

100 East Divinity Hall: corridor from the Elm Street entrance. YM&A. Image no. 4848.

101 Marquand Chapel in the 1870s. YM&A. Image no. 4144.

102 Divinity School: plan of the ground floor drawn by Harrison W. Lindsley, 1893. YM&A. RU 1/Drawer 60/Folder 305.

103 Trowbridge Library in the 1880s. Photo: Phelps. YM&A. Image no. 6549.

104 Day Missions Library. YM&A. Image no. 4863.

105   Day Missions Library: interior and plan. YM&A. Image no. 4861.

106   "The Yale Boat-House," ca. 1875. Wood engraving after a photograph by William Notman, Montreal. YM&A. Image no. 6462.

107   Frederick Law Olmsted, "Plan for Laying Out the Yale Athletic Grounds, New Haven," 1881. From W. E. DeCrow, *Yale and "The City of Elms,"* 2nd ed. (Boston: W. E. DeCrow, 1885). YM&A. Image no. 6463.

108   Grand Stand at Yale Field in the 1890s. YM&A. Image no. 6465.

109   Kent Chemical Laboratory and Sloane Physical Laboratory, before 1907. YM&A. Image no. 4855.

110   Kent Chemical Laboratory and Sloane Physical Laboratory: plan of the ground floors drawn by Harrison W. Lindsley, 1893. YM&A. RU 1/Drawer 60/Folder 305.

111   Kent Chemical Laboratory: ground-floor laboratory in 1889. YM&A. Image no. 2131.

112   Sheffield Scientific School in the late 1890s. YM&A. Image no. 4873.

113   Hillhouse Avenue (west side) in 1895. YM&A. Image no. 4138.

114   Hillhouse Avenue (west side, contiguous to FIG. 113) in 1895. YM&A. Image no. 4851.

115   North Sheffield Hall in the early 1870s. YM&A. RU 703/Box 33/Folder 706.

116   North Sheffield Hall: drawing room for Mechanical Engineering. YM&A. Image no. 6474.

117   North Sheffield Hall: students posed on the steps of the entry porch. Photo: C. A. Gulliver. YM&A. Image no. 6472.

118   Winchester Hall in 1928. YM&A. Image no. 2353.

119   Sheffield Chemical Laboratory (now Arthur K. Watson Hall), ca. 1900. YM&A. Image no. 4879.

120   Demolition of North Sheffield and Winchester Halls in 1967. YM&A. Image no. 4874.

121   Winchester Observatory. Photo: Pach Bros., New York. YM&A. Image no. 4221.

122   Main Building of the General Hospital Society of New Haven in the 1890s. YNHHA.

123   Farnam Operating Amphitheatre and East Ward. YNHHA.

124   Farnam Operating Amphitheatre. YNHHA.

125   Hospital buildings from the northeast in 1898. YNHHA.

126   Hospital buildings from the southeast in 1899. YNHHA.

127   Map of the hospital buildings, 1922. From *Yale University School of Medicine, The Past, Present, and Future of the Yale University School of Medicine and affiliated clinical institutions* (New Haven: Yale University, 1922). Historical Library, Harvey Cushing/John Hay Whitney Medical Library, Yale University.

128   Peabody Museum: perspective drawing by Josiah Cleveland Cady, ca. 1872–73. From *The Yale Record* 2 (1873–74). YM&A. Image no. 2219.

129   Peabody Museum in 1880. Photo: Pach Bros., New York. YM&A. Image no. 2222.

130   Peabody Museum: plan of the ground floor drawn by Harrison W. Lindsley, 1893. YM&A. RU 1/Drawer 60/Folder 305.

131   Peabody Museum: lecture room, ca. 1890. YM&A. Image no. 6473.

132   Othniel C. Marsh House (now Marsh Hall): south elevation by Josiah Cleveland Cady, 1878. YM&A. Image no. 2289.

133   Dwight Hall and Alumni Hall after 1894. YM&A. Image no. 4860.

134   Dwight Hall after 1912. YM&A. Image no. 6725.

135   Chittenden Library in the 1890s. YM&A. Image no. 4876.

136   Chittenden Library: presentation drawing by Josiah Cleveland Cady, ca. 1889. YM&A. Image no. 2213.

137   Chittenden Library: main reading room in the 1890s. YM&A. Image no. 6720.

138   Osborn Hall, ca. 1890. YM&A. Image no. 4535.

139   Osborn Hall after 1894. YM&A. Image no. 4146.

140   Osborn Hall: plan of the ground floor drawn by Harrison W. Lindsley, 1893. YM&A. Image no. 5078.

141   Osborn Hall: north and west facades. YM&A. Image no. 4859.

142   Demolition of Osborn Hall in 1926. YM&A. Image no. 6724.

143   Welch Hall: east (College Street) elevation by Bruce Price, 1890. YM&A. RU 1/Drawer 2/Folder 17.

144   Yale Infirmary in the early 1900s. YM&A. Image no. 4877.

145   Hendrie Hall: perspective drawing by Josiah Cleveland Cady, 1894. Photo: Phelps. YM&A. Image no. 4201.

146   Donn Barber, "Here's to Good Old Yale," with Gandolfo's perspective of the University Gymnasium, 1891. From *The Yale Record* (28 November 1891). YM&A. Image no. 366.

147   University Gymnasium, ca. 1894. Photo: A. B. Corbin, New Haven, Conn. YM&A. RU 703/Box 27/Folder 566.

148   University Gymnasium: plan of the ground floor drawn by Harrison W. Lindsley, 1893. YM&A. RU 1/Drawer 60/Folder 305.

149   University Gymnasium: Trophy Room, ca. 1895. YM&A. Image no. 4864.

150   University Gymnasium: Main Exercise Room in 1906. YM&A. Image no. 4878.

151 Berkeley Oval: south facade, after a presentation drawing by Josiah Cleveland Cady, 1893. YM&A. Image no. 4849.

152 White Hall and Berkeley Hall, with gate lodge on the right, around 1895. YM&A. Image no. 4862.

153 Berkeley Oval before the addition of Haughton Hall in 1909. YM&A. Image no. 2237.

154 University (Blount) Avenue before 1912. YM&A. Image no. 4856.

155 Haughton Hall: preparatory drawing by Robertson and Potter, 1908. YM&A. Image no. 5381.

156 Sterling Memorial Library with the buildings of Berkeley Oval split in parts and flanking the open space of Cross Campus: proposal by James Gamble Rogers. YM&A. Aperture card 2103.

157 Demolition of the Berkeley Oval in 1933. YM&A. Image no. 478.

158 Yale from the sky, flying south, in 1925. YM&A. Image no. 4869.

159 R. Rummell, "Yale University," 1905. From a photogravure of Rummell's drawing published by F. R. Nichols Co., Boston. YM&A. RU 703/Cabinet B/Drawer 19/Folder 63.

160 Map of Yale University, 1912–13. From *Catalogue of Yale University 1912–13* (New Haven: Yale University, 1913).

161 Bicentennial Buildings: presentation drawing by Carrère and Hastings, 1899. From *Yale Alumni Weekly* 9, no. 18 (31 January 1900). YM&A.

162 Bicentennial Buildings: presentation drawing of the interior view by Carrère and Hastings, 1899. From *Yale Alumni Weekly* 9, no. 18 (31 January 1900). YM&A.

163 Bicentennial Buildings: plan by Carrère and Hastings, 1899. From *Yale Alumni Weekly* 9, no. 18 (31 January 1900). YM&A.

164 University Commons set for a dinner, ca. 1906. YM&A. Image no. 4927.

165 University Commons in 1909. YM&A. Image no. 4928.

166 Woodbridge Hall: presentation drawing by J.K.J. for Howells and Stokes, 1900. From *Yale Alumni Weekly* 9, no. 35 (30 May 1900). YM&A.

167 Noah Porter Gateway: competition-winning drawing by Howells and Stokes, 1912. YM&A. Image no. 6454.

168 University Commons after completion of the Yale Alumni War Memorial colonnade, ca. 1928. YM&A. Image no. 4924.

169 Byers Memorial Hall in the early 1930s. YM&A. Image no. 2349.

170 Kirtland Hall: presentation drawing by Kirtland Kelsey Cutter, 1902–3. From *Yale Alumni Weekly* 22, no. 16 (21 January 1903). YM&A.

171 Hammond Hall: side elevation by W. Gedney Beatty, 1904. YM&A. Image no. 4883.

172 Hammond Hall in 1918: interior with concentrator plant. YM&A. Image no. 6470.

173 Sprague Hall: presentation drawing by Coolidge and Shattuck, 1916. From *Yale Alumni Weekly* 26, no. 9 (17 November 1916). YM&A.

174 Olmsted Brothers, "Plan for the Developement [*sic*] of the Hillhouse Property," 1905. YM&A. Aperture card 9649.

175 Vanderbilt Hall: presentation drawing by J. K. James for Charles C. Haight, 1894. YM&A. Image no. 5248.

176 Phelps Hall: sketch by Charles C. Haight on a letter to William W. Farnam, 1895. YM&A. Image no. 4932.

177 First Vanderbilt-Scientific Hall: presentation drawing by Hughson Hawley for Charles C. Haight, 1902. From *Yale Alumni Weekly* 12, no. 16 (21 January 1903). YM&A. Image no. 6721.

178 Yale from the sky, Shefftown, in 1925. Photo: Yale Co-op. YM&A. Image no. 2360.

179 Mason and Dunham Laboratories in 1918. YM&A. Image no. 4145.

180 Sloane Physics Laboratory in 1912. YM&A. Image no. 6457.

181 Osborn Memorial Laboratories. YM&A. Image no. 6458.

182 Linsly Hall: competition drawing by A. M. Githens for Charles C. Haight, 1905. YM&A. Image no. 2212.

183 Daniels Memorial Gateway: drawing by A. M. Githens for Charles C. Haight, 1911. YM&A. Image no. 5078.

184 Brady Memorial Laboratory in the 1920s. YM&A. Image no. 6459.

185 Central Power Plant: preliminary design for the York and Ashmun Street elevations by Day and Klauder, 1917. YM&A. Image no. 5247.

186 Yale in China College and Hospital, Changsha, China: bird's-eye presentation drawing by T. F. H. for Murphy and Dana, 1916. YM&A. Image no. 807.

187 Wright Hall from the Old Campus: perspective view by Delano and Aldrich, 1911. YM&A. Image no. 4880.

188 Construction of the Yale Bowl, October 17, 1913. YM&A. Image no. 4911.

189 Playing fields and the Yale Bowl after 1928. YM&A. Image no. 5926.

190 Adee Boat House on the Quinnipiac River, New Haven, in 1910. YM&A. Image no. 4854.

191 Yale Armory and Stables in 1917. YM&A. Image no. 4139.

192 Lapham Field House: drawing by D. O. Stebbins for Charles Klauder, 1923. YM&A. Image no. 5077.

193 Charles E. Coxe Memorial Gymnasium (Coxe Cage): drawing by O.R.F. for Lockwood, Greene and Company, 1926–27. YM&A. Image no. 4882.

194 Bob Cook Boat House: watercolor of the original proposal by James Gamble Rogers, 1924. YM&A. RU 703/Cabinet C/Drawer 26/Folder 84.

195 Bob Cook Boat House on the Housatonic River, Derby. YM&A. Image no. 4853.

196 Sterling Chemistry Laboratory: south elevation by Chester B. Price for Delano and Aldrich, ca. 1920. YM&A. Image no. 4933.

197 Excavation of the Sterling Chemistry Laboratory site, September 7, 1921. YM&A. Image no. 6468.

198 Sterling Chemistry Laboratory in an aerial view of the Pierson-Sage Square in 1954. YM&A. Image no. 1373.

199 Sage Hall: perspective drawing by Chester B. Brice for William Adams Delano, 1922. YM&A. RU 1/Drawer 53/Folder 251.

200 William L. Harkness Hall: drawing by Chester B. Price for William Adams Delano, 1926. YM&A. Image no. 4857.

201 Department of University Health. YM&A. Image no. 2195.

202 High Street Bridge. YM&A. Image no. 1271.

203 Art Gallery: proposal by Egerton Swartwout for the complete Chapel Street facade, 1926. From *Yale Alumni Weekly* (16 April 1926). YM&A.

204 Art Gallery: plan of the ground floor by Egerton Swartwout, 1926. From *Yale Alumni Weekly* 35 (16 April 1926). YM&A.

205 Art Gallery: proposal by Egerton Swartwout for the Chapel Street facade as built, 1926. From *Yale Alumni Weekly* 35 (16 April 1926). YM&A.

206 Peabody Museum, ca. 1925. YM&A. Image no. 5168.

207 Sterling Hall of Medicine before 1929. YM&A. Image no. 4930.

208 Sterling Hall of Medicine: plan of the ground floor by Day and Klauder, 1921. From *Yale Alumni Weekly* 31, no. 15 (30 December 1921). YM&A.

209 Map of the School of Medicine, showing proposed additions in black, 1922. From *Yale University School of Medicine, The Past, Present, and Future of the Yale University School of Medicine and affiliated clinical institutions* (New Haven: Yale University, 1922). YM&A. Image no. 5544.

210 School of Medicine and hospital buildings in 1926. Photo: Lieut. P. P. Hill, U.S. Air Corps. From *General Hospital Society of Connecticut, 1826–1926. Centenary* (New Haven: Tuttle, Morehouse and Taylor Co., 1926). YM&A.

211 School of Medicine and hospital buildings in the early 1930s. YM&A. Image no. 4923.

212 Institute of Human Relations and Sterling Hall of Medicine: perspective study of the Cedar Street entrance by John Tompkins for Grosvenor Atterbury, 1929. YM&A. Image no. 4931.

213 Clinic Building: model by Henry C. Pelton, 1929. YM&A. RU 685/Box 7/Folder 157.

214 Sheffield-Sterling-Strathcona: presentation drawing by Schell Lewis for Zantzinger, Borie and Medary, 1929. Photo: Simonds Commercial Photo Co. YM&A. Image no. 5491.

215 Construction of Sheffield-Sterling-Strathcona, September 24, 1931. YM&A. Image no. 6469.

216 Sterling Divinity Quadrangle: bird's-eye view by Schell Lewis of Delano and Aldrich's first proposal, 1930. YM&A. RU 1/Drawer 54/Folder 260.

217 Sterling Divinity Quadrangle from the west. YM&A. Image no. 1191.

218 Sterling Divinity Quadrangle: sketch by Floyd Yewell of Delano and Aldrich's proposal for the buildings and terraced area behind the chapel, 1931. YM&A. RU 1/Drawer 54/Folder 260.

219 Sterling Divinity Quadrangle: west entrance. YM&A. Image no. 1596.

220 P. Kingham, "The Old Order Changeth," 1931. From *The Yale Record* 59 (25 March 1931). YM&A.

221 Weir Hall, ca. 1924. YM&A. Image no. 6456.

222 George Dudley Seymour, "An Open Letter," *New Haven Register,* 2 June 1907. George Dudley Seymour Papers. YM&A. Image no. 5518.

223 "The City of New Haven, Connecticut," 1879. Facsimile of a print after a drawing by O. H. Bailey and J. C. Hazen, Boston. Courtesy Office of Facilities, Yale University.

224 New Haven in 1907: looking west from Chapel and State Streets. Photo: T. S. Bronson. NHCHS.

225 Cass Gilbert and Frederick Law Olmsted, Jr., "Preliminary Plan: Improvement of the City of New Haven," 1910. From *Report of the New Haven Civic Improvement Commission to the New Haven Civic Improvement Committee* (New Haven: New Haven Civic Improvement Commission, 1910; henceforth cited as *Report of the New Haven Civic Improvement Commission*), no. 32. YM&A.

226 Cass Gilbert and Frederick Law Olmsted, Jr., "Birdseye [*sic*] view of proposed Avenue from the Station to the Green through the proposed Public Square," 1910. From *Report of the New Haven Civic Improvement Commission,* no. 31. YM&A.

227 Cass Gilbert and Frederick Law Olmsted, Jr., "Sketch view…showing how the Avenue would connect the Station with the City," 1910. From *Report of the New Haven Civic Improvement Commission,* no. 30. YM&A.

228 Hillhouse Avenue looking north toward Sachem's Wood, ca. 1868. YM&A. Image no. 2078.

229 Cass Gilbert and Frederick Law Olmsted, Jr., "City of New Haven: Map showing areas [in black] in which are needed more small parks for local purposes," 1910. From *Report of the New Haven Civic Improvement Commission,* no. 10. YM&A.

230 Cass Gilbert and Frederick Law Olmsted, Jr., "New Haven [Regional park plan]," 1910. From *Report of the New Haven Civic Improvement Commission,* insert. YMC.

231 Frederick L. Ford, "Map showing approach proper to new station," 1912. From *New Haven Union,* 8 October 1912.

232 New Haven Green from the colonnade of the United States Post Office and Courthouse around 1918. YM&A. Image no. 6653.

233 Bird's-eye view of the "New Campus," 1919. Frontispiece from John Russell Pope, *Yale University: A Plan for its Future Building,* illustrations by Otto R. Eggers (New York: Cheltenham Press, 1919; henceforth cited as *Pope Plan*). Private Collection.

234 "Yale University: A General Plan for its Future Building," 1919. From *Pope Plan.* Private Collection.

235 "A General View of the Proposed Plan," 1919. From *Pope Plan.* Private Collection.

236 "The New Campus," 1919. From *Pope Plan.* Private Collection.

237 "The Campus," 1919. From *Pope Plan.* Private Collection.

238 "The Gymnasium," 1919. From *Pope Plan.* Private Collection.

239 "The Square," 1919. From *Pope Plan.* Private Collection.

240 Synthesis of the New Haven Civic Improvement Plan of 1910 and the Pope Plan of 1919. Drawing by Erik Vogt. Watercolor and graphite on board, 40 x 86 inches. © Erik Vogt.

241 "The Hillhouse Group," 1919. From *Pope Plan.* Private Collection.

242 Advisory Committee design sketch, 1920. From Bertram Goodhue, William Adams Delano, and Paul F. Cret, *Report of the Advisory Committee,* 19 February 1920. YM&A. Image no. 6558.

243 James Gamble Rogers, "Sketch plan no. 3," ca. 1922–23. YM&A. Image no. 4534.

244 James Gamble Rogers, "The Corporation's Plan," 1924. From *Yale Alumni Weekly* 33, no. 20 (1 February 1924). YM&A.

245 James Gamble Rogers, "Bird's Eye View of New Cross Campus," 1924. From *Yale Alumni Weekly* 33, no. 20 (1 February 1924). YM&A.

246 Harkness Memorial Tower: detail of High Street elevation, September 1918, with revisions from May 1919 to June 1921. Drawing by E. Donald Robb. YM&A. RU 1/Drawer 19/Folder 77.

247 Memorial Quadrangle: presentation drawing, ca. 1918. YM&A.

248 Memorial Quadrangle: plan of the ground floor. From *Architecture* 44, no. 4 (October 1921).

249 Peabody Square, July 21, 1917. Photo: James S. Hedden. YM&A. Image no. 683.

250 Construction of the Memorial Quadrangle, July 16, 1918. Photo: James S. Hedden. YM&A. Image no. 5291.

251 Construction of the Memorial Quadrangle, July 10, 1920. Photo: James S. Hedden. YM&A. Image no. 5292.

252 Construction of the Memorial Quadrangle, November 1, 1918. Photo: James S. Hedden. YM&A. Image no. 5293.

253 Memorial Quadrangle: Branford Court looking southeast toward Harkness Memorial Tower in 1921. Photo: James S. Hedden. YM&A. Image no. 6691.

254 Memorial Quadrangle: Branford Court looking northwest toward Wrexham Tower in 1921. Photo: James S. Hedden. YM&A. Image no. 6728.

255 Harkness Memorial Tower: detail showing the statue of James Fenimore Cooper. YM&A. Image no. 4561.

256 Memorial Quadrangle: Memorial Gateway from High Street in 1921. Photo: James S. Hedden. YM&A. Scan 5294.

257 Memorial Quadrangle: preliminary sketch of the Memorial Room, ca. 1918. YM&A. RU 1/Drawer 19/Folder 77.

258 Memorial Quadrangle: fan vaulting in the Memorial Room. YM&A. Image no. 4562.

259 Sterling Memorial Library: preliminary sketch by Hugh Ferriss for Bertram Grosvenor Goodhue, ca. 1923. YM&A. RU 1/Drawer 33/Folder 123.

260 Sterling Memorial Library: original plan by Bertram Grosvenor Goodhue, ca. 1923. YM&A. RU 1/Drawer 33/Folder 123.

261 Sterling Memorial Library: plan of the ground floor by James Gamble Rogers, ca. 1925. YM&A. RU 1/Drawer 34/Folder 126.

262 Sterling Memorial Library: High Street elevation by James Gamble Rogers, ca. 1925. YM&A. Image no. 2002.

263 Sterling Memorial Library: east (High Street) facade, June 20, 1930. YM&A. Image no. 6726.

264 Sterling Law Buildings: plan of the third floor. YM&A. RU 1/Drawer 42/Folder 161.

265 Sterling Law Buildings: High and Grove Street facades. YM&A. Image no. 4564.

266 Sterling Law Library in 1931. YM&A. Image no. 4539.

267 Hall of Graduate Studies: east (York Street) elevation. YM&A. Image no. 663.

268 Looking west on Wall Street toward the Hall of Graduate Studies, ca. 1935. YM&A. RU 623/Box 2/Folder 1.

269 Map of Yale University: detail, 1935. By A.H.S. after William Addison Dwiggins. From *Bulletin of Yale University. General Catalogue Number for the Academic Year 1936–1937.* (New Haven: Yale University, 1936).

270 Construction of the York Street section of the Sterling Quadrangle (Trumbull College), February 22, 1930. YM&A. Image no. 521.

315 Claes Oldenburg, B.A. 1950, "Lipstick (Ascending) on Caterpillar Tracks," 1969–74: installation in the courtyard of Morse College. Cor-Ten steel, steel, aluminum, cast resin; painted with polyurethane enamel, 7.2 x 7.6 x 3.3 meters. Fabricated by Lippincott, Inc., North Haven, Connecticut, and members of the Colossal Keepsake Corporation. Engineer: J. Robert Jennings. Photo: Attilio Maranzano. Courtesy Claes Oldenburg and Coosje van Bruggen.

316 Yale Center for British Art: perspective view looking west on Chapel Street. Louis Kahn Collection. YM&A. Image no. 3489.

317 Yale Center for British Art from the Art and Architecture Building. Photo: Michael Marsland. YOPA.

318 Yale Center for British Art in 1975. Photo: William B. Carter. Yale Department of Public Information. Courtesy Yale Center for British Art.

319 Yale Center for British Art: Library Court. YM&A. Image no. 5379.

320 Seeley G. Mudd Library. Photo: © Steve Rosenthal, B.A. 1962. Courtesy Roth and Moore Architects.

321 New Residence Hall. Photo: Patrick Pinnell, B.A. 1971, M.ARCH. 1974.

322 Henry R. Luce Hall. Photo: Patrick Pinnell, B.A. 1971, M.ARCH. 1974.

323 Class of 1954 Environmental Science Center. Photo: Patrick Pinnell, B.A. 1971, M.ARCH. 1974.

324 Boyer Center for Molecular Medicine. Photo: Terry Dagradi, MedMedia Group, Yale School of Medicine.

325 Yale Psychiatric Institute. Photo: Terry Dagradi, MedMedia Group, Yale School of Medicine.

326 Anlyan Center for Medical Research and Education: east and north facades. Photo: © VSBA, by Matt Wargo. Courtesy VSBA.

327 Anlyan Center for Medical Research and Education: south facade. Photo: © VSBA, by Matt Wargo. Courtesy VSBA.

328 Monterey Place: Hope VI Dixwell Neighborhood. Photo: Vincent Scully.

329 Monterey Place: Hope VI Dixwell Neighborhood. Photo: Vincent Scully.

330 Betts House. Photo: Michael Marsland. YOPA.

331 Gilder Boathouse. Photo: Richard Cadan. Courtesy Turner Brooks.

332 Irving S. Gilmore Music Library. Photo: Richard Benson.

333 Present Campus Plan, Yale University, 2000. Courtesy Cooper, Robertson and Partners.

334 8 Prospect Place. Photo: © Norman McGrath. Courtesy Centerbrook Architects and Planners.

335 Broadway, looking north from its intersection with Elm Street. Photo: Michael Marsland. YOPA.

Index